RAINCOAST
CHRONICLES
SIX/TEN

The Coastal Steamer Princess Mary, by E.J. Hughes, 1968. Oil, 81 x 122cm.

Crofton Beach, by E.J. Hughes, 1964. Oil, 61 x 91.5cm. Courtesy the Glenbow Museum, Calgary. See the article on Mr. Hughes on page 264.

Preceding page; *Logs, Ladysmith Harbour,* by E.J. Hughes, 1949. Oil, 76.2 x 101.5cm. Courtesy the Art Gallery of Ontario, Toronto; gift from the Albert H. Robson Memorial Subscription Fund, 1950.

RAINCOAST CHRONICLES SIX/TEN

Collector's Edition II

Edited by Howard White

HARBOUR PUBLISHING
Madeira Park, B.C.

Raincoast Chronicles Six/Ten: Collector's Edition II

Harbour Publishing
Box 219
Madeira Park, BC
V0N 2H0

Canadian Cataloguing in Publication Data

Main entry under title:

Raincoast chronicles six/ten

Reprints of issues six to ten of the periodical
Raincoast chronicles.
Includes index.
ISBN 1-55017-067-8

1. Frontier and pioneer life – British Columbia.
2. British Columbia – History. I. White, Howard.
II. Title: Raincoast chronicles.
FC3803.R342 1983   971.1   C83-091342-4
F1086.R342 1983

Illustrations pages 15-20, 26-27, 29, 110, 122-126, 130, 144, 149, 151, 166, 249, 261-262, 272-274, 278 by Robert Jack. Illustrations pages 22-25, 54-57, 76-80, 165 by Belinda McLeod. Illustrations pages 28, 50, 52, 108-109, 282 by Linda Prine. Illustration page 37 by Ed Whitaker. Illustrations pages 59, 68, 113, 129, 131, 132, 182, 190-193, 195, 200-203, 225-226 by Stephen Jackson. Illustrations pages 134 and 135 by Bus Griffiths. Illustrations pages 156-164 by Jacqueline McKay Mathews. Illustrations pages 177-179 by Dave Burggraf. Illustrations pages 237-245 by Gaye Hammond. Illustrations pages 254-255 by Bryan Wert. Illustrations pages 276-277 by Howard White.

Photographs page 32 courtesy of Frank White. Photographs pages 61-66 courtesy of Special Collections, University of British Columbia Library. Photograph page 61 Ayame Sakata courtesy of Tamio Wakayama. Photograph page 63 K. Kadota courtesy of Les Peterson. Photographs pages 71-75 courtesy of the Public Archives of Canada, Ottawa. Photographs pages 89, 95 and 98 courtesy of the Maritime Museum, Vancouver, B.C. Photographs pages 91, 93, and 97 Bill White. Photographs pages 99 and 102 Mrs. Anne Haig-Brown. Photographs pages 115-121 Jim Spilsbury. All other photographs courtesy of the British Columbia Provincial Archives. Photographs pages 168-169, 171, 173, 175 (bottom) courtesy Vancouver City Archives. Photographs pages 231-236 Gilean Douglas. Photographs pages 258 and 260 Ray Phillips.

Our thanks to E.J. Hughes and to Dr. Max Stern of the Dominion Gallery in Montreal for permission to reproduce works on pages 264, 265, 267, 268 and 269; to the National Gallery of Canada for permission to reproduce *The Car Ferry at Sidney, British Columbia* (page 268) and to Patricia Salmon, Kenneth G. Heffel Fine Art Inc. (Vancouver) and the Equinox Gallery (Vancouver) for their considerable help.

Many thanks to the following for their assistance and generous support: George Brandak, Mrs. Anne Haig-Brown, Allan Haig-Brown, Joe Simson, Tamio Wakayama, Frank White and Ann Yandle. Special thanks to Edith Iglauer for her excellent editorial assistance.

Printed and bound in Canada

Contents

Contents, continued

Dedicated to the memory of Kay White

Foreword

IF YOU BE A READER new to *Raincoast Chronicles,* you are, friend, akin to the wedding guest who is about to be told the story of the albatross.

The wedding guest of Mr. Coleridge's poem did not know the adventurous voyage of mind and spirit which lay before him when he met the ancient mariner. He was a man on his way to a good party and had not the slightest interest in cursed birds or bright-eyed ancient men with strange powers of speech. But once the story was begun, he could not choose but hear. He missed the wedding, but received a richer gift in its place.

It is with the same sort of barnacled impertinence that *Raincoast Chronicles* lurches out of the slick, anonymous run of published and broadcast entertainments which take up one's time these days, to command one's attention. Whether it be the separate softcover journals or this bound collection—the voices which rise from these printed pages are strangely compelling and sometimes compellingly strange.

In *Raincoast Chronicles* an intensely subjective oral account may appear with no speaker's name attached to it. The name may sometimes be hunted down in the index or contents page but seldom are we told precisely who that hoary storyteller is or why he has chosen this occasion to stop us in our way. True, many of the authors in *Raincoast Chronicles Six/Ten*—George Woodcock, Earle Birney, Edith Iglauer, Hubert Evans, Susan Musgrave, to mention a few—are familiar to many of us who still read print, with or without moving our lips. But there are others who remain, to readers, perhaps even to the editors, as mysterious as the nameless mariner.

Reading these stories, one senses that many of these writers are appearing on the public stage for the first and last times in their lives. They have a story and have recognized it. There is at least one story in almost every human being but most don't recognize it and of those who do, most go to the grave without telling it. Here a few such undiscovered Miltons get their moment before the footlights. Then they vanish and leave the image of their experiences, though not of themselves, etched in our minds.

On page 111 there appears a touching letter to the editor of *Raincoast Chronicles* from the daughter of one unlettered bard who died shortly after being given his shot at immortality in issue six, thanking the journal for giving her "a look into his youth which many parents never get around to telling their children."

We note the speakers' names briefly in passing but it is, I think, praiseworthy that *Raincoast Chronicles* puts its emphasis not on the teller's name so much as on the story he has to tell us. This is precisely the reverse of the guiding strategy devised by the television industry. A typical television series begins with a famous actor, proceeds through a formula called a theme (single mother copes with eight children and three Hungarian Partridges at veterinary hospital) and, these presumed essentials having been set in place, the matter of filling the time between commercials with stories is delegated to hack writers who do it all in paint-by-numbers style.

If you think today's television shows are good, throw away this book. You are going to be disappointed.

Should you be devoted to half vast poets who use strange words and explain them by saying that their thoughts are none of your business, this is not for you either. On these pages all the language and the thoughts are clear. There may be mystery in the stories that are told. There is mystery in all our lives. But there is no doubt about what a writer wants to say to you.

These are stories of real people who are also interesting people. What is common to them all is that they helped populate the rain forests on the western coast of Canada and had ways, manners and morals which were peculiarly their own.

Much of *Raincoast Chronicles* is history, some ancient, much recent. It has been said, by Voltaire as well as others, that history is nothing more than socially acceptable fables. Perhaps. But we all live by a sense of our history: personal, family and regional. If a man claim that nothing except the immediate present is of interest to him, ask him if he would be happy as a victim of amnesia.

Raincoast Chronicles history is less burdened with data and statistics than most, and the better for it. The thoroughly ribald but undeniably authentic story of "Bunkhouse Betty," in this collection, tells me more about what really goes on in a coast logging camp than could all the collected annual reports of the logging industry. "Searching for Cape St. Elias" is the story of a wonder-filled voyage to the land of emerald ice not unlike Coleridge's, told by an old sailor who appears to be a dead ringer for the original, to judge by the portrait accompanying his piece. "Floatplanes and Snow" is a comic bush flying tale with a plot outlandish enough to have been concocted by Baron Munchausen, but its real charm lies in the fact it is obviously being told just as it happened by the man it happened to.

Insanely detailed logging cartoons, earnest testimonials to the existence of sea monsters, revelations of back-woods murder kept secret since World War I, affectionate eulogies over famous old tugboats gone to the worms, century-old scandal about the sinking of the S.S. *Beaver,* supernatural doings among starfish, engine foundry nostalgia—a remarkably diverse list of poems, paintings, stories, studies vie for mention.

But varied as the contents of this book may seem, they are closely tied in one respect. They all contain the stuff of real life and are peopled with real men and women. They are told plainly but touched, almost always, by the grace of mystery, the mystery of human conduct. It is this compelling quality they share with Mr. Coleridge's ancient mariner.

PAUL ST. PIERRE

Viola Wood

WHENEVER I THINK OF ENOCH RICE, I THINK OF BLACK ROSES. It was Enoch's ambition in life to create a black rose. His house in Port Clements was buried in flowers and shrubs, but the closest he ever came to realizing his ambition was a rose of deep navy blue. To Enoch it must have been almost black, because he treasured that flower over everything else in the garden.

I think of old Enoch Rice quite often, because my first home was a little house Mom and I rented on his grounds. The property was sheltered from Masset Inlet by a solid wall that was entered not through a gate, but a high door. Inside was a creek, a merry clear creek often filled by the tide, and a tiny float where Enoch kept a boat. And there was a rose pagoda, where in my romantic years I used to sit and read poetry.

My own daughter Fern had to grow up without seeing the Queen Charlotte Islands and when she first proposed we return for a visit, I demurred. "God gave us memories that we might have roses in December," I read somewhere. I had the roses, and December was just around the corner.

It was my long absence that had preserved my Charlottes memories so fresh and clear I knew, and I feared what seeing those time-sequestered places after nearly half a century of harsh change might do to me. But Fern had heard too much — her own name comes from my love of the Islands' ferns — and I had to give in.

It's hard to believe how completely some things, taken for granted fixtures of our world then, have disappeared, how helpless the poor memory is left when the forest moves over on a trail or drifting sand makes some invisible change in the very shape of the earth. And stumbling on moss-cushioned remnants of buildings one remembers standing new and strong and full of hopeful activity in clearings, one has the chilling sensation of almost feeling the bony hand of Father Time on the shoulder. Surely it's not that long, one thinks, hurriedly ticking off the decades — but the moss does not lie.

Just as remarkable though are the things that have remained exactly — the most solid and fluid of things, expressions frozen in stone, blushes of wind on lagoons . . . in them the old spell lives on as strong as ever.

IN OLD PORT CLEMENTS, IF ONE CONTINUED ALONG THE ONE LONG GRAVEL ROAD that started at the wharf and meandered inland past the Dunroes, Mayers and Minakers, past the road at Crocker's Corner that linked up with the famous plank road out to Tlell on Hecate Straits and past Enoch's to the top of the hill, one used to come to

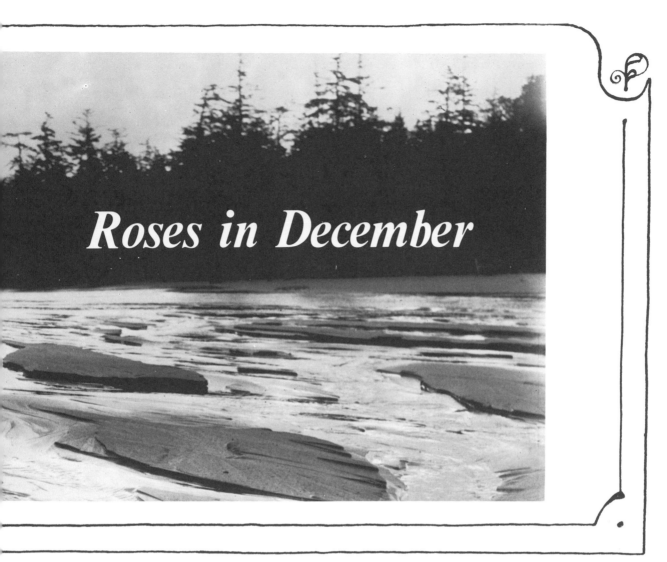

Roses in December

the driveway that led into Bill Vyse's place. Bill built, in most laborious shovel and wheelbarrow fashion, a pretty little road down to the beach, and one of the great disappointments of my visit was to find Bill's road choked with alder and used as the local dump.

Port Clements was no longer the pretty, sleepy little town I had known. Enoch's wall is gone and the rose pagoda as well, the merry little creek is sluggish, and the navy blue roses may as well have never been coaxed into existence. But I can still go down to the wharf and look toward the mouth of the inlet and remember how we used to watch so intently every two weeks for the first appearance of the "boat" on the "lake", as Masset Inlet was called, and how we would look at the clock and give her an hour to make the wharf, then leave a little more for Mrs. Mallory to sort the mail. For those few moments standing with my back to all her changes and my face to the beach, its sight and sound and smell never changing, Port is still the Port of my dreams.

When I first knew the little town (they say there were 50 people then within a radius of three miles) several people kept cows. The cows were allowed to roam, and it wasn't at all unusual to stumble over one in the road if it was dark and one forgot a flashlight. Not that the cows were a traffic hazard, because there wasn't any traffic.

Bill Rennie had a truck and a car. Mr. Dyson

owned a car too, which served as the local taxi. Usually his passengers wanted to go to Skidegate or Charlotte, or perhaps to Tlell, where "The Dunes" was a summer resort. Vacationers from Prince Rupert disembarked at Port and were driven across the old plank road at a very moderate speed.

A year or so later there were more vehicles in town. Frank Pierce and Harry Ross, the two General Store keepers, acquired trucks to haul freight. One or two youths bought cars, which widened their range of travel to include dances held at Lawn Hill, Skidegate and Charlotte. It took two-and-a-half hours to drive from Port to Charlotte and the destination was seldom reached without going off the planks at least once. Or having a blow-out. Every passenger became an expert, mending inner tubes and changing tires. But it was always worth the effort to arrive at Charlie Miller's Hall, where the sound of the Delco lighting plant was soon drowned out by the local orchestra. The only times the lights were dimmed was when a moonlight waltz was announced. Then the boys chose their favorite girl and danced to the music of "Down the River of Golden Dreams."

Mrs. Crocker became the proud owner of a car — using the term loosely — at about that time too. It was a strange looking contraption, resembling something an over-zealous schoolboy might have constructed for a soapbox derby. She never drove it herself, to my knowledge, but goodnatured Ed

Crawford was elected to chauffeur. She liked to go out the plank road to pick cranberries. She must have been well into her eighties then, for she lived to be a hundred or close to it and she's been gone a long time now.

There was one outstanding peculiarity about that car of Mrs. Crocker's. It took elaborate preparation to get it started. Ed would place a block at the rear and set up a kind of see-saw arrangement using a plank under the axle. I was usually called upon to sit on the other end of the plank while Ed set the different gadgets and proceeded to crank. Sometimes Mrs. Crocker's chariot took off prematurely, and Ed would have to leap out of the way and squeeze into the narrow cab as it jolted by. As often as not he missed, and the little black Lizzie would trundle off into a clump of salmonberry bushes to sulk, while I, in complete disarray, ended up on the ground.

The Islands felt like home to me almost from my first glimpse of them, but they didn't have the same effect on Mother. She definitely preferred city methods of shopping and city ways of living. She saw nothing romantic about a coal oil lamp, the gas lights frightened her, and she was terrified of bears.

When my mother decided to leave, it was arranged that I would stay and board with Mrs. Dunlop. Although she hadn't been blessed with children of her own, she had raised Gloria from infancy. She took me under her wing too and became my "other" mother. I know Gloria shares my sentiments when I say that to Mrs. Dunlop we owe memories of ginger cookies hot and spicey, party dresses, black kittens, picnic baskets and laughter. We owe her thanks for sympathetic understanding, gentle nursing, a garden with delphiniums and candytuft, for the homey room under the sloping roof where the scent of honeysuckle tangled with the smell of salt spray outside our window. She was always there. We never came home to an empty house.

Yet she took a very active part in Port social life, such as it was. Ladies turned to her for their dresses of fashion and bachelors depended on her to mend or alter their clothes. She was called upon to administer first aid, for there wasn't a doctor within miles. Naturally there wasn't a florist either, and Mrs. Dunlop made wedding bouquets, funeral sprays and wreaths. If there weren't any garden flowers available she created realistic blossoms from crepe paper. She decorated bridal cakes, raised chickens and sold big brown eggs. She made "home" something special for her husband Oscar, Gloria and me.

THE WATUN, SANGAN, TOW HILL, TLELL, SHANNON BAY, CAPE BALL — the sands mix so gradually with the sea, the dusty low horizons grey so vaguely into sky, the sunlight that filters through curtains of moss eases so greenly into shadow — nothing is sharply focused on these soft islands where even the present sometimes seems like memory, and names serve to locate one only approximately. The Watun, or Woden to use the white name, was a little settlement scattered around the mouth of the Watun River which runs into Masset Sound about two-thirds of the way from Port to Masset. I stayed a short time with the Ormbraks in their comfortable two-storey home there during the early thirties. Their second daughter Alice and I were close friends and we had the romantic notion of some day owning Ship Island in the Lake up Port way. Oh! the plans we made! But in the meantime we spent our days working in the cannery for 25c an hour or digging clams at Tow Hill for 80c a box.

Remembering the Watun as it was, so many pictures crowd my memory. I see little Esther's swing by the woodshed, and remember pumping it higher and higher until I felt I was flying clear across the inlet! Or on cold mornings, a delight to hug the oven! The stovepipe from the heater housed an oven where Mrs. Ormbrak baked delicious loaves.

Or excursions we made to the old school house where the blackboards were indeed boards painted black, and the chalk marks had left ghosts of yesteryear's lessons. The desks were intact and there seemed to be a kind of hush, as if the old school waited for

· Port Clements ·

pupils who would never come again. Leaving the school, we walked the long, straight Echo Lake Road that crossed the eerie muskeg. There were deserted homesteads on either side of the road. Signs of painstaking labour to make homes were in evidence, but also of the hopelessness which had caused the settlers to abandon personal belongings, such as trunks, as though left swiftly with no time to look back.

I remember Ethel, the eldest Ormbrak girl, and how we worked with the tide to peavey some logs to the water's edge, stapling each one and securing them all with ropes. The plan was to tow them to Art Robertson's mill in Masset and try to sell them for ten dollars. We borrowed an anchor from Ed Finney and set off confidently, edging into midstream where the current would carry us. We made the tow in record time and pulled our precious logs into Delkatla Slough. Then we ran into problems. We could not find the channel. As I was wearing my perennial hip gumboots, Ethel suggested I get out and search for it, so there I was, rope in hand, walking around in shallow water, pulling the boat with Ethel perched on the centre seat and the boom obediently following, searching in vain for the channel that would lead us to the mill. Then I did a foolish thing. I looked up and glanced around. It was the craziest feeling, like being in mid-Pacific, and walking *on* the ocean! I can't swim, so I suddenly froze with fright, imagining that at any moment the water would give way beneath me.

Sensing something amiss, Ethel terminated the search by deciding we would anchor the logs right there in the shallows and make a more thorough search in the morning. We used Ed's anchor to secure the boom and rowed to shore where we presented ourselves to a kind friend for shelter for the night.

That's the closest our logs ever came to Art Robertson's mill, because a wild storm cut loose in the small hours of the morning and we never saw them again. Or Ed Finney's anchor, which troubled us most of all. That left us with nothing to do but go to Martin's General Store, order a month's supply of groceries, and head up the inlet for home. Neither of us ever mentioned beachcombing again.

Usually we rowed the ten miles from Watun to Masset, using the tide to our advantage, and sometimes it was dark as we pulled up the inlet for home. Depending on the swiftness of the tide, we more or less went by guess and by God to estimate when we were approaching the Watun, craning our necks over our right shoulders to seek the lamplight in the window that would guide us home. It wasn't a trip we exactly enjoyed. The weather was unpredictable. and the way was long. We were always on the lookout for a lift and when we heard Ed Finney was borrowing the cannery tug *Carolina B* to tow some logs to Masset some time after our beachcombing adventure, we wasted no time arranging passage.

They landed the boom at the mill after what seemed hours crawling down the inlet with the back eddy, then, as we headed for the wharf, the engine went dead. Ed, as engineer, thought it was mechanical trouble and started tinkering with the motor, then tinkering with the motor and swearing. Mr. Coalthirst the captain, a very mild and quiet soul, went below

to investigate. Then both men came up top and threw the anchor over the side, telling Ethel and me to watch for drift logs and avoid them, then disappeared below again.

Thus abandoned on deck, Ethel and I had little trouble steering clear of the logs that came torpedoing towards us with the swift waters. Hours passed, and curious peeks down at the engine room revealed Ed filling a bucket with bits and pieces of the *Carolina*'s engine while the muffled explosions of his curses rumbled continuously in the background.

As dusk approached it became increasingly hard to see the driftwood. Finally a big one hit us square on the bow and went clean under, breaking loose the anchor — and away we went! The tide, running swiftly as a river, bore us rapidly along. The moon had come up and showed the silhouette of the trees literally streaking by! Old Masset, as it was known then, was growing closer by the minute; and the mouth of the inlet with its violent open water, too close to think about comfortably. Just then, Ed appeared with heartening news — we were out of gas. But also at that moment, as if in answer to our silent prayers, a small troller putted up the inlet from Old Masset and Ed put all his pent-up frustration into one thunderous halloo. By the time the little boat answered and came alongside with a gas can on an outstretched arm, the light at the mouth of the inlet was too close for me. I turned to Ethel and said, "I don't know about you, but that boat's going, and this one isn't," and with that I jumped. Ethel hesitated but a moment and followed suit. Our startled saviour said not a word, though he must have thought plenty. He was still speechless as we left him at the Masset wharf, never knowing who he was.

ANYWHERE ELSE ON THIS UP-AND-DOWN COAST TOW HILL MIGHT NOT EVEN RATE ITS OWN NAME, but the whole north beach of Graham Island is such a prairie the round 300-foot bump serves as a landmark for miles in all directions. The Hi-Ellen River winds past its foot and here Captain Simpson had built his cannery for canning razor clams in the twenties, a quarter mile east of Anderson's old store. There were dozens of little cabins clustered about like chicks around a hen and here the diggers were boarded, two to a cabin — two boys or two girls. On my 16th birthday Alice and I got special permission from the forelady to have girls *and* boys in our little shack and we stayed up till the wee hours eating from scallop shells and dancing to the comb-and-tissue.

One cabin was occupied by two older girls who'd been driven north by the Depression, and one of them I remember was a Lancashire lass named Annie who kept the whole camp in stitches. Neither of them had a clue what they were letting themselves in for, but Annie made a joke of everything, especially herself. I suppose I idolized her, for there wasn't anything I wouldn't do for her. One thing she didn't like to do was get out of bed in the morning and light the fire, and one time I elected myself to the task. The wood was wet, so I tried what I'd seen others do and splashed in a little gas from one of our digging lanterns. I might have gotten away with it if there hadn't been live coals in the bottom, but the next thing I knew stove lids were bouncing off the ceiling and my poor ringing head felt empty of the few brains it had. I never volunteered to light any fires after that.

The second season at Tow Hill my partner was Doreen Dunn, whose father, Dr. Dunn of Masset, had a lovely rustic home near the mouth of the Sangan River. We stayed there when the tide was wrong for digging, which might last three or four days, and it was a welcome relief. On dig days we had to rise with the falling tide, whatever the weather, climb onto the open Model T trucks and set out up the beach in search of the lucky spot. When we wanted off we'd bang our shovels on the deck, jump down and the drudgery would commence, relieved only periodically over a quick bonfire where cold winds and salt-roughened hands might be momentarily forgotten.

digger reaches swiftly into the small hole, grabs the clam by the neck and pulls hard! The razor clam has a powerful digger, and his channel leads to the sea. If at first you don't succeed, don't dig for *that* clam again. You're wasting time, and though you may eventually capture him, the shell will likely be mashed — and you may have been able to dig two or three successfully in the meantime.

I learned the technique from Charlie Minaker, and my first attempt came near to being my last. What I took for the neck of a clam turned out, when fully extracted and dropped squirming about my terrified feet, to be an extraordinarily menacing sandworm. It took Charlie a lot of talking — and he a boy of few words — to convince me that this would probably never happen again. It was only when he said with final exasperation, "Do you want to dig clams for a living or go hungry?" that I was convinced. I liked to eat.

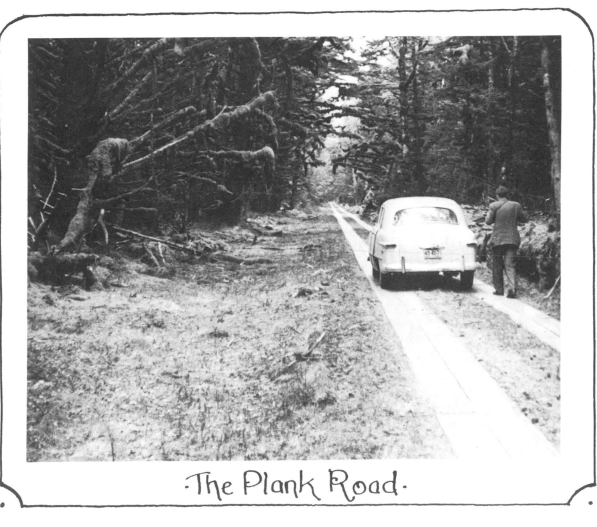

·The Plank Road·

Digging the razor clam is a unique occupation. They are not dug as the butter clam, using an ordinary shovel and turning up several at a time. The razor clam requires a special shovel, narrow and sharp, with the handle at an angle. The razor is a wary fellow, and one is required to work deftly, capturing each clam, one at a time. The blade of the shovel must be inserted about one inch from where the clam has shown his presence — usually appearing as a slight indentation in the sand. One quick scoop, and the

I NEVER DID GO BACK TO SHANNON BAY. If there have been changes there, I know I couldn't bear to see them. Shannon Bay, on the south end of Masset Inlet, was the site of the largest cannery ever built in the Charlottes, and the winter I spent there with the Crawfords stands out as one of the most pleasant periods of my entire youth. Ed Crawford had been a fairly big logger at one time, but when I met him in Port he had a troller called *Miss Pat*. It was said he invented the floating A-frame but unlike Otto Davis, he didn't bother to patent his invention and eventually went broke.

Ed was one of those people everyone came to when they were having troubles, especially personal troubles, and his company always proved rich and effective tonic. Some people called him Peter Pan because he would always be young. Others turned to him for leadership, but Ed had no ambition in that direction. His great ambition, he said, was to have an income of $50 a month and live on Jimmy White's place at the Oeanda River below Rose Spit.

While we were still in Port I often kept Mrs. Crawford company, while Ed was out on the *Miss Pat*, in the big house that still stands opposite Chapman's store, and neighbours were always leaving vegetables, eggs and home-baked bread on the verandah in return for kindnesses Ed had done.

Then Ed took the job watching Shannon Bay over the winter and I went along to be company for Mrs. Crawford. It was amazing how quickly and serenely that time flew by.

Ed showed me how to handle a .22 and Jim May, the maintenance man, loaned me his rowboat to make excursions around the small islands. My favorite spot was an almost landlocked lagoon where I could ship the oars and note an eagle soaring overhead, or watch a deer mincing to the water's edge, curious and un-afraid. Perhaps a bluejay would scold my intrusion, and I would laugh back at him. I belonged there too, no matter what he thought.

Evenings never varied at Shannon Bay. The radio was our entertainment. Fred Allen, Jack Benny, Fibber McGee and Molly would send us into hysterical laughter. Richfield News told us what was going on in the outside world, and we felt grateful for our isolation from its miseries. When the news was over, Jim would produce a pitcher of blueberry wine which tasted quite delicious with hardtack and cheese. Ed would aim a cigarette butt at the coal scuttle, and proceed to roll another from his favorite brand, Chateau Quebec. And I, having successfully dodged the last of numerous cigarette butts all evening (my chair, drawn close to the heater, was in the line of fire), would head for bed enjoying the last strains of Jesse Crawford's organ music, the programme that rounded out the evening. Ed would leap out of his chair — he never moved slowly — and dash out to turn off the lighting plant. He had it timed so that we were able to climb into our beds before the lights flickered and went out. The last sounds of the day would be Ed whistling "Little Grass Shack" as he made his way back to the house.

DOROTHY AND FRANCIS RICHARDSON IN-TRODUCED ME TO CAPE BALL in October '35, when they invited Dorothy Rennie and myself to share the holiday they planned to spend there. The fall chores at the ranch were completed: sacks of carrots, turnips, and potatoes were bedded in the fresh sand of the root house. Jars of mangle tops, beets and other garden produce as well as home-canned beef and salmon filled the preserve cupboard. Francis had smoked sides of pork for breakfast in the winter months and now it was time to relax for

a few days before winter set in at Tlell.

It was with high spirits that we piled into the wagon, which was already packed with supplies for our nine-mile ride northward up the beach. The floor of the wagon was well cushioned with a huge pile of hay to be used as feed for the team, Daisy and Kipper, as well as bedding for Gary, the Richardsons' young son, and Dorothy's brother George. Although there were six of us and we expected to be gone close to a week, packing food to satisfy enormous appetites for that length of time was simple. A sack of mixed vegetables, a side of bacon, plenty of flour, sugar, coffee, tallow and fresh-churned butter was all we required. The rest would be supplied by the boys as we needed it.

Travelling by wagon was very slow, and you had to plan carefully to get beyond the high bluffs before the tide came in again. The Tlell River had to be waded through, water rising higher under the wagon box, with Daisy and Kipper breasting the current, stumbling occasionally, and snorting their displeasure. Then having gained the opposite shore, we settled down to enjoy the sights and sounds, periodically launching into song. We seemed to sing a lot in those days.

When we reached a certain spot in what seemed a sameness of sand dunes Francis turned the team inland and within a few yards we reached our desti-nation. As far as I can recall it was always known as the trapper's cabin. With its back to the sand dunes separating it from the sea, it faced a clearing and a pond. In the five days to follow, we would go there to splash the sleep from our eyes, then, waiting for the rings of disturbance to settle, use the mirrored surface to arrange our hair; spending little time on vanities, much more eager to begin the new day's adventures.

The cabin contained a big double bed, a table and a bench. The small cook stove was always pulled aside from the stove pipe opening when one vacated the cabin to prevent the rain from rusting the pipes. We set it back up, cleared the window facing the sea and the dunes of sand to let the daylight in, and we were in business.

We tramped the beach, hunted, and explored the Geigerich homestead, lingering by the baby's grave in a clearing dotted with daisies. The crude cedar slab was often trodden down by cattle or other wild creatures, but always re-erected by a passing friend who understood and cared. Actually it had been less than three decades since the Geigerich family had attempted to settle there, but to youth it was far back in history. We visited the site of the old Haida camp, a ring of stones marking the place of their fires. It was such a lonely tranquil spot it was hard to imagine the activity, the living, that must have gone on there.

Such mornings! Waking up to the tantalizing smell of home-cured bacon, a quick splash in the pool, tackling the bannock . . . And when the boys shot a goose! making a stew in the biggest kettle, adding the vegetables one at a time as it simmered . . . Every drop and scrap disappeared first sitting. It was there I learned how to cook liver — half a tabletop covered with venison liver, acres of chopped onions, the liver slightly under-done — but perhaps the semi-darkness was the most important ingredient. We played cards in the evening or just talked of "shoes and ships", and the warmth of friendship made each day very special. Even the horses seemed a part of the family. Daisy was aloof, but Kipper had a chummy habit of sidling up and nudging your shoulder as you walked along. It took a little getting used to, until you realized he was just an affectionate horse.

On two or three occasions I had the opportunity to visit Cape Ball again, herding cattle out to forage in the early spring, and I was to spend one more night in the little cabin before I left the Islands to be gone so many years.

It was the late spring of '36 and Anna Geigerich had come from her home in the United States on a sort of pilgrimage to the homestead of her father Nick. If it hadn't been such a busy time at the ranch likely the Richardsons would have hitched the team to the wagon and made another family camping trip of it, but as it was I had to accompany her on foot with one of the boys to guide us.

We walked over to the homestead first. What thoughts crossed her mind as she looked at the cook stove disintegrating into layers of rust and the newspapers yellowed with age, she didn't say. The lonely grave certainly struck a note of sadness, but the age and decay did not seem to daunt Anna. I believe her dreams and hopes were only strengthened, and I admired her.

Our companion and guide built a fire for us by the little pond in front of the cabin and left. It was with sinking heart that I watched him disappear into the shadows of the trees, homeward bound. Night was approaching and I realized Anna and I were alone with the elements as the first sigh of the wind made itself known.

We sat by the fire waiting for our supper. Potatoes were roasting in the hot sand beneath the bed of coals while Anna dreamed aloud of bringing the old homestead to life again. That night Cape Ball belonged to just us.

As we toasted wieners and munched the scorched potatoes with youthful healthy appetites the sigh of the wind became a moan and then a cry and the sound of the sea grew louder. When the first drops of rain fell Anna and I ran to the cabin where we bedded down for the night. The howl of the wind and the crash of the waves didn't disturb our slumbers but just before drifting off to sleep a small splash heard from the direction of the trapper's mouse trap sent us bounding out of bed, flashlight in hand, ready to rescue the unfortunate creature. The rusty sides of the coal oil tin had given the little fellow enough traction to climb out however, and the only evidence of a near tragedy was the tiny wet footprints crossing the cabin floor.

It was still blowing a gale when Anna and I started back to Tlell the next day. We leaned on the wind as we pushed our way down the beach. Poor Anna, who had insisted on wearing Cuban-heeled oxfords, was limping badly from the pain of her blistered heels, which must have caused her more misery than she would admit. I was more fortunate, wearing boys' leckie boots and thick wool socks, only complaining that the wind and rain prevented me from rolling a decent cigarette!

The storm abated about the time we reached the banks of the river and when we were opposite Ralph Ward's place Carl Severson rowed across to pick us up and invite us in for a meal. Whenever I think of chicken dinner I remember the one Carl served us. It was the most delicious chicken I have ever eaten. Although Carl explained how he had cooked it and I've followed the directions he gave me, it has never been the same. And all it was was boiled whole, with no fancy trimmings or spices!

Funny the things one remembers, looking back. A baby's grave in a patch of daisies, the sigh of the wind, Anna's face in the firelight, driving rain and a sodden cigarette; a neighbour's hospitality and finally the sun sparkling on the river as we continued on our way home to Tlell.

When I went back to Cape Ball last summer, 38 years later, I couldn't find the old landmarks. The pond was there, yet it didn't seem as big or clear. The sand dunes seemed to have diminished and rough grass sprouted from the hummocks. There were new tenants on the Geigerich homestead and the baby pioneer's grave was clearly marked with a slab of cement, but close by a discarded washing machine struck an incongruous note. I couldn't find the daisies. But the biggest disappointment was the trapper's cabin. It simply wasn't there. That gave me a desolate feeling. The lonely hominess of the cabin had been a kind of talisman during intervening years, and I had dearly wanted to brush the sand from the window and hold the wild beauty of Cape Ball close once more.

Then I learned from good authority the cabin is still there . . . and just the way it was. It is buried beneath the sands of time, where the years will never change it.

And yes, I have moved back to the Charlottes.

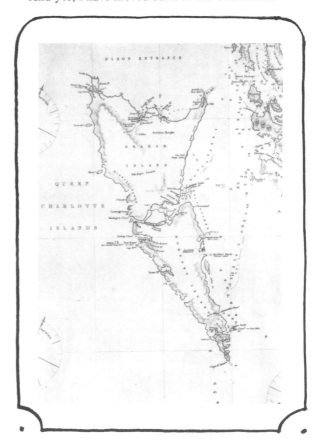

Mother Holly

A short story by Sean Virgo ~ Illustrated by Robert Jack

 see her occasionally. Or a suggestion of her presence. She's not much more than a dim squat shape, vaguely swathed in a cloak like pale moss. She's something like those old Haida Indians in blankets and tall rain hats. Anyway, she always stands at the edge of the forest, looking out. In under the branches of a spruce or hemlock tree, where it's too dusky and green-filtered for you to be really sure.

Some Indians were taking a missionary up the Nass river. They needed meat, and they saw a bear a short way upstream. They beached their canoe and stalked through the trees. When they got there it was only a rotten tree stump. "The bear turned himself into that stump," the Indians explained. "What strange minds," the father noted afterwards, "having to explain a simple optical illusion by magic."

Of course Mother Holly has no place here. She's German, we all know that, standing at the wood-cutter's door and handing down just desserts to his assorted daughters. But she's here now, and she's certainly not the only immigrant like that. I mean, Newfoundland probably swarms with Kelpies and Banshees at Halloween, and there must be farms on the prairies where Swedish grandmothers put out a saucer of milk in the barn for the Tomten. Of course, as the missionary would have been quick to point out, it's the farm cats that get the milk.

I think I know how Mother Holly came to be in the west coast forests, or rather who she came with. I was working my summer vacation in a logging camp up north. Better than three bucks an hour plus travel time and more food than I'd ever seen. You can take any kind of job when you know it's only for three months, and I was getting strong, lugging 50-pound dynamite boxes over the slash, and learning to talk like a logger. Getting better at that all the time. Someday there'll be only one word left in the language. A choker boy who'd had his lunch bucket stolen that evening, burst into the showers and declaimed "Some fucking fucker's fucked me fucking fucker." Everyone knew what he meant.

This week they weren't blasting and the grade foreman loaned me out to a falling crew. It was different riding out on the mainline in a crummy full of fallers. They don't talk much — for one thing they're mostly foreigners. Pete the Greek and Lars the Black Swede. John was a Bohunk and Luigi and A-Frame were just DPs. Behind their backs. Fitting in with fallers isn't a simple matter of swearing a lot and saying that university's just bullshit anyway and you're just going to please your parents. Fallers' eyes focus differently and they sit hunched in the jolting crummy with weird contemplative expressions. And you know they're strong, and make incredibly good money, and some of them are going to die pretty soon, and they've no feeling left in their arms.

When we reached the site the bullbucker told me to watch the road for a couple of hours and hold the warning sign. After that he'd let me go up and help one of his men. So round about ten o'clock he told me to go and watch Kurt — "He's safe and you'll learn a lot if you keep your eyes open."

Kurt was about fifty, pretty old for a faller. He just nodded when I came up and I sat on a stump at a safe distance while he got on with it. A short-legged, stocky guy, working at a steady determined pace. But with those big 18-horsepower chain saws, there's always a feeling of frenzy and menace. The two lines of the undercut take about a minute each. Then a piece of the tree flips out: fresh, clean wood like a neat slice of cake. For a little while the tree's wound gapes like a bird mouth in the direction she's going to fall. Then the last severing cut from the back of the tree — again it takes a minute at the most.

That's with a tree four or five feet across. Not long to get through something that's been there for two or three hundred years. There's just this hungry cloud of sand-coloured woodchips and oilsmoke, smelling of resin and blasting your ears numb. And the faller's crouched in there, like a money's shadow, swirling in the panicky roar. There's a little pause and then the tree creaks and starts to lean — a solid, 100-foot yellow cedar tree going headfirst down the hillside, suddenly pathetic and girlish as it comes down almost inverted into its foliage. Like a lake image. Then the ground shakes and a minute later the idling saw starts to roar again.

When Kurt's tree fell away from him he took off his hard-hat for a moment. He looked much older without it — white hair and nearly bald. He took off his hard-hat every time a tree went down and he never looked at me till the bullbucker blew the lunch horn. I thought he'd go down to eat in the crummy — they do on all the other jobs — but some fallers like to keep to themselves. He told me not to go fetch my lunch bucket, he had plenty to share in his. It seemed incredibly quiet in the woods without that saw: you could hear the ravens again, like you always do when a machine shuts down. They know when it's about food time.

We sat on a hemlock stump. Down the hill from us lay the bodies of all the trees he'd killed that morning. I was counting the rings on our stump — three hundred and thirty-seven years. "Pretty long time, ja?" he said, smiling, "Sure is," I said, "How long before all the really big trees are dead?" "Not long, Paddy, not long *is* for shoore."

It's probably a bad habit of all students: to attack the basis of their summer jobs. I gave my speech about murdering trees to make the New York Times, and screwing up the world and eroding the hills. Kurt didn't come up with any of the stock replies. He patiently chewed his sandwich, very deliberately, and when he'd swallowed his mouthful he nodded his head a few times. "Ja — Mother Holly is not like this for shoore." "Who's that?" I said. This was like being one of the Grimm Brothers.

"When I was a boy we was taught she is queen of the woods. She look after the — how you say? — well, the living things onyhow. You be good boy or Mother Holly steal you 'way. Hein?" And he laughed quite loudly. His face and the boyish laugh made me feel

sad somehow, something about the pale blue eyes
and the funny, inconsistent accent. After thirty years
in Canada.

"Do you still believe it then?" I asked.

"What you think?"

I shrugged.

"Yes, well she is here for shoore. I tell you. She is
from the trees watching. Everything. It's a bad business."

"Why do you do it then?"

"What else I am good for, Paddy boy? When I
come here I say I am good farmer. Is true. They say
'Where's your land?' So I go for work to farm in the
interior. Twenty bucks a week and lay off in winter.
I say 'fuck you, sonsabiche'. Hah. But I am always
strong since I was a boy. So I take this work. Am I
wrong?"

"I don't know," I said. "I don't see how you can spend your life doing something against your conscience."

He looked at me very levelly across the stump. "Someday you will be great man, huh?" But he was kindly. He took me for what I was, like I should have done.

Maybe he was annoyed, though. He didn't offer to talk anymore. He kept holding out his hand with food on and making a little chirrupy sound. You'd have thought he was coaxing canaries, not ravens. They were up in a tree just behind us, yelling away and jumping from branch to branch. "Don't know what the matter with dem damned birds," he said, "Always they come down for food now."

"Maybe they don't like me," I said.

His eyes twinkled. "No, I think they have nest hereabouts. Feeling worried."

There was a huge white scar between his thumb and his wrist. It must have laid his hand right open. "A saw do that?" I asked.

"Ja. Damn lucky she not take my fingers off. Four months I was on compensation. Money no damn good."

"What do you do with all your money?" He didn't seem like a high liver and it costs nothing to live in the bunkhouse.

He only grunted and spat one of those long logger's spits that comes out of a perfectly straight face.

But at the end of lunch break he turned to me as he was pouring gas into his saw. "You see," he said, "I have mother and grandmother in old country. Last year I went for visit. And my brother. He did not come to Canada in time. He was hurt in the war. Was in Dieppe and he get bullet in his back. Now is in wheelchair. But got five children all the same. Ja, plenty for both of us." And that funny over-boisterous laugh again.

"I got to get good money together before I'm too old for this job, you know. Then I think they come out and we all have house together in Bee Cee."

Halfway through the afternoon he shut his saw down and called me over. He was standing with his hard-hat in his hand and jerked his head upwards. "There. See?" It was a huge mulberry-coloured spruce and about eighty feet off the ground a big branch went out horizontally with a bend like an elbow. There was a nest there, a great bundle of sticks that must have grown there year by year with the tree. One raven was hopping nervously from nest to branch and back, the other kept planing out above our heads, croaking. "They got young vons there, you know?" All across the valley the other saws were snarling away. "So we go round this one, ja?"

At the day's end the tree was on its own, standing twenty yards out from the new tree line. Kurt dumped his saw and gas can under it and unhooked his chain. "O.K. Hein?" he said, "This one not on my conscience yeh?"

I nodded enthusiastically. "Fucking rights," I said.

He called out to me after dinner that evening from his window. "Come pass the time a while." His room was number nine and I walked into its still, old smelling gloom. It wasn't much like most of the men's rooms. No Stag Mag pinups, no corny posters, and the table and windowsill were crawling with plants, tinting the room green. Climbing geraniums and other flowers I didn't know.

"Bull-cook hate me like hell," he said, handing me a beer. "Says my place impossible to get clean!"

"You're lucky to have a room of your own," I said.

"I been in this camp twelve year. They have to give me some privilege."

I sat on his bed and he played records on a cheap phonograph. Some tinny Brahms and a German choir recorded in a Bavarian church. Then we just sat for a while. He didn't turn on a lamp though it was getting dark inside. Down the hallway a door opened with a burst of laughter. For a moment the singer's voice "Oh my daarling, Knock three times on the ceiling if you want me . . ."

I knew I didn't have to make conversation. He didn't smoke and hardly touched his beer though he got me a new bottle every time I finished one. Till about ten o'clock we sat there listening to the loons out on the inlet and the occasional car outside, swinging its lighthouse beam round the walls above us.

"How do you really feel, Kurt, working at the most dangerous job on the claim?"

"Shoore, you know," I couldn't see his face very well now, I was facing the green window, "Every time I come to a tree, I say 'One of us going to die, you or me.' They know that I think."

"What if you did get hurt again? Badly I mean."

"Not hurt, no, is no good. If a tree do me in, Paddy, that's O.K. you know. Company have to pay 8000 bucks. I have insurance too."

"Not much consolation to your family," I said, "What about the house you're going to get for them?"

"Oh that is the bullshit, I'm sorry, my young friend." I felt the pale eyes considering me. "You see my brother is cripple and my mother have the Tee Bee. Ony way they don't like to come here. Just I like to think about it."

"I'm sorry," I said, aware that the beer was getting into my voice.

"Well, tough luck onyway," he said cheerfully, "Is all a mess every way around, ja? You get the education. Will be O.K. for you huh?"

"Fuck," I said, "How would I know?"

He leaned over on the bed and punched my shoulder gently. "Is O.K." he said, "No more talk, huh? You want another record on?"

"No, I've got to get some sleep."

"Ja. Goodnight then."

"Gute Nacht," from the door.

He laughed boisterously.

Next morning the bullbucker came up into Kurt's quarter with me. "What the fuck's that tree doing there?" he demanded.

Kurt shrugged, "Nest there, boss. The blackbirds. Have young ones this time."

"Oh shit," said the bullbucker and raised his eyebrows at me. "Look you old fart, it you hadn't been on the job so long I'd have you off right now. *I'm* paid to do the thinking, right? So you get that fucking tree down right now, first thing."

Kurt was hooking on his chain. "No dice, boss," he said without emphasis. "She don't need to go."

The other took a breath. "There's four thousand board feet up there," he said, "and you're going to get it down. We don't run a goddam charity school here. You want your money, Kurt, you do your job."

"No," said Kurt, "and don't give me a bad time boss." His eyes passed to me for a moment. An expression I couldn't translate.

"Jesus," said the bullbucker, "Fucking Krauts and Bohunks. No sodding good. O.K. Kurt, I'll forget it. Just be an old woman and give me that fucking saw."

But when he reached to take it, Kurt swung away from him. "You no understand," he said, "I no slacker, I do my job. Is my quarter — if she have to go, I take her. So fuck you."

"Alright then," the man said. "Then get to it. And fuck you too," he added, laughing.

"You go also boy," said Kurt. "I'm not in mood for company."

I went back down towards the road with the bull-bucker. "Funny old guy," he said to me, "full of funny ideas. But what the hell, he's a damned good logger. The older ones aren't afraid of work." I grunted agreement. I was safely hating him. Safely outraged by it all. And a bit contemptuous of Kurt maybe.

His saw started up, drowning out the screaming of the others. One long, chewing, worrying whine. Then another. Now he'd be going round for the last cut. I decided I wouldn't watch, even though I wanted to. It would have been too much like watching a public execution.

The saw cut in again and then there was that few

seconds of silence as the tree gets ready to go. "Holy shit," said the bullbucker, and then I heard the creak, the whispering swing and the hill shaking under our feet. The bullbucker was still standing there, looking back. His face was sweaty and white. He took off his hard-hat.

"?"

"The dumb fucker knelt down and put his head in the undercut," he said, "I saw him."

The ravens were beating slowly along the tree line and I saw her squat figure for the first time, silently raising a thick, draped arm towards the birds.

Or, as the missionary would have said, I thought I did.

Mill Town

First
and always foreground
the mill
like an experiment
in the logic of ugliness
pins down the town,
billowing smoke   steam
white grey grey-white
into the low sky.
Its robot extensions everywhere
penetrate the town:
a valve is opened
— "Pish — steam
seeps out of the postoffice roof;
hot water drips from the church
— "Whoof — a cartoon balloon
of smoke pops up
on the foul line
in the ballpark.
And always of course
the pulp&sulphite stink
(burnt cabbage with nuances
of urine and tar)

Then the neat wooden houses
strung between mountains,
another generation's
summertown houses
painted pink yellow green
verandahs thick with roses,
each with a lush old-fashioned garden
(nourished perhaps by steam).
In the evenings families gather
in their livingrooms
to hear Fred Allen;
they play monopoly;
they have peacock feathers
in a vase on the mantel.
And the late-model cars
parked at the curbs
the TV antennas
planted among the sweet peas
are all a mirage
an atmospheric joke:
they'll vanish any minute
with a pop
and a puff of steam.

But what I wonder is,
the kids:
do they ever see the sun
as we do
bare naked
and bellowing yellow warmth?
Or is its light fractured
in cloud cover of steam,
a skyful of crazy rainbows?
It may be
it's told like a legend,
older child to younger,
a secret of childhood
discarded with the first high heels
or mail order two-pants suit:
"Up there,
  over the rainbows,
  is a huge ball of gold.
  If people see it,
  it changes the color of their skin,
  or burns them.
  It's very beautiful
  and dangerous."
And of the sulphite stink
that lives in their pores,
that clings
even to the tiniest
damp tendrils
of the babies' hair:
"Out there,
  over the mountains
  in other places,
  the air smells funny."

Pat Lowther

LOST IN THE RAIN FOREST

Alex Kean

Illustrated by Belinda McLeod

MY NAME IS ALEX KEAN. I'M SIXTEEN YEARS OLD. I'm rooming in Vancouver. This is 1918, the year of the big flu epidemic. People are dying by the hundreds. I decide to leave the city before it gets me too. I hire out as signalman for the Robert Dollar Logging Co. at Union Bay on Vancouver Island. On arrival, I hand my workslip to the timekeeper. "Okay," he says, "go over to Number Six bunkhouse, you'll find an empty bed there."

Next morning we take the logging train to the woods and it lets us off at the spartree. I head out with the rigging crew. Soon the mainline is coming back with the chokers dangling. The rigging-slinger hollers to the punk to stop. I blow the whistle. The crew hooks the chokers onto a couple of logs and jumps out of the way. He yells for me to go ahead.

This half of the setting, the logs have to be yarded over a deep ravine. As the turns are yarded in, they shoot into the ravine and hang up on the other bank. The donkey-puncher opens the throttle of that powerful compound machine. She winds herself right off the ground in line with the bull-block. This is damn dangerous.

The donkey-puncher calls in the hooktender and says, "When in hell are you going to do something to stop this machine lifting off the ground?"

The hooker goes over to the loading-crew and points to a big fir butt-log lying in the pile. They throw the tongs on it, pick it up and swing it across the front of the yarder's sled. This done, the donkey-puncher is much happier.

The hooker comes back to the woods and stops to talk. "How's she going, kid?"

"Fine," I say. "By the way, Red, how's the hunting

22

around here?"

"Real good," he says. "I'm going hunting Sunday. Want to come along?"

"Damn right."

We log right through to the end of the week and after supper Saturday night Big Red the hooker says, "Come on punk, we're going to town."

We land up at the old Union Bay bar. Big Red calls for drinks on the house. I sip mine. Dave the rigging-slinger says, "Drink up, kid," and pushes me over another shot. Down it goes. Somebody pushes me two more drinks. Slowly I get them down. Feeling awfully groggy, I go over to a corner of the barroom, sit down against the wall and fall asleep. When the boys are through drinking, they pick me up and throw me into the taxi they've hired to get back to camp. Arriving there, we stagger into the bunkhouse, throw our clothes off and roll into our bunks. I fall instantly asleep.

Sunday morning we are awakened by the breakfast bell. It's raining cats and dogs. Getting up, we dress, run over to the bathhouse and have a good wash, Again we run to the cookhouse to get breakfast. When I'm finished, I ask Big Red if he's going hunting today.

"Hell, its too damn wet. You going, Alex?"

"Sure," I say, "I've got the clothes for it."

Before I start out he says, "Remember what I told you about me getting turned around back in that valley. Better keep out of there."

"Sure," I say and off I go up the railroad track, through the logging slash and into the tall timber. After a bit I sit down for a rest. On a ridge about a hundred yards away, I spot a big buck deer. Bringing the rifle quickly to my shoulder, I take aim and fire. Down he goes. I climb up to the ridge but there's no deer. Looking around, I see blood spots on the moss. I follow the spots along the ridge, through some snow and down into the valley.

The snow peters out and so do the blood-spots. I decide to give up. Turning around to go back, I get the shock of my life. There are mountains all around me and all the same size. Just where in hell did I come in here? If I hadn't been so eager hunting for that deer, I might have known my way out. I take the draw directly behind me, follow it up to the top of the mountain and run into snow. I hear a whooing sound and know it's connected with civilization. It seems to come from the right. I walk that way for a while and listen again. Dammit all! now it seems to come from the left. Back and forth I go and decide at last that the sound must be echoing all through the woods. To hell with it! What I want most right now is a drink of water. Ahead, I see a grassy clearing and a beautiful pool with ferns growing round it. As I come close to the spot, it disappears. I can't believe my eyes. Either I'm going crazy or it was some kind of mirage. Off I go again and again run into snow. I fill my mouth with it and keep on going. Suddenly I come across footprints. Somebody must be around here. I fire three shots and wait. No answer. That gets me thinking. I place my boots in the marks and they fit perfectly. I've just crossed my own tracks.

I look at my watch. It's four o'clock and the rain's coming down in buckets. I should have reached the logging-slash by now. I come to a big windfall with enough room at the butt end to crawl under. Beneath it, I find enough dry twigs to make a fire. I bring out my matches, strike one on a dry rock and the head comes off. They are all soaking wet. Disgusted, I crawl under the windfall. Placing my rifle handy, I curl up and go to sleep.

In the night I am awakened by something prowling around. I grab my rifle and wait. Whatever it is gradually moves off into the darkness. I fall asleep again. In the early hours of the morning I wake once more, this time from the cold. I'm damn stiff and sore. Looking at my watch, I see it has stopped.

Rolling out from under the windfall, I stagger to my feet and jump around a bit to warm up. Then I head downhill. Shortly, I come to a river deep down in a gorge. To the left and above me is a beautiful falls. As I stand there watching the tumbling water, I make up my mind to follow this river. It's got to lead to a lake or the saltchuck. Maybe a prospector's or trapper's cabin. I head downstream and run into a valley, thickly overgrown with giant devil's club eight feet tall. I don't want any of those thorns in me. I know they are like fishhooks and just as hard to get out. Gingerly I work my way between the prickly stems and under the giant leaves for what seems like hours. Eventually, I manage to move sideways up a hill and get above the devil's club. I'm back in big timber again. The ground is covered with moss four inches deep and it's a lot better going. After a long time, it begins to get dark again. I come to another huge tree that has fallen with age and decide this is as far as I'm going today. I'm damn tired. Stacking some of the moss on the lee side of the windfall, I lie down on it and am asleep before I know it.

I wake the following morning, stiff, cold, hungry and damn sore. I try to get up from my moss bed. Nothing doing. Trying again, I get on one knee, bring up the other leg and down I go. Good God! I think, surely this can't be it. Reaching up, I get my fingers in a deep crevice of the thick fir bark and manage to pull myself to my knees. Reaching higher, I get a new hold, pull with my arms, push with my feet and finally manage to get up. Leaned against the log, I kick my feet to get some blood circulating again. Keeping a hold on the log I work my way along to the end. Letting the log go, I take a few shaky steps. I feel like a robot.

Gradually I manage to get going and soon come to the river again. The rock ridges on the opposite side are quite high. I figure if I could get over on top of them, I ought to be able to see right down the valley. Following the river down, I reach a place where it widens out. This usually means shallow water. I wade across to within eight feet of the other side. The water's above my waist and doing its damndest to sweep me off my feet. I notice something here I don't like. The river has dug a deep channel against the bank and the water is rushing through at terrific speed. It sure looks dangerous but, dammit all, I'm not going back if I can help it. I spot a willow-root sticking out of the bank about three feet. It looks solid. I back up against the current ten feet or so, throw my rifle-strap over my shoulder, hit the water and manage to catch the root on the way by. The current swings me into the bank. Pulling myself out, I just lie there for a minute. My God, that water's cold! I have to get up or I'll freeze to death. I force myself to rise and slowly make my way up the high ridge till I reach the top. Exhausted, I collapse on the rock. Lifting my head, I take a look down the valley, rub my eyes and look again. Sure enough there's a log house away off in the distance.

Getting up, I work my way down to the river's edge, pushing my way through the thick brush. Suddenly I break into a small clearing and there's the log house. It's small and, looking inside, I can see it hasn't been used for years. Going around the back, I discover a trail. Someone has walked over it recently with caulk-shoes. This cheers me up. Following it, I come out on a sandstone bluff and right below me is the small coal town of Cumberland. I'm out of that damn valley at last.

Climbing down to a gravel road, I follow it to the Island Highway. I'm awful thirsty. Noticing a woman working in her garden, I go over and ask her for a drink of water.

"You wouldn't by any chance be the signalman from the Robert Dollar camp, would you?" she asks, looking at me curious.

"That's right," I say. "Why?"

"My husband came in Monday morning to get his rifle. He was going out with the crew to look for you." She invites me inside. "Guess your clothes must be soaked."

Sure are."

She offers me a chair and goes into a back room. "I've laid out underwear, a shirt, pants and a jacket for you," she says returning. "Go change."

I sure don't argue. Putting on the dry clothes, I

roll the wet gear in my raintest jacket. I go back to the kitchen and she hands me a glass of hot rum. I drink it down, feeling the nice hot glow of it in my body.

"How does that feel?"

"Gosh lady, you've saved my life. Thanks a lot."

"You must be hungry too." She makes two big sandwiches of homemade bread with lettuce and boiled ham. I'm sure not long in finishing them up. We sit talking. Suddenly she jumps up and runs out the front door. Curious, I look out the window. She is on the side of the highway talking to somebody in a car. She comes back and says: "There's a ride for you to Union Bay. Leave the clothes you got on at the company office. My husband will pick them up."

I thank her again, carry my damp bundle out to the car and get in. The driver is a Jap. He drives along the highway for a bit and stops at a crossroad. "Me no go any further," he says.

I look at him. "You told that lady you were going to Union Bay."

"No go."

I start to climb out with my bundle of clothes. "You give me money, I take you to Union Bay," he says.

I can hardly believe what I hear. When people go hunting they don't pack money. "If you take me to the logging camp, I'll pay you what you want."

"No take camp."

I feel like punching him in the nose but I realize I have to play it his way. "You know John, the owner of the store at Union Bay? Well he's my friend. You take me there, I'll get him to pay you."

"Okay, you jump in."

Away we go again. I think, "What a dirty son of

24

a bitch he turned out to be!" We reach the Bay and I get out of the car.

"You get money now."

"You go to hell!" I say. "Two can play at this game, feller!"

He jumps out of the car and comes at me. I swing my rifle straight at him. "One more step and I'll blow a hole right through your belly!"

I've got him scared. He stops and stands looking at me. I tell him to climb in his car and get the hell out of there. He does too – digs holes in the road getting away. I try to call a taxi but they're both out. I phone the camp. Let them know I'm back in civilization again. Tell them I'll be back in an hour.

After another long hike up the camp road, I arrive at the bunkhouse. Inside of ten minutes, the place is plugged with men and a lot more standing outside. They want to know where I've been and what the hell happened. I tell them quick as I can. Then I escape to the bathhouse for a good hot shower. When I come back, I roll right into bed. It sure feels good. I sleep through till the breakfast-gong, roll over and go right back to sleep. Sometime later the camp cook comes in and asks if I want something to eat. I tell him I'm too tired to eat but maybe I'll feel better by noon. I go over at noon and have lunch with the cook. Back at the bunkhouse, I climb back in bed and sleep till the crew comes home at five-thirty. Feeling better, I get up and go eat supper with them.

Later in the bunkhouse, I talk with the boys who tell me what happened while I was gone. When I didn't show up Sunday evening, Big Red had told the super. He'd got the engineer to go out to the yarder and blow the whistle three times every fifteen minutes on the chance I might hear. They'd done this for the next couple of days. Monday, forty-five men had gone looking for me and the super had sent a telegram to my parents telling them I was lost. He'd also phoned my brother Bob at Cowichan Lake but he was out hunting for one of his own crew.

Big Red comes in. "Guess you got into that valley, eh?" he says.

"Yes," I tell him, "but it was accidental." I tell him about the deer.

"Consider yourself lucky you got out of there," he comments. "Never forget the day I got turned round in that valley."

I remember the whooing sound I'd heard on the first day and ask Red if he knows what it was.

"Sure, that's the big air-fan down at the Cumberland mine." He goes out.

A few minutes later, the blacksmith comes in. "Old Bob and Jim are coming down the railroad tracks," he says. "Get under the bunk, Alex, we'll have some fun with the old fellows."

I roll under the bunk and Bob and Jim enter. "Where's the kid?" they ask, looking around.

"We don't know yet," says the blacksmith straight-faced.

All of a sudden Old Bob throws the bedspread back, catches me by the legs and pulls me out. I get up and he hugs me like I was his own son.

"How in hell did you know he was there?" asks the blacksmith.

"Easy," says Bob. "His clothes are hanging on the line over the heater."

Bob and Jim go trapping every winter after the camp closes down. They know the country. The super had asked them to go back to the mountains and try to head me off from crossing the range. If I'd done that, it would have been the last of me. The oldtimers had heard the arranged whistle signal that I'd been found so they'd come back.

About a week later I'm giving signals for the crew when I begin to feel dizzy. I fall off the stump I'm standing on. The rigging's coming back with the chokers swinging. The rigging slinger hollers stop but there's no whistle. Everyone on the rigging crew starts yelling and waving. At last the chaser sees them and hand signals the engineer to stop. Catches her just short of tearing out the tail-block.

The hooktender comes over hollering his head off. "Hey punk, you asleep or pulling your goddamn wire?" Then he sees me laying there and he knows there's something wrong.

The rigging slinger and his chokermen come over. "What's the matter with him?"

"Don't know, Oley," Red says. "Better go down to the tree and get the engineer to phone for the locie. And fetch back the stretcher."

The boys lay me on the stretcher and pack me in to the spartree. The locie comes up with one flatcar. Red tells the brakeman to watch me till they get to camp and hand me over to the first-aid man. The first-aid man can't figure what's wrong so he phones the sawbones at Union Bay. Up he comes and has a look at me. Then he heads for the office to see the super.

"Have you got any empty bunkhouses?"

"We got three just built," says the push.

"Well you're sure going to need them. The kid's got that bad flu that's going around the city."

The sawbones is right. Damn near the whole camp goes down with it.

About ten days later I'm feeling better aside from being a little weak. After all the tough luck I've been having, I decide to go over and draw my time. The cheque's not very big but its enough to get me home to Sechelt.

SEAGULLS

I

As soon as the sun pokes a bloody finger
through the venetian blind
I raise it
let the day in
and the two gulls
do a flypast
skimming over the waves' skip-rope

I see them   skydancers
who, at the most judicious moment
settle, mother and child
on the boathouse roof
and cry for food

If there's a crust left
I'll throw it
She will swoop, devour
while he huddles on the roof
mewing
until she returns
regurgitates
and stuffs her bread-laden beak
into his beak

Such hunger
I've never felt such hunger!
My sight is blurred
their eyes carry the sun

II

On a rare day
clear as crystal
Mount Baker is suddenly there
pure thought
iced under white crown

But the islands
cower down
brood
like my grey child seagull
who cannot attack
even when I throw bread
onto the stones

O how he mews, he mews!
opening and closing
his beak
a creature (he says)
on the edge of starving

The crows descend
three, four
dart at the crusts of bread
until the miracle happens:
bold white and grey
the mother gull swoops round
calling and calling
her kith and kin respond
whirl in and down
fling wings against the crows
who jaggedly veer off
squawking

The field is clear
and four white gulls
hover and cheer
as the grey young one
head down, quick as a flash
gobbles

Dorothy Livesay

Robert Jack

No Flood Here

Rev. G. C. F. Pringle

Ian McKechnie

AFTER ALMOST SEVENTY YEARS OF RESI-
DENCE ON THE COAST OF BRITISH COLUMBIA
this scribe, with an almost total recall of events and
conditions on the "Rain Coast" has, I believe, some
right to comment on said happenings.

Our weather is often disparaged by short-term
visitors. Many go away with the idea that it never
stops raining in these here parts. It is true that at
times we have an over-abundance of moisture preci-
pitated upon us. But apart from that, where else in
the world can one go that has a climate and conditions as moderate as ours? We do not have cyclones,
whirlwinds, tornadoes, earthquakes (a few minor
ones), volcanoes, and other ruinous furies of nature.
There are few poisonous snakes and a bearable number of stinging and poisonous insects. Nearly every
other place in the world that is touted as a Paradise
on Earth has one or more negative features that
cancel out all the euphoria that is credited to them.
Our winters are sometimes colder than we want, but
are of short duration and the differences of tempera-
tures in the various seasons make for healthier bodies
and longevity.

The following yarn was told to me by a man whom
many older residents of the coast will remember. His
name — Rev. George Pringle. For many years he was
associated with the Presbyterian Coast Mission, travelling the length of our coast in the good ship *Sky
Pilot*. There were few coastal residents in bays, inlets,
small or large settlements that did not know George
Pringle. As well as attending to his church duties as
a saver of souls he was also in many cases a saver of
bodies. Although not a medical doctor, he was very
adept at first aid and administering various common
drugs. He could prepare an accident victim for a
journey to a doctor or hospital and often he was the
one who transported the patient to one of these.

I met him on several occasions in logging camps
and my family knew him well. He would come ashore
with his portable organ and put up a sign that a
meeting would be held at a certain time in the cookhouse. We never had the feeling that we were in
church. He would read a few verses from the Bible,
tell a simple story like the Prodigal Son and have a
sing-song with a few well known tunes. "Where is my
Wandering Boy tonight" was one of his favorites. I
am sure he often stimulated feelings of a deeper sense
of living, even in the rougher types of men and
women.

On one occasion he was at a small settlement
about two hundred miles northwest of Vancouver
where the population was almost entirely of native
extraction, that is, Indians. At that time the natives
were not as well educated as they are now, in fact,
the older ones had none of our so-called modern
education. George always conducted his services to
suit his congregation. He would talk in pidgin English
and use his hands a lot to convey some of the
meanings of his "sermons".

As this place was noted for the heavy rainfall, he
chose the Biblical story of the Flood as the subject of
his sermon. He started thusly:

"Long time ago when world was very young, many
people lived in the Bible country, far far away. Some
were good people that God loved but very many were
very bad and would not obey God's laws. Every year
there were more people and soon most of the people
were bad. Pretty soon there was only one man and his
family who God liked. So He said to this man whose
name was Noah, 'You and I know that most of the
people in this beautiful world are bad and do not
obey My laws. So I am going to get rid of all these
bad people and leave you and your family alive to
start a new race on the earth who will do My will.
I want you to build a big boat called an Ark and you
must build it the way I tell you. When you have got

it built, I want you to put on board the Ark two of every kind of animal, bird, snake, and every thing that lives on this earth, one male and one female of each kind. Then I want you to take all your family, your wives, sons and their wives, daughters and their husbands and their children and their children's children and get into the Ark. Then I will kill all the other people on the earth and you will start a new world.' "

"Now Noah was a good man and he knew that what God told him was true and because he loved God he did everything that had been told to him.

It took many months but finally it was all ready. As soon as the last person was aboard and the Ark sealed tight, God made the rain start to fall. It rained and poured for forty days and forty nights and then the whole world was covered with water and everybody on it was drowned, except Noah and his family."

The congregation had sat in rapt attention during this narration so far, but at this point the old chief, who had been sitting in the front row, arose and started to leave. I asked him why he was leaving and he turned to me and said, "Your story big lie. This place it rain forty year and no flood yet!"

Robert Jack

MONOLOGUE AT SEA

I'll tell you, mate, I
Give this lecture often—
Every year—
To anyone who isn't here,
And you're one more
Who's no exception.

"Watch them move
On their boats, everything,
Swaying into holds always there. A grace
Born of custom. Easy going, here:
These men stumble on shore."

Brief existences at sunrise
Or sunset, wedged
In the arc of a rainbow.
Always
By surprise
And always alone.

Drop the hooks. Set the nets.
There's worlds to be caught
Finning under that surface: only
Who's the captive of
These nets I set and set.

John Skapski

The Written Woods

Peter Trower

There is, to put it mildly, a dismaying dearth of books that deal in any sort of authentic way with the west coast logging camps. I find this dismaying because of the exciting and colourful nature of the material but I suppose it's understandable. Logging is a hardboiled business, frequently practised in wretched weather on ground better suited for mountain goats. Danger is omnipresent. Such a trade is unlikely to attract many cerebral types. In all the years I worked the woods, I never met another writer – or at least none who would admit to the fact. Most loggers could read – there was little else to do on windy inlet weekends and at night – but few of them ever wrote more than their names or the occasional labourious letter. However they would spin yarns like nobody's business at the drop of a dirty sock.

Of course the woods have been written about, but very sketchily in comparison with the Klondike or the Old West. And much of this writing has appeared in specialized trade or historical journals with limited circulation outside the industry. Such pieces are often austere overviews written by academics and too technical to be of much appeal to the average reader. The true logger is reduced to a shambling statistic peering from the wings of such bloodless essays, his legend unrecognized, his rough laughter muted. Much fascinating folklore has been lost forever or reduced to beer-parlour garrulities more fancy than fact.

Fortunately, there exist a handful of books written or compiled by people who were close enough to the real action to tell it like it honestly was. Such a book is *Holy Old Mackinaw* by Stewart W. Holbrook, later reissued as *The American Lumberjack*. It is an epic attempt to cover the entire development of logging in North America from the earliest masting camps in New England, through the days of riverdriving and whitewater men; the plunder of Michigan and Wisconsin; the Big Wheels of the Idaho pine camps, to the west coast rainforests where modern highlead logging came into its own. Holbrook writes wittily and well of such outrageous characters as Jigger Jones who worked barefoot and commenced his days with a stiff snort of high-proof liniment. The book's main fault is that it attempts to cover too vast a subject in too few words. Some regions are dealt with rather cursorily and British Columbia, scene of some of the toughest logging that ever was, is almost totally ignored. This oversight is rather ironic since Holbrook spent three years in various B.C. camps in the early Twenties before moving to Oregon and a long career of writing for and editing various lumber journals. Holbrook wrote many books about the Pacific Northwest, several of which contain logging material but *Holy Old Mackinaw* with its sprawling scope and unquenchable good humour will undoubtedly remain his best-known work.

A monastic camplife was the rule in the early days; tales of floating whorehouses that sometimes serviced the oldtime camps are difficult to substantiate. For the most part, the loggers worked from stake to hard-earned stake in the absence of female company. All this began to change as married quarters were introduced and female flunkeys began to replace the growly winos and skittish fags. The presence of women did much to humanize the camps although many an erstwhile romeo received his comeuppance for sneaking through the wrong window. Some of these women, after years of close proximity to the rugged brush-apes, wrote books of their own. One of the best of these is *Tough Timber* by Myrtle Bergren.

Tough Timber is essentially the story of how unionism came to the B.C. woods despite the strenuous efforts of the timber barons to prevent it. The monumental difficulties encountered by the early organizers, frequently compelled to enter the camps by night over murderous terrain, are grippingly described. The sheer remoteness of many outfits and the transient habits of loggers complicated their task, but these were stubborn, dedicated men. Bergren captures their spirit admirably, tells movingly of the loyal wives who backed them up and with skillful images paints in the rugged country around them. She embellishes her central theme with colourful anecdotes about the freebooting ramblers who prowled the early woods, such as the eccentric brawler called Redwig and Eight Day Wilson, king of the camp inspectors. The book's chief weakness, if such it can be called, is the almost-microscopic attention paid the Cowichan Valley area to the neglect of other parts of the coast. The bias is understandable since this is the author's home district but one would like to hear more for instance about the legendary "Logger's Navy," dealt with only sketchily here. It falls short of being a fully-rounded overview in this regard but as it stands *Tough Times* is an engrossing, well-written saga of lost years and hard-won causes.

Ralph W. Andrews of Seattle is responsible for three watershed books about the woods. They are respectively: *This Was Logging*, *The Glory Days of Logging* and *Timber*. The first is essentially a showcase for the logging photographs of Darius Kinsey, the Matthew Brady of the Pacific Northwest. The text is secondary and while interesting, rather undistinguished. *Glory Days*, by far the best of the three, is quite another matter. Here a fine balance is struck between pictures and prose. Included are Stewart Holbrook's fine sketch "King of the Bullcooks," two excerpts from M. Allerdale Grainger's classic *Woodsmen of the West* plus other hard-to-come-by pieces including a series of profiles on famous B.C. woods characters by the well-known woods poet and whistle farmer, Robert E. Swanson, Swanson is also represented by a couple of his better-known logging ballads and another bunkhouse bard, Charles O. Olson, provides additional verse. *Timber* is a bit of a letdown, being a return to the format of the first book with all text by Andrews himself for the most part but it does contain some excellent pictures and prose about forest fires.

A book that falls roughly into the same category is the recently-published *Timber Country* by Earl Roberge. It is certainly the largest book on the woods ever published as well as the most expensive. Fortunately, the excellence of the contents justifies the lavish format. Roberge's subject is the modern-day woods and his coverage is awesomely comprehensive. He is a fine photographer and his dazzling pictures are impeccably reproduced in full colour. They are quite the best logging pictures I have ever seen, imaginatively composed, almost stereoscopic in their clarity. Mr. Roberge also writes well and his text is very engrossing. Each of the western logging areas from Idaho to Alaska, including B.C., is the subject of a long chapter while other sections deal with gyppo camps and reforestation. Such latter day methods as balloon and helicopter logging and grapple-yarding are fascinatingly dealt with. The book is a labour of love in every respect.

Woods Words by Walter F. McCulloch occupies its own unique niche among logging books. Published by the University of Oregon, it is essentially a dictionary of timber slang and contains a mind-boggling four thousand words and phrases. Even at that, some of the raunchier terms are omitted due to the finicky restrictions of the mid-Fifties when the book was published. Apart from the exclusion of these commonly used words, it is a remarkable compilation and some of the definitions are fascinating little essays in their own right.

Numerous novels have been written over the years that employed woods backgrounds. The majority were superficial potboilers that have deservedly slipped into oblivion. Some, such as the late Bill Sinclair's *Big Timber* and *The Inverted Pyramid* are essentially transplanted westerns slanted for the Zane Grey market although the second contrives to dig a bit deeper. *Timber* by Roderick Haig-Brown (not to be confused with the Andrews book of the same title) is a creditable attempt at something more substantial. Haig-Brown was no stranger to the logging camps in his early years and the background details are dead on. Yet somehow the book is not as good as it should have been. The characters are curiously remote and lacking in real depth. Roughly the same criticism can be applied to yet a third book that bears the title *Timber*. Written by Edwin Parker, this novel is set in Washington and deals with the efforts of the Wobblies to better conditions in the woods, climaxing in the outrage known as the "Everett Massacre." This is exciting material but it is treated in a rather austere and academic fashion that lessens the impact. *The Timber Beast* by Archie Binns is also set in the Washington timber country and has a few good moments but again, the characters seem to be simply going through the paces and there is an abundance of mundane and boring dialogue.

A much better novel than any of the foregoing is *The Kingdom Carver* by E. G. Perrault. Reputedly based on the early career of Gordon Gibson, the well-known B.C. lumberman, the novel is set in the period immediately following World War One and takes place mostly on the west coast of Vancouver Island. Fast-moving and full of authentic local colour, it follows the adventures of young Dave Laird as he quite literally carves himself a kingdom from a remote tract of timber. The many characters both Indian and white, are well-drawn and believable. It is a highly enjoyable yarn.

I am not going to dwell too long on Ken Kesey's tour-de-force of the Oregon timberlands *Sometimes a Great Notion* since it has been reviewed exhaustively elsewhere and was the basis of an interesting movie. Suffice to say that Kesey spins one hell of a tale, full of poetic imagery, smoulderingly real dialogue and gritty conflict. The monolithic Stamper family and their roughshod world linger on in the mind long after the book is finished. It is a work of singular excellence.

Woodsmen of the West by M. Allerdale Grainger is one of the earliest and best of all logging books. First published in 1908, it was out of print for many years, but has been reprinted by New Canadian Library. It is described as a novel but its lack of contrivance and the natural flow of the narrative suggest that it is almost wholly autobiographical. Told in the first person, it follows the journey of a young Englishman to a remote logging camp in the Knight Inlet country. His experiences in this camp under the tyrannical tutelage of its owner, a slavedriver named Carter, are described in detail as are his stopovers in Minstrel Island and other upcoast communities. The chief power of the book lies in Grainger's compassion for and understanding of the rough-hewn loggers he describes. The delineation of Carter is a minor work of art. The book is one of the true classics of the genre.

The Superior books have a recent imitator in Hancock House of Victoria, who have put out a picture book using only B.C. material. Unfortunately *Logging* by Ed Gould is one of those books you can visualize flying out of bunkhouse windows into the rain, notwithstanding that it's twice the price of *Glory Days of Logging*. Gould plagiarizes with truly astonishing openness from the other work discussed here and seems to have had no qualms about fabricating what information he couldn't pilfer. I recall one passage where he explains the phrase "tin pants," commonly used to refer to the old-style canvas rain gear, as meaning loggers' work pants which have become stiff with pitch. The book is replete with rancid rhetoric of the "legendary breed of he-men" brand, and abounds with throwaway photo captions like the one which describes the ungainly barge tug Haida Chieftain as "pretty as a picture but far more efficient." But for me the high point of the book was on the first page, where Gould anchors his opening statement on a claim that the man who drove the ox-teams was called the "bull pusher." As any logger's four-year-old daughter could have told him, the term is "bullpuncher." A bull *pusher* is someone whose facts you can't exactly trust, which tells the prospective reader all he needs to know about Mr. Gould.

This summary of the written woods has made no attempt to be all-embracing. I apologize in advance for any serious omissions but by and large, these are books I have found indispensible. I have not touched on the subject of logging poetry, of which there is a surprising amount, but will deal with this in depth in a future article.

The Day Joey Came

Howard White

DINAH HAD A CHAIR PULLED BACKWARDS
up to the cookhouse window and she was kneeling
on it leaning out on her elbows. "The tide's almost
up to the floor," she said. Sammy was kneeling on
the bench at the end of the table playing with
plasticine.

The bay was so full the water was touching the
brush all the way around the shore and the bluffs
across from the camp you could barely see for rain
and mist. Outside, the broken eavestrough was plop-
ping rainwater into the chuck and somewhere else a
great big drip was hitting one of the washtubs: ting-
tang, ting-tang, tong! Raindrips were scooting down
the windows like streams with lots of twists and
branches like tree roots and the glass was misted
over from the roasting pan on the stove that kept
opening its lid like an oyster and blowing out big
whooshes. It was almost as dark as nighttime.

"Mummy will you please make some homemade
bread today?" I said.

"If I get time dear," she said.

I was at the other end of the table drawing boats.
A great big tugboat making piles of black smoke and
a bow wave big as Niagara Falls. All boats I drew had
big bow waves and big stern waves. Daddy always
said making big waves was cowboy stuff and good
boats like Archie Nichol's could skim the water like
a seagull, but I liked big waves.

I drew a picture of the Clarke truck. That was our
big logging truck and it was always broke down. It
was homemade and for power it had two Chrysler
Crowns side by side, so I made one that had two
Easthopes in it instead of Chrysler Crowns. That was
so it would never break down. We had an Easthope
on our boom winch and it never broke down.

"Frankie's drawing logging trucks," Sammy said.

"You better put that plasticine away before Daddy
comes home and catches you," Mummy said. Sammy
was rolling the plasticine into snakes, rubbing her
hand back and forth on the table real fast till the
snakes got long pointed tails that whipped around
and snapped off. Then she made a jacket of it around
a pencil and rolled it till the jacket was big and loose.
She had plasticine all stuck to the table and the
bench and her hands.

"You're getting the colours mixed up!" I said.

"I am not," she said.

Me and Dinah tried to keep the colours in separate
balls but Sammy always got it into one big ball the
colour of mud, like when you mixed all the poster
paints together. Then the ball would shrink smaller
and smaller till we were out of plasticine again, like it
had evaporated. I never did figure out where plasticine went to and I never figured out where the fuzzballs came from. The fuzzballs were under Daddy's
big easy chair and he'd get mad and make Mummy
sweep 'em all up but pretty soon they'd be back like
tumbling tumbleweeds scooting around, and Dad'd
be mad again. He got even madder at plasticine
because it got stuck to the floor. All around the
table there'd be flat circles of plasticine squashed
onto the floor and he'd yell for Mummy to scrape
'em up with the pancake flipper and tell us the next
time he saw plasticine in the cookhouse it was going
straight out the window, but Mummy always bought
us new stuff and when you used it your hands would
get nice and clean and smell all day like plasticine.
Me and Dinah would make the new cars out of the
Saturday Evening Post and good airplanes with windows and rivets showing even, except the wings always
sagged, and Sammy'd whimper that we were taking
too much plasticine, but all she could make was
snakes.

"Mr. Black is back," Dinah said. We all went over
to look out the window.

"Quiet Sammy," I said, "You'll scare 'im."

"I will not," she said, and pushed in front of me.

"Over there, under the gangplank," Dinah said.
You could just see a black shadow on the bottom.
Mr. Black was a black stranger fish who came every

year to our beach and rested on the bottom just below the low tide line. He wouldn't bite any kind of bait and Daddy said he must be an Alaska Black Cod.

"Must be wintertime in Alaska," I said.

"Gangway!" Mummy called out and came between us with a bunch of peelings in a basin. The rockcod all took off, then when the peelings settled down they came twitching back from rock to rock and started gobbling and tearing, stirring up the bottom.

"Here comes Bulldog," Dinah said. Bulldog was a big black and white rockcod that chased the other guys away and we could never get him to bite either. He'd grab a bacon chunk if you dropped it down but not if it was on a hook. He was mean but smart too. The littler cods were so dumb we could catch them anytime, but we never bothered fishing unless there was some big stranger fish around. I caught a big lingcod out the window one time, and one time we looked out and saw something that looked like somebody'd dumped a tub full of deer guts kinda flowing along over the garbage and after a while Dinah figured out it was an octopus. Dad and Jack Cummings came with a pike pole and stabbed it but the old octopus just wrapped an arm around and around the pike pole, lifted both of 'em up and scooted away. That's how strong octopusses are.

There was a bunch of clumping on the porch and Sammy grabbed her plasticine and ran into the back room but there was a big lump of it where she was sitting with cloth marks pressed into it and other bits scattered around so I yelled at her and she was back digging at it with a knife when Daddy banged the door open and said, "Lil, will you throw something down on the floor?" The porch didn't have any roof and he didn't want to stand out in the rain to take off his cork boots. Charlie and Tommy Gray and Ivan Purdy were with him, and Charlie said, "I hope the coffee pot's on," but it wasn't. Mom busted open a cardboard box for them to walk over to the table on but Ivan Purdy's corks stuck to it because they were new so he took two big tip-toe steps out on the linoleum. The corks made a sticky sound and Mummy gave him a cross look.

Charlie rubbed Sammy on the hair and said, "How's Mrs. Bad Keeky today?" Mrs. Bad Keeky and Mrs. Good Keeky were two pretend characters of hers and the men always joked about it because they thought she was cute but she wasn't really. She just had fuzzy hair.

"Mrs. Keeky's asleep in her house," Sammy said.

"She better wake up, it's time to put supper on," Ivan Purdy said.

"She's gointa wake up in a minute and put supper on," Sammy said.

"Where is this house of hers, I don't think I've seen it," Tommy Gray said.

"That's because it's over in Chair Bay," Sammy said.

"Chair Bay, where's that?" Charlie asked.

"That's around the first point where that reef comes out," I said.

"How come you call it Chair Bay?" asked Ivan Purdy.

"Dinah named it that," I said. "She named everything."

Dinah kept looking out the window because she didn't like to pretend in front of grownups anymore. Lately she didn't want to pretend much with me and Sammy either. She was starting to have private stuff and be by herself a lot. Mummy said it was because she was a big girl now, but she wasn't that big, and besides I didn't see why we couldn't have just as much fun as always.

"Did the fallers stay out in the woods, Bud?" Mummy said.

"Yeah, we came down with the load," he said. "They'll be here pretty quick."

He saw the plasticine but didn't say anything. He never got mad where there was people around.

"Would you put some coffee on, Lil," he said. He was a little bit mad that it wasn't ready already or he would of said Love.

"I thought you looked more like Good Keeky today," Tommy Gray said, bending down to Sammy who was still digging at the plasticine.

I pushed my drawings over to him. "See my boat drawings," I said. They started looking them all over real interested which made me start to have a swelled head. Whenever somebody like that started to pay attention to me thousands of tiny tickles would rush up the back of my neck to my head like little bubbles when you bang a glass of 7-Up. It felt better than just about anything.

"By God that's a good one of the old truck," Charlie said. "What's this here on the front?"

"I put Easthope motors in it so it won't break down all the time," I said. That made them laugh. Charlie banged the table and said, "There you are Bud, maybe that's your answer." Dad grinned a little and said, "Yeah, we'll never be short of answers as long's we got Frankie around."

"This boy of yours is quite the artist, Mrs. White," Tommy Gray said. He was the only one who kept calling Mum Mrs. White. Dad always said he was a real little gentleman.

"The way you can draw you should be a naval architect and design boats for people. Then you'd make lots of money," he said.

"Frankie doesn't want to make a lot of money. What would he do with a lot of money?" Charlie said.

Charlie always treated me like a little kid. He never let you hold a sharp knife or walk on the boom. Daddy would even have log rolling contests with me and get me to run the dump winch when there was no men around. He'd say I was as good as having another man in camp, and my head'd swell for two days. Even Dinah couldn't do things like that.

"If I made a lot of money," I said, trying to sound as much as I could like Daddy, "I'd pay off all the bills so a guy could get some sleep at night around here." The men laughed longer at that than anything, and Charlie banged the table and said, "By God Bud, you've done a good job on this kid," but I could tell by Daddy's look I'd done it wrong again.

"You kids pick up this mess and go into the back room," he said. "Lil, is that coffee on?"

I hated it in the back room. It was dark and cold and Dinah wasn't there. She got to help Mum in the kitchen. Dad went out and started the light plant because it was so dark and Sammy wanted to go see movies. Dinah had a projector that showed pictures on the wall and whenever the light plant was on we'd get it out and shine pictures of new cars or Tugboat Annie stories from the Saturday Evening Post. Sometimes we'd shine a new Fox & Crow comic book and Dinah would read it out like a real movie. But that was way over at the Yates house where us kids slept and it was raining outside. Besides it was no fun doing anything with Sammy. She was too dumb. The only fun I had was with Dinah. She was about the smartest girl in British Columbia and she was my best friend.

"You're as dumb as a bum," I said to Sammy.

"You said a bad word. I'm going to tell Mummy."

"A bum is an old man," I said. She ran for the door but I grabbed her and she started hollering. I let her go but the talking in the kitchen stopped and I heard Mum say to Dinah, "Maybe you better take the kids over to the Yates house till the men have eaten."

The hard raining was ending and the chuck wasn't in grey patches anymore, it was glassy black with just light pinpricks like cork boot prints on the ripples. The tide was changing and there was a crooked line of driftwood right across the bay.

"Let's go over to the Yates house and show movies," I said to Dinah.

"Yeah, let's," Sammy said.

"No, you have to stay here and have your afternoon nap," I said.

"I had it already," she said.

"You never did," I said.

"She can come," Dinah said. Whatever Dinah said we did because we wanted her to play with us. We never did what Mum said.

There was a bright flash like a tugboat searchlight at the window and sunlight came shooting in in yellow stripes of turning dust just like when it came through the float cracks fishing perch, lighting up the teredo dust that was sifting down.

"Sunshine!" Sammy squealed.

"Now we can't show movies," I said.

The men were still sitting around the table drinking coffee and arguing. Dad was leaning forward pointing at Charlie saying, "Say you're a Chinaman now Charlie, just for a minute," and Charlie was making a funny face saying, "A Chinaman! I don't know . . ." and Ivan was pulling on Daddy's shoulder saying, "Look here Bud . . ."

Outside one whole side of the sky was crackling saltchuck blue and the side that was still black you could tell was losing out. The wharf was steaming already and the air was so sharp with the smell of elderflowers it hurt your nose. It was like a different day. It was fresh like morning and the sun hurt our eyes.

"We should row out to Chair Bay and see if anything good drifted in," Dinah said.

"I'm going to come!" Sammy said.

"You don't have your life jacket," I said, but she ran into the cookhouse to get it.

Chair Bay was the best place to look for junk that drifted in because it was the only place in Green Bay — except Cover Point — that had a flat beach. The shore everywhere else was either straight bluff or else big boulders and things didn't get hung up easy. Chair Bay also had a huge granite boulder to climb up on

with a brown rain pool on top and behind that a crabgrass flat and lots of good places to play. We all ran down the float and piled into the dinghy.

"I'll be Dinah of the Stores and you be Seward Billington," Dinah said. They were my favourite characters because Seward Billington was sort of Dinah of the Stores' boyfriend. "And say this is a two-hundred-foot luxury cruising yacht that I own and you're my guests," she said.

"Well this is a very nice ship you have here, Dinah," I said in my Seward Billington voice. "How did you get ahold of it, because as I recall last time we were speaking, you were broke."

"Who should I be?" Sammy said.

"You be the motor," I said.

"You be my handmaiden, Mamie," Dinah said. It didn't matter because whatever Sammy tried to be she always came out like Mrs. Bad Keeky.

"I said how did you get the boat and you haven't answered yet," I said in my real voice.

"I know," Dinah said in her real voice, then put on her Dinah of the Stores voice. "Well, I certainly wasn't broke and I think it's most rude of you to bring it up, but since you did, I will say that I've had some rather good luck with my oilwell explorations and in fact there have been two gushers on some property I hold up near Goose Lake this week."

"I'm very glad to hear that," Seward Billington said. "I'm doing pretty good myself since I just put in about a hundred sections of number one fir from my show up by the shop there and I think I'll get me a fancy ship like this myself when I get back from this here luxury cruise we're on."

"I'm going to get one two times as big as you guyses," Sammy squawked in her Keeky voice.

"You can't do that!" I said. "Ol' Keeky can't be a millionaire!"

"She can too, if you guys can," Sammy said.

"How'd she get it then? You've got to have a proper way."

"She went around her house cleaning up and got all the money out from under the cushion on the easy chair and off the window sills, so there!" Sammy said.

"Ha!" I said, "That wouldn't even come to one dollar!"

"I hear a boat," Dinah said for real and held the oars up to listen.

"It's not the Suez," I said, "It's a Chrysler Crown though."

"Maybe it's Ed Wray. It's sure close to the shore."

The boat came out from behind the point under the leaning snag where the eagles always sat and it was Archibalds, from the next camp down Agamemnon Channel. As it went by us they slowed down and waved and there was a big boy standing in the back. "Hey, that must be Joey," I said. Archibalds had a big boy who went to boarding school in the city that we'd never seen before.

"We better go back to camp," I said when we could hear them going in reverse at the wharf.

"To see *him*?" Dinah said. "He's creepy. I don't want to see *him*."

I didn't see how she could tell that from so far away. "Mrs. Archibald said she was going to bring Joey up to play with me sometime, so I have to go back," I said.

It was funny for Dinah to be that way because we always went to meet anybody who came in in a boat, especially if there were kids on it. When we got to the wharf they were all up on the cookhouse walk talking and laughing with Mummy and Daddy and the men, and the boy was with them. Mrs. Archibald saw us and started screeching in her real pointed voice, "Oh there they are! Hello there children. Come up and meet Joey!" But Dinah turned and went towards the Yates house, scooting along with her head down and her arms folded across her front.

He was a way bigger than me and after Mrs. Archibald said our names to each other and told us to go off and play but not to get where we couldn't hear her if she called, we just kind of stood around and it wasn't till the grownups went inside we said anything.

"Let's get outta here," he said. "I need a drag."

"What'd you say?" I said.

"A fag . . . a smoke . . ." he said, holding a flat tailormade cupped in his hand so I could see.

"Do . . . do you smoke?" I said.

"Yeah, but my old lady don't know and I don't want her to find out. My old lady's a bitch."

"Is . . . is she?" I said. I never thought I'd hear anyone call their own mum a word like that.

We went along the boardwalk past the storeroom and toolshed and onto the trail up around the Little Bunkhouse, curling around the cliff where the Big Dome stuck out and down past the light plant.

"This is a keen trail," he said, tripping on a root, "It's just like Lynn Canyon Park. Have you got any keen sights to see around here?"

"What's keen?" I said.

"Boy, you ain't too hep are you?" he said. "Keen is . . . nifty . . . sharp . . . *fun?*"

"Oh sure," I said. "We got lots of stuff like that."

"Keen," he said. "Wait'll I get a light and let's go see some of it."

I took him to see the rivers behind the Yates house where the rain had built up some new sand bars with little feather designs like brown frost on the mud full of gold flecks, but he thought that was dumb. Then I took him to see the monkey tree behind the Yates house, a crooked cedar tree that hung out of a cliff like a camel's neck with branches looping down curled up at the ends like monkey tails, but he said there were lots of real monkey trees in the city and they weren't anything like that.

We went back to the float and I took him all around the bay in the dinghy. I showed him all the stuff we collected in our pretend store at Chair Bay and the hermit crab pools at Cover Point. I kept going further and further looking for something he'd think would really be keen. Finally we went right around Eagle Point under the snag that looked like a nightmare bird to Mrs. Henry's stumpranch to see their cow, but it just got worse and worse.

"What's so great about *that* cow," he said. "In Richmond there's more cows than there is seagulls. I wanna go back to your camp. My Mom might be looking for me."

I was ashamed because I didn't know anything keen. We'd been out so long by the time we got back to the wharf the sun was going down, burning a hole like a welding flash in the mountain, but the grownups were still inside laughing and drinking beer so we

started walking back over towards the Yates house. I was trying my hardest to think of something to do, then I remembered before he came thinking of going up to look for the grape hyacinth, so I led him up to the top terrace of the old rock garden. Sure enough there was one out, poking up through the crabgrass and marestail.

"You brought me up here to see a stinking *flower?*" he said.

"It's the grape hyacinth," I said. I thought the grape hyacinth must be the keenest thing in the world, with its little purple balls like toy grapes. "It comes here every year, just by itself."

"Big deal!" he said, "Don't you do anything around here besides sniff posies and play stinkfinger with your little sister?" He got out the butt of his flat cigarette.

"Do you ever pretend?" I said.

"Pretend, what the hell's that," he said, making the cigarette bounce between his lips. The smoke went up in his eyes and he squinted them just like a grownup.

"Pretend . . ." I said, "Go around and pretend you're made-up characters . . ."

"No, is that what you do?" he said, like it was the stupidest thing he ever heard. "That's for little kids." He held the cigarette out to tap the ash off, but it was too short and fell on the ground. The way he swore scared me. He was madder than just at it.

"Look out, you're stepping on the grape hyacinth," I said as his boot touched the purple flower.

"Big deal," he said and stomped it flat. I couldn't believe it and jumped up, opening and closing my mouth without any words coming out.

"You shouldn't of done that . . ." I said.

"Why?" he said with a mean grin.

"It was my Mum's . . ." I said.

"Well how'll she know who did it," he said, "Unless you tell her? This isn't a garden anyways, it's just a weed patch."

"You shouldn't a done it," I said, bending down to try and fix it. "I liked it."

The little grapes were smashed open and bleeding purple blood, such a beautiful dark purple a lump came up in my throat and I had to close my eyes. If I started crying I wouldn't be able to stop.

"Where's that broad?" he said.

"What broad?"

"That ginch — *girl*, you dipstick. I saw a girl come in with you in the rowboat, an older one. Is she your sister too?"

"That's Dinah," I said.

"Dinah, like Dinah Shore?" he said laughing. "How old is she?"

"Twelve."

"Twelve! Wow, are you sure? She's really stacked for twelve. I'm twelve and nunna the broads in my class are that stacked."

"She'll be thirteen on June 6th," I said.

"Hey, izzat right?" he said. "I'm eight days oldern her. Where is she?"

"Probably up in her tree reading," I said. "Over by the waterfall."

"In her tree! What a blast! You guys are really flakey. Let's go bug her." I didn't know quite what to say. It gave me kind of a funny feeling to hear anybody talking that way about Dinah but I was glad to find something keen before he got any madder. I was quite scared of him.

We crawled up through the bushes on the cliff where we could look down at the big maple where Dinah was sitting with her book picking lint off her blouse.

"Wow, she's stacked!" he whispered. "Have you ever seen her boobs? You must've."

"You mean breasts?" I said. I could tell what that meant. He nodded, grinning. "Nope, ever since she got 'em she doesn't bath with us anymore," I said.

"Wow, I'd sure like to bath with her," he said. "Have you ever felt 'em?"

"Nope, except I punched one of 'em," I said.

"Didja? What happened? What'd it feel like?"

"Oh, it worked real good. She doubled all up and went away holding it, but Daddy told me to never do it again. It was soft and squishy like a sea anemone."

"Keen," he said, "that's really keen." My head started to swell a little.

"Holler and tell her to come and play hide and seek," he said.

"Hey Dinah, Joey wants ya to come and play hide 'n seek," I yelled, and she looked up startled.

"You dipstick!" he said, grabbing my shoulder. "I'll tear your head off. Don't say I want her to. Say you want her to."

"No Joey doesn't wantcha to, I wantcha to," I hollered again and Joey got so mad I got ready to run. I knew he couldn't catch me in the bush.

"Well I don't want to play hide and seek with either of you," Dinah said. "I would appreciate it if you just left me alone."

Joey pulled loose a piece of moss and heaved it down at her. It smashed up in the branches and dirt dropped on her.

"Go away and leave me alone!" she screamed. It was funny, because I'd played worse tricks on her before and she didn't get that mad. It was something to do with Joey but I didn't know quite what.

"You throw one," Joey said, handing me a clump of juicy moss. It hit the same place as his. Dinah jumped up and started climbing fast down the tree. We threw some more, but we could see she was going to get away before we could get down off the bluff.

"Let's cut her off so she can't get to the cookhouse," he said, and we started crashing through the salal, running with our arms and our legs almost like swimming, and getting almost as wet too. We got to the trail a little bit after Dinah but we were closer to the cookhouse so she turned and ran back towards the Yates house. There were no locks on the Yates house, but she jammed a table knife in the crack and it took us a few minutes to bash it out. She ran out the back door and up the trail towards Mum's vegetable garden. Joey stumbled on a boulder and hit the funny bone of his knee and by the time it stopped we couldn't see her anywhere. The path to the garden went up a dry creek through a thick stand of alder trees for about ten minutes, then opened into a big clearing of green grass. The sun was almost down and the shade made the wetness of the brush so cold my teeth started clacking. The garden was in the middle of the clearing, with a tall wall of skinny poles with points at the tops to keep out deer. Part of the back wall was a tall hollow stump so brown and buggy its bark had all fallen off from us kids playing around it.

"I bet she's hiding in there," I said. We walked up to it and the hole at the bottom was covered with a board. "She's in there," I whispered.

"Tell her we'll quit if she'll come out and play hide and seek," Joey whispered.

There was no answer. We stood there and looked at the stump. We kicked at the board but she had it jammed good. Joey tried climbing up but just got orange goo all over his good clothes. "I've got matches. Maybe we could light a fire and smoke her out," he said, but I knew there'd be nothing dry enough to make a fire with. I had an idea I didn't want to tell him, but I got afraid he'd get mad again. I grabbed a handful of grass, pulled up a sod, and lobbed it up on to the top of the stump. It went down the hole.

"Hey!" Joey said, and we started tearing up sods and lobbing them in, yelling and making Indian noises till there were hardly any good sods left. Then I heard a funny noise.

"Hey stop," I said. "I heard something."

We held still and listened.

There was crying coming out of the stump.

"Let's quit now," I said. In an eyeblink it had gone from where you could see to where it was all dark shapes you couldn't tell how far you were away from. I felt scared in a very weird way. I'd never made Dinah cry before.

"Are there any cougars or bears around here?" Joey said. He was just a voice coming out of the dark.

"No, not very many," I said. I could hear him brushing off his shirt.

"I better get back," he said. "I'll be in hell," His voice was sorta shaking and he started running and stumbling down the crunchy gravel. I was starting to get the feeling of something more happening than just what happened. The dark shape of the stump was gone into the dark of the forest and the sad sad crying just seemed to be coming from everywhere. I tried to think but I just didn't know. I couldn't believe I'd gone on some stranger boy's side and ruined my best friend in the world.

I closed my eyes and opened them. It was so dark it didn't make any difference. I didn't feel like I was where I was. It was like it was all a dream, like the real day ended when it was dark before and the men came home, and Joey coming was all a dream, only I couldn't wake out of it. Things wouldn't go back the same.

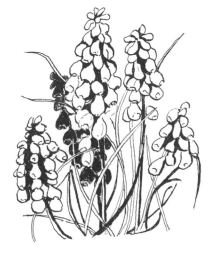

Ed Whitaker

BOOBY-TRAP

As though two hands held it bending
the small alder curves tight
over the thin creek that goes dry in summer —
It is spring — we blunder about
pretending to be fallers
through eleven acres of boggy bottomland.

Powersaw grumbling —
our own grumbling —
the slap of that rotten rightofway timber —
No matter which way we notch the bitches
they keep dropping crooked and counter —
No trusting those devious trashtrees.

Steady dribble of rain —
vague argument by the thin creek —
I stand back twisting a smoke —
He touches the chain to the bowed tree —
The tension explodes —
It splits like a sprung wolftrap.

Fourteen feet
that mulekicking alder barberchairs back —
Catches me clean in the crotch —
Tears the fly right out of my jeans —
Flings me flat on my ass —
Vibrates above me dangerously humming.

"You okay?" he yells running over
our minor dissension forgotten —
"I guess so" I mumble uncertainly
so close to a eunuch it doesn't bear dwelling on —
We are two green fools falling —
Around us the windy woods hiss disappointment.

Peter Trower

OUR HERO, AL RICHARDS, IS NOW TENDING HOOK ON THE *"TRACKSIDE" REPLACING THE INJURED HOOKER, JIM HENDY — AL'S SIDEKICK, RED HARRIS, IS PULLING RIGGING FOR HIM, AND THE TWO PALS SEEM TO BE THE CATALYST THAT MOULDS THE TRACKSIDE RIGGING CREW INTO AN EFFICIENT HIGH-PRODUCING UNIT, A "LOG-HUNGRY CREW", MUCH TO THE SATISFACTION OF BOSS-LOGGER, JIM BRADLEY AND HIS ROUGH, TOUGH FOREMAN, ART DONNEGAN —

IN THE LAST EPISODE, AL IS INFORMED THAT IN FUTURE HE WILL HAVE TO HANDLE THE HIGH RIGGING CHORES, IN ADDITION TO HIS JOB AS HOOKTENDER — UNDER THE EXPERT GUIDANCE OF FOREMAN DONNEGAN, HE TOPS HIS FIRST SPAR TREE, A THRILL HE WILL NEVER FORGET —

THE "OLD MAN" IS SURE IN A FOUL MOOD — HE'S GROWLIN' LIKE A BEAR WITH A SORE PAW —

OH! WHAT'S HIS PROBLEM?

HE'S MIFFED 'CAUSE THE LOADERS HAVEN'T GOT ALL THE LOGS LOADED OUT FROM THE OLD SETTIN' AN' WE CAN'T *"STRIP TH' SPAR TREE" UNTIL THEY FINISH —

WELL, WE'VE GOT THIS NEW SPAR NEARLY RIGGED, AN' WE'LL BE LOGGING TO-DAY! WHAT'S HIS BEEF?

HE WAS MAD ABOUT THE LOGS PILING UP ON THE LANDIN' AN' THOUGHT THE TRUCKS COULD HAUL AN EXTRA LOAD OR TWO, OR MAYBE "CHILLIWACK" COULD PILE MORE WOOD ON EACH LOAD

I SHOT OFF MY FACE, A BAD HABIT OF MINE, AN' TOLD HIM WHAT I THOUGHT OF THEM IDEAS -- HE'S GETTIN' MORE PRODUCTION THAN HE'S EVER HAD---BUT THESE BOSS LOGGERS ARE ALL ALIKE --- THEY SEE A BIT OF A HANGUP SOMEWHERE AN' THEY GET *"PANICKY"!

I'LL GO UP AND HANG THAT BULL BLOCK STRAP AND SHACKLE, AND THEN YOU CAN SEND UP THE BLOCK— OKAY! GOING UP!

THINK YOU CAN HANDLE IT OKAY?

IF I CAN'T I'LL HOLLER-AN' THANKS FOR HELPING ME HANG THE GUYLINES —

HELL! I HAD TO MAKE SURE IT WAS DONE RIGHT, DIDN'T I ?

LOGGING TERMS

*TRACKSIDE — A LOGGING SETTING WITH SPAR AT ROAD OR TRACK
*"STRIP THE SPAR" — TAKE DOWN ALL THE RIGGING -- BLOCKS, LINES, ETC.
*"PANICKY" — EXCITED ----

BUS GRIFFITHS —

WHEN YOU SEND UP THAT STRAP AND SHACKLE FOR THE HAULBACK BLOCK, SEND UP MY AXE AND A COUPLE RAILROAD SPIKES

GET THAT SHORT PIECE OF ROPE OFF THE MACHINE, HOWIE!

WHEN YOU'RE SENDIN' SPIKES UP TO THE RIGGER, THIS IS THE WAY TO DO IT — JUST TWIST THE ROPE TO OPEN THE LAY OF THE STRANDS AN' PUSH THE SPIKE BETWEEN THE STRANDS···THEN THERE'S NO CHANCE OF THEM SLIPPING OUT—

WE LEAVE THE RIGGING-UP CREW, AND JOIN RED AND HANK, WHO ARE PACKING OUT THE TAIL BLOCKS —

IT'S A SHAME THESE BLOCKS AIN'T A BIT HEAVIER — A GUY SHOULDN'T BE COMIN' OUT HERE HALF LOADED!

I KNOW YOU'LL BE HEARTBROKEN TO KNOW YOU CAN SOON PUT YOUR LOAD DOWN

HANG THAT "WATCH FOB" YOU'RE PACKIN' ON THAT FIR STUMP AT THE TOP OF THE HILL! I'LL GO OVER FOUR ROADS AND GET RID OF MINE!

LOOKS LIKE AL HAS THE HAULBACK BLOCK HUNG, AN' IS ABOUT READY TO COME DOWN THE TREE

OKAY– *"MEAT ON THE HOOK··· PICK UP THE SLACK"! START PULLING SLACK ON THE STRAW-LINE — I'LL BE THREADING THE LINES NEXT!

LOGGING TERMS

*"MEAT ON THE HOOK, PICK UP THE SLACK"— MEANS THAT THE RIGGER IS READY TO COME DOWN ON THE PASSLINE, AND IS A SIGNAL FOR THE ENGINEER TO TIGHTEN THE PASS-LINE AND TAKE THE RIGGER'S WEIGHT ON THE LINE—THEN THE RIGGER WILL FREE HIS ROPE FROM THE TREE AND COME DOWN ON THE LINE —

Bus Griffiths—

YOU NEEDN'T BOTHER PUTTIN' THE MACHINE *"IN LEAD"—I CHECKED HER, AN' SHE'S OKAY! YOU CAN GO AHEAD AN' THREAD THE LINES

GOOD! THAT'LL SAVE A LITTLE TIME

SHEDDING HIS BELT AND SPURS, AL TAKES THE END OF THE STRAWLINE, SITS IN THE PASS CHAIN, AND IS PULLED BACK UP THE SPAR TREE—

PULL LOTS OF SLACK ON THE STRAWLINE

THE STRAWLINE IS THREADED THRU THE HIGH-LEAD, OR BULL BLOCK, FROM THE MACHINE SIDE, THEN DOWN THRU THE HAULBACK BLOCK FROM THE OPPOSITE SIDE —

AL MAKES THE END OF THE LINE FAST TO THE SHELL OF THE BLOCK, THEN PULLS SLACK ON THE BIGHT OF THE LINE BETWEEN THE BLOCKS—

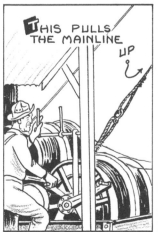

PUT THE BIGHT OF THIS LINE IN THAT BLOCK, AN' THEN PULL LOTS OF SLACK SO AL CAN COME DOWN WITH THE END OF THE LINE —

AL COMES DOWN ON THE PASSLINE AND HOOKS THE END OF THE STRAWLINE TO THE EYE OF THE HAULBACK LINE, AND THE *"DONKEY-PUNCHER" ENGAGES THE FRICTION-TYPE CLUTCH ON THE STRAWLINE DRUM OF THE BIG *"DONKEY"— THE LINE STARTS TO WIND ON THE DRUM, AND THIS PULLS THE HAULBACK LINE OUT THRU THE BLOCKS AND BACK TO THE DONKEY —

Bus Griffiths—

THE STRAWLINE IS UNHOOKED, AND THE EYE OF THE HAULBACK IS FASTENED TO THE EYE OF THE MAINLINE WITH A SMALL SHACKLE THAT WILL PASS THRU THE SHEAVE OF THE BULL BLOCK---THEN THE PUNCHER "GOES AHEAD" ON THE HAULBACK-

THIS PULLS THE MAINLINE

UP

THRU THE BULL BLOCK AND DOWN

TO THE BLOCK ON THE LOG, IN FRONT OF THE SPAR TREE-

THE LINES ARE THREADED!

LOGGING TERMS

*"IN LEAD"—THE HOOK-TENDER CLIMBS BE-TWEEN THE DRUMS ON THE WINCH AND SIGHTS FROM THE UNDERSIDE, ALONG THE FLANGE OF THE DRUMS TO THE BLOCKS IN THE TREE, TO MAKE SURE THE LINES WILL SPOOL PROPERLY— IF THE MACHINE IS NOT IN LEAD, THE NOSE OF THE SLEIGH IS MOVED TO ONE SIDE OR THE OTHER TO MAKE THE ADJUSTMENT—
*"PUNCHER"-ENGINEER
*"DONKEY"—A SLEIGH-MOUNTED MACHINE WITH DRUMS FOR SPOOLING CABLE— POWERED BY STEAM, GAS, AND LATER, BY DIESEL —

WHILE YOU CLEAR UP THE PASSLINE, I'LL TAKE OUT THE STRAW-LINE AND START STRINGIN' YOUR ROADS—

GOOD! MY FIRST ROAD WILL BE ON THE SQUARE LEAD AN' THE CORNER BLOCK WILL BE FOUR ROADS OVER— I'LL DROP IN WITH EACH ROAD, AN' THEN SWAP LINES TO GET HAULBACK ON THE UPPER SIDE—

THAT'S TH' IDEA! NOW LISSEN, *"CHASER" YOU WATCH THE PASSLINE ON THE DRUM WHILE AL'S IN THE CHAIN, BUT AS SOON AS HE'S DOWN THE TREE, YOU COME AN' PULL STRAWLINE—WHEN TH' FIRST EXTENSION COMES OFF TH' DRUM YOU HOLLER AN' CUT HER OFF

SURE

WHEN DAN *"CUTS HER OFF" I'LL START OUT ON SQUARE LEAD WITH TH' NEXT EXTENSION

EVERYTHING WENT SMOOTHLY— AL GOT THE PASSLINE CLEARED UP AND TIED OFF TO ONE SIDE, CLEAR OF THE CHAFING OF THE YARDING LINES —

MEANWHILE, ART AND THE REST OF THE CREW ARE PULLING OUT THE STRAWLINE

*"THAT'S LINE"

THAT'S LINE, ART— THE EXTENSION'S OUT—

GOOD!

OKAY, YOU GUYS! HEAD IN AND GIVE AL A PULL ON THE OTHER EXTENSION—

*"CHASER"— HE UNHOOKS THE CHOKERS FROM LOGS AT SPAR TREE— GENERALLY REQUIRED TO BE A GOOD CABLE SPLICER
*"CUT HER OFF"— UNHOOK--- DISCONNECT
*"THAT'S LINE"— MEANS ENOUGH LINE HAS BEEN PULLED BY HAND —

AL PULLS THE END OF THE STRAWLINE OUT ON SQUARE LEAD, THRU THE TAIL BLOCK AND ALONG THE *"BACKLINE"— HE COUPLES UP HIS END OF THE LINE TO THE EXTENSION THAT ART HAD PULLED OUT —

THAT'S LINE! GO AHEAD ON THE STRAWLINE WHENEVER YOU'RE READY, CHASER---- YOU WATCH THAT BLOCK DON'T FOUL, RED —

*"BACKLINE"— THE LINE THAT RUNS BETWEEN THE WOODS' BLOCKS

DAN, THE CHASER, HOOKS THE STRAW-LINE TO THE EYE OF THE HAULBACK LINE, AND AT HIS SIGNAL THE DONKEY PUNCHER ENGAGES THE FRICTION ON THE STRAWLINE DRUM, SLACKS THE BRAKE ON THE HAULBACK AND OPENS THE THROTTLE ON THE BIG *"STEAM POT"— WITH A THROATY STACCATO, THE HAULBACK LINE IS PULLED OUT THRU THE WOODS' BLOCKS AND BACK IN TO THE FOOT OF THE SPAR TREE —

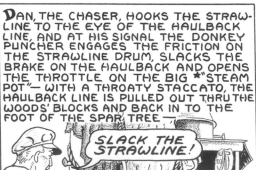

SLACK THE STRAWLINE!

*"STEAM POT"— A DONKEY POWERED BY STEAM —

WHILE THE RIGGING CREW IS STRINGING OUT THE YARDING ROADS, HOWIE, THE *"WHISTLE PUNK" IS TAKING OUT HIS WHISTLE WIRE — HE OPERATES A JERKWIRE WHISTLE, WHICH CONSISTS, SIMPLY, OF A TAUT WIRE STRETCHED FROM THE VALVE ON THE WHISTLE TO A SPRINGPOLE ON THE ROOF OF THE DONKEY, THEN OUT TO THE WOODS — A SPRING HOLDS THE VALVE CLOSED AND ANY JERK ON THE TAUT WIRE OPENS THE VALVE AND OPERATES THE WHISTLE —

BEING A RATHER INGENIOUS LAD, HOWIE HAS INCORPORATED SOME OF HIS OWN IDEAS INTO THE SYSTEM — HE HAS THE WIRE ON A SPOOL WHICH IS MOUNTED ON THE FRAME OF A PACKBOARD — AS HE WALKS OUT FROM THE DONKEY THE WIRE UNWINDS, CONTROLLED BY HIS GLOVED HAND —

HE HAS THREADED A NUMBER OF OLD, PORCELAIN INSULATORS ON THE WIRE, AND EACH HAS A PIECE OF CORD ATTACHED — WHEN A LENGTH OF WIRE HAS UNWOUND FROM THE SPOOL, HOWIE TAKES OFF HIS PACK, AND GOES BACK AND STRINGS UP HIS WIRE, ATTACHING THE INSULATORS TO ANY CONVENIENT SAPLING, ETC. —

REACHING A VANTAGE POINT, FROM WHICH HE CAN BOTH SEE AND HEAR THE RIGGING CREW, HOWIE TAKES THE PACK FROM HIS BACK, WINDS THE WIRE TIGHT WITH THE CRANK ON THE SPOOL AND JAMS THE CONTRAPTION BETWEEN ANY CONVENIENT OBJECTS TO KEEP THE LINE TIGHT —

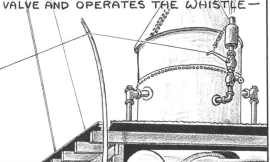

WHEN HOWIE WANTS TO "PICK UP" HIS WHISTLE WIRE HE JUST REVERSES THE PACK, SO THAT THE SPOOL IS IN FRONT OF HIM AND WINDS THE LINE UP, UNTIEING THE INSULATORS AS HE COMES TO THEM —

AND NOW, HOWIE HAS HIS WHISTLE WIRE STRETCHED OUT, THE CHASER HAS COUPLED THE HAULBACK TO THE BUTT RIGGING ON THE END OF THE MAINLINE, AND, TRUE TO ART'S EARLIER PREDICTION, THE CREW IS LOGGING IN HALF AN HOUR —

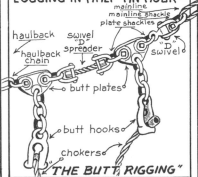

mainline
mainline shackle
plate shackles
haulback
swivel "D" spreader
haulback chain
"D" swivel
← butt plates →
butt hooks
chokers

"THE BUTT RIGGING"

LOGGING TERMS

*"WHISTLE PUNK" SIGNAL MAN ON YARDING CREW — HE RELAYS THE SHOUTED ("SCREAMED") SIGNALS FROM THE HOOKTENDER AND RIGGING SLINGER, IN TO THE ENGINEER ON THE DONKEY, BY MEANS OF HIS WHISTLE WIRE —

BUS Griffiths —

45

DON'T PUT THE CHOKERS IN THE BUTT HOOKS, DAN— WE'LL GET "SLACKLINE" TO STAND THE RIGGIN' UP!

GIVE 'EM A *"TIGHTLINE", HOWIE! WHOO-WHOO-WHOO-WHOO-WHOO-

TOOT TOOT TOOT TOOT TOOT TOOT

THREE JETS OF STEAM, CLOSELY FOLLOWED BY TWO MORE, SHOOT SKYWARD AS THE SHRILL WHISTLES PIERCE THE AFTERNOON AIR, AND ECHO ALONG THE HILLS—
THERE IS A SHARP BURST OF POWER FROM THE BIG YARDER AS "SLACKLINE" THE ENGINEER, OPENS THE THROTTLE, AND THE LINES SPRING CLEAR OF THE BRUSH, TO STAND QUIVVERING FOR A MOMENT, LIKE STEEL RIBBONS ETCHED AGAINST THE SKY--- THEN THE LINES ARE SLACKED DOWN AND DAN, THE CHASER, CLICKS THE CHOKER KNOBS INTO THE BUTT HOOKS—

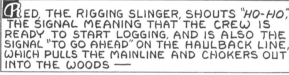

RED, THE RIGGING SLINGER, SHOUTS "HO-HO", THE SIGNAL MEANING THAT THE CREW IS READY TO START LOGGING, AND IS ALSO THE SIGNAL "TO GO AHEAD" ON THE HAULBACK LINE, WHICH PULLS THE MAINLINE AND CHOKERS OUT INTO THE WOODS

HI!---SLACK 'ER DOWN!

TOOT TOOT-TOOT-TOOT-TOOT-TOO TOOT-TOOT-TOOT-TOOT

ONCE THE BOYS GET THESE BASTARDS CLOSE TO THE TREE PICKED UP, SHE'LL BE CLEAR SAILIN'

YEAH--- BUT WE DON'T WANT TOO BIG A PILE AT THE TREE UNTIL WE GET THAT LOADIN' RIGGIN' UP HERE!

THEY'LL FINISH LOADIN' OUT AT THE OLD SETTIN' TO-DAY— WE'LL STRIP THE TREE TO-MORROW

GOOD! THEN WE CAN GET THE BOOM AN' THE REST OF THE LOADIN' RIGGIN' UP HERE AN' GET DOWN TO SOME SERIOUS LOGGIN'!

IT DON'T TAKE DAN LONG TO SNAP THE CHOKERS OFF! HE SETS THE LOGS OUT GOOD FOR THE LOADERS, TOO!

YEAH, HE'S GOOD-- HE TAKES PRIDE IN HIS WORK- THAT'S A BIG THING IN A MAN, HAVING PRIDE IN HIS WORK--- WITHOUT IT HE DON'T AMOUNT TO A PINCH OF SNOOSE!

LOGGING TERMS

*"TIGHTLINE"— SIGNAL FOR ENGINEER TO "GO AHEAD" ON BOTH MAIN AND HAULBACK— THIS TIGHTENS ONE LINE AGAINST THE OTHER, AND "STANDS THE RIGGING UP," CLEAR OF ALL OBSTRUCTIONS

"THE CHOKERS SAIL OUT, AND RED, THE RIGGING SLINGER, BARKS HIS SIGNALS TO THE WHISTLE PUNK—WHITE JETS OF STEAM SHOOT SKYWARD, TO HANG LIKE MISTY PLUMES AGAINST THE DARK TRUNK OF THE SPAR TREE, AND THE SHRILL WHISTLES ECHO ALONG THE HEAVILY TIMBERED HILLS— THE CLINK OF METAL ON METAL CAN BE HEARD AS THE CHOKER MEN DRAG OUT THE STEEL CHOKERS AND SET THEM ON THE BIG BROWN LOGS—

A SINGLE SHOUT FROM RED, ONE SHRILL BLAST FROM THE WHISTLE, AND A JET OF STEAM SHOOTS UP— THERE IS A BURST OF POWER FROM THE BIG YARDER AS 'SLACKLINE' OPENS THE THROTTLE— TWO LOGS LEAP FROM THE BRUSH, CRASHING DOWN SNAGS, UPROOTING SAPLINGS, BOUNCING OFF STUMPS, AS THEY FOLLOW THE PULL OF THE MAINLINE AND BUMP AND SLIDE IN TOWARDS THE SPAR TREE— THE TURN REACHES THE LANDING AND THE SHARP JANGLE OF THE BUTT RIGGING CAN BE HEARD AS THE ENGINEER SLACKS THE LINES— THERE IS A SLIGHT PAUSE, AND THE CLINK OF METAL, AS THE CHASER GOES OUT TO UNHOOK THE TURN, THEN THE QUIETER SOUND OF THE HAULBACK WORKING AS THE CHOKERS SAIL OUT TO THE WOODS AGAIN—

ALL AFTERNOON THE CHOKERS SAIL OUT AND THE LOGS THUMP AND CRASH IN TO THE LANDING, UNTIL, FINALLY----

TOOT-TOOT-TOOT--TOOT-TOOT-TOOT--TOOT-TOOT--TOOT

THERE'S THE *"SLACKOFF"! LET'S GO, BOYS!

YOU RIDE WITH ME IN THE PICKUP, AL— SURE HOPE WE DON'T GET HELD UP TOO LONG WITH 'EM LOADIN' OUT AT THE OLD SETTIN'

MAYBE WE'LL BE LUCKY, ART! THEY MIGHT BE ALL FINISHED!

WE'RE IN LUCK! "CHILLIWACK" IS PUTTIN' THE *"PEAKER" ON BARNEY NOW— GOD! THAT'S ONE HELL OF A LOAD !!!

BARNEY WHEELS THE BIG TRUCK OUT OF THE LANDING, AND STOPS OPPOSITE THE *"TURNAROUND" TO ALLOW THE FOREMAN'S PICKUP AND THE CRUMMY, BEARING THE REST OF THE YARDING CREW, TO PASS—

THAT KNOTHEAD MUST HAVE DRY ROT BETWEEN HIS EARS, THROWIN' A LOAD LIKE THAT ON OL' BARNEY--- I THINK I'LL JUST STOP A MINUTE AND SMARTEN THAT BASTARD UP!

LOGGING TERMS
*"SLACKOFF"—
QUITTING WHISTLE

*"PEAKER"—
TOP LOG ON THE LOAD

*"TURNAROUND" (TURNOUT)— A WIDE SPOT IN THE ROAD WHERE THE TRUCKS CAN TURN AROUND, OR PASS

Bus Griffiths—

47

ART STOPS IN THE *"LANDING" TO "CHEW OUT" THE *"HEAD LOADER"~

WHAT TH' *HELL* YOU TRYIN' T'DO, "CHILLIWACK", PUTTIN' A LOAD LIKE *THAT* ON POOR OL' BARNEY? YOU MUST HAVE ROCKS IN YOUR GODDAMNED HEAD!

WELL, YOU GUYS ARE *ALWAYS BELLYACHIN'* FOR *MORE* BLOODY LOGS

LISTEN, YOU SMART-ASSED *BASTARD*--DON'T GIVE *ME* ANY OF YOUR GUFF-- *I'LL* SHARPEN YOUR FEET AN' DRIVE *YOU* INTO THE GROUND! YOU'LL BUST THEM GODDAMNED TRUCKS IF YOU PUT ON MANY LOADS LIKE *THAT!*

ER--A--- WELL--A--- I WANTED TO FINISH UP, ART! THAT LOAD DOES IT---THAT'S WHY I WOODED OL' BARNEY DOWN!

MAYBE I WAS A BIT ROUGH ON HIM--- I SUPPOSE OLD JIM HAS BEEN RIDING HIM HARD ABOUT GETTIN' THEM LOGS LOADED OUT-- BUT HE'S KIND OF A *MOUTHY BASTARD,* ANYWAY~

THANKS FOR LETTIN' US PASS BARNEY-- THAT'S A *HELLUVA LOAD* YOU'VE GOT! MAYBE I *SHOULD* RIDE ALONG BEHIND YOU---BUT I DON'T FANCY EATIN' YOUR GODDAMNED DUST ALL THE WAY DOWN TO CAMP!

THAT'S OKAY ART! IT'S SURE A HEAVY LOAD, BUT I'LL TAKE IT EASY!

YEAH— *YOU* MAKE SURE YOU *DO THAT!*

*J*HE END OF A DAY'S WORK, AND THE CAVALCADE OF TRUCKS WINDS DOWN THE ROAD TOWARDS CAMP— THE SUN SINKS BEHIND THE DARKLY TIMBERED MOUNTAINS CASTING LONG SHADOWS OVER THE *"OPEN SLASH," HIGHLIGHTING THE STARK RAPE OF THE LAND ~

LOGGING TERMS

*"LANDING"~ AREA AROUND SPAR TREE WHERE LOGS ARE LANDED AND LOADED OUT

*"HEAD LOADER" HEAD MAN ON THE LOADING CREW— IN A TRUCK SHOW HE STANDS ON CAB OF TRUCK AND PICKS THE LOGS FOR HIS LOAD

*"OPEN SLASH" LOGGED-OFF COUNTRY

Bus Griffiths~

A FEW YEARS AGO A LOT OF THE GUYS SAID TRUCKS WERE NO GOOD IN THE WOODS — THEY FIGURED TRAINS WAS THE ONLY THING —

THE BIG OUTFITS ARE USING *"LOCIES" AND THEY'RE LOGGIN' IN THE BIG VALLEYS — THEY LAY THEIR STEEL IN THE BOTTOM AN' REACH UP THE SIDEHILLS AS FAR AS THEY CAN WITH THE *"SKIDDERS", OR SOME KIND OF BIG STEAM POT USING A SKYLINE SYSTEM — THE TIMBER THEY CAN'T REACH, THEY LEAVE!

"MOST OF 'EM LOAD WITH A *"DUPLEX" AN' THEY'RE USED TO SLAMMIN' THE LOGS AROUND — IF THEY KNOCK A CAR OFF THE TRACK THEY JUST GRAB IT WITH A LOADIN' TONG AN' SET IT BACK ON THE TRACK — YOU SURE AS HELL CAN'T HANDLE TRUCKS LIKE THAT!

NO — THEY'D FALL APART

A LOT OF OUTFITS TRIED TRUCKS, BUT THEY WASN'T GETTIN' ANYWHERE — THEY THOUGHT THEY COST TOO MUCH, BROKE TOO EASY, AN' WOULDN'T PACK ENOUGH WOOD — BUT THEY WAS ALL FOOLIN' AROUND WITH SINGLE-AXLE JOBS — THEN SOME OLD FARMER FROM THE FRASER VALLEY STARTED HAULING LOGS OFF VEDDER MOUNTAIN WITH TRUCKS, AN' HE SHOWED EVERYBODY HOW TO USE 'EM —

I GUESS HE WAS A MECHANIC, AN' A GOOD ONE — ANYWAY HE MADE SIX-WHEELERS OUT OF HIS TRUCKS AN' THAT WAS THE ANSWER!

THE BACK AXLE DIDN'T DRIVE, BUT IT MADE THEM INTO A BETTER TRUCK, AN' THEY'D HAUL NEARLY TWICE THE LOAD — THEY'VE COME A LONG WAY SINCE THEN, AN' IT'S JUST A MATTER OF TIME UNTIL THE TRUCKS TAKE OVER FROM THE RAILROAD SHOWS!

SINCE THE START OF THE DEPRESSION THERE'S LOTS OF *"GYPPOS" — MOST OF 'EM ARE USING TRUCKS!

MEANWHILE, THE BIG TRUCK, WITH ITS HEAVY LOAD OF LOGS, BREAKS OVER THE BROW OF THE LONG HILL ABOVE CAMP, LESS THAN A MILE BEHIND THE CRUMMY, AND THE PICKUP TRUCK, BEARING AL RICHARDS AND ART DONNEGAN —

MY GOD! THE BRAKES WON'T HOLD HER — SHE'S TOO HEAVY!

Bus Griffiths —

LOGGING TERMS
*"LOCIE" — A LOGGING LOCOMOTIVE
*"SKIDDER" — A YARDING DONKEY WITH A SKYLINE SYSTEM FOR ROUGH GROUND — ABLE TO REACH OUT 1200 ft. ON SQUARE LEAD AND 1600 ft. ON CORNERS OF THE SETTING —
*"DUPLEX" — A LOADING DONKEY WITH DOUBLE, REVERSING ENGINES —
*"GYPPOS" — REFERS TO SMALL OUTFITS — SOME WERE GOOD CAMPS, AND SOME WERE WHAT THE NAME IMPLIES — HAYWIRE FROM THE LOG DUMP TO THE TAIL BLOCKS —

49

Linda Prine

A VERY ORDINARY LIFE

Reviewed by Howard White

The most unusual local book to come our way this year has a brown paper wrapper bearing on the front a crooked snapshot of a heavyset man with a genial, unfocussed look, one hand in his pants pocket, the other stroking the family Alsatian. Beside him is his moderately overweight middle-aged frau, smiling awkwardly at the brownie as a backyard breeze plays with her calf-length print skirt. The text is on light newsprint and in the middle is a further cluster of motheaten snaps – tenement washlines, marching soldiers, dancing 1920's hippies called "Wandervogel", the woman again, younger, posing with a life-ring, the man again sitting on top of a Depression boxcar, both of them with another Alsatian beside a very crude log cabin with a Model A parked in front, the woman on the porch of a small house above Vancouver Harbour with an extravagantly beaming boy, men flocking to a camp cookhouse, the woman much later hoeing a backyard vegetable patch.

The book is called *A Very Ordinary Life* and it is the woman's story, beginning in the dank "cellar air" of a pre-first war Berlin tenement, continuing through such misadventures as panning gold in Lillooet in the thirties, working an endless succession of upcoast camps with her baker husband, ending "rusted in" by age and illness in a Burnaby apartment. Her name is Phyllis Knight and she tells the story, sensitively encouraged and edited by her boy, now an anthropologist at the University of Toronto.

In form and content the book is a tour-de-force of the commonplace. But the irony underlying it is that there is really no such thing as the commonplace. Things, like the lives of immigrant working people and books about such lives, which seem dull from where we sit, when studied closely invariably prove to conceal astonishing intelligence.

A world so nervous with rumours of war and depression as ours couldn't fail to be captivated by the accounting Phyllis Knight gives of the two world wars – seen from both sides – and three depressions she has lived through already this century. Her telling makes them as real as they could ever be for anyone who wasn't there, because she remembers them in such bread-and-butter terms:

Towards the end of the (first world) *war the government started to recruit anyone who could carry a rifle, from sixteen year old kids to men of fifty. My father was 45 when he was called . . . The upshot was he lost the printing business. All those years he scrounged and sold his soul, and he lost the whole shebang. For three years we were almost constantly hungry. Each family was entitled to a pound of bones each week – if you could get it. You'd crack the bones open with an axe and boil the marrow out of them. Talk about stone soup . . .*

In his introduction and notes Knight stresses the political implications of the story, and it does give a very clear picture of what economic oppression is in our culture, but in the end both political and historical considerations are overshadowed by the tremendously moving personal story of Phyllis Knight. By drawing his mother's personal experience out to the full extreme that he has, Knight has effectively pushed oral history technique into a literary dimension not approached by the Terkels and Broadfoots, and created a book with the emotional force of a great realistic novel.

One can go even further and argue that a book such as *A Very Ordinary Life* has an impact born of total credibility that no fictional work could equal. The thing is, this remarkable company of girlfriends, boyfriends, workmates *did* exist, and you could go to Vancouver and shake the hand of this woman to whom these all-too-real things happened – or could have until a few weeks ago. Phyllis Knight died in her Burnaby apartment this July at the age of 76, fortunately not too late to see her ordinary life made into this extraordinary book. One is tempted to hail her as a great woman and this book as a great monument to her, but the truth is she really *was* a very ordinary woman. The greatness readers will feel impelled to credit her with is the greatness that lies taken for granted, like the opal inside the dull stone, within all ordinary life.

A Very Ordinary Life, by Rolf Knight.

AMOR DE COSMOS

Reviewed by Robert Wishlaw

The writing of Canadian history has suffered from official containment with much the same loss of vitality as the making of Canadian history. Where the American style was to throw territory open to the flood and leave settlers to make order of their own chaos, it was always our way to fence the land off by official decree and establish corporate monopoly control at the outset, the better to avoid un-British developments and make certain profits went into the right pockets from the start.

In the same spirit B.C. schoolchildren have over the years been persuaded that the lordly corporation bureaucrat Douglas virtually fashioned the province from Dover clay, deviating admirably little from the blueprint handed down by Queen Victoria, while Amor de Cosmos, the local boy who threw the monkey wrench in Douglas' corporate works and opened the land to the people, has spent a hundred years waiting in the footnotes.

After such a wait it is doubly gratifying to have de Cosmos' story introduced by a biographer the stature of George Woodcock, who has made his usual hard-packed amalgam of the widely scattered facts in *Amor de Cosmos*, put out by Oxford University Press.

Amor de Cosmos was a native Canadian — a rare thing among our founding fathers — born in Nova Scotia in 1825 under the rather less inspiring name of William Smith. He went to California in 1853, too late for gold, but found a living providing courts with photographs of disputed mining claims. Woodcock does not delve at length into personal motivation, noting simply that "to change one's name is in a way to change one's life," but it was in this lowly station that William Smith became somehow infused with cosmic ambition, transformed himself Superman-fashion into "Amor de Cosmos", joined the new rush to Vancouver's Island, and began advising that colony on all aspects of its public life as first publisher of the *Colonist* newspaper.

With the example of wild-west republicanism fresh in his mind, de Cosmos found a natural enemy in the monarchic Douglas, declaring in his first issue, "Douglas is alone responsible for the corruption, speculation, wrongs, outrages, depopulation, destruction, mistakes and losses entailed in these colonies through corrupt and unfit officials . . ." He immediately proposed "the union of these colonies, the Pacific railroad, the overland wagon road . . . and, the introduction of responsible government, a system long established in America, by which the people will have whole and sole control . . ."

By 1871 he could look back and see all of these objects gained, along with one not on the original list; one bitterly opposed by the aging Douglas but more fiercely championed by de Cosmos: confederation of "these colonies" with Canada.

De Cosmos was elected to office both provincially and federally — simultaneously — and when the Douglas-backed John McCreight failed to survive his first vote of non-confidence in 1871, was chosen B.C.'s second premier. One of his first acts was to throw land open to all comers, raising the maximum pre-emption to 250 acres.

It was at the height of his power on February 7, 1874, while speaking in the legislature, that de Cosmos was interrupted by Douglas' son-in-law Helmcken at the head of a mob of 2,000 people chanting, "We'll hang de Cosmos from a sour apple tree." He escaped with being hung in effigy from a lamppost that day but the next morning his old paper broke a story charging him with serious misdealings in developing the Texada Island Iron deposits.

De Cosmos was forced to resign, and the sudden infusion of vision that had delivered him from clerk-dom 16 years earlier seems to have as suddenly forsaken him, for though he was cleared of all charges by a royal commission, he never returned to an active role in provincial politics. He became reclusive and with an obsessive fear of electricity — he wouldn't enter a building that was wired — and took in his last years to wandering the streets of Nanaimo making incoherent pronouncements in an insane parody of his former circumstance. His death in 1897 was so pathetic even his old nemesis Helmcken was moved to write,

"*. . . that such a man should come to this . . . such a funeral is neither worth living for nor dying for . . . governments, corporations and the public seem to have no hearts, no sentiments, no memory . . .*"

Like Riel, de Cosmos was just too blood-coloured, to messily real to have been fitted into the drab weave our official mythmakers seem to have wished our written history to be. Although one might have wished for more on the complex and intriguing personality behind the name, Woodcock has made a well documented case for now recognizing de Cosmos as a major influence in this province's making.

Amor de Cosmos by **George Woodcock**

THE COWICHAN

Reviewed by Peter Trower

Working men silhouetted against the risen sun
Like dancers lifting the steel bite of heavy boots
From log to log with rapid step and leap
Or balancing, walk a long pole
Cross the plunge of a deep ravine

A kind of ballet
A kind of circus act

This is how it can begin.

That's the dance of the woods all right and the opening poem in David Day's fine collection of logging verse *The Cowichan*. David did that rough dance for five years in various Vancouver Island camps and knows whereof he speaks. He crafts his material with a spare clarity, counterpointing the caught immediacy of his own experiences with poems that speak in the earthy argot of the old-time brushape. This balance works very effectively — old and new woods images intermingling to move the reader back and forth between past and present. Conditions in the pre-union

51

camps — the low wages, animalistic living quarters and disregard for human limb or life — are spelled out in tough, uncompromising verse that often hits like a belly-punch. Yet there is humour too and passages of haunting beauty inform the more lyrical pieces. This is a masterly grouping of deft, accessible poems that describe the logger's predicament in no uncertain fashion. I recommend it wholeheartedly both to lovers of good poetry and *Raincoast Chronicles* readers in general.

The Cowichan by David Day

WHISTLE UP THE INLET *and* THE PRINCESS STORY

Reviewed by Howard White

You'd get on the boat, get your stateroom and all, snoop around to see if there was any babes on board, maybe get together in somebody's room for a drink and a bit of b.s. you see. Well before you know it the boat's comin', let's say, into Lasqueti Island, you'd all go out and hang over the rail, everybody on the Island'd be there on the dock, there'd always be someone you'd know. Charlie Klein'd be trying to talk you into gettin' off to help him for a couple weeks, women'd be shouting scandal back and forth, some gyppo maybe would be there catchin' freight and guys up on the boat'd after him about work, he'd be sayin' well have you ever run a Skagit, yup, well there'd be last minute wage negotiations, the skipper'd be listening from the bridge to see which way it went, maybe hold the boat a bit, people'd be stumbling along the dock still yappin' as the boat eased back, shoutin' and wavin', and this would go on all the way up the line to Rivers Inlet, at every stop. That kinda kept things stuck together you see, the coast was like a buncha people along a street seeing each other on the way by all the time. It got to be kind of a family affair. It seemed all a lot closer together than it does now."

Jim Mackay, 76, Minstrel Island, July 30, 1974

Mention of the Union Steamship Company recalls for most people an era when the B.C. coast was in its heyday and every bay from Bowen Island to Portland Inlet was occupied by camps, ranches, canneries, Indian villages all welded together in one long unlikely community by the common lifeline of the steamer route. It is an era now established in memory as a kind of golden age of the coast, and like all golden ages there is a bottomless nostalgic fascination with it among those who survived it. The Union Steamship Company, on whose back so much of the adventure was borne, is central to any picture of those days, not because of anything special about its boats, but because of the trips that were taken on them; not because of the people who built and managed the boats, but because of the people who used them.

It is this point that Gerald Rushton neglects in his book about the Union Steamship Company, *Whistle Up the Inlet*. Rushton, whose father was in the parent Welsford company in Britain and who himself spent most of his life working for the B.C. company, makes passing mention here and there of pioneer families like the Thulins of Lund or the Calvert Simsons of Thormanby Island and periodically lists the Pacofis, Brems and China Hats that sprang into being as steamer stops, but the greater part of his book is concerned with the official machinations of the company. Chapters begin with quotations of speeches by company directors and the tone consistently verges on and frequently plunges into corporate hagiography: ". . . the torch of Union traditions handed on to Harold Brown from Gordon Legg, Henry Darling, John Barnsley and Ernest Beazley was still alight, even if it flickered a bit during the thirties . . ."

But it's a waste of time to criticize books for what they aren't. *Whistle Up the Inlet* is an extremely evenly textured piece of writing considering it's Rushton's first effort and the book does detail the origins and work histories of the boats with a thoroughness and authority that will delight the maritime history buffs. If he leaves the better part of the Union story untold, Rushton is nevertheless to be admired for making a start where no one else has.

Norman Hacking and Kaye Lamb approach the job similarly in their history of the Canadian Pacific Steamship Company, but *The Princess Story* seems to work better. The Canadian Pacific can trace its blood directly to the *Beaver* and *Otter* of the early Hudson's Bay Company fleet and its corporate genesis is much livelier than that of the stodgily colonial Union Steamships. The direct forbear of the modern Canadian Pacific line was Canadian Pacific Navigation whose founder and chief inspirer, John Irving, is developed by Hacking into a character of Falstaffian dimensions. Hacking is of course one of the most respected maritime writers on the west coast and he has seldom turned in a better job, managing even to restore life to the legend of the *Beaver*. The section by Kaye Lamb covering the period from 1900 to the present is necessarily less dramatic although it throws interesting light on several of the famous disasters, particularly the loss of the *Princess Sophia* with 343 people in October 1919 — the worst wreck in the history of coastal transport. The book is a must for ship lovers.

Whistle Up the Inlet by Gerald A. Rushton

The Princess Story by Norman A. Hacking and W. Kaye Lamb

SHADOW-SHAMANS

Koyah the Raven and Ninstints of the Eagle Crest were two powerful Haida chiefs during the 1800's. They lived on Skang'wai (Red Cod Island), what is now called Anthony Island, off the south-west coast of the Queen Charlottes.

Their bones sleep
in the forest
fallen behind the
rain-wall.
I heard laughter
and a
ghost-raven,
his skin was like a
pale sea-flower.

I heard it was
Koyah,
chief of
Raven-town.
He told me
this story:

*Skulkinance was a great chief who had
two sons. These were called Koh and
Skindaskun. They lived in the village
called Cadadjans where everyone was
always talking.
Skulkinance was returning to his village
with his two sons. They had been hunting
for seals up the coast.
They stopped at night to make a fire and
cook some devil-fish. Skunkinance felt
the presence of enemies.
"Koh" he said, addressing his eldest son.
"go to the canoe and get me my harpoon."
Koh replied that he had no use for it and
besides that he was too hungry.
"Skindaskun" he said, addressing his
younger son, "go to the canoe and get me
my harpoon." Skindaskun replied that he
had no use for it and besides he was too
sleepy.
Skulkinance addressed each of his sons a
second time.
Again they disobeyed him.
Then Skulkinance jumped up, ran down to
the canoe, climbed in and pushed himself
far out to sea.
He looked back over his shoulder and saw
his sons lying with their throats cut
open. In the firelight he could see one
arm of the devil-fish they had just finished
eating. One arm was reaching out of both
their throats.*

I saw
armbones in the
rock-pools,
heard thunder
in the dark.
I saw it was
Ninstints,
chief of the
Eagles.
He told me
this story:

*Once I was nobody.
I went to the top of a mountain and
stayed there for a long time. I ate
devil's club. I ate whatever I could find.
I wanted to know what my name would be.
Then I came down from the mountain and I
was sick for a long time. The shaman sang
for me and I opened my mouth to tell him
what I had seen. Some rats just came
running out of my stomach. The last one
to run out of me was white.
The people in the village gathered there
to see it. "Give me back my own" I cried
to them. The last one to come out of me
meant that I had eaten a small spirit.
Then I was somebody.
My people called me a chief and
told me what my name would be.
My people called me their chief,
He-who-is-equal-to-two.*

I found
rain-stones
under the
tree roots,
fire-pits in the
ghost-lodge.

I went to sleep
in a nest of
ravens
but woke up holding
the claw of an eagle.

Susan Musgrave

HIGH COUNTRY BURN

Peter Trower

Illustrated by Belinda McLeod

IT'S HIGH SUMMER IN THE HIGH HILLS and several degrees more torrid than the hobs of hell. The scale on the humidity gauge dips ever closer to the danger level. There hasn't been the barest dribble of rain in well over a month. Trees rustle thirstily in bonedry breezes. The coastal timberlands have become tinderlands and orange fingers are scratching through the green in countless places. The situation is beginning to be described as critical and a total forest closure appears certain. I'm blowing whistles for a gyppo camp in a steep, narrow valley. I've seen fires from a distance before but never actually fought one. I vaguely hope the Forestry will shut the woods down before I'm obliged to learn how.

Finn Billy, fearless highwire artist of spartrees, is tending hook. He's a small, ruddy, excitable man who runs a tight hill but keeps off your back as long as you do your work with reasonable competence. At the moment, he's struggling with a hung-up fir log a few hundred feet below me and I listen intently for his falsetto signals, interspersed with lower-pitched but quite audible cursing. I don't blame him for blowing his top. It's uncomfortable enough just sitting in this heat, let alone moving around. My brother, who's pulling rigging, takes a grateful break with his chokermen about halfway between. They're smoking like I am, roll-your-own cigarettes made with Chantecleer papers that don't burn worth a damn but are all you're allowed to use when the brush is this dry.

Billy gets the choker re-set, runs clear and goes ahead on her with an exasperated hoot. The log rolls free and kicks on down the hill. The mountain throbs and simmers in the sun. I'd get in the shade if I could but I have to stay out in the open where I can see the crew. I'm squatting on a high first-growth cedar stump about twenty feet outside the roadline. The haulback cable unreels tight as catgut, lean and silver, braking the huge paylog as it crunches in to the landing. I'm only fifty-some feet from the tail block that hangs on a fir at the timberline. It needs oiling, and whines and rasps evilly as the haulback rushes through it, spinning its weary wheel. The line grates against the block-shell and I see the sparks flash free.

I've seen that old block throw sparks before. Finn Billy's always talking about bringing out the grease-gun and socking some oil to her but he's never gotten around to it. It's too late now because this time the sparks hit something dry as guncotton and all of a sudden, flames are tonguing up from the bracken. I watch them, half-drowsily for a second until the significance of what has happened snaps me awake. Goddamit! What's the signal for fire? I can't remember so I blow four or five longs on the whistle and head over to the block. Already it's too widespread to stamp out. There's supposed to be a backpump full of water around here someplace. I locate it but it's fallen over on its side and most of the water's leaked out thorugh a loose cap. Nothing's left in the damn thing but a few rusty feeble streams that have about as much effect as spitting in the sea. The fire's already become a ten-foot circle that expands visibly. The machine's shut off and the others are heading up. "Hey, we need water!" I holler helplessly.

"Jesus! She's sure spreading fast!" pants Chris as he arrives at the back end with his chokermen close behind.

Finn Billy's up on a stump waving his arms like a madman at the landing crew. "Hey, we got a friggin' fire here! Skin us some water back quick!"

They're running around like a gang of headless chickens down below. Finally they get a drum of water and two or three full back-packs tied to the rigging and start running it up mountain. It's hopeless. There's sixty square feet of ground already burning and the flames are expanding like ripples. A contrary wind has sprung up from nowhere to whip it ever wider and wilder. Billy and the others start cutting loose the gear but the thing's already beyond control

54

and heading down on me like a hungry dragon with that badluck wind behind it.

"Hell with her!" says Billy. "May as well run this stuff back in and get down to the tree. We ain't about to stop that whore now!"

The flames have almost reached the stump where I was sitting. I head over there and start winding in the whistle-wire. Behind me the ever-spreading flames crackle and spit. I stumble downhill, looping the black rubber coils round my neck. It's like an enormous black collar by the time I reach the donkey and thankfully hang it up on its peg at the back. My neck's sore from the pinching weight.

The rest of them are running in the lines before the fire ruins them. Ab Halsam, one of the owners who doubles as cat-operator along with his younger brother Roy, stalks about lividly. "Goddammit Billy, how did that sonofabitch start?" He turns, his bald head gleaming and fixes me with a baleful glance. "Started right close to where you was sittin', punk. You been watching them cigarettes?"

"Sure, Ab," you gulp, as he's a formidable-looking man with thick black eyebrows and a menacing wrestler's glare. "It was sparks from the tailblock. I seen them hit the ground." I tell him about the spilled watercan.

"Oh yeah." He can't lay the blame directly on anyone. The fire's there just the same, widening fast like a crackling red rash over the splintery hill. It's largely a cedar show and the claim's littered with combustible wreckage. The flames eat into it like hungry animals. Now they've found the fat juices of the standing timber. In a popping burst, they crash up like water through the boughs, laugh wildly in the crowns. "Jesus! She's into the bloody trees. We'd better get the hell organized here!"

All at once there's a bedlam of frenzied and half-confused activity, the main purpose of which is to get the donkey moved out of range. No time to drop the high-lead blocks. She's roaring down the sidehill like Niagara Falls with that ill mountain wind still pushing her. A singed fir log with the ground eaten out from under it comes barrelling down the slope like a juggernaut, crashes by about thirty feet uproad from the spar, down and down to echo away in the creek bottom. But it's hard to hear echoes above the angry crackling.

"Hey, come on there!" urges Finn Billy. "Let's get them tie-up lines cut loose. Fetch the spike bar and hammer, kid!"

I locate them on the cluttered deck of the machine and four of us bang and tug free the railroad spikes from the two stumps to which the donkey's anchored. The machine's an early model diesel-fake on an extra heavy sled. Roy backs his cat up and hooks on. He pulls the donkey a short distance but it's much too slow for Billy.

"Mister Jesus! Hook the other cat on her for Christ sake! Them flames'll be hitting the landing any damn time!"

Ab, who's been bulldozing the landing free of debris to make a better firebreak, glowers blackly and seems about to make some retort. He and Billy have almost come to blows on several occasions. But this is no time for fighting. He swallows his annoyance, brings the cat over and Chris hooks his line on

the other lug. Together they manhandle the giant donkey away at a good clip till they hit the slope where one cat can manage it. Ab jumps off his machine, grabs the old Army four-by-four they use for a crummy and, commandeering the two chokermen and the chaser, rares off down the hill to phone the Forestry and borrow pump equipment from the nearby pulpmill. The rest of us are left to keep an eye on things which is about all we can do, and from a healthy distance. A fiery root, its last ties with the ground burned free, comes whirling crazily like a cockeyed, sideheavy wheel, a deadly sparkspitting tumbleweed that crashes across the landing and over the spot the donkey has just vacated.

"Sure didn't get her out of there any too soon, eh?" says Billy to Chris, shaking his head. The donkey's safe for the time being, a thousand feet down the road and still going. No telling how big this bastard's going to get.

"If the wind takes her over the hill," says Chris, "the damn thing could burn right through to town!"

"Sure hope that don't happen," I remark with some concern. The stump ranch where we both live with our mother and younger brother lies in bottom country between here and the milltown and will get hit first if the fire heads that way. They must be able to see the smoke from down there by now if they're looking in this direction. It's pouring and roiling up the sky above the snarling inferno the hill's become. Even from where we're standing, a couple of hundred feet down the road, we can feel the intense, withering heat through the lesser heat of the day. I back off from its fierce breath. Roy, who's walked back up the hill, jumps aboard Ab's cat and rattles it away from the immediate danger.

The flames are in the landing now, chewing at the chunks and cold-decked logs with impatient appetite. Now the spar itself, a pitchy, secondgrowth fir, is on fire. Red claws swarm up it like a gang of high-riggers from hell till its a blazing pillar against the blazing slope. It's a perversely exhilarating sight. We watch fascinated as the guylines blacken and the highlead blocks sizzle in their own grease.

"Well, I guess you'll never have to strip that one now, Bill," says Roy, impressed and seemingly unconcerned that its his timber going up in smoke. "Look at the old bitch burn!"

There's a strange sense of futile unreality as I stand there with the others, watching that raw energy cutting loose. It's pure force, unleashed and greedy, and nothing can quell the fury of its first onrush. All you can do is watch, wait and back further down the road as the heat intensifies. So far it's not burning in our direction to any marked degree as there's an old creekbed between that's acting as a natural firebreak. But it's a narrow gap and the fire'll leap it like a broad jumper if the wind switches direction. In that event, there'll be nothing to do but run.

Somehow several hours have slipped away since this all began. It's getting to be late afternoon. Far off down the road, I can hear the four-by-four returning, struggling up the steep grade with every ounce of its power. It roars and strains into view. Ab floorboards her to the top and jumps out, wild-eyed.

"Let's get these pumps and the hose unloaded!" he shouts urgently. "We got to get some water on that bastard. Maybe we can save a bit of this goddamn timber!"

Everyone flies to it. It's a relief to be making some sort of positive move, however futile it may prove to be. The immediate task involves getting the pumps down to the creek, which is several hundred feet below in the V of the valley. We struggle with them along old deer trails and no trails at all, tripping through salal bushes, down slippery banks, over windfalls toward the remote gurgle of the water. It's an awkward bitch of a job and we're all getting snarly by the time we reach the bottom. Roy stays there to get the pumps running. The rest of us puff back up to the road and start stringing hose.

Finally we get everything connected and functioning after a fashion. They've strung one line clear to the top in an effort to kill the flames in the standing trees. But there's little pressure because of the slope and the distance. It's a token gesture at best. The fire snarls savagely on the ridge and seems a sure cinch to burn over the top.

The Forest Ranger pulls up now in a green truck with government decals on the doors. He's an adenoidal type with glasses who looks to be fresh off campus but he speaks with crisp authority as he sizes up the situation. Ab obviously doesn't much enjoy being told what to do by this wet-behind-the-ears dude but he's a logger not a fireman so he listens dutifully. The guy wants to know how it began and I repeat my story. "You fellows should check those back-packs once in a while to make sure they're full," he says but doesn't pursue the matter any further.

There's a third pump and a couple of miles more hose in the back of the Ranger's truck. Again we make the awkward descent to the creek, everyone straining and bitching worse than the first time. It's beginning to get late and we've been out in the weeds since five this morning. We're starting, now the initial excitement's worn off, to feel tired and hungry. Someone's supposed to be fetching sandwiches and coffee from the mill cafeteria but they haven't arrived yet. At length they get there and we break from stringing what seems like interminable coils of canvas pipe, to eat. I sit down beside Chris on a roadside log.

"Wonder howinhell long we're going to have to stay out here?"

"Heard them saying something about a crew from the mill coming out at eight o'clock to relieve us. Guess the brass down there are getting panicky. She's still burning bad in the top timber."

"Christ! That's another three hours yet! Well, we're getting paid for it anyhow, that's one consolation."

"Sure," says Chris, "and we're getting our regular rate too. No lousy Forestry six bits an hour. You only get paid that if they call you out themselves."

"Hell, that's okay," I say, feeling better.

The dry creekbed is still effectively preventing the fire from spreading down valley but it's backburning furiously and snapping among the trees on the fateful ridge. So far the wind has been against any really serious advances in that direction but the wind may change. It's still in the lap of the gods.

I finish eating and man one of the hoses for a bit but with the low and erratic pressure, it only amounts to a feeble nibbling at the edge of the hard-dancing blaze. Finally, near eight, the relief crew from the pulp mill shows up. They climb out of the truck and cluster in a bunch, gazing about dubiously. One or two of them have managed to scrounge caulk boots from someplace. The rest are ill-shod for scrambling around mountainsides. But that's their problem. I'm too bushed to care one way or the other. I pile thankfully into the four-by-four with the others, leaving the fate of the country in the hands of the bookish-looking Ranger and a motley crew of mostly greenhorns.

They drop Chris and myself off near the stump ranch where our mother and brother wait worriedly. Years later, my brother will recall us kicking down the darkening road that evening, caulks striking sparks from the pebbles as though we're bringing a bit of that fiery mountain home with us. The red glow beyond the ridge is frighteningly visible in the gathering dusk and it seems to be breaking over in a couple of places. But there's nothing much we can do about it. If the thing takes off it takes off. We eat a belated supper, down two or three bottles of beer and hit the sack. Despite the long day, it's difficult to sleep. We talk for some time before drifting off.

My dreams are busy, nervous, full of incendiary after-images and continuing extrapolations of flame and smoke ravening unstoppably across the land. I'm running glue-footed down a slippery, treadmill road that leads only to another relentless palisade of waiting fire. The mountains go up like haystacks on every red horizon. I'm alone in a self-consuming universe. There's no escape.

I wake sweating, unable to separate reality from nightmare for confusing seconds but all seems quiet. Only the soft tick of the clock, the normal, small forest sounds from the black woods around me. I slip on my shoes and pay a quick visit to the moonlit outhouse. There's still a crimson glare on the mountain shoulder but the air is motionless, without the faintest suspicion of a breeze. None of the horrific visions have come to pass. I'm relieved and obscurely disappointed at the same time.

Since I've been working early shift for over a week, neither Chris nor myself is able to sleep much beyond five a.m., despite the knowledge that we don't have to relieve the night-shift till eight. We throw some breakfast and sandwiches together and sit around listening to the radio and waiting. It proves to be a futile exercise. No one comes at the usual time and it's getting on for nine before Finn Billy shows up in the crummy.

"Guess you guys can go back and catch some more shuteye," he says. "Ab wants you to switch shifts and go on fire watch tonight."

"Goddamn!" says Chris, "I wish they'd let us know earlier. I guess that's what we get for not having a phone."

"How's the fire going?" I ask Billy.

"Seems to be dying down pretty good. It's still burning further up the valley but it's just about out in the timber. Pure shithouse luck! Looked for sure it'd spread this way. You guys must live right."

"Hardly," says Chris. "Say, how did that gang from the plant make out with no caulk shoes?"

"Pretty fair considering. Took one of them home with a twisted ankle but the rest seemed to hack it

all right." He revs the motor. "Well, take her easy.
I think Roy's going to pick you up in the evening."
He throws in the clutch and roars away.

I return to the cabin somewhat frustratedly. Now
I've got a whole unexpected day to deal with. There's
an odd feeling of somehow being left out of things.
Chris and I end up, of course, in the local pub,
discussing the fire with the gang of the regulars, but
we have to keep a rein on the boozing because of the
night duty. All too soon it's evening and Roy, who
lacks his brother's overbearing manner, picks us up at
the roadside.

"Just the three of us going out," he says, grinning.

"She's still burning some but looks like the worst is
over. Think we'll even be able to salvage some of the
logs. Lot of the stuff around the edges only got
scorched a bit."

Chris makes a wry face. "I logged a burn around
Minstrel, a couple of years back," he reflects. "Pretty
messy job!"

"Ah, it ain't so bad. We'll give you an extra buck
a day dirty-money."

And then we're back on the mountain with night
falling. Billy and the others have all gone home. The
spar's still standing, a gnawed, black monolith, ghostly against the sky. The fire's still smouldering over

several sloping acres of ruined wood and the landing's cluttered with smoking debris. The steep burn's a wasteland of ash, skeletal trees and innumerable shells of stumps like squat chimneys with fire deep in the roots, spitting forth fitful sparks. Occasional flames leap to life along the perimeters as the heat ignites some overlooked bush or chunk, but mostly the crisis is past. The front ranks of the timberline trees are branchless and ravaged on the ridge but they've withstood the onslaught. The fire has scoured the valley but the forest beyond is out of danger.

I make a cursory tour around the edges of the burn, hosing down the odd hot spot that seems to need it. Roy climbs down to the creek to check the pumps. Darkness is falling rapidly and by the time we reconnoitre at the truck, it's getting difficult to see clearly. The air is sour with smoke and the stench of cremated wood.

"Well, I guess that's about all the damage we can do," says Roy. "May as well make ourselves comfortable. I brought along a little something here to make the night go easier."

He produces a full twenty-sixer of rum from a rolled-up coat. I eye it in pleased surprise. Maybe this won't be such a bad stint after all. Ab, who's not much on drinking, would never approve but what Ab doesn't know won't hurt him. The charred hill sputters and fumes. We begin to pass the bottle back and forth.

STEVESTON: POEMS AND PHOTOGRAPHS

Reviewed by John Skapski

As a twenty-two year veteran of Steveston, fifteen of that around fishing, and somewhat of a poet too, I must confess I was taken aback by someone coming into my territory and presuming to tell me about it after what amounts to a cursory glance. "Tourist poems", that's what I expected.

After reading a few poems however, I began to recall things as I'd known them, experiences I considered intimate to my relationship with the area, and Daphne Marlatt had me. Somehow she'd guessed right, she'd managed an empathy with the place.

Through a litany of repetition and cataloguing these poems manage to build up a loose picture of Steveston as a lusty, bustling town that reminds me of Carl Sandburg's Chicago . . . "Steveston, fish packer of the world . . ." But that's not the end of it, there's also a sense of time, of a place once overcome with the Fraser, fish, fishing, fishermen: a gutsy rural town that never became a city, filled with various races each making their separate places, and then the slow urban crush of Vancouver, carrying Steveston before it like a glacier, wedging it precariously into the southwest corner of Lulu Island. That progression, from frenetic boom town vying to be kingpin of the northwest to washed-out industrial bust (Steveston as ribs rotting on beach and: the memory-imagination of the fine ship she was.)

There is another sense even more pervasive, what T. S. Eliot spoke of — "I do not know much about gods but I know that the river is a strong brown god."

By midnight we're all half-loaded and the bullshit is flowing freely.

"Goddamn her," says Roy, "I remember a cook we used to have at the old camp. The guy was an awful booze-artist, into the extract all the time when he couldn't get anything else. Well, one time, he comes back from town with the shakes, the snakes and everything else in the book. The old fart was deadly afraid of cats for some bloody reason so a bunch of us got together to play a joke on him. There was a mangy white tom used to hang around the bunkhouse. We dipped him in some pink dye and sneaked him into old Dan's shack when he was sleeping. Should have heard the hollering and yowling when he woke up and saw the damn thing. Packed his gear right smartly and caught the next boat out. Just as well. He was a piss poor cook anyhow, even when he was sober!"

On the strength of that tale, Roy miraculously produces another half-bottle to replace the one we've killed. We drink on through the night like three delinquent sentries guarding some sleeping encampment where a hundred banked fires glow fitfully. Perhaps, as forest fires go, it wasn't all that much but it was my first and I saw it grow from a few random red motes into an awesome thing. Like your first woman, you know you'll never forget it.

I know a good deal less about gods than Eliot but I do know that it's the strong brown Fraser god that ultimately reigns over Steveston, perhaps that river's most ornate shrine, a place that comes from and turns away toward the Fraser. This book hums with the river's presence.

The poems have the fragmentary, garbled syntax characteristic of Marlatt's style, which I had to more or less ignore to overcome, but after that the poems began to work and the fuzziness gave them a fading memory quality which lends to the historic as does, say, a sepia print.

For me the photographs don't work as well mainly because they fail to consider these matters of time and river. The photographer is stuck in the present to begin with which imposes a fairly severe limitation in a place as historically alive as Steveston, like using pictures of graves to represent people. Perhaps in an effort to escape this problem the pictures tend to be portraits, all rather tightly, even monotonously cropped. The physical presence, the masses of boats, cannery buildings, cannery houses, machinery, the "strong brown god" and its trappings, seem to be left to a few pictures of Finn Slough which are not enough to carry the weight.

The book easily survives on the poetry's strength however, and as a Stevestonite, or whatever you call us, I commend it. About time we got beyond historical pamphlets.

Steveston by Daphne Marlatt and Robert Minden

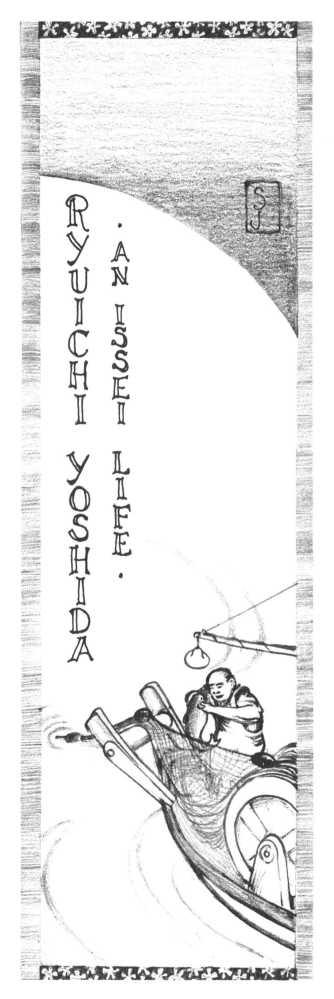

RYUICHI YOSHIDA
. AN ISSEI LIFE .

RYUICHI YOSHIDA'S STORY

I WAS BORN IN 1887, IN A VILLAGE OF BOSHU. My family owned about 130 acres: they were old landowners. I had studied law at Hosei University and thought I would become either a lawyer or a civil servant, but I failed the bar exam. So I decided to go to America, without any definite purpose in mind. My mother was against me going, but I told her that I would come back soon and she accepted that.

When I came to Canada in 1910 the jobs that most Japanese had were fishing, sawmill work, logging and pulpmill work. Some worked on small farms and some on building railways. Japanese had only the bottom jobs. The professional associations had rules which excluded orientals. Maybe they could become a merchant or a doctor or teacher among the Japanese.

I could not find any suitable jobs. I heard fishermen talking and it sounded interesting. My native place in Boshu is by the sea. It was very rough water and I was used to waves.

First I worked for the Balmoral Cannery in the Skeena, in the spring of 1911. Because I didn't know anything about fishing I was made the partner of another man. We both worked in a cannery boat. A double-ender, 28 feet long and five, maybe six, feet wide, with a sail. They were open boats with no cabin.

The sail was very simple. Just some canvas and rope, some poles and a few pieces of iron. I didn't have any dangerous experiences with those sailboats; they didn't upset very easily.

One partner rows the boat: he's called the boat puller. The boss is the netman, he sets the net. But my boss was physically weak, so I did the rowing and a lot of the net work was well. We divided the boat into half. From the centre to the bow was for rowing and for us to live and cook in. From the centre to the stern was for fish and for working the gillnet.

The canneries had engine boats that pulled twenty or more fishing boats to the fishing grounds. They would take us to the spot we wanted to fish. We used to fish six days of the week then, and come back to camp only on Sunday. We cooked rice and we had bean paste, soya sauce, vegetables. We always had lots of fish to eat. I really like fish so it was a feast. At night we put up a tent to keep us dry when we were sleeping.

Fishing is quite complicated and that's what is interesting. You have to find where to go and when to put in your net, you have to think how best to use it each time and place, for high tide and low tide, when the wind is blowing and when it's calm. We could only get up-river on the tide, even with the sail. Going down-river, we usually put down the nets twice.

After the first year I became netman myself. There weren't many white fishermen on the Skeena but there were as many Indian fishermen as Japanese. When I started, most of the Japanese worked under the "attach system." The government gave a number of fishing licenses to the canneries. Canneries issued the license to the Japanese fishermen. In this way they were bound to the different canneries.

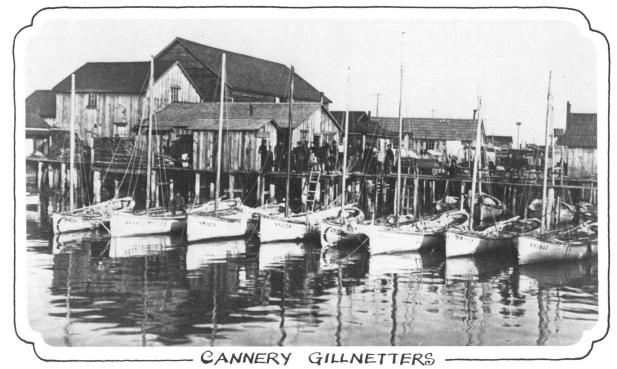

CANNERY GILLNETTERS

The canneries had a quota system for dividing the licences between the Indian and Japanese fishermen. Japanese fishermen were also restricted in the areas they could fish and the gear they could use.

In terms of yearly income, workers in sawmills and pulpmills could earn more money than fishermen. But for the summer, fishing was the best money. I could make one hundred and fifty dollars by the end of the season after the fares up to the Skeena and all the expenses and food were subtracted. But fishing was ups and downs. In a poor year I sometimes made only ten or twenty dollars for the season.

All the canneries who had Japanese fishermen had a Japanese "boss." His job was dependent on how he got on with the boys. The boss was the only one who had his wife in the camp, and she would do the cooking and the laundry for the crew. He would also see that those men who wanted to fish took out the boats and that others took work in the camp mending nets and such.

The fishing boss distributed everybody's income from the cannery, since most first generation fishermen couldn't speak English. In my experience, the fishing boss didn't receive any kickback from the fishermen.

When the fishing season was over, at the end of September, all the fishermen went to town by steamship. From there Indian fishermen went back to their villages and the Japanese fishermen went to Vancouver.

During those years I spent every year almost the same way. In the summer I did salmon fishing on the Skeena. When the fishing season was over I went to the logging camps until the next fishing season opened.

I was a faller. I liked falling too, even though it was dangerous work, and many people I knew died in logging accidents. You have to always think how to do it, think about various ways to fall the tree; if you fall it in the wrong place it gets wasted.

We were almost totally separated from white society, especially those of us working in the camps. We were young men, and the memory of our families and what we had been doing at home haunted us most of the time. Many of the Japanese who came to Canada were from farming villages. They were different from the people I used to know in Japan as a student. They weren't the type of people who spoke about the meaning of life and so on. We talked about women and drinking and fights and what we hoped to do. I started to drink a lot after I came to Canada. There were no other pleasures.

They were all extremely proud of their home places and planned to go back after they saved enough money. But they were often far from reaching their goal. They usually ended up inviting a wife from Japan and settling in Canada. Those were the days of picture brides. A man would exchange pictures and correspondence with a potential bride and if they decided to, they could marry on a document. The husband then brought the bride to Canada.

Many of the people I worked with could not read or write Japanese, so some men would ask me to write letters for them. They wanted me to say good things about their life in Canada so that their girls would marry them and come over.

After fishing in 1919 I did not go logging. I took a job at Ocean Falls. There were about five hundred Japanese workers there, the largest number of any at one place in B.C.

We were hired and paid our wages by the company but there were two Japanese bosses in charge of room and board. After a while we realized that they were cheating on the food. The boss told the company, "So much for the food this month," and the company deducted that from our wages and paid the boss. With five or six dollars unearned profit a month per head the boss was making a lot of money. On top of it, he got commissions from the stores he bought the food at.

There was another papermill nearby, at Swanson

· FALLERS · HILLCREST LUMBER C⁰ LTD. JUNE 1940 ·

Bay. In 1919 the Japanese workers in that mill went on strike and were all fired. These people all came down to town and organized a Labour Union (Nihonjin Rodo Kumiai). It took the form of a general union of all Japanese workers. Japanese workers were too few, too scattered to develop unions according to occupations.

The person most responsible for establishing the Labour Union was a man called Etsu Suzuki, a writer for the *Continental Times (Tairiku Nippo)* in Vancouver. The Anti-Asiatic League was starting to become very influential: discrimination was worsening. Suzuki thought that if the Japanese workers unionized they could approach the white unions and slow down the anti-oriental movement.

The Anti-Asiatic League blamed the Japanese for unemployment, for low pay; they blamed us for working for low pay. They blamed us for everything. It became very strong after the First World War. There was a general anti-oriental feeling in B.C. but it was the Anti-Asiatic League that led the open attacks.

The positions and views of the Union were publicized through the Union's *Labour Weekly (Rodo Shuho)* and sometimes through articles which Suzuki still wrote in the *Continental Times.* I read those publications at Ocean Falls. I came down to Vancouver, talked to Suzuki, and became a member of the Labour Union. Soon after, Suzuki asked me to be editor of the *Labour Weekly.*

The next years I was very busy in building up the Labour Union and working with the Skeena Fishermen's Association. I was always giving talks, going to meetings, doing research and writing.

Most Japanese organizations, including the Union, were branches of the Japanese Association. The Japanese Association (Nihonjin Kai) used to be dominated by the Japanese Consul and run by merchants and the like. They had important influence over the life of Japanese in Canada. As long as the Association followed the Consul's ideas it could give "authorized approval" for legal documents. For instance, there were many Issei living here who were still liable for the draft in Japan. Without the Consul's permission one would have to return to be drafted. On applying to bring wives to Canada one needed the Association's approval. But they did nothing for the Japanese worker here.

The Labour Union reached the conclusion that it was absolutely necessary to break the Association's control. After many struggles, we voted to make the fishermen's associations independent of the Association. At that point the executives of the Association resigned and were replaced by members and supporters of the Labour Union.

I got married in 1922, when I was thirty-five years old. I first met my wife when she was a girl, the daughter of the man I used to buy sake from (I hadn't thought of her as anything but a young girl then.) Our daughter was born a year later, in 1923. My wife was very ill after she had the child. The doctor said she might die if she got pregnant again.

The old executive of the Japanese Association, through the Japanese business community, forced the *Labour Weekly* out of circulation. Our only chance was to buy a press and go daily, which we did

in May, 1924.

The name of our paper was *The People (Minshu).* It was a daily paper and took the form of a regular newspaper into which the views of a union paper were woven. I was the editor for two years.

For a short while I received a wage from the Labour Union and then from *The People*, but mostly it wasn't paid because the Labour Union had no money. So it was very difficult for us financially. I only got just enough for food. We lived on debts. For almost three years we shared an apartment with Suzuki. It was communal living, but communal life wasn't particularly convenient. Because of the responsibility of supporting wife and daughter I stopped drinking as much, and started working as a gardener.

I was still active in the Labour Union. The practical problem was that the Union didn't increase in membership. It wasn't possible to strengthen the Union because we couldn't achieve any gains in wages and conditions. It was too small, and without the cooperation of the white unions we could achieve nothing.

In 1926, after six years of trying, the Union was admitted to the Vancouver Labour Council as the "Japanese Camp and Millworkers Union." We worked closely with C.C.F. people like Ernest Winch, and Angus McInnis was especially helpful.

The Labour Council quit its support of the Anti-Asiatic League, and soon after the League was dissolved. However, the truth might be that anti-oriental feeling was so widespread by then that the League wasn't necessary. Now discrimination came not only from the unions but from the general public. Politicians took advantage of that feeling to get themselves elected. They had no policy or platform, just hatred of orientals.

The B.C. government brought in a law forbidding us from buying farm land. Even Japanese born here could not vote. There were laws passed that barred us from contract work in the government forests, and many other jobs. Then the provincial government convinced the federal government to cut off the licenses for Japanese fishermen. The Skeena Fishermen's Association carried on a long court case for years against that, and finally won. But by 1928 half the Japanese fishermen had lost their licenses.

The Japanese Consul, Mr. Comyo, had been understanding about our Union and had some progressive attitudes. But in 1926 he was replaced by a very conservative and imperialistic Consul who thought he should convert Vancouver Japanese to become ardent nationalists.

The supporters of the Union soon started to suffer from pressures by this Consul. For instance, he didn't give permission to Union members to bring their families from Japan.

The Consul gave instructions that the former directors should work to regain control of the Japanese Association, and he gave them his support. Finally, in August, 1927, the Labour Union supporters resigned. The Union then broke completely with the Japanese Association and became autonomous.

About 1929 Japan started to take a hard approach to socialism and Japanese people in Vancouver were influenced by that policy. Japanese militarism

·ART OF KENDO · ENGLEWOOD 1930·

became even more influential following the Manchuria incident and the war with China. The problem originally was the education of the Meiji era that the Issei of my generation received in Japan: "Be faithful to the emperor and love your country." We were stuffed with nationalistic teaching and military training.

The Japanese in Canada were very resentful about discrimination at this time and they were influenced by Japanese militarism. The more discrimination they received the more dependent they became on Japan. That's clear to me looking at the post-war situation.

The Union advised people to get adjusted to Canada. We didn't mean that Japanese culture was bad, but that we had to adapt in order to stay in Canada. Men working in the camps and the countryside understood this position better than those living in the very closeknit Japanese community. In town, not many people were in agreement with our position. They were very old style Japanese, perhaps more so than people in Japan. Like the first generation at Steveston. Those people were maintaining the old habits and styles that had existed in their little villages in Japan. They weren't interested in anything new.

As the depression got worse people couldn't pay me for gardening anymore. Fishing didn't seem so badly affected. So when my wife was a bit better I went fishing again. There was a quota on licenses for Japanese fishermen. Though I had been a Canadian citizen for almost twenty years, I couldn't get a license at first; only those Japanese who were veterans from World War One had the same rights as white fishermen. I worked as somebody's partner at first. The next year I managed to get a license from a man who was quitting fishing.

Gas boats had already come in at the Skeena by 1932. White fishermen had started to come in after the Japanese lost their licenses, and they used engine fishing boats, so the canneries had changed over. With those Easthopes and Palmers there was only one man to a boat. I didn't like those early gas boats too much, they were dangerous. Also, the numbers of the fish weren't what they were before — the canneries got bigger and our catch got smaller. Gradually fishing days dropped from six days a week to five days and then four days during the season. Still, I was a good fisherman and I did quite well.

Once I started fishing I became active in the Skeena Fishermen's Association again. I continued my visits to various camps giving talks about the principles of the labour movement and the Labour Union.

The white fishermen had a small group in Prince Rupert, more like a fishermen's club than a union. There were other little groups like that at Pender Harbour, Victoria and Nanaimo. On the Fraser River I think there were about three different unions of white fishermen, all negotiating with the canneries on their own. Only after the war did all these little groups get together in the U.F.A.W.U.

My daughter was going to school then. We didn't demand any special thing of her. She only went to Japanese language school for about two years. She could understand and speak Japanese quite well but she couldn't read or write much.

It was impossible for our generation to discard Japanese habits. But I didn't think that the generation born here should be indoctrinated with Japanese culture. I have warm feelings about Japanese ways but I don't think that they are better than any other. They may be good to keep but if we have to discard them, it's alright for the next generation. Those generations born here are very different from us. We Issei were basically Japanese. But the first generation born here are more than eighty per cent Canadian in their outlook and life. Only a few Nisei were strongly influenced by the Japanese language schools.

Well sure, discrimination affected our personal lives. It's difficult to pick out all the particular incidents, but it was a constant thing. Like the White Lunch: they didn't allow orientals to eat there for many years. Whenever I would try to get people to fight racism they would say, "No. I'm not going to stay here very long." That was their excuse. But almost all who said that stayed in Canada the rest of their lives and raised their children here.

·SEIZED VESSELS AT ANNIEVILLE DYKE·

I was still on the Skeena fishing when the war started with Germany in 1939. At that time the Vancouver Japanese were very much influenced by the Showa period militarism from Japan. Only a small minority of Issei were not. Most people were hostile towards the Union and our supporters. If I weren't a fisherman I couldn't have made a living.

1941 was a bad fishing year and I didn't even make the advance money. So I went straight from the Skeena to work on a packer that collected cod and dogfish and delivered them to Lake Bay on Vancouver Island to be made into cod liver oil and fertilizer for the war effort. I was working on that boat when the war broke out with Japan. The captain yelled for me to come up to the bridge and hear the news on the radio. The next day we got into Nanaimo where the captain was told that any boat with Japanese on it had to come in to Vancouver. At Vancouver a Navy boat took me off for investigation.

When I came home the Japanese community was in great confusion. All Japanese fishing boats were towed to Annieville, near New Westminster, where they were tied up and later sold. There was a curfew on Japanese; we could not be out at night after eight. People who looked suspicious were arrested.

What I was afraid of was a riot like in 1907, but worse, because anti-Japanese feeling was much higher than ever before. I thought that if we did anything to provoke trouble something really horrible would happen.

All the Japanese associations and groups were dissolved as soon as the war started. All the Japanese language newspapers were banned from publishing, except the *New Canadian*. I wrote an article saying people should stay calm and cooperate with the regulations. There were many rumours. The Issei were very quiet but some Nisei were furious, protesting that it was unfair to treat them that way when they were born here. Some of the teachers and students of the Fairview Japanese Language School became extreme nationalists and most of them were sent to special internment camps — they all went back to Japan after the war.

Then the government decided to collect all Japanese from the countryside at Hastings Park. People in Vancouver were allowed to wait at home. In March,

1942, the government announced that Japanese had to move away from the coast. Younger Nisei men could go to the east to work. All other men and those Nisei who didn't want to leave their families were to go to road camps and their families to relocation camps.

We were allowed to take only 150 pounds of luggage with us to camp. One man we knew had a concrete warehouse in Vancouver. We and about ten other families stored our other things there, but the watchman of the building sold or destroyed most of them.

I really didn't have time to feel very much. We didn't own anything, like a house or a boat or a shop, so we didn't have that to worry about. I thought that as soon as we were away from·the city we would be safe.

We left Vancouver at the end of May. All Japanese were gone by the beginning of November. My wife and daughter were moved to Kaslo with many other women and children. There were many deserted towns through there used for camps.

The road camp I was sent to was at Three Valley Gap, about fifteen miles west of Revelstoke. We lived in tents and they gave us plenty of food. Our job was to make a highway out of a very rough road. We chopped trees and burned them, and cleared the right of way. That work was less than what I was used to.

At the end of August married men were sent to the New Denver and Hope areas to build camps. I was sent to Rosebery. We cleared the land and built houses to receive our families. Most of those shacks are still standing today.

We had a Japanese foreman for each camp. Foremen understood English and they followed government supervisors' advice on managing each camp. In Rosebery the foremen were hated and there was a continuous turnover of foremen. Some people thought it was better if they didn't follow any advice from the government. They wouldn't even cooperate to bring in the water system or cut firewood for our own use. I was a foreman in charge of cutting down trees for firewood for a while, but these people insulted me all the time, so I quit.

After I got a house my wife and daughter came

JAPANESE WERE COLLECTED IN VANCOUVER...

AND SENT TO CAMPS IN B.C. INTERIOR

WINTER IN CAMP · TASHME ·

and we lived there for the next four years. They brought pots and kitchenware along. Beds and furniture we made ourselves. The stove was provided by the goverment. During the first winter it was extremely cold.

At the beginning there were many passes required for everyday life. Control was quite strict. Later that was loosened up, because the Japanese were quiet in general.

I didn't have much personal contact with white people during those days. At Silverton they were hostile and didn't want any Japanese there. Other places they were kind. There was a farmer near New Denver who was very kind to us.

Life in those camps was not so bad. Everybody made a garden. But we couldn't get enough fish to eat.

I wasn't bored. We had our clubs and each camp had a public hall. We had performances of stage plays and amateur shows. We built several public baths in Rosebery and we took a bath every day. We got used to that kind of life after a while.

Our daughter started to have boyfriends and we began to worry about her. There were a lot of young men and women together in camp; it was a carefree life for them. I told my daughter not to go to dances and things like that. "Don't use makeup. Makeup is not for young girls," I said. I was a strict father, I suppose, but at the time I thought I was quite liberal.

We knew of the progress of the war by reading newspapers. There were two Japanese papers published in the States that had articles that came from the bureau of the Japanese Army. It was obvious what was happening. But most people didn't believe it.

Before the end of the war the Canadian government started a program of repatriation of Japanese.

· THEATRE IN CAMP ·

Naturalized citizens were to choose whether they wanted to go to eastern Canada or go back to Japan. The government would pay the fare and give two hundred dollars for expenses. At first we weren't allowed to stay in B.C. The B.C. government hoped to get rid of the Japanese that way. The Conservative M.P. from Vancouver South, Howard Green, I think he wanted all Japanese to be sent back.

I and about ten others at Rosebery went around and told people we had to decide how to deal with this, that Japan would be defeated and the war would soon be over. I was called a betrayer and a traitor. People threw rocks at our house and insulted us on the street. It was impossible to describe the amount of hatred there was toward us. Despite our efforts, I think most of the Issei signed those repatriation papers at first. The Nisei, not very many. When the news came that Japan had unconditionally surrendered, people were in a complete shock. But they began to think more clearly and about half the people wanted to cancel their signatures for repatriation. We hired two influential white lawyers and started a cancel movement. In the meantime, most of the Nisei were sent to the east. My daughter left for Toronto about one year later. All her friends went east so she followed them.

One thing: because of the internment all of our friends are scattered. Some went back to Japan, many went east, others are scattered around B.C. But discrimination against us began to disappear shortly after the war.

In August, 1946, we moved to the east. We first lived in an old prisoner-of-war camp in northern Ontario. It was a temporary accommodation for the Japanese going east.

Our daughter was living in Toronto and working in a big cleaning shop. We were worried about her. But we found that young men and women were living quite happily by themselves, free from parental restrictions. In Vancouver the parents had had lots of influence over their children, even when they were grown.

I worked in a steel mill in Hamilton for five years. My job was very dusty. Workers were supposed to wear masks but it was hard breathing with the mask so I didn't put it on. The air pollution was terrible and I finally quit when it became difficult to breathe at all.

Japanese were first allowed to vote in Ontario in 1946. I worked for the C.C.F. campaign in Hamilton. We won, and it was very satisfying. When I voted, for the first time in my life I felt like I could finally join the human race.

After 1951 Japanese were allowed to fish in B.C. again, and B.C. Packers came east to recruit experienced Japanese fishermen. I was sixty-five years old but when I talked to the cannery people I decided to come back and fish on the Skeena.

I fished for Sunnyside Cannery for nine years. If we'd been using the old way of fishing I couldn't have done it for long, but when I went back to the Skeena the work was all done by the engine.

Many fishermen were buying their own boats, but I didn't know how much longer I'd be able to fish, so I used a cannery boat. My wife took up mending and fixed the small holes in the net herself.

If you hired somebody to do that it was expensive and they didn't do a particularly good job.

Gradually more Japanese fishermen came back. There were no restrictions against us. We could fish offshore. We could catch shrimp or crab all the winter. The big change was that most Japanese fishermen now had their own boats and came up from Steveston and Vancouver to fish.

When we came back the Indians didn't like it. They caused us trouble and corked us a lot. But they mostly fished in the river and at the mouth, so we went to fish offshore to avoid disturbances.

When I went back to the Skeena I wasn't as good a fisherman anymore. I was too old. I didn't have any problems in the daytime but I lost my sense of direction at night. I couldn't tell how close I was to shoals or to the beach. The tide is fast there and you can get into lots of trouble.

Once you know how to fish and where and when to fish, success depends a lot on how much you work. When the fish are running you might only get three or four hours sleep. When I was young I often didn't sleep for three days. I just couldn't do that anymore.

I was almost drowned once. I was working near the Standard camp, at the mouth of the Skeena River. Somehow I got my feet caught in the anchor line and I was thrown in the sea. I couldn't get my rubber boots off. So I swam with them on; it was hard. I got to the boat and I couldn't reach up to the deck, but there was a rope hanging down into the water from the bow and I swam to that. The water was so cold and I was so tired that I couldn't pull myself up. After fifteen or twenty minutes a boat came by. I shouted, but they couldn't hear me over their engine. It had already passed when the fisherman's wife saw me waving in the water. They came, and saved my life.

In springtime I worked in the cannery doing net repair work for wages. In the wintertime I did a little trolling from a rowboat, and I used to give the fish away. It was really a lot of fun.

We stayed in a cannery house on the wharf, but my wife didn't like that life in a small Japanese community, with all the interference into each other's personal affairs. It didn't bother me at that time but it seemed to bother her very much. So we moved to New Denver. We bought an old house there and fixed it up. The house had been abandoned since the war and it was very cold and draughty. I fixed everything up and it's fairly nice now. It was the first time we'd ever owned our own house.

I have never been back to Japan, though my wife went back once. When I was younger I wanted to go for a visit but I never had the money. My family sent me money to come back after I had been in Canada six or seven years but I didn't want to go back then. Now, it's too much trouble to go. My family and the people I knew, they're all dead.

GUMBOOT NAVY

Capt. Donald Peck

WE CALLED IT THE GUMBOOT NAVY. THEY CALLED IT THE F.R.S. It had been rather hastily pasted together in the frantic weeks following Pearl Harbour to provide a kind of first line of defence along the B.C. coast, where the regular naval forces were hopelessly inadequate, and it was properly titled the Fishermens' Reserve Service. I served as a Commanding Officer in it through till the time it was disbanded in May, 1944.

I suppose it's a natural fate for any irregular force to become endowed in time with something of a clownish legend, but it often seems that the Fishermen's Reserve, when it is remembered at all, is thought of as a species of wartime boondoggle, and its men given little more credit than draft dodgers.

Of course it is popular in many circles these days, since we have all become so wise with hindsight, to belittle all wartime defence preparations on the west coast, the Fishermens' Reserve along with the gun emplacements, blackouts and the rest. When Pearl Harbour was being bombed out of the sea to the south of us and Japanese troops were occupying Atu and Kiska in the Aleutians to the north of us however, this blithe attitude wasn't nearly so evident amongst the general public. It was not a bit evident among F.R. recruits who, in the course of sailing small, lightly armed, wooden-hulled vessels through water known to be occupied by enemy subs and

mines – not to mention the natural hazards, which were extreme – certainly felt no more secure than their well-provisioned and protected colleagues in regular service.

The popular image of the F.R. doesn't gall me so much, since our men cared little about public recognition, as the attitude of military officialdom, which was one of towering disdain not in the least tempered by their own incompetence in dealing with our problems.

The strategy behind the F.R.S. was to establish a full time reconnaissance patrol of the whole coast using the available experience and equipment of the commercial fishing fleet, and men were mainly recruited from the fishing and towboat industries. The vessels were also largely conscripted seiners and packers, though some were specially built. At the peak there may have been 40 in total.

The boats were skippered by reserve personnel but directed by regular naval authorities out of Esquimalt – and there was the rub. Actually when I first started in the F.R. Captain Jimmy McCulloch was in charge and he had been to sea with many of us, understood what we were up against and kept an open door. He was tremendous. Unfortunately he was soon transferred and a real calamity in Navy uniform we shall call the Brown Bomber arrived from Halifax to take charge. If the Brown Bomber had any previous experience with wooden-hulled ships he showed little evidence of it. His ineptitude was soon demonstrated. When the H.M.C.S. *Ekholi* was damaged on the rocks off Macau'?*y* Point he ordered the workers to bore through the two parts of the stem that had been split and pull it together with bolts, completely ignoring the stopwaters between the stem and the forefoot that were either missing or shattered, thus negating their purpose. I had the misfortune to captain this flawed vessel on her next voyage and spent the worst night of my experience.

We started out in mildly threatening weather that rapidly worsened as we proceeded upcoast. By the time we reached the vicinity of Pachena Point the wind had howled itself to gale force and the waves were green mountains of gigantic size, rolling in from the open sea, as we passed the lee of Cape Flattery, and striking us almost dead abeam. It was one of the most furious storms I ever encountered and water poured in through the faulty repair area. Two of the ratings were cleaning up the galley after the evening meal and having great difficulty keeping their feet, as the vessel was rolling rails under with each sea. Suddenly a particularly titanic wave struck and broke almost simultaneously, leaving the vessel literally in mid-air and on her beam ends. Both sailors lost their grip on the sink where they had been washing dishes and fell headlong to the lower side of the galley. Fortunately, neither was injured but every dish and drop of water had left the sink, proving the vessel had been pitched more than 90 degrees from an even keel. Further evidence of this was found in the forecastle where mattresses and other spare gear were flung from the top port bunk to the starboard with nothing hitting the deck.

Shortly, the asdic watch picked up a sonar ping. It worked out to the equivalent of 24 fathoms and indicated we were too close to shore for safety. I immediately altered course and hauled further off. The vessel had taken on a temporary magnetism while lying in Esquimalt and both compasses were out as much as 16 degrees. We were steering by guess and by God with no real idea of our position. My nerves were beginning to fray under the strain.

I decided to try and get into Bamfield as we had eighteen inches of water on the cabin floor and the pumps were barely coping. But now, to add to our problems, it had begun to snow, reducing our visibility to practically zero and blacking out the lighthouses. Repeated blasts on the whistle failed to raise an answering hoot from their foghorns and I realized my signals were getting drowned in the whining fury of the wind and the boom of the breakers. There was nothing to do but stay well offshore and hope we could ride out the storm. Before long a gigantic sea roared aboard, burying the whole after end of the vessel and washing the rubber mats off the bridge. It was obviously time to heave to and I did so. The boarding sea had told me one thing — that we were probably in the tide rip off Amphitrite Point caused by the ebb tide out of the Ucluelet area. It was reassuring to have some idea of our position. The compasses were still malfunctioning. It often took 24 hours for a wooden ship to shake off the magnetism.

After we had been hove to for nearly three hours,

the snow stopped and it became possible to see at least as far as the next trough. We got underway again but had not gone far before the wind once more hit gale velocity, bringing another onslaught of gargantuan waves. The behavior of the waves suggested that we had reached the shallower stretch of water off Estevan. Spume blowing from the wave tops had again brought zero visibility however and it was decided to heave to a second time and wait till daylight. We spent an uncomfortable night.

By ten a.m. the following day the visibility had improved somewhat. Putting a small cross on the chart to mark our present position, I plotted a course for the entrance to Nootka Sound. I was confident that, should my calculations be faulty, the sound of the breakers would warn us in time. After running this course for upwards of an hour a breaker was spotted about four points off the port bow. I kept to my original course after checking the chart and finding a reef indicated in that precise location. After running another few minutes, I spotted a sharp pinnacle, again off the port bow. As it was impossible to determine the distance or size of the object, my first thought was that it might be the highest peak in the mountain range behind Nootka. We drew closer and I suddenly realized with a surge of relief that it was the peak of the Nootka lighthouse. I hurried to the wheelhouse and ordered the helmsman to adjust course three degrees starboard. Word spread quickly around the ship and the crew was jubilant. The chief engineer, an oldtimer on the coast, who had been convinced we were in the vicinity of Esperanza, was heard to mutter, "Well I'll be goddamned!" as he left the bridge. Months later my son, who was a rating on the *Ekholi* at the time, repeated a remark overheard in the forecastle — "Your old man is a pusser old bugger but he sure can navigate!" Little did he know that I'd been just as surprised as the rest of them.

A second near disaster in the shipyard came about when Dave Ritchie's command ripped off all her ironbark sheathing in heavy seas, leaving several hundred nail holes fountaining water into the hull. A lesser man might have abandoned ship under these circumstances but Dave was made of sterner stuff. Although the bilge pump and the engine circulating pump (which had been rigged to take water from the bilge rather than the sea) could barely keep ahead of the leaks, Dave finished his patrol and returned to port as originally planned. The vessel was immediately hauled out on the slip. The repair was no difficult matter — simply locate every nailhole, plug it and replace the ironbark sheathing. The Brown Bomber had other ideas. "Take axes and cutting tools and cut away that inner ceiling," he commanded. "If there's a bilge clamp in the way, cut it off too!" The inner ceiling is an important part of the vessel's strength. This would have weakened the ship irrevocably, ruined her for all time. Dave Ritchie wasn't standing for that. When he saw what was about to happen, he gave a howl of rage, took out after the startled Bomber and chased him ashore. Fortunately, saner heads prevailed. The repairs were effected in the accustomed fashion.

I was put teaching navigation but I was anxious to get back to sea. When I was asked to go to Bella Bella and take command of the H.M.C.S. *Spray*, I jumped at the opportunity. I hadn't joined up to polish the seat of my pants. On arrival at Bella Bella, I sailed almost immediately to take up examination duties off Kiwash Island on the Inside Passage route to Alaska. There was a tremendous amount of shipping as the Americans were using the offshore islands as a screen against possible submarine attack. The open stretches like Queen Charlotte Sound were patrolled by Corvettes and Bangor-type minesweepers of the R.C.N. All vessels received escort across the un-shielded water. As a result of my report regarding the lack of any protection for Hakai Pass — very familiar to the Japanese — a vessel was placed there with asdic submarine detection equipment on 24-hour patrol.

After a month on this duty the *Spray* was relieved by another of the F.R. fleet and returned to Esquimalt. I was quickly reappointed to the H.M.C.S. *Merry Chase* on her maiden voyage as a member of our fleet. Going down the straits we kept company with the *Fort Camosun*, just out of Vancouver with her first cargo. We separated near Cape Flattery. Some time later I learned the freighter had been torpedoed off the Cape. Luckily her cargo was lumber and plywood and kept her afloat despite a completely flooded engine room. The torpedo had entered her hull on an angle at the No. 3 hold, caromed off the plywood and punched its way out again a few feet further aft. After a sufficient part of the cargo had been discharged the holes were closed up and the vessel returned to sea, little the worse for her hair-raising experience.

Most of our patrols in fine weather were pretty routine. We'd simply cruise along the coast, poking into every nook and cranny in search of hidden subs. On one particular occasion we were three nights out and anchored in Hot Spring Cove after a careful search of Sidney Inlet. The Japanese had operated a copper mine there and, so the rumour went, had established a hidden fueling facility in anticipation of the coming war. It was a beautiful evening, windless with a full moon throwing silver in the water from a cloudless sky. As it was June 15 and nearly the longest day, it never really got dark that night. Suddenly, the tranquil atmosphere was shattered by a series of violent explosions somewhere to the west. Estevan Point lay in that direction. We learned via radiophone that they were being shelled by a Japanese sub. I immediately took to sea in hope of getting a fix on her so I could report the location to the Navy. I had already gotten a report away to Naval Headquarters and it was the first they had heard of the shelling. As we had no armament aboard there was no way of coping with the sub ourselves. We could only wait and hope, but the sub slipped away before help arrived.

Next morning I was in company with H.M.C.S. *Moolock*, which had been instructed to evacuate the women and children from the lighthouse and wireless station. The captain, Norm Flander, had also been instructed to relay a hand message to H.M.C.S. *Sans Peure*. This he asked me to do, as he was anxious to get his passengers to the Port Alberni hospital. Some of them were suffering from considerable shock.

No damage was done at Estevan by the shelling and it was held by many to have been a futile effort

on the part of the Japanese. But I have always believed they got the information they were seeking when there was no defensive reaction to their shells. The Estevan Station was, before the war, a strategic point for North Pacific shipping. It was there they made their first wireless contact with North America. I feel the Japanese were just testing to see how well we were equipped to handle an attack. Failing to draw a response from Estevan, they could pretty safely assume the coast to be virtually unprotected. They would have been largely right. We did have guns at Mary Hill near Victoria and others at Ucluelet but that left a 125-mile corridor between that was open to any invader. At this time the western representatives in Ottawa were pressing for more adequate protection. Their efforts were hampered by idiotic argument. One defense department genius declared the coast to be indefensible. "In case of an invasion, the population of B.C. will have to retire behind the Rocky Mountains!" Not without cause did Bruce Hutchinson once write, "Although Ottawa is only three thousand miles from Victoria, Victoria is thirty-three thousand miles from Ottawa."

ESTEVAN POINT LIGHTHOUSE

The rendezvous with H.M.C.S. *Sans Peure* was arranged for 1200 hours on the day after the shelling at a position 10 miles southwest of Estevan Point. When 1600 hours arrived with no sign of the *Sans Peure* I decided to abandon the vigil and proceed to Nootka. There was a fuel depot there and it was possible the sub might attempt to replenish her fuel supply.

At any rate, we ran in from the position off Estevan and approached Escalante Reef. I was busy calculating the compass deviation and instructed the signalman to keep a sharp eye peeled while I worked out the problem. When I finally looked up, the first thing I saw was a vessel trailing us about a half-mile astern. It seemed initially to be another F.R. boat or a fishing vessel of similar size but on closer examination, I saw the deck structure was oddly narrow. "Where the hell did that vessel come from?" I queried the signalman. "Dunno," he replied looking mystified and vaguely guilty, "She must have come out from the shore." This was patently impossible since there is no place to come out from between Sunday Rocks and Escalante Reef. The mystery was soon answered when she simply dived. We had just sighted our first sub! I got an immediate signal away to Naval Headquarters. On arrival at Nootka, I was amazed to find they knew nothing of Estevan being shelled. It was after sunset and every light in the village was ablaze. I ordered a complete blackout and posted an armed guard on the wharf near the fuel tanks. I was afraid the sub might sneak in to top off her tanks. The Japanese Intelligence was undoubtedly aware of this fuel depot. But nothing happened and it was just as well. We would have been no match for the sub.

The next day, after a thorough combing of the channels and inlets, I anchored in Queens Cove near the entrance to Esperanza Inlet. The following morning, we resumed patrol westward. On leaving the inlet, we encountered high winds and a rain squall that reduced visibility to a few hundred feet. Some time later I learned an R.C.A.F. plane had spotted a sub on the surface just south of the whistle buoy where I had altered to a westerly course. Because of the low visibility I hadn't seen the plane and it was doubtful he had spotted us. Radar was still in its infancy and available sets were going to higher-priority areas.

This had turned out to be considerably more than a run-of-the-mill patrol and it wasn't over yet. The next day, while checking a deserted Indian village at the mouth of Ookanish Inlet, someone noticed that a board in one of the shacks had been recently disturbed. On further investigation, we uncovered a cache of modern rifles and ammunition. I reported this find and was instructed to turn it over to the Indian Agent at Alert Bay. He was at a loss to explain the arms cache; I don't believe anyone ever came up with the answer.

On returning to base I was signed off the *Merry Chase* and shuttled through several temporary appointments. In August I was appointed to H.M.C.S. *Burrard* as special recruiting officer. My duties were to recruit young men of the right background and ability to take commando training at Comox under Commander Windyer and other tough officers. Of the nearly five hundred men who were screened through our offices, only three failed to complete the course — not a bad average. But I soon grew bored with desk work again.

When my recruiting duties were finished, I was given command of the H.M.C.S. *Moolock* and made several uneventful patrols on the west coast. One day in Seymour Inlet the boss's wife at a logging camp we were visiting was stricken with a heart attack. I was asked to take her to Port Hardy where she could get transportation to a hospital in Vancouver. There was a gale blowing and we were the only vessel in the area equipped to weather it so I didn't hesitate. I radioed my intentions to Esquimalt and, receiving no reply, left the inlet early the following morning when the tide allowed. At the mouth of Seymour lie the notorious Nakwakto Rapids which have a slack period of less than five minutes. At peak flow the current reaches a speed of twenty knots. It is a treacherous piece of water and seldom run at night. But this was a high-order emergency and since I knew the channel well, there was not that much danger involved. We negotiated the rapids successfully and I pulled into Port Hardy feeling rather proud of myself. This sense

of well being was rudely shattered by a curt command: REPORT FORTHWITH TO CAPT D. ESQUIMALT. Since my small breach of protocol had involved the saving of a human life, I was somewhat mystified but I complied with the order.

When I confronted Captain D., a singularly unpleasant man, he immediately accused me of having carried a woman aboard the *Moolock* contrary to Navy orders and when I denied this he declared me a liar. His hostility was undisguised and quite out of proportion to the incident. When he ran out of breath, I asked him why he had not signalled me to the effect that my action was improper. I was again accused of lying, this time in regard to the message I had sent. I demanded a search of the communications office and my signal was turned up. It had not even been delivered. The obnoxious Capt. D., however, offered no apology for his unfounded accusations. I was simply dismissed from his presence. To say that I was rankled by this high-handed treatment would be an understatement. Since, during the run from Seymour to Port Hardy, I had found and plotted a hitherto uncharted reef, perhaps preventing some future shipwreck, I was doubly annoyed. But there was little I could do.

LAUNCHING THE MOOLOCK

Some time later, while patrolling the area between Pachena and Estevan Points, my signalman came down with the mumps. I was granted permission to land him at Ucluelet for hospitalization. I remained at the R.C.A.F. base for no more than half an hour and then resumed patrol. A day or two later, I was advised to proceed again to Ucluelet, land the boy's personal possessions and pick up a replacement signalman who had been dispatched there. On this occasion, I was docked for no more than ten minutes. Shortly after, to my considerable bewilderment, came another terse summons to appear before Capt. D. At the Esquimalt gate, I was handed a further order restricting all leave for H.M.C.S. *Moolock* and taken under escort to the office of Capt. D. I was quite in the dark as to what it was all about. The disagreeable Captain was in an even viler mood than on the previous occasion. I noted that the M.O. was in attendance, looking as though he had given up all hope of survival. There was no doffing of caps as is usual at such meetings. D. launched into a wild harangue, accusing me of being a disgrace to the Navy along with a lot of other things of which I had no knowledge whatsoever. After he had run out of insulting things to say about me, I asked him what the hell this was all about. D.

informed me that the M.O. was going to inspect myself and my entire crew for venereal disease. My patience snapped completely. I accused D. of making malicious and unfounded statements and insulting me beyond endurance. When the dust finally settled, the story came out. A letter had been received from the M.O. at Ucluelet. Two of their men had contracted venereal disease and, when questioned, both had named the same woman. They claimed she had been spending nights on one of the F.R. vessels. Since we had been in Ucluelet on those two brief occasions, the *Moolock*'s name had somehow been brought up. I knew damn well who the real culprit must be as one of our vessels was stationed on examination duty at the port entrance. How we had come to be blamed for their indiscretions I couldn't imagine. I insisted the M.O. go through with the examination anyway and my entire crew received a clean bill of health. But again there was no apology from the insufferable Capt. D.

Back on patrol, still seething from the pointless incident, I was directed to Ahousat to investigate a submarine sighting. It had apparently been spotted by an old Indian out fishing in his dugout in the early morning. Two other C.O.s were sent along to sit with me. The Indian's name was simply Old Samuel. The chief was acting as interpreter and I became suspicious that we were getting his version of the story rather than the witness's. The inquiry was being conducted in English and Old Samuel couldn't understand a word of it. I had no knowledge of that particular dialect but I was quite familiar with Chinook Jargon. I addressed the witness directly in this tongue. It was a lucky guess. He turned to me as though he had found an old friend and gave me his own story. It convinced me that what Old Sam had seen with his failing eyes was simply a basking shark on the surface with its huge dorsal fin extended. Foggy weather and poor visibility had further confused him. I was satisfied that we had the truth of the matter and imparted my information to the others. The writer made out the report, we signed it and the affair was settled.

Soon after this, the *Moolock* was assigned to work out of Prince Rupert and I went thankfully. I'd had more than a bellyful of Captain D. and his half-baked accusations. On arriving at Rupert, *Moolock* was assigned to the Queen Charlotte Islands and Hecate Straits patrol. It was midsummer and we enjoyed three weeks of exceptionally fine weather. When our victualling bills came in at the end of the first month however it was apparent that something would have to be done to economize on the grub. I was already deep in the red. Although the Navy allowed 95 cents per man day on its own ships, the F.R. vessels were only alloted 85 cents mess money for officers and a ridiculous 50 cents for ratings. Why this dichotomy existed I have no idea, but exist it did. Working out of Esquimalt, it was possible to scrape by on this pittance with careful planning. While in port, a good many of the crew ate in restaurants or with family or friends. This situation did not apply in Rupert. There were 10,000 Americans based there and prices were sky high whenever you could get into one of the constantly packed restaurants. The grocery prices were the same. The town was a Yankee enclave and the money flowed like rain. It was difficult to even go to a movie. The lineups were endless.

I had to compromise somehow and we turned to a diet consisting largely of venison, fish and shellfish. The crew griped a lot at first but they got used to it. The food in Rupert was simply beyond our price range.

Shortly after my assignment to the new post, I was granted compassionate leave. My wife had suffered a nervous breakdown in Winnipeg and my signature was required before she could receive treatment there. On the train I struck up conversation with several western M.P.'s on their way to Ottawa who were greatly interested in my involvement in the Estevan affair. They had at the time demanded and got an investigation of the incident. Representatives from the Army, Navy and Air Force had been called in to give an accounting of themselves. But the whole thing had broken down into a buck-passing farce and nothing had been resolved. The Navy representative had gone so far as to question whether the shelling

· Van Isle · Valdes · Western Maid · Cape Beale · San Thomas ·

had ever actually taken place, since it was obvious on any map of Canada that Estevan was in Saskatchewan! The Air Force had sidestepped the issue of why the one available bomber at Patricia Bay had not been dispatched by claiming bad weather. It had ended up just one more east-west snafu bogged down in misinformation and cross purposes.

In Winnipeg, after treatment, my wife was released from hospital under strict orders that she be kept completely quiet for a week or two. I took her to her sister's farm west of the city where I was reasonably sure we would be undisturbed. Around midnight of the second day we were awakened by a loud hammering at the door. It proved to be her brother with a telegram from Prince Rupert. It ordered me to return immediately to the west coast and report to Captain D. at Esquimalt for court martial. I could think of nothing I had done to warrant such action but I was highly annoyed that the message had come via C.N. Telegraph rather than Naval wire service with no attempt at discretion. The message so disturbed my wife that any benefit she had derived from the treatment was completely nullified.

In due course I arrived at Esquimalt and presented myself immediately to my old adversary. Neither Captain D. or his staff would tell me what was going on but simply turned me over to Security. They agreed not to hold me in close confinement on the promise that I appear at Work Point Barracks the following morning where Lt. Col. Gardner would conduct the proceedings. I spent an uncomfortable night. I still had no idea what any of this was about.

I arrived at the inquiry the next day with some sense of foreboding and was introduced to the Colonel. I relaxed somewhat on noticing that he didn't appear hostile. We went into preliminary conference and I found to my relief that I had simply been called as a witness. Two Army men were accused of having some Russian pencils and a pencil sharpener in their possession. These items were said to have come from a Russian vessel wrecked at Pachena Point which had been placed under Army security. One of the men was also accused of pilfering a sack of flour from the same source. I stated to the Colonel quite frankly that I failed to see that such a heinous crime had been committed. A ship ashore and abandoned was fair game for plundering before it was lost to the sea. The Colonel inclined to agree with my point of view and the men were let off quite lightly.

Around this period a vessel of the R.C.A.F. fleet went missing. The ship was called the *Midnight Sun* and had left no clue to her disappearance. My friend Curly Auchterlonie, then C.O. aboard H.M.C.S. *Ripple*, had been drifting in the vicinity of Cape Swaine on the night the *Sun* had vanished. He had been lying with his lights out in hope of discovering a surfaced sub and had heard a violent explosion. It had come from the general area that the *Sun* would have been crossing on her course from Milbank Sound to Cape St. James. It was not till some time later that we learned of the disappearance, since the R.C.A.F. preferred to handle their own problems. Auchterlonie and I got our heads together and decided there was very likely a link between the two events. I reported our suspicions and was assigned to investigate.

On arriving at the western entrance of Higgins Pass, I put a party ashore to search the beach. Within fifteen minutes I could see from the bridge that they had discovered bits and pieces of something and were collecting them. When the various items of wreckage were brought aboard and reassembled, it was obvious that we had recovered part of a pilot house with pieces of its floor as well as other debris that could have come from the missing *Sun*. More careful examination showed the flooring to be part of a false floor built over the engineroom hatch. On the splintered ends of the boards the slivers were all turned upward, and the shattered condition of the wood suggested extreme force from below. We took the wreckage back to port and were ordered to turn it over to the Air Force at their Seal Cove base. They were fortunate in being able to come up with a member who had served at one time on the missing vessel. He was able to find parts he had actually painted and there was no doubt that we had located the remains of the *Midnight Sun*. It seemed very likely that the vessel had collided with a drifting mine.

The theory was further substantiated on my next patrol. I had returned to my regular assignment area and was cruising through turbulent seas in a half-gale off the northwest tip of Graham Island. The west coast of the Queen Charlottes is no picnic ground at the best of times. Through the heaving waves and drifting fog, I spotted what appeared to be an oil drum drifting sluggishly in the distance. On closer examination it proved to be beyond question an enemy mine. I worked up as close to it as I considered safe from collision, then made notes of its size, shape and general characteristics. I then decided to detonate it with rifle fire, since it would remain a constant hazard to shipping if left adrift. I radioed N.O.I.C. at Prince Rupert: HAVE SIGHTED AND SUNK DRIFTING MINE BY RIFLE FIRE and gave the exact location. The message was worded in the past tense as I had no way of telling what damage might be suffered by our vessel when the mine went off. A severe concussion near a wooden hull could open the caulking and sink the vessel out from under us. The lifeboats were made ready and preparations taken to abandon ship at short notice should we need to. Fortunately my fears were unfounded and the mine was dispatched without a hitch. I wired again in fifteen minutes as was customary to say that *Moolock* had resumed patrol. We then headed for the tip of Langara Island where our position could be definitely established by the lighthouse foghorn. When we reached Naden Harbour I got busy making a sketch of the mine from my notes. There was no way to ascertain its type since we had not been issued with an identification book. Just as I completed my sketch, I received a signal from N.O.I.C. instructing me to abandon patrol and report to Rupert forthwith.

Upon our arrival, the mine experts and other knowledgeable officers were assembled. I was subjected to a real grilling. The sketch I had made showed the mine to have three prongs or triggers. This had struck me odd at the time but I was sure of my observations. After considerable search, a print of a Japanese mine was produced that fitted my drawing exactly. Our kill was duly accredited.

Winter weather closed in on us with its attendant

hardships and each patrol began to seem tougher than the last. Often, for days at a time, we were unable to sleep in a dry bunk or eat a hot meal. Tossing endlessly through storm-churned waters, it was impossible to get proper rest and the food situation was particularly grim. The cook assigned to *Moolock* had no sailing experience whatsoever. He got seasick the moment we left harbour and remained that way for the duration of each voyage. The ratings soon nicknamed him Charcoal Charlie, declaring the only way he knew anything was done was when it burst into flame. Prior to joining the Navy, he had been a blacksmith's helper at an interior mining community. Few cooks were entering the Navy and fewer still applying for sea duty. A story circulated as to how the Navy was dealing with this shortage. They simply made up a squad of new recruits and ran them up and down the area around H.M.C.S. *Naden* to the point of collapse. Then they were brought to a halt and volunteers for the galley advised to drop out. If there were no volunteers, the run was resumed at an even faster pace. When one considered the end results, it was difficult not to give some credence to this yarn. But all in all it was no laughing matter. I became so exhausted I went to the M.O. and asked for a tonic. After checking my physical condition however, he assigned me to a month's rest in hospital. I didn't argue with him.

I returned from my rest cure in considerably better condition and reassumed command of the *Moolock*. The weather had not improved during my absence but we managed the first run without mishap. At the Skidegate area however, where our patrol should have ended, I was ordered to make a 150-mile detour and pick up a signal book from Masset. No one aboard, including myself, was much pleased by this instruction as it would shorten our time in port but such extra duty was often imposed. We could only grin and bear it. As we approached Rose Spit the wind out of the inlets reached gale force. We passed the Spit and I found to my alarm that the southeast gale that had plagued the earlier part of our journey was continuing in Hecate Straits. We were caught in the middle of a gigantic floodtide created by the cross sea and the current was breaking wildly in every direction. We climbed to the top of one colossal swell and then were hit broadside by an equally enormous sea from the southeast. The waters exploded against one another and the *Moolock* was left momentarily in midair. She hit the trough on her beam ends with shuddering impact as though she had been dropped from a three-storey building. The force of our landing was such that the mast was snapped clean off above the stays like a rotten twig. I received an immediate alarm call from the engineroom. The terrific jolt had shifted the engine and broken the circulating discharge pipe. As a result water was pouring into the bilge where certainly none was needed. Fortunately I had a very efficient engineer. Temporary repairs were effected, we got underway again and I headed for the lee of Rose Spit. This is a very risky position. If the wind switches to the westward one can be caught in a trap. Many vessels seeking sanctuary there have failed to fight clear and gone ashore in the breakers. But we had little option under the circumstances. We cast anchor and waited nervously for daylight.

As soon as it was possible to see, a boat was dispatched for material to shore up the engine. It had been found that both engine beds were split in two and only its own weight was holding the engine in place. The tail shaft was taking a beating each time the engine leaned over and was badly out of line. There is never any shortage of flotsam on Rose Spit. It gathers most of the material driven up Hecate Straits from points as remote as the Oregon coast. Suitable wood was secured from the beach and two braces rigged, extending over the wing fuel tanks and coaming level to the top of the engine. These were secured with wedges and we were in business again. We hauled anchor and set out for Rupert but as soon as we hit the first bad sea the wedges fell out. It was found the vessel was working so badly that the distance spanned was not constant. It remained for an engineer to shoulder the engine end of the brace and jam the engine each time it rolled toward him. In this half-crippled and jerry-rigged condition we finally limped into Rupert some five hours later.

I turned the *Moolock* over to the port engineer for repairs and we went gratefully ashore. But he underestimated the extent of the damage. His men simply screwed the holding-down bolts to the end of their threads, reported repairs completed and the ship ready for sea. My engineer, in whom I had complete faith, took me down and showed me these so-called "repairs". I was then handed my sailing orders, which I flatly refused to accept.

The roof fell in. I was immediately hauled before the top brass to explain my actions and some most disagreeable threats were flung in my direction. Our routing officer came to my defence, suggesting that the matter was too serious to go unheeded and that a more careful survey should be made in line with my complaints. I would settle for nothing less than that the sixteen-ton engine should be lifted and moved to one side and a proper examination made. Against considerable objection, this was finally done. The report originally given by my engineer proved correct in every detail and a thorough repair job was ordered.

When the engineroom had been put right again I accepted my sailing orders and we returned to sea. On this patrol, I was pushing toward Skidegate Bar through foul weather and poor visibility. The sea was breaking heavily and I was anxious to clear the bar before darkness came down. I spotted a near-tidal-wave-size breaker bearing down on us through the murk but judged it would spend itself before it reached the *Moolock*. My judgement proved wrong and it continued to build up. We were just rolling to port when the great wave struck like a wet sledgehammer. I was standing in the pilot house and the front of it suddenly crumpled and came in on me, wall, windows and all. By some miracle I received no injury but the steering wheel was jammed. The vessel had to be stopped and the wreckage cleared away. The channel is narrow at that point with little room to drift, so this task was accomplished with the utmost haste and the ship gotten underway again. Fortunately we had just reached a patch of easier sea. Proceeding at reduced speed, we reached Alliford Bay safely. Here a canvas was stretched over the broken front of the wheelhouse and we were able to complete our patrol around the Charlottes. Inspection revealed that instead of the uprights being mortised into the coaming, they had been simply toenailed with no more care than the uprights on an outhouse. There were six vessels in *Moolock*'s class, built two apiece in three different yards. *Moolock* and her sister ship *Leelo* had the misfortune to be built in the poorest yard of the three. The Army had similar problems with her *General Lake*, built in the same yard. Her engine fell off its bed in the same manner that ours had. There were no such complaints of our other sister ships.

The war was drawing to a close. I was appointed to H.M.C.S. *B.C. Lady* and given command of a five-ship convoy. One of these was being towed to Esquimalt for decommissioning. When the F.R. vessels had come into the Navy, all the fishing equipment and other unneeded gear had been stripped and stored on a small island in Esquimalt. Now it was time to return these vessels to their owners and it was soon discovered that the earliest dischargees had absconded with all the best equipment. The picked-over gear that remained was largely useless and it was clear that some compensation would have to be made to the short-shrifted owners. After discussing the matter with some of the justifiably incensed men involved, I suggested that $4,000 be offered to each man in

lieu of his missing gear. This was found acceptable to both sides involved and the remaining vessels were soon demobbed. The Gumboot Navy was being phased out.

I had not been paid for nine months as a result of the Navy having mislaid my ledger sheet. I expected this situation would have been rectified by the time I arrived at Esquimalt but such was not the case. In addition I found that a $150 clothing allowance, intimated in a general order, was not to be forthcoming either. In some anger I took my troubles to the Paymaster. He lent a sympathetic ear and after a lengthy discussion, I thought to tell him of my compassionate leave in Winnipeg. This seemed to jog his memory and he got in touch with the H.M.C.S. *Chippeweyan*. It turned out that they had received a signal at that time drafting me to their establishment but no subsequent one as to my disposal. They forwarded my ledger sheet and the matter was resolved. After taking a long overdue leave, I was finally discharged on May 10 1944. I left the service with a slightly bad taste in my mouth. It was difficult to forget the inequitable pay, the injustice of the food allowance, the general lack of respect accorded our branch — both officers and men — by the regular Navy.

And yet, I by no means regret my service in the Fishermen's Reserve. It was a highly rewarding experience in many ways. I held more commands than any other C.O. during my two-year hitch yet I never had what could be termed a poor crew. I believe the Navy assembled a fine group of officers and ratings in the F.R. They probably possessed collectively a greater knowledge of the B.C. coast than the rest of Canada combined. The following signal, received from Ottawa as the Service was being disbanded surely proves that there were some who appreciated our efforts.

NAVAL MESSAGE

To: ALL FISHERMEN'S RESERVE PERSONNEL: AIG #163.

From: COPC.

RESTRICTED.

THE FOLLOWING SIGNAL HAS BEEN RECEIVED FROM THE CHIEF OF NAVAL STAFF AND IS HEREBY PROMULGATED:

"TO EVERY MEMBER OF THE FISHERMEN'S RESERVE, NOW DISBANDING, I WISH TO CONVEY SINCERE APPRECIATION AND THANKS FOR THE EXCELLENT JOB YOU HAVE DONE. IN CARRYING OUT THE ARDUOUS PATROLS OF THE WEST COAST EFFICIENTLY AND WITHOUT COMPLAINT, IN ALL WEATHERS AND UNDER THE DIFFICULT CONDITIONS NECESSITATED BY THE SIZE OF THE SHIPS IN WHICH YOU HAVE SERVED, NO HIGHER PRAISE CAN BE EXTENDED TO YOU IN THAT YOU HAVE LIVED UP TO THE BEST TRADITION OF SEAMEN IN DEFENCE OF THEIR COUNTRY. I WISH YOU ALL SUCCESS IN THE FUTURE AND TRUST THAT YOU WILL CONTINUE TO MAINTAIN YOUR INTEREST IN THE NAVY".

the Shakers

Yvonne Klan

"SHAKER DEVIL, SHAKER DEVIL, SHAKER DEVIL!" the older children taunted in singsong. I stared at the passing Indian and wondered how so ordinary an appearance could conceal such sinister purpose. A real Shaker devil!

When I was a very young child we lived on Vancouver Island, in a dingy little house on a hill by the Koksilah (Coke-SIGH-lah) River. I was already well acquainted with the usual childhood terrors – ghosts, darkness, kidnappers, the bogeyman – but most dreaded of all my terrors were the Indian Shakers. Often I heard the adults (possibly as uneasy as I) talk of Shaker medicine-man rituals performed by candle-light, of Shaker possession by the devil and, most frightening of all, of Shakers raised from the dead. The noise of Shaker bells, it was said, drowned out cries for help.

Some nights the sound of distant Shaker bells reached up the hill, into our house, into my bedroom. "The Shakers are at it again," someone would say, "they're really going crazy down there." And talk turned again to stories of unholy Shaker powers. Fearful, I would call out for a drink of water, actually hoping for attention, comfort, reassurance. "Get to sleep," I was told, "or the Shakers will come and get you." And I lay owl-eyed and apprehensive in the darkness while the devil bells grew louder, and louder . . .

These long-forgotten terrors surfaced recently when a chance remark was made about Indian Shakers. What did they actually do, I wondered. Who were they? Do they still exist? I researched, I interviewed, and I learned. I learned of the Indian Shakers' bizarre beginnings near Mud Bay, Washington . . .

Big Bill, a Mud Bay Indian, made the first prophecies in 1880. Wasted by tuberculosis, des-

pondent, and unable to work, he attempted to hang himself. At the point of death he had a vision of his dead brother, who urged him to live and gave him important news to tell his people. Big Bill's despondency vanished. His cries for help brought rescue and he lived to spread his revelation. God would give a great power to someone in the area, he prophesied, and when that person appeared everyone must listen to him and help him because those were God's wishes. In June, 1881, Big Bill died.

Four months later John Slocum, an illiterate logger who managed to support his family despite his weakness for drinking, gambling, and horse racing, died. Uneasiness hung over the mourners gathered around Slocum's shrouded body, for there were dark suspicions that he was the victim of a medicine man hired by his wife's family to kill him. Then, in full view of the gathering, a startling thing happened: Slocum's body stirred beneath its wrappings. He sat up, opened his eyes, and spoke to the awed assembly.

He spoke of his death, and of his soul's journey to the judgment place of God where it was stopped by an angel. The angel forbade Slocum to enter Heaven because of his wickedness. His only hope of getting to Heaven, said the angel, was to return to earth and give up his sinful ways. Further, he must instruct others, by word and example, in Christian living; only by renouncing their sins could the people hope to reach Heaven. A church must be built where Slocum could hold meetings. Indian medicine men were evil, the angel continued, and must be avoided. If the people believed in what Slocum said, God would give the Indians a new kind of medicine.

The Indians sorely needed a new kind of medicine. Indian doctors were evil, the missionaries said and the government passed laws banning Indian doctoring. As yet the Indians had little confidence in white medicine, for it was common knowledge that whites were immune to shamans' powers and had no medicine against them. Nor did whitemen's souls go astray and get lost as Indian souls did. Meanwhile Indian villages were being ravaged by tuberculosis, smallpox, and measles — diseases which fell upon white people with a lighter touch.

The Indians also had their social problems. Mud Bay Louis remembered those early days:

Well, my friend, we was about the poorest tribe on earth. We was only tribe now full blood and nothing else. We would not believe anything. Minister came here but we laugh at him. We lived bad habits — stealing — and John Slocum died. He was not a religious man — knew nothing of God — all of us same . . . I was worst of lot. I was drunkard — was half starving — spent every cent for whiskey. I gambled, raced horses, bet shirt, money, blanket — did not know any better . . . We lost by drowning — our friends drink whiskey and the canoes turn over — we died out in the bay . . .

Slocum's resurrection, Mud Bay Louis recounted, changed all that.

Long ago we knew nothing at all. When Slocum came back from God we found out there was a God. From that time we have prayed for anything we want. We follow God's way. God teaches us if we do bad we will go to hell. That's why we pray and avoid bad habits. If we don't ask grace, bad things come when we eating. When we drink water, we think about God before drinking. If we don't think of him, may be we get sick from water. If traveling, maybe we die if we don't think of God. We are afraid to do wrong against God . . . God put people here to grow — put our soul in our body. That's why we pray so much. If we quit, like a man quit his job, he gets no pay. We would go to fire in hell. We have no power to put out hell fire.

Now I have quit swearing — my heart is upside down — it is changed. . . . I will remain a follower of Christ as long as I live. [1]

News of Slocum's resurrection and of the angel's instructions spread. People from neighbouring reserves came to hear him preach. He gained converts. Clearly drawing upon his early Catholic and Protestant training, he instructed his congregation to confess their sins and repent, to pray before eating, and to cross themselves on frequent specified occasions. But Slocum was not an inspired leader. His services were dour, dull, lengthy affairs. Worse still, he began to slip back to his old vices and thought less and less about God. His congregation dwindled and the whole episode may have vanished from memory but for a yet more startling event.

About a year after his resurrection, Slocum lay ill and was expected to die. His family wanted to hire a powerful medicine man but his wife, Mary, mindful of the angel's instructions, bitterly opposed this. In spite of her opposition John's father hired a medicine man and threatened to kill Mary should John die. Distraught, Mary left the house, returning shortly in the throes of a hysterical seizure. Sobbing, praying, trembling violently, she circled her husband's body. As she brushed past the assembled relatives they, too,

started shaking. She touched John and he immediately revived. Mary declared that shaking was the new medicine God had promised the Indians. The Indian Shaker religion was born.

Excitement ran high as news of the "shake" medicine spread. Regular curing meetings were held where converts came to confess and renounce their sins; people went into trances and were revived; miraculous cures were brought about. A big meeting called in August, 1883, sparked tremendous excitement. Two logging camps closed for the event and many people came from outlying areas. There were rumours that the world would end; that the unconverted would go straight to Hell; that Jesus Christ would appear at the meeting; that the dead would be restored to life. Reverend Eells, the Presbyterian missionary, learned of the event and recorded:

Visions were abundant; four people, it was said, died and were raised to life again; women, professing to be angels, tried to fly around . . . It was reported that they saw myself . . . and others in hell; that I was kept on the reservation to get the lands of the Indians away from them, and that I told lies in church. [2]

During the frenetic proceedings of a subsequent meeting it was revealed to Big John of Skokomish that he was Jesus Christ Incarnate and that his wife was the Virgin Mary. The Shakers were so enthralled with the revelation they decided to spread the news to the townsfolk of Olympia. With his arms extended like the crucified Christ, Big John and his wife rode horseback through Olympia, followed by at least fifty enraptured Shakers. For leading this disturbance Big John was promptly jailed by the authorities.

Most missionaries were appalled by this corruption of Christianity and enlisted the support of Indian Agents to abolish the spreading movement. Their various manoeuvres served only to drive the Shakers underground until 1889, when Washington became a state and its inhabitants were granted American citizenship. Eells noted morosely:

Lately the Shaker sect has revived considerably. This singular freak is a new religion . . . and when it first originated was kept under quite firmly by the agent. Lately, however, they have learned that the freedom of citizenship allowed them this religion as much as they wished, and consequently it has revived quite strongly. Some things about it have been rather discouraging to me. [3]

The Shakers still had to contend with a government edict banning Indian doctoring (convicted medicine men were sentenced anywhere from 30 to 45 days' labour). The difference between Shakers and traditional Indian doctors was not as clear to the agents as it was to Sam Yowaluch, an early Shaker healer:

I take power and cure people when they are sick. Long time ago I knew nothing — just like an animal. No doctoring, no medicine — no good. I was a drunkard, was a thief, and a robber. When I joined this religion I was told to be good . . . I heard that if I prayed I would have power and be a medicine-man, and could cure the sick . . . There is lots of difference between this power and old Indian doctoring. This is not old power. I can cure people now. I have cured some white men and women, but they are ashamed to tell it. I cure without money . . . One man offered us twenty dollars – but no, we refused it. God will pay us when we die. This is our religion . . . I believe this religion. It helps poor people . . . We were sent to jail for this religion but we will never give up.[4]

The Shakers shunned and ridiculed medicine men, whom they considered particularly evil because they used their power to bring sickness and death to people. When shamans did cure, they charged large fees for their services. (This criticism was also levelled at white doctors.) Some medicine men retaliated by shooting malicious powers into Shaker meetings in order to disrupt proceedings. However, other medicine men became converts and restricted the use of their power to benign purposes.

Some Shakers satisfied old grudges by making indiscriminate and unfounded charges of shamanism practised within the congregation. The frightening witch hunts and cruel persecutions which resulted alienated many Indians from the young church. Other Shakers withdrew because of the constant bickering, the internal turmoil, and leadership struggles. Ironically, one of the main sources of discord was the Bible. One faction felt it should be used in Shaker services as an inspired book. Another faction maintained Shakers didn't need the Bible because God's will was made known through Slocum's revelation and, more directly and personally, when one got the shakes. Today's Shakers may be very familiar with the Bible, but they do not use it in services.

By the early 1900's the movement had spread into California, Oregon, Idaho and B.C. Several churches were built in the Victoria area, one was built in Koksilah, and another in Duncan. Small but enthusiastic congregations held meetings in Nanaimo, Squamish, Musqueam, and North Vancouver.

With the help of sympathetic whites, the Indian Shaker Church was incorporated as a religious body in Washington State in 1910. Until very recently the church was not recognized in Canada. If Canadians wanted a ceremony performed by a Shaker minister they had to cross the border to obtain the services of an American Shaker. Permits had to be obtained to hold meetings. This has changed now. A Shaker told me recently:

About two or three years ago this fellow came from Victoria. He wanted to see what went on in the church. He watched what went on in the church. He watched what people did in the church. He stood there for two hours. He got so shook up he walked out. He told one of the men, "If I had stayed in there any longer I would have been jumping around like the rest of you people." They gave the Indians a license to perform weddings, burial ceremonies and baptisms, and this was put on a trial basis. So we're on trial now.

Shakers perform their ceremonies in simple, unadorned churches of wood-frame construction. One end of the building is formed into an alcove which contains a prayer table and, on the wall above the

table, a large cross. The table holds handbells, candles, and perhaps a simple floral arrangement. (Most Shakers have similar, though smaller, prayer tables in their homes.) The congregation sits on benches, those for observers set apart from those for participants. A large open area accommodates the processions and the shakers. A few chairs for those who seek healing complete the furnishings.

Church services are supervised by the floor manager, who may call upon anyone in the congregation to lead a procession, a song, or a ceremony. Services vary in different churches but usually include prayers, testimonials, singing, elaborate processions, the ritual handshake, and frequent signs of the cross. When a Shaker goes to church he expects to participate rather than observe. Curing ceremonies may be included in a service, but usually special meetings are held for this purpose.

One cannot be a Shaker until one has got "the shakes" – the outward manifestation of power. Shaker power comes from God. It gives vivid insight into His will and makes clear the nature of all things. It restores, regenerates, soothes, and leaves a profound sense of well-being. "Under power" a Shaker may become clairvoyant, have meaningful visions, receive inspiration. But the most important thing about the power is that it gives not only the ability to know the nature of a malady, but also the ability to cure oneself and others. The power may "hit" during church services but it is most intensely experienced during curing ceremonies.

During the procession at church services, or at the beginning of a healing ceremony, someone starts a rhythmic song. The song is the expression of the singer's spirit. The spirit wells up inside until its power can no longer be contained, then bursts forth as song. Should the song falter after its initial outburst others in the procession will try to pick up on it, to encourage it, to "help it out." Soon the whole congregation is singing, the voices swelling with each repetition of the song. The floor manager signals with his handbells. People who brought bells pick them up and, holding one in each hand like a rattle, shake them in unison to a steady, driving rhythm, while circling the room. The heavy tramp of feet, the deafening noise of bells, drown out the song. People stop singing, close their eyes, and give themselves up to the pulsating rhythm. The walls throb with the pounding, unrelenting din. Spectators help by beating time. The power hits. As the shake spreads through the congregation one member after another begins to tremble violently. Each individual becomes lost in his own ecstasy, all the while making brushing, scraping gestures over his (or his neighbour's) body to "get the sin off."

A prospective initiate may at this point join the throng, his arms uplifted in an invitation to the power to hit him. Miss Ober, an early missionary, gives an eyewitness account of a young man's initiation:

They clustered about him, dancing frantically, ringing many bells close to his head, making hypnotic passes over him, stroking, rubbing, whirling him round and round . . . I saw women whirling round and round him for over an hour, until I could scarcely distinguish their separate figures, so rapid were their dizzy evolu-

tions. Then they whirled him about with them, till severally they fell out, exhausted, and only one was left, a small woman whose head did not reach the boy's shoulder. How she did it I cannot tell, but she whirled that stiff, motionless body round and round, and all over the room, and he never moved even his feet . . . The boy was like a wooden statue, without sign of life or motion. Finally both fell to the floor, the boy's head striking with an awful crash. The woman was soon resuscitated, but the boy lay without life or motion, in the very same attitude that he had taken at the beginning. For an hour the Shakers continued their performances, until at 4 a.m. I left. But the next morning . . . there was (the youth), as lively as a cricket, dancing away, and full of happiness for he had "got the shake."[5]

Curing ceremonies are the most dramatic demonstrations of Shaker power and give a clear example of Christianity blended with old Salish shamanistic beliefs. Almost every Shaker can tell of miraculous cures he has witnessed or experienced. One does not have to be a Shaker to seek Shaker help and it is against Shaker principles to accept payment for curing. Those who seek healing seat themselves in the centre of the circling Shakers, and the group "works on" them. If a patient is too ill to go to church, Shakers are called to the home. Curing sessions last as long as the supply

of patients and enthusiasm dictate. Some cures take only an hour or so; more difficult cases involve several nights of hard shaking.

Though the Shakers reject Indian doctoring, they maintain some of the old Salish concepts of sickness and cure. When someone becomes despondent or loses the will to live, Shakers believe that he has lost his vital essence (or soul). In the old days the soul might have been kidnapped by a malicious medicine man. The days of the medicine man are past but other hazards remain to threaten the hapless soul. It might accidently become dislodged by a fall or a psychological shock to the system. Sometimes ghosts, yearning for those left behind, kidnap a loved one's soul to keep them company. Some Shakers under power can see lost souls, which are light, fluffy, and "like a fog." Others are led to the soul by a thread "like a cobweb," or by an invisible guiding force. When the wayward soul is found the group restores it to the body with smoothing and patting motions.

In the old days one could hire a medicine man to shoot a deadly object into an enemy. This was usually a small, sharp bone with a bit of hair or feather attached. It was infused with such power that it flew faster than the eye could see. Most dangerous of all was the personal power a medicine man could shoot into a victim. If it was strong enough nothing could be done and the victim died. Shaker power was pitted

against shaman power in a dramatic struggle. The intruded evil must be located and extracted. It was distinguished from the soul by feel: whereas the fog-like soul is soft and gentle, the evil is tough, black and rubbery. When grasped, the thing writhed, squirmed and contorted in its efforts to escape. Once extracted the enraged evil hurled its captor around in an awesome display of power. An eye-witness account reports:

The "disease" dragged the captor about despite the efforts of the others, who held him about the waist, into a corner near the altar. There his hands, still held together, could be heard knocking rapidly on the wall. One of the group was dispatched for a crock of water into which they put the captured "disease," hastily screwed on the lid and carried it out to be buried.[6]

Modern Shakers are more likely to attribute the presence of such malevolent power to an accumulation of sin. Today sin is recognized as the main cause of illness and misfortune; alcoholism is one of the most frequent complaints. Present-day battles with sin are seldom as dramatic as those battles of the past. Bells still pound and feet still stamp as entranced Shakers work on the sufferer. However, various brushing, scooping and scraping motions made over the patient's body usually suffice to "get the sin off." True, there are backsliders, but if they present themselves for help the congregation willingly shakes and prays over them. Chronic backsliders may find themselves handled none too gently.

The shake is God's gift to Indian people. It was not intended for whites because whites aren't afflicted with the disorders which plague Indians. However, there are many instances where Shakers have been called to shake over white patients when all else failed, and there are reported cures. Today a small number of whites are participating members in the Indian Shaker church.

Shakers are not given to meditation and philosophical discourse. Generally speaking, they are content to let such concepts as the Trinity, atonement, redemption and original sin, remain mysteries. The essential element in being a Shaker is having faith in God, Jesus Christ, and the power. Without faith one cannot cure or be cured. Without faith there can be no shaking; the emotional release described as "rapport with God" cannot be experienced. Shaker faith is continually fortified by the intense feeling of well-being experienced while shaking, and by cures either witnessed or experienced.

When derided by people of other denominations, Shakers take pride in pointing out that they don't drink, smoke, or gamble. This is viewed as evidence of moral superiority and effectively silences most critics.

Nowadays camp meetings are the most popular form of Shaker service. The larger congregations take turns hosting the weekend affairs on a rotating basis. Shakers from California, Oregon, Washington, and B.C. unite in worship and fellowship. Feelings of regeneration are more profound, cures are more spectacular, as the congregations join forces to help sufferers with a demonstration of the power of simple faith.

Many years later — an adult now — I visited a Shaker home. A white-haired Shaker with a soft voice talked to me; his young grandchild listened attentively. In a corner of the room stood a prayer table holding a cross with candles and the family's handbells.

(Devil bells . . . Shaker devil . . . The resurrected terrors of my childhood seemed remote and unreal.)

He talked of his religion and conversion, of a lost faith suddenly found, of the beneficent changes wrought in him since conversion. Yes, he said, he had witnessed many miracles . . .

We talked about miracles and other things until it was time to leave. I paused at the door. "You know," I confided, "when I was a little child I used to be afraid of Shakers."

He nodded slowly, and replied, "There's lots of people today still afraid of Shakers."

References

1. Mooney, James. "The Ghost-Dance Religion and the Sioux Outbreak of 1890." **Fourteenth Annual Report, Bureau of American Ethnology, 1892-93. Part 2.** Washington D.C., 1896. (University of B.C. Library)
2. **Ibid.**
3. **Ibid.**
4. **Ibid.**
5. Ober, Sarah Endicott. "A New Religion Among the West Coast Indians," **The Overland Monthly.** Series 2, LVI (1910). (Olympia Public Library)
6. Waterman, T.T. "The 'Shake Religion' of Puget Sound," **Smithsonian Institution Annual Report for 1922.** Washington D.C., 1924. (Vancouver Public Library)

Bibliography

Barnett, H.G. **Indian Shakers — A Messianic Cult of the Pacific Northwest.** Southern Illinois University Press. 1957. (Vancouver Public Library, Northwest Room)

Spier, L. **The Prophet Dance of the Northwest and its Derivatives.** University of Washington Ph.D. thesis. 1935. (University of B.C. Library)

Suttles, Wayne P. **Economic Life of Salish of Haro and Rosario Straits.** 1951. University of Washington, Ph.D. thesis. (University of B.C. Library)

NOW YOU'RE LOGGING

A STORY BASED ON LOGGING IN THE "HUNGRY YEARS", AND ABOUT THOSE COMPLEX, AND INTRIGUING CHARACTERS, THE LOGGERS, PRODUCTS OF A SPECIAL TYPE OF WORK, AND WAY OF LIFE----HARD, TOUGH MEN, BECAUSE THEIR LIFE WAS TOUGH, AND BECAUSE OF THE VERY NATURE, AND THE DANGER OF THEIR WORK—

THEY LIVED, AND QUITE OFTEN DIED, WITH THE WIND AND THE RAIN IN THEIR FACES, AND THE PUNGENT ODOR OF THE BIG WOODS IN THEIR NOSTRILS—

AND OCCASIONALLY, FOR NO APPARENT REASON, THEY WOULD "PULL THE PIN," AND UNWIND WITH A HELL-ROARING SPREE—

TRUE, THEY WERE A HARD-LIVING, HARD-DRIVING BUNCH······AND SURE, THEY WERE QUITE CRUDE AT TIMES·····BUT EVEN AMONG THE CRUDEST, MEANEST, AND THE TOUGHEST, THERE WAS A GENTLER SIDE, AND A GREAT LOVE OF NATURE AND THE OUTDOORS—

THESE WERE THE LOGGERS, MEN OF STEAM AND GAS DONKEYS, HIGH-LEAD LOGGING, AND THE BIG TIMBER OF THE RAIN FORESTS OF THE FOG-SHROUDED PACIFIC COAST······MEN WHO TOOK A PRIDE IN THEIR WORK AND SKILLS, AND WHO WERE ARTISTS IN THEIR OWN RIGHT·····

by BUS GRIFFITHS

THE PICKUP TRUCK ROUNDS THE CORNER INTO CAMP—

WHY IS THE *"CAT" CLEARING OFF THAT CHUNK OF GROUND, ART?

THE "OLD MAN" WANTS SPACE FOR MORE BUILDINGS---- LOOKS LIKE DOUG IS GONNA WORK OVERTIME—

ART PULLS IN AT THE SIDE OF THE TRUCK SHED, AND AS AL CLIMBS OUT OF THE CAB, JIM BRADLEY APPROACHES—

HI, JIM!

'LO, AL--- SAY, ART, YOU GOT A MINUTE?

SURE, JIM--- CLIMB IN—

MEANWHILE----- WHAT OF BARNEY?

THE ROAD IS PRETTY FLAT THRU CAMP--- IF I CAN JUST HOLD HER ON THE ROAD!

JUST LISTEN TO THAT MOTOR HOWL! SOUNDS LIKE IT'S GONNA FLY OUT AN' HIT ME IN THE FACE!

BARNEY CAN FEEL THE RUNAWAY TRUCK LOSING SPEED AS HE NEARS THE CORNER HEADING INTO CAMP—

I BETTER LAY ON THE HORN-- IF I CAN HOLD HER ON THIS CURVE I MIGHT GET HER STOPPED ON THE FLAT STRETCH THRU CAMP!!

*"CAT"— CATERPILLAR TRACTOR—

STRONG ARMS GUIDE THE RUNAWAY TRUCK ON THE CURVE, AND HORN BLARING, THE BIG TRUCK ROUNDS THE CORNER INTO CAMP—

GOOD GOD!! THE CRUMMIES! !?!

UNAWARE OF THEIR DANGER, AND UNABLE TO HEAR THE BLARING HORN ABOVE THE ROAR OF THE *"BULLDOZER" WORKING IN CAMP, THE BANTERING CREWS PILE OFF THE CRUMMIES, WHICH SIT IN THE MIDDLE OF THE ROAD, SQUARELY IN THE PATH OF THE RUNAWAY TRUCK—

Bus Griffiths

*"BULLDOZER"— A TRACTOR WITH AN ANGLE BLADE USED FOR ROAD BUILDING—

CURSING SAVAGELY, BARNEY WHEELS THE LOGGING TRUCK OFF THE ROAD— THE TRUCK CAREENS WILDLY, AND THE "PEAKER," OR TOP LOG, FALLS OFF—

THE BIG LOG HITS THE GROUND BEHIND THE PICKUP, AND ONE END SWINGS UP HITTING THE BACK OF THE TRUCK—

THE SMASHING BLOW DRIVES THE PICKUP TRUCK THRU THE WALL OF THE TRUCK SHED—

THERE IS A MUFFLED EXPLOSION, AND THE BUILDING IS ON FIRE —

THE LOGGING CREW STANDS IMMOBILE, STUNNED BY THE SUDDEN, DRAMATIC EVENTS OF THE PAST FEW MOMENTS— AL, WHO HAD JUST LEFT THE PICKUP TRUCK, AND HAD STOPPED NEAR THE CRUMMIES TO TALK TO HIS PAL, RED, IS THE FIRST TO MOVE —

RED-- FOR GOD'S SAKE, C'MON! JIM AND ART ARE IN THE FIRE!

THEN THE CREW EXPLODES INTO ACTION

I'LL GET THE FIRST-AID MAN!

WE BEST MOVE THEM BLOODY CRUMMIES!

WE BETTER CHECK ON OL' BARNEY!

C'MON—LET'S GIT THEM FIRE HOSES!

Bus Griffiths

WHILE IN THE FIRE—

WOW! WE CAN'T GET NEAR THAT TRUCK, AL!

DON'T THINK THEY'RE IN IT! LOOK! BOTH DOORS ARE OPEN!

OH, GOD! GET US OUT OF HERE !!!

THEY'RE IN THE *"GREASE PIT"!

THEY FOUND THE TWO MEN IN A DAZED CONDITION, HUDDLED TO-GETHER IN THE GREASE PIT, THEIR CLOTHING SMOULDERING, BUT SAFE FOR THE MOMENT FROM THE CHOKING SMOKE AND SEARING FLAMES—

RED?--- IS THAT YOU, AL ????

I'LL HELP 'EM UP THE LADDER, RED!

THANK GOD!

YEAH, IT'S ME — RED'S WITH ME-- WE'VE GOT TO GET YOU OUT OF HERE ! CAN YOU WALK?

SURE I CAN WALK--- BUT--- I CAN'T BLOODY WELL SEE!

NEITHER CAN I !-- I'LL HANG ONTO YOU

YOU HELP JIM! PUT YOUR COAT OVER BOTH YOUR HEADS AN' KEEP LOW--- I'LL TAKE ART!

OKAY, AL— I'LL KEEP AS CLOSE TO YOU AS I CAN!

LET'S GET TH' HELL OUT OF HERE !-- WE-- HAVEN'T GOT--- MUCH-- --TIME---!!

Bus Griffiths

*"GREASE PIT"— A PIT DUG INTO THE FLOOR, MADE SO A TRUCK CAN STRADDLE IT, AND DEEP ENOUGH FOR A MAN TO STAND UP AND WORK ON THE TRUCK'S UNDERCARRIAGE —

MEANWHILE, THE TIMEKEEPER, WHO ALSO DOUBLES AS FIRST-AID MAN, IS GETTING THE CREW ORGANIZED, AND ISSUING ORDERS LIKE A FIELD MARSHAL—

TAKE THE STRETCHERS OVER CLOSER TO THE BUILDING--- *HANK,* YOU FETCH ANOTHER BUCKET OF THAT WARM SALT WATER FROM THE COOKHOUSE! HEY- YOU BOYS- HOSE DOWN THE REST OF THE BUILDINGS SO THE FIRE WON'T SPREAD!

SUDDENLY, A SHOUT GOES UP FROM THE MEN OUTSIDE THE BURNING TRUCK SHED —

LOOK! THEY'RE COMIN' OUT!

THEY'VE GOT JIM AND ART!

THEIR CLOTHING IS AFIRE-- USE THOSE BLANKETS THE WAY I SHOWED YOU!

THE MEN WERE UNCEREMONIOUSLY ROLLED IN THE BLANKETS TO SMOTHER THE FLAMES, BUT MOST OF THE FIRE PROVED TO BE IN THE COATS THEY WERE HOLDING OVER THEIR HEADS FOR PROTECTION —

Bus Griffiths

GOOD WORK, BOYS!

THAT *SURE* TOOK GUTS!

YOU SURE YOU GUYS ARE ALRIGHT?

YEAH, THANKS-- WE'RE OKAY-- WHAT ABOUT JIM AND ART?

I DUNNO- ARCHIE IS WORKIN' ON 'EM!

LET'S GET AWAY FROM HERE, RED- LET'S GO AND SIT ON THE *"WOOD LOG"*—

YEAH--- BOY! I COULD SURE GO A COLD BEER RIGHT NOW!

GOD! THAT WAS CLOSE IN THERE, AL! I DON'T--THINK I COULD--HAVE LASTED---MUCH LONGER—

ME NEITHER! I DIDN'T THINK-- WE WAS--GONNA MAKE IT, PARTNER'!

I WONDER HOW BAD ART AND JIM ARE?---WONDER WHAT HAPPENED TO BARNEY AN' THE TRUCK?

WE'LL SOON KNOW-- HERE COMES ARCHIE!

LOGGING TERMS—
"WOOD LOG"--A LOG THAT HAS BEEN DEPOSITED IN CAMP, TO BE CUT UP AS FUEL FOR THE COOK-HOUSE AND BUNKHOUSES —

THEY'RE ASKING TO SEE YOU BOYS— THAT WAS A *GREAT JOB* YOU DID—— GOING *INTO THAT FIRE* AND *PULLING THEM OUT*—A *TERRIFIC JOB!!*

THANKS! HOW BAD ARE THEY, ARCHIE?

I DON'T THINK THEY ARE TOO BADLY BURNED, BUT I'M A LITTLE WORRIED ABOUT THEIR EYES——IN THE FLASH OF THE EXPLOSION THEIR FACES AND EYELIDS WERE SCORCHED— THEY'VE LOST ALL THEIR HAIR, EYE- BROWS, AND LASHES!

I SURE HOPE THE POOR BASTARDS ARE GONNA BE ALRIGHT!

I'VE SOAKED THEIR CLOTHING WITH THAT WARM SALT SOLUTION IN CASE OF BODY BURNS, AND WRAPPED THEM IN BLANKETS TO KEEP THEM WARM— THAT WILL COMFORT THEM UNTIL WE GET THEM TO THE HOSPITAL—BUT YOU HAVE *NO IDEA* WHAT A *DIFFICULT MAN* ART DONNEGAN IS!

WHO SAYS WE DON'T!

WHAT ABOUT OL' BARNEY? WAS HE BADLY HURT?

I CAN'T REALLY SAY! THINGS HAPPENED SO *FAST*, AND I'VE BEEN BUSY WITH THE BOSS AND ART—— I HAVEN'T HEARD A *THING* ABOUT BARNEY!

NOW, DON'T TALK TO THEM *TOO LONG*—- WE'VE GOT TO GET THEM TO THE HOSPITAL AS SOON AS POSSIBLE! THE BOYS ARE HERE, ART!

YOU GUYS ARE *SURE SOMETHIN'!* I THINK I'M SPEAKIN' FOR JIM, TOO, WHEN I SAY I'LL *NEVER FORGET* WHAT YOU *DID*— WE'D *NEVER* GOT OUT ON OUR OWN—— HELL—IT HAPPENED SO BLOODY FAST!

ART'S RIGHT, LADS—-BUT WE WERE LUCKY— WHEN THE PICK- UP WENT THRU THE WALL IT HIT A POST— WE GOT THROWN OUT, JUST AS IT EXPLODED—— WE WERE ON FIRE, BUT MADE IT TO THE PIT—WE ROLLED AROUND—AN' THEN YOU COME— *JUST THANKIN'* SOMEBODY FOR SAVIN' YOUR LIFE *DON'T SEEM TO BE ENOUGH!*

AW, HELL—-WE'RE JUST GLAD WE MADE IT IN TIME!

Bus Griffiths—

86

WHAT TH' *HELL* HAPPENED, ANYWAY? WE WAS SITTIN' IN THE PICKUP---- I STILL HAD THE ENGINE RUNNIN'--- AN' THEN I SEEN BARNEY GO FLYIN' BY --- THERE WAS A *HELLUVA CRASH,* AN' WE WAS IN THE SHED, AN' ON FIRE --- *WHAT TH' HELL HAPPENED TO BARNEY ?*

GUESS HE HAD A RUN-AWAY--- HE COME SNORTIN' AROUND THE CORNER AND THE CRUMMIES WERE UNLOADING THE MEN!

BARNEY JUST WHEELED HER OFF THE ROAD AND A LOG FELL OFF AND HIT YOUR PICKUP---- I DON'T KNOW HOW *HE MADE OUT*----

GOD! HE COULD HAVE *WIPED OUT TH' WHOLE CREW!* I HOPE THE OLD BASTARD'S OKAY!

HI, AL! I HEARD YOU MENTION BARNEY--- HE'S OKAY! I JUST LEFT HIM!

THAT'S SURE GOOD NEWS!

WHO THE HELL IS THAT?

IT'S *ME---!* CHILLIWACK!

BARNEY RUN THE TRUCK INTO THAT BUSH BACK OF THE SHED, AN' HE NEVER GOT A SCRATCH---- BUT THE TRUCK'S BUGGERED UP A LITTLE----

TO *HELL* WITH THE TRUCK! I'M GLAD OL' BARNEY'S OKAY!

WE PARBUCKLED THE LOAD OFF WITH THE CAT, AN' DOUG PULLED THE TRUCK FURTHER FROM THE FIRE--- BARNEY'S GONNA CHECK HER TO SEE HOW BAD SHE'S DAMAGED--- HE SAID HE COULDN'T HOLD HER ON THE LONG HILL--- GUESS THE LOAD WAS TOO HEAVY--- SHE RAN AWAY---

BUS Griffiths-

ALL THAT, AN' HE JUST LOST *ONE LOG* OFF THE LOAD! WHEN I LOAD 'EM, *THEY'RE LOADED!*

IS THAT ALL HE LOST? WELL, HE COULD HAVE *LOST HIS LIFE,* AN' HE *COULD* HAVE WIPED OUT THE WHOLE CREW--- *YOU SONOFABITCH---YOU* BETTER GET YOURSELF A JOB LOADIN' HAY, 'CAUSE YOU SURE AS *HELL* AIN'T GONNA BE LOADIN' *NO MORE LOGS* AROUND *THIS OUTFIT--* YOU CAN GET YOUR GODDAMNED TIME IN THE MORNIN'--- SEE ABOUT IT, ARCHIE!

I CERTAINLY WILL, ART!

EASY, ART!

87

I WISH I COULD SEE WHAT THE HELL'S GOIN' ON! IS THE WHOLE SHITEREE BURNIN' UP?

THE TRUCK AND BLACKSMITH SHOPS ARE A TOTAL LOSS, BUT THE BOYS KEPT THE REST OF THE BUILDINGS WET DOWN AND STOPPED THE FIRE FROM SPREADING!

WHAT ABOUT THE OTHER TWO TRUCKS? WERE THEY IN TH' SHED? AND WHAT ABOUT THAT *"MASTER MANIAC", AN' THE BLACKSMITH?

THE TRUCKS ARE OKAY, ART-- THEY JUST GOT BACK FROM THE *"LOG DUMP"-- CASEY HAD TROUBLE DUMPING HIS LOAD AN' HELD THINGS UP--- THE MECHANIC AND SMITHY ARE OKAY--- THEY HAD JUST GONE TO THE COOKHOUSE, FOR A *"MUG UP"--

BUT WE BETTER GET YOU CHAPS DOWN TO THE VILLAGE AND INTO THE HOSPITAL—

I WISH TO HELL YOU'D SHUT UP, ARCHIE--- NOW LISTEN, AL— ALL THAT LOADIN' RIGGIN' STILL HAS TO BE STRIPPED OFF THE OLD SPAR AN' HUNG ON THE NEW TREE---

I'LL TAKE CARE OF IT, ART!

I'LL BE LAID UP FOR A FEW DAYS, SO WE'LL SHUT DOWN TH' LOGGIN' 'TILL I GET BACK-- BUT I'LL GET WORD TO CAMP--- LOOK AFTER THINGS WHILE I'M GONE---DOGGONE IT-- YOU GUYS----I---

SURE, ART— YOU GUYS TAKE CARE OF YOURSELVES, AN' GOOD LUCK!

GO EASY ON THOSE NURSES, ART--- AN' WATCH OL' JIM WITH THAT HEAD MATRON

IT'S TOO BAD YOU FIRED "CHILLIWACK"— I GUESS I'M PARTLY TO BLAME---I WAS RIDIN' HIM PRETTY HARD ABOUT NOT KEEPIN' UP WITH TH' YARDIN' CREW!

WHATTA YA MEAN, "TOO BAD"? IF I COULDA SEEN TH' SONOFABITCH I'DA BIT TH' FACE RIGHT OFF HIM--- AN' LISTEN, YOU OLD GOAT-- IN FUTURE, WHILE I'M PUSHIN' CAMP, I DON'T WANT YOU INTERFERIN' WITH TH' CREW--ALL YOU GOTTA DO IS SIGN THEM BLOODY CHEQUES--- I'LL LOOK AFTER TH' LOGGIN'!!

THEY'VE GOT 'EM ABOARD! LET'S ROLL!

ART SOUNDS OKAY, BUT I DOUBT THAT HE'LL BE BACK IN A FEW DAYS!

YEAH— IT DON'T SEEM LIKELY--- BUT YOU NEVER KNOW WITH GUYS LIKE HIM---THEY SURE DON'T COME ANY TOUGHER! WE'LL JUST HAVE TO WAIT AND SEE---C'MON, LET'S GET SOME SUPPER

LOGGING TERMS
BUS Griffiths—

*"MASTER MANIAC"— A SARCASTIC NAME FOR THE HEAD MECHANIC
*"LOG DUMP"— WHERE THE LOGS ARE UNLOADED AT THE BOOMING GROUND
*"MUG UP"— HAVING A CUP OF COFFEE

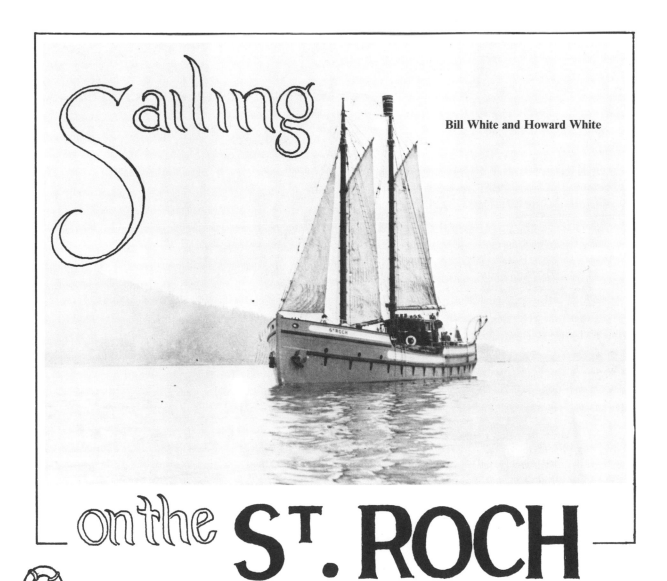

Sailing
on the St. ROCH

Bill White and Howard White

N THE MORNING OF JUNE 17, 1930, A DECKHAND FLOPPED OUR STERN HAWSER into the chuck alongside the old Evans Coleman dock in downtown Vancouver and the *St. Roch* was off to the Arctic under Henry Larsen for the first time. I was glad to be on the way at last, but if anybody'd come up to me then and said fifty years later that ship would be inside a museum or that jittery character on the bridge would be established as a national hero, I'd have thought they were nuts.

I sure don't remember much fuss being made about us at the time. If there were writeups in the papers I never saw any and there was no sendoff party other than the usual handful of waterfront bums who got quite a kick out of watching us "horse marines" get our feet wet.

What was probably taking up most of my thoughts at the time were misgivings about being the only one of the crew who admitted to having no prior sailing experience whatsoever. My total sea time consisted of the several ten-minute trips we'd made across Burrard Inlet on the old North Van Ferry, which I might add made a deep impression on me. I was fresh off the farm and I could drive six up on a gang plough like nobody's buisiness, but if anybody saw the *St. Roch* go by during my first few tricks at the wheel they must have figured we were taking evasive action.

The *Roch* was a tubby, blunt-nosed 104-foot schooner built at Burrard Drydock in North Vancouver and launched in 1928. She'd been specially designed for Arctic service and she was supposed to do a number of jobs.

At the time the RCMP was the Canadian government's only official presence in the north. There was no local government, no game wardens, no social workers, no military — the RCMP did it all. This is what the old Northwest Mounted Police was originally established for in 1874, to represent the Dominion Government in the Northwest Territories when that meant everything between B.C. and Ontario — but by 1928 the Northwest Territories had been cut back to the 53rd parallel where it is now.

So the *Roch* was supposed to carry mail, ferry Eskimo children to school, run sick people to the hospital, explore new shipping routes and perform all manner of official chores. In addition she was to serve as a mobile RCMP detachment and winter in areas not served by existing posts. But mainly she was to free the posts in the Western Arctic from their dependence on ships of the Canalaska and Hudson's Bay Companies for supplies.

Originally and for the larger part of her career the *Roch* had flush decks with just the pilot house, captain's cabin and radio shack up top. The super-structure she has now was added in Halifax just before her second trip through the Northwest Passage at the same time they put the big engine in. In my time she had a 150-horsepower Union diesel but in 1944 they put in one twice that size. For accommodation she had the two bunks above decks — the skipper's and the radio operator's — then four more in the stern behind the engine room, galley and saloon, and up front in the foc's'l where I bunked there were eight more bunks, two uppers and lowers on each side. In between the foc's'l and engine was the cargo hold, which was always too full of stores and cargo to get through — you had to go outside to get from the saloon to the foc's'l. The deck was pretty well loaded too, with drums of oil, lumber for a new post at Cambridge Bay, dog sleds and whatnot.

There were seven crew on this trip and one deadhead: Larsen, Fred Farrar the mate, Jim Davies the radio man, Bob Kells the engineer, Dad Parry the cook, and myself and Dinty Moore, seamen. The deadhead was Sergeant Fred Anderton, who had a strange kind of position on the *Roch*. You see the *Roch* was two things at the same time — a ship with a crew with the skipper in charge and an RCMP detachment with an NCO in charge. When you looked at it as a ship the boss was Larsen, and everybody took orders from him — not that Henry gave orders, he just got you to do things — but when you looked at it as the RCMP, well then Larsen was just a green corporal and Anderton was boss. It could have been a pretty sticky situation if it's been anyone else but Larsen, because Anderton was a stuffy officious bugger, but Henry was so easy going there was never any squabbling between them. Anderton was no sailor at all and when the ship was on the move he pretty much kept out of sight.

I forget when I first met Henry but I know I liked him right from the start. He'd been around. He'd worked on ships since he was fifteen, on this coast and in the Arctic as well as deep sea, and he'd worked on shore as well. It gave him something career cops didn't have and he and I always got on better together than we did with them.

The last time I saw Henry we went out on an all night booze-up together. Me, Henry and that big dog he used to take everywhere, dragging around to every bootleg joint in Vancouver. For years you never saw Henry except with that dog.

I gave Henry that dog. I'd raised him from a pup up at Cambridge Bay. I broke him in as a lead dog pulling sled and he was a good one too, but he turned killer and I was going to shoot him when Henry came along and said he'd try to train him out of it. I asked him if he ever had any trouble with him in town, and he told me this story about the two old maids.

Henry was living in Victoria and these two old maids next door had an old ginger tomcat they pampered and doted on something terrible. This one day Henry was sitting on his porch and they were sitting on their porch, yakking back and forth between the two yards, and this ginger tom came strolling up and poked his head through a hole between the fence pickets. Henry's dog spotted him and pricked his ears up, and the cat saw this, but just furred up a little and came on through, rubbing his sides against the fence, strolling very regally into Henry's yard. Well, the dog let him get in about fifteen feet, then rushed him and flipped him up in the air with his back broken. Henry felt pretty stupid because he had watched it all happen, just sitting there talking, but it came about so innocently he didn't think to do anything about it, and all he could do was take the cat and kill it as quickly as possible by swinging it by the tail and knocking its brains out in the dirt — right there with these two old girls shrieking and wailing. It was years before that this happened, but you know Henry as he was telling me the story, he was all sort of coloured up and misty-eyed — almost crying remembering how he'd had to kill these old maids' cat. Henry was a soft guy you see, he had a very good heart. He loved animals and loved people. All this stuff you read about his Viking blood and iron will is just so much malarkey. He was never comfortable being in charge of other men.

WE HAD GOOD WEATHER ALL THE WAY UP THE INSIDE PASSAGE, and by the time we got to the top end of Vancouver Island I'd decided there wasn't all that much to becoming a sailor after all. I'd gotten over wanting to say "gee" and "haw" for "port" and "starboard," I'd discovered the secret of getting the boat to go straight was to hold the wheel straight, and I hadn't had a thought of seasickness. Then we rounded the north end of Vancouver Island and I saw what looked like a vast range of green hills ahead, except they were moving.

Wellsir, whoever named that boat knew what they were doing. There's not a boat been built that knew better how to rock. She stood on her head and stood on her tail and rolled with rails under all in one motion. The green seas crashed aboard and within a few minutes I was just as green as they were.

The only consolation I found as I crawled to the rail was that all my seafaring colleagues — with the sole exception of Larsen — were lined up there ahead of me. We made our contributions to the fishes with increasing regularity for three days, proving, as Kells pointed out, "that no matter how weak your somach is, you can heave as far as a man with a strong stomach."

The only one of us who maintained any pretence of devotion to duty and loyalty to the King was the cook, Dad Parry, a great bulky man who never gave up his battle with the flying pots and pans in the *Roch*'s tiny galley.

After three days some distinct signs of recovery were beginning to make their appearance among us. Some attempted to shave. Others became curious as to what the smell of food might do to them, and went so far as to poke their heads into the saloon. Dad was still losing his battle with the pots however, and we existed for the next week on bully beef and hardtack. After five days the crew was good as new, and I for my part have never been seasick since.

The seas would die down for a while then spring up worse than before. She'd really be sticking her nose into some big ones, and to get from the wheelhouse to the foc's'l you'd have to time yourself between dives and run like hell. To make things even more pleasant, the foredeck leaked and the whole foc's'l started to get damp and clammy. One morning when Farrar and I were coming off watch he fired up the coal heater we had in there to try and dry things out. Well, the foc's'l wasn't that big, I suppose eighteen feet long and ten feet wide on the average, and after we were in there for half an hour it was so hot we were just stewing in sweat. I remember seeing Farrar get up and there was a door at the top of a few steps that you came in by, and he latched that open and went back to his bunk. It wasn't too rough at that point but a few hours later I woke up and found the ship was in a dive.

I knew there was something bad about that but before I could wake myself up enough to figure just what, a square column of water came driving down at us the full size of the open door. I scrambled up to a top bunk before I got very wet, but we'd taken in a good thousand gallons and with every pitch of the boat it sluiced from one bulkhead to the other, bowling over everything in its way. One of the things in its way was a collection of paint cans Henry'd stowed under the steps, and within a few pitches the water was all colours of the rainbow.

There was still a little water slopping in through the door from the deck too, and there was danger of another big one coming over the bow, but neither of us felt like enough of a hero to get down in that soup and walk back, so we just crouched there on our bunks, watching it slosh and getting sick on fumes. Finally a couple of the other guys made it back with a pump and bailed us out, but you never saw such a goddamn mess. There was paint over everything — woodwork, bedding, stove, gear — and the smell of turpentine was so strong it was worse than being seasick, but there was nowhere else to lie down on that bloody boat and we were too tired to get up.

Henry had made a straight shot from the north tip of Vancouver Island up to the Aleutians, bypassing the Queen Charlotte Islands and Prince Rupert, so our first port out of Vancouver was Dutch Harbour on Unalaska Island.

COMING INTO DUTCH HARBOUR AFTER TWO WEEKS OF TUMBLING OUR GUTS OUT IN THE *ROCH* WAS LIKE ONE OF THOSE OLD SAILOR'S DREAMS of mermaid cities or paradise islands full of man-hungry women. There was a U.S. Army radio base in Dutch Harbour but there was also a very large fish cannery, which had a staff of better than a hundred Seattle girls who'd come up for the summer and seemed quite hard up for excitement. They were dressed for work in look-alike shirts and jeans with their hair tucked up in scarves, but there was apparently no fish in that day, and we

DUTCH HARBOUR

FARRAR, DAVIES, WHITE, & FRIENDS

hardly had the boat tied up before they were swarming over it like termites. There were girls in the saloon, girls in the galley, girls in the wheelhouse and girls in the foc's'l. There were even a couple sticking out of the crowsnest.

That night they put on a dance for us and when we arrived you could hardly recognize them, all in their best dresses and their hair down. One especially nice-looking girl had spent a lot of time in the radio shack with Davies earlier, and when he didn't recognize her she said, "You've forgotten me already." Davies, who was painfully bashful, stammered, "Aw, I'm sorry . . . I didn't recognize you with your dress on . . ." Everybody roared of course, and poor Davies blushed so hard I thought he was going to pop an artery. The girl must have been the motherly type and taken pity on him though, because they soon disappeared and we didn't see much of Davies the rest of the visit.

Before we left Vancouver we were given permits to buy certain commodities out of bond, that is, tax free. There was very little variety in the commodities most of us chose to stock up on: whisky, rum and smokes, and smokes, rum and whisky. A case of good whisky was $22 and a gallon of rum could be had for $6, and we put in a pretty good store.

Well it didn't seem likely we'd ever have a better chance to make use of it than now, and we made sure enough got around to oil all the social gears and remove whatever lingering inhibitions there might be. By the time we left there wasn't a bottle left, but nobody was complaining.

The second morning we were visited by a crowd of men from the base. I don't know if they figured we were infringing on their territory or what, but they seemed a bit chippy. There were jokes about "how many screws on that there boat," and so on — there's nobody in the world as mouthy as Yanks in a big gang like that. Well, they wanted us to defend ourselves. They had a fella there with gloves on and they were waving another pair around for one of us to come up and take him on. I was never a guy to stand around when there was a scrap in the offing, but this guy was an absolute giant. He must have been well up in the 250 range.

There was a bit of shuffling around, and finally Davies steps out of his shack and says in his quiet voice, "I'll try." Well Davies was easy the smallest guy on the crew and we thought maybe his romancing had affected his brain, but he was quite sure, so up the ladder he went. "Too small, too small! Throw the little one back! Give us a man!" they were hollering.

Well you know, Davies could've killed that big bugger. Jesus, he was good. Just jab and jab and jab, he'd get the guy backed up, then whistle a trip-hammer past his chin — he could just as easy have hit him but he didn't want to. The big fella didn't hardly get a punch off. He took it in good part mind you, but after that nobody else felt much like fighting. We were as surprised as anybody, and later when I got to talk to Davies I found out he'd been in the ring a lot, he'd fought many many fights. He was one tough monkey, but you'd never have suspected it.

We made pretty good friends with these army guys after that and the rest of the trip was pretty much a contest to drink up everything on the island. The last night we ended up in a hell of a drunk up at the wireless camp in one of the rooms with these two Yanks, Toban and Chicago. I don't know what Chicago's name was — we called him that because that's where he was from. All our liquor was gone and we were down to scraping the scum off a batch of green brew they had going there, and drinking that, when these two Swedes came in. I don't know who these two Swedes were but they had a bottle of this Alaska Mule with them, which is about as wicked a type of screech as you can get. We were setting there nipping away at that — and it was nipping back at us now; that stuff has real teeth in it — and Bob Kells, he was leaning back against the wall with his chair tilted on two legs, right out of the blue he says to these two Swedes, "You two guys better take off." Well normally Bob Kells was the friendliest, most good natured guy you could hope to run across and this was just someone else talking out of his mouth — I guess it was the Mule. Everybody kinda ignored it and kept on talking and carrying on, but about five minutes later he says again, "You guys better take off." Still there was no action, so a few minutes later he says, "Well, I told you guys to take off and I gave you your chance, so now I'm going to throw you out myself." His chair banged down on the floor but instead of springing up like we expected he pitched on forward and dove under an army cot across the room with a tremendous crash, then he laid still. This was alright with us, but someone noticed a bit of fur where he'd cleared under the bed rail so we dragged him out into the light and found he'd lost a piece about the size of a silver dollar off the back of his scalp.

We slung him on top of the bed and took a sheet and tucked it in all around so he looked like a corpse, drank him a few toasts and told him what a good stiff he was and so on, watching with interest as the sheet gradually turned red all around his head.

The next one to get bit by the Mule was Chicago. He stood bolt upright and said, gravely like he was delivering a prophecy, "Boys, it's time to wreck this joint." Well, that seemed like one hell of a good idea, and out we went into the next room and tried to turn over their pool table. It was too heavy for us but there were some big heavy chairs there which we threw out the windows. In the kitchen we got into a contest. The living room was lined with donnaconna and you stood at the doorway and tried to throw things through the wall. Plates, coffee mugs, a meat cleaver went through with no trouble, and one guy heaved an alarm clock which not only went through

but kept on running afterward, which we thought was truly marvellous. Now I'm telling you, by the time we were done, that place was a writeoff. The walls were still up but that was just about all you could say for it.

The next morning Henry went ashore to round up the crew, and when he finds Bob wrapped in his bloody sheet in the midst of all this wreckage he figures there's been a real battle. So he comes running back to the boat all steamed up, hollering for us to roll out, the bastards got Bob and we're going up there to settle up with them. "They damn near killed him, but he must of put up an awful fight," he says, "he tore the house apart damn near." I think that's the only time I ever saw Henry quite that fired up. He was quite ready to lead us up there and do battle.

I told him what happened. "Oh, oh, well alright," he said, "A couple of you guys come up and help me get him then. We better get out of here before *they* come after *us* if that's the case."

Well Kells didn't remember a goddamn thing about what had happened. He figured he'd been in a fight and kept wanting me to tell him who the bastard was that clobbered him with that bottle. I just put him off, but he kept after me about it all the way north. "You son-of-a-bitch," he said, "who're you covering up for anyway?" Finally I said, "I'll tell you Bob. It wasn't a bottle. You don't know how goddamn lucky you are. That guy swung at you with a meat cleaver. You just ducked in time or he'd have taken your head clean off." That satisfied him. When we got to the post at Herschel Island where Bob was quite well known, they all wanted to know what happened to his head and I heard Bob telling them, "Oh I had a little disagreement with a guy down at Dutch Harbour and the bastard come at me with a meat cleaver. I was just lucky I ducked in time, or he would've had my whole head."

Bob Kells died just a few years ago and as far as I know he went to his grave thinking that was just what happened. He probably told it to his grandchildren many times, believing it was God's truth. I've often wondered what those fellas at Dutch Harbour thought when they woke up and saw that house though. I'm sure that when the reports were written up most of the credit went to the RCMP although we never heard anything about it. Maybe they found that Alaska Mule bottle and put the credit where it belonged.

HENRY IN HIS BOOK HAS A STORY ABOUT SPOTTING A WHALE back during the first few days in the open seas, and a certain recruit fresh from the prairies who comes running up on deck with a loaded shotgun "in nothing but his union suit, flap open, face covered with three days beard and still pale, but the look of the hunter in his eyes." He had to convince me you couldn't kill a whale with a shotgun, he says,and sent me back below, "somewhat dashed."

Well now I was green as a sailor, but I had been hunting for years, and no one needed to tell me that a shotgun wasn't the best weapon to take after a whale. If it was anyone but Henry telling it I wouldn't give the story a second thought, but its possible he remembered some incident I have completely forgotten. You can do a pretty good job of forgetting something when it doesn't show you up just the way you like to see yourself, and an incident Henry figured in right around this same period offers good proof of that.

We were about three days out of Dutch Harbour in the Bering Sea bound for the Bering Straits. The weather was completely overcast and Larsen was unable to get a sight, either by night or day, but he and Farrar worked out a course and we ploughed ahead confidently. This night Farrar relieved me at the wheel just as it was breaking daylight and before going below I stopped to take a leak over the side. As I was looking down something caught my eye — something funny about the water. It was one of those things you weren't sure you were seeing it or not, but to my eye it seemed sort of roily and muddy. Just on a hunch I climbed up the rigging to have a look around. I don't know what I expected to see, but my gut just clenched like a fist. We were driving fullbore straight into a low, dark spit. I yelled for all I was worth and Farrar started bringing her about but it sure seemed to take a long time. The spit wasn't 500 yards away with seas breaking all around and I could almost feel the crunch. Larsen's cabin was immediately behind the pilothouse and he felt the change of motion in his sleep and was up with his nose in the compass before I got down to the deck. The first thing he always did was look at the compass before he even spoke, and there was nothing that brought his temper up quicker than finding it reading something else than it was supposed to. Right now it was pointing exactly the opposite way it was supposed to and that made Henry mad. Farrar still didn't know what was up so Henry came after me.

"What the hell's the idea?" he yelled.

"Well, what were you planning to do back there, make a portage?" I said.

"Portage?" he said. "There's no land within a hundred miles of here."

"You climb up there and tell me that," I said. He had to look astern because we were heading away from the spit then, but when he came down he was looking pretty sober.

"Well you saved the ship, Bill," he said.

We had come within a few minutes of ramming into Cape Mohican on Nunivak Island. He and Farrar both wore pretty long faces for the next few days, and from that point on I figured I had my passage pretty well paid for. I didn't hear any more ploughboy jokes, at least not until I read Henry's book. He doesn't say anything about running into Cape Mohican there and one time a lot later when I was out of the force I asked him, "Hey Henry, do you remember the time I saved the ship?"

"No," he says, "I don't remember that." He didn't want to remember it, either.

Henry was an old sailor and never missed a chance to "get the rags up" as he put it, although his enthusiasm wasn't shared by anyone else in the crew. The *Roch* with her bathtub lines was no *Bluenose* and it took a good eye to see any difference either in her speed or her stability between when her sails were up and when they weren't, but the difference in the amount of work involved was obvious. With bare masts all you had to do was hold to the course, but under sail you needed men out on deck to fight the rigging and the steersman had to really work the ship. The first few times it was fun and everybody helped, but pretty soon the guys got tired of it and poor old Henry got so he was afraid to bring the subject of sailing up, even when the wind was fair. I liked to have something to do besides lie on my bunk or sit in the saloon and slurp Dad's coffee, so I used to say, "Hey Skipper, don't you think we're missing out on some good air here?" No amount of black looks from Moore and Farrar would bother Henry if he had one friend on his side, and a moment later we'd be out hoisting canvas. It got so I was the only one who'd help him with the rigging at all. None of the other

· ST ROCH UNDER SAIL · BILL WHITE IN FOREGROUND ·

93

guys would go aloft even to repair broken lines, and any time there was climbing to be done Henry had to come looking for me.

One time we had the wind behind us so Henry decided to show us what sails really could do and put them goose-winged, out both sides. That really made the old tub pour foam, but it's dangerous as hell because running wing on wing like that, unless you keep the wind dead astern, she'll jibe — one sail will slam around to the other side like a door caught in a draft, and it can gear the mast right out of the boat. It can be done safely, even in a big sea with the ship yawing around like we were, but the guy at the wheel has to be right on the bit. Normally Henry would take it himself but this time it was Moore's watch and being the kind of guy he was of course he decided his reputation as a great sailor was at stake and he wouldn't step away. If it had been me in Henry's place I would have swatted him out of the way, or else took the sails in, but you see Henry couldn't do that, he just stood back and looked worried. Well Moore did pretty good. He held her straight in till the wind rose up about double, then got up right on top of a big sea and yawed around bloody near beam on. The foresail came booming around like thunder and I expected to see the deck pop out like the top of a keg of nails. I let the sheets go and Henry ran for the wheel and brought her about, then came back to check the damage. The shrouds had held and the mast was okay but the collar that the halyard was anchored to had been twisted right sideways on the mast so that when the boom was brought back straight the block fouled. This collar had stayed hooked to it besides the halyard, so when it twisted around these stays screwed it down and burned it into the mast wood. In order to turn it back we first had to take the weight of the lines off it with a temporary block hung higher up and shim it back in the right position. This meant climbing up to the small part of the mast above the shrouds and clinging there with one hand and trying to work with the other. The foremast on the *Roch* was 60 feet high and all this time the boat was pitching in heavy seas. I remember taking comfort in the thought that if I slipped I'd probably be thrown well out into the water instead of smashing like an egg on the deck.

Most jams like that a few years later you can laugh at, but thinking of hanging out there in the sleet and spray jerking around busting knuckles and pinching frozen fingers in the lines, it still hurts. Like that episode with the turpentine, if I think about it enough, I start to feel a bit of a headache creeping into the back of my brain. That was the story with that goddamn boat — she seemed to be designed in every detail to give maximum discomfort to any poor bastard unlucky enough to be caught aboard. You never got a full cup of coffee — the floor always got half. There was always a bolt where you went to set your head. Even tied up at the dock you'd be stubbing a toe or backing into a sharp edge to let somebody wiggle past. Even Henry, who must have come as close to loving her as anybody did, said she was the crankiest and most awkward ship he'd ever set foot on.

But I guess she was right for her work. Egg-shaped like she was, any time she got caught in a pinch she would pop up like a slippery seed — there were no corners where the ice could get a hold on her. I don't know whose stroke of genius that was because not every boat that was sent up to the Arctic was made like that.

In 1937 Henry was coming out through Dolphin and Union Strait alongside the Hudson's Bay ship *Fort James* when a northwester pushed a bunch of heavy ice in from the open sea. The *Roch* sat up and rolled over like she was supposed to, but the *Fort James*, which was straight-sided and had a deep keel, just sat still while the ice closed in and crushed her to bits. You couldn't have a better test than that.

She was strong too. She was double planked with ribs that mut have been a good six inches square, and not more than a foot apart. She was a rock in more ways than one.

OF ALL THE BAD PLACES IN THE WORLD TO TAKE A SHIP, from the Cape of Good Hope to Juan de Fuca Strait to the Bermuda Triangle, there isn't one that can touch the Arctic Ocean in terms of the incidence of disaster, and this is of course because of the ice. Threading a ship through the sea ice of the Arctic is like walking through a herd of wild caribou which might at any moment stampede in any direction. All the usual problems of wind, tide and hidden reefs are there in quantity, but they become secondary to the problem of outmanoeuvring the ice. It is a science of squeezing around edges, and seizing openings of the moment, but avoiding openings that lead into traps. Probably Henry Larsen's most outstanding skill as an Arctic navigator — and he had many — was his ability to read the ice. His knack for knowing when to drive into the pack and when to run for shelter was uncanny, and this was plain even on his first trip as skipper.

We started to run across drifting ice as soon as we left Dutch Harbour and as we neared the pack a noticeable tension began to build up amongst all the men on the boat, with the exception of Anderton, who took no interest in the work of sailing and strolled around the deck whistling like the guest of honour on a pleasure cruise.

The job of steering became much harder, what with having to keep both eyes peeled and constantly dodging the drift. We didn't get into our first heavy floe ice until we were leaving Wainright, and just below Point Barrow the pack became too heavy to go any further.

If you look at the map of Alaska with your bad eye you can see it as the head of a walrus in profile, with Anchorage at the mouth, the Aleutians for the tusk, Nome at the bulging eye, and the North Slope running down the back of the head towards the Yukon border. Nunivak Island is a large island about the size of the larger of the Queen Charlottes, just off the walrus' nose. The Bering Straits, marking the division between the Bering Sea and the Arctic Ocean, are a 50-mile wide constriction formed where the eye bulge, or Seward Peninsula, juts toward Siberia. The whole head is 1,500 miles around and the North Slope makes up 400 of that, with Barrow at the most northerly extreme, a small topknot that juts out just as you make the turn to go down the North Slope. With this picture in mind you can see

how it is here that the Arctic ice pack hangs up as it begins to break up and drift westward each summer, making Point Barrow one of the worst bottlenecks of the Northwest Passage. Although navigation of the Northwest Passage from the east had come halfway across the continent by the time of William Baffin's voyage in 1612, exploration from the west remained blocked here at the western end until Collinson and McLure finally battled around Barrow on the Franklin search in 1850, and no one repeated their feat until the whalers came around the turn of the century.

Every spring boats would be lined up below Barrow waiting to make the first run of the season into Herschel Island, which the whalers had established as the main trade centre of the Western Arctic. Later into the summer the ice often drifted miles off shore leaving clear passage, but it would be blocked again by September and if you planned to cover much ground inside you had to get an early start. The traders had another motive since the first boat into Herschel could get better trade for her goods than the second boat. At least these were the excuses given out for the race around Barrow every spring. In the minds of the skippers the biggest thing was the prestige that went with being first boat, because the competition involved boats like the *Roch* which didn't figure in the trading.

There were three ships waiting ahead of the *Roch* that year – the Hudson's Bay Company flagship *Bay Chimo*, the Canalaska trader *Patterson* and the *Old Maid*, also for the Hudson's Bay Company. The *Chimo* had been specially fitted out for Arctic use and was the reigning Queen of the North at that time. Her skipper Sidney Cornwall, who had an experienced ice pilot on board, considered the race his for the taking and had laid on some fairly hefty bets to that effect. He obviously didn't consider the *Roch* in the running, with her rookie skipper and horsesailor crew, and even went so far as to offer Larsen some fatherly advice.

Shortly after we arrived the wind eased off its pressure on the pack and the race was on. The *Roch*

had one thing in her favour, and that was her shallow draft. The land around Barrow is very low, with gradually sloping beaches and in some places the pans ground quite a ways off shore, leaving a narrow but dangerous corridor along the edge. Larsen made the most of this, easing inshore till we had sometimes less than a fathom clearance while the larger boats waited for leads to open in the deep water.

If you ever go down to look at the *Roch* in the museum there you'll see up by the bow on the starboard side a little platform sticking out. It's just a short plank with a break in the rail so a man can stand out clear of the side, and unless you had it pointed out to you you might not notice it, but I can't look at the ship without that thing pokes me in the eye like a sharp stick.

It's the sounding deck. The *Roch* didn't have any depth sounder – well it had one alright but it wasn't like the ones today that you turn on with a switch. The *Roch*'s depth sounder was a round hunk of lead with a dimple in the bottom and a ring in the top with a jeesus long piece of rope tied onto it, and you operated it by standing out on that board and throwing it over and pulling back till you got too beat to know what you were doing, then you crawled away and somebody else took over.

What you were supposed to find out was how deep it was straight down you see, not down on some crazy angle, and this took pretty good timing in how you threw the thing. You had to give it a pretty good boost and get it a good ways out ahead of the ship so by the time the ship came up on it, it was just touching bottom. In the kind of water we were in around Barrow everything depended on the man swinging the lead; the boat was steered according to what he said. Hour upon hour upon hour I stood out there heaving and yarding on that goddamn thing. It only weighs eight pounds but after a few watches of swinging on it, it's the heaviest eight pounds in the world, I'll tell you. In the shallow water you don't have to pull it quite so far but that's more than made up for by the fact you have to heave it ten times as regular. And the water up there, oh she's cold. It's down sometimes well below freezing. And when that line's coming in there's a roostertail of icy brine just peeing all over you, you'd be a solid block if you stopped long enough to let it set. It's your hands that finally give out, because you have to feel the fathom markers and you can't wear gloves, so what with the chafing of the rope and soaking all the time the skin started to crack up pretty bad and when the salt got in that, it was about all a guy could take.

As it was we were making damn good progress in this shallow water and had taken quite a lead over the other boats. Whether or not Henry had actually started out figuring he had much of a chance of beating old Cornwall of the *Chimo* would be hard to say because it was overreaching a bit to go for the title your first time out, but there was a quiet determination about Henry you only got to see at times like this. Normally he'd back off from an argument and keep his thoughts to himself, while underneath he wasn't backing off at all, he was just waiting for the chance to make things work out his own way. Here he was now, not acting panicky or showing any sign that this contest meant anything really important to him; yet he had quietly worked our schedule out so we arrived at the pack just the right moment, and started right off ferreting out leads and crowding the shore in a pretty daring way.

We still hadn't got the worst point – Point Barrow itself – behind us yet, and as we got closer to it the ice got heavier and tighter and more menacing.

It's pretty hard to give an idea of the Arctic ice-pack around Barrow to someone who hasn't seen it because there's nothing on the same scale you can compare it to. You could try maybe thinking of floodwater from a burst dam, the Hope slide as it was coming down or a runaway glacier. Awesome would be a good word for it if it wasn't used on things a lot less awesome. You see chunks the size of skating arenas flip up miles away in the distance, and from it to you and who knows how many hundred miles around is all ice, great pans jostling and roaring like trapped dinosaurs. It makes you think of dinosaurs and the formation of the world to look at it, it's so slow and ponderous and the force is so enormous. The way it buckles and piles up is exactly the way mountain ranges are formed, and whatever the ice is doing it seems permanent as the mountains, but changes do come over it – the floes will be one time crowding the beach, then it'll back off and start the other way, or just fall loose like the life went out of it. Experienced ice men will claim to see the tide and wind behind all this but to the ordinary guy its bloody mysterious.

To make things more mysterious at this point a dense fog rolled in over the ice reducing visibility to nil. All we could hear were muffled crashes like far-away thunder and creaking sounds like the hinges of the universe sagging open. It made you feel like being careful.

But Henry, he kept poking back and forth like a fly on the window. Sometimes he would probe down a lead for several miles, then turn and run like hell, just getting behind a grounded pan in time to see all the ice we were in come grinding and crushing past us at several knots. Other times there'd be a lead that looked wide enough to take the *Roch* through

sideways and he wouldn't go near it. We'd wonder why, then we'd see it clamp shut like a vise.

After we'd been stopped like this for a couple of watches we heard a different noise, a low thrumming sound, and a bit later we could see the lights of the *Chimo* working her way into the ice further out. So all that work we'd gone to trying to make time inshore with the leadline was gone to waste.

Finally a small lead that Henry liked the look of showed and he rang for full power. We were down into it several miles when it looked like it was coming to a dead end, but Henry just slowed down a little and just before we got to the blockage the lead jogged off to the side and we swung down that. Before long we were into it too far to get out but the lead kept giving us these last-minute reprieves, sometimes narrowing to the point it seemed we'd never fit, but Henry just stood there looking grim, ploughing into it. Maybe that was the Viking stuff coming out in him then, it's hard to say. The guys didn't take him too serious a lot of the time but for those few hours off Barrow they were meek and obedient as frightened children, staring into that fog with their eyes wide open. Gradually we could notice the lead opening and things loosening up and you could feel the tension easing off.

"We've got 'er," Henry said a bit later, and Point Barrow was behind us.

THIS WASN'T THE END OF THE ICE BUT OUR SHALLOW WATER PASSAGE APPEARED AGAIN along the beach and we were able to chase it all the way to the Flaxman Islands, halfway to Herschel. I took the lead line up again with a will. We had no idea now whether we were ahead of the *Chimo* or not but it seemed a good chance we'd have the advantage making slow but steady way inshore while they waited on leads out in deep water. By this time most everybody was getting caught up in the chase and everybody was helping out on the leadline – except Anderton.

There was just once on that trip Anderton got interested in what the boat was doing and that was down near Bernard Harbour when we ran into the *Nigalik*. We were in a wide lead and a ways further down we could see this boat – at first we thought she was underway, and then we decided she must be anchored. When we got close we could see it was the Canalaska trade schooner the *Nigalik*, and she was up on the rocks.

Well now these guys were in a real panic. She wasn't a big boat, the *Nigalik*, but they were trying to get out to meet the *Patterson* with the season's first fur and they had her loaded with a quarter million dollars' worth of white fox. The weather was mild for that time of year which meant there was a storm on the way according to Henry, but what really had them worried was that the *Chimo* would catch them there, and since she was a derelict old Cornwall could claim salvage on ship and cargo both. Competition between the two companies was such that they would probably rather lose the ship than see the opposition get it.

Anderton's ears perked right up when he heard all this and he immediately took charge. After a short conference in Henry's cabin with the skipper Hugh

Clarke it was announced we'd try to pull the *Nigalik* off. We got out a long piece of three-inch manilla line and pulled for all the old *Roch* was worth but the *Nigalik* didn't even wiggle. Henry took a run at it and the line snapped in the middle like a shoelace. Maybe it was from having Anderton in his hair, it's hard to say, but Henry at this point became completely flustered and backed over the line, tying it up so tight in the propeller the engine stalled out. With only a few feet of clearance under our own keel and a strong current running we were in prime shape to go around ourselves and just managed to get an anchor down in time.

The problem then was whether or not we could free the prop, and Moore, who claimed to be an old pearl diver, volunteered to take a knife in his teeth and swim for it. We encouraged him cheerfully, but he was only in about a half second before he bobbed up and grabbed the side of the boat, speechless.

Henry in his book tells how Bob Kells was the next to try and how we had to cover the big scab on his head with waterpump grease for insulation, but he makes no mention of that scab's fascinating history. The grease was a washout, and Bob surfaced roaring like a grampus in faster time even than Moore. Our final solution was to dig away at the rope from above with a chisel tied to a pikepole, and after a few hours we were back at the *Nigalik* with a wire line and finally jerked her free.

In Henry's version this whole effort was carried out in the spirit of good Samaratinism on the high seas, but the fact was, Anderton had made a deal with Clarke and we got paid for the job. The take was to be split up evenly amongst the crew with dire warnings to keep mum, since of course it was totally illegal. We got thirty bucks each, but later I learned from the Canalaska trader at Cambridge Bay, Carson Winswold, that Clarke had given Larsen and Anderton $3,000 — meaning they'd held back on us for better than 2,500 bucks. That would be all Andy's doing of course, Henry would never pull anything like that on his own, but the trouble with him was he wouldn't stand up to Andy either.

At the Flaxman Islands the ice and fog disappeared together and we found ourselves clipping along in sparkling sunshine. It was the first time since below Barrow we'd been able to see and we were eager to have a look around and find out what kind of a world we'd entered into, but the land was just as low and featureless as it had seemed in the few glimpses we'd had, except now we could pick out a range of mountains far inland. Henry said we'd be back on the ice before long, pointing to something over the horizon that looked like weak flashes of light. This was what was known as "ice-blink," he said, and it only happened when there was ice ahead. Sure enough, a few hours later we were back cruising up and down a solid icepack looking for leads. There wasn't nearly as much of it as last time and at one point the barrier was less than forty feet wide. When Farrar and I came on Larsen said to keep cruising up and down waiting but with clear water just forty feet away that got pretty hard to put up with. After an hour or so Farrer said, "The hell with this, let's hit it at that thin spot." I was on the wheel and circled back for about a quarter of a mile, then aimed her full ahead for the notch. She struck with a slight jar then slid up on the ice cake and lay hard over on one side. A few very long moments later there was a loud crunch and we sailed free, encountering no more ice all the way to Herschel Island.

We could see masts sticking up from the boat harbour behind the island but none of them were tall enough to be the *Chimo*'s. Henry leaned on the whistle and within ten minutes every man, woman and child on the island was down on the beach shouting and waving.

We were the first boat of the year. We'd beat 'em.

The first thing we did as soon as the anchor was down was get on the radio and pass the good news on to the police base at Aklavik. Captain Cornwall, who was still in the ice, overheard the call on the *Chimo* and got so excited he broke a blade of his propeller trying to get free. This was a bad setback since there were no drydocks in that part of the world and he was bound to spend the whole season limping around his route, then make the long haul back to Vancouver at half speed. When he reached Herschel the next day he was still screaming mad.

"Goddamn you Larsen, you had no business diving into that ice like that," he yelled. "You didn't even know where you were in that fog. You don't even know enough to know how bloody lucky you are."

Henry grinned and said that was probably right, he'd try to not let it happen again. But old Cornwall was a pretty good salt at bottom and proved it later by calling Henry over for a sampling of some Hudson's Bay rum. First boat of the year always made for festive spirits on Herschel and all bitterness was soon forgotten. Eskimos and traders came in from hundreds of miles around to trade their catches and pick up their orders — most of which took full advantage of the twelve-bottle liquor ration white men were permitted in those days. Gossip flew, partnerships were made up, great schemes were laid, marriages were performed and liquor was consumed in great quantity.

To add to the excitement this year at Herschel, right in the midst of the furor a pod of beluga whales cruised into the harbour. Belugas were among the more prized game at that time and the festivities had a time out while everyone who could lay their hands on a gun staggered down to the beach and opened fire. This is one whalehunt I do remember taking part in, and in fact I was one of the few to actually hit one. I didn't do it with a shotgun either.

At one point someone out for an early morning visit to the rail spotted Captain Cornwall on the deck behind his cabin with nothing on but a T-shirt, dancing some crazy kind of a jig. Memories of his defeat at Larsen's hands must have lingered on in the back of his mind though, because next spring, as if to make sure he was at least the first boat *out* that trip, he drove into the ice off Barrow too early and *Chimo* got caught. They abandoned her with a full cargo of fur but the odd thing was she wasn't crushed like they expected and drifted intact out into the polar sea. It must've frozen into a big pan that kept it protected, because years later, it was still appearing out of the fog to parties of wandering Eskimoes like some frosted-up *Flying Dutchman* of the north. The ice pack doesn't all melt you see, the bulk of it stays up there, circulating around, returning year after year. It wasn't so long ago I heard the *Chimo*'d been sighted again, and she may still be up there, drifting around with the floes, haunting the old course.

The *Roch* of course kept going and by the time she was officially turned over to the City of Vancouver for a museum display in 1954 she had survived more seasons in the ice than any other ship afloat. She had also won a permanent place in the history books by making the first trip west to east through the Northwest Passage, by making the first return trip through the Northwest Passage, and by being the first ship to circumnavigate the North American continent. Henry for his part became recognized as the foremost Arctic navigator of the time, and died knowing his name had become a household word in this his adopted country. I always took a special satisfaction in that, though I quit the force early, because Henry wasn't the sort of guy who usually makes it into the history books — he was just a quiet, easygoing Norwegian who got ahold of a job that suited him and hung onto it. You could say that about the *Roch* too. There was nothing great about her either, but she was right for the work. They both were.

ST ROCH · CHIMO · OLD MAID · PATTERSON at HERSCHEL ISLAND

$\mathcal{R}$emembering RODERICK HAIG-BROWN

George Woodcock

WHEN RODERICK HAIG-BROWN DIED LAST YEAR, it was suddenly and quietly in the garden of his house on Vancouver Island, beside the river which he had loved and about which he had written so often in his books on fishing and in his discursive essays. To us who knew him, as a man of quiet wisdom, as a good friend, as a fellow in the craft of writing, it seemed a fitting passage.

It was through the craft of writing which we shared that I came to know Haig-Brown, and I remember very vividly the unusual combination of humility and assurance with which he approached it. His emphasis was always on the craft, on the minimal need to perform the task in a workmanlike way. "And if one practices the craft with diligence,"

I remember him saying as we sat one night years ago in his great study beside the river, "then the moments of art come to one, gratuitously, as a reward."

I believe that in the thirty-odd effective years of Roderick Haig-Brown's writing life the moments of art came in fact quite often. Yet his name has not been one spoken loudly by Canadian critics during the recent upsurge of interest in the writers of our country, and this neglect, this lack of critical perception, has seemed to me particularly unfortunate, since I can think of few Canadian writers who have written a more subtle and adaptable prose or have responded with a more immediate sensitivity to the texture and feeling of the Canadian land. Recently there has been a pronounced turning of younger poets, particularly in western Canada, towards an almost topographical verse into which a direct response to the land and its qualities is emphasized, and among novelists since Margaret Laurence there has been an equally pronounced turning to a kind of local historical fiction into which physical landscape qualities enter very deeply. In all this I feel the poets and the fiction-writers are actually building on the work of essayists — Haig-Brown prominent among them — who have developed a Canadian version of the kind of country writing which one associates with the great line of English rural writers from William Cobbett down to W.H. Hudson.

Prominent among such Canadians have been Frederick Philip Grove, who remarkably evoked the look and feel of the prairies in volumes of essays like *Over Prairie Trails* and *The Turn of the Year*, and Hugh MacLennan with books like *Cross-Country*, his book of travel essays, and *The Rivers of Canada*, which is really a rich collection of historico-geographical essays.

It is among such writers that Haig-Brown should have found a high place, for he has been for thirty years one of our best essayists, yet his most considerable reputation has never existed among writers, who ought to have responded naturally to his mastery of a difficult prose form, but among outdoorsmen — hunters, fishermen and environmentalists — who read him primarily for the subjects he treated, which on the more obvious level were mainly fishing, hunting and conservation. Yet I am sure that many even of the outdoorsmen sensed the artistry of Haig-Brown's prose, and that his success among them was due in very large part to his literary quality, to his extraordinary power of making one experience not only the feel and smell and look of the natural setting but also the sheer excitement the angler feels when he has made a catch with proper skill, using his wits against an adversary he respects and in a strange oblique way loves. I will come back later to that point about the beloved adversary, for Haig-Brown's books tell us some very interesting things about the curious relationship that exists between the hunter and the hunted.

But for the moment I'm still concerned with the question of why Haig-Brown was not more widely accepted by Canadian literary critics, and I think it springs less from his subject matter than from the curious paradox that, while Canada has produced a remarkable succession of fine essayists from Joseph Howe down to the present, at the same time there has not been any wide Canadian readership for essays. As a result, the sheer economic problems of making a living by writing have forced natural essayists to concentrate in other fields, so that both Hugh MacLennan and Frederick Philip Grove became not entirely successful essayists in fiction, while Haig-Brown in his turn seemed to swerve away from the essay in a purely literary sense when he found that the fishing and hunting which had been his passion since boyhood provided him with a readership that lay mainly outside the perimeters of the orthodox literary world.

What the critics missed was that in the process Haig-Brown was achieving some very interesting effects by reconciling his expositions on the craft of fishing with his inclination to reflective and evocative prose by becoming something of a twentieth-century North American Isaak Walton. For, like Walton, Haig-Brown quickly learnt the ability to give the reader a feeling of total experience when he wrote of fishing, a feeling that even someone who was not a fisherman — and even someone who was theoretically opposed to fishing — could sense and respond to. This was partly because he wrote so often in terms of personally experienced and vividly transmitted episodes, and partly because, like Isaak Walton, he always regarded fishing as "a contemplative man's recreation," with the consequent fringe benefits. "A man," he said in *Fisherman's Summer*, "should think when he is fishing, of all manner and shapes of things, flowing as easily through his mind as the light streams along its rocks." Some of this free and flowing thought Haig-Brown introduced into his writing, so that his fishing books, like the central tetralogy of *Fisherman's Spring*, *Fisherman's Summer*, *Fisherman's Winter* and *Fisherman's Fall*, contain many things that would have no place in an ordinary angling text book. In fact, of course, they are not text-books, but books of experience, and out of experience comes reflection, and out of reflection distilled and processed comes what one recognizes as the art of prose.

And indeed, by the time you have finished the four books I have just mentioned, you recognize that thinking about his experiences while fishing has made Haig-Brown a great deal more than a fisherman only. Among other things, it made him into what, if he had given a slightly different form to his books, we would call a very evocative travel writer, for many a British Columbian lake and stream comes to vivid life as he takes us to its waters. Then there is *Fisherman's Winter*, dealing with a journey Haig-Brown made in the early 1950s to investigate trout fishing in Chile and Argentina. There emerged a narrative reminiscent of the Victorian naturalists' books, which Haig-Brown admired so much. Just as the best of those writers, like Charles Darwin in *The Voyage of the Beagle* and H.W. Bates in *A Naturalist on the Amazons*, evoked· vividly the physical look and native life of the countries whose fauna and flora they investigated and collected, so Haig-Brown, in describing the game fish of the Andes, gave an unforgettable picture of the the mountains, lakes and rivers of Chile and the Chilean people at a stage in their development which recent Chilean history makes seem remarkably idyllic. Similarly, in what is perhaps the best of all his books of essays, *The Measure of the Year*, Haig-Brown wrote an unusual kind of static travel book, in which he takes one through time rather than space as he tells the cycle of his yearly life in the then small village of Campbell River, where he functioned not merely as a writer and fisherman but also as local magistrate and as a highly respected community leader.

But even more than making him an unusual kind of travel writer, Haig-Brown's passionate interest in fishing also turned him into a fine naturalist in the same manner as the Victorian field naturalists he admired, carefully observing in their natural settings the creatures that fascinated him. He did not neglect modern biological discoveries; in fact he was remarkably well-read in them, but he never sought the total objectivity of the professional scientist, and he distrusted the temptations of specialization. What intrigued him in his observations, as it did in the practice of fishing, was — as he expressed it — "the strangeness and beauty of the fish, their often visible remoteness, their ease in another world, the mystery of their movements and habits and whims."

There were some striking changes in Haig-Brown's attitudes over the years towards the wild creatures which he had pursued ever since his boyhood fishing in the chalk streams of the England where he was born, and here we come back to that interesting question of the beloved adversary.

In a public way the theme emerged when Haig-Brown became an ardent conservationist many years before environmentalism became a radical fashion, and only a few weeks ago, just before his death, I read with a degree of amazed recollection some pages he wrote in *Fisherman's Spring* as long ago as 1951 and which would have seemed freshly contemporary twenty years later from the pen of a young ecologist. Haig-Brown fought publicly and often with very little support against many of the hydro and industrial developments in British Columbia which he argued would be harmful to wild life and the environment in general; in almost every case events proved him right, and a lot of harm was done to the environment for little real advantage.

Of more intimate interest than Haig-Brown's public actions as a conservationist was the growing empathy towards game animals and fish which he evidenced in successive books. At first he appears to have hunted and fished with zest and without much apparent reflection. Then he began to become conscious of that strange sense of identity with the quarry which often occurs among hunters, and in this way he drew close in sympathy with the native Indians of British Columbia, whose hunting magic was based on a belief in the bond of affinity between man and the creatures necessity leads them to pursue. This was shown in what I think is the best of Haig-Brown's several novels for children, a book called *The Whale People* which portrays the life and the hunting methods of the Nootka Indians of western Vancouver Island, who went out in canoes to chase the whale and, with great skill and courage, and using elaborate sympathetic magic, often succeeded in killing the great creatures and towing them home to land.

As early as *Fisherman's Spring* in 1954 Haig-Brown remarked: "it is the imponderable and the unpredictable in the ways of wild creatures that unites us and makes our common ways. We try to become one with the creature we pursue, to know its ways and anticipate its actions." In Haig-Brown this process led not only to a sense of identification with the quarry but also to an acceptance of the often atrocious-seeming fatalities of their natural life cycles. Like anyone who sees it for the first time, he was appalled by the apparently meaningless waste of lives when the Pacific salmon, having ascended the river and spawned, invariably die. But once one has developed an empathy for the creatures whose strange fate it is to die through the process of giving life, then acceptance can come. "Now," says Haig-Brown in *Fisherman's Fall*, "I have lived so long with this fact of collective, simultaneous death that I no longer resent or question it. Instead I find it fitting and beautiful, certainly useful in ways that are not entirely clear, and a yearly occasion of high drama. I am still curious about the manner and meaning of it, but I do not question that it has manner and meaning."

What one observes in all these stages of Haig-Brown's changing attitudes towards the world of wild nature is the steady shedding of barriers between the human and the animal world. The final stage comes in the extraordinary terminating chapters of *Fisherman's Fall*, Haig-Brown's last important book, in which he told of his experiences when he took to scuba diving and began to spend hours underwater in the familiar river outside his house which hitherto he had known only from the other side of the surface film. He found that in fact he was not only seeing the fish's world with a fish's eye, but that he was also experiencing in a tactile way the sensations of being a fish. The experience intensified the sense of identification, and turned the fish from an alien being inhabiting the other side of the water surface into the denizen of a shared environment. "I find," said Haig-Brown in what is a remarkable confession for a lifelong fisherman, "that I have practially no desire to go out and catch the fish I have seen while diving; I would rather go back and have another look at them. By the time I have watched the same fish twice, he is an old friend and I wouldn't dream of going out to kill him; I would even hesitate to disturb him by catching him and putting him back."

At the end of *Fisherman's Fall*, Haig-Brown tentatively raised the question whether this book, published in 1964, would be his last writing about fish and fishing. It was in fact the last book written with the special sense of total involvement that had marked his fishing books up to this time, and the last decade of his life was — for his admirers — disappointingly scanty in terms of literary creation. It was not inactive; in fact, it tended to be filled with community service of many kinds. But Haig-Brown's true vocation was writing, and the reason he became almost silent on paper during these final years must be found in the way his writing developed, moving constantly towards that point of empathetic identification with the subject which meant that writing no longer seemed necessary.

Such considerations circle one back from Haig-Brown the fisherman, the naturalist, the environmentalist, the servant of the community, to Haig-Brown the writer, which, as he himself well knew, was his central role. And as a writer there is one more important thing to say about him. He wrote for a wide audience, and probably had more readers in the United States — and presumably more in Britain — than he had in Canada. But his appeal was based on his intense apprehension of a particular locality. He did not write about streams or lakes or forests in general. There was never any doubt that he was writing with a specific vividness about certain actual rivers, mainly in British Columbia, though occasionally in childhood England or traveller's Chile. In other words, he made the vital connection between regionalism and universalism, and this in part is why he has been misunderstood by Canadian critics who have been bemused by nationalist myths. Haig-Brown was never in the narrow sense a nationalist, though he was a good Canadian patriot. But he realized that patriotism has its roots in the intimate locality, the *patria chica* or little fatherland, as the Spaniards call it, and once he said: "I am not at all sure that provincialism is such an evil thing at that. No man becomes a great patriot without first learning the closer loyalties and learning them well: loyalty to the family, to the place he calls home, to his province or state or county . . ."

Even in the way he forged his craft, Haig-Brown was an intensely local writer. He began to write in his teens while he was working in Pacific Coast logging camps. Unlike many other writers, he never served an apprenticeship in the literary world of some capital city; he remained on the Pacific Coast, immersed in its local life, and there he became the writer we all have known. But when as an editor I once asked him for an essay on the writer in isolation, which appeared as the first item of the first issue of *Canadian Literature* nearly eighteen years ago, he came to the conclusion that even his remoteness from the grand cultural centres did not mean that he had ever been in a real sense more isolated than other writers. Like them he had been influenced by books and by the people he met and the experiences he underwent, and like them he faced the ultimate task of creation — as we all face birth and death — on his own. Or, to put it in his words: "In the end, all writing is isolation. A man observes and absorbs readily enough among his friends. He may test ideas or sharpen argument or search for encouragement in talk. But he must mature his thought, develop and control his emotions, plan his work, alone. And he must write alone."

Yet at the same time Haig-Brown felt that a writer was perhaps better off if he added just a little more to this inevitable isolation of creation, and there is one passage from his *Canadian Literature* essay which I have always felt singularly timely in our present generation when writers are constantly tempted to become public exhibitionists, reading their works to audiences, signing their books in bookstores, appearing on television, and doing everything but write. "Any writer," said Haig-Brown, "who has the necessary minimum of integrity can readily afford to expose himself to influences of all kinds without fear of loss and with some real chance of gain. Yet talk is a danger to writers. More than that, talk is a positive, ugly menace. Talk is much easier than writing, its satisifactions are so immediate, that some of the need to write is all too easily lost in it. It may be true that no man will talk himself out of being a writer if he has it in him to write, and no doubt some men have capacity for both. But I think the frustration of enforced silence is good for most of us."

I remember now the good sense of those words, and of so much else that Roderick Haig-Brown wrote, and even spoke, though mostly in private, and I realize once again that he was not only a good writer; he was also that much rarer kind of being, a man made wise by the patient observation of nature and of life.

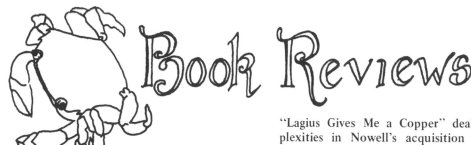

Book Reviews

SMOKE FROM THEIR FIRES

Reviewed by Rolf Knight

I was born at Fort Rupert in the year 1870. It was coming on to winter. Soon after I was born the Walas Kwakiutl lost forty men in front of Fort Rupert. They got upset in their canoe and all got drowned.

So begins the life history of Charles Nowell, as told to anthropologist Clellan Ford in 1940. Largely unknown outside a small circle, *Smoke From Their Fires* is the most illuminating and probably the best autobiography to come from a native person in B.C. Dealing as it does with detailed recollections from fifty to over one hundred years ago, there will be no other such account.

What raises Nowell's story far above analogous biographies is the honesty and gusto of his reminiscences (and Ford's resolution not to tamper with them). *Smoke From Their Fires* is neither a fashionably romanticized and bowdlerized tale of an Indian chief, nor was it written to support the political mythology of professional native organizations. Speaking near the end of a long and eventful life, Nowell has few regrets and no apologies to make. For instance, he recounts a "love affair" of his younger days which misfires when the grandparents of the girl catch them in the act:

They hollered out, "Hello there! Who's there?" and I got so scared I just ran in the house. My undershirt was so short I had to pull it down over my pecker. The next day we was invited to a feast, and all the Fort Ruperts went. And while I was at the feast, the men that saw me spoke, and one said he saw a naked man who got so scared he ran into one of the houses. I felt so bad I slid down in my seat. He also says we ought to keep watch because some men from other places that don't know enough to wear clothes is coming into our village and prowling around.

Alongside the current crop of hymnals to native spirulaity this kind of thing is very refreshing.

Throughout his adult life Nowell was a knowledgeable and unequivocal supporter of traditional Kwakiutl ways. In the context of his own experiences he weaves descriptions of the nature and power of sorcerers and Kwakiutl spirits; of how the intricacies of kinship and inheritance are learned and work; of marriage and child-rearing, of myths and menstrual taboos; of proper Kwakiutl ambitions and social etiquette and much more. The chapter entitled

"Lagius Gives Me a Copper" deals with the complexities in Nowell's acquisition of an important social rank and is one of the classic descriptions of the potlatch system.

At another point he describes the elaborate stagecraft that went into mounting the Winter Dances, stagecraft which would stagger American audiences when Nowell and half a dozen other Kwakiutl performers attend the St. Louis World's Fair in 1904. A fragment describes his earlier initiation into the "secret" of a Towidi dance:

They put her in the box while all the people saw her put in there in her blue blanket and tied the box, and they put the box on the fire and poured on the oolachen grease. The fire burned and the box burned, and she was still singing inside, and then the box go up in flames, and they can see her burning in her blue blanket, and all her relatives just cry and cry. Although they know it is not real, it looks so real they can't help it. It was all a trick. There was a hole under the box with a tunnel leading out of the house, and the woman went out of the box and put a seal in her place wrapped in a blue blanket, and then someone sang into the fire through a kelp tube, her song. Oh, it looked real.

Although a "traditional" Kwakiutl man, Nowell was capable of meeting the industrial world of that era head on. In 1887, as a young man who has been to school in Metlakatla a few years, he travels to a job in the Fraser River canneries, along with hundreds of other upcoast Indians. After the end of the salmon run there he works briefly in the hop fields of Washington State and then on to the bright lights of Seattle. "Dead broke," he returns to Vancouver and gets a job as a stoker in the North Shore sawmill, and later does a stint as a longshoreman and then load checker on the Burrard Inlet docks.

The same winter, back at Quatsino, Nowell and a crew of already well-travelled Kwakiutl sealers ship aboard the schooner *Rosie Olsen*, bound for a one-year sealing cruise in Japanese waters. They are in Yokohama for about a month to refit.

During the time we was there I stayed with a Japanese girl, and all the boys had their Japanese girls. When the carpenter built us canoes, we began to seal hunt. Charley Wilson was the hunter and I steered the canoe. When we got through hunting there, we went inside to Hakodate. While we were going through the inlet, we ran against a sandbar during the night. It was foggy and raining that night, and our schooner got wrecked.

During the three-month layover in Hakodate they haggle with rickshaw drivers, scout the city for a restaurant they like, round up the rest of the crew and find a boarding house advertising "'All Europeans Welcome,' that means sailors there." After various adventures they arrange with a shipping agent for passage to B.C. and work their way back on another schooner which plays hide-and-seek with American patrol ships guarding the seal rookeries of the Aleutian Islands.

Charlie Nowell's combination of traditional knowledge and understanding of the non-Indian world made him popular with the anthropologists, and through his association with Dr. C.F. Newcombe he became well travelled as an "Indian dancer." He was called upon to dance before King George during a royal visit to Vancouver, but says, "I wasn't feeling well and didn't go." One request he did accept was that of the World's Fair in St. Louis.

At the time all the big people of the Fair came to see us, we was given notice about a week beforehand that they were going to come. So we got everything ready – our dancing blankets, and a headdress with ermine skins on the back, and Bob Harris made everything ready for himself, because he was a Hamatsa. We kept Dr. Newcombe busy at that time, getting all the stuff that we wanted. There was a little African pygmy that used to come and see us. He liked to come because we always had bananas, and this little fellow loved bananas. He didn't seem to want to eat anything else; as soon as he come in, he look at the bananas hanging up and say, "Huh – Banana!" Bob Harris wanted to make a little man just like him, so I told him to come in every day and sit down and eat bananas while Bob Harris was making a little man with some bones and mutton flesh. He made it just like him, and when it was finished it was put in an oven, and Bob Harris looked after that while it was baking. Bob Harris take it out and hold it up alongside of the little man, and the little fellow would offer it a banana. Bob Harris was making a whistle; he pinch the little fellow to make him squawk, until he made a whistle that sounded just like him. He made the mouth of this thing to move; when he pinch the little fellow, he watch how he open his mouth, and he put the whistle under the skirt of the little fellow he made, so that every time he presses where the whistle was, he make the right noise. He filled the inside with a tube of blood.

We went to the place where all the people was – they say there was about twenty thousand people that came that time. We was put to start first. We had a screen that was painted in a square – about eight feet square. We told the little fellow how it was going to be done, and not to tell his friends about it or we won't give him any more bananas. We had this baked mutton as a man inside the screen, where all our dresses are. We begin with a Bella Bella dance; the West Coast people all knew the songs, and they was singing while Bob Harris and I was dancing. When we got nearly through with one song, Bob Harris made a mistake in beating, and then he says, "Hap-hap-hap." I got behind the screen and dressed as an Indian and came back and told the people in English that the Cannibal is mad now, because they made a mistake in beating the board, and we don't know what he is going to do, because he is so fierce. The two young men from West Coast came and held him – trying to keep him from going toward the other people. Bob

Harris was struggling to get free from their hold. Finally he got away from them, and he ran around. When he got to where this little fellow was sitting, he picked him up and ran behind the screen and left him there. Then he took hold of this thing he made just like him and make it squeak and yell, and when he came out in front of the screen, it was yelling loud. Bob Harris came in front of us and set this little fellow in front of us and push his head down and bite the neck until out came the blood all over his face. All the little pygmies got up with their spears and was coming to kill Bob, and all the people in the audience thought sure he had bitten his neck off, but the guards just pushed them back and told them to sit down. The little pygmies just went home while Bob Harris was eating the mutton. I was the one that was cutting the flesh in strips while he was eating them, and crying, "Hap-hap." When he got through eating – some of us helped him because we were hungry – I looked around and saw there was no Indian in that place; they had all got frightened and went home.

I told the men in the hall that we had done a great thing that is only done in the wintertime, and that we are going home to our Indian house where we will try to bring him to life again. Dr. Newcombe never came near us, he was so scared of what Bob Harris had done. That was a murder, he said; that means he is going to be hanged. I told him to keep away from us. "You are a white man," I says, "and you better not come near us." I told the guards to go and put fire into our Indian house. While he was gone, we kept on singing songs, turning around as we go. People come with their kodaks taking our pictures; the guards couldn't keep them away.

It was evening when we get to our house and the house was already full of white people. Last of all the people that owned the Fair came in and sat in the front of the house. All the ladies and gentlemen were sitting right on the ground with their silk dresses on – right on the dirt – because they were told by the guards that is the way the Indians sit. Dr. Newcombe came over to us and want to have a talk with me. I look at him with a strong fierce look on my face and told him not to come near.

So we begin with one song and sing it, and Bob Harris get up and go around the fire singing with the rattle in his hand. Then he go to see the body that he had eaten and say, "The bones are all stuck together now." I interpreted to all the people in the house. Then we sang another song, and then he got up and went around the house and went up to where this little fellow was lying on a table. It was the little pygmy himself, lying under a mat. He says, "He has flesh on his bones now; the whole body is in good order." Then we sang another song, and he went around again, lifted up the mat, and felt. "He is quite warm now," he says. He came back and we sang the last song. then the West Coast men was dancing over the dead man with their hands shaking while we were singing. When we got through, Bob Harris went around the house, still using his rattle, singing, and went toward to where the little man was lying and lift up the mat. He took the mat off, and took the little man up and sit him up on the table, and he begin to look around stiff like as we told him to do. Bob

104

Harris took him down from the table and took him around the house, holding him by the hand. And all he say is, "Banana. Banana!"

Then they came back and sit down, and I got up and spoke to all the people: "I am very glad to learn that our friend here, Bob Harris, done this great thing. You all saw him when he ate the flesh of this little man that is standing by his side. This is the same man that was dead, and his flesh was all eaten up. Now he has his flesh and his life back, and now he is alive. And I am glad that there will be no law that will come against us." Dr. Newcombe slapped his knee and say in a loud voice, "Smart boys!" Then he got up and made a long speech, telling the people about the Indians in British Columbia and how they could do wonderful things.

After experiences such as these, Nowell and his compatriots were not easily overwhelmed by culture shock at developments in B.C. Such luxuries were left to a later age. Indeed, in the late 1880's and the 1890's native people were working in and holding their own in virtually every major industry in the province. During the next forty years Nowell himself worked as a fisherman, sawmill worker, labour recruiter for Brunswick Cannery and as an assistant to the Provincial Museum.

Smoke From Their Fires recalls dozens of native men and women of that era. Their doings are woven through the story, as are the places they worked and lived: Matilda Hunt, Stephen Cook, Tlakodlas and many more. These are not the textbook stereotypes of a "primitive" society where all activities are governed by custom and everyone follows the pre-scribed rules. They are real people, very much like people we all know today. Another stereotype Nowell assaults is the one that asserts that in the "good old days" every native person was part of one big happy family. Charlie Nowell was an important Kwakiutl chief, yet even he describes, with dismay, the treatment of "commoners" in some of the coastal villages.

Nowell's story is deceptively simple and straight-forward. But it yields additional insights with successive readings. Twenty years ago, when I first read *Smoke From Their Fires*, I saw it as another, better than average, life history of a man coming of age during the last phase of traditional Kwakiutl society. Now I see that it is much more.

Smoke From Their Fires, by Clellan Ford (ed.).

SPIT DELANEY'S ISLAND

Reviewed by John Faustmann

Reading this book of ten short stories is like noon hour at the pulp mill. Turning the pages, you open your lunch box to see what the wife sent today. Two cold meatloaf sandwiches and a package of cheeze doodles. Again.

Set on Vancouver Island, Jack Hodgins has peopled this book with very ordinary folk. Spit Delaney, who appears in the first and last stories, is an average guy, about forty, with an average family. His teenage daughter eats chocolate cake and watches a lot of television. His son doesn't say much, and reads all the time. His wife is leaving him. Theirs was the only marriage among their friends to have lasted this long, and now that it's over, Spit doesn't know what to make of any of it. His only real thrill in life was driving the old steam locomotive at the mill, but the company sold it to a museum in Ottawa. Now all he has left is the tape recording of his locomotive, and his room at the Touch and Go Motel. Every now and then a friend comes by and they crack open a couple of beers. You can almost hear the caps flip, clinking onto the worn linoleum floor.

The rest of the stories have much the same flavour, inhabited by people whose lives seem to roll over them. The sad ketchup of their passions drips onto the wax paper of their days. They exist, like daytime television, in the weary lookalike houses that line the island highway. Standing at the rain-smeared picture windows, they watch the cars going past in intent, maniacal bunches. Perhaps they wonder about the people going by, what their lives must be like. But then, maybe they don't.

Hodgins' caricatures rest on a lumpy reality, the faces are familiar. The hitchhikers out on the road slump unconcernedly, thumbs extant. The middle-aged women pull bread from the oven and reminisce about family reuinions. Three mindless adolescents motorcycle around the cowpastures. Logger husbands come home drunk and hit their wives. Car doors slam, calves fall down the well, and American tourists arrive in the summer to litter the landscape with gum wrappers.

Unfortunately, the action here borders on the banal. In "The Trench Dwellers," the main character is a hotline radio announcer, irritating his listeners into calling the station. His wife leaves him, too, taking the kids he never really knew. In "The Religion of the Country," the small bookstore owner, who, for years has inveighed against crass commercialism, marries a go-getter woman from up the island. He ends up selling rock-and-roll records, and dabbling heavily in real estate. In "Other People's Troubles," a rural Mary Worth is always there to listen to her neighbour's problems. But when her husband comes home, injured in a logging accident, she is impotent at the prospect of her own misfortunes. Leaving him bandaged at the kitchen table she runs off to her bedroom for a good cry. This sort of thing is a little too bland to sustain our interest too long.

Sensing this, Hodgins peppers a few stories with a minor sensationalism. One woman, on an isolated farm, has a ten year old son with brain damage. She hides him in the attic. A man passes by another farm, and stops to chat with the spinster lady there. Before an afternoon has passed the two of them are sitting on the roof of her house. He's doing a water-colour painting of the mountains while she talks and sips her homemade dandelion wine. By the time they come down they've decided to go into town and get married. Trying to work his way out from under the glaze of banality, the author reaches in all directions at once. The result is a verisimilitude pocked with fabrication.

Still, these stories are well written. The progression in them is tight, and aside from a few extraneous touches, they proceed solemnly from beginning to end. The author exhibits a control that is admirable, and he limits his subjects, fleshing out the narrative fully in most cases. He offers well-carved slices of ordinary lives.

Unfortunately, his choice of characters leaves him little room to move. His people are drawn well, but the scope of their possibilities is exceedingly narrow. The folk that dot these pages, that support the burden of society by going off to their dehumanising jobs, are, finally, rather dull. One can feel sorry for them, but it's hard to take any sort of interest in them. Further, one gets the impression that the author himself doesn't much care for the people he's written about. It seems as though he offers them up for our delectation, inviting us to look down our noses at his characters. Seeing the muddle they've got themselves into, we are left to shake our heads sadly.

This is unfortunate. Jack Hodgins demonstrates a palpable expertise in the writing of these stories. They do manage to evoke a certain widespread quality of life on the coast — the pickup camper consumerism with the gun rack in the back, the quiet desperation of a top-tidy arborite kitchen and the decay of society to a valueless norm. If only his characters were people we could care about. Cold meatloaf sustains us, but it fails to inspire.

Spit Delaney's Island, by Jack Hodgins.

STEVESTON RECOLLECTED

Reviewed by John Skapski

To quote from the introduction to this book: "This is not a history of Steveston in the conventional sense. Rather, it is an attempt to understand the role of the Japanese-Canadians in this community through the words and thoughts of the Japanese-Canadians themselves."

Since the book's premise is history through "words and thoughts," the authors have had to talk to the older Japanese, who know little English, and most of the book is translations of interviews in Japanese. Besides a short introduction and further introductions to the speakers by Marlatt, these interviews are pretty well allowed to speak for themselves. They are edited to generally group together, usually around one topic or idea. Because of this there's no real form or structure to this book, and certainly no detailed sense of historical progression. Throughout, there's a mixture of modern photographs and old archive prints. What results is a collage, a montage into which past and present are loosely interwoven. It's more like actually sitting and talking to a group of oldtimers: loose assocations

a sense of what lifestyles were, vague histories and geographies mixed in with anecdotes, personalities and the inevitable contradictions and differences of opinion, there's an impressionistic sense of what Steveston and the Japanese are about, but no strong statements, no precise definitions. In the end I find this rather pleasing. Anything else might spoil its fitting poetic effect and shatter the sense of tranquility that lies over the book like stillness over open waters.

And I choose that metaphor carefully, to point. Here is a past obviously filled with racial tension and conflicts and the now glaringly shoddy treatment of the Japanese during World War II, a grand opportunity for some vitriolic and embarrassingly righteous tub-thumping. But none of that. It comes out in typical style: low-key, pragmatic; over and done with and best forgotten, let's get on with today. But behind it the undertones of both bitterness and guilt. (At any rate, I managed to live in Steveston for over ten years, with Japanese friends, and never really find out about the happenings of the internment until I started to question why most of my friends, who seemed to have roots well back into the community, were born in eastern B.C. and Alberta.) It's something quite simply stated, but facts which make one feel embarrassed for the people who let it happen to them and the people who did it to them, even as one begins to realize the insularity and the closeness of the community, which probably lent to its mistrust and misunderstanding by the white community. The same restraint as in their views on internment and racial troubles also relates to their recollections of fishing disputes and strikes: just facts: prices, names, dates, but no dogma of the proletariat. And the hard times. The same. Just it was hard. It was cold. No complaints. No regrets.

It's a good book I'm sure, even if I can't sort out how much of what I like about it is just a reverberation of some hidden chord inside me, touched by memories of the old cannery houses on stilts where I used to deliver newspapers, and stare into strange-smelling houses full of exotic-looking Japanese dolls in glass cases where I went to collect the paper-money. I know it's not an overpowering book, but in its gentle, pervasive way it's probably stronger than a louder, more direct book would be. It leaves one, I think, with a sense of the personality of the Japanese-Canadian subculture, and the town central to them.

Steveston Recollected, by Daphne Marlatt.

IMAGES: STONE: B.C.

Reviewed by Mark Budgen

The late Wilson Duff, in his writing, teaching, and Provincial Museum responsibilities, made a large contribution to our understanding of the native civilisations in B.C. His writing was remarkable for its lack of anthropological jargon, his ideas were original and cogent, his influence will endure. This book, written as an accompaniment for an exhibition of northwest coast Indian sculpture, has the right mixture of scholarliness, elucidation, inspiration, and guess-work for its likely readership. With the excellent photographs by Hilary Stewart, it is a significant and inventive contribution to the scholarship of northwest coast Indian art.

In essence, Duff set himself an impossible task, as he well knew – "we do not have any way of 'knowing' what the stone sculptures really 'meant' to their makers and users." Quite gratuitously one can add that we also have no way of knowing if they were supposed to mean anything, although Duff, following Levi-Strauss, would insist that they are the products of a "scientific" mind. He tries, and to a limited extent succeeds, to demonstrate that many of those images in stone seek to resolve the perpetual antagonisms of life and death, male and female, physicalness and spiritualness, etc. Whatever the case, Duff has begun a chain of thought which will inevitably be continued, and deservedly so.

Images: Stone: B.C.: Thirty Centuries of Northwest Coast Indian Sculpture, by **Wilson Duff**. Photographs by **Hilary Stewart**. Hancock

BACKROADS OF B.C.

Reviewed by Frank White

It has been many a day since any book so delighted me as this travelogue of our own backyard.

It was a good many years ago that my youngest daughter laid down the law – we would see B.C. first. As she said with her grade seven wisdom – it has everything and it is ours. Since then there have been many trips together and separately, experiences and discoveries throughout the length and breadth of this province.

What a pleasure then to open this book and rediscover some of the beauty and sense of discovery of those long ago summers. Here are twenty-five trips through the real British Columbia. Backroads they may be to some but front roads to others of us, and most have been there many times longer than the highways. In terms of beauty and interest the highway may be regarded as only the means to get to the experiences laid out for us here.

Each trip is historically researched, beautifully documented with colour plates galore and replete with clear easy-to-follow maps.

For those mainlanders who know Vancouver Island and the west coast only in terms of its well-advertised tourist meccas, why not a leisurely weekend or any day spent learning the charm of the Saanich Peninsula, whose beauty is unique among the attractions of B.C.? Although many of the trips require a larger commitment of time there are others such as this which can be taken in on a spare afternoon or by sacrificing the few hours a direct route might save, rewarding the traveller with vistas to remember and enjoy for a long time.

This book will be as indispensable to the family just starting to discover B.C. as it is gratifying to one who has travelled its back country since the twenties.

Backroads of B.C., by **Liz** and **Jack Bryan**.

FIRST APPROACHES TO THE NORTHWEST COAST

Reviewed by Mark Budgen

A book on this subject is long overdue. Previously histories of European exploration of the Pacific Northwest coast have viewed the voyages of Bering, Perez, Cook, and Vancouver in isolation from other world events. Pethick, in this book and a forthcoming sequel, puts these and other explorations into the total context of European expansionism and mercantilism. His first chapter describes the preliminary Spanish and British voyages in the fifteenth and sixteenth centuries, his second the Russian movements to Alaska, and the rest of the book shows these three imperialist powers vying for territory and hegemony in this part of the globe in the last quarter of the eighteenth century.

While governments in Moscow, Madrid, and London were worried about which flag had laid claim to which latitude, more enterprising persons were beginning to exploit the fur trade to Asia. Many of these latter merchantmen – Meares, Barkley, Colnett, Douglas, et al. – named parts of our coastline and were, in fact, the precursors to the Hudson's Bay and Northwest Companies; it is their initial enterprise, together with Fraser's and MacKenzie's travels overland, which eventually decided that this coast would become part of the British, instead of the Russian or Spanish empires. This is not to say that they were entirely honourable men – they sailed under flags of convenience, frequently stole furs if they could not trade, and destroyed native villages for the flimsiest of excuses. New England traders were equally at fault, it should be added.

The book is handsomely illustrated with reproductions of contemporary prints and paintings. The only complaints are that the author neglects the Indian side of things almost totally and that he is occasionally guilty of some crass overwriting – "Royal France has fostered science, purified manners, presided, if somewhat reluctantly, over the emancipation of man from superstition; but in 1789 it was to strike upon a hidden reef and quickly disintegrate." Fortunately such sentences are few and not germane, on the whole, to the central theme. Also one wonders why Erna Gunther's excellent book on the same period, *Indian Life on the Northwest Coast* etc. (Univ. of Chicago Press, 1972) is ignored in the bibliography.

First Approaches to the Northwest Coast, by **Derek Pethick**.

Lucy Moon

The Last of the Long-Head Indians

Lucy Moon lived in Quatsino, B.C. and died around the time of the first war. Binding girl-babies' skulls to produce a back-tilted, elongated shape was an ancient Nootka practice, and Lucy was its last surviving example. According to Wenatchie Becker the Provincial Archives in Victoria offered her $1,000 to be paid on delivery, but Lucy's husband Frenchie insisted the payment be in advance, then buried her according to custom in a hollow tree and refused to tell which one.

She takes the freshly baked
Quatsino buns out of the oven
to be eaten hot with butter
and chicken breast.
Frenchie directs this preparation.
As he eats, she tucks
her chewed fingernails
inside the palms
flashing the rings he made her
hiding the gnawed skin
at the fingertips.

Lucy Moon bends over the tidal pool
poking a finger at cockles
and snails, urging these to hurry
on their one-footed way.
Spider-legged insects nip
at each other.
Two snails press stubby soles
each to each
their Chinese feet bound
like her head
hide-bound at birth
Lucy, the last of the Long-Heads,

her tunnel-shaped head
funnels the surf,
turns the volume
up or down, as though she moved
close and away and
close and away
on a schedule of tides
of her own.

Above the tide
shelled things on rock sides
dry out in the sun
pink, purple and hard
bleached white
like old skulls
monuments on the volcanic rock.

In the pool, the spiny
shell of a sea urchin
houses a mushy worm.

Each day a gift —
a coloured stone carved by the waves,
snake flowers in the woods,
the bleeding hearts of spoiled love;
kittens abandoned in a ditch
dead, an unnatural mother
slinking off through the tall
yellow grass;
sour grass or honeysuckle
blackberries, a sand cookie
she knows where to look
for them all.

The day the man came
lilacs hung heavy
with purple beads,
clusters of tiny grapes
sweet in the warm, still air,

the kitchen hot from the oven
made the man sweat,
his shirt sticking to his back,

mopping his face
with his napkin,
a few damp crumbs
of Quatsino bun
stuck to his forehead

"A thousand dollars
for Lucy's skull
payable on receipt," he said.
"What good could the money do
when I'm dead?"
she said, fondling her small-mountain head
with affection
not flattered with thoughts
of her skull behind glass
bleached and preserved,
a barnacle in the sun.
"Better pay now," chuckled Frenchie.

The head was all
and not inside
the smooth, white contour
of bone
a conch to lift to the ear
to hear the sea in,
the wind could whistle in
the empty eye sockets
the jaw a grotesque grin
the absence of a nose
eroded by the wind
and the waves.
She touched her head,
an object to find buried
in the sand.

Stiffly Lucy Moon gathers the shellfish
she'd come for
in an instant sees the sun
tip the silver waves gold
and slip back to its place
losing breath
behind clouds
shrouding her eyes.

Dead bones of ancestors
old scattered bones
picked clean
the birds begun eating
before the flesh is cold.

How do you sever a head?
One sheet over her trunk,
a smaller white sheet covers her face
leaving a thin line of neck
a circle to mark the incision,
an acrid skull boiling in a pot.

Frenchie washes her gently,
oils her skin, dresses her,
then carries her, head intact
to the hollow tree
in the mountains
and packs the opening
with clay.

What could the museum say?
It was Lucy
who didn't deliver.   **Lois Gubbe**

OUTHOUSE

Nothing left in sight
but that crazy sentrybox outhouse
a simple man's totem
standing guard
over oysters cobbling
greengray rocks —
starfish orange and purpling
the lost bay's bottom —
wary seal backsliding
into the calm deeps quick with fish.

Brush has buried the rest —
thirty years of wild growth put paid
to the garden in the gully —
the garbage-heap tells how long —
bottles and cans from bellyup companies
gleam and rust in an alderthicket.

Time's had its way with this homestead —
those fragile skulleyed shacks
hard to find on a tanglewood ridge
are empty as a whore's smile —
no trace of who or why —
a few more snows and winds will flatten them —
ground-rot chew their boards to mulch.

But not the outhouse —
it'll stand for a while yet —
built for the wars, that crapper —
fashioned solid and lovingly
with even scrollwork around the eaves —
straddled on two skookum logs
over the narrow creekmouth —
self-flushing —
an ingenious joy of a john.

It must have been his favorite place
to sit with ruminative pipe
on bird-rustling evenings
planning a confident kingdom
to last at least forever.

Peter Trower

I would like to write to you people on the very good book, the *Raincoast Chronicles First Five*. It sure is good reading and the pictures are real good. I myself am an ex-towboater and the tugboat article is very good, the pictures you have of all the tugs. Well, the *Prospective* tug you have in the book, she was steam when the picture was taken, I was captain on her for ten years when she was a diesel tug and then she was sold to American interests and went to Alaska. I heard she was sunk up there.

By the way, I live with John (Baldy) Martell. I have been with him for 15 years here in Loughborough Inlet, he is the longest and oldest person in the inlet, 50-odd years. He fished in Rivers Inlet 40-odd years up to 1968 and was very interested in the story of Rivers Inlet. He is now 86 years young.

Well I guess that is all for now and I want to thank you for a very good book.

Doug Cliff
Campbell River, B.C.

My father, Alex Kean, passed away very suddenly on December 21st. In the past weeks, remembering Dad's last few years and of the things that were important to him, you came to mind many times.

The day he received your letter to say you had accepted his story "Lost in the Rain Forest" for the *Chronicles*, he was elated and from that day on his interest in writing grew, which gave him a lot of pleasure. Also many proud times, when people read the story and asked for his autograph.

I just had to thank you for giving him those special times and thank you also for giving him the interest to write many more pages, which have given me a look into his youth which many parents never get around to telling their children.

Kathy Fraser (nee Kean)
West Vancouver, B.C.

In answer to your request for memories of Panicky Bell, last of the bad old bastards—

Lost now is a 20-verse Swanson-style ballad I wrote of crossing Kicking Horse Pass in 1948, flying over to the Charlottes and Panicky Bell's Aero camp, too bad. He met us at the dock, not a big guy, maybe 5'8", skinny, face browned, wrinkled, neck distinctly red, kind of ugly beneath a huge hard hat. Scowling always. Hard nasty humour. Wanted hard workers, "men" only in his camp. Voices around me — "there he is" — afraid kind of, but with affection too. He kidded with those he knew, spoke with new men only to ask them what they did, looking them over. He put me chaser on a cold deck with Bullshit George, more a character than Panicky, a huge hairy bear yelling at his donkey all day. Also did some second rigging with Snowball, a Haida highrigger who could beat his hat down the tree.

Saw Panicky throw a shackle at a catskinner and fired guys by the dozens because he didn't like the way they worked. Always did it with style: he'd say to some guy innocently, like he wanted an errand, "Know where the plane docks?" "Yeah," the guy would say. "Well the next time it comes to you go down and get on it." Fired a kid getting off the crummy in the morning because he didn't have suspenders. "You'll be pulling up your pants all day." Then the famous one of the incompetent rigger who took all day to top a tree. "Can you see Vancouver from there?" Panicky yells up from the ground. The rigger scans the horizon and yells down, "Nope!" "Well, you'll see 'er tomorrow," Panicky hollers.

Really it wasn't a bad camp, comfortable and good grub. We worked on the last railroad show, then pulled up tracks to be sent to India for telegraph poles. Were given steel measure tapes with Aero Camp and date stamped on at a get-together when we wound up. Pictures of Panicky Bell? I doubt you'll find any. The legend is probably better off without them anyway.

Peter Blue Cloud
Assistant Editor, Akwesasne Notes
Bombay, New York

I recently acquired a copy of your *Raincoast Chronicles First Five* and read through it with great interest. One article which caught my attention particularly was "A Fir Tree of the Mind," which purports to expose British Columbia's entry under tallest trees in the Guinness Book of Records, the 417-foot Douglas fir reputedly cut by George Cary of Lynn Valley in 1895, as "a nuisance legend in no way authenticated by any proof whatsoever . . . a fiction invented to appease the need of B.C. people to have a claim to a world's record."

The writer, Tod Carney, implies that a tree of such dimensions is well beyond the realm of the possible and traces the legend to a doctored photograph of a redwood tree used by a group of turn-of-the-century Vancouver lumbermen to "put one over" on their colleagues in Washington State. He quotes two U.B.C. silviculturists and the late Vancouver archivist Major J.F. Matthews in his support and no doubt feels he has closed the book on the issue.

While I do not dispute Mr. Carney's findings regarding that particular much-used photograph, which indeed seems spurious, I think his other statements do a disservice both to the people of B.C. and to the Douglas fir. In short, I do not think his conclusions reflect accurately either on our gullibility or on its size, and I am hoping your readers can help me prove that a fir tree of record size was in fact cut on Burrard Inlet in 1895, whether or not it was cut by George Cary or had the exact dimensions of the one credited to him by Guinness.

To begin with, just how naive would it be to believe that the Douglas fir, growing under ideal conditions, could reach heights in excess of 400 feet? According to Mr. Carney this would have made the Cary tree a hundred feet taller than the largest specimen elsewhere reported. A tree of such size may well seem unimaginable today, but our sense of scale in this matter has diminished over the years.

I remember visiting the Vancouver Museum with my father in 1920 and seeing a photograph there of a Douglas fir which had been measured at 410 feet. To us, living in the Fraser Valley at a time when many stands of giant fir were still extant and having personally heard of specimens well over 300 feet being felled, 410 feet seemed exceptional but quite realistic.

William H. Harlow, professor of Wood Technology, State University of New York, states of the Douglas fir in his *Textbook of Dendrology* (1958), "...heights of 325 feet and diameter of 8 to 10 feet are not uncommon. The tallest known specimen in the United States stood near Mineral, Washington and was approximately 385 feet in height and 15 feet in diameter." This tree, which presumably inherits the record if the "Cary Fir" is disqualified, would have been only 32 feet or 7.6% shorter than the one considered fantastic by Mr. Carney. In a virile, genetically plastic species known for giantism like the Douglas fir, I would not consider this a fantastic degree of variation.

My principal reason for taking issue with Mr. Carney, however, is the photograph I mentioned seeing above. This photograph, which is not the one discussed in your article, would appear to offer tangible evidence that a tree tall enough to be the world's record was indeed cut on the North Shore of Burrard Inlet, whether or not it is the same tree at back of the Cary Fir legend. As I say I viewed this picture in the old Vancouver Museum at Main and Hastings one day in 1920 while visiting with my father, who was very interested in such things. It was, as I recall, about five inches by ten inches with typed caption and was prominently displayed. Along and in front of the butt was a scattering of people standing but no ladder as in the discredited picture of the redwood. I remember it being pointed out to me that one individual was the then Vancouver mayor. There were other dignitaries too, of the city of that time. I also seem to remember that the tree was felled in or near Capilano. But what I do remember very clearly were the measurements of the tree: diameter 25 feet and height, not 417 feet, but 410 feet.

The Vancouver City Archives are now unable to find any record of this photograph. I am not entirely surprised considering that the museum remained in the very cramped Main and Hastings quarters until 1968 and much discarding of material must have occurred. Forty-eight years is a long time for a photo to last on display.

I might have been convinced to let my memory rest had I not come across an item in a book entitled *The World of Trees* by H. L. Edlin during a recent trip to England. I quote "In 1895 lumberjacks in the Capilano grove felled a Douglas fir which proved, after measurements on the ground certified by the mayor and sheriff, to have been the tallest tree known anywhere on earth! It scaled 417 feet (127 m.) and was 50 feet (15.2 m.) round." This information seemed to coincide quite nearly with my memory of the old photograph so I contacted Mr. Edlin at the Forest Research Station in Farnham, Surrey and he agreed to send me anything of use he could find among his references. Nothing has come of this yet, but it occurs to me that readers of "Notes and Queries" may be able either to throw some light on what has become of this old photograph or at least corroborate my own memory of having seen it. Either way we may be able to strengthen B.C.'s claim to having had the world's tallest tree in fact and not just in wishful fiction.

Dr. A. C. Carder
Victoria, B.C.

And now we've got two requests of our own. Up the coast in the vicinity of Princess Royal Island there are two sights that never fail to beguile passers-by. On the mainland side of Graham Reach in a place called Swanson Bay rears a great concrete chimney, its base in anonymous bush. This is the sole memorial to B.C.'s pioneer pulp mill, first run in 1909. On the other side of Princess Royal Island the first-time boater is startled coming around the final bend of Surf Inlet to see his way blocked by a huge concrete dam which stretches from shore to shore. This abandoned structure holds back a ten-mile lake once used to barge out rich gold-silver ore from the Belmont Mine, which may have employed a thousand men around the end of World War I. No one seems to know much about it for certain. There's nothing in the libraries or archives. This is the kind of challenge we seem to be here for, and we'd like your help in putting some facts about both of these forgotten company towns on the record.

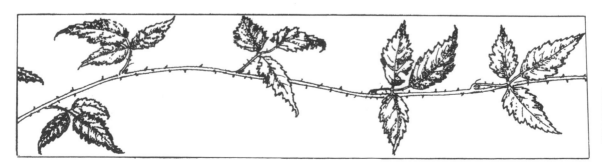

Robert Jack

THE BRUNETTE 1890-1979

Howard White

Everyone agrees — it was no fit ending for the grand old lady of the B.C. towboat fleet.

As recently as 1975 the 36-ton wooden tug *Brunette,* pictured on page 113 in a drawing by Steve Jackson, was being cited as one of the wonders of the west coast. Not only was she the oldest towboat afloat, she was arguably the prettiest — and she was still working a full shift. She was stately and tall in the old style but her condtion was so good people found it hard to believe she'd been launched in the year 1890.

The *Brunette* was built for Brunette Sawmills of New Westminster at a shipyard operated on the mill property by the transplanted New Brunswick boatbuilder Wesley Peck, the grandfather of *Raincoast Chronicles* contributor Captain Don Peck. She was designed as a log tower and with her original wood-fired John Doty engine she could tow four sections. When M.R. Cliff converted her to diesel with a 275-horsepower Buda in 1953 she found herself pulling up to 40 sections, a fact that would have no doubt amazed her builder.

Captain A.C. "Simmy" Simpson, who skippered the *Brunette* for twenty years from 1925 to 1945, says she was a wonderful boat to handle and an exceptional towing boat because of the fineness of her lines. She wasn't particularly fast with steam, running a shade under 8 knots, but when they put in diesel she came into her reputation as a speedster and was sent down to the towboat races in Seattle. She did well but didn't win.

"They might have won if they'd had her trimmed right," says Simpson, who had left Cliff by this time. "I asked 'em how they had 'er trimmed and they said, well, they'd lightened 'er by having the fuel tanks empty. So I told 'em that was their mistake. The fuel tanks were forward, and she always went better loaded. It put 'er down by the head and lifted 'er aft, made less stern drag. That's what made 'er go, the *Brunette,* she was so clean aft."

"That was her failing too, she was so fine back there she had no lift in a following sea. Running from a sou' east gale in a snow storm out off Halfmoon Bay one time we took a boarding sea that caved the winch deck right in. Left the top of the winch down just level with the bulwarks. You had to watch 'er like a hawk."

For most of her working life the *Brunette* was a "delivery boat", picking up logs at the Howe Sound booming grounds and delivering them to the mills of Burrard Inlet and the Fraser River, but she did enough outside towing to become well known up and down the coast. She was sunk once up the Fraser, the result of a drunken skipper taking her inside some pilings, and later she was put on the beach by one of her owners, Robert Smith, but otherwise she led a charmed life.

Simpson calls her "a lucky boat that brought good luck to all who had her." Not the least of her good fortune was in finding owners who knew her value and gave her the special care that allowed her to outlast every other vessel of her time. She was in the Smith and Dollar fleet for a time, and Simpson thinks it was J.W. Pike who replaced her original low house with the higher one that became her trademark. In 1920 she found the love of her life in one Murray Robertson Cliff, a Vancouver towboater who built the once-considerable M.R. Cliff Tugboat Company around her. It was as a Cliff boat Simpson put in his two decades as skipper and he often warned Cliff never to sell the boat. "I told him he'd go broke. She was his lucky talisman." In 1953 when others of her vintage were being led off to the boneyard, Cliff treated the *Brunette* to a complete rebuild and gave her diesel power, but a few years later he sold her. In 1958 he went broke.

After several years in limbo the *Brunette's* good luck in 1964 led her into a second longlasting affair with Captain Vic Di Castri of Westview Towing Company at Powell River. "I looked after that boat," says Di Castri. "Anything that needed doing, I got it done right now. If she had to come out for a bunged-up wheel, I always got her painted at the same time, even if she'd been done the month before. Just before I gave her up I had her out for steamboat inspection and they wanted me to raise the hatches and put on steel doors to meet the new rules, but they passed the hull. She was sound."

Di Castri kept her fifteen years, doing a variety of jobs including outside towing and rescue work, but mostly handling scows and docking ships around the Powell River pulp mill.

"She was a lovely boat. Around the dock she was good because she could just lie in there and *hang on.* And towing, well, she could get down into the water and just *pull.* She was 'way ahead of any steel boat. Often they had to get us to come in and do things they couldn't do."

In 1975 the *Brunette's* luck ran out. Di Castri fell ill and sold the business to Lloyd Wade of Lund, who brought the old tug back from his first trip with a bad split in the hull, then decided she wasn't right for the work and stood her down for a steel tug. She lay at her berth unpainted and deteriorating for upwards of a year when she was taken to Lund and stripped down for living on. Three years later Wade's successor Jim Arnold took out the engine, stripped her hardware and sold her to Spirit Cove Oyster Farms for the princely sum of one dollar. It was in this group's hands she finally met the fate she had eluded for 89 years, but by this time she was no more than a worm-eaten hulk.

"It was a damn shame," says Di Castri, "If I'd known what was going to happen I never would have let her go. She could have gone on a long time yet if she'd been given the chance."

His regret will be echoed up and down the B.C. coast for many years to come.

Floatplanes and Snow

A.J. Spilsbury and Howard White

APART FROM AIR CANADA, WHICH WAS CREATED BY AN ACT OF GOD, most airlines in Canada were started on shoestrings by overweening bush pilots. Ginger Coote started West Coast Airlines, Grant McConachie started C.P.A., and so on. Queen Charlotte Airlines, or P.W.A. as it later became, was a different story. It was started on a shoestring rightly enough, but by a confirmed passenger, namely myself. I didn't learn to fly until quite well on in the game.

I guess I wanted to fly but I was too darn busy trying to keep things together to take the time. However, when the airline got well going and we had two or three hundred people there and twenty

or thirty aircraft I got enough time off that I went to the Aero Club and took lessons on a Tiger Moth with Len Milne as instructor. I went up a few times but I just couldn't run the thing. I couldn't find any connection between the stick and what happened to the aeroplane. It seemed like there was a missing link there or something. I had a hell of a time with it and I was most unhappy.

The fifth time I was out there Len said, okay, next time you're on your own. Well *no way* was I ready. I hadn't managed to land that thing yet without bouncing it or putting it on its nose. I never went back. It scared the heck out of me.

About a year later I was talking to Stan Sharpe at Brisbane Aviation and he took pity on me. He said, look, we won't charge you the full rate, come on over and carry on with your lessons. They had a different kind of aircraft. I learned then on an Aeronca tandem — the student sat forward and the instructor behind him. It was much easier to fly. Very forgiving. It made me wonder why they ever persisted in trying to teach people on Tiger Moths. They killed hundreds of people in Tiger Moths during the war. They were dreadful things it seemed to me, but the oldtimers swore by them. My instructor this time around was a bit more of a psychologist. After he'd taken me on a few runs through he said, you just keep on like that, I'm going to go have a smoke. I was 500 feet in the air before it dawned on me just what was happening. I was solo! I got my licence, I flew on wheels just enough to get checked out on floats and from then on I used to fly a little four-place Stinson Station Wagon that the company had, CF-FFW. I could putter up the coast on my own, go up to Savary Island with the family, and I really enjoyed it.

All in all I think I have less than 250 hours accumulated time as a pilot but I could go back and fill a book with all the engine failures I've had, troubles I've got into and so on. When they came out with the new licences and everybody had to go in and rewrite, that's when I decided to hell with it. I had better things to do. It was just as well.

During the time I was flying I was very involved in trying to get an airstrip built at Powell River. We

to Al Alsgard, the publisher and owner of the Powell River News, who died only recently.

I should mention I was also active in these years as a manufacturer of radio equipment and I had to fly on up the coast this day and do some repairs at the Wilcox Store on Stuart Island so I said to Al — I'd known him since we were kids together on Savary Island — I said, "Al, I'm going up all by myself, why don't you come along for a ride?"

"My gosh yes," he says. "Fine. Do I need anything?"

"No, nothing. Come just as you are. Bring your camera."

We drove down to the Lake, got in FFW, took off, went up to Stuart Island, flew back and my god, the view was overpowering. I got up to a fair altitude and you could see clear over the Gatineau Range right back to Garibadi. It was the sort of day that just put mundane cares out of your mind and fired your imagination. I had an inspiration. I turned to Al and said, "You know Al, what I really feel like doing right now is flying straight over there to Lake Garibaldi. How would you like to come over with me, then come into Vancouver and I can put you on Flight Three in the morning. You'll be back in your office by nine a.m. What do you say?"

"Well how'll I let my wife know? She'll be worried," he said.

"Oh heck, that's no trouble," I said. So I get on the radio and called our agent in Powell River, please

were flying into Powell River but we were landing on Powell Lake with Stranraer flying boats and Norseman seaplanes, and we wanted to get on land. We had the Board of Trade, we had the municipality, we had the local flying club, we'd meet once a month in the old Westview Hotel to try and promote this thing. This particular day I had to be up there at twelve o'clock so I flew up in my Stinson and it was a fine day, a beautiful day, you could see to the ends of the earth. After the meeting I found myself talking

advise Mrs. Alsgard that Al Alsgard will be in Vancouver overnight, returning tomorrow morning. This was checked okay, and Al was happy.

Now, I wasn't being entirely frivolous. I had a reason for wanting to make this trip. We had a forty-year agreement with the Garibaldi Parks Board to develop air transportation between Vancouver and Garibaldi Lake and we had built a lodge in there. We flew in with seaplanes during the summer but it's a high, glacial lake, ice-free only a comparatively short time, and the question we were hung up on at this point was how to get in after freeze-up. You might think we could use skis and land on the lake, but to land on skis you have to take off on snow and we were taking off on water.

So how do you take off from water and land on snow? This was the problem we were mulling over in our idle moments.

We might have gone on mulling for years, but as they say, necessity is the mother of invention, and the previous winter we'd found ourselves in a postion where we had to find an answer. This was the very harsh winter of '48 or '49 when the temperature at Vancouver Airport stayed around zero for weeks and the Fraser River froze over. We woke up one morning and found ourselves out of business, because our seaplanes couldn't take off on theice. We realized that if we could get them over to our base in Nanaimo Harbour we could shuttle passengers back and forth between Vancouver and the Nanaimo airstrip using a wheel plane, and continue flying up the coast with floats, but meanwhile how do we get our seaplanes out of Vancouver airport?

It was our operations manager, Johnny Hatch, who hit on it. There was a good cover of snow alongside the runways and he taxied a floatplane out of the hangar, pulled off the beaching gear and sat the bare floats down in the snow. He taxied around, it moved along nicely, then he pushed the throttle forward and took off. Nothing to it. So we took all our seaplanes off in snow and my golly we landed them on snow at the Nanaimo Airstrip. We didn't even have to use Nanaimo Harbour, we just met the land shuttle at the airstrip and flew up the coast directly. It worked *fine*. Except of course it was illegal, and we didn't dare tell the D.O.T. about it.

It wasn't long before someone said, "Here's the answer for Garibaldi Lake! We can just land in the snow on floats! Fly in there all year round." The only question was how the snow was going to be. Would it be level enough, or all hummocky? Would it be ice or powder? This was burning a hole in my head. I wanted to get on with the thing. It was now June and we only had a few weeks before the lake ice stated to break up for that year.

I explained all this to Al Alsgard and said, "This is what I want to find out today. I just want to take a low pass over the lake and see." He was very interested. He got his camera ready. We went in over the top at ten thousand feet, you could see all the way to the Rocky Mountains, I found Garibaldi Lake, circled in past the Sphinx Glacier, did a beautiful let-down over the Sentinel Glacier, levelled out and flew low over the surface of the lake. It was as smooth as a billiard table, sparkling umblemished white. I pulled out at the end and went up.

"Al, are you nervous?" I said. "Because I'd like to put my floats down on that surface, just to feel it. I want to know how solid it is."

"Go ahead, " he says. "I'm having a wonderful time."

I went around, came down over the glacier again, did a let-down, a bit of a sideslip, and levelled off about twenty feet over the lake. Then gradually, gradually let down til the float was skimming the snow. It was so smooth I couldn't tell my floats were

down. I eased the throttle back, it was soft, soft powdery dry snow and we glided to a gentle, perfect stop. I shut the engine off. It was stunning. The sun was brilliant, the snow was sparkling, the lake was impeccable. We opened the window and outside of the engine cooling making a ticking sound and gyro instruments still spinning it was the quietest thing you ever heard in your *life*!

~ GARIBALDI LAKE ~

"By God!" Al said, "What a country! I'm going to get a picture."

He was just in his light clothes, no overcoat, and Al was a big man. When he stepped off the float with his press camera he went in up to his armpits. Just powder and air. But he got his picture, came back in, said, "Boy, that's enough for me." It was June but it was still damn cold. I'd found everything I needed to know so I started up, opened the throttle gradually — and nothing moved. I opened it full up. Still didn't move. I rocked it. I tried the ailerons. I tried everything but the aeroplane wouldn't budge. I sat and thought about it for a minute. Somewhere sometime I'd heard a bushpilot talk about skis warming from the friction of landing, then freezing into the snow. I thought I remembered what you were supposed to do. I turned to Al.

~ ALSGARD and the STINSON ~

"I hate to ask you to do this, but you will have to get out again and take the aircraft by the tail and shake it up and down while I open the throttle. If she starts moving, try to scramble up on the float. If you can't catch up I'll circle back." He went out, I opened the throttle, he shook and she started to move. And he couldn't get near it. He was left there looking like a lost snowman. It blew powdered snow in his pantlegs and out his collar. Oh, he looked miserable. I went around in a big circle half-a-mile wide, came back and missed him. I went as slow as I could without getting stuck again. It took me about three tries. Finally I got slow enough and close enough he was able to lunge and catch a strut and pull himself up onto the float while I put on power, and he clambered into the plane.

"B-b-boy, will I ever be glad to get w-w-warm," he said. I opened 'er up, and waited, and waited, and waited — and eight miles an hour was the best I could do.

I kept going and headed for the lodge. The lodge was a three-storey cabin and the peak of the roof and one little window was all that was showing. There was about twenty-eight feet of snow. I stopped the plane, wallowed over to the cabin, got the window open, got the oil stove going, and got poor Al Alsgard in there. I had further plans for him, but I wanted to get him warm before I told him. It was pitch dark inside so I lit a lantern.

"Al," I said, "it may be that I can get airborn with just myself aboard. I'm sure if I can get back to base and talk this over with the boys we'll be able to come up with something, perhaps a different aeroplane with more power. But you're going to have to shake me loose again."

Well, what choice did the poor bugger have? I got him out there while we still had some light, he waggled my tail, I got moving, and bygosh, without Alsgard's extra weight I got her up to speed and lifted off.

I'd been in touch with Vancouver all through the ordeal, keeping them posted, and they had been taking it all without making any comment. When I taxied up to the float in Vancouver there was Johnny Hatch standing there, looking very grim. He had originated the floats-on-snow technique and he had wanted the honour of testing it on Garibaldi Lake. He didn't say anything but if he had said what he was thinking I suspect it would have been, "You're lucky to be alive, you damn fool," or something along those lines. He was very brittle with me.

Johnny had our best-performing Norseman CF-CRS ready to take off and didn't want to hear any of my explanations. He had it all figured out. "The difference between your aeroplane and CRS is you're not supercharged," he told me. "That lake is five thousand feet up and your darn little Lycoming motor only has half its power at that altitude. There'll be no trouble in CRS because it's supercharged and it's got full power at five thousand feet." I was still carrying my briefcase, still dressed for my meeting in Powell River, but there was no time for anything but to climb in and take off to rescue Alsgard.

It's a twenty-five minute flight from Vancouver straight over the Lions to Garibaldi Lake. Johnny said, "Now watch. I'm just going to put the keels of my floats in and feel it." I couldn't bring myself to tell him that was exactly what I'd done. He comes down over the Sentinel Galcier, levels off, touches the keels of his floats which on the Norseman are very deep-veed, slows down, then says, "Good enough, way we go," and opens the throttle up again.

And the aeroplane goes slower and slower and slower and stops! The floats are sunken clean out of sight! The Norseman was a much heavier machine than the Stinson and didn't work half as well. I was vindicated, but much too alarmed to take any pleasure in the fact.

This is a good half-mile from the lodge and we're sitting there trying to appreciate all the implications of these last developments when we notice something moving in the snow away over on the far shore of the lake. It's Al Alsgard struggling out to meet us holding his press camera over his head. All we can do is wait. Oh, it took him ages and when he finally got to us he was dead beat.

"Boy am I ever glad to see you guys," he gasps. We said, well, we didn't know why because we weren't going anyplace. We gave him a chance to catch his breath while we radioed Vancouver that we were Garibaldi R.O.N. — Remaining Over Night — then all three of us started out for the cabin. We didn't know what on earth we were going to do but

- The CABIN -

we knew we weren't going to do it in what was left of that day. There was something funny with Alsgard and as soon as I smelled liquor I knew what it must be, although I found it hard to believe. There was only one bit of liquor in the cabin, an emergency bottle of rye which I had hidden in the rafters down behind the wall plate and out of sight the previous year. But sure enough, he had gone over that building til he found it, and he'd killed the thing! He was higher than a kite!

We got the fire going again, relit the lamp and started to look for something to eat. The cabin was well stocked, but of course everything was frozen to the consistency of young granite. There was frozen soup, rocklike pork and beans, concretized canned milk which we thawed for coffee — but once canned milk has been frozen it's very strange. There were eggs which bounced like golfballs. We didn't feast, but we didn't starve.

Tobacco was another matter. We were all smokers — Al and Johnny cigarettes and I a pipe — and we were through what we had with us before we realized what we were in for. They were soon retracing their steps collecting butts and emptying out the ashtrays in the aeroplane, salvaging the used tobacco and rolling it in writing paper. This didn't appeal to me so I experimented drying tea on top of the stove and putting that in my pipe. I was happy enough with it, but Al and Johnny said the smell of it made them sick and objected most piteously.

All night we talked about what to do in the morning and it was obvious to both Johnny Hatch and me that we had to somehow increase the surface of the aeroplane's floats. We had to construct some kind of toboggans and then contrive to get them under this two-ton Norseman which was sitting six feet down in this deep powdery snow. We were up early. In the cabin I found a double-bitted axe, a carpenter's hammer, a handsaw, a keg of spikes and a few common nails. There was no lumber, but the spikes reminded me that we had just recently built a dock down at the lakeshore using rough cedar two-by-twelve planks, eight feet long, which we'd flown in. After some exploring we figured out where the dock was and dug a great long shaft 20 feet down through the snow, which was in layers like a layer cake — layers of slush, layers of powder and layers of re-frozen slush like ice. We exposed the boards, pried them loose with a peavey and passed up about ten of these heavy planks. That took the morning. I sawed two of these planks in half, giving me four pieces four feet long, and these I attached at an angle to four full-length pieces so I had two sleds two feet wide and twelve feet long with the forward four feet angled upward. I put sides on them for strength and then took some short pieces on edge and veed them out with the axe till they fitted the bottom of the floats like lifeboat chocks. To lift the aeroplane we had to cut trees down for pries and drag out a bunch more planks to act as the fulcrum.

You had to get surface area so it didn't punch into the snow, then place blocks of wood on that. We had to do this not once but many times because every

- PREPARING the NORSEMAN -

morning we'd find the aeroplane had sunk down from the warmth of the sun and frozen in again. It was brutal work. It took us five days, which included one day of blizzard when the thermometer went down to twenty-five below and we couldn't get outside.

Alsgard had started off in a great flap about getting back to put out his newspaper but this concern was soon supplanted in his mind by one simply of getting out alive. He tried to be of help but he was not terribly practical. Johnny and I did most of the work and Alsgard, I think, prayed. At least he mumbled a lot.

The morning of the day came when we finally had these toboggans finished. We took aluminum sheeting off the cabin roof which we nailed to the bottoms of the rough planks and coated this with rancid Crisco. We lowered the plane onto them, it held up, and we decided to try it. Johnny had very thoughtfully drained all the lubricating oil out of the crankcase when we arrived, which we now heated on the stove and carried very carefully out in buckets and poured into the frozen motor. We got Alsgard aboard, Johnny got the engine going and I stayed out to wiggle the tail. Our labours were now about to be put to the test.

- The TOBOGGANS -

These toboggans must have weighed about half as much as the aeroplane. They were the most ungainly-looking things you ever saw. But they moved. I leapt for my life, Johnny eased the throttle ahead, the motor laboured and we very sluggishly gathered speed. We had three-and-a-half miles of lake ahead of us. Johnny had the throttle wide open now. We were doing twenty miles per hour, less than a third of what we needed. All three of us had our eyes rivetted to the airspeed indicator. Twenty-five, thirty, thirty-five — it flickered and faltered, and our hearts flickered and faltered, but it started rising again and after an eternity it reached seventy-five. Then and only then did Johnny pull back on the control column and without a hitch the plane lifted into the air. As he circled back we could see the toboggans, still clipping along about thirty miles an hour for the other end of the lake. They floated around the lake for years and I used to see the kids paddling around on them having a great time, blissfully unaware of their history.

We got back to Vancouver, loaded Al with my sincerest apologies back on a plane to Powell River, and I went back to my office. On my desk was a telegram from Dan McLean, the Director General of Civil Aviation in Ottawa. It contained a very curt message. The DGA wanted to know if I could show any reason why John Hatch, operations manager, should not lose his pilot's licence and Queen Charlotte Airlines should not lose its operating certificate for illegally flying passengers in a non-approved aircraft.

This was serious. We were the third largest airline in Canada, and here we were being threatened with dissolution. What happened was, at this time we were flying in fierce competition with other operators on the coast for the lucrative freight and passenger business into the Alcan smelter project at Kitimat. They used to monitor our radio channels so that when they heard we had passengers waiting at a certain location they could try to get an aeroplane in ahead of us. They had heard all of our calls from Garibaldi Lake and seen it as a chance to make trouble for us, which was standard practice. They had reported us to the DOT and made sure it got the attention of Ottawa.

I climbed on a plane and was in Ottawa the next morning. I went in through the green baize-covered door in the Number Three Temporary Building and found Dan McLean waiting for me. The Overlord of all civil aviation in Canada, from whom there was no appeal. The Godhead. He told his assistant to leave the office and close the door. He was in a serious mood.

"Alright Spilsbury," he said. "What is going on?"

I played innocent. I said I really didn't know what he was referring to. "You do know what I'm referring to," he said. "This flying in and out of Garibaldi Lake without properly equipped aircraft."

"We landed in Garibaldi Lake in two different aeroplanes," I told him. "Our Stinson CF-FFW and our Norseman CF-CRS. We landed in both cases on regulation floats and we took off on regulation floats."

"They tell me you used skis," he said, "and that they were non-approved skis."

I said, "Well, I'm sorry but your information is incorrect. We taxied on two toboggans but we never flew with them. I'm not aware that there was any contravention of flight rules."

"Well read your Air Regulations, Spilsbury," he said.

"I have done, sir," I said.

He reached over and got out the little red book, opened it up at page whatever it was, and I think I can remember the wording: "Seaplane, definition: A seaplane is an aircraft designed for landing and taking off a water surface."

"Now Spilsbury," he said, "do you see anything there that would give you reason to believe it is permissible to land a seaplane on snow?"

"I see nothing that rules it out," I said.

"How do you figure that?" he asked.

"Well, snow is water, only at a low temperature," I said. "And it doesn't say here what temperature the water is supposed to be." Fortunately, Dan McLean had a sense of humour. He tried not to smile and said to me, "This is just a play on words. Now let's get down to it. The fact is, you people have been fooling around with irregular equipment, and what's worse, you've been doing it with a passenger on board, name I believe Mr. Al Alsgard. Now, I'm not going to put up with any more of this. If you people want to experiment, apply to us and get an X-licence. Then instead of CF-CRS it's CX-CRS, it's an experimental aircraft and you can risk your neck all you want as long as you don't carry any passengers." He gave me a good talking-to, then he leaned back in his chair and smiled a slow, fatherly smile. "You

know," he said, "part of the trouble with you west coast people is you always think you're the first people ever to do anything. It never occurs to you others have run into the same problems and already worked out perfectly good solutions. There is such a thing, you know, as the "Federal Wheel Ski." It is an aluminum ski with slots for your wheels to go down and you have a hydraulic hand pump. You pump the ski up four inches so you can land on wheels, you pump it down and you can land on a snow surface. They are approved and with them you can take off from Vancouver airport and land on Garibaldi Lake and carry passengers to your heart's content. Now for godsakes, quit fooling around and get yourself a set."

So for six thousand seven hundred dollars I bought a pair of Federal Wheel Skis custom fitted for a Norseman aircraft. We put them on the next year when the lake was again frozen over and Johnny Hatch flew in with our chief of maintenance Dick Lake, a commercial photographer by name of Harold Vandervort, and two other passengers. There were five of them. They circled past the Sphinx Glacier, let down over the Sentinel Glacier, touched down on the lake and plunged down, not just to the depth of the floats as we had done, but right up to the belly of the aircraft. The propeller was in the snow. They were twice as far from the lodge.

Some second guessing had been done by now and this time it occurred to me to have toboggans built in our shop in Vancouver which could be flown out

- SPILSBURY and WHEELSKIS -

to the lake. They were constructed out of aircraft-grade birch plywood by our Chief Engineer Charlie Banting, who did the job in jig time with great flair and precision. We took them out in an Anson along with a lot of winter gear — warm clothing, mukluks, food, even snowshoes and dropped them from the air. Johnny and his party went to work with their pries and finally, five days later, they got out. But there was a hitch.

Charlie Banting's professionally-built toboggans had been designed to hook onto the tips of the skis with the idea that after they got airborne the pilot could shake them off by doing a quick flip. Well, Johnny flipped half the way home and one dropped off but the other just wouldn't let go. So how do you land?

- DIG and PRY -

There was some snow on the ground at Vancouver and they didn't know whether to land all in snow or partly in snow and partly on the runway. Johnny chose the latter, thinking this would equalize the drag better, and landed with the toboggan on the snow and the ski on the grass. He went right up over a snowdrift left by the snowplough, broke the belly out of the aircraft and headed straight into the hangar and slammed the door before the D.O.T. had a chance to see what happened.

The lesson we learned from our experience in Garibaldi Lake was that floats were quite as practical as skis for landing on snow but it was not practical to let Dan McLean find out about it. We later hauled tens of thousands of gallons of diesel fuel from Stewart in Northern B.C., taking off in salt water and landing on the glacier at Granduc Mine. We even carried the fuel by pumping it into the centre compartment of the floats. We'd land uphill, stop, pump out the fuel, swing the aeroplane around by hand, and take off down the glacier. We kept the mine going all one winter. This snow-float technique was picked up in nearby Alaska and as far as I know they're still using it up there. But it's still very illegal in Canada.

FOG

Today after finishing my Saturday chores
I went hand trolling for late fall cohoes
and was a mile or so off shore when fog rolled in.
Tide running every which way, water too deep to sound
I completely lost my bearings and would probably
have drifted the Gulf all night in an open boat
except that I chanced to hear what I took to be
our old rooster crowing. Lucky for me it was.
I turned the boat, followed the sound to shore
and landed home in time for supper.

This forenoon if I could have laid hands on him
that rooster'd be in the pot right now
simmering for our Sunday dinner.

Strange sometimes how things work out.

Hubert Evans

121

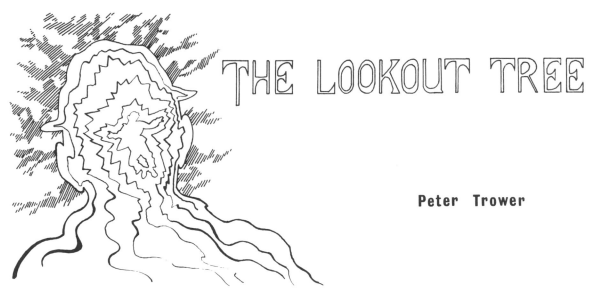

THE LOOKOUT TREE

Peter Trower

Note to the Reader:

The following is a true account of certain events known to have taken place in the village of Gibsons Landing around the time of the first great war and some years after. Because it involves a murder in which neither the victim nor the perpetrators were ever made known to the authorities, and because certain of the principals and their descendants are still living in the area, we have taken the precaution of altering some names. The other facts have been gathered and put down as accurately as is possible given the passage of time and the understandable secrecy which has shrouded the event from its occurrence to the present day.

SURE, I REMEMBER WHEN CAL BRADLEY DONE HIMSELF IN. That was way back around 1921 but I can still see it clear as yesterday. I was only a kid then – ten years old. Me and a couple of other young fellers was walking along the road by the cemetery one afternoon when we heard the shot. Could have been someone out hunting except it come from the graveyard and who the hell would be hunting there? We was a bunch of curious young buggers and we walked over to see what was going on. Didn't see nothing at first but grass and gravestones. There was an old gravedigger's shack there then and as we got close to it, I began to get a funny feeling in my belly. We sneaked up and peeked through the window. Next thing, we was scooting away from there as fast as we could damn well dangle. You'd figure we'd seen a ghost, but what we seen was Bradley. He was sitting sort of slumped over with a rifle between his knees, all duded-up in his best suit like he was going to a wedding. Might have figured he was asleep except for the blood. Scared the Jesus right out of us. I can still see him sitting there. Heard later, he'd got a haircut that morning. He was always a neat, fussy kind of guy. Guess he wanted to die that way. Anyways, we told the first grown-ups we ran into. They said they'd take care of it and that we'd better get the hell home. It wasn't no business for kids.

"No one was all that surprised when we got to thinking about it after. Cal Bradley had been acting odd for two-three years, ever since the War. Got a couple of younger guys to go up on the mountain with him once. Said he wanted to hunt for hibernatin' bears. Didn't make any sense. It was the middle of January in a bad winter. There was about eight feet of snow. Used to be a big burn there then and he insists they spend the night in the middle of it with no tent or nothing. He did a lot of crazy things like that. Word went round that he'd had a brain-tumour and it had messed up his thinking. There was a lot more to it than that but they kept things all hushed up. I was a grown man before I finally heard the real story."

* * *

1917, the fourth blood-sodden year of World War One: across the carnage-ground of Europe the blind armies wrestle from trench to trench – salient to salient – stalemate to stalemate. Back and forth they stumble over the muddy corpses of the fallen to fall by the countless thousands in their turn. The War is the most relentless killing-mechanism that man has yet unleashed. Its insatiable mouth has swallowed millions already and still it hungers. The calls go out ceaselessly for men and yet more men. In Canada, an ocean remote from the hostilities, a Conscription Act is passed to pressgang the reluctant into service. Opposition to the draft is strong in the maverick frontier province of British Columbia. Some take to the hills, construct well-hidden camps and live a fugitive existence – emerging seldom and always by night – under constant threat of discovery by the vigilant Provost patrols. Their motives are various. Some have definite ideological objections to the war; others are pacifists of one sort or another and some are simply averse to becoming cannon fodder in a cause they can't understand. They band together these disparate men, in dark clearings on remote mountainsides. They watch and wait. Many condemn them as traitors and cowards. Others are sympathetic. The war grinds on without them.

Twenty miles upcoast from Vancouver, the

mountain broods behind the still-rustic village like a great, squat spider. Loggers have not yet felt the need nor summoned the effrontery to invade its upper reaches. It hides behind an unbroken green hood. Several years earlier, a forest-fire had ravaged its lower slopes. The enormous scar of the burn stretches for barren miles, a spectral disasterscape, punctuated with jagged black snags, healing slowly. Along its upper perimeters, the face of the virgin timber rears like a stockade wall. Deep in that dark, high forest, four men toil in a hard-won clearing. They are Finns, wiry, smallish men, born to the woods. They wield their axes deftly. Slowly, the refuge takes shape — two neat log cabins, their corners impeccably dovetailed, scarcely an axe-mark showing. At the clearing's edge, a tall fir stands. It will become the lookout tree. They nail a ladder of boards ninety-feet up it and build a small platform there.

* * *

"Yeah, it was those four Finns mostly built the camp. They was all related. Think a couple of them was brothers. Not local fellers. They smuggled them up from Vancouver in fishboats late at night. It was kind of like an underground railway, you might say. They was all members of some communist group which I guess ain't no surprise, coming from so close to Russia and all. Anyways, they was the first. Got the whole deal set up. Only a few people in the village knew about it — mostly other Finns. They kept them supplied with grub and whatever else they needed. There was a stumprancher — old man Heinke — who was some kind of cousin of theirs. They could see his spread from the lookout tree. Used to signal them by hanging his wash on the line in certain ways — they always knew when the coast was cleared to come down. Sort of a morse code of bloomers and long-johns. The Army Provost used to come snooping around the village at least once a week. They knew damn well here was men hiding out someplace. They just didn't know where.

"More guys started coming in on the fishboat shuttle. They say sometimes you could see lanterns crossing the burn in the dead of night. Folks who didn't know what was going on figured it was either some kind of phosphorus or ghosts. These other men was mostly Canadians or English who'd took up with the Finn commie outfit in town. Think a couple was actual deserters. Never heard many names but there was this one guy called Ambrose Wood. He was some kind of remittance man, a black sheep. Chased him out of England for raising hell in the wrong places. Say he was a big man — powerful as an ox but well-educated too. Hated the British Empire like the bloody plague. He became sort of the leader what with having strength and brains both. He could put things into words better than any of the rest of them. Used to give lectures on philosophy and stuff like that. Suppose most of them listened. Wasn't buggerall else to do except read, sleep, bullshit, hustle fire-wood, go hunting or whittle chains out of cedar wood.

"They had a few close shaves. One time, three of them was out looking for deer when they run into a couple of guys from the village doing the same damn thing. These village fellers didn't know about the camp and was surprised as hell to find three strangers prowling around the hills. Don't recall any words was exchanged. They just stood staring at each other for a minute, all of them packing rifles. Looked like there might be a shoot-out but the camp fellers must have thought better of it. They just turned around and took off into the underbrush. Guess there was some mighty nervous guys around the hideout for the next few days. Lucky for them, the village boys couldn't have told too many people about it. Leastways, it never got to the Provost. They would have searched the mountain for sure."

* * *

What might be the camp's most serious problem — procuring supplies — is made easier by co-operation from an unexpected source. There is only one store in the village, and the owner, an Englishman named Winn, has distinguished himself in the forefront of local flag-wavers. The great parliamentarian Grace McInnis is a girl in the village at this time and she refers to Winn in *A Man to Remember*, the excellent biography of her father, J. S. Woodsworth, who served during the war as village pastor:

"He (Winn) was superintendent of the Sunday School and kept a close eye on the church services. He and my father clashed when the latter refused to read war bulletins from the pulpit on Sundays and would permit no one else to do so. The storekeeper thought of himself as a patriot, but the Finnish people shook their heads and smiled cynically. It was a closely-guarded community secret that in the black vastness of Mount Elphinstone there was a draft-evaders' camp. No one knew much about it till later, but sometimes men from the Hill would carry away huge loads of groceries from the Landing store and disappear with them away up the mountain trails. The storekeeper had never sold such quantities of supplies to those Hill families before. But he asked no questions."

* * *

"One night they was packing up the supplies and a sack of rice got torn open. When they finally reached the camp they found they'd left a clear trail just about all the way back to old man Heinke's farm. Took them till damn near dawn before they got their tracks covered up.

"Sometimes when they was feeling real reckless a few of them would even sneak down and go to the Saturday night dances. Must have got damn lonesome up in those woods without any women. Folks who wasn't in on the secret used to ask who the hell they were but their friends would cover up for them. Say they was just visitors from some other settlement.

"Anyways, by the start of 1918 there was twelve of them holed up in the camp. They was all from out of the area except for two local boys who was good friends with the Heinkes and had kind of gotten themselves duked in. One of them was Bobby Foster. He'd grown up on a stumpranch — bit of a simple kid who didn't know nothing about wars and politics.

His dad was real anti-English – got out of the Old Country one jump ahead of a poaching warrant – but Bobby had no axes like that to grind. Just wasn't fussy about getting his ass shot off.

"*The other feller was Cal Bradley. He was a different kettle of fish.*"

* * *

Bradley is a man of confused emotions. This cold day in mid-January, 1918, he crouches like a shaggy, shivering bird on the lookout tree platform. Eight of them rotate this chore. The remaining four are afraid of the height and compensate by doing other work. The crows nest is manned faithfully, rain or shine, as long as there's visibility. Only at night or when fog lays a ghost mantle over the mountain do they fail to keep watch. Bradley huddles in his mackinaw against the chill and broods dourly. Voices drift up from the cabins in the clearing. Finnish accents mingle with English and Canadian in a profane babble, dominated as usual by Ambrose Wood's cultured pronouncements. Unlike the others who are mostly practicing atheists, Bradley is a devout, fastidious man, a regular churchgoer prior to his self-exile. The blasphemous prattle of the others constantly makes him wince. He has felt out of place from the beginning among this rough, godless group. Only his fervent pacifism holds him here. Sometimes he prays for them secretly. Bradley is only an eight-year English immigrant himself but, unlike Wood, he retains strong feelings of loyalty toward King and Country. His younger brother has recently enlisted in the Army. Guilt struggles with principle in Cal Bradley's mind. Can it be truly Christian to cower in a forest like this while other men are risking their lives overseas? Chewing this rubbery dilemma, he gazes out over the winter-pinched country.

The land tumbles away before him. There is little snow. The weather has been merciful to this point. Across the eerie blasted heath of the burn, the outlying farms are clearly visible, most importantly the Heinke stumpranch with its cryptic clothesline. The village itself is largely hidden by trees and the angle of the shoreslope. Only a few faraway housetops and the protruding brown tip of the steamship dock are visible. Bradley studies the Heinke farm through binoculars. The colour arrangement of the hanging clothes proclaims that all is clear but Bradley has never much trusted this system. What if the Provost should steal a leaf from their book and enter the area secretly? – Heinke would never know. He suppresses the paranoid fantasy and turns his thoughts to Foster. What can have become of him?

Bobby Foster had left the camp two days previously against the advice of the others. Word had reached him that his mother was seriously ill in a Vancouver hospital. He had determined to try and see her despite the considerable risk involved. The city is reputedly crawling with military police.

Bradley hopes sincerely that he hasn't been caught. Bob Foster is the only person in camp he regards with any sort of affection. He couldn't care less for the heathen rest of them but he and the slow-spoken farmboy have been friends for years.

Bradley's concern is not motivated wholly by friendship however. Foster is a naive kid who's scarcely been out of the village in his life. Under interrogation he could quite conceivably be tricked into revealing the camp's existence. Bradley worries on through the cold vigil.

The minutes crawl sluggishly by. In the clearing below two of the men are bucking and splitting firewood. They have many cords already cut and stacked under lean-tos – enough for months – but it's a method of getting exercise and eases the monotony. The thud of the axe mingles with the nasal grinding of the swede saw in haphazard rhythm. The wrangling in the main cabin, which also serves as cookhouse, has quietened. Ambrose Wood has captured the floor and is pontificating on one of the more obscure theories of Karl Marx. Bradley is heartily sick of that booming, know-it-all voice. He has little tolerance left for the renegade Englishman and his obscene, treasonous talk. He fumbles for his pocket watch. Only fifteen minutes more. Then that little weasel of a deserter Ryan can take his turn at playing sentry.

Aimlessly his eyes rove the downmountain trail. He can see along the narrow, shadow-dappled corridor for some distance. Suddenly, Bradley stiffens. A figure has detached itself from the tight ranks of the virgin timber; is moving purposefully up the path. This would not necessarily be cause for alarm, as visitors sometimes dropped up from the village. But this is no social call. The man is wearing an Army uniform.

Panic surges through Bradley like a drug. All his direst forebodings have come to pass. Foster must have given them up. Almost without conscious thought, he snatches the rifle from the platform beside him, tucks the butt to his shoulder, draws a bead on the intruder's chest and fires. Bradley, his prissy ways notwithstanding, is a competent hunter and a good shot. His aim is dead accurate. The uniformed man gives a startled gasp of pain, topples forward and lies in a crumpled khaki heap. The sound of the shot echoes off into the trees.

The woodsplitters drop their tools; gaze startledly upward. The rest of them burst from the cabins, led by Ambrose Wood, his theorizing forgotten. "I say what the bloody hell's going on?" he shouts angrily. "Do you want to give us away to the whole bloody country?"

"We're already given away," stutters Bradley. "Just shot a soldier on the trail. May have us surronded!" He is conscious of an unhealthy excitement. Slinging the rifle strap over his shoulder, he starts down the ladder as rapidly as his stiff limbs will allow him. Up this tree he's a sitting duck.

By the time Bradley reaches the ground some of the others have already got their guns. The rest shuffle about in a quandary, obviously weighing the consequences of a pitched battle against trained soldiers. The possibility of such a raid occurring has been discussed many times. The vote between battle and surrender is about evenly divided. Now the crisis has finally arrived, even the usually pragmatic Wood seems at a loss. They simply cluster there, listening, waiting. For several minutes there is only the sound of their breathing; the fingering of the wind in the tree crowns; the furtive rustling of small animals and birds.

Bill Heinke, the oldest of the brothers and chief spokesman for the Finns, breaks the impotent deadlock. "If dey vas coming, dey would have come by now!" he states flatly.

"Quite right" says Ambrose Wood, recovering his decorum. "Let's have a look along the path. Perhaps our friend Bradley here has just been starting at shadows again."

Bradley, bewildered, feels the primitive emotions dwindling in him. "I tell you, I shot a soldier!" he insists. He has begun to wonder himself if it was all an illusion. Desperately, he heads for the trail.

But there's a body on the path all right, a still-breathing, uniformed body that fitfully groans. Bradley, aware for the first time that he has perhaps mortally wounded a man, walks up to his victim and freezes, afraid to move. The cap has fallen off. There is something about the hair . . .

Wood pushes past him. "Let's have a look at the bloke," he says. Very gently, he turns the injured man over.

"Why did you do this to me?" whispers Bobby Foster, his ingenuous farmboy face contorted with pain and disbelief. "You're my friends. They caught me at the hospital. Made me enlist. Gave me twenty-four hours. Was just coming up to say goodbye." He tries to say more but something chokes him. The voice falters. The eyes extinguish. The head drops sideways.

Bradley begins to suddenly pant like an animal in agony. He lifts up his head. "Jesus! Jesus! Jesus!" he cries. It is a primal scream, an irrational wail with

no trace of piety in it whatsoever. He falls on his knees beside the limp body of his friend; cradles the lifeless head. His anguish is a naked and terrible thing. The others can only look on in shock and sympathy. Finally Heinke and Wood take the distraught man by the arms and lead him stumbling back to camp. The lookout tree pokes at the clouds like a mocking finger.

* * *

"That's pretty much the way it happened, according to the oldtimers. I've heard the story from several of them and the facts don't vary much. Damn sad business. They buried young Foster right up there on the mountainside. Bradley got himself together enough to say some words over the grave but he was half out of his mind for weeks after. Claim they had to keep him tied up some of the time. He wanted to run down into the village and confess all their sins. That would have sunk the lot of them for sure. The war was still on and now they had more to hide than just themselves. They finally got Bradley calmed down by telling him it could have been any one of them up that tree. And they swore a pact to keep silent about the shooting. Wood told them they was all accessories to murder in the eyes of the law.

"When Armistice Day finally come that November they began to drift back down to the village, a couple at a time. Some of them got jobs at a local sawmill for awhile. Then they headed back to wherever they come from. Cal Bradley, he went home and stayed there but I guess that godawful guilt must have kept festering inside of him. Suppose in the end he just couldn't live with it no more. Some say he left a letter confessing everything but it never turned up. Reckon his family must have burned it. They didn't want no scandal with cops and reporters snooping around.

"That's about all there is to tell. The empty camp sat up there in them woods for years. Sometimes hunters or kids out hiking, would come across it by chance and wonder what the hell it was. Finally, the loggers got there and by the time they was through pulling trees over top of the spot, wasn't nothing much left at all but a heap of trash. Guess they must have yarded right over Foster's grave without even knowing it. Timber's come back and been cut several times since. They could bring the whole army in to search the place and never find it now. It's gone — completely gone. Except in peoples' minds. There's a kind of a myth about that you can see lights moving up there on the mountain some nights, and the story keeps coming back like the ghost of a soul done wrong. I guess it'll haunt this town forever.

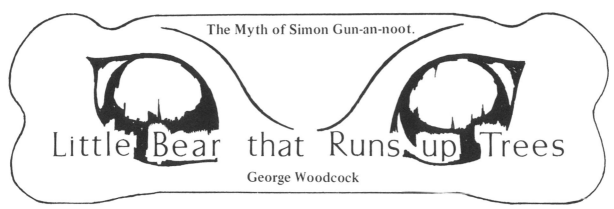

The Myth of Simon Gun-an-noot.

Little Bear that Runs up Trees

George Woodcock

SIMON GUN-AN-NOOT IS PERHAPS THE MOST FAMOUS OF BRITISH COLUMBIAN OUT-LAWS. He was one of the Gitksan people who inhabit the villages of the Upper Skeena where many totem poles still stand to commemorate a lasting devotion to the old ways of the Coast Indian cultures. Accused of the murder of two men at different localities on the same night of 1906 in the locality of Hazelton, he fled into the bush, and for thirteen years he eluded his pursuers. In 1919 he walked out of the wilderness and gave himself up; by this time such witnesses as spoke at the coroner's inquest of 1906 were either unavailable or forgetful, and Simon Gun-a-noot was acquitted.

During the years that have followed, Simon Gun-an-noot has become and remained a hero in the Upper Skeena country and a legend in the rest of British Columbia. Even before he surrendered in 1919, his ability to live in the bush and evade pursuit had aroused admiration among the very white settlers in the Hazelton area who had been ready to condemn him in 1906. With his acquittal, the idea emerged that he was an innocent man wrongly condemned in 1906 by a white jury because he was Indian and vindicated by a more enlightened jury in 1919; he fled, it was now thought, not because he was guilty, but because he believed he would never get a fair trial. Simon Gun-an-noot was hailed — and still is hailed — by white liberal and radical writers as the martyr of a racially weighted legal system who finally escaped its injustices; it was not questioned that he was an innocent man who would have been framed and probably unjustly hanged if he had not escaped at the right time and remained hidden for so long. His fellow Indians appeared to concur in this opinion. One myth of Simon Gun-an-noot was established, and like most myths it obviously contained a good deal of truth.

But myths are the crystallizations of social passions, just as dreams are the crystallizations of individual passions, as social attitudes change the myths are modified. In recent years our Indians, like many peoples in the Third World, have tended to shed the image of themselves as submissive victims that was imposed by missionaries and other well-meaning white men. The Indian still sees himself as a victim, it is true, but a defiant victim who takes as his model the guerilla fighter. There is no need for me to go into the various permutations of this model in North American Indian life; the point I make in the present context is that now, in the 1970s, the Indians of the Upper Skeena, who once acquiesced in the liberal white argument that Simon Gun-an-noot was an innocent man, wrongly accused of two sensational murders, are now inclined to claim that he was a kind of early pioneer of the Indian liberation movement who really did kill two obnoxious white men and, after his thirteen splendid Robin Hood years, returned defiantly to confront his accusers and win his freedom, not because he was technically innocent, but because the law was despicable.

To go back over the case and weigh the probabilities involves one in an intricate story that not only arouses the basic question of guilt and innocence but also poses conflicting systems of morality (sometimes existing within the same person) and, beyond all that, provides such an extraordinary record of endurance and self-restraint on the part of Simon Gun-an-noot, who never fired a shot at his pursuers during his thirteen fugitive years, that one is amazed no novelist has ever seized on it as a basis for a western Canadian prose epic.

Let us begin with the given facts. The central figure of the story was born about 1874. The Upper Skeen was subjected relatively late to the intrusion of white men. The Tsimshian cousins of the Gitksan, who lived on the Coast near what is now Prince Rupert, had encountered Spanish, English and American mariners and traders in the 1780s, but it was not until the early 1860s that the first Hudson's Bay trader penetrated to the locality of present-day Hazelton. Later on white trappers moved in, and then missionaries of several sects and a few settlers. But the real white influx did not begin until the 1890s, when the Skeena lay on one of the overland routes to the Yukon and, shortly afterwards, the Yukon Telegraph line was laid through the region, which resulted in an influx of workers, packers and various other transient white men, including prospectors who vainly hoped to find in the Skeena region something resembling the goldfields of Cariboo, Omenica and Klondike.

When Gun-an-noot was born the traditional Indian way of life was still almost intact. His father Na-gun was a respected chief, and among the Gitksan the links between fathers and sons were stronger than among the coastal Tsimshian; nevertheless, Gun-an-noot belonged to his mother's Wolf Clan and was given one of the names of her lineage; it meant The Little Bear That Runs Up Trees.

At one time during his boyhood Gun-an-noot was threatened by the rigours of the customary law by which his people continued to live. One day he and his elder brother Din were playing with some other boys in the village of Kitanmax where he was born, a now vanished place between the present site of Hazelton and the Hagwilget Canyon. Din played the hunter with one of his father's guns and the other boys were supposed to be the bears he hunted. He fired at one of them, the gun turned out to be loaded and the boy was killed.

The traditional law of the Gitksan on such matters was clear enough, and as yet there were no white lawmen to interfere. The Indians made no difference between manslaughter and murder; a life must be paid for with a life or an agreed equivalent. The maternal family of the dead boy could claim Din's life or that of any matrilineal relative of equal standing, and since Din fled into the woods and was later found to have hanged himself the threat of death shifted to Gun-an-noot. Perhaps because the influence of the missionaries was already spreading along the river the aggrieved family decided to waive physical revenge, and instead they accepted as compensation a pile of blankets as tall as the boy. But there were many traditional Indians who prophesied that Gun-an-noot's family would not escape the debt of blood.

There seems to have been very little from that point on in Gun-an-noot's early career that pointed towards a violent turn in his affairs. In fact, according to the standards of the time, he turned into the model of a Good Indian, peaceful, industrious and money-oriented. He was converted to Catholicism and baptized as Simon Johnson; henceforward he was generally known as Simon Gun-an-noot but rarely, even officially, as Johnson. He married his equally devout wife Sarah in church, baptized his children and always wore a holy medal around his neck. He was a good hunter and fisherman, a superb marksman and a diligent trapper. He also had a very shrewd sense of business; he would take his furs down to Vancouver or Victoria where he would get a better price than the traders in Hazelton would offer him. With his profits he established a little store on the outskirts of the Indian village of Kispiox.

Gun-an-noot was not a very gregarious man and he had few friends who were not close relatives; rather than live in Kispiox he built a log house on a bit of land where he grazed horses and cows and kept the dogs that he used for winter hunting. Many of the Indians envied the prosperity that came from his careful way of life, though it is probable that given enough time Gun-an-noot would have distributed a great deal of it as gifts at potlatches according to the custom of his people; by this time the potlatch was illegal, but the Gitksan were far enough from the centres of authority to ignore the law with relative impunity. Many of the tough and arrogant white men and half-breeds from other regions who then gathered around Hazelton as packers and trappers and settlers regarded Gun-an-noot as an Indian who was getting too big for his mocassins, and this attitude undoubtedly contributed a great deal to the events that followed.

On the night between the 18th and 19th of June, 1906, two murders took place in the locality of Hazelton. Early in the morning of the 19th Constable James Kirby, who ran the British Columbia Provincial

Police post in the village, was awakened by some Carrier Indians who told him they had found a man's body about a mile out on the trail to Babine Lake. Kirby aroused the coroner and the local doctor and they went out to find a half-breed named Alex McIntosh lying beside the path. The tracks indicated that he had been riding at the time of his murder and his horse was later found in the bush. He had been killed by a shot that must have been fired by someone kneeling on the ground, since the bullet had entered his body in the lower part of the back and had travelled upwards to emerge below the left collarbone. His face was bruised as if he had been fighting and the little finger on his left hand had been gashed and dislocated; he did not appear to have been robbed.

While the three men were examining the body a trapper rode up with the news that he had found another dead man beside the trail leading from Hazelton to Kispiox, and the investigating trio made their way there. The second murdered man turned out to be a professional outdoorsman named Max Leclair who had recently moved into the Hazelton area from Kamloops; Leclair, a quiet and rather reserved man who preferred the wilderness to the haunts of men, had written articles on wildlife and hoped to establish himself in the Skeena area as a guide for well-to-do hunters and fishermen. He was killed in the same way as Alex McIntosh, with a gunshot that had sent a bullet running up through the body from low in his back to the region of his shoulder; his horse was grazing beside the path and he too did not appear to have been robbed.

If there was any close relationship between the drunken, aggressive, womanizing McIntosh and the restrained and taciturn Leclair, nobody knew of it then or subsequently found evidence of it. Nor was there any evidence, except the manner and time of the killing, to link the two deaths, and in the case of Leclair no likely motive for the killing ever emerged.

It was different in the case of McIntosh, for on the evening of the 18th he had been involved in a violent situation at a rough kind of tavern called the Two Mile House between Hazelton and Hagwilget, kept by James Cameron, who was due to stand trial in two days on a charge of supplying liquor to the Indians. McIntosh himself, who lived by many devious ways as well as his nominal occupation as a packer, had just emerged from jail on a similar charge, and he and a few other rather unruly figures were celebrating at the Two Mile House when Simon Gun-an-noot entered with his brother-in-law Peter Hi-madan.

Gun-an-noot had just come in from a successful trapping tour and had been squaring up his jawbone at the Hudson's Bay post, where the prices this year were more competitive. He was flush with money and ordered drinks all round; Cameron, who does not seem at this moment to have taken his forthcoming trial very seriously, provided them after a slight show of reluctance.

Alex McIntosh was inclined to get cantankerous in his cups, and appears to have held a long-standing grudge against Gun-an-noot. An ugly situation developed as the two men set out to prove themselves against each other. The argument turned to marksmanship, and Gun-an-noot showed his prowess by smashing a bottle which he shot at blindfolded in the tavern yard. This seemed to incite McIntosh's rancour, and he began to boast of the women he had possessed, and of how many Indian women he had bought. Gun-an-noot protested, and McIntosh went on further to claim that all Indian women, including Sarah Gun-an-noot, were purchasable and had been purchased. The men then began to fight, and Gun-an-noot, having the advantage of the first blows, wreaked considerable damage on McIntosh. Cameron and some other white men ended the fight and pushed Gun-an-noot and Hi-madan out of doors; they departed, as far as one can tell from the confusing evidence later given, in the direction of Kispiox. Before he left the tavern Gun-an-noot, it was remembered, threatened that he would "fix McIntosh proper." McIntosh left shortly afterwards, went to the packer's camp where he was employed, and then rode towards Hazelton to get treatment for his injured left hand. He never reached his destination.

When the inquest was held a day later neither Gun-an-noot nor Hi-madan appeared, but what was said by those who had witnessed the quarrel through an alcoholic haze led the jury to return a verdict that in the case of Alex McIntosh it was a matter of wilful murder by "a person of the name of Simon Gun-an-noot (Indian) of Kispiox Village," and another verdict that there was strong cause to suspect that Max Leclair's murderers had been Gun-an-noot and Hi-madan; it is unclear why Hi-madan's name was included in the second verdict and not the first. One of the important witnesses, James Cameron, vanished from Hazelton on the following day, and was never seen there or heard of again.

Undoubtedly the absence of the two Indians added to the jury's certainty of their guilt, but the verdict – quickly passed on through the native community – ensured that, whether guilty or innocent, they would continue to keep away, which is what they did. They kept away for the thirteen years until Gun-an-noot's surrender in 1919, followed by Hi-madan's a few months later.

The evidence against Gun-an-noot was never more than circumstantial. No witnesses to the killings ever appeared, Constable Kirby seems to have turned up no clues on the spot that might help to identify a killer and the bullets used in the killing were never matched to a gun. Gun-an-noot had a possible motive for the first killing, but none was known for the second. All the advantage we have seventy years later over the jurors in 1906 is a certain amount of hearsay evidence, by its nature never completely reliable.

On her death-bed Peter Hi-madan's wife is said to have asserted that she killed Leclair, who had made advances to her. Bus since she did not claim to have killed McIntosh, and the two men died in the same way and evidently by the same hand, her confession is highly suspect, if indeed she made it. The shootings were obviously the work of a good marksman used to shooting at moving targets such as large mammals, and Gun-an-noot was the best marksman in the Hazelton area.

Later hearsay evidence links him more closely with the killings. Until a good while after his death

in 1933 the local Indians were very tight-lipped about the case, but gradually they began to talk about it, and in 1951 the *Northwest Digest* published the account of an old Indian, Abraham Nikal, who asserted that Gun-an-noot had shot McIntosh out of jealousy and had shot the second man because he met him on the path as he was returning home to Kispiox and mistook him for a policeman. However, this account is so inexact in other details (Nikal called the second man MacDonald instead of Leclair and gave a garbled report on the incidents leading up to the murder) that one cannot pay it very much attention.

Somewhat different was the article – claimed to be "the authentic story" of Simon Gun-an-noot – which Constance Cox contributed in 1958 to the centennial edition of the *Native Voice*, as near as one can find to an official organ of the Indians of British Columbia. Constance Cox was the daughter of Thomas Hankin, for many years in charge of the Hudson's Bay post at Hazelton; she spoke all the local Indian languages, was for years Court Interpreter, and served as interpreter for Marius Barbeau on his Skeena expeditions. The Gitskan probably trusted her more than any other white person in the region. And she stated categorically – with no Indian contradicting her – that after the quarrel at Two Mile House Simon Gun-an-noot went home, got his rifle, and shot Alex McIntosh on the trail where the body was found. Later, on his way back to Kispiox, he encountered Leclair and shot him also.

Hearsay evidence continues to crop up; recently, for example, Pierre Berton appears to have encountered descendants of Gun-an-noot who claimed that he used to talk proudly of the two killings. Tales recounted thirty years after the event by people who were not present are always suspect, no matter who the teller, but the account of Costance Cox, who was in the Skeena country throughout the time when Gun-an-noot was on the run, certainly deserves attention. Though later events show Simon to be far from a man of violent inclinations, and the evidence that now exists would still not be sufficient for a conscientious jury to bring in a verdict of guilty, the fact remains that of all the possible killers of McIntosh and Leclair, Gun-an-noot seems the most likely.

Yet, granting the possibility that he did kill the two men under the influence of rage and of the kind of dubious liquor that James Cameron served to Indian customers, one still admires the extraordinary restraint combined with endurance which Gun-an-noot practiced during that long period on the run. He may have been a killer of men under extreme provocation, but he did not act like one after he fled into the wilderness.

Whether they were guilty or not of the crimes they were accused of, Gun-an-noot and Hi-madan had little faith in their chance of acquittal by an all-white jury, and Gun-an-noot's father, Na-gun, seems to have argued strongly in favour of a flight to the wilderness where, as expert hunters, they could subsist indefinitely. By the time the coroner's jury reached its verdict they were miles from Hazelton.

After the inquest, Constable Kirby consulted the Provincial Police in Victoria and recruited a posse of special constables. They set off first of all to Gun-an-noot's store; the contents were undisturbed and the place had been left as if someone would return at any moment. Nobody did, and they rode on to the holding, where they found Gun-an-noot's four horses lying dead, his ammunition gone, and his wife Sarah totally uncommunicative. A short time afterwards, on the banks of the Kispiox River, they found thirteen tethered dogs, which one of the posse identified as belonging to Gun-an-noot; Kirby ordered them to be shot so that they could not be of use to the fugitives. Shortly afterwards he saw an Indian crossing the river in a canoe and disappearing into the woods. The posse gave pursuit and eventually caught up with Na-gun, who refused to answer questions, whereupon Kirby took him back to Hazelton and locked him in the police post. This diversion, which Na-gun had evidently planned, enabled Gun-an-noot to get away safely. After a couple of days Na-gun managed to escape by prying some boards off the wall of an outhouse recessed into the post's stockade. He alerted his own wife, as well as Sarah Gun-an-noot and Hi-madan's wife, and they set off to join the two fugitives at the rendezvous near Kisgegas, to the northeast of Hazelton and not far from Bear Lake in Carrier Indian country.

had left for winter hunting at the head of the Nass. They contained ammunition, traps, fishing nets, axes, provisions and even canoes, so that the party was able to build little cabins in hidden valleys and to begin living by hunting and fishing.

The authorities imagined that by spectacular manhunts they could catch Gun-an-noot and bring him to the courts. But they were dealing not only with a resourceful man who knew the country from years of hunting and trapping, but also with the kind of country that co-operated with the fugitive. It was a wilderness as large as France, with no roads, and trails that were passable only in good weather. In August 1906 a party led by the government agent Berryman went to Kisgegas and the locality, but found no trace of Gun-an-noot and his party. In September Constable Otway Wilkie arrived from Victoria and searched as far as Fort Connelly to the east of Bear Lake, and then went over the mountains in the direction of Telegraph Creek, but returned as winter came on. He was back in the summer of 1907 and mounted a two-pronged expedition, one party going up the Stikine and the other up the Skeena. He covered vast stretches of territory, almost always on foot, and braved the winter until February, 1908, when he gave up and returned to Victoria without

Steve Jackson

Reunited, the group of three men, three women and two children headed farther north into the mountainous region where the great rivers of northern British Columbia — the Skeena, the Stikine and the Nass — have their sources. Through this wilderness of fir and spruce forests, barren ridges, valleys tangled with briar and devil's club, muskeg and mountain tundra, Gun-an-noot led his party to the caches he

having seen Gun-an-noot, though Gun--an-noot, alerted by Indian trappers, had seen him and followed him, walking on the ridges while Wilkie and his men went along the valleys. Once, when Gun-an-noot and Hi-madan went to check their traps in a box canyon without an exit, Wilkie almost trapped them, coming to the canyon's entrance and turning back as Hi-madan was about to shoot him despite Gun-an-noot's

129

attempts to restrain him. And in the end Wilkie enabled the fugitives to stay on. The winter of 1907-8 was an especially hard one, and Gun-an-noot, watching Wilkie's camp from the mountainside above, was starving and so dispirited that he thought of surrendering. But that day Wilkie turned south, leaving a cache full of supplies that tided the fugitives over until the spring. The last effort of the authorities was to hire American Pinkerton agents at a cost of $11,000, but again there was no result, and after 1910 the police sent in no more search parties and contented themselves with offering rewards for the capture of Gun-an-noot and Hi-madan, beginning at $1,000 and eventually reaching $2,300. But there were no takers, and no policeman caught sight of either of the two men for thirteen years.

Other people did, however. Gun-an-noot and Hi-madan began to appear on the outskirts of Indian villages whose inhabitants had already been leaving food and messages for them. And some of Gun-an-noot's friends, like Solomon Dick and Dan Skewill, began to meet him and bring his furs out to sell on his behalf. Part of the returns they would spend on ammunition and provisions which they would take in to him, and the rest they gave him as cash, for which Simon had a purpose in mind. The fugitive party slowly changed in its composition. Old Na-gun died, and they carried his body for three days to bury it beside a lake he loved in the far interior. His wife followed him and so did the three children that were born to Sarah Gun-an-noot in the bush. Hi-madan's wife went back to her village to die, and Sarah Gun-an-noot eventually went home with her surviving children. But a number of young men joined Gun-an-noot either because they admired him or because they had got into trouble with the police, and at times the band seems to have numbered a dozen or more.

Eventually — and particularly after the outbreak of war in 1914 when the police had fewer men at work — Gun-an-noot began to appear on the edge of white settlements. He was seen at Stewart and Telegraph Creek; when Constance Cox was staying on a ranch outside Hazelton he appeared and asked her for medicines, which she gave him without telling anyone of his visit. He would appear at the camp fires of linemen working on the Yukon Telegraph and talk to them but vanish when they began to ask questions. Prospectors encountered him, and sometimes he would exchange game for delicacies like tinned jam. A Salvation Army missionary who went to Kisgegas with Solomon Dick found himself in Gun-an-noot's company; Gun-an-noot was anxious about his children and asked the missionary to make sure they were educated so that they would not be at a disadvantage in a white man's world.

In the end, adept though he was at wilderness living, Gun-an-noot began to find life in the bush unendurable, and to long for his village and his people and the world. At this time, in 1918, he met a man named George Beirnes who was working for a supply contractor on the Telegraph line. After appearing several times at Beirnes' camp, Gun-an-noot began to develop a trust in him. He told him who he was — which Beirnes knew already — and talked about his desire to give himself up if only he could be sure of a fair trial. Beirnes remarked that a fair trial depended on a good lawyer, to which Gun-an-noot replied by revealing that he had been saving the cash brought to him for his furs in order to pay for his defence. Beirnes suggested a highly successful criminal lawer from Victoria named Stuart Henderson and Gun-an-noot calculated that by the next year he would have the money to pay him. Beirnes returned to the Skeena in 1919, found Gun-an-noot ready to surrender himself, and sent for Henderson. On the 24th of June, 1919, the three of them walked into the police post at Hazelton, and Gun-an-noot surrendered himself to Constable John Kelly. The most celebrated outlaw in British Columbian history had come in out of the cold.

Henderson orchestrated the rest of the story in a masterly way. A first hearing was held at Smithers, but he succeeded in getting the venue changed to Vancouver. Once the trial took place, it was found that many of the original witnesses at the inquest had vanished, and others were unable to sustain their shaky memories against Henderson's cross-examination. The jury returned a verdict of not guilty, and Simon Gun-an-noot walked out of the court a free man, innocent in the eyes of the law.

A free man, but not a happy one. His wife died soon after his release, and the years in the bush had scarred him, so that he became a sad and solitary man as he continued his hunting and trapping until, in the autumn of 1933, he collapsed and died on the trap line. He was buried in the wilderness, where a mountain was named after him by the surveyors who were grateful for the information he had given them about the north country while he was awaiting trial in Vancouver.

Simon Gun-an-noot was the wisest of the outlaws. He may — or he may not — have killed two men on one dark night of his life. But he knew that violence was no way out of his predicament, and he followed the only course that would eventually set him free. He had the sense and the courage to trust to time and men's forgetfulness. I suppose one could say that he showed the triumph of character over impulse, the triumph of will over the resignation to which so many Indians of his generation succumbed. And that is why we remember him with admiration.

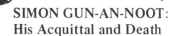

SIMON GUN-AN-NOOT:
His Acquittal and Death

Simon Gun-an-noot
walked out of freedom
into justice.
A jury condemned him;
another acquitted him.
Did that even the score?
Did it balance
his years of hard exile?
Did it make him any more
innocent? Did it
liberate him? He was
innocent and free already.

The voices of manmade law
claimed virtue and merit
for releasing this outlaw,
but the outlaw lived
in another law:
the law of nature, not
to kill without reason,
not to waste life like
polluted water.

In the wild distances
beyond systems, beyond
codes and courthouses
lie the heart's solitudes,
were life is sucked from
the sands of adversity
and wisdom's a thirst
quenched only by those
who lose their worlds
and find their own beings.

And wisdom is sadness
before it is joy.
Gun-an-noot was sad
and his sadness a burden
carried back to the Skeena,
to the trapline and trading,
not young any longer
and marked by loneliness,
claimed by the bush.

Simon Gun-an-noot
escaped once again
from life into peace.
They buried him
beside his father
by a green lake
in the far beyond
and called a mountain
Gun-an-noot.

George Woodcock

SWEET WORT & SOUR KROUT: COOK'S RECIPE FOR DISCOVERY

Tom Stitt

IN TERMS OF EXTENDING THE RANGE OF MANKIND'S TRAVEL CAPABILITY CAPTAIN COOK WAS THE WERNER VON BRAUN OF HIS DAY. Ironically his greatest contribution to the travel technology of the eighteenth century is the one which is now most often overlooked. Sea travel of Cook's day had run into the same block as space travel of our day: how to extend the range, not of the vehicle, but of the crew. Bringing men back from their discoveries alive was every bit the problem to the navies of two hundred years ago that it is to the space programmes of today, and the breakthrough that brought the world's nether reaches into the great navigator's grasp was his mastery of this problem. The name of the problem, in Captain Cook's time, was scurvy. While it was suspected that diet probably had a bearing on the outbreak of this disease during lengthy voyages little was actually done about it due to the utter lack of facilities for the preservation of fresh foods aboard ships of that era. On Cook's first voyage this malady broke out aboard the *Endeavor* and by the time he got back to England thirty men out of his total complement of eighty-four had succumbed. The horrors of that experience made such a lasting impression on the young lieutenant that he vowed to find some method of combatting it on future voyages.

For this reason he took special precautions when he began the preparations for his second voyage. He was of the opinion that both diet and cleanliness had a good deal to do with his crew's general health so, with the co-operation of the Admiralty, he provisioned the *Resolution* with a supply of what he hoped would be antiscorbutic or scurvy-preventing foods. In addition to this he laid down stringent regulations with regard to his ship's cleanliness and insisted they be obeyed throughout the voyage. His efforts proved so successful that only one crewman died during the whole venture despite the fact that he had a complement of 118 aboard and the voyage lasted three years and eighteen days. And even that one death was not attributed to scurvy!

On his return to England at the conclusion of his second voyage, Cook delivered a paper before the membership of the Royal Society in which he explained in detail the precautions he had employed in combatting scurvy on the ship. This earned him the Sir Godfrey Copley gold medal for the best experimental paper of 1775 and, in addition, a Fellowship in that very exclusive scientific body.

In his paper Captain Cook listed several of the provisions he felt had proven particularly advantageous. What was known as "Sweet Wort" was made from the supply of malt that had been on board. This was actually an unfermented beer that was issued to every man showing even the slightest symptoms of scurvy in amounts that varied from one pint to three quarts per day. It was, in Cook's opinion, the most effective antiscorbutic he had on board. The ship had also been stocked with large quantities of "Sour Krout" (sic), and this too Cook considered very useful. This was a particularly meaningful discovery because it could easily be stored over long periods without spoiling. One pound of this was served to each man twice a week or oftener while the ship was at sea. "Portable Broth," which was a congealed meat stock, was added to vegetables as well as to oatmeal and wheat porridge three days a week. Cook credited this with encouraging his men to eat more vegetables than they would normally have consumed. The ship's surgeon, he indicated, also made use of the "Rob of Lemons and Oranges" that was on board. This was prepared by boiling the fruit juice to the consistency of a syrup and preserving it with sugar. Considerably more sugar than usual, but much less oil, had been taken on the voyage because Cook felt sugar was an antiscorbutic whereas he was certain the oil was not. He also had wheat added to the oatmeal and this too, it was considered, assisted greatly in the control of scurvy. The Captain refused to allow the crew to use any of the fat that was boiled out of their salt pork and beef. This fat, he believed, was not really good for them and actually contributed to scruvy in the long run.

Captain Cook operated his ship with three watches rather than the customary two; this saved his men from unnecessary exposure to the elements and served to avoid their wearing wet clothing over the longer periods caused through working watch on watch. He insisted on the crew keeping themselves as well as their bedding, hammocks, and clothing as clean and dry as possible.

Special efforts were employed in cleaning and airing the ship as well. Stagnant air below decks was moved by means of fire pots twice a week, and when this could not be done the interior was smoked with a mixture of gunpowder and vinegar or water. The slightest neglect in airing the ship in this manner "produced a putrid and disagreeable odour below decks" and Cook insisted it was extremely important that this routine be adhered to.

Fresh water was taken on each time the ship dropped anchor in an area where it was available. Cook was of the opinion that fresh water was much more wholesome than water that had been stored on board for any length of time so he continually replenished his supply even when it was not really needed. Because a great portion of that second voyage had been in cold latitudes he had, fortunately, been able to obtain plenty of fresh water through melting down ice, so the ship's company had never experienced any real shortage. Fresh provisions, too, were taken on at every available opportunity in whatever form was to be found where the ship anchored.

The general knowledge of hygienics in the Cook era is demonstrated in a letter written to Sir John Pringle by Captain Cook just prior to embarking on his third voyage. It was dated July 7th, 1776, at Plymouth Sound, and contained the following comments:

"I entirely agree with you, that the drearness of the Rob of Lemons and Oranges will hinder them from being furnished in large quantities. But I do not think this is so necessary; for, though they may assist other things, I have no great opinion of them alone. Nor have I a higher opinion of vinegar. My people had it very sparingly during the late voyage, and, towards the latter part, none at all; and yet we experienced no ill effect from the want of it. The custom of washing the inside of the ship with vinegar, I seldom observed; thinking that fire and smoke answered the purpose much better."

Despite his living in a world that had little or no knowledge of vitamins or their bearing on matters of general health, Captain Cook was surprisingly accurate in his theory. While the Captian had no way of knowing it, what he really required in the crew's diet was "ascorbic acid" (Vitamin C), named (though few people think of it today) for its very "antiscorbutic," or scurvy-preventing, property.

Actually the most valuable antiscorbutic he had on board was the sauerkraut, which normally contains fourteen milligrams per hundred grams of ascorbic acid. At the rate of consumption described in Captain Cook's paper (two pounds per man per week), each man was receiving the benefit of about nineteen milligrams per day. It is now known that as little as ten milligrams per day is sufficient to prevent scurvy.

The rob of lemons and oranges was also a useful substance in preventing scruvy but much of the ascorbic acid (normally about forty milligrams per hundred grams, depending upon the type and the degree of ripeness), would have been lost in the cooking required to reduce this fruit to a syrup.

While beneficial to the overall health of his crew, most of the other food listed in his paper was not actually antiscorbutic. Salt beef and pork contain from zero to a mere trace of ascorbic acid while dried peas, wheat, oatmeal, and sugar contain none at all. Modern authorities in the field of vitamins feel the "sweet wort" or unfermented beer probably contained very little ascorbic acid.

The importance of Cook's policy of using fresh food from the country and especially of taking fresh greens aboard wherever possible can be appreciated in light of comments by one of the leading modern authorities on scurvy, the Canadian explorer-scientist Vilhjalmur Stefansson:

"Fresh vegetables if raw have marked antiscorbutic value, but this is lessened or destroyed by either cooking or storage, and especially by a combination of the two. There are probably few foods which do not have antiscorbutic value when raw, whether they are vegetable or animal, fish, flesh or fowl. That is the secret of preventing and curing scurvy."

Cook throws some light on his own understanding of this secret at the conclusion of his paper:

"It was my first care to procure (fresh foods) whatever of many kind could be met with, by every means in my power; and to oblige our people to make use thereof, both by my example and authority; but the benefits arising from refreshments of any kind soon became so obvious, that I had little occasion to recommend the one, or to exert the other."

It is curious that in spite of the notice taken of Cook's methods and the recognition given him, this most important of his discoveries was neither incorporated into standard medical practices nor into official naval policy for another hundred years. Instead the British Admiralty clung steadfastly to the policy of relying on provisions carried aboard ship, only supplemented with "antiscorbutics" such as preserved vegetables, vinegar and lime juice. Stefansson writes:

"It was believed for more than a century that lime juice was a specific against scurvy. But every polar expedition during the nineteenth century was outfitted with lime juice and nearly all of them had scurvy."

The case in point, according to Stefansson, is the Franklin Expedition, in which 129 men perished in the late 1840's. Franklin was well provided with lime juice, but as Stefansson says, "while the effect of lime juice on scurvy is positive and rapid if freshly bottled, juice several years old has no appreciable preventative or curative value." Had Cook's dietary emphasis on fresh food been put into general practice Franklin's voyage may have been completed as successfully as Cook's, and the lives of hundreds of British sailors in all parts of the world could have been saved.

In light of the above, we may discover a saddening irony in the words of Sir John Pringle, presenting the Copley Medal to Elizabeth Cook on November 30th, 1776, after the great mariner had departed on his third and final voyage:

"For if Rome decreed the Civic Crown to him who saved the life of a single citizen, what wreaths are due to that man, who having himself saved many, perpetuates in your Transactions the means by which Britain may now, in the most distant voyages, preserve numbers of her intrepid sons, her Mariners; who, braving every danger have so liberally contributed to the fame, to the opulence, and to the maritime empire, of their country."

MOON DOWN ELPHINSTONE

Larry woke his girlfriend
  — Jan, your brother's smart.
Till this war's over
  I'm hiding out with Bart.

Larry took his compass,
  slid into his pack.
— When the shootin's over,
  love, we'll be back.

Moon up Mount Elphinstone
  lit a world of trees . . .
Made it somehow through to Bart
  on feet, hands, knees.

Bart shot another squirrel.
  Broiled it on a rack.
Then they crawled under blankets
  in their brushwood shack.

Moon down Elphinstone
  lit a world of bough.
— Bart, I just got to see
  What Jan's doin' now.

Moon down the mountain
  bright going south,
but dark words only
  from her soft mouth.

— The war goes on and on, Larry.
  I'm only young now.
My new boy's comin' to supper
  I don't want a row . . .

Said the cop down in Skidroad —
  When you've slept off yer toot
you'll look a lot smarter
  in a noo khaki soot.

Day before his first leave
  the Sarge slung him the phone —
My ma's dyin', Larry;
  Bart should come home.

Sun on the tall firs,
  soldier up the slope.
— If Bart don't believe me
  he can read what Jan wrote.

Bart on the lookout snag
  sky building stormy.
— Only soldier I'm goin' to kill
  is the first one comin' for me.

Deergun in the shadow,
  cap-badge in the light.
— Hafta send more than one
  to take me to fight . . .

Bart turned him over,
  found his sister's note,
wrote P.S. in blood
  bright from Larry's throat.

Cocked his gun, took a boot off
  stuck the letter on a limb
— "Just dig a hole deep enough
  to bury me with him."

Rain down Elphinstone,
  on bough, wave and shore,
and two boys' faces
  safe from a war.

Earle Birney

NOW YOU'RE LOGGING

Reviewed by Tony Robertson

Once in a while a book comes along that seems by its very existence to make up for the general run of junk that comes out of so many presses disguised as literature and entertainment. *Now You're Logging* by Bus Griffiths is such a book. It is simply the best thing that has happened between book covers for a long time.

Now You're Logging is a 119-page, 700-panel comic strip, but it is no ordinary comic strip. Granted it does have adventure, derring-do, suspense and a love story. Woven through these elements though, is a remarkable history of logging in the early thirties as seen through the lives and work of the characters in the story. The hero is a young logger named Al Richards. He and his friend Red Harris go to work for a small west coast truck show and Al in particular learns to be more than just another hewer of wood. He is a natural logger, able to bring together men, machinery and trees in that perfect combination of muscle and knowhow that get trees out of the bush safely and efficiently. Al Richards learns quickly because the work is as important to him as breathing. In his work is the rhythm of his life, and even if there were no other reasons to find this book wonderful, the way in which Bus Griffiths connects work and man is itself worth the price of admission. If there is a balance between man and nature that can work even when man is taking from nature then it works in the kind of relationship Bus Griffiths describes.

I make so much of this because work as work and as something from which satisfaction can be taken is a rare subject in our literature. It is as if we were afraid of it and yet in *Now You're Logging* it is celebrated. Al Richards and a lot of the men he works for and with know what they're doing and take pride in their work.

Bus Griffiths, now in his sixties, was a logger at the time in which the story of *Now You're Logging* is set. Personal experience and some research have given his book the added dimension of authenticity. The way things are done in the story is the way they were done at the time and the drawings emphasize the authenticity in their accuracy. But beyond that the drawings also show a deep affection for the men and their equipment and machinery, for the whole business of cutting down trees and taking them out of the bush to mills. The genuine artist can take us to another place and yet keep us in touch with where we are. Folk art seems to have the unique ability to do that with a directness that passes right by all the normal stops of qualification and consideration. Folk art seems to go to a simple part of us, to break through sophistication or hesitation about seriousness or value right into an immediate apprehension of the connection between ourselves and what we are seeing.

In *Now You're Logging* I don't think Bus Griffiths so much creates a myth about logging and the bush as he does give language and images to one that already exists in the atmosphere of this place. Our history as distinct from its native counterpart is brief in time, but such is the nature of the place that that history is from the beginning bound up with trees and water. In an imaginative sense, the first man here was a logger and from then until now the fact and fancy of logging have been inextricably a part of this place. The chief distinction of Bus Griffith's book is that it weaves fact and fancy, myth and history into a whole which flickers in the memory as if it were a part of one's own individual experience and not a story composed from the elements of a shared past and the author's own experience.

Now You're Logging is a romance. In the end Al Richards gets to do what he wants and he gets his girl. They will be happy because it is their nature. The reader gets part of that happiness in the pleasure of having read about it. He also gets the pleasure of having learned in the nicest way possible an enormous amount about logging. He will also have the paramount pleasure of having read a unique work of art which expressed the enduring spirit of connection between man and trees. Bus Griffiths has his subject "by the face" and he's "catty" too. If you want to know what those terms mean you're going to have to go out and get *Now You're Logging* and read it. Don't waste any time doing it either. The book is just too damn good to stay on the shelves for long. It's the real thing and we all know how rare that is.

Now You're Logging, by Bus Griffiths.

The Old Shingle Bolt Camp

Bus Griffiths

AFTER WHAT SEEMED HOURS TO AL AND RED, THE LITTLE BOAT GAINS THE ROCKY POINT AND ROUNDS INTO THE EASIER WATERS OF THE BAY—

LOOK! THERE'S A HOMESTEAD UP AT THE SIDE OF THE BAY!

YEAH, AN' SOMEBODY IS COMIN' DOWN TO THE SHORE! GUESS THEY WERE WATCHIN' US BATTLE THE STORM!

THERE MUST HAVE BEEN SOME KIND OF BIG OUTFIT IN HERE!

YEAH—PROBABLY AN OLD SHINGLE BOLT CAMP--- IT LOOKS LIKE THE REMAINS OF AN OLD FLUME, OVER THERE!

Bus Griffiths

YOU BOYS HAD A ROUGH GO, OUT THERE! WE WERE UP ON THE BLUFF, AND WE'VE BEEN WATCHING YOU FOR OVER AN HOUR!

I--- I WAS SCARED!

YOU'RE NOT THE ONLY ONE! IT WAS GETTIN' DOWNRIGHT DRAFTY OUT THERE!

— YOU'RE NOT KIDDING!

ARE YOU LADS FROM AROUND HERE?

WE WORK AT BRADLEY LOG, FURTHER DOWN THE SOUND— I'M RED HARRIS, AND HE'S AL RICHARDS—

HI!

H-HELLO!

THIS IS MY DAUGHTER, DEBRA! I'M JOE BROWN---YOU LADS COME UP TO THE HOUSE--- YOU'VE HAD A ROUGH MORNING—MA SHOULD HAVE SOME OF HER GOOD COFFEE ON THE STOVE, AND YOU'LL HAVE LUNCH WITH US!

THANKS-- WE DON'T WANT TO PUT YOU OUT NONE---BUT IF YOU INSIST, I'D LIKE YOU TO HAVE A FISH!

SAY, JOE—WHEN WE WERE COMIN' IN WE NOTICED ALL THE OLD PILING, AND THE REMAINS OF AN OLD FLUME, OR SOMETHIN'...

YOU'RE RIGHT! IT WAS A FLUME, AND A DANDY! THERE WAS A BIG SHINGLE-BOLT CAMP IN HERE, AND THAT FLUME WAS OVER FIVE MILES LONG!

Bus Griffiths

IS THERE MUCH OF THE OLD STUFF LEFT?

WELL, THERE'S NOT MUCH LEFT OF THE FLUME OR BUILDINGS--WE GET SOME HEAVY SNOWS AT TIMES---BUT THE SKIDROADS ARE STILL OKAY!

WE'D SURE LIKE TO LOOK AROUND!

I WORKED HERE BEFORE THE WAR AS A *"TEAMSTER", AND THEN AGAIN WHEN I CAME BACK! SHE SHUT DOWN IN '26 AND I WENT TO VANCOUVER-- WHEN THE DEPRESSION HIT, THINGS GOT TOUGH! THIS PLACE WAS ALWAYS GOOD TO ME, SO I CAME BACK AND TOOK OUT A HOMESTEAD---I'LL SHOW YOU WHAT THERE IS, AND TELL YOU THE REST!

CAN I COME, DADDY?

WHEN WE CAME HERE, THE TIMBER STARTED AT THE BEACH--- CEDARS LIKE YOU WOULDN'T BELIEVE!

THE FIRST THING THEY DID WAS BRING IN CHINESE IMMIGRANT LABORERS AND BUILD A CAMP ON THE BEACH OF HAND-SPLIT CEDAR—THE GRAIN IN THE TREES WAS SO STRAIGHT THEY COULD SPLIT A 24-FOOT LOG WITH WEDGES, AND MAKE THE LUMBER THEY NEEDED!

THEN THEY STARTED TO BUILD THIS SKIDROAD FROM THE BEACH TO THE BACK END OF THE CLAIM, A DISTANCE OF OVER FIVE MILES!

THEY SURE DID A FINE JOB!

THE ROADS WERE CERTAINLY WELL MADE—THE GROUND WAS GRADED BY HAND-- PICK, SHOVEL, AND MATTOCK, THEN THE CUT TIMBER WAS LAID—THE STRINGERS WERE SET IN PLACE, AND EVERY FOUR FEET A PEELED SKID WAS DRIFTED TO THE STRINGERS — BETWEEN THE SKIDS, HAND-SPLIT *"CEDAR PUNCHEON" WAS LAID —

LOGGING TERMS
• • •
*"TEAMSTER"— A MAN WHO DRIVES HORSES-

*"CEDAR PUNCHEON" ROUGH-SPLIT PLANKS, WHICH MADE A DRY, AND EVEN SURFACE FOR THE HORSES TO WALK UPON-GENERALLY SPLIT FACE GRAIN, AS LESS LIKELY TO CRACK THAN EDGE GRAIN PLANKS—

BUS Griffiths-

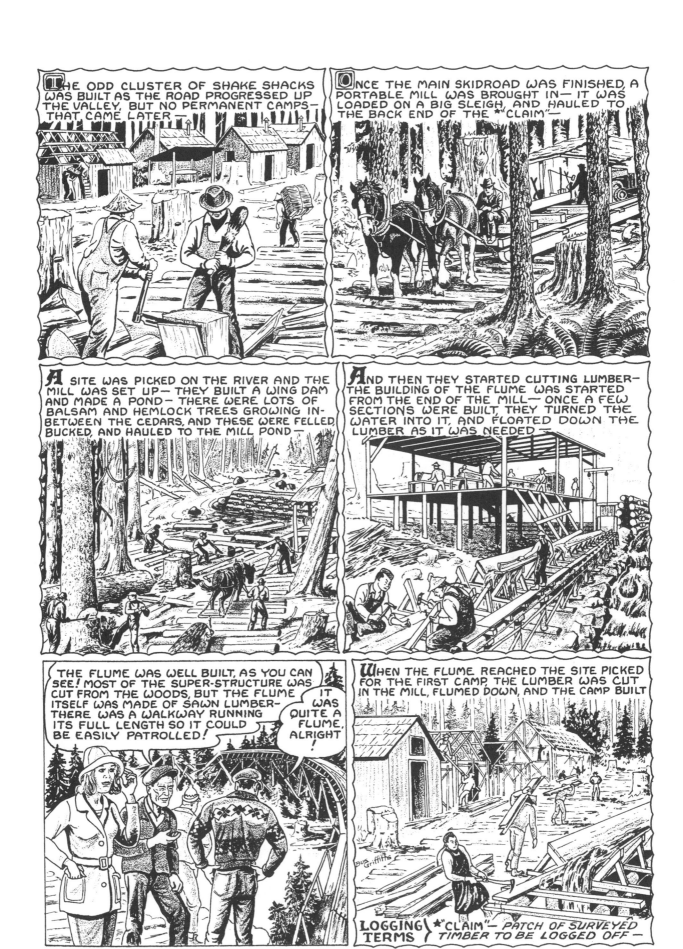

THE ODD CLUSTER OF SHAKE SHACKS WAS BUILT AS THE ROAD PROGRESSED UP THE VALLEY, BUT NO PERMANENT CAMPS— THAT CAME LATER—

ONCE THE MAIN SKIDROAD WAS FINISHED, A PORTABLE MILL WAS BROUGHT IN— IT WAS LOADED ON A BIG SLEIGH, AND HAULED TO THE BACK END OF THE *"CLAIM"—

A SITE WAS PICKED ON THE RIVER AND THE MILL WAS SET UP— THEY BUILT A WING DAM AND MADE A POND— THERE WERE LOTS OF BALSAM AND HEMLOCK TREES GROWING IN-BETWEEN THE CEDARS, AND THESE WERE FELLED, BUCKED, AND HAULED TO THE MILL POND—

AND THEN THEY STARTED CUTTING LUMBER— THE BUILDING OF THE FLUME WAS STARTED FROM THE END OF THE MILL— ONCE A FEW SECTIONS WERE BUILT, THEY TURNED THE WATER INTO IT, AND FLOATED DOWN THE LUMBER AS IT WAS NEEDED—

THE FLUME WAS WELL BUILT, AS YOU CAN SEE! MOST OF THE SUPER-STRUCTURE WAS CUT FROM THE WOODS, BUT THE FLUME ITSELF WAS MADE OF SAWN LUMBER— THERE WAS A WALKWAY RUNNING ITS FULL LENGTH SO IT COULD BE EASILY PATROLLED!

IT WAS QUITE A FLUME, ALRIGHT!

WHEN THE FLUME REACHED THE SITE PICKED FOR THE FIRST CAMP, THE LUMBER WAS CUT IN THE MILL, FLUMED DOWN, AND THE CAMP BUILT

LOGGING TERMS \ *"CLAIM"— PATCH OF SURVEYED TIMBER TO BE LOGGED OFF—

CHINESE BOLT CUTTERS WERE BROUGHT IN AND THE CUTTING STARTED— WHEN FALLING A TREE, THEY FIRST MADE A SAW CUT ON THE UNDERCUT-SIDE, AND THE SNIPE WAS CHOPPED UP FROM THE UNDERSIDE TO MEET THE SAW CUT— THIS WAS DONE SO THERE WOULD BE A SQUARE CUT ON THE BUTT OF THE TREE, AND THEREFORE NO WASTE IN THE BUTT BLOCK—

THE BLOCKS WERE CUT 56 INCHES LONG AND SPLIT WITH HAMMER, STEEL WEDGES, AND A SPLITTING BAR— EACH BOLT WAS ABOUT FOUR FEET IN CIRCUMFERENCE— THE BOLTS WERE STACKED ON END SO THEY COULD BE TALLIED— IT TOOK ABOUT 32 BOLTS FOR A CORD, AND THE CUTTER RECEIVED 75 CENTS PER CORD—

WHILE THE CUTTING WAS GOING ON, MORE SKIDROADS WERE BEING BUILT THRU THE TIMBER— THE BUILDING OF THE FLUME WENT AHEAD, AND TWO MORE CAMPS WERE BUILT— EACH CAMP HAD BARNS WITH STALLS FOR 30 TO 40 *"HAY BURNERS"

FINALLY THE FLUME WAS FINISHED AND THE PILING DRIVEN FOR THE BOOMING GROUNDS— 16-FOOT SLEIGHS WERE BUILT, WITH RUNNERS MADE OF GUMWOOD, AND EACH SLEIGH COULD HAUL TWO CORDS OF BOLTS— NOW THEY WERE READY TO START HAULING OUT THE SHINGLE BOLTS!

THE SKIDROADS WERE BUILT SO THAT TWO OR THREE ROADS WOULD CONVERGE AT ONE SPOT ALONG THE FLUME— THESE WERE LANDINGS, AND PLACED WHEREVER THE TOPOGRAPHY OF THE LAND WAS CLOSE TO THE LEVEL OF THE FLUME— THE LOADED SLEIGHS WERE DRIVEN ALONGSIDE, AND PARALLEL TO THE FLUME—

MEN WITH PICAROONS PULLED THE SHINGLE BOLTS OFF THE LOADED SLEIGHS INTO THE FLUME, AND THEY WERE ON THEIR WAY TO THE *"SALT CHUCK"— OVER 1000 CORDS OF BOLTS HIT THE CHUCK EVERY WEEK—

LOGGING TERMS} *"SALT CHUCK"— SALT WATER--TIDEWATER *"HAY BURNERS"— HORSES

THE SHINGLE BOLTS WERE LOADED ABOARD CRIBS—A JACK-LADDER, POWERED BY AN OLD AIR-COOLED ENGINE, WAS USED TO LIFT THE BOLTS OUT OF THE WATER—

A CREW ABOARD THE CRIB STACKED THE BOLTS, AND IT WAS A VERY EXACTING JOB—GREAT CARE HAD TO BE TAKEN TO LOAD THE CRIB EVENLY, OTHERWISE IT WOULD FLIP OVER, AND DUMP THE LOAD— THE MEN WOULD GO FOR AN INVOLUNTARY SWIM, AND THERE WAS ALWAYS THE DANGER OF BEING TRAPPED AND CRUSHED IN THE MASS OF BOLTS

THE LOADED CRIBS WERE TOWED AWAY BY A BIG STEAM TUG, BOUND FOR THE MILLS SCATTERED ALONG THE BANKS OF THE MIGHTY FRASER RIVER—HERE THE BOLTS WERE CUT INTO SHINGLES, PACKED INTO BUNDLES, AND SOLD TO COVER THE ROOFS OF HOUSES THROUGHOUT THE WORLD—

THESE ARE THE BUILDINGS OF CAMP ONE--- THEY HAVE LASTED BECAUSE THE SNOWS AREN'T QUITE AS HEAVY HERE AS THEY ARE FURTHER UP THE VALLEY!

THIS WAS *SOME OUTFIT* WHEN IT WAS GOING FULL OUT--- OVER 200 CHINESE WORKING, BESIDES THE WHITE TEAMSTERS AND BOSSES-- AND ABOUT 100 HORSES!

MUST HAVE BEEN A BUSY PLACE!

THANKS FOR SHOWIN' US ALL THIS, AN' TELLIN' US WHAT IT WAS LIKE--- IT SURE WAS INTERESTIN'!

THE WAY YOU TOLD IT, MADE IT SEEM LIKE WE WAS BACK THERE WITH THE CHINAMEN!

YES, IT WAS QUITE A PLACE! I CAN'T WALK TOO FAR ANYMORE, BUT I LIKE TO WALK THE OLD SKID-ROADS---IT BRINGS BACK LOTS OF MEMORIES!

ENDINGS, by Hubert Evans
DEEP LINE, by Kevin Roberts
BUSH POEMS, by Peter Trower

Reviewed by Ira Bruce Nadel

In his new work, *Endings,* the octogenarian British Columbia poet Hubert Evans conveys his experiences through definitive imagery and a mature voice. His themes are aging, writing, nature and history and his form is conservative, as in the poem "Still Life":

On this coast
in this season of straight-down rain
cedars in winding sheets of tattered mist.
Hunched raven on a bough, black on black.
Amid enveloping salal, weathered wooden dove
on rusted wire legs
marks the fallen grave house
of some long-forgotten chief.

But Evans can gently, comically, look at himself and take pleasure in his efforts at poetry:

Inept old would-be poet
your huffings and puffings amuse me.
You remind me of that half-drunk glass blower
at our county fair. I paid him ten cents —
all of my weekly allowance — to blow me a swan
but the best he could do was a lopsided bubble.

Endings is a book traditional in its language and method but original in its treatment of themes. There is an engaging brightness and gentle humour in the volume whether Evans confronts the fearful reality of death or the joyous blessings of memory.

Kevin Roberts writes poetry about working, specifically fishing, in his book *Deep Line.* In vivid but spare imagery, Roberts applies the qualities of the imagist poem to the experience of commercial trolling. Influenced also at times by the *Maximus* poems of Charles Olson, Roberts succeeds in presenting the danger and thrill of fishing through plain but carefully fashioned language:

nothing but time spent
like a fine coiled line
knot that will not give
tells you the rhythm
of fish or
fishermen

casual flick of
spoons
uncoiling
out of the box
one leg
on the tiller
picking lines
set to come
regular as waves

("For Charles Olson")

Deep Line is a strongly realized book of poems, successfully and powerfully rendering the experience of the sea.

Bush Poems, a new collection of forty poems by Peter Trower, illustrated by Bus Griffiths, demonstrates a rugged but traditional talent. A self-taught poet who has published four previous books, Trower concentrates here on logging and the physical and metaphysical experience it generates. There is a strong Dylan Thomas quality of vivid imagery and physical power in these poems that transforms the labour, danger, skill and satisfaction of lumbering into poetic form. Surprisingly, Trower finds great similarities between his two occupations:

loggins's a bit
like writing poetry.
Mind-cables wrench loose
the sluggish ideas,
sometimes to wedge them
in hopeless canyons
and knowing just when
to blow the whistle
and cut them off
is a knack
of no small importance.

("In the Gully")

Many of the poems in this collection were published in Trower's previous book of logging poems, *Between the Sky and the Splinters,* but the addition of such successful new pieces as "Early Shift", "The Mountains/The Valley", "Dreamshackles", "The Reclaimed" and "The Ravens", along with some judicious rewriting and weeding out make this a much stronger collection than the earlier book. The fourteen plates by Griffiths, a man whose understanding and love of the logger's world equals Trower's, surpasses the merely illustrative role to the extent that *Bush Poems* becomes a work of graphic as well as literary art.

FROM DESOLATION TO SPLENDOUR

by Maria Tippet and Douglas Cole

We finally have a useful, reliable book about British Columbia landscape art, a book which catalogues the artists' changing perceptions both of the coast and the exotic unexplored mountain areas. Maria Tippett and Douglas Cole emphasize that they did not set out to make *From Desolation to Splendour* a history of art in B.C. "Our purpose is to write about the idea of landscape," they say in the preface. "This is an essay into cultural and intellectual history, not into art history."

Well, fidelity to their stated purpose is one of the few areas in which I might find fault with the authors of this book because it does serve as an absolutely invaluable history, not of B.C. art in its entirety, but of B.C. landscape painting. I think that the authors have made only very obvious points about our cultural and intellectual history, but that the rich information they have given us about B.C.'s landscape painters and paintings is thoroughly fascinating.

The book is organized chronologically (it deals exclusively with white pictorial impressions of B.C., and not native ones) so that the first landscape records of the area were coastal, made by the artists who accompanied the 18th century explorers – men like John Webber who has been much celebrated (and deservedly so) in exhibitions dealing with the Cook voyages. The explorers' esthetic reactions to the coastline were, with few exceptions, to find it "dreary and inhospitable" (George Dixon), or "as gloomy and dismal an aspect as nature could well be supposed to exhibit" (George Vancouver).

These views, of course, reflected contemporary European tastes conditioned to the enjoyment of gracious and garden-like harmony in their landscapes. European tastes continued to dictate artistic response to the outdoors throughout the early years of settlement right into the post WWI period. Then more individualistic traits grew strong through the native genius of such people as F.H. Varley, Jock Macdonald, Emily Carr, W.J. Phillips, Paul Rand and W.P. Weston.

Slowly, inevitably, these artists began to look for and find their subject matter in the spiritual qualities of nature, specifically in the rawness and ruggedness of the land which, only shortly before, had been ignored or seen fit merely as material for illustration. While the spiritual heartland of landscape was usually found in the mountains, all the abovementioned painters also worked extensively with the more subdued, subtle coastal scenery.

By the 1940's, a new generation of artists, including E.J. Hughes, B.C. Binning and Jack Shadbolt, had come to fairly comfortable imaginative terms with their natural surroundings, and was soon chasing down the emerging paths of abstractionism. Many modern B.C. artists have been successful at combining abstract ideas with ideas derived from landscape, as can be seen from the internationally known work of Gordon Smith and Toni Onley. Tippett and Cole do not cover the modern period, however, in nearly as much detail as they do the century prior to WWII.

The authors' modest description of their efforts as an "essay" should not lead people to overlook this volume as cursory or light-weight. It is a solid, hardcovered book, only 160 pages it is true, but beautifully printed with 74 illustrations (including 31 in colour) and well worth the $20 price tag. The text is scholarly yet readable, the notes voluminous, and Jack Shadbolt has contributed a thoughtful forward.

From Desolation to Splendour: Changing Perceptions of the British Columbia Landscape, by **Maria Tippett and Douglas Cole.**

EMILY CARR

Reviewed by John Faustmann

Written by Doris Shadbolt and produced by the Vancouver Art Gallery, this 96-page book is a crisp, balanced catalogue of Emily Carr's work. The short biography in the front contains some good old photographs as well as an interesting text. The more than thirty colour plates are of good quality, and Doris Shadbolt's accompanying commentary is actually readable, unlike the usual inane verbosity one often encounters in this sort of book. The chronology, bibliography and black-and-white plates at the back round this work off nicely.

Small prints such as these can never do justice to the actual paintings they represent. Half of the enjoyment of looking at an Emily Carr painting comes from the palpable texture she achieved. Then, too, her canvasses are quite large, some of them as tall as fifty-one inches. Still, for those unacquainted with her work, these prints are as good as any to serve for an introduction. For those who know something of her work, they're an accurate reminder. Scaled down as they are, the brilliance of her art manages to shine through.

Emily Carr was the strong-faced genius of her age, and possibly the most talented artist Canada has ever produced. Her inordinate depths of intuitive passion arrive on the canvas complete. Her deep colours, with their brooding, primitive, mysterious associations cannot fail to have a powerful effect on even the most casual viewer. Her skies swirl with movement, gathering up the landscapes below them. Her dark totems devour the light, and her trees actually seem to grow on the paper before you. Her interior forests contain the mystical, ominous presence that must once have inspired our ancestors to the creation of a protective religion.

It has been remarked that Emily Carr erred on the side of the pathetic fallacy – imbuing nature with a human sentimentality. I suspect that this is less true than it appears. This is the art of animism, rather than anthropomorphism. The spirit which emerges in this work belongs less to the artist than it does to the trees she painted. With an intuition reserved only for genius, she sensed the dark power that sways all living things. In *The Book of Small* she writes: "These paintings are the sound of that silence."

Emily Carr, by **Doris Shadbolt.**

Smoke in the hills

Myrtle Bergren

R.I. Jack

THE OLD MAN DRESSED NEATLY IN THE MORNING AND PUT ON HIS SNEAKERS, and after the early lunch when no one was watching, he went down the long hallway, past the elevators, to the back stairs exit of the new hospital. Heavy double doors blocked the stairway but he pushed with his shoulders and opened them, and holding carefully to the railing he made his way down the two flights to the ground. Almost always he could get out without being noticed.

The hospital grounds were still green with salal brush and coniferous trees, like the surroundings of his cabin in the bush. Far away through the trees on the south side was the highway, its traffic a whisper; and on the other side cut the railway track, straight into the bush, the same one that ran the loaded log trains past his cabin in the woods.

He found a spot behind an outbuilding, in the warmth of early afternoon. A muffled shot in the forest to the west reminded him that the autumn hunting season had begun.

He sat on the springy ruin of a stump at the edge of the woods, out of sight of the strange place he had been staying in all summer. A soft breeze slid through the dry grass, and the branches of the yellowing vine maples moved languidly. He heard a faint rustling of fir needles and grasshoppers clicking in the sun, and smelled a light smokiness in the air.

He leaned back and received the sun. The swallows had gone, impelled by the same mystery that stirred in him, and he knew that today he would take the long walk along the railway track and into the woods.

Those moments of special awareness came more seldom now, and were usually connected with memories, and were very private. There was hardly anybody left to talk about anything any more.

He found a yellow plastic pail hanging on the shed wall to pick the wild blackberries into, for that was the greatest joy of the walk, and nobody would know where he was. The track would guide him when he needed people.

It was a while before he found himself there, with a voicy sigh of satisfaction. The wooden ties felt solid under his sneaker soles, and when he stepped on the hard ground between them he felt the pebbly texture of the earth under his toes.

Branches of wild berry bushes reached almost to the track here and there, and he only needed to step off the embankment into the easy places to reach the berries, full of purple juice. His lips and fingers were blue with squashing them as he ate.

The logging railway cut through the forest, with trees close on either side. Occasionally, a good distance away, he heard a muffled shot, and hoped wryly it wasn't one of those trigger-happy city slickers at large. It did not occur to him to be nervous.

The sun shone into the right-of-way and he did not notice how far it had moved in the sky. A whistle of the train in Sparks village two miles to the west caused him to look up. It was only a signal. But he felt it would be time now for the first log train of the afternoon to be heading down the track. He mildly resented having to interrupt his thoughts to watch out for the train, but his legs weren't what they used to be since the accident.

He had been so preoccupied that he had to stare hard both ways to figure out where he must be. There was nothing behind but the track disappearing around a bend in the timber, and ahead, the rails leading west around another curve into the shadows. There was no sign of habitation.

A feeling of eeriness came over him, and he tried to judge how far he had come. He used to know, when he walked from his cabin, but that was farther out. His foot slipped suddenly on the gravelly incline and his heart raced with shock. He was dismayed with himself but only because he was vague about his cabin, he thought, and the distance. Things changed so fast these days, and the only way you could tell was by the shape of the mountains, and the timber. The alders especially grew up so fast a man couldn't tell where he was any more.

His bucket was about a third full of berries, and he didn't want to think about moving off the track until he had to. Ahead was the rock cut, steep and black, on one side; and on the other, a steep, rough drop, tumbling in to the logged-off slopes below.

He brightened up then, remembering like a flash of light in the shadows of his mind that he was picking berries for Grace. It was nice to be able to take his daughter something. The berries were something from his own two hands that he could give. She would be surprised.

But this trip was something different. If he walked real slow maybe he could make it. He had never doubted himself before. It wasn't the hip so much as the pain between his shoulders that drained him. It was connected to the old head wound where the limb had come down and nearly killed him in '39 when he was logging at Menzies Bay.

Nothing stayed in his mind for long any more, and he was soon beckoned farther along the track by the long dark berries.

Down below the slopes he knew, somewhere, was the river. And higher up now he saw the blue sky, hazy from the smoke of slash fires in the west. The logging outfits were burning the waste of the past. It seemed risky on days like this, when everything was crackling dry.

He heard the shots of the hunter again and remembered when it got too dry the government closed the forest even to hunters because of the fire hazard.

The smell of the smoke excited him, and the orange cast of the sun on the ground. He could see it, a round, deep orange ball screened by the haze.

He had come to a small, logged-off area that swept down from the track in unforeseen hummocks and holes, and grown-over slash. Forest was all around the edges of the clearing. He sighed, and setting his bucket beside him on the railway bed, lowered his ropy frame to the ground.

His eyes weren't so good any more, but it seemed to him that the trees up ahead and into the distance were of the colossal size of the timber he had felled at Pender Harbour so many years ago he couldn't remember. Six and seven-foot fir logs.

Looking for a long while in the sultriness of afternoon, something happened. He saw the donkey engine, with its hissing plume of steam, yarding logs on the hillside below him. He saw the donkey engineer and heard the shouts of loggers through the woods, and the piping whistle of signals. He watched, absorbed, and fancied he saw it all going on along the face of the timber.

Suddenly he was shocked into action by the approaching whistle of the lokie in the distance. Grabbing the bucket of berries he lodged it behind a bush, and began to inch his way carefully, in his seated position, down the sidehill, filled with the wreckage of ancient logging, sticks and roots and holes and snags, like a carnage of bones, and obscured by new growth and dry grass and bushes. He lay in the weeds with a branch sticking into his ribs, and none of the train crew saw him as the tons of iron and steel thundered down the track above him. The long string of empty flatcars rumbled away into the distance, heading for camp and another load of logs.

In the years he had passed his life in his cabin by the track, he had grown to look on the train crews as his connection to outside. They were young men. He had known all the old crews before them. But who had been at the throttle today? — Things from the past seemed clear, but lately his mind seemed to be playing tricks.

He heard the shots again, and wondered if there really was any game around any more.

Working his way up to the track with the utmost care, he resumed picking, feeling a mild flash of triumph at having hidden from the train crew. Nobody knew where he was. Out in the wild, in the trees again, all alone; and after a time, a short way off the tracks, walking through sky-reaching woods, on soft paths under his thin soles, slippery with old brown fir and hemlock needles, between ancient black rocks covered with moss and lichen.

"Jesus, Jesus," he murmured, looking up into the heavy swaying cedars and through a space the hazy autumn sky, and saw the distant mountains across the strait. There never had been anybody he could talk to about things like that, and he never really wanted to.

His cabin came into his mind, where he could live alone, independent. It was a one-room log cabin he had built himself, chinked with moss, and now lined with styrofoam. It had one window, a double bunk, a small table and two chairs, and he did his cooking on a propane stove, welcoming the new that was unobtrusive.

He trod along the track slowly, with a longing for his old routine, which he seemed to have missed, although he wasn't too clear in his mind how it had happened, or even how he missed it. The well-loved books, the familiar view, the pictures on the wall, the little radio. And the television. But the television puzzled him, like so many other things lately, and he didn't really know if he was thinking of home, or somewhere else, with other people, in a big room, when he recalled the box of shadows in the corner. All the shooting and noise, and a picture that swam into his brain, the head of a president, an aircraft carrier where his ear should be, and the line of his brow melting into the sands of some country far away. There was so much confusion nowadays.

When he was young there was a war too, and he was in it. He thought of that programme on his radio when they played "Goodbye Dolly I must leave you . . ." and it petered out to a faint playing of Taps that raised the goosepimples on him. It was some time around then he'd met Edith, and married her, and then she'd died, so soon. He heard the echo of taps again in his mind. He had almost forgotten her, except for her picture on the wall.

. . . There were two pictures . . . yes . . . and he remembered the other one on his cabin wall. It was an enlargement of two young loggers, him and Curly Gronlund, standing outside the old Europe Hotel in Vancouver. — New roll brim hats, fresh shaves, boots all shined, dressed fit to kill. In for the summer shut-down, and they were just heading in for a beer when this street photographer appeared. He saw Curly so clear in his thoughts, blue-eyed, wide-browed, with a head of fair, tufty curls, and an easy grin.

He'd been hurt in a logging accident and afterwards, somehow, he remembered, Curly had got enough money from someone to start a little hotel in Campbell River, and he used to do a little bootlegging after prohibition came in. Before he went broke.

"There never was a man went hungry around that place," the old man muttered to himself as he went along, because he had said it so many times before. "Whether he knew them or not, Curly says, 'Come on in, boys, come on in and eat.' He says, 'It was cork shoes built her up, boys, and it's cork shoes'll tear 'er down.'"

A wheezing chuckle broke from him as it always did at a story of good times, for those were the kind of men he had known.

He looked ahead again. The train would be returning with a load of logs. A plume of purple smoke rose from behind the nearest mountain where the village would be. A new fire. And the sun was a crimson ball.

His limp held him back, and he began to wish he was at Grace's. His forehead furrowed at the idea of needing anyone. He wanted nothing from anyone; and he even, once or twice, contemplated getting himself lost in the woods if the time ever came when he couldn't look after himself.

He was stiff now, and he began to worry how far it would be. He had to cross the bridge first, and soon he would see the first houses in the village.

There would be Parnell's, then Tonkins, and then, a little farther on — it opened like a light in his mind, across the shadows of remembering — the image of Inga Petersen, who lived in the little brown shingled shack by the side of the crossing. Years ago, he had lived near there, and the memories crowded into his thoughts — the parties, where she was soft and small and laughing, and dressed in a blue dress, with twinkling beads around her neck. He recalled her homemade wine, and the Norwegian coffee she used to make.

Grace and all else left him now as if it had never mattered. He was filled with a new, glad purpose, to visit Inga.

He heard the shot again, closer this time, followed by a volley of three cr four, and he began to hope that some asshole out there knew what he was shooting at.

"I hope you know I'm here, mister," he muttered, "I'm not ready to kick off yet . . ."

He came to the high wooden railway bridge which was the threshold to the village. It was an old bridge, high off the water of the river, and constructed of timbers, long and immensely strong. He felt a bond with the bridge for he had helped to build it. But the great feeling of comfort came from the knowledge that across the bridge he was going to see Inga.

He remembered her little house, one of the earliest ever built there, where she had spent her life. An ancient grape vine arched over the doorway, and in the front yard was a plum tree. When you went in through the tiny dark kitchen, she would set you down in the small front room, crowded with bric-a-brack that she had brought out from Norway, or collected over the years. When she greeted you with her courtly ways and the intense smile and piercing look, she would go and put on something different, to honour you, and left you there with a glass of wine that she had made herself from the grapes of her garden. And you looked at a very old painting of a young girl, costumed, in the mountains of Scandinavia, calling the cattle home with her long birch pipe.

You sat and took in the crowded room, the old chairs, the table, the old-fashioned heater, the high sofa with its row of hand-embroidered cushions on the back, and the two round, beaten copper trays standing on the back of the seat, reflecting hazily the golden room, as there was nowhere else to put them on display.

She would come with fruit cake, dark and good, and she cut off wide, thin slices to go with the wine, and then they'd sit and talk and laugh about old times when her Osmo and his Edith were still alive and they were all young.

Ahead, one more curve in the track was obscured by the long shadows of heavy timber. He felt every pebble beneath his feet now, but soon came upon a scene he had never imagined. The whole place was different. Where Jake Tilleen's lot used to be, stood a square white gas pump with three hearts whirling in the wind, green, yellow and red, saying Cars Love Shell. Near it was a strange building, Don's Low-Cost Foods. And a small cafe called "Dora's Coffee Shop." Two cars were parked outside and a couple of T-shirted strangers stood talking at the gas station. Indignantly, he saw that they had even put some blacktop on the old gravel road below the track.

He trudged on down the grade, ignoring all but the third house which he knew to be Inga's. Footpaths led off the track to the homes. He saw no one until he came to the little brown house behind the plum tree. He limped through the rickety wooden gate and down the short pathway to the door. The grape vine was still there, but leafless now. It looked dead.

His skin felt the old cedar as he knocked, and his heart quickened as he heard someone approaching. The door opened and a young woman he had never seen before appeared, with a small yellow-haired boy peering at him from behind her thigh.

"Is — is Inga in?" he heard his voice husky and tight.

The woman stared. "I know you!" she said finally, "You're Mister Milligan." He felt she was evading him somehow. "Inga's dead," she said, her eyes big. "I saw you at the funeral, don't you remember? You were there." Her tongue flicked at the corners of her mouth.

He stared, not able to comprehend, labouring to make his mind connect with the truth of it. There was nothing he could do to stop the shaking of his chin. He turned at last and began to move uncertainly away.

"Would you care to come in, Mister Milligan?" the stranger said.

His tongue worked in a dry foam. "No, no thanks. I've got to get back." And then he remembered the berries, and turned. "But please — take these!" He offered them with outstretched hands. "I picked them for her."

When he had climbed back on the track he heard the loose metallic closing of the old latch in the distance, as it used to be.

He felt stunned and insecure. Curly's house was nearby too, over the track on the other corner. He shuffled across, not quite able to control his feet now and feeling every stone. The air was cooling though the sun had not quite gone down in the scarlet smoky sky.

Curly's white-painted place looked the same. There never had been curtains, even after his alcoholic wife died. It seemed deserted, glowing and empty in the sunset. He limped past the west window, catching sight of his own head reflected golden red now in the sun's last rays. He climbed slowly up the old wooden back steps and knocked. Nothing stirred. He noticed the tangle of raspberry canes in the garden. Curly had always kept them trimmed.

He knocked again, apprehensively. Once, twice, and then turned to go down the steps.

A neighbour woman who had been watching him called out, "Looking for Mr. Gronlund? He's in hospital."

He peered across the blank, pink face. "In hospital, you say? What — what's the matter with him?" His throat cut with dryness.

"He's pretty sick." She came over to Curly's fence, bare arms wrapped into each other across her breast. "He's in Victoria hospital."

He looked at her, scarcely noticing. "Oh . . . I'll have to go and see him, I guess." But he couldn't think how he was going to, as going anywhere wasn't what he did, ever, anymore.

The woman was shaking her head. "It's no use. He doesn't know anyone any more. He's just a vegetable."

He held the rail and came down slowly, while the enormity of it sank in. Then he said, "Thank you," and noticed how suddenly the air had chilled.

Turning his back to walk away, the voice reached his ears. "Say, mister, are you the old gentleman they're looking for at the hospital?" But it seemed to be meant for someone else. When he passed the window again, his reflection was lost in grey shadows.

A hunter in a red jacket came down the road from the track carrying his gun and two dead grouse held by the neck. He looked at the old man sharply as if to speak, but passed on by. The old man scarcely noticed.

He never knew how long it took to limp back to the track. He was going to the cafe to get something to eat.

Part way there he heard the stupendous rumble of the locomotive returning with its load of logs, but even that was not enough to rouse him from his shocked reverie. He crossed the track, but he was too disinterested to raise his eyes as it shrieked and thundered on behind him.

THINGS UNSAID

The forms simply demand, "Occupation?" and
You just print, "Commercial Fisherman".

You don't say, "I know they're down there
Waiting for me . . ."
Or that

You piece together what happens in the sea
By what you interrupt with your nets: guess rabbit worlds
By what you pull out of that hat.

Bad times, the stern rises and smashes back
With a boat length shudder, every wave, and
Some mad judoist throws you on a wet mat
Again and again, all night long. Or some times
At some point long past exhaustion or caring
You're still there in your stern, up
To your ass in scrap-fish or weeds
And only half your net picked up.

But it only seems that bad
When it's happening: some days it's
Flat beautiful calm and sunshine all through.
Good days and bad days, and
Bad days you swear off it, sell your boat:
Become a prairie farmer
Until it's safely past and you can laugh.

John Skapski

"— if such a frightful apendage can be called ornimental......."

Beth Hill

THE WORDS WERE WRITTEN BY FRANCES BARKLEY, the lively young lady with the red hair, the first European woman to visit the Northwest Coast of North America. She came to Nootka in 1787 and returned to our coast in 1792. It was on her second visit, when she walked in the villages at Yakutat Bay and Sitka Sound, that she saw the type of labret she describes as "a frightful apendage." Her response to the labrets was a form of *culture shock*. If a motion picture showing Australian aborigines eating worms upsets your stomach, or if you are a Canadian tourist appalled by some Yugoslavian outhouse, you are experiencing culture shock. It is caused by unfamiliarity, egocentricity, lack of understanding, and as it is a fundamental problem for us all, the story of Frances Barkley and the labrets is a cautionary.

Frances was only eighteen years old when she first examined the peoples of the coast and wrote her impressions in spidery letters in her Diary. She was accompanying her husband Captain Charles William Barkley, a handsome, courageous and competent young man who had courted her in a whirlwind romance during the six weeks when his ship, the *Imperial Eagle*, was being outfitted in Ostend, and who had then carried her away on the perilous trading venture to the North Pacific. When they returned to the Northwest Coast in 1792 in the 80-ton brig *Halcyon* she was twenty-three, and her young son Willie played on the deck. Her one-year-old daughter Patty had died of a fever on the voyage, a grief only five months eased when the *Halcyon* appeared off the Alaskan coast.

Although Frances was probably the first English-woman to arrive, she was not the earliest European visitor, nor the only one to be repelled by the ornament called a labret. Infinitesimal specks on that vast salt water landscape, the wind-blown ships came. Long before the rest, in 1592, came the Greek pilot Juan de Fuca, dispatched by the Viceroy of Mexico on a voyage of exploration. In 1741 the Russians Bering and Chirikof arrived. The summer storms of 1774 frustrated the Spaniards under Perez. The following year there were more Spaniards under Bodega. 1778 was the year of Captain Cook's arrival and after Cook all the world knew there was money to be made in the Northwest Coast fur trade. Hanna came in 1785, and in 1786 there was La Perouse in a French ship, Meares from India, Dixon, Portlock, Lowrie, Guise from England. None of them rediscovered the fabled Strait of Juan de Fuca, and Cook categorically stated that it did not exist. However in 1787 Charles and Frances Barkley came to Nootka, purchased furs, then sailed south and east and were much surprised to find the great gaping mouth of the strait exactly where Juan de Fuca had recorded it. The first American vessels came the next year, and more Spanish ships, and the Russians Ismylov and Bocherov reached Yakutat on the Alaskan coast. Not long behind the Russians, in 1792, Charles and Frances Barkley made their second journey, this time in the brig *Halcyon*, just a year ahead of the methodical Captain Vancouver.

Of course we cannot be certain that there were no women below decks in the trading ships of Spain, France, Russia, Britain and America, so we must only say that Frances was the first European woman to be plainly recorded, the first to be standing visibly on the deck. And not only can we see the women of Alaska through her eyes, but we have some idea of how Frances looked to them, for Frances' descendants, in every branch of the wide-spreading family tree, have legends of the interest and surprise expressed by the native peoples when Frances arrived among them. Her long red-gold hair was myth-making. Her children's children's children were to tell of Frances unpinning "a shower of golden hair" and releasing "a cloud of hair to her feet," and they insist that the natives worhsipped her as a goddess. That is most unlikely on the Northwest Coast, but certainly they must have observed her with every bit as much curiosity as she regarded them.

It was on the 17th of August, 1792, that Frances blew into Yakutat Bay, having departed from India on December 29th of the previous year, visiting Kamchatka (the peninsula on the Asian coast) in their search for furs. The day was fine "with Mount St. Elias and Mount Fairweather in view . . . their heads covered with snow. The weather at this time tolerably warm," she wrote, "but misty and like the weather we met with on the Coast of Asia, very changeable and at times chilly." The anchor splashed into the sunlit water of Lord Mulgrave's Harbour (Yakutat Bay) and Frances noted that "the country looked green and pleasant to the eye" and "the anchorage safe and snug. Several canoes soon hove in sight, some from fishing and some with women on board. They appeared most disgusting objects covered with greasy sea otter skins, with the fur to the skin and the leather tanned red, and beyond description dirty! — it was here that we first saw women with those pieces of shaped wooden lip orniments which are discribed in Cap. Cook's Voyages — if such a frightful apendage can be called ornimental . . . the piece of wood is inserted into a slit made in the underlip when the females are about fourteen yers old, and it is replaced from Year to Year, larger and larger until in Middle Age it is as large as the bowl of a table spoon and it is nearly the same shape in appearance, being concave on the inside of the Lip, which it presses out from the gum, thereby shewing the whole of the teeth and gums, a frightful sight."

Presumably, if it had been the ear and not the lower lip which had perforations to take an ormaent, Frances would not have been so abusive, since she herself probably had her ears pierced for the wearing of "orniments." Nor did she realize that the labret had a status significance for the Alaskan women. Holmberg (1856) tells us that "As soon as the first signs of maturity appear in a girl her lower lip is pierced and usually a bone point is inserted in the opening, though sometimes silver is used. As long as she remains unmarried she wears this, but when she gets a husband a large ornament of bone or wood which is slightly grooved on the gum side is pressed into the opening. Through the years the ornament is enlarged so that the old women wear them over two inches long." The important point is that the labrets denoted the status of the women and were worn with pride. Slaves were recognizable by the absence of this conspicuous decoration.

Since Frances has so emphatically recorded her reactions to the generally dirty appearance of the women, we must pause here to point out that the Tlingit painted their faces for good reasons. Krause says that both sexes painted their faces red and black, using a charcoal of fir pitch, soot or graphite mixed with seal grease, or a brown powder was made by burning a sponge to charcoal and pulverizing it, or red ochre was powdered to make a red cream. The Tlingit said they smeared their faces to protect the

Holmberg says a wealthy Tlingit painted his face daily. Some women nowadays would feel "undressed" if their skin and lips were not coloured, and our brilliant lipsticks would make the Tlingit ochre appear pale. Frances Barkley probably had her own creams and ointments for the protection of her English complexion. In Europe at that time the women were foolishly painting their faces white with a dressing containing lead, which proved devastatingly destructive to their skin. Perhaps Frances would have been less upset by the Tlingit "dirt" if she had recognized it as a cosmetic.

To return to the "frightful apendage": It is not known how the labret came to be used by the peoples of the coast, or whether the ornament may not have originated here. An unpublished study by Grant Keddie of the B.C. Provincial Museum summarizes what is known about labrets. He writes:

Labrets occur archaeologically in small numbers from the northern tip of Japan to the Kurile Islands and north to the southern Kamchatka Peninsula. The earliest labrets may have occurred at the latter location 4000 years ago but the dating is uncertain in this case. Labrets were not being worn west of Bering Strait by historic times except in the case of peoples displaced from the east at a late time period.

On the Pacific Coast of North America labrets occur by 3000 years ago in sporadic locations from northwestern Alaska and the Western Aleutians to Puget Sound. In some of these regions the custom persisted until historic times while in others, such as the Gulf of Georgia area, it disappeared for unknown reasons nearly 2000 years ago. Labrets were not worn by the Nootka, Bella Coola, or southern Kwakiutl and have not been found archaeologically within the territory of these groups.

Another major occurrence of labrets in the new world is not found until the northern Gulf of Mexico,

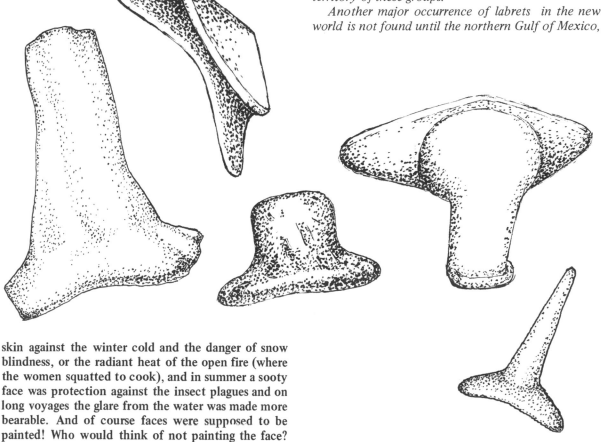

skin against the winter cold and the danger of snow blindness, or the radiant heat of the open fire (where the women squatted to cook), and in summer a sooty face was protection against the insect plagues and on long voyages the glare from the water was made more bearable. And of course faces were supposed to be painted! Who would think of not painting the face?

over 4600 miles southeast of Puget Sound. The distribution extends south from this area through parts of Central America to Peru and the Amazon Basin of Brazil. They date back 2500 years in Coastal Ecuador and are still being worn today by an increasingly small number of people in parts of South America.

The only other area in the world where labrets have been known to be worn is West and Central Africa where they occur in scattered locations between Central Mali and Northern Kenya.

their complexions could not be ascertained, for their skins were besmeared with soot and Red ochre. Their hair, however, is dark and shiney, and appeared to be kept in good order, parted in the middle and kept smooth on each side behind the ears, and tyed at the top in a knot." Undoubtably Frances approved of the style of hairdressing, since it was so like her own, and she appreciated the cleanliness because of her own problems in caring for her extravagantly long tresses, when the water for the ship had to be laboriously brought aboard in barrels hoisted by the sailors.

Courtesy of the British Columbia Provincial Museum, Victoira, British Columbia.

Thus we see that labrets have a fairly limited distribution: Japan to Puget Sound around the North Pacific, parts of Central America and south to Peru and the Amazon, and that strange line of labrets across Central Africa, a distribution dominantly coastal and riverine. Dating is not yet detailed enough to permit conclusions as to the origin of the ornament.

On her first voyage to the territory of Chief Wickananish on the west coast of Vancouver Island, Frances saw no labrets because the Nootkan people did not wear them, neither in the historic period nor archaeologically. In the Gulf of Georgia area the first visitors did not observe labrets, but the ornament is commonly found at a level dating three thousand to two thousand years ago. At a recent dig at a Gulf Island site six labrets were found in a variety of sizes and shapes, but none of these six is the same style as the round spoon-bowled ones which upset Frances. Hilary Stewart's book *Artifacts of the Northwest Coast Indians* includes a page of labrets, with almost every type represented.

Frances wrote: "this odious Mouth piece so compleatly disfigured them that it was impossible to tell what they would have been without it, for even

If only the women of Alaska had been able to record their impressions of Frances, to give us the view from the canoes as the furclad, face-blackened, labret-wearing women examined this weird pale female creature on the deck of the foreign ship, with her hair as dead as winter grass and her clothes flimsy like eagle-down. Frances describes her own dress as "being nothing more than a white Bengal Muslin dress with a broad China ribbon sash which is now the fashion, the ends (of the ribbon) reaching the ground, and the dress has a long train which must have appeared odd to them."

Did the Tlingit women, gossiping later by the fires, describe with horror the appearance of Frances Barkley? . . . "How revolting to have such a pale face, as if she were made of fog" . . . "She is like a white worm found under a stone! And she has no labret — she must be only a slave." No doubt such remarks were made, for we are all alike under our powder, whether white lead or red ochre, and egocentricity is not the exclusive attribute of the European visitors.

Yes, to the women of the Alaskan coast the labret was indeed ornamental — and the bigger the better!

SUMMER RUNS DOWN CREEKS

The creek grows smaller,
murmurs beside the porch
and under the plank
that bridges the banks.
afternoon grows hot behind the house,
out of its shelter
the air comes cool off the sound
moving up the narrow cleft of the beach.
high up in the trees on the ridges
the sound seems larger,
whistling out of a vast sky.
the sun keeps my company
while i thin lettuce, pull grass
out of the beds,
and watch the beans grow
to their poles.
way across blackfish sound
past layers of hills,
the snowline moves up the mountains
leaving black-edged crags
burnt out of the ice.
my mind falls open
watching water
run down the creek.

Julia Moe

'CAPI' BLANCHET

Edith Iglauer Daly

WHEN I CAME TO LIVE ON THE BRITISH COLUMBIA COAST I WAS GIVEN AS A SORT OF SPIRITUAL INTRODUCTION a remarkable little volume entitled *The Curve of Time* by M. Wylie Blanchet. The book was a particularly appropriate choice; my summers were spent on a fishing boat, the *Morekelp*, with my husband John Daly, a commercial salmon troller, and the area he regularly traversed partly followed the path travelled by Mrs. Blanchet and her five children on their tiny motor launch, the *Caprice*.

The five Blanchet youngsters, led by their indomitable mother, spent four summer months for fifteen years — the older ones less time as other commitments pressed in — on a twenty-five by six-and-a-half foot boat made of half-inch cedar, traveling around the west coast of Vancouver Island and as far north up the Inside Passage as Cape Caution. They explored the inlets and bays, sometimes following the trail broken by that earlier intrepid mariner Captain George Vancouver, with whom they felt a great empathy; their experiences finally written down in a series of sketches that encompassed all the years of their journeys as if they were one. The title *The Curve of Time* refers to the capacity of any one of us to stand on the highest curve of the Present in Time and look back into the Past, forward into the Future or to wander at will from one to the other. Which is precisely what M. Wylie Blanchet did in this brief account that has triumphed over Time to become one of the classics in British Columbia literature.

The Curve of Time is now in its fourth edition and has had two publishers: William Blackwood & Sons Ltd. in Great Britain, who let it go out of print, and subsequently Gray's Publishing Ltd. in Sidney, B.C., with sales that now reverse the usual pattern by showing a slow, steady increase. Four of the chapters previously appeared as separate articles in *Blackwood's Magazine* and it is M. Wylie Blanchet's only book, originally published in 1961 when she was seventy years old. That same year she died of a heart attack, sitting at her desk where she was found slumped over her typewriter. She had lived just long enough to enjoy being a published author with a small reading public that wrote her admiring letters.

M. Wylie Blanchet. At first, she tried using just "M. Wylie." *M.* was for Muriel, the author's given name, which she hated; *Wylie* was borrowed from a grandparent; and *Blanchet* was acquired by marriage. Altogether it was the impersonal sound that she intended: she hoped the author would not be recognized by the people up the coast about whom she was writing, who knew her simply as "Capi" Blanchet. As to the nickname — wasn't she the Captain of the *Caprice*?

In the last chapter of the book, entitled "Little House," Mrs. Blanchet comes off the *Caprice* to write about the family's land base on seven secluded acres of Vancouver Island's coast, from which they departed each June and to which they returned in October. For an ordinary family this would have meant cutting two months from the school year, but the Blanchet children received their early education at home under their mother's guidance. In the first edition of the book, Mrs. Blanchet confined herself in this final chapter to a poetical narrative evoking the wild and beautiful setting of Little House. Later editions include the beginning of a second unfinished manuscript and add mysterious shadows, with the suggestion of personal tragedy in a cryptic statement, "the legacy of death often shapes our lives in ways we could not imagine." *The Curve of Time* manages to be sentimental, imaginative, and often strays into whimsy, but it is reticent about hard facts; it reads like an impressionist painting. Its characters, whose physical appearances are never really described, are shadowy figures against the lush and brilliant scenery of the British Columbia coast. We know what they do and how they feel but not what they look like or who they are other than a mother and five children, three girls and two boys, the youngest around three at the time Mrs. Blanchet chose to locate her story.

Despite the reticence we do know the important things about this remarkable woman. She comes through as extremely courageous, innovative and as a kind of mechanical wizard compared to most women. Without formal training or experience she could make an engine that failed at an isolated anchorage start chugging again. She could steer a small craft over shoals, through narrows and rapids, read charts correctly and arrive where she intended to be, while she was providing food, proper shelter from whatever winds were prevailing and adventure for her children. Yet readers close her book with a scratchy feeling of curiosity. Who *was* M. Wylie Blanchet? What was she like?

Her Canadian publisher Gray Campbell, a fellow British Columbian who was both neighbour and friend, has described her as having "a delightful shyness," as a serious person with "a delicious, dry sense of humour." Campbell first became acquainted with her when the *Caprice* was berthed next to his boat at Canoe Cove, a short distance from the Blanchet house, which was five miles from Sidney. He too was writing, and Capi Blanchet used to sit in the cabin of his boat and read the chapters of his uncompleted manuscript. He has said since that it was the lack of success of the first edition of *The Curve of Time*, whose English publisher never bothered to see that it was stocked in bookstores either in Victoria or Vancouver, that helped to convince him that there was a need for regional publishing. Only six or seven hundred copies even got as far as Toronto. The author had to loan a local bookstore the money to get copies of her own book for her friends.

Muriel Blanchet was born Muriel Liffiton in 1891 in Lachine, Quebec, into a well-to-do family with High Anglican principles. The Liffitons were English but the Snetsingers, on her mother's side, were pre-Revolution Dutch settlers in the Hudson Valley. They crossed the border into Canada during the

American Revolution, settling in the St. Lawrence valley with a land grant well located downstream from the town of Cornwall. Grandfather Snetsinger was a warden of Cornwall and Member of Parliament for the area, and left a considerable inheritance whose final distribution was made only a year ago. The ancestral home is now under sixty feet of St. Lawrence river water and all the original land has been sold.

Muriel was the middle one of three sisters and something of a tomboy. She customarily carried squirrels and mice around in her pockets, to the horror of the girls' tutor, described as "a kind of retired clergyman." Their father was a prosperous customs broker who announced from time to time at breakfast that he was departing and would then disappear for a year or so. The only hint of his whereabouts would be a casual remark later when he helped his daughters with their geography lessons, that he had just been in Alexandria, Egypt, or once, in Timbuctoo. Later he sent the three girls to St. Paul's private school for girls near Montreal, where Muriel developed a strong sense of competition with her sister Violet, five years older and a prize-winning scholar. Muriel set out to surpass her in the same determined manner with which she later approached the mysteries of the gasoline engine. The results of this four-year scholastic campaign are still evident in a row of small red leather Temple volumes of Shakespeare in the library of Mrs. Blanchet's youngest son David (called John in the book). Each volume was given her as a prize for top honours in a different subject, and she never stopped until she had the

graduation. One year she was awarded a special prize *(Antony and Cleopatra)* for top excellence in "All Subjects." Her older sister Violet, known in the family as "Auntie Teake," subsequently married a banker, was widowed, and at ninety-six lives in a nursing home in Windsor, Ontario. Until very recently she still continued a lifelong habit of writing letters all night to the family. The youngest sister Doris, remembered by her nieces and nephews for her charm and erudition, studied at Oxford and the University of Rome, converted to Catholicism and became a nun, entering the Order of the Sacred Heart. When she was Mother Superior of the Sacred Heart Convent on Point Grey Road in Vancouver the two oldest Blanchet girls, Elisabeth and Frances, attended high school there for two years.

With a scholastic record like hers Muriel Liffiton was expected to go on to university but instead at eighteen she married Geoffrey Blanchet, the brother of a school friend — a decision she is said to have regretted later. The first Blanchet in North America arrived from France in 1666 but Geoffrey, although bilingual, was only about one-sixth French. He was from Ottawa, the youngest of eleven children, and his father was a minor civil servant.

Geoffrey and Muriel Blanchet started married life in Sherbrooke, Quebec, where he was a bank manager. Later he was placed in charge of foreign exchange at the Toronto headquarters of the Bank of Commerce. He was a clever, somewhat artistic man with a highly emotional, nervous temperament. In his early forties he became ill and took early retirement. The family by that time included four children,

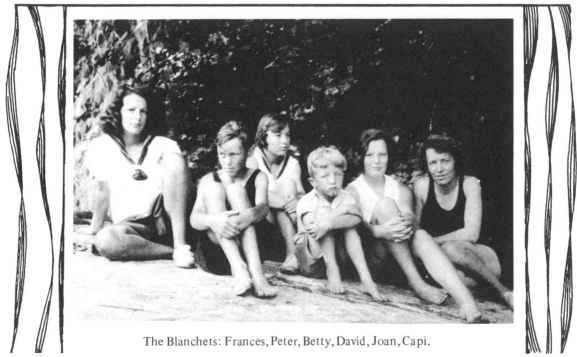

The Blanchets: Frances, Peter, Betty, David, Joan, Capi.

whole set, inscribed to Muriel Liffiton in the heavy black script of R. Newton, Rector of St. Paul's, and bearing the motto *Non Sans Droit* with the school's coat of arms. Between 1905 and 1908 Muriel Liffiton repeatedly captured first prizes in Latin, French, spelling, astronomy, history, geography, geometry (Euclid), algebra and English, beginning with a modest two her first year and winding up with six at

and when he had sufficiently recovered he packed them all into a Willys-Knight touring car which, according to one of the children, "had flapping curtains and a great top that folded like an elephant sitting down," and started driving across the country looking for an island to live on. They drove and drove until they came to Chicago, where the Blanchets parked their car on a city street while they all slept.

David had not been born yet and Peter, then aged three-and-a-half, remembers sleeping in a hammock strung from the roof of the Willys-Knight. A policeman woke them up and they continued across Canada and the States until they came to Vancouver Island.

Peter Blanchet, whom the family calls by his middle name, Tate, is now a grey-haired geological engineer in his late fifties. Sitting in his office in Vancouver, he can still remember clearly how they found their new home. "We came to a locked gate with *Clovelly* written on it, got out of the Willys-Knight, climbed the gate and had supper on the other side," he recalled. "Intrigued, we packed the gate off its hinges and drove a quarter of a mile to a house built of log slabs with the bark still on it." Clovelly, named by a previous owner after a place in Cornwall, became Little House, purchased by the Blanchets in 1922. It had been empty since 1914, part of a one-hundred-acre real estate scheme that collapsed during World War I. The Blanchets were able to buy seven acres at the extreme tip, Curteis point, overlooking the Gulf of Georgia, and they kept it until Mrs. Blanchet died in 1961, although Little House was torn down in 1948. It was an unusual house, a strangely mystical English cottage covered with ivy, with a big fireplace and a billiard table on the first floor and four bedrooms up a rickety flight of stairs on the second floor. "It was designed by a celebrated architect, Sam McLure, and built by a crook," said David Blanchet, who was born there. "It was a beautiful design on wretched foundations and full of dry rot." By the time he and his mother tore it down after World War II the foundations were so far gone that the house had a tremendous list and dining room chairs were sliding every which way.

Their boat the *Caprice* was purchased in 1923 for six hundred dollars. It had been build the year before, a cold year and the Brentwood Ferry, near which it was anchored, managed to shove a cake of ice into the side of the *Caprice*, sinking it. It was hauled out on a nearby dock and the Blanchets bought it on the spot, with water still dribbling out of it. "This was probably when my mother learned to deal with engines," David has commented. "It had to be cleaned out immediately, once it had been in salt water. We had that same engine for twenty years, until it was changed in 1942."

Peter Blanchet remembers the first time his mother took the *Caprice* out on her own. It was in March, on his sixth birthday, and she had promised to take him to Shell Isand, a favourite spot where she liked to say she would spend her hundredth birthday. She and Peter got in the boat, which they kept at Canoe Cove, and "she cranked and cranked that darned engine, and still it wouldn't start," Peter recalled. "She could see my father sitting on the Point watching to see if we would get off and she had to go and get him, which really irked her. Then she and I went fishing for the day off Sidney Spit. We caught a couple of fish which we cooked over a fire on the beach at Shell Island. It was very good salmon!"

Geoffrey Blanchet died in 1927. He had gone off on the *Caprice* by himself for the day, stopping at nearby Knapp Island, where he anchored and set up his cookstove. He was never seen again, but his boat was found by a Chinese gardener working for the Harvey family, who lived on the island. Blanchet had had heart problems and was presumed to have gone for a swim, had an attack and drowned.

The second summer after his death, Mrs. Blanchet rented Little House and took the children off on the *Caprice* for the first of the venturesome trips that as a composite memory became the substance of *The Curve of Time*. With the money she received from renting Clovelly in summer to a wealthy family from Washington and her own small income, she was able to manage. The two oldest girls, Elisabeth and Frances, missed several summers on the boat when they were sent east to live with an aunt and uncle on their father's side in Ottawa; and later when they went to the convent in Vancouver, their holidays were shorter, eventually shrinking to two weeks when they both studied nursing. Elisabeth started nursing on the B.C. coast, married and went to England, where she still lives. She became a freelance journalist and the successful author of over thirty published books. Her mother's attitude towards her writing was a mixture of pride and a tendency to regard her daughter's books as pot-boilers. Most of them are novels with a documentary background, often based on Elisabeth's hospital experiences, and many are still selling. Frances married two years after she started nursing, and she and her husband, Ron King, raise Hereford cattle on their ranch near Golden, B.C.

The three younger children, Joan, Peter and David, were educated almost entirely at home, by correspondence, by their mother, and by a Scottish engineer who was a mechanic at the Canoe Cove boat works, who taught them math, chemistry and physics. Joan, known as the rebellious member of the family, went to art school in Vancouver and then continued her art studies in New York. When she left Vancouver, she bought an old Indian dugout canoe for five dollars and paddled home. It took her five days, and she crossed the Gulf of Georgia at night, to avoid traffic and heavy seas, a remarkable feat since it required at least nine hours of steady paddling. Frances King vividly recalled hearing about her sister's arrival. "When she rounded the point in her dugout, wearing an old red sweater, Capi and the boys were sitting on the bluff, wondering who the Indian was! Joan had expected some commendation, and was amazed at Capi's anger. "Just because I'm a fool doesn't mean you children have to be!" Capi said. Later the boys reported that Capi laughed herself to sleep. Joan later confided to a friend that she was testing herself; she felt if she could cross the Gulf of Georgia alone, she would have the confidence to face New York. She subsequently married Ted McFeely, from whom she is now divorced and lives in a remote spot on the already remote Queen Charlotte Islands.

Peter, who had an inventive mind and was working on a memory rod before he ever heard of computers, entered the University of British Columbia at sixteen, and managed one more summer on the boat before the pressures of adult life took him away. David, who inherited his mother's imaginative sensitivity, after one year in a local school and a year in university joined the army when the Second World War began. After the war he returned to Little House, which by now was literally falling apart. He and his mother proceeded to tear it down, starting at the top, and together they designed and built her an attractive white bungalow directly overlooking the sea. David went on to construct another house for a friend and began one for himself, meanwhile returning to university to study architecture. By then he was married to Janet Patterson, a handsome woman of great character and the daughter of writer R.M. Patterson. They had one child, Julia, and when she was four David was stricken with poliomyelitis, which left him partially paralyzed, confined to a wheelchair. They live now in North Vancouver.

In appearance, Capi Blanchet was of medium height, with very fine blonde hair brushed upwards so that it formed a kind of haze around her head. She had a strong rather than a pretty face, round and pleasant. Her normal attire was a pair of khaki shirts, an Indian sweater and sneakers that sometimes had holes in the toes. She had begun wearing shorts in the nineteen-twenties, long before they were fashionable, and her daughter Elisabeth has recalled that a journalist writing about people he had met on the B.C. coast in *The Saturday Evening Post* "commented on her shorts and how suitable they seemed for what she was doing – running a boat." In 1957 Capi went to England to visit Elisabeth, bought a Land Rover, and the two women went camping. "We were shopping in Chartres, France, and she was wearing blue jeans, clamdigger length," Betty said. "A white-haired Frenchman walked slowly around her, smiled and bowed. 'Très chic, Madame!' was his comment." What impressed Mrs. Blanchet however on her trip was the lack of wood on the beaches, since this was her main source for firewood at home.

Mrs. Blanchet's children and friends were enormously fond of her, somewhat in awe of her all-around competence, and thought her fair-minded but domineering. "She was a challenge for any child, but slightly dampening," her eldest daughter has written. "She could do almost anything that men did, and still be feminine."

"She had a lot of courage or self confidence, but she did not over estimate her mechanical ability," a writer friend, Hubert Evans, has said. "On a run from Sidney to Vancouver, the *Caprice* was overtaken in the Gulf by a late season southeaster, and the little boat took quite a dusting," he related. "Capi had several children aboard. 'I told the Lord I could take care of the boat but would he please keep the engine running,' she said to me afterwards."

Capi Blanchet does not seem to have been particularly light-hearted or spontaneous, and she was somewhat arrogant about anyone she considered her inferior. "Like many English of a certain class she had a stiffness and tended to classify people," another friend has remarked. "She had a slightly Church-of-England attitude, even talking to fishermen, who were never sure how to take her. She had a good sense of humour but a rather studied laugh. I think there was a good deal of repression there. Even when David was desperately ill she never permitted anyone to see her upset, and said to her daughter-in-law, 'Oh heck, he'll get better in no time!'"

A description from her daughter Frances exemplifies the quality of character her children and friends remember best: "She was capable of handling any situation. If she was worried she didn't let us know."

On the boat Mrs. Blanchet was even-tempered under what must often have been trying conditions at such close quarters; her method of discipline was to separate her children, not argue. David remembered his mother losing her temper with him only once, when he was about twelve. "It was some silly mistake, something about an anchor, that I did my way instead of what she wanted," he said. "Normally her eyes were brown, but suddenly they were a turquoise colour and blazing. It was unbelievable!"

She was one of those rare women who are mechanically inclined, and enjoyed tinkering with engines and working with tools. Every so often she took apart the *Caprice* engine, a four-cylinder Kermath, cleaned and painted it and put it back together again, grinding the valves herself. Frances King remembers the first time she took her husband to meet her mother. The morning after their arrival he found Capi in her workshop. She had taken the old engine out of the *Caprice*, had ground the valves and was putting in new rings and checking the timing. "Having worked in a garage, Ron could appreciate with amazement what his mother-in-law was doing, whereas this was everyday stuff to me," Frances said.

An intimate friend of Mrs. Blanchet's, Kathleen Caldwell, has described her as "not excessively domestic, but interested in people and politics, which she loved to discuss. Her house was comfortable and pleasant, and Capi could produce a beautiful meal with what looked like no effort." In their close circle Capi was renowned for her roast beef, Yorkshire pudding and mouth-watering pastry. Oddly enough, although she liked to eat fish, she never cooked it except outdoors on a beach because she couldn't stand the smell.

Mrs. Blanchet liked to draw sea creatures in pen and ink, and once illustrated a fairy story she wrote with drawings in the margin. She was also a fair pianist, and in later life enjoyed playing a violin that her grandfather gave her when she was twelve. It now hangs on the wall of David's living room, but his mother used it often; she had joined a small orchestra at Deep Cove, playing second violin, reputedly a quarter-tone flat.

Children found her very understanding. She treated them like adults, and when David contracted polio she took care of their daughter Julia for two years while he was in hospital in Vancouver and Victoria and his wife Janet worked. Grandmother and grandchild got on very well, and it was a mutually beneficial relationship; by then Capi had become somewhat reclusive – having Julia with her forced her to go out.

David fell ill before the interior of Mrs. Blanchet's new house was completed and it never seemed to advance beyond that half-built stage. She lined the whole interior with vertical cedar planks herself, but doors were a late addition to the bathroom and kitchen and knobs usually came off in hand. Her firewood was never quite dry and Kathleen Caldwell once delighted her by bringing a gift of Presto logs. When Capi's doctor prescribed a drier climate for a cough that later developed into emphysema she ignored him and instead sat with her head as far into her oil stove as she could get it for twenty minutes a day. "That's my high, dry climate," she said. She had an ingenious system of heating water in the morning before she was ready to light the oil stove. She turned an electric iron upside down, supported it with stones, set it at its highest heat, put a pan on top of it and boiled her water for breakfast there.

As for the *Caprice*, it was never meant to have any other owner than Capi Blanchet. After the war she planned to build a new boat and sold the *Caprice* for seven hundred dollars — a hundred more than she had paid for it — to the owner of a boat works in Victoria, who hauled it up for repairs. While it was on the ways the entire boat works burned down, including the *Caprice*. Mrs. Blanchet did have another boat after that, the *Scylla*, but she never really used it.

Mrs. Blanchet's children, now older than she was when they made their wonderful odysseys along the coast, look back on that faraway time with wonderment and affection. "They were exciting; something we looked forward to," Peter commented. "It was a fairly normal life for us, however, because we always seemed to be doing it."

"I loved the summer journeys but I doubt if any of us appreciated quite how unique our childhood was. We just knew Capi was doing something unusual," Elisabeth writes from England. "She used to get a bit tense if we were taking green water over the bow or wallowing about in a following sea or running the Yuculta Rapids. Otherwise she took everything in her stride — whether crossing the Straits of Georgia at 4 a.m. to beat the sou'wester or exploring new territory."

"Only fools seek adventures," David has remembered his mother as saying at one time or another. However foolish Mrs. Blanchet's adventures may have seemed to her (which is doubtful), they have a dreamlike charm for an increasing number of readers. *The Curve of Time* has had a separate and ongoing life of its own, achieving its own small immortality.

Recently David, who is his mother's executor, received a request to permit the publication of *The Curve of Time* in Bulgaria. David is mystified by the sudden Bulgarian interest in the book, but thinks it may somehow be involved with a Wylie relative who once grew roses in Bulgaria to make attar of roses perfume. Closer to home a Canadian film producer has proposed to make a short feature film of the book that would combine a narrative with dramatization of the events his mother wrote about, against the scenic beauty of the British Columbia coast, hopefully catching the family's spirit of exploration and adventure and Mrs. Blanchet's enterprise and expertise.

Henry Finds the Roar

M. Wylie Blanchet

Sechelt Inlet is a long slender body of water with two arms, Narrows Inlet and Salmon Inlet, branching off the eastern shore, several small islands, a shallow bay named Porpoise Bay at the head and a narrow, violent tidal rapids called the Skookumchuck at the mouth. This is a story about a killer whale named Henry who got accidentally pulled through the rapids into Sechelt Inlet and had his troubles getting out again. You may be able to understand Henry's problems better if you follow his wanderings on our map.

"PUH-PH . . . E . . . E . . . W!" BLEW HENRY IN DISGUST, as he just missed another salmon that sprang out of his way with a violent twist.

"Puh-ph . . . e . . . e . . . w!" blew Henry in alarm, when a few minutes later he tried to swim back the way he had come. The current was certainly terribly strong and he didn't seem to be making any headway at all.

"I'm getting mad!" sputtered Henry, "I won't stand much of this!"

"Won't you!" roared the Skookumchuck, filling him up with water and tossing him sideways into a jagged point of rock.

"Won't you!" roared the Strong Waters, spinning him about and standing him on his head.

And they all pulled and tore and fought and laughed over him as they tossed him along, until with ill-concealed regret they threw him into the quiet inland arm of the sea called Sechelt Inlet, where he lay bruised and bleeding, a great battered hulk of a killer whale.

However, the next day Henry moved his tail, and as it wasn't so very bad, he tried moving his eyes too, and found that he could still see.

Then he tried thinking. He knew what must have happened . . .

Words came back to him, lessons learned years before and repeated over and over to an anxious mother: "It's better to keep away from the Skookumchuck Rapids altogether, but if you do go through, wait for slack tide." He could remember the directions for if you did go through – drift slowly down until you come to the Indian village and wait there until the Roar stops. Once the Roar stopped that meant that it was slack tide. But even then you had to hurry – no fishing or dawdling going through – for in five minutes the Roar started again. Henry had had a very clear impression at the time that once the Roar started there was not much hope for anyone in it. Then the last words of the lesson had been, "And wait for a slack to come out again."

Henry groaned. Yes, he remembered it all now, word for word. Not that he had altogether forgotten, but he thought he didn't need to bother with lessons and directions and things now that he was so big. He had been diving and rolling along out in Jervis Inlet with his brothers and friends when a big school of salmon, great silvery fellows, had suddenly appeared almost under his nose. Instead of giving the call of his kind to let the rest of the whales know that food was in sight, Henry had slipped off, intending to keep them all for himself . . . and this was the result. Henry groaned again and wallowed deeper

157

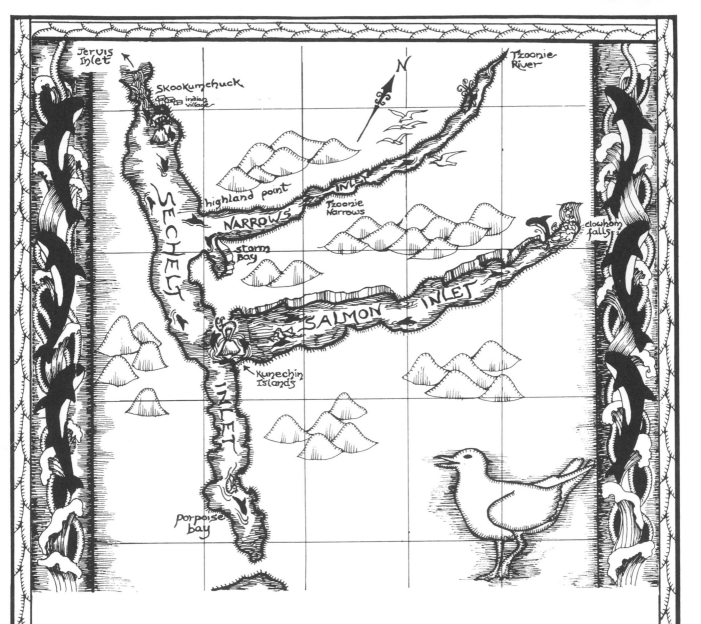

in the soothing leaves of the busy kelp bed where he'd come to rest.

But the next day he felt decidedly better. Trying his mouth and finding that it still worked, he decided that he was hungry. With a couple of gulps Henry made a light dinner of the kelp bed's population of rock and spider crabs.

"That feels better!" sighed Henry. "Now I'll be going to find the others."

Away he cruised, but there was no sign of the place to get out, and whichever way he turned, sooner or later he bumped into a cliff. He repeated the instructions carefully, especially the last part — "and wait for slack to come out again." Well, he was going to wait for slack, but he had to find the place before he could wait.

"It's quite simple," said Henry firmly, "You wait for —" ... bump! "— slack, and then you go out." ... bump!

"This is getting tiresome," worried Henry, "I'll have to find a quiet place to sit and think about this."

A rocky island hove in sight, rising with straight sides out of deep water. Twisted juniper and stunted pines braced themselves sturdily on its uninviting crest, while mosses and stonecrop clung to the lower rocks out of reach of the tide.

Henry eyed it with satisfaction. "Just the place for a think," he said. Cautiously warping himself in, he stopped beside a shelving rock and rested his chin on the seaweed.

"Now," said Henry, "what was I going to think? Oh yes, yes. Two things. First the Place, then the Roar."

Henry rested his chin more comfortably on his flipper. Instead of trying to find the Place, which was difficult when you didn't know what it looked like, and then waiting for the Roar to stop, he would look for the Roar first. Once he had found the Roar, he would have found the Place — for of course where the one was, the other would be too. Then he would get rid of the Roar by simply waiting for it to stop.

"So now," said Henry, "all I have to do is to swim along on the surface and listen. Then, once I hear the Roar, why I'm practically out." Henry was very pleased with himself. "I'm rather good at thinking," he thought.

HENRY DID NOT KNOW ANYTHING ABOUT SECHELT INLET, except that as far as he knew there was only one way in or out. So he decided that if he always kept the cliffs or shores on his left side, then he would always know that the next cliff was another cliff, and not the same one. So every point he rounded Henry would say, "And this is another cliff," and then listen very carefully. However, after he had gone along for some time he got very bewildered, for the Inlet got very narrow and he could see two cliffs, one on each side of him and very close together.

The current was rather strong here, which made navigating a little difficult – especially as he was trying to keep one ear above water. Then he began to get excited –for current suggested Roar. Suppose this was the Skookumchuck he was in now, and suppose it suddenly began to roar . . . !

He was decidedly nervous now and his whole tail was trembling. Then to make matters worse, some seagulls commenced wheeling and calling to each other just above his head, as though anticipating a good meal. Henry glanced apprehensively at them. He felt more and more sure that this must be the Skookumchuck, and finally he raced ahead, to get through before it began roaring.

Now it broadened out rapidly, and Henry's last doubt vanished.

"Out, I'm out!" he shouted. "Thought I was going to be eaten by a lot of seagulls, did you?" and he smacked his tail and glared at them with his big, white, make-believe eye. Now to find the rest of his brothers. No need to listen any more. And he raced full speed ahead, diving deep to make better time.

Overhead the seagulls shrieked and laughed. "He'll go aground! He'll go aground! What a meal we'll have! I bags first bite! No, I do, I do!"

Suddenly Henry shot up to the surface with a groan, hastily swallowed some water and blew it out with a frightful "Pu-ph-e-e-e-w!", which made the seagulls duck and wheel.

"This water is going queer," said Henry. "Rotten funny taste!" And a moment later he bellowed, "And it's full of dirty, stinking, dead jellyfish!"

A couple of yards further and he gave a terrific blare and backed water with all his might. The water churned and got dark and muddy as Henry wallowed and blew, realizing with terror that he must have come up a blind arm that ended in a fresh water river.

He hardly dared to breathe until he was safely back in deep water once more. There he rinsed his mouth again and again with the clean salt water, sending huge showers of it high up into the air. He had never noticed the taste of clean salt water before . . . "Pu-ph-e-e-ew!" Wasn't it treat! Off in the distance the seagulls called and shrieked, "Who cares! Who cares! Who cares!" but nobody paid any attentin to them at all.

Now NIGHT CAME ON AND THE CLIFFS GREW DARK AND TALL. The sky gradually filled with stars. And finally up over the cliffs rose a slightly lopsided moon. On and on Henry swam, listening and watching the stars. He had never thought much about stars before. If he thought now, it was probably just to wonder why there should be so much phosphorus up there tonight when there was none down here. Henry liked phosphorus. He liked to see the wonderful spreading paths he could make through the water on a night

when there was plenty about. And the fishing . . . ! Henry smacked his lips at the memory. For every fish, big or small, made a phosphor-flash when it moved. And all you had to do was race around swallowing the biggest flashes and you had a meal in no time.

Henry gave a prodigious yawn . . . no sleep for him though; always this wretched listening for the Roar that never came. However, he heard a great many things that he had never bothered, nor never had the opportunity, to listen to before. It was strange how many noises there were in the night, like the p-p-p-ppput of the little brown owls that flitted around and the funny hu-hu-hu-hush of their wings.

Lighter and lighter it grew. He could make out a deep bay just ahead of him now and decided that it would make a good place for breakfast, as he cold hardly get lost in a bay.

Rather an awkward thing for a bay, to have a thirty-foot whale drop in for breakfast. And of course very much more so for the inhabitants, which in this case were mostly rock cod. Nasty, wormy things, was Henry's usual opinion of rock cod, who lazed around in the shallow water and gossiped with the spider crabs in the kelp beds. But Henry was not in a position to be particular this morning, he simply *had* to have a meal. So . . . green cod, grey cod, brown cod, in they all went. The whole bay tossed and heaved with the commotion Henry made over his breakfast. It gave Henry rather a squirmy feeling to think of all those wormy things inside him so he broke his rule and went on a big dive. The cool deep water washed the feeling away but when he burst to the top again he couldn't decide which side was which.

He stopped in front of a rocky point to think, and just as he was about to get it all thought out a white goat came down on the point and made the kind of noise a goat makes at him. Henry stared. This was something new to him. The creature came down nearer the water and stared at Henry. He didn't know what Henry was either, but whatever it was, it was company — and wherever it was going, he was going too. And he jumped and hopped and capered over the rocks, making a clack-clack-clack with his sharp little hooves. And whenever Henry stopped, he'd stop too and watch him, his head with its ridiculous beard tilted to one side. Henry didn't like it at all, this strange creature pacing him along the shore. He tried blowing at it, but it was just a waste of time. The goat seemed to like it.

"I'll race and leave it behind," decided Henry, when finally he got to the stage where he could stand the sight of it no longer. So away he tore with the goat following. He soon left it behind bawling on a point. But Henry raced on, taking no chances with a creature like that.

"Ye gods! Another goat!" Well, he wouldn't give this one a chance to get familiar. Past he tore at full speed, and the goat only had time to turn its head futilely from side to side. Nor would he give it a chance to catch up; on and on he raced.

This was a strange part of the Inlet he was in. Every mile or so a narrow channel and great frowning heights, and then always opening out again. It was getting tiresome.

Another goat! This was too much! Henry stopped with a lurch, and the whole world, with the goat standing on top, proceeded to go round and round and round in huge circles. Gradually the circles got smaller and finally they stopped, and everything swayed gently in front of him. He felt very sick.

Yes, the goat was still there, and Henry looked at it weakly. It looked awfully like the first goat that had paced him along the shore. But that had been miles and miles back. An angry kingfisher screamed at him from a dead branch, "Look here! What are you racing round and round our island for?"

Henry stared . . . "Island?"

"Yes, island! You've been round it half a dozen times now, and it's upsetting everything!"

"An island . . ." said Henry slowly. All too clear was the meaning of the recurring strait with its cliffs, and the never-ending goats . . . The goat said whatever goats say, in a consoling kind of way, and Henry glared at it.

He must have mixed his sides — that was the only thing he could think of. "When I took that dive," Henry thought. "Yes, that is when I mixed my sides and this miserable goat came along before I could think them straight again."

"No more dives!" said Henry, thinking aloud.

"No more dives!" echoed the goat, or whatever a goat echoes.

"Oh, get lost!" bellowed Henry, and the goat made a quick retreat up the rocks to escape the splashing of Henry's great tail as he headed back to his left-side cliff.

Henry had a feeling now that the cliff was not as friendly as it might be, that it might trick him again if it got the chance. Well, there wouldn't be a chance — Henry would take care of that. And he eyed it fiercely and was *very* careful.

Towards evening his carefulness was rewarded, for he *heard* something. At first he didn't know what it was, but he knew it was a sound that hadn't been there before. He went very cautiously. The Inlet was narrower now. Everything was more or less as he had expected it would be, and it certainly was beginning to sound very like you-know-what! He didn't dare say it, in case it made the sound stop. Round another corner . . . still narrower . . . still louder. And then he was *sure* — it was his Roar!

"I'm out!" he said, trembling with excitement. "Practically out! Nothing to do now but wait for the Roar to stop."

And warping himself in closer to the cliff, Henry settled down to wait . . .

Henry shifted himself and sighed, put one flipper up and the other down for a change. Then wriggled his big spar fin to get the pins and needles out of it.

How long should Roars take to stop? It seemed to him that he had been waiting a very long time. Still, with freedom so near, one must be patient. He let out a terribly deep sigh, and yawned – tremendously! This was the most monotonous thing he had ever done in his life.

Morning came at last. The sun rose up in a heavy mist, a sure sign of a hot day to come. Everything big and little had been up for hours about their various affairs of the day. And what was more, everything was fed and comfortable – except Henry. He still lay beside the cliff, pale and haggard, red of eye and tired of ear, listening, ever listening to his Roar.

Hotter and hotter grew the day. His big fin began to drop like a tallow candle that has been left in the sun. All the water around him warmed up to the temperature where fat becomes, well, less solid. And as Henry was encased in great layers and rolls of fat, he felt decidedly limp and fluid. Henry put his head under the water to try to thicken up his brain again. Thoughts, he knew, shouldn't be quite as liquid as this – fairly running all over the place. Down in the cooler water things gradually straightened out, and the vague idea became a horribly solid thought – *something was wrong*.

There was nothing for it, he decided as he came up to the surface again, he would have to risk everything and go and look at the Roar. Find out what had happened to the *stop* of it, or rather what *hadn't* happened.

Slowly he started toward the Roar, peering cautiously around each point before he rounded it and never leaving one safe point until he was sure he could reach the next one. It was getting nearer and louder. He carefully swung his tail out to try the force of the current –but he could feel none at all. Goodness, this was nerve-wracking!

The next point jutted out very far. It looked as though anything might happen and happen suddenly once you rounded it. He measured the distance with his eye and picked out a likely place for a probable back-current when he got there. Then he dashed for it. Safe!

When his heart stopped pounding quite so fiercely he very warily looked around the point. Straight across the Inlet was a deeply fissured, rugged cliff, framed in a mass of evergreens. And from the fissure poured a beautiful, roaring waterfall, churned to a snowy whiteness that gleamed against the dark rock. Henry stared dully, the beauty quite lost on him. It was a roar that never stopped and never would stop – the roar of Clowhom Falls!

At first Henry was very mad. He blared like a steam engine letting off steam that should have been let off some time ago; he leapt out of the water; he ploughed back into the water, smacking his tail with a thunderous bang that drowned for a moment the roar of the falls; he bit the bellies out of three innocent seals, then flung them aside, so mad he forgot to be hungry.

B UT GRADUALLY HENRY QUIETED DOWN and became more reasonable. The evening was cool and everything around was calm and peaceful. He began to like it up here on top of the sea. He had got so used to it now with all his listening that he rather missed it when he went down below. So he stayed up and settled down to a quiet, steady roll-along, roll-along, going nowhere in particular at all, when suddenly, right in his path, he met Timothy. And Timothy opened his mouth and squawked at him.

"What!" said Henry, rather taken aback. Things, especially small things, didn't usually squawk at Henry.

"Squ-a-a-awk!" said the little seagull once more, and held out his beak. Henry wriggled his tail. "Look here!" he protested. "Don't you realize what I am? I am a very large and fierce and frightening killer whale. What's the matter with you anyway. Why aren't you flying?"

"I can't," answered Timothy. "See, I have a broken wing. A man mended it for me but it's still no good. He was a nice man and he named me Timothy."

"Timothy!" echoed Henry. "Why did he call you that?"

"Because my toes are pink," answered Timothy.

"Oh!" said Henry, wriggling his tail. He wasn't used to such young grey and pink things, and he eyed it nervously. As he did, Timothy opened his mouth wide and once more squawked for something to eat.

That is where Henry made his first mistake. For he said alright, he would get him one small fish if he kept quiet. Then he dived and presently appeared with a nice grilse in his mouth, which he put in front of Timothy and hastly backed away. Whatever his problem catching fishes, Timothy was quite equal to eating them! He tore it viciously to pieces, clutching, grabbing and bolting all he could hold. When he had finished, and had rinsed his beak and ruffled up his feathers as best he could with his broken wing, he turned confidently to Henry and said, "Well, what shall we do now?"

Then Henry made his second mistake – he should have left at once – but he stammered, "Wha-at?" and was lost.

He tried to mend matters when the seagull repeated the question by saying he had to find the way out, remembering as he said it that he had almost forgotten he was looking for it anymore.

"What way out?" asked the seagull.

"Oh, the way out of this Inlet," said Henry gloomily. "You wouldn't understand," he added, and turned away.

"Oh yes I would!" said Timothy. "I've often been out of here. Often."

Henry turned and stared at him. "And you'll show me?" he asked eagerly. "You'll show me the way out?"

"Yes, but tomorrow, not tonight. I'm sleepy." And without even bothering to say goodnight, Timothy tucked his head under his good wing and went to sleep.

Henry was left there looking at him and wondering if it were safe to trust a seagull who was called Timothy because his toes were pink. But, as there was nothing he could do about it anyway, he decided that he would have a sleep too. So, side by side, out in the widest part of the Inlet they slept – Timothy, full once more and happy in spite of his broken wing, and Henry, worn out with listening and disappointment.

It WAS QUITE LIGHT – COLD, GREY, SHIV-ERY LIGHT – when Henry woke up next morning – or rather was wakened up – and looked about him trying to decide what had roused him.

"Squ-a-a-awk!" said a voice suddenly in his other ear, and then he remembered – Timothy, of course!

"I wish you wouldn't do that before I'm awake," grumbled Henry.

Most very small things would have felt rather alarmed to be grumbled at by a whale. But Timothy had no sense. He merely ruffled up all his feathers, and looked so soft and downy that it gave Henry a peculiar, weak feeling. Then Timothy opened his mouth wide, very wide, and kept it open – and Henry knew what he had to do . . .

When he had finished gorging himself Timothy rinsed off his beak and said, "Well, come along and I'll show you the way out now." So on down the sun's path they went, Henry trying to keep from slipping along too quickly, and Timothy paddling and paddling and paddling with his little pink toes to keep up.

But they had hardly gone more than half a mile before they were both exhausted, Henry from going so slowly and Timothy from going so quickly.

"You'll have to give me a ride!" gasped Timothy, stopping and holding his sides.

"Me!" said Henry. "Me, give a ride? I've never given anything a ride in my life!"

"You'll have to!" panted Timothy, "or I can't show you the way out."

"Well, how'll I do it? In my mouth?" asked Henry sulkily.

"No, on your back of course," said Timothy. "I'll climb on."

"Oh, alright," groaned Henry.

Then pat-pat-pat-pat, cold pink toes pattered up his back, accompanied by much squawking and fluttering of the one good wing, for Henry was *very* slippery.

"Now go slowly," said Timothy, trying to balance himself. "There's nothing to hold into."

Henry gave a cautious roll forward. Timothy slid squawking down his back towards his head. Just as he reached his blowhole, Henry let out his breath and up shot Timothy high into the air.

"You – you stupid, overfed fool!" Timothy spluttered as he flopped down into the water with a splash.

"Sorry!" said Henry cheerfully, "it wasn't my fault."

"Of course it was!" squawked Timothy. "Who ever heard of anyone having a waterspout in the top of his head, anyway!"

"Perhaps you had better swim after all," offered Henry hopefully. But Timothy wouldn't swim another inch. Henry could stay there for the rest of his life for all he cared.

"But I can't help it if I'm slippery," said Henry. "If you're so stupid that you can't stay on, you'll *have* to swim."

"I *won't*!" said Timothy.

"Well don't then!" said Henry. "I'll find my own way out!" And he blew savagely.

And Timothy . . . Timothy just ruffled up his feathers and put his head underneath his good wing. Henry's heart missed a beat. The last time Timothy had done that it had meant a whole night's sleep before he had stirred. Still, Henry was darned if this miserable bird was going to boss him.

"Alright, goodbye!" he called, watching Timothy anxiously.

Not a sign from Timothy. Henry backed slowly away. When he was about fifty yards away he sang out, "Well. So long!" and raised himself in the water to watch the effect.

But not a sign from the round grey ball, rising up and down gently on the little waves.

"Darn him!" said Henry.

He decided to try frightening him – making him squawk for mercy! He raced toward him, then he tore round and round him, making huge tide-rips whose waves leapt in all directions at once. But, up and down, up and down, crest and trough, bobbed Timothy. Head over heels he turned at times, little pink toes looking so limp and helpless; and Henry hated himself . . . Then he hated himself for hating himself . . . Miserably soft this Inlet was making him! No way for a he-whale to feel at all! But he could stand it no longer!

"Alright!" he shouted. "You can ride!"

Timothy, very pleased with himself, clambered up and steadied himself against Henry's big spar fin before he answered. "Do you see that point, the far one?" he asked.

Yes, Henry saw it quite clearly and calculated that with Timothy on his back it was going to take three hours to reach it, whereas by himself he could do it in about three minutes.

"Well, around that point is Porpoise Bay, and that is where the way out is," explained Timothy.

Henry pricked up his ears – porpoises were good substantial eating. "Are there any porpoises in there?" he asked eagerly.

"I don't know," answered Timothy impatiently, "I've never seen any. Do hurry!"

So somewhat damped in spirits, Henry started his miserable crawl and wriggle toward the distant point.

Henry felt that something was not right. He knew by the feeling that the water was getting shallow, and still no sign of Timothy's way out. He was just about to say as much when there were excited squeaks from Timothy.

"I can see it! I can see it! Straight ahead to your right!" Henry turned and went cautiously forward, trying to see in the darkness. But as far as he could see, trees loomed in an unbroken circle against a quiet sky. And what was more, the water got still shallower and Henry more uneasy. After all, Timothy was only a seagull. Then he felt weeds tickling his tummy, and he knew his vague fears had been correct.

"What are you stopping for?" shrieked Timothy, stamping with his pink toes.

"Because there isn't enough water," said Henry darkly.

"That doesn't matter!" stamped Timothy. "It's only fifty yards across here and then we are right out in the straits."

Henry caught his breath. "Fifty yards of *what*?" he asked with dark politeness.

"Sand!" cried Timothy. "Nice soft sand! What more do you want?"

So that's what soft pink toes led to – nice, soft sand! He might have known . . . There was a south wind blowing and from their sheltered bay he could hear the wind out in the straits piling the waves up against some unreachable shore. When you are a thirty-foot killer whale fifty yards of nice, soft

sand might as well be fifty miles of horrible, hard mountains.

He was very quiet, considering. "Get off my back," he said. And Timothy got.

"Now go on out into your straits," he said bitterly, and Timothy started off obiediently. But looking back over his shoulder in a bewildered way he asked, "Aren't you coming too?"

"I can't swim in sand!" bellowed Henry. "Do you think I'm a seal?"

"Oh!" said Timothy, wildly trying to shield himself from the furious splashes with his one good wing. "I didn't think of that."

"You wouldn't." said Henry, and added, "Get out of here."

And Timothy got . . . as fast as he could. Off across the nice soft sand he pattered, very wet and miserable, his broken wing trailing along the ground. Pad, pad, pad, went the little pink toes, and pathetic he looked, fading away into the darkness . . .

When Timothy had disappeared quite out of sight Henry began to back out. It took him some time, as it was very weedy and also he wasn't at all sure which way he had come. Then to add to his troubles he didn't know whether the tide was high or low and he knew he might be in very real danger of being stranded. And all because of . . . No! He'd never think of him again as long as he lived – or

any of the ridiculous things he had made him do. He shut his eyes tight to keep out the unpleasant thoughts. But immediately a procession of little pink toes and fluffy grey feathers padded across his mind. In the end he found that the best way not to think of him was to think of something else. He thought of being free.

Fast and furious came the wild free thoughts as he rolled steadily and surely along. In fact they came so fast that it was hard to think of anything else. He was through with cliffs that led to nowhere and roars that never stopped and seagulls that . . . never mind what. He'd depend on nothing and nobody but himself in future.

This was very narrow! Henry stopped and looked about him. A most queer place and a most peculiar feeling about it! Henry raised himself a little further out of the water and eyed it with his new bold look. The surface of the water was covered with tiny ripples. Each little ripple seemed to be trying to push the next little ripple, lip-lip-lipity-lap-plup, and then it would leap over and start pushing the next one. Along the shore, the water was making soft gurgling noises, climbing up the stones as far as it could reach and then suck-suck-suck, as it drew back again and pulled all the water out of the crevices as it went. Then it would try again a little further along, then suck-suck-suck, and then hurry off. Henry just lay there wondering and thinking how persistent they were, these tiny ripples, as they tore and fretted against his sides to get in. Then everything kept getting louder and louder and stronger and more insistent. And still Henry lay there, rather enjoying it all.

"It's certainly making enough noise about it! he chuckled. "Roaring like anything!"

Not until he said it did he realize what it was. Roaring! Of course it was Roaring! There was only one thing he knew of that could roar like that – and when it did, he wasn't supposed to be there!

With a terrified bellow he struck out for safety in the only direction he could, the way the water was going. He knocked the ripples over and sent them flying in all directions. He played havoc with the whirlpools, who were only beginning to feel their strength; and he made the waters suck still more greedily at the shores with the tumult of his going. And all the time the Roar grew steadily louder. Soon it began to be doubtful whether Henry was knocking the ripples or the ripples were knocking Henry. And although the whirlpools were not strong enough yet to suck him down, still they could hold their own. And as for the shore, the water had no time to suck now, it raced past and forgot all about it.

Suddenly, into sight came the straggling Indian village. The same village mentioned in his mother's lesson, the village where you waited until the Roar stopped. The village where Henry hadn't stayed, and so had got into all these troubles. At the sight of it, Henry knew that not only was he safe, but that he was safe at the right end of things. This time the Skookumchuk had not dragged him *in*, it had spat him *out*.

"Out!" he shouted. "Why, I'm out!"

"Pu-ph-e-e-ew!" he blew joyfully as he raced toward the small round islet that marked the entrance to Jervis Inlet.

Up rose the tall spar fin . . . then sank . . . then one pointed flange of the great tail . . . and sank . . . and Henry was gone. The waters of Sechelt Inlet roared louder and louder as they tumbled and foamed behind him and their roaring echoed on in Henry's ears. To him it seemed rather an angry kind of roaring, as though the strong waters were in a rage at the clever way he escaped them. To others perhaps it might have sounded more like the roaring of very loud laughter.

Sailing a Tow

Capt. Donald Peck

Back in 1921 I was captain and owner of a little steam tug engaged in general towing out of Vancouver. She was the *Topaz,* one of two built by the British Admiralty as a mine layer for Esquimalt Harbour.

The *Topaz* was later declared surplus and subsequently sold to the North Coast Towing Company of Prince Rupert, from which firm I bought her in 1917.

It was in the *Topaz* that I had a rather hair-raising experience. I had taken on a scowload of 470 tons of coal at Ladysmith for Woods & English, a pioneer logging camp at the mouth of Nimpkish River across from Alert Bay. Everything went along fine until we reached Camp Point in Johnstone Straits. Then on my watch, about eleven o'clock on a dirty black night, I hit a submerged log and lost the port propeller, knocked off clean at the hub. Of course the port engine ran away until the engineer got its throttle shut off. As we still had the starboard propeller we were able to proceed after tying down the towline on the starboard to balance up the strain and make her steer.

When my very capable mate, Mell Oreer, came on duty at midnight, we discussed the situation and agreed that we should, in the interests of safety, slow down the remaining engine in case we had the misfortune of hitting another log. There were acres of drifting debris everywhere as is often the case in the vicinity of York Island. The wind had freshened to a southeast gale by now and it was snowing a blizzard, reducing visibility to practically zero.

I laid down on the shelf in the wheelhouse with one eye and both ears open (this is the way towboat skippers usually get their rest) and then it happened. There was a resounding bump, the engine ran away like crazy and we were adrift with a scow of coal behind us.

I leaped to my feet, taking my blankets with me. As I went out on deck I saw the light of Cacroft Island through the snow. Since we were obviously favouring the Cracroft shore and since the tide had just turned to ebb, I immediately was concerned with the danger of being carried out through Blackfish Pass and then winding up goodness knows where or even being swept down on Swanson Island. All these calculations spun through my head in a split second. I had made up my mind what I must do in an effort to keep clear of the beach as long as possible.

First I called to the mate and asked him to put his wheel hard to port in order to get her into the trough and heading offshore while we still had steerage way. Then we rigged blankets between the funnel and the mast, and between the mast and the anchor davit, tied together with rope yarns and supported by pike poles. As there was a strong wind still blowing there was considerable strain on our improvised sails. So I was greatly encouraged to find, after I shortened the towline, that we were actually reaching ahead and moving through the water.

Now if someone would only come along that would take us in tow. As there were no radios in those days I was unable to call for help and as shipping was few and far between the chances of being picked up were rather remote.

However, after sailing for over an hour we sighted surf breaking on the shore a little forward of the starboard beam. She had reached clean across Broughton Straits and what we were sighting was Blinkhorn Island, too close for comfort. I ran aft and released the brake on the towing winch to give her better steerage while the mate swung her before the wind; then I again set the brake and proceeded to adjust the blankets across the bow. We cleared the island by a narrow margin. As we passed Beaver Cove daylight came in, the snow let up, and I saw that we were heading straight for the end of the breakwater at Nimpkish. I began to hope that no one would come along to claim salvage as I was confident that we had everything under control and that we would bring her to a safe anchorage behind the breakwater. This we did.

I must say we put in an anxious few hours. We became disabled at 3:25 a.m. and dropped anchor at 9:15 a.m.

My reward for a successful effort, besides the satisfaction of winning, was a very nice letter from Captain Cullington, who represented the underwriters, commending me for my action.

This was only one of the many trips made by the *Topaz* to Nimpkish, as she towed most of the equipment for Wood & English in setting up the original Nimpkish operation. However, none of the other trips were anything but routine.

Notes and Queries

Three cheers for Dr. A.C. Carder and his spunky defence of the Cary Fir legend in your last issue!

(Ed. note: It is on the basis of the Cary Fir, a 417' x 25' Douglas Fir allegedly cut in Lynn Valley near the turn of the century by one George Cary, that the record for the tallest tree ever cut is granted to British Columbia by the Guinness Book of World Records. *Experts quoted by Tod Carney on page 143 of* Raincoast Chronicles First Five *claim the Cary Fir is "a nuisance legend invented by the people of B.C. to appease the need for a world's record" and flatly state there is "not a shred of evidence any such tree ever existed," but Dr. Carder has challenged this claim on the basis of a photograph he remembers seeing in the Vancouver City Museum as a boy.)*

I can't help Dr. Carder in his search for this missing photograph but I have some evidence of my own which leads me to believe Dr. Carder is right and the experts are wrong.

In the fall of 1930 I with two friends was taking out split cedar bolts on Grouse Mountain. During our daily travel back and forth we decided one day to go and see the reported giant fir stump located not far from Lynn Valley centre. We found the place and were amazed to see the stump, planed, polished, and with a railing built around for a dance floor. Steps had been made for getting up on it and a bandstand built along one side.

The stump had been cut down to about four feet above the ground and the three of us took careful measurement of its diameter. To the best of my recollection it measured 27 feet.

One of my partners, Bill Crabbe, has passed away, but I have reason to believe the other, Babe Nugent, is still alive and could verify the above facts.

Incidentally, I believe there were other fir trees in B.C. that reached heights in excess of 400 feet. It is a matter of record that one was taken out of Copper Canyon by MacMillan Export Co. in fairly recent years.

Ernie Dalskog
Fanny Bay, B.C.

Peter Blue Cloud's reminiscence of Panicky Bell in Raincoast Chronicles No. 7 rang a bell for me because I was in Aero Camp at the same time as Peter and still have the steel tape measure he tells of being given when the railroad show wound up. Now he writes a letter to you from Bombay, New York, and I read it in Kuching, Sarawak. Strange how things work out.

Aero was an old camp when I went there in 1955. The big two-storey bunkhouse at the end of the railway line had been worn away by so many passing generations of caulk boots we used to joke there wasn't a plane surface or right angle left in the place. I met Panicky in the engineering office and he looked so much as Peter described except that Peter didn't mention Panicky's teeth. He didn't have any, which gave his face a "caved-in look" and caused him to lisp slightly. I should add that this did not in any way diminish the force of his words.

My job was to assist in laying out the truck roads and highlead settings and I remember Panicky standing squarely in front of our wall map, thumbs hooked in suspenders, scowling at our weeks of careful surveying and plotting. Occasionally he would take a tape measure out of his hip pocket, stretch it out on the map and "prove" that certain spurs or spars could be eliminated. The logging engineer certainly had to be ready on the comeback.

It is true Panicky never fired a man without cracking a joke and we often suspected that certain obvious candidates for his attention were enjoying a few days reprieve while Panicky thought up a suitable line with which to speed them on their way.

Panicky was one tough hombre, but he did have another side. One thing he was very interested in was introducing pheasants to the Queen Charlottes, and I remember on one occasion being attacked by an angry cock he'd set out in a patch of cutover. Later I was transferred to the company's Alliford Bay camp and when the subject of my accommodation came up Panicky told me to make my own arrangements. I retorted that I'd thought this was the kind of thing he was being paid to do, and Panicky jumped as if stung by twenty horseflies. He didn't say anything though, and I was too young to realize I hadn't won a show of strength but had been spared by an act of mercy. I had occasion to reflect on my good fortune at Alliford that spring, where we had as cook a fine old man from the Peace River country named Fraser Nicholson. He enjoyed our company and turned out first rate food for us, but the crew kept expanding and without anybody's realizing it, poor Fraser was becoming overworked and edgy. One day at mealtime he too answered back to Panicky, but in front of the men. He was fired instantly, with no thought of cracking a joke. Fraser stood there very straight, his white head erect and looked down on Panicky.

"Clear out of here," he said. "I want to be alone with my boys." Panicky pursed his lips, turned on his heel and left without a word. Later as I was walking down the corridor I heard him growling at the caretaker.

"Why the hell didn't you send for a flunky?" He said. "If that cook hadn't been plumb tuckered out this never would have happened!"

Panicky Bell a hard man? No doubt about it. A heartless man? No sir.

Those were wonderful years. I have always felt privileged to have spent them as I did. Dave Hansen and I worked out from Alliford, surveying road lines and looking for quarry sites. When we began the streams were jammed with spawning salmon. The following spring I was cornered against a cliff by an irate mother bear but scared her off by hammering my hard hat on a rock. On weekends we went down to Sandspit where square dances were held with recorded music in the social hall. The men viewed this with little enthusiasm, tending to stand around the walls, so that the women in spite of being in the minority often had to dance the male steps themselves. I remember approaching a lady I took to be my new partner only to have her skip by me saying, "Excuse me, but I'm a man!"

On one memorable day Dave and I were out on a steep slope from which we could see the channel separating the two main islands; we could see Queen Charlotte City, we could see Skidegate Village with its row of totem poles along the beach miniaturized by distance, and tugs with their big rafts gaining inperceptible way down the coast. It was one of those magical moments when time stands still, and became more so when I put my eye down for a compass sighting and espied in a clump of hemlock saplings directly ahead a Haida canoe. A cedar log dugout, laying unfinished and overgrown with moss where it had been abandoned by its carver untold years before. The outside was perfectly shaped but the inside had never been begun. The wood was totally rotted and a young hemlock grew out of the middle as if it were a mast.

I did not realize what wonderful times those were until several years later when I was setting chokers in the Willamette Valley above Molalla, Oregon. There I listened to the stories of logging adventure that seemed marvellously familiar until one day it dawned on me the Americans were talking of events which had taken place in the time of their fathers while I, in the Queen Charlottes, had been living with such things happening all around me.

Ian D. Hutchinson
Kuching, Sarawak
Malaysia

KYUQUOT DREAM: RUNNING THE OUTSIDE DOWN

There's a huge slide scooped out
Of that night mountainside
Steep and high inside. Time past.
Emotions returned. And high on the ridge
One tree stands out sharp and taller.

Near: the silent radars, domed and white.
Waiting: watching. Thin
Filaments of x-rays spidering out
This web which only touches. They
Note the motion and continue, turning
In their phosphorescent dream. And

I sense our voices centred high
In that circle of radio masts
Ringed desolate like some new Stonehenge
Mystic electrons flitting like bats or swallows
Beneath the night constellations
Pin-wheeling above inexorable, rising
Into the full-moon dawn. Enter

A brash roar under my hand
Like a float-plane driving off the water
As my boat breaks the stillness
Mind and water had gently merged.

John Skapski

STANDING among the towering buildings of downtown Vancouver or driving for mile after mile through the city's ever expanding suburbs, it is difficult to imagine that less than 100 years ago this was little more than a watering hole for a handful of loggers and mill workers.

In the following article Joe Simson describes the village of Granville as it was when his father, Calvert Simson, arrived here a century ago. At that time the population of Victoria was 12,000 and New Westminster was a thriving town of 4,000 souls. The total white population of Burrard Inlet, however, including the villages of Granville, Hastings, Moodyville and Port Moody, was less than 500.

When Calvert Simson died in 1958, the view from his home on Barclay Street in Vancouver's West End already was disappearing behind a wall of highrise apartments—but in his memory he held a clear picture of Burrard Inlet as it existed on the first day he saw it, June 25, 1884. On that day, a Wednesday, he had caught the morning stagecoach from New Westminster after finishing the night shift in the sawmill where he'd worked since his arrival in B.C. a month earlier. The air was fresh and clear, cleansed by a spring rain.

Like almost everything else in his life, the chain of events leading Calvert Simson to the south inlet shore that day was ordered and reasonable.

Born in 1861 in Penrith, Cumberland, in Northern England, and apprenticed to a merchant, Simson decided at age 22 to emigrate to the New World.

Joe Simson

Accordingly, he went for advice to his father, Captain George Simson, a shipowner engaged in a profitable trade between Australia and New Zealand. Although Captain Simson had never seen North America, he had heard seafaring associates describe Burrard Inlet as one of the best natural harbours in the world. Among the vast collections of maps, charts, coastal pilots and sailing guides in his library were charts of the lower B.C. Coast prepared some 20 years earlier by Admiral Sir George Henry Richards. These confirmed the inlet's advantages.

As well, Capt. Simson was aware of developments within the Empire which might affect the shipping business. He had heard of an agreement whereby the Canadian Pacific Railway Syndicate was to receive $25 million and 25 million acres of crown land in return for building a transcontinental railway to tidewater in Burrard Inlet. Although the exact location of the terminus had not been decided, it was then widely assumed to be Port Moody. His shipmaster's eye however, led Capt. Simson to nearby Granville with its deeper water and the potential to become one of the finest harbours in the world. He told his son that if he intended to settle in the New World, he could not do better than to choose the obscure village of Granville.

Calvert Simson had duly followed his father's advice, travelling via South Africa, New Zealand, San Francisco and Victoria. He arrived in New Westminster and worked nights at the sawmill until he heard of an opportunity to clerk in Granville.

Simson arrived that Wednesday at Granville's Sunnyside Hotel in time for lunch.

Gastown:

Gastown circa 1884

BEFORE calling on Ben Wilson, the owner of the waterfront general store, Simson made a tour of the village, which took all of 15 minutes. He found that it extended for about one block on Front Street (now Water Street). On the south or land side was a row of wooden buildings, some two storey but most little better than shacks. The larger buildings included "Gassy Jack's" Deighton Hotel and the Granville Hotel. On the water side was the Sunnyside Hotel, along with the home of George Black, the "Laird of Hastings", and his butchershop and slaughterhouse. There was nothing further on this side of Front Street until Ben Wilson's store and the Methodist parsonage. The water side buildings were constructed partly on piles over the water, which supplied a salt water sewage system. When the tide was low, the exposed mudflats were invaded by pigs rooting up clams, closely followed by the seagulls who cleaned up after.

There were three floats, one at the Sunnyside Hotel, another in front of the Granville Hotel and one at Ben Wilson's store. Almost all traffic, freight and passenger, was by boat. That was why Front Street was levelled and planked for only half a block. There was, however, a wooden sidewalk as far west as Ben Wilson's store.

The whole village boasted less than a dozen homes. There was an Indian church, a lawyer's office, a doctor's office, a telegraph office, a customs house, a jail and jailer's cottage.

Village commercial activity included a shoemaker, a Chinese laundry, a small drygoods store, Black's butcher shop, a small Chinese wash house and drygoods store, and two general stores. The village had 38 men employed within its boundaries, one of whom gave his occupation as "gentleman" — no doubt a gambler. There was a total population of 130, including those who worked at the Hastings Sawmill half a mile to the east, and others as far away as the Fraser River. The entire female population could be put in one big rowboat, as had been done for a picnic a few days before Simson's arrival.

The village was surrounded by tall stands of timber. Logging operations were in progress nearby, with oxen dragging the logs down greased skidroads to the shores of the inlet.

The most lucrative business in town was the sale of liquor to the thirsty loggers, mill hands and fishermen, who were well accomodated by the three hotels with their spacious saloons and by the "Hole in the Wall" saloon.

At the end of his tour of inspection, Simson applied for the clerk position at Wilson's general store. He was hired and put to work immediately, at a salary of $60 a month plus board at Joe Mannion's Granville Hotel. Wilson paid Mannion $10 a month, in groceries, to cover the boarding.

One of Simson's first customers was Ada Blair, the 14-year-old daughter of W.T. "Billie" Blair, across the street. Blair had been manager of the Deighton Hotel, while his wife had rented out the rooms at 25 cents a night. Now Blair was engaged in setting up his own establishment, the Terminus Saloon. He was a good saloonkeeper, enthusiastic about the product he sold — and consumed himself — and popular with his customers.

Everybody Knew Everybody

Simson was behind the store counter 12 hours a day and found the business vastly different from the English version for which he had been trained. Many of the customers were native Indians who spoke Chinook. Blair gave Simson a Chinook dictionary and corrected his pronunciation in the second language of the area. The two men struck up a friendship; one was a garrulous saloonkeeper who had seen it all in his 15 years in British Columbia; the other was a shy newcomer, a non-drinker and a greenhorn. They were an unlikely pair, but they respected each other's knowledge.

During the long summer evenings, Simson would visit the larger Hastings Mill store, where he was intrigued by the amount and variety of the stock. There he met Henry Harvey, who had been the mill store manager for many years but was ready to quit and go into business for himself. Simson also became friendly with Ainslie Mouat, bookkeeper at the store, and R.H. Alexander, the mill manager. In September, three months after his arrival, Simson took over as manager of the mill store.

THE HASTINGS Mill store carried clothing, including men's suits, overalls, flannel underwear from Victoria (red was popular as a supposed cure for rheumatism), shirts, socks, men's work shoes and fine boots, hats and caps, Indian shawls, cotton prints and blankets, bought largely from Victoria wholesale merchants.

A selection of patent medicines was sold, including Thomas Eclectic Oil, Peruna, Pains Celery Compound (the latter two being 75 percent alcohol and much in demand in the logging camps after a big drunk), Jamaica Ginger, St. Jacob's oil, scented hair oil, red rouge for Indian face colouring, liniments, cough mixtures and many others. These were bought from Victoria wholesale druggists.

Hardware included tinware from a New Westminster tinsmith, heavy unbreakable English crockery for camp use, ropes, axes, saws, nails, files, locks, hinges, oxbows, ox shoes and hickory goad sticks for the bull punchers, who were very particular as to quality.

Groceries generally came from Victoria, Portland or San Francisco on the ships arriving to load lumber. Shippers' agents would wire Simson when they had a boat ready to sail to Burrard Inlet, and he would inform them of the store's current needs by return mail.

An order of goods received at the Hastings Mill Store on September 3, 1883, consisted of 330 sacks of flour, 452 sacks of ground barley, 25 sacks of wheat (sold for chicken feed), 25 sacks of beans, five bales of salt, 10 kegs of pickles and 20 boxes of dried apples. Other orders included canned fruit, condensed milk, rolls of butter in brine, canned meat, china tea, and Alaska dried cod in bundles. A lot of corned beef and pork in barrels was sent to the logging camps, along with green salt sides of bacon to make pork and beans. Fresh pork was plentiful as each camp usually had a lot of hogs feeding on the swill.

The store did a good business with the logging camps and settlers up the coast, Indians and mill workers. An express wagon delivered to town customers.

The mill workers were paid a monthly wage plus board. The single men ate in the cookhouse. Wages were low and hours long. There was little to do but work and eat and sleep, with Sundays off, three holidays a year, and Granville's saloons, an ever-present refuge.

The Hastings Mill store also functioned as the post office. It had long counters down two inside walls. At the left counter was a small desk used for issuing money orders. Behind this, one of the window panes had been removed and replaced by a slotted board for drop letters. The mail arrived at Granville by stage and rowboat. On mail day many townspeople would gather in the store. Simson handed out their letters and put the other mail in a rack made of cigar boxes.

As postmaster, Simson had many inquiries from people trying to locate relatives who had neglected to write home. He got to know the hometowns of many loggers, who might come from Maine, the Maritimes or Quebec. Many of them were illiterate, and the postmaster wrote letters for them and then read the answers from their wives or sweethearts. On the rare occasion when an Indian received a letter, it was quite a task to translate it into Chinook so that he could understand it.

All outside accounts were paid by postal money order, and all savings were deposited in banks, usually in New Westminster or Victoria, by the same method. Simson was in effect the village banker, and soon discovered which citizens spent their pay in the saloons, saved it or sent it home.

BURRARD Inlet was still heavily wooded. Logging was selective, with only the biggest and best Douglas fir and most cedar being taken. Hemlock, smaller fir and most cedar were left standing. There were two large local camps supplying the Hastings Mill: one at Jericho, run by Angus Fraser, and the other near Little Mountain. There were also a number of small camps and handloggers on Burrard Inlet and the north arm of the Fraser River. These loggers felled trees directly into the water, and several steam tugs owned by the mill were engaged in towing booms of such logs. Prices paid for these number one logs were: four dollars per thousand board feet up to 40 feet in length, five dollars per thousand up to 55 feet, six dollars up to 70 feet, and seven dollars up to 85 feet. No log could have a knot, and all were over three feet in diameter at the small end. Today the worst logs in the boom would be worth at least $350 per thousand. The Moodyville and Hastings mills each produced over a million board feet of lumber per month, almost all of which was exported.

The Hastings Sawmill employed 100 men, including the gangs of Indians who loaded the sailing ships with lumber, and another 100 in the logging camps. Loggers earned $30 a month plus board. If it rained too hard, they did not have to work, but sat around the bunkhouse playing cards and getting paid for it. They came to town twice a year, at Christmas and July 1. All got into as much alcoholic trouble as possible, so they would have something to talk about the following six months.

The Indians lived in their own villages near Granville. There was one east of the mill, another in modern-day Stanley Park, and a third at Snauq, near Kitsilano beach. Most of the natives were customers at the mill store, where they would tie their dug-out canoes to the float. Simson soon got to know the Indians, who had names given to them by the white men for some distinguishing characteristics. There was "Pieface", "Dummy", "Howe Sound Jim", "Jimmy Jimmy", (son of the first Jimmy), "Mowitsh Jim", "Jim Grouse", and "Skookum Jim". There was Charlie Hundred, who always had a lot of small silver and gold coins. Jericho Charlie, father of the famous weatherman Domanic Charlie, owned a big canoe and freighted loads of barley and groceries to Angus Fraser's logging camp at Jericho.

The Indians had their own names for the whites. Simson, who had a healthy beard but little hair even in his twenties, became known as Halo-Yakso-Tyee, literally no-hair-chief or Chief Baldhead.

The mill store did a wholesale business with the merchants and hotel owners of Granville, who employed a boatman to freight over their supplies. He had a small scow with long sweeps which travelled between the village floats making deliveries. The boatman also han-

Hastings Sawmill,1885,reputed original mill 1865-7,burned Oct 1898.L to R;-"Dumps"
Baker(forearm bent);English foxhound;Chas Coldwell,sideways next to Calvert Simson,
hand in vest pocket,A.J.Mouatt,white waistcoat next. Peter Cordiner(tools in left
hand) next to "Silly Billy"Frost(both arms bent)   JSM

The Hastings Mill.

Hastings Mill Store,ft Dunlevy,new shop front conceals old store on right,new addition
on left.Cookhouse bell & ventilator,mill wharf & shed,plank roadway,Calvert Simson,
storekeeper(beard,before window) approx date 1888. C.S.Bailey & Co photo.   JSM

Hastings Mill Store.

dled the cargoes from Victoria, Puget Sound and New Westminster, which were unloaded at the Hastings Mill wharf, the only one on the south side of the inlet.

The sawmill property was a complete company town with an Anglican church, a library and reading room, and a school building which doubled as a community centre. There were about 20 children in school when Simson arrived. The married employees and executives of the mill had homes supplied, including a cottage for the store manager. There Simson lived with Mouat, the store bookkeeper.

Simson soon found that he had not only to speak the trade language of the Indians, but also had to talk knowledgeably with visiting ship masters about ship chandlery. The sailing ships loading at the mill were large square-riggers, unlike the small coastal vessels Simson had supplied during his apprenticeship in England. While he was familiar with hull and deck fittings, the rigging aloft was mostly beyond him. He solved this problem by importing books from San Francisco and memorizing the names, positions and functions of all blocks, lines, yards and standing rigging of full-rigged ships, brigs, barques and barkentines.

Sometimes a captain preferred to work out a ship chandlery order in the grog shop, with liquid refreshment instantly available. This posed a problem for a man who did not drink, but Billie Blair soon remedied this. His Terminus Saloon always kept a special bottle behind the bar for Simson, who drank quite a bit of cold tea when necessary on these occasions. So the captain suffered no pain, Blair was glad of the business, and the mill store got its order without embarassment to the storekeeper.

SIMSON had barely arrived in Granville before his father's prediction began to be borne out.

By 1884, the land speculators of Port Moody were about the only people who still believed that the transcontinental railway would terminate there. In June, W.C.Van Horne, vice-president and general manager of the C.P.R., formally opened negotiations with Premier Smithe of British Columbia for the extension of the rail line to Granville, with a right-of-way to Kitsilano via False Creek. It was first proposed to erect the terminal docks just west of the present Burrard Bridge.

By November, the terms of the agreement had been approved. Meanwhile, the C.P.R. was pushing the preliminary survey of the right-of-way west from Port Moody to Granville with Major Rogers (of Rogers Pass fame) in charge. At dusk in a snowstorm on Christmas Day, 1884, the survey crew reached Granville and drove a stake at the waterfront.

By this time, the village was being called Vancouver, a name selected by Van Horne, who wanted the Pacific end of the railway identified with Vancouver island, a name known throughout the world. In Granville and around the Hastings Mill it was accepted that the terminus of the railway would eventually be Coal Harbour, almost a mile west of the village. At that time Coal Harbour (named for its surface coal seams) had heavily wooded shores with a rough road linking the village to Spratt's Oilery, a floating cannery and reduction plant.

For 10 years there had been little change in the operation of the mill and the neighbouring village. Now a sense of change began to grow, and a strange face at the bar was less an occasion than before.

One stranger who was welcomed to Granville at this time was the pioneer boatbuilder, Andy Linton. No waterfront was ever more in need of a man who built a good boat. Linton was from New Brunswick, where he had been trained as a master shipwright. After his apprenticeship, he had moved west on the Union Pacific Railway to San Francisco and had gradually worked his way up the Pacific coast. Linton worked as a carpenter in the Moodyville mill for a few months, then went to Granville where he began building rowboats on the beach, living in a tent on the site. In the spring of 1885 he built two large decked-over floats with shake sheds on them to be his workshop and living quarters. The floats were anchored in deep water beyond the low tide mark and connected with the beach by a long approach float near the foot of present-day Carrall Street. Linton built double-ender clinker rowboats with hand-made spoon oars for which purpose he obtained edge-grain cedar from the Hastings Mill, specially cut to his order.

Linton's float soon became the centre of waterfront activity. It was the marina of its day. Rowboats were bought, sold and rented and Linton was soon building sailboats and organizing races. His establishment became a young men's club, with Linton the host. Almost everything started at Linton's float, including funerals, with the cemetery at that time being on Brockton Point. The coffin and mourners rowed from the float to the burial ground, the only alternative being a five-mile trek on a trail through the woods.

Linton built himself a sloop, the *May,* with which he won many local races. Often on Sundays he took Simson for a sail around the inlet, a new experience for the young man, and one which he found so enjoyable that he commisioned Linton to build him a 26-foot sailboat. This boat, of contemporary design, was a gaff-rigged sloop, very beamy, with a round chine, nearly flat bottom, and a centreboard. Simson named his boat the *Marcia,* after a favorite cousin in England, and kept it at the mill store float.

Every Sunday, weather permitting, Simson, Mouat and Ed Caulfield, the engineer at the mill, spent all day sailing. An ebbing tide in the morning would carry the yachtsmen west through the First Narrows, past the Point Atkinson lighthouse, and allow them to cruise around Howe Sound all day and then return with the flood tide in the evening. Often they stopped at Deep Bay on Bowen Island, and on a few occasions sailed along the weather side of Bowen Island to Tunstall Bay, where Joe Mannion, the "Mayor of Granville", had bought a large block of land. This area abounded in willow grouse, which could be killed easily with a slingshot.

On alternate Sundays, the tide would usually be flooding in the morning, and so the trio would sail east through Second Narrows, occasionally as far as the head of Indian Arm. However, this was an area of light winds, so a sail to Port Moody was preferred. There it was possible to tie up at the floats and dine at the hotel, then spend an hour or two looking around the C.P.R. dock where vast quantities of railroad construction materials had been unloaded and stockpiled from deepsea ships. Three mixed freight and passenger trains a week left Port Moody, as well as work trains running east to the end of the steel, and several steamships a week traded between Port Moody, Victoria and New Westminster.

If conditions were not favourable for sailing through either narrows, Simson and his companions would sail over to Moodyville, on the north shore of the inlet, and visit friends at the local sawmill. Another favourite outing was a sail into the mouth of one of the many rivers emptying into the inlet. The centreboard of the *Marcia* could be raised so that she could be beached. In time, Simson got to know all the local streams. He wrote: "In the fall, all of those streams were full of dog salmon. On the salt water there used to be two or three acres of ducks swimming off the Hastings Mill wharf eating the herring—the water was just black with them. Sometimes at night they made so much noise you could not sleep."

Any sport fishing at the time would have been for trout in streams, but it was no fun; there were too many trout. No white man trolled for salmon, although the waters were full of them. Why bother, when a salmon could be bought from an Indian for ten cents? The same applied to deer. Venison was five cents a pound.

Linton had started boat building at an opportune time: as fast as he could build rowboats, they were rented by the C.P.R. survey parties. From Hastings Mill to Coal Harbour, it was planned to lay most of the track on trestles over the water. The rest of the surveying had to be done through heavy bush and forest along the shoreline.

THE SURVEYORS finished work on the right-of-way in March, 1885, 15 years after the village of Granville itself had been surveyed.

There was still the 2,00 acre City of Vancouver to be laid out as called for in the C.P.R. agreement with the Smithe government. All this railroad activity brought quite a few men, some with their families, to the village of Granville. It also convinced some farsighted New Westminster businessmen to open branch offices and stores in Granville. Land speculators were also arriving. The boom was beginning.

The New Westminster and Port Moody Telephone Company ran a line to Granville and soon had over 30 subscribers. The village was expanding away from the waterfront. Dwellings were being built on Trounce Alley and Willow Street (now Cordova). School enrollment doubled by the end of the spring term, and was expected to reach 80 pupils in the fall. The increase in population and commercial activity was felt in the post office. At the end of the 1885 fiscal year, its gross revenue came to $750 as against $148 for the previous year. Simson spent much more of his time in his capacity as postmaster. The hotels and saloons of Granville were exceptionally busy, some being open seven days a week. They were the employment bureaus and meeting places of businessmen, surveyors, loggers and mill hands. Women were not allowed in the bars.

Nearly all the exclusive social functions of Burrard Inlet were held in the Mechanics' Institute building in Moodyville, on the north shore. In Granville, mixed gatherings such as dances, meetings and theatre were held in Blair's Hall. It was ideally located, being only a few feet from the back door of Blair's Terminus Saloon, and a small door was cut in the corner of the wall through which drinks could be placed, unseen, on a screened-off shelf. Very handy for a husband who wanted refreshment without his wife's knowledge.

One Friday evening late in November, 1885, Blair was rather startled to serve a Roman Catholic priest at the bar of the saloon. This was Father Patrick Fay, who had lately been ministering to the C.P.R. construction crews in the mountains and had hitched a ride in the caboose of the first transcontinental train to arrive at Port Moody. Over a glass or two of stimulant, Father Fay mentioned that he was seeking a place to conduct religious services, with the result that the First Roman Catholic Mass in Granville was duly celebrated in Blair's Hall on the following Sunday and for many Sundays thereafter. Father Fay—known as "the merry priest"—became a great favorite in the village and Blair's Hall became interdenominational. After Mass it was used for the Baptist's Sunday school.

The first newspaper in town, The Vancouver Herald, was established by William Brown. The first issue, published on January 15, 1886, reported the large meeting held at Blair's Hall, 250 being in attendance to hear John Robson, provincial secretary, urge the appointment of a committee to prepare a bill to incorporate the City of Vancouver. Ten prominent citizens were

Hastings Sawmill cottage, built prob.1870, formerly occupied Harvey, 1st storekeeper; then; 1885, by Calvert Simson, storekeeper & postmaster and Ainslie J.Mouatt, acct. Simson on chair, Miss Simson(sister) in door, gardiner(barrow) gard's son(watercan). Old hawthorn hedge planted by Harvey; cor.new office(old office burned winter 1884-5) Hastings Sawmill store exactlyopposite this cottage. photo taken 1885.Authority Calvert Simson. JSM

elected to the committee, which named R.H. Alexander as chairman. Advertisements were placed in the papers giving notice of a proposed act to incorporate the city, an area of more than 6,000 acres.

At about this time Simson submitted his resignation as postmaster (he was dissatisfied with his wage of 50 cents a day) and a new post office was established. Simson was thus the last postmaster of Granville.

The City of Vancouver was incoporated April 6, 1886, and held its first civic election May 3. By this time the population was just under 1,000, mostly transient workmen released from the C.P.R. mainline construction. Many were engaged in clearing the forest for the new C.P.R. townsite west of the old Granville boundary. Those who could qualify as carpenters were building substantial frame structures to shelter this population explosion. In less than three months, 150 new buildings were erected, until there was accomodation for over 600 men in eight good hotels.

THE MONTHS of April and May had been exceptionally dry and warm, ideal weather for the land clearing method of the day, which was to fell all standing timber and burn it. Hundreds of acres were on fire day and night. A dense cloud of smoke hung over the area, and at night the glow could be seen for miles. The clearing fires spread with the wind and there was no firefighting equipment to arrest them.

The Vancouver Daily Advertiser reported on May 26 that "Several building in the city were threatened with destruction by fire this afternoon. A change in the wind averted so serious a disaster. A few tents, blankets, etc. were burned before their owners could get near them. Afterwards the employees of the Hastings Sawmill were kept in readiness to prevent a wandering blaze from alighting on those buildings. A calm in the wind brought quietude to all."

The next day, "The slash fires near the foot of Burrard Street burned out of control today. Spratt's Oilery almost went. John McDougall's clearing camp also had a narrow escape; one tent burned and a small shack belonging to a shingle maker containing his effects was burned up. The wind died down and a light rain saved the other tents of the camp."

By June dozens of slash fires were burning day and night in an area from Cambie Street to Burrard and from the inlet to False Creek. As the fires got nearer, the businessmen of the city became apprehensive and held a meeting at Blair's Hall. One hundred dollars was subscribed to organize a hook and ladder company, with Blair as foreman.

Sunday, June 13, 1886 was the 94th anniversary of Captain Vancouver's charting of Burrard Inlet. By a strong coincidence, the weather conditions were similar to those described in Vancouver's log. For two days the wind had been blowing a moderate southwest and at daylight on the 13th had changed to a light westerly with fast-moving mare-tail clouds also from the west and a rainbow at sunrise.

Captain Vancouver would have next expected violent westerly squalls during the hottest part of the day, but if anyone amongst his successors to the place thought of this, they kept the fact to themselves.

Near the corner of Homer and Hastings Streets was a large pile of slash, in places 30 feet high. It was set afire at 7 that morning. The village air was thick with the smoke from such fires.

Billie Blair and his family left their rented home on Cordova Street that morning and strolled south across the False Creek bridge to a wooded site near the present Main and 7th Avenue where they were having a house built. Thankful to escape the slash fire smoke overhanging the village, they had a leisurely lunch, and

afterward Blair climbed down into his new well to work at a seam of coal which had been found at the 20 foot level.

While he was in the well, the gale struck. A blast of wind knocked a pile of lumber on top of the well, trapping Blair inside. It took him only a short time to climb to the surface and free himself, and by then the wind had subsided. In those few minutes, however, Blair lost everything he owned on the north side of False Creek, including his hall and the Terminus Saloon.

Simson and Mouat, also seeking escape from the town's smoke that morning, had left their mill cottage for a day's sailing. In the afternoon, they were near the north shore of the inlet when the westerly winds increased to a full gale, with squalls of hurricane force. The pair reefed all sails and beat back into the screaming storm for the mill. It took less than half an hour for them to cross the inlet, but in this short time the numerous runaway fires, fanned by the wind, had become one roaring inferno voraciously consuming the settlement's dry wooden buildings.

Simson and Mouat could only watch in horror while their town vanished in flames.

Then, suddenly, the wind shifted and dropped. The fire was over. In 20 minutes 700 buildings had been razed and 20 people burned to death.

HASTINGS Mill had been spared, so the two young men were able to land at the mill wharf, crowded with the stricken survivors of the holocaust.

By late afternoon, wagonloads of mattresses, blankets, food and medical supplies were arriving from New Westminster. The Blair house became an emergency ward for those who were not badly burnt, while those with more serious burns were taken to the Royal Columbian Hospital in New Westminster.

From his float, Andy Linton sent 20 rowboats to search Coal Harbour for survivors who had escaped the fire on makeshift rafts. The injured were taken to the Hastings Mill Store, and the others to sailing ships on the wharf. During the gale the barque *Robert Kerr* had dragged her anchor from the vicinity of Deadman's Island, and now lay conveniently just off the mill wharf. She took aboard 300 of the homeless.

When the *Marcia* had landed, Alexander, the mill manager, ordered Simson to keep the mill store open day and night. The cookhouse was opened on a 24 hour basis; nobody was turned away during the emergency.

Granville was gone, years of hard work turned to smouldering ruins in one afternoon, but rebuilding began in earnest the next day. Hastings Mill had over seven million board feet of lumber which was not good enough for export, and it was from this stockpile that Vancouver began to grow on the still warm ashes of Granville.

Seldom have the pioneer and modern phases in a city's history been so clearly demarcated as was Vancouver's by the fire of 1886. The flimsy little milltown at the edge of the world that Calvert Simson had followed his father's advice to in 1884 was to be rapidly transformed into a metropolis in which the young storekeeper would secure his fortune.

Was he content with this success, a future he had travelled half way around the world to gain? Three quarters of a century later, Simson wrote to Vancouver Archivist J.S. Matthews: "At first coming from the cities of Manchester and Salford, with a joint population of 900,000, one felt lost, but after awhile, one hated to see strangers coming in. It seemed to break up a pleasant community where everybody knew everybody."

Andy Linton · Boatbuilder

The Harbor

Hastings Mill Store wharf, spring, 1886. only dock for passengers and freight. Bqe" Robert Kerr" in stream. freight shed, and corner new addition mill store; schooner with deck load hay; barge with towing bits on beach. man with wheelbarrow. Indian Klootch name board old tug "Maggie" nailed to boathouse. pleasure yacht, rowing boats; horse and wagon collecting Victoria and Port Moody package freight. Paddle wheel tug "Mermaid" on marine ways. tow rope. fence. flowers. piledrivers. Steamship "EVANGEL", from Roche H'b Alderman C.A. Coldwell, first City Council, possessed this photo, and gave date as "Spring 1886." Appears to be H.T. Devine photo J. S. M. marine ways 100 feet due west Dunlevy Ave. "EVANGEL", 77 tons, 13 men, every 3 or 4 days from San Juan Is'ds with farm produce, etc. Aug. Sept. 1886. Yacht "Marcia" owned Calvert Simson, mill storkeeper. "Mermaid" owned R.H. Alexander, mqr. and Ainsley

The Pork-Pie Hat

D.W. Higgins

YOU want me to tell you something about Burrard Inlet in the early days. Well, although I can tell you a good deal, I did not get here until 1865, when Stamp put up the Hastings mill, but the first sawmill was built by Hicks & Graham in 1863. The first white men who settled on the site of Vancouver were John Morton, William Hailstone and Sam Brighouse. About Christmas, 1862, they located 550 acres, and when the government came to survey the land it was sold to them at one dollar per acre. Morton and Brighouse afterwards divided their land, which lay west of Burrard Street and took in English Bay, by tossing a coin—head or tail. The land which had been bought for $550, and was disposed of by the toss of a coin, is now worth between five and six million dollars. A single lot has been sold for $45,000! I was employed as a hand logger at that time. Most of the hands at the mills were Americans and Indians. There were no Chinese or Japanese then. The little village which sprang up near the Hastings mill was called Granville. Deighton's hotel was the only place of entertainment. Its owner was called Gassy Jack, for the reason that he was such a gas-bag, always talking and blowing. After a while people got to calling the place Gastown, after Jack. He used to keep his money in a "safe," as he called it; but it was in reality a cigar-box, such as holds a hundred cheap cigars. This "safe" used to rest on a shelf back of the bar during the day, and at night Jack would lock it up in a drawer and go to bed. No such thing as a robbery being possible ever entered his head. He was honest himself, and imagined every one else was the same.

At the time of which I am speaking I worked at Hastings. Captain Raymur was in charge, with Mr. R. H. Alexander as his assistant. I was on the day-shift, and one evening—it was at the close of a beautiful day, warm, clear and still—I came up to the hotel from my work. I was just tuckered out, I was that tired and hungry, and was taking a swift wash in a tin basin that stood on a packing-case near the hotel door. Half a dozen other hungry men were waiting their turn to wash and dry themselves upon the one towel, when I heard the clattering of horses' hoofs on the hard road. Looking up I saw two Indian ponies, on which were seated a gentleman and a lady. The gentleman was dressed in a suit of dark clothes that looked worn and dusty. He was light complexioned, and his hair, which was parted in the middle, was streaked with grey. He wore a long, heavy, tawny moustache which swept across his face and almost lost itself in his ears. I remember I thought at the time that but for the hairy ornament he would be quite good-looking. The lady seemed to be about eighteen. She had the loveliest black eyes, large and lustrous, and fringed with the longest lashes that you ever saw. She had on a dark-green riding-habit, and on her jet-black hair was perched a little turban of a style then much worn, and known as the "pork-pie." She had a sweet, engaging face, and sat her horse gracefully. The man dismounted, and assisted his companion to alight. She leaped down, with the skirt of her riding-habit gathered in her hand, and after taking in the crowd with a quick glance of her glorious eyes, she busied herself with beating her habit with a riding-whip, sending up little clouds of dust from the folds.

"Gentlemen," exclaimed the man, in a soft and pleasant voice, as he removed his hat, "good evening."

"Good evenin'," returned one of the boys.

"Kindly direct me to the landlord," said the new arrival.

"You will find him at the bar mixin' lickers," said the spokesman.

At this moment Gassy Jack appeared at the door, and seeing the gentleman and the beautiful lady, removed his hat and bowed almost to the ground, for he was awfully soft on the woman question.

"You are the landlord, I presume," said the gentleman.

"I ham," replied Jack.

"Well, my daughter and I have ridden over from New Westminster, and she is very tired. Can we get two rooms, with supper to-night and breakfast in the morning?"

"Sure!" cried Jack, in his most effusive manner. "Yer can have the best the house has got, and what it hasn't got I can get yer."

"We heard," said the gentleman, "that there is a vacancy here in the school-teaching line, and as my daughter is a teacher we thought we would cross and look at the surroundings before applying for the place. We like the appearance of things. My name is Crompton—Lionel Crompton—and my daughter is

Miss Crompton.''

"By gracious!" said Jack, striking his fat thigh with his hand, "it's just what we want—a schoolmarm—and I'm a trustee, and I'll help your gal git the job."

"Thanks, awfully," returned Mr. Crompton. "We'll stay here overnight, and perhaps two or three days longer. Kindly have our horses looked after."

Jack summoned the Indian hostler, and the animals were led off to the stable. While this conversation was in progress Miss Crompton continued to dust her habit, occasionally raising her pretty eyes to survey the group that stood spellbound by her beauty.

"Come, daughter," said Mr. Crompton, "we will remain here," and giving her his arm he conducted her to the parlor, as Jack called his best room. The parlor was small and low-ceilinged. Its walls were adorned with cheap pictures of uproarious color and design, and a card bearing the legend, "God bless our home." There

were two or three books, among which was a hymnal, for Jack allowed church services to be held there on Sundays. In one corner was a piano with a few sheets of music lying upon it. The girl laid down the whip, removed her "pork-pie," and went to the piano. After running her fingers over the keys she began to play, and, oh! the music that she brought out. It swept through the house in a great gust of melody, and floating outside filled the woods with delicious sounds. It was a great treat, in the midst of that wildwood, to hear such strains. Presently she sang in a clear and strong contralto several popular airs, and when supper was announced, she was in the midst of "Robin Adair." Didn't the boys who were gathered at the door just go mad with excitement, and didn't they clap, and whoop, and shout for more. Some who were due on the night-shift at Hastings wanted to stay and listen all night.

As father and daughter passed into the diningroom we

yer can have the best the house has got...

177

regular borders sheepishly followed, and took our seats on either side of the table. The evening meal never amounted to much. The food was generally wholesome enough, but on that occasion it was rich. Pork and beans were not in evidence for a wonder, and there was cold chicken on the list, and Jack, who could not take his eyes off the beautiful vision, waited on the pair in person and saw that they wanted for nothing. We boys supped high that night, and when the meal was over and the party had gathered on the verandah, Deighton passed around the cigars. As daylight faded the girl returned to the parlor, and again attacked the piano, to our intense delight. In the meantime a few of the boarders managed to pluck up courage and spoke to her, and found her affable, but very prudent and sedate.

Some one in a burst of enthusiasm proposed a dance, with Indian girls as partners; whereupon the young lady said she did not play dance music, and dancing was sinful; besides, it was bed-time and she would retire. Wishing all a sweet goodnight, she again swept the group with a glance from her expressive eyes. Then she kissed her papa, and gathering up her long skirts with the remark, "Don't be late, dear, and don't drink any more," she walked toward the stairs. There were two coal-oil lamps burning on the table, and I seized one and volunteered to light the girl to her room. She thanked me, and we went upstairs, and I led the way to the door. Then she said:

"May I ask your name?"

"Certainly," I replied; "my name's Simmons—Bill Simmons."

She laid a little hand on my arm and looked long and searchingly into my eyes. I trembled like a leaf on a tree. The floor seemed to be giving 'way beneath my feet. All things were in a whirl and my knees just knocked together. In my excitement I almost dropped the lamp, and how I refrained from falling at her feet and telling her that I loved her, I cannot say. Perhaps I did—I don't know—I was so upset. In a few seconds I recovered myself, and then I saw that her sweet eyes were filled with tears. In broken accents she said:

"Oh, Mr. Bill—Simmons, I mean—can I trust you?"

"You can," I remarked; "hope I may die if you can't," and I drew a cross on my chest with my finger as a mark of fidelity.

"Oh! my poor, dear father," she moaned.

"What's the matter with your old man—I mean your daddie?" I asked.

The poor thing just leaned her head on my arm and my body shook with emotion, while I trembled and felt like sinking through the floor. I wanted to put an arm about her, and tell her that she was dearer to me than life, but I couldn't, for she held one arm, and the other was occupied with the lamp. At last she said:

"How can I tell you? But I must. My father is addicted to drink. When he gets among a lot of nice, handsome young fellows like you and Jack he never knows when to stop. I want you to promise me that when you go downstairs again you will do all in your power to get him to bed."

"All right," I said, "I'll do it."

The dear girl murmured her thanks, and resting her hand again upon my sleeve gave my arm such a squeeze that the blood seemed to leave my heart and fly to my head. Again everything seemed to give 'way. My head went round and round like the great fly-wheel at the mill, and a buzzing sound, as of a circular saw ripping through a plank, filled my ears. At this critical moment the girl released my arm and opened the chamber door. Then I recovered myself and said, in faltering tones:

"Don't thank me—you are quite welcome."

Again she murmured her thanks, again she placed her hand on my arm, and again the hot blood flowed

like a current of electricity through my veins. The door stood open behind her. She gave me another long, searching look, and then, quick as thought, she sprang backwards and slammed the door in my face! Then the key was turned in the lock, and when I came to I found myself standing alone on the threshold. I pulled myself together with difficulty, and tumbled, rather than walked, down the stairs. In the bar I found the strange gentleman "shouting for the house," as they say in Australia, or "standing treat," as British Columbians put it. All hands lined up at the bar, and Jack, who was very much "on," insisted upon toasting the strangers.

"'Ere's to the new boarders!" he shouted, "'specially to the young 'un. Her father's a dandy, but she's a peach."

The toast was drunk with cheers. The health of the old 'un was next washed down the parched throats of the millmen and loggers. The Jack got his share of toasting, and before midnight all were in a state of how-come-you-so? and wobbled on their legs. The old gentleman had to be assisted to his room, where he was put to bed with his boots on. While we were tucking him in the covering he knocked on the partition of his daughter's room and called out:

"Alish—Alish, dear (hic), are you all right (hic)?"

"Yes, papa."

"And (hic) are you very, very comfor'ble (hic)?"

"Yes, papa."

"Then good-night, my sweetheart (hic), pl-pleasant dreams to you (hic); may good digestion wait on appetite (hic)."

"Oh, fie, papa!" cried the girl.

"Yesh, dear (hic), what ish it?"

"You've been drinking again. Oh, my! What will poor mamma say?"

"Shay? Why she'll shay, 'I'm a jolly good feller, which nobody can deny.' Good-night (hic). Shay, Alish, to-morrow I'm to be Queen of the May (hic). and they're going to kill the fatted calf in my honor (hic)."

Alice, apparently disgusted with her father's condition and incoherency, made no reply, and he presently turned over and went to sleep. Then the house fell into a deep slumber, broken only by the snoring of inmates as they slept off their heavy potations.

The morning broke brightly. The sun was high in the heavens, and the little birds in the woods had break-fasted and were caroling their thanks, when the Indian hostler, who had joined in the revelry, awoke from his drunken stupor and proceeded towards the stable to look after the horses. He stopped at a spring to cool his parched throat, and then dragged his aching head and unwilling limbs to the barn. He opened the door and peered into the stalls. To his surprise they were empty! Where he had fed and bedded two ponies the night before there was a void. Scarcely trusting his eyes at first he stood open-mouthed, gazing into the untenanted stalls. Then, uttering the one word "Clattawahed" (Gone), he rushed to the hotel, and knocked up Jack, who, in turn, ran to the stable, and then back to the house. He ascended the stairs two steps at a time and knocked at the door of the old man's room, gently at first; but meeting with no response he gave a thundering bang and shouted:

"Beggin' your parding, Mr. Crompton, but your horses is stolen."

Still no reply. Then Jack turned the door handle and slowly pushed his red face into the room. The bedclothes were tumbled and the room was in disorder. The window was wide open, but the gentleman, like his ponies, was gone!

Jack flew to the room to which the girl had been conducted. He tapped gently. Then a little harder, and still meeting with no response, he softly opened the

Jack tiptoed into the room...

door. The blind was closely drawn down, and the light in the room was uncertain, but he could discern the beautiful black hair which he had admired so much the evening before straggling over the pillow, and, what struck him as most singular, resting on what seemed to be her head, was the pork-pie hat!

"Strike me lucky," he shouted, "I'm jiggered if the gal hasn't gone to bed with her hat on for a nightcap! Miss," said he, "wake up! Your daddy's gone, and the horses is stolen."

There was no answer, and, with an air of becoming modesty, Jack tiptoed into the room, and advanced to the side of the bed before he discovered that there was no girl there! She, too, had gone, leaving behind her a wig and a hat. On a chair was spread her dark-green riding-habit. Jack beat his head with his clenched fist, and bounding downstairs to the bar ran straight to the drawer in which he nightly deposited the "safe." The drawer had been pried open and the "safe" was gone, too.

"Robbed, done up, buncoed, ruined!" he wailed. "there was four hundred dollars, nearly, in that 'ere safe, and that man and that girl is the thieves."

A hue and cry was raised, and a party was soon on the trail of the supposed robbers. A short distance away were found eight gunny sacks that had been tied about the horses' feet to muffle the sound of their tramping as they were led past the hotel; and near the same spot the "safe," rifled of its contents, was picked up. The pursuers reached New Westminster quickly, but the robbers had got away by crossing to the American side and reaching Washington Territory. It was afterwards learned that they were male members of a strolling theatrical company, who, learning of Jack's careless habit with money, had disguised themselves for the purpose of robbing his "safe." The fellow who acted the part of the girl and captivated the lumbermen was one of the most expert impersonators of female characters then on the Coast. They were never caught.

Jack returned from the search a wiser man. He bought a real safe and became a woman-hater. The wig he committed to the flames and the pork-pie hat adorned the head of the wife of the Indian chief of the tribe for a long time. When it became so dilapidated that even the Indian woman would not wear it, the hat was sent to a museum as the cooking utensil of a prehistoric race, unearthed on the shore of Burrard Inlet. It was classified and may still be seen there.

THE WRECK OF THE BEAVER

The Truth Comes Out

THE *S.S. Beaver,* launched at Blackwall, England, in 1835 and brought the following year to the northwest coast to serve as a supply vessel for Hudsons Bay Company trading posts, is much celebrated as the first steamship on the north Pacific.

In the 50 years she plied these waters she served as a gunboat, a survey vessel, a mobile trading post, a floating courtroom, freighter, passenger ship and later as a log tug and camp tender — so far surpassing original expectations of her that a biographer was able to subtitle his account "The Ship that Saved the West."

The wreckage of the 109 ton sidewheeler, stranded on Prospect Point at the entrance to Vancouver Harbour on July 26, 1888, provided Vancouver with an enduring historic image, a signature of place that has long outlasted the actual hulk, which was disloged by the wake of the steamer *Yosemite* in 1892.

The demise of the *Beaver* also left Vancouver with a mystery of sorts, namely how this remarkably fortunate and durable vessel, which had survived half a century in some of the most treacherous waterways in the world, managed to come to grief on the very doorstep of her home port.

The authorized version of the accident, handed down by the late Vancouver archivist Maj. J.S. Mathews and quoted in the book referred to above, states simply that the ship was leaving the harbour late one night and somehow got too close to shore.

Capt. William Cates, an accepted authority on Vancouver waterfront history, has elaborated on this story, pointing out that the *Beaver* had poor steerage at best and in this instance was crowding shore to take advantage of the outrunning backeddy that forms there on the incoming tide. He quotes his pioneer father Capt. Charles Cates as saying, "On this trip the crew were sober and therefore not normal."

Captain George Marchant, whose unfortunate fate it was to skipper the *Beaver* on her last trip, in a 1919 magazine article stated in his own defence that there was a thick fog at the time of the accident.

I have reason to believe, however, that the fog was in Capt. Marchant's head.

In 1941, more than 50 years after the wreck of the *Beaver*, I took my father to Prospect Point to attend a dedication ceremony. The authentic "walking beam" of the *Beaver* was officially presented to the city of Vancouver. There were speeches praising the courage and spirit of the *Beaver's* pioneering crews. As the ceremony ended, an elderly member of the audience got up on the speaker's platform and delivered an impromptu address of his own.

He identified himself as William H. Evans, second engineer on the *Beaver* when it was wrecked. This caused quite a stir. He said he remembered the event very clearly, for he had been the only sober man aboard. Being too young to drink, he had been left on the ship to keep up steam while the other crewmen had gone to the Sunnyside Hotel.

The crew returned and set out for Thurlow Island in high spirits, singing as they went. The *Beaver* had gotten as far as the First Narrows, Evans said, when someone discovered that the ship's stock of liquor had been left ashore. That called for immediate action, and the wheel was turned smartly. Unfortunately, it was turned to port instead of to starboard, and the old ship was ridden onto Prospect Point by the outrunning current.

My father was probably the only listener who took this information calmly. He had been storekeeper at Vancouver's Hastings Mill store when the *Beaver* had met her end, and the engineer's story dovetailed with accounts of the incident he had received at the time. In particular, it coincided with what he had been told by George Weeks, then manager of the Hudson's Bay wholesale operation in town. The night of the grounding Weeks had been in the Sunnyside Hotel, and he told my father he had seen the crew of the *Beaver* assembled at the bar enjoying themselves in fine style. They finally left around midnight, in good spirits, but returned two or three hours later, announced the ship was stranded on Prospect Point and resumed drinking. The bars in those days were open 24 hours.

Shortly after the 1941 dedication, I was able to corroborate the engineer's statement by talking to Billy Clark, a Vancouver businessman who was probably the only witness to the *Beaver's* demise. In 1888, Clark had been working as a boom man for a logging operation at the mouth of the Capilano River. Clark told me that on the night of July 26, he had heard singing and looking east he saw the *Beaver* passing Brockton Point on her way out of the inlet. He could hear "Sweet Adeline" and other melodies of the day being sung with great gusto, the choruses carrying over the noise of the steam engine. When the old tug came out of the narrows, Clark saw her turn to port and run aground.

I think this leaves little doubt about how the most historic ship ever to sail out of a B.C. port met her end. Certainly, it has a more realistic ring, according to my understanding of how things were done in those days, than the story that is told in most history books.

by Joe Simson

Hoffar H-1. Note water-cooled boat motor complete with radiator

Vancouver's First Aeroplane

*U*NLIKE *their cautious branch-plant counterparts of today, Vancouver's pioneer business people would try just about anything once—and none were truer purveyors of this spirit than the Hoffar brothers, Jim and Henry.*

Operating on pure gall Henry Hoffar founded the original Coal Harbour shipyard at the age of 19, an enterprise which has prospered in various forms to the present day.

A less successful but even more audacious undertaking was the brothers' venture into aviation. With no experience in the field and with none of the technical knowledge supposedly indispensable to such projects, the Hoffars in 1915 built and flew British Columbia's first airplane.

*The H-1 was a two-seater biplane equipped with floats. It was copied from a picture in **Flight** of the first Avro tractor biplane, a construction method which obviously left more than a few details to the Hoffars' ingenuity. The motor, for instance, was a two-cycle, six-cylinder Roberts marine engine which previously had resided in a speed boat. Instrumentation consisted solely of one ignition switch to short the magneto.*

Despite all odds, the H-1 flew. Henry Hoffar, the Christopher Columbus of Vancouver flight, tells his own story.

As we were operating a boat building shop, the aircraft was a part time job and took about four months to complete.

Having built it, we then had the problem of learning how to fly it. We figured the safest way to do this was to taxi up and down the harbour, gradually getting the feel of the controls until we could get her flying about 10 feet off the water. Then we would practice turning and landing, etc. However, things did not work out as planned.

My brother Jim and I tossed a coin to see who would have the first crack at it, and Jim won. He climbed into the cockpit; I made a line fast to our speed boat and we cruised to the centre of Burrard Inlet. I cast off and Jim proceeded to prime the six petcocks on the cylinder heads. Then he climbed down to the float behind the prop, hanging on with one hand and turning the prop with the other. The motor fired and Jim climbed back to the cockpit, no easy feat with the plane in the meantime turning in a tight circle.

As I watched, the plane straightened up and ploughed down the inlet at about 10 knots. About a mile away, Jim swung around and headed back towards the boat. I could hear the increasing bark of the motor, and as the plane passed about 100 feet away I could plainly see that the float was clear of the water. Then suddenly it was climbing and finally levelled off at about 100 feet.

Needless to say I was scared stiff, as we had not planned it this way. We decided we should do *at least* an hour of taxiing before taking off.

However, Jim seemed to be flying straight and level, and I could see him make a wide, flat turn over by North Vancouver. He appeared to be losing altitude and I figured that he was going to attempt a landing. This he did about 100 yards away. He simply flew onto the water at full throttle, and a beautiful landing it was, not at all like the bouncing around when I made my first attempt some days later.

feet. It contained the propeller and the Roberts motor out of the H-1.

The H-2 was chartered to the B.C. Forestry Department for use on forest patrol, and after Jim had test flown it for about an hour it was immediately turned over to forestry officials, who had secured the services of a student pilot from Trenton.

The following day this chap took off from Burrard Inlet and circled over English Bay. At an altitude of about 1,000 feet above the West End, the motor cut out, whereupon he went into a nice flat spin. The pitched roof of the residence of Dr. Farish provided an ideal landing strip and the pilot found himself in a bathroom which had just been vacated by the maid.

The pilot suffered only minor bruises and scratches and no reason was given for his failure to pull out of the spin. After souvenir hunters took over that evening, there was little beyond the engine to cart away.

This ended the B.C. Government's first attempt at forest patrol by air.

The following year I designed the "H-3" flying boat which was equipped with a six-cylinder, 150 hp Hall Scott engine. The life of this aircraft proved to be quite short. While taking off on a projected flight to Victoria, we struck a deadhead off Burnaby Shoal and the ship was a total loss. Fortunately our injuries were not severe.

We cooled down our avocation for some time. Then in 1919 we bought 3 surplus JN4s and equipped them with floats along the lines of the H-1. As far as I know, this was the first Jenny conversion for seaplane use.

We sold them from Canada to Manila; one of the Canadian sales was to Price Bros. in Quebec.

This was the last aircraft activity by Hoffar Bros. We had a lot of fun, but realized that as aircraft builders and pilots *we were damn good boat builders.*

He stopped, I towed him to the float and made fast. Then, being his elder, I gave him hell for not following our plan.

Jim explained it this way. "I was going along on the water fine and then it did not feel so bumpy and I looked down and the water seemed a long way off. I kept going and near North Vancouver I turned slowly and decided that the best way to get down was to keep flying lower and lower, which I did till I felt the pontoon hit, then I switched off the motor."

We operated the H-1 for about a year until the steel bracing wire was becoming very rusty, and we decided that the aircraft was not too safe. Actually it must have had a structural safety factor of *minus* 100 percent.

We removed the motor, which was in fine condition and had never failed, and such fittings as turnbuckles, etc. The rest was buried at sea. We did retain the centre float, and some years later it was being used on Coal Harbour as a canoe.

The Hoffars' next two airplanes had briefer and more unfortunate histories.

The H-2, completed during the summer of 1917, was a two-seater flying boat biplane with a wing span of 34

STEVESTON 1926

Mr. Minami's house stands on piles. When the tide is low he goes down the wharf ladder to his fishing boat. When the tide is high, or when the Fraser is in flood, he can step into his boat from his veranda.

The outside of the Minami house is not much to look at but its inside is pleasing. It has grass floor mats, some low bamboo stools, a shiny black stove, a table and a dwarf evergreen in a tub beside its door. The room is very, very clean.

When Mr. Minami laughs, his eyelids flutter like the wings of tiny birds. Mrs. Minami only smiles, bows slightly and clasps her hands, one above the other. The Minami children play on the narrow wharf. When I asked Mr. Minami if he was not afraid one of them would fall into the water he shook his head and laughed. When I said one might, he shook his head again and laughed again.

One afternoon when I came to visit, Mr. Minami was shaping small, oblong pieces of wood. He sawed with a saw which sawed backward and planed with a plane which planed backward. After finishing the pieces he painted Japanese writing on them with a brush which had a bamboo handle. "My cousin going Japan. These for his baggage, say where."

"Your cousin goes on a visit?"

"No. Go home. Sick here." Mr. Minami tapped his robust chest.

"Too bad."

"Yes. Too bad. Oh well..."

When Mrs. Minami is mending nets her fingers move quickly and sometimes as she works she sings, not a song, not a tune, just small high notes, circling around and around not going anywhere. Her children sing only school songs. Her eldest daughter goes to high school and is learning to be a stenographer. She makes marks on smooth paper with a graceful pen.

When the salmon are running strongly, Mr. Minami is very happy. When there are not so many salmon he is not unhappy. But when a snag fouls his net, or when a steamer ignores his riding lights and ploughs through his net he is very unhappy.

One evening before Mr. Minami went fishing, he took me into the cabin of his boat. He showed me his Easthope engine and his galley stove with cedar kindling and fir bark laid ready. A narrow roll of paper with Japanese writing in gold and black hung from the ceiling above the steering wheel. When I asked, he said the writing was of Japanese prayers. "Camasami, like this." He bowed his head and rubbed the flats of his hands together. "Every day camasami, good. This boat not sink. Other men only some days camasami not so good. Big wind come. Those men, Oh Camasami, camasami. Too late. Those boats go down sure. Every day camasami good, only some days camasami, no good." He paused, eyes partly closed, head tilted, considering. "I think this country no camasami. Yes?"

"No. But plenty good men, plenty church men.."

"Hah, not so good." He shrugged. "Oh well..." He was leaving churchmen to their fate. Fate would deal with them. He must go fishing.

WILL VIVIAN
Pioneer Engine Builder

David Conn

"The power behind the Pacific Fleet."

EVER since the first Hastings sawmill at Vancouver, this province has most often found itself in the role of primary resource hinterland, with reprocessing and manufacturing carried out elsewhere. However, in the earlier part of this century, homegrown secondary industry also flourished in unique B.C. fashion, producing equipment for local enterprises. One of these industrial pioneers was the Vivian Engine Works of Vancouver, which expanded beyond its local market to become a worldwide exporter.

When you come to think of it, virtually every power plant on the coast, every logging donkey, and a good majority of fishboats all had Vivians at one time. Name any village up in the interior and it'd have a Vivian power plant. They all had our power. *

Will Vivian has been called the Henry Ford of the Canadian diesel industry—a self-taught tinkerer who began with an idea and built up an international marine engine business that helped motorize the B.C. fleets. But the Ford name is still with us, while the Vivian name has faded into obscurity.

Will Vivian grew up in 1890's Vancouver. His father was a carriage painter and the family was poor. Young Will left school at the age of nine and went to sea as a cabin boy on the trans-Pacific *Empress of China*. Later he worked on fishboats in the Gulf and in the Fraser, and as a mechanic's helper at the Easthope Engine Works in Coal Harbour.

Still in his mid-teens, Vivian went to San Francisco in 1906 and found a job with an early machine shop, the Imperial Engine Works. There he picked up engine lore and tinkered with his own designs at night. The precocious Vivian had chosen a career. He returned to Vancouver and set up a tiny shop at 1090 West 6th Avenue, on the south shore of False Creek. His first engine was finished in 1909, when he was nineteen. It was the milestone from which he measured his progress. To prove that the single-cylinder, six-horsepower kicker was no toy, he installed it in boatbuilder Henry Hoffar's first Columbia River fishboat. It was still running in 1950.

Vivian was in the right place at the right time with a simple reliable engine. The west coast cannery fleets were converting from oar and sail to power, and Vivian

Vivian foundry in the 1930's.

Vivian staff, 1934, at 1090 West Sixth Avenue. Vivian extreme left, standing.

was able to get orders. His staff and shop expanded piecemeal to keep up with demand. The Vivian engine series grew, but the principle remained: four-cycle, long-stroke, slow-turning marine engines, large and heavy by modern standards, with every phase of design and production under Bill Vivian's direct control.

One time we had to come in on a Saturday morning, and some little gillnetter had come in, and he was tied up against a boom of logs down in False Creek. We got a five-horsepower engine and we took it apart, and I can still see Bill Vivian carrying the base with the crankshaft in it, and Fred Nelson had the cylinder, and I had the cylinder head and some shafting. The three of us hoofed it down and walked out on this float and into this boat—and before one o'clock, putt-putt, away he went. This would be in '29.

We used to have a handtruck, used to take a lot of them engines down to the wharves by hand. Five-horsepower, but the damn things still weighed over three hundred pounds. The flywheel alone weighed a hundred and fifty.

Seeking improvement, Vivian began experimenting with the diesel principle, as various U.S. engine builders were doing. He became convinced that its simplicity and efficiency would pay off in the marine market. The resulting all-enclosed Vivian diesels supplemented and eventually replaced their line of larger gasoline engines.

Once tooled up, the diesels cost no more to build, burned cheaper fuel, and greatly reduced the danger of shipboard fire and explosion. The Vivian Engine Works was the first Canadian company to build a marine diesel, and was able to compete successfully against foreign engines. The first production Vivian diesel was a three-cylinder, ninety-horsepower rig which powered the tug *Totem* for many years. The diesels were an immediate success, and sales increased gradually through the '30's.

Sandy Watt, the pattern-maker, did the first 6 by 10 engine without drawings. Bill Vivian did some sketches and told Sandy to go ahead and make an engine. Then they'd take drawings off Sandy's patterns. They finally got a good engine out of it. You couldn't do that nowadays, but there was no money around, and we had to go the cheapest way. There was a good bunch of fellas working, and everybody'd come up with an idea or something. There were no rules or regulations.

Building up a business, even with orders in hand, was a difficult process. Capital was needed to buy new equipment and to expand the plant. Getting it, both before and during the depression, was a constant struggle.

The companies just started out, worked from hand to mouth. This was true of all manufacturers in western

Vivian eight cylinder diesel being installed in fisheries patrol vessel.

Canada at the time. There was no financing. You went to the bank and scrounged as much as you could, and when that ran out you did your best to get some more.

The old man used to tell us not to cash all our paycheques in one place or he wouldn't be able to make the payroll. Or the power would go off and he'd come out and say, "I'm sorry boys, you'll have to take a few days off. B.C. Electric pulled the plug on us."

Though forced to lay off workers during the depression, Vivian managed to find enough orders to keep the company going, and never cut wages. A 1938 company catalogue boasts medium, semi-heavy and heavy-duty marine diesels from one to eight cylinders, with horsepower ratings from 10 to 240, plus a similar selection of stationary diesels. They also continued to manufacture a line of gasoline engines. Will Vivian still supervised production personally.

I never saw anybody who could walk around the shop like that, and if somebody had made a screwup on a machining job, he could spot it. It could be a boxful of stuff, and if one wasn't right, he could pick it out, every time. He used to live upstairs then, above the machine shop.

By the end of the depression, Vivian engines had found their way into various locations and capacities: they were used to generate electricity, pump out mines and drydocks, power sawmills and logging donkeys, as well as aboard fishboats, tugs, yachts, ferries and auxilliary schooners. A contemporary newspaper cartoon pictures Will Vivian as "The Power Behind the Pacific Fleet." The engines were selling to maritime nations belatedly experiencing the push to power, especially Australia; in fact, one of the first Sydney harbour tugs was named *Vivian*.

Engine production in the Vivian shop wasn't the sophisticated operation we expect from diesel manufacturers today:

Six hundred r.p.m. was the maximum—otherwise the engine'd shake itself apart. Nothing was balanced—they didn't even weigh the pistons. We built one engine, the 7 by 10, that would turn over at twelve hundred r.p.m., but it gave nothing but trouble. The minute they'd rev it up, she'd start flying apart.

One fella started in on the lathes, and asked how tight he should machine the pistons. The answer was, "machine the piston and hammer it into the liner with this sledgehammer and a wooden plug. When you get down to the post down there, if it's halfway through the plug, you're just about right!"

World War II brought a great boom to Vivian, as it did to most other manufacturers. Foreign engines were all needed for the war effort, so Vivian stepped in to fill the gap. Vivian diesels powered many of the vessels built in Canadian shipyards: minesweepers, tugs, tankers, escort and patrol vessels and landing craft, including the leading boats in the Normandy invasion. The Vivian works expanded to more than eight hundred employees, turning out an engine a day. Subsidiary companies were formed to produce gunsights and distribute munition orders.

Meanwhile, the American and British diesel builders were stepping up research and development along with war production.

During the war, the American diesel r.p.m.'s were rising almost on a yearly basis. They got up to a thousand r.p.m. and you thought that was it. Then twelve hundred, fifteen hundred, eighteen hundred. We were left in the dust. When the war ended, they had a modern engine and we had the same beast we had in 1939.

Vivian could have used the war years, the government money and knowhow to develop a high-speed engine like the rest. But he didn't budge. Within himself, he felt he'd reached the point where he should be. The rest of the world would circle around the slow-speed engine.

He had a chance to build diesel locomotive engines, and even whole locomotives. They offered to put a spur track right through the plant from Clarke Drive, but he turned it all down. Just at the tail end of the war. We had a plywood pattern for a locomotive crankshaft, and he just let it hang on the wall behind the big lathe for years. He was the first guy ever given a chance in this country to do that. It could have been all Vivian locomotives, but no, no---"If you don't like my engines, to hell with you."

SPECIFICATIONS

VIVIAN
MARINE GASOLINE
ENGINES
5 h.p. to 60 h.p.

Details of Larger Sizes up to 300 H.P. on application.

BRITISH EMPIRE ENGINES
MADE IN CANADA

VIVIAN ENGINE WORKS LIMITED
1090 West Sixth Avenue, Vancouver, B.C.

Although Vivian didn't want to change the product, he was willing to sell it in new ways. Facing the postwar depression, he decided once again to push exports to countries that seemed ripe for the switch to engine power. He dreamed up a daring marketing idea: a joint venture of Vivian Engine Works and Star Shipyards Ltd. financed and built a very special fishboat. The *Arauco II* was launched in 1946, in the same week as Vivian built its thousandth diesel. The *Arauco II* was a

Vivian 6¾x10 diesel engines (80 horsepower at 600 RPM).

1949 trade fair exhibit.

Vivian-powered floating trade mission to South America. It carried equipment for purse seining, dragnetting, trolling and longlining in order to demonstrate all the B.C. fishing methods. The plan was that the largely sail-powered South American fishing interests would be impressed enough to order B.C. fishboats, gear and engines to improve their catches.

There was the small matter of getting the sixty-foot boat down the coast from Vancouver, however. Captain Fred Kohse and a four-man crew spent a month taking the *Arauco* south, with various stopovers. When they left Vancouver in April, 1946, every crevice was jammed with food, fishgear and spare parts. At steamy San Salvador they wired Vivian for "a new thermometer with more numbers on it" and continued on to give demonstrations for authorities in Columbia, Peru, Argentina and Chile. The mission was a success: the crew caught tons of local fish, the officials were duly impressed, the *Arauco* was sold to the Chileans, and Vivian received orders for seventy-eight diesels to upgrade the South American fishing fleets.

Due to Vivian's aggressive exporting policies, much of the post-war engine production was sold abroad and ended up in all sorts of places — news photographs show crates of Vivian generating plants being poled into Shanghai, part of a United Nations aid programme to repower China's war-shattered industries.

On the face of it, the postwar future of the Vivian Engine Works seemed assured. The market for spare parts for the wartime engines alone was substantial; Will Vivian had successfully lobbied for a government tariff to protect domestic diesel engine manufacturers from foreign competition; the works had a loyal staff and a reputation for quality, service and prompt delivery.

But things weren't quite that rosy. There was the chronic capital shortage, the missed opportunities for new contracts if they involved any outside control, and dissension over engine design. Will Vivian, the self-made man, was stubborn and wilful, reluctant to delegate authority. He resisted his engineers' advice about engine modifications, even to such proven items as shell bearings and split ring oil seals, which would have greatly simplified servicing and overhaul.

At the same time, the companies building the new high-speed automotive type diesel engines, with the trucking market assured, were converting them to marine use. Light and compact, they were more powerful, easier to install and service, and had all the benefits of mass production and the latest metals technology. Like Ford's Model T, the Vivian design was kept frozen past its prime. For economic reasons, many of Vivian's longtime friends and customers found themselves switching engine brands.

Ih 1949, the company celebrated its fortieth anniversary with a gala reception. Less than a year later, Will Vivian sold out his controlling interest in the Vivian Engine Works, retaining a consultant position with the new owners, the Brush-Able Group of England. This was essentially his retirement, at sixty.

It was a typical corporate move, where they bought Vivian and they decided in a board meeting in England that the best engine to be built here was their National brand. So we stopped building Vivians and tooled up for the National. We spent a million dollars — which has got to be five million today — on tooling that was never used; never even got off the shelf. It ended up they could export three engines to Canada for what it was going to cost us to build one.

While we were in with Brush, building National engines, is when the ferry came over from Britain — the **Princess of Vancouver.** *They had National Engines on it. I remember our boys spending half their time going back and forth from here to Nanaimo, trying to keep them engines running. In fact, we had to fly a crew down to Panama to get the ferry up here in the first place.*

The company continued on, making munitions for the Korean War and doing repair and servicing on Vivian and Brush engines. The Vivian name disappeared in the early '50's, when Hawker-Siddeley bought out Brush and handed the Vancouver works over to its Canadian subsidiary, A. V. Roe. The former Vivian men and equipment are now with Canadian Car in Surrey, B.C., currently the world's largest sawmill equipment manufacturer. They still make spare parts for the surviving Vivian engines all over the world, and are searching for a small Vivian gasoline engine to display in the plant lobby. The Vancouver Maritime Museum has four Vivian engines in storage, of which two are intermittently displayed.

Will Vivian himself died in 1965, and his engines are gradually being retired. The real legacy of the Vivian enterprise was to train much of the present generation of waterfront industry leaders, and to begin, against all odds, to put Vancouver on the map as an industrial centre for customers all over the world. As the motto in Will Vivian's office read, 'The damn fool didn't know it couldn't be done, so he went out and did it.'

*Italicized passages are quoted from a taped discussion with former Vivian employees Charlie Folting, Orton Frank, Walter Mould, John Minot, Jim Fullerton, Charlie Christian, and H. M. (Blackie) Robinson in June, 1977.

SHIPYARD MACHINIST'S TIME CARD

8:00 — at my bench
by the slipway, I spin
the hours on a company-
coloured lathe. Time
contracts in proportion
to the size of the job:

10:00 — small billets leave
moments to regard the midship
bulk out my latticed casement,
a calendar's graph superimposed
on a glacial parade of hulls.
I know them all by now:

12:00 — how they ride up, landed
amid the dockmaster's shouting,
silica drifting in the door
from the sandblaster's hose.
welders' cold arcs flicking on,
painters and their layers of tinting:

2:50 — I polish propellor shafting,
which goes on turning like this
inside the ships far at sea,
while I traverse the machine shop,
content now with the heft of tools
in the hand, with beginning the turning:

4:15 — I make out my time card. The machines
fall silent. For the first time this
afternoon, we hear faint broken rain
on the roof, the calling of sparrows
nesting high on whitewashed rafters,
under the dimming skylights.

David Conn

TOOLS OF POWER

by William L. White, President
Marine Workers and Boilermakers Industrial Union of
Canada, 1944-1955

IN THE old days when a union guy started to shape up as a threat to the establishment, they'd kill him. Early union leaders in the U.S. were shot and hung by the dozens. When the B.C. dockworkers went on strike in 1903 the C.P.R. hired armed strikebreakers, shot organizer Frank Rogers and smashed the strike. In 1918 Ginger Goodwin, who was vice-president of the B.C. Federation of Labour, was shot and killed by a hired union-fighter after he'd helped organize the C.P.R.-owned smelters in Trail.

The trouble with this method was it could backfire. Goodwin's killing brought on the first general strike in B.C., and his name is a powerful rallying cry for labour still today. So what they do instead is go for harassment through the courts.

It is still possible for an employer who's being picketed over some dispute to phone up a friendly judge and get an ex parte injunction to stop the picketing just on his own word, with no argument from the union until

later. A lot of judges are all too happy to crimp a union too. There used to be a story about old Judge Mason, the Hanging Judge. Someone phoned him up in the middle of the night and said, "Sorry to disturb you, your Honor, but we need an injunction." "Injunction granted!" Manson said. "What union is it against?" I don't doubt for a minute but it's true either.

There was another dandy, a dried-up little shit who always wore a string bow tie. He was a police court magistrate and the cops on night patrol used to pick him up passed out in the gutter, but any of the guys came up before him on a drunk charge, Jesus, would he ever come down hard on 'em. Another judge was a strong Catholic and anybody the least bit left wing had a hard time with him.

Dealing with prejudice like this all the time it's easy to see how unions got to forming up in flying squads and dishing out their own brand of justice. Often it was closer to the mark than what was being served up in the courts.

When I was union president in the forties and fifties, I practically lived in court. I couldn't look sideways but I was being nailed for some damn phoney thing or the other. It damn near came to the point Ivy'd have to look in the papers to see if I was going to have dinner at home or at the pokey.

One time there I got charged with assault for saving a guy's bacon.

This was over at Celtic, the B.C. Packers boatyard on the North Arm. We were in a real pickle there, and the worst thing about it, we brought it on ourselves.

We'd just won a new contract in the steel yards and got a good boost on wages, but the contract with the wooden yards didn't come up for another six months and it was bugging us that the guys there were going to have to go all that time working at the old wage.

Bill Stewart, who'd been defeated as party president in 1944 then banned from holding union office for two years for stuffing ballot boxes, was back on the executive by this time and he proposed we break the contract. That was typical for him. He was great at setting up battles from behind the scenes, as long as it would be somebody else going out to fight them. I wouldn't fall for that, but I agreed to try and get the contract opened some other way because I felt pretty sure we could get the guys a raise. It was stupid, you see, because we didn't have to do it. We were just doing it because we thought we could get away with it.

We started by asking the companies to open their contracts. Naturally, they refused. I didn't want to get into a confrontation over it, so I ruled out any illegal stuff like sitdowns or walkouts. Our position wasn't strong enough for any of that. We needed something that would be legal but would cause just enough of a nuisance these employers would say, "Aw, what the hell—we're going to have to put through this raise eventually, let's do it now and get on with business."

I went over the contract looking for an idea, and I noticed nowhere in it had the men committed themselves to working more than eight hours a day. There was nowhere it said they had to work overtime; overtime was voluntary. Well, the wooden yards had to work with the tides a lot and they really depended on the guys working overtime. So I thought, we'll call a halt on overtime. I checked with the lawyers to make sure, and they said we were in the clear as far as the law went. So I called a meeting and the guys agreed to put a freeze on all overtime.

There was an instant bloody uproar. The companies charged us with an illegal strike because we were too greedy to wait for our contract to come up. The papers gave us shit. I said we weren't on strike, we were just working "to the letter of the contract." The term "work-to-rule" wasn't known in those days, and as far as I know this was the first time the tactic was used in B.C. In any case, it wasn't an accepted practice like it is now, and the companies right away took it to the Labour Relations Board.

THE L.R.B. was another one of these three-man boards with one labour rep, one employer rep and a neutral chairman who was neutral as hell on the side of the boss. The chairman at this time was Colonel something, but the board was actually run by Fred Smelts, who was the employer nominee. Smelts, there was no gettin' to him at all. And smart, boy, he had a bloody brain. He was the toughest guy I ever set across a table from, bar none. When him and I got together the other guy's ears would be ringing for a week after.

At one of these hearings there was quite a crowd, a whole bunch of lawyers and 15 or 20 people around this long table all waitin on me—I was a few minutes late. When I come in old Fred said some goddamn sarcastic thing; he always had some scorcher right on the tip of his tongue, you know. And rough talking? Christ, he'd made a bull-puncher blush. Fock this and fock that, right in formal hearings. Great big guy, just like a frontline football player. And he was quite a noted horseman, he got up every day at 5 a.m. and rode his horse around Point Grey for an hour or two before he come to work. So I said to 'im, "Bygosh, Fred, you learned to ride in Alberta?" I knew he come from Alberta.

"Yeah, that's right. I did," he said, "Why?"

"Oh, I run into a guy the other day that knew you. Told me that's where you'd learned to ride."

"Oh, is that so? Did he say his name?"

"No, he didn't," I said. "He said you run a big cattle spread there raising purebred cattle. He said you shipped purebred bulls all over Canada."

"Are you sure?" he said. He was really puzzled, who could of said this.

"Oh yeah, it was you," I said. "In fact he said you had the reputation of being the biggest goddamn bull-shipper in all of Canada."

None of 'em was expecting it, you know, it was so serious in there. It really caught 'em, and they all broke up to beat hell. Fred was so disgusted he just about turned purple. "Fock you, you sonofabitch," he growled. You didn't often catch him with his guard down though.

Usually we just gave up when we went up before the L.R.B., but this time we couldn't see how they could find against us, because all we'd done was follow our contract to the letter. That didn't bother them though.

"In the opinion of the board it is more than a coincidence that the decision of all employees to refuse and to continue to refuse overtime followed hard upon the decision of the employers not to re-open the wage clause of the unexpired contract," the decision read. You won't get away with it, even if it is legal, is more or less what it meant.

But the bombshell was, the Marine Workers were declared "de-certified" in all the wooden yards.

It turned out they'd lined up the A.F. of L. to come in and take over from us and they figured they'd just wipe us out with a stroke of a pen and deliver the men over to the Carpenters Local 506. Smelts told the papers the Marine Workers Union was no longer recognized as the bargaining agent in any of the city's wooden boat yards and invited "any other union" to come in and sign them up.

This was so heavy-handed even the Canadian Congress of Labour was roused to take an interest. It was haywire as hell you see, because what if the men refused to jump? The Labour Code provided that any union that had a majority of the workers in a plant was legally entitled to certification and the company was legally bound to bargain with it. So what happened when you took the certification away but the union still continued to hold the majority? Could the men just go back to the way it was before the Labour Code when it was force against force? Could you go on strike and force the company to bargain outside of labour code provisions?

The L.R.B. said no, you can't go on strike because to call a legal strike under the labour code the union has to be certified. It was Catch-22.

I figured as long as we held the men we had them over the barrel just as bad as they had us, so we sat tight and held onto the men. Then the companies locked us out and got the A.F. of L. to bring in scabs.

We found out when the scabs were coming and made

a pact they wouldn't get through. Stewart was to take a gang of pickets to Macdonalds Shipyard on Coal Harbour, Jack Lawson, the business agent was to cover the next biggest yard, Bensons, and I went out to Celtic, which was the biggest. It did all the work for the B.C. Packers fishboat fleet. We had to stop the scabs or we were down the tube.

OUT AT Celtic there was a little bridge about 12 or 14 feet wide going into the yard and we just set up on that. They had several carloads of scabs and they would come up and start to push on us with their bumpers but we wouldn't move, just hammer on the hood, you see, so they'd back off.

There was an old guy there, about 60, name of Bob Newlands. Nice old fella, too. He didn't want to be at the front so he was back behind us a little. And there was a car come along driven by a strikebreaker named Roy Loop. He had two other guys in with him and they all had these ironbark clubs about two feet long and an inch and a half square. We wouldn't let 'em through, so the bastard, he backed up and took a run at us. Some of the guys jumped up the hood of the car and rolled off the sides. Loop just rumbled through and nailed this old guy, who'd been running away with his back to us. Hit him from behind so he went backwards over the hood and was carried for 247 feet—the cops measured it after. Then he fell off and they run over him with the front wheel and up on him with the back wheel and stopped right like that so he was pinned under the back wheel of this car full of strikebreakers.

I was the first there and I thought the old guy was dead. He was just as white as could be.

I yelled at this scab to back off so we could get him out, but instead of backing off he locked all his doors and windows and set his emergency brake.

I hauled off and hit the car window on the driver's side. It was this damn shatterproof glass and I cut hell out of my hand but the glass caved so I quick pushed it in and unlocked the door.

Loop grabbed his club and swung himself around with his feet on the ground ready to come out, but he had to kind of duck his head through the doorway and right as he was ducking I unloaded on him. Jesus, I lifted him too. I don't think I ever hit a man so hard in my life. Split his jaw and he just dropped. I flung him into the ditch, released the brakes and the bunch of us pulled the old fella out. I was sure he was dead.

This was right in front of the shipyard office and every window had a head in it looking out. I just run over and bust in there, never asked 'em or anything, and phoned for an ambulance.

No time at all, out come the ambulance. We loaded the old guy in and one of the attendants seen this other guy, still laying in the ditch. This was about 20 minutes after.

"What about that man?" he said.

"That ain't a man, that's a scab," I said.

Away they went. The office staff was still all plastered to the windows, and when they seen we didn't grab their scab, they phoned for an ambulance, too. That ambulance come, and they had to drag this guy out of the ditch. He still wasn't moving.

Then we hear the music coming and here's two carloads of harness bulls.

"What happened here?"

I told 'em. They got out their tape measures, took pictures, amd one guy come up behind me. "Good for you," he says. "Ida done the same thing." I thought, Jesus, this is pretty damn good. Maybe we're homefree, you see. Couple minutes later out come another coupla guys in a car. I stopped 'em.

"Who're you?" I said.

"Who're you?"

"I'm Bill White."

"You're under arrest!" They were plain clothes detectives.

The buggers wouldn't even let me take my car back down town. They loaded me in the wagon and down to the slammer I go. The guys sent word up to the union and they come down to bail me out, but the cops said, "We don't know any Bill White. He isn't here." When cops get hold of somebody they like they hate like hell to let go, you know.

ALL this time I was feeling pretty good because, after all, we stopped the scabs. We'd done what we had to do and as long as things went okay at the other yards we had the situation pretty well saved. Then I got out and they told me we hadn't held the other yards. Apparently the scabs just walked in and neither Stewart nor Lawson lifted a finger to resist them. So we lost the wooden shipyards to the A.F. of L. It was a major setback to the union. And it was my fault. It was up to me to tell the men to wait til their contract was up, and that's what I should have done. I accept full blame.

Because of how I decked that strikebreaker Loop I was charged with assault. At the trial there was testimony from a dozen guys that I was acting in defence of human life, which was backed up by the attending officers' report and medical evidence. But the judge rejects this for the testimony of the company and its scabs and pronounces in his decision that I beat this strikebreaker senseless while union thugs pinned his arms.

That was Judge O'Halleran. I just about fell over when I heard that. It wasn't even in the evidence. He fabricated it on the spot. The papers carry this story and not one person in a thousand questions it, because it's the words of a judge quoted in the newspaper.

So you see how the establishment works. The law, the government, the press are all just tools of power. There was no investigation at all, except the harness bulls who figured I done the right thing. But somebody made a call to somebody else and bam! I'm in jail. The company strikebreaker who creates deliberate injury with his car goes free while I'm brought before a labourhating judge and convicted of assault. I'm made into a bloody villain and for crushing their workers' legitimate union the company comes out smelling like a rose. This is the modern way to run the country. Beside this, assassination is crude and ineffective. There's no general strikes this way.

OLD COAL HARBOUR

On the 1700 block of West Georgia Street, in downtown Vancouver, the last Coal Harbour marine industries have now disappeared, to be replaced by high-rise offices and apartments and, hopefully, some open park. The waterfront shops and shipyards that once crowded the adjoining blocks have gone broke or moved to the industrial fringes on the lower mainland. Once the busy hub of local fishing, yachting and towing activities, the Coal Harbour yards produced and maintained many boats, and even some airplanes. They also brought to prominence names like Hoffar, Easthope, Menchions and Benson. The Coal Harbour Oldtimers' reunions of 1976 and 1979 seemed to be an acknowledgement that an era had ended in Vancouver, an era of industrial pioneering, trial-and-error techniques and colourful characters.

Jim Campbell remembers: he is the oldest active Coal Harbour worker. Semi-retired now, he owns a busy propeller business across Georgia Street from the vanished waterfront buildings and docks. He designed a line of airfoil-section propellors for sailboats in his seventy-second year.

I CAME to Vancouver in 1912 from Scotland with my family. I quit school before I was fourteen, in 1920. The first time I came to Coal Harbour was to look for work. In those days you had to find your own jobs. You'd starve otherwise; there was no relief of any kind. You'd start off at seven o'clock in the morning walking to the company gates, where there'd be a lot of other people looking for work.

I left town and worked all over B.C. firing steam shovels on the railway from 1923 to 1927. Everything was steam in those days. But in the winter, when the ground froze up, you were out of a job until the spring again. Well, after five years I was no further ahead than I had been at the beginning. So I decided I'd become an apprentice down at the shipyards in Coal Harbour.

Dunc Hood, the blackgang foreman at Hoffar-Beeching Shipyards, said he could get me a job down there. This would be around February, 1928. I started in as an apprentice at 25¢ an hour. Well, I knew how to fit pipes and thread pipes and do metalwork and all that. They could see I got on pretty well, so they gave me a nickel raise, and another nickel raise, until I was up to 45¢ an hour within a year.

In 1929 Bill Boeing, the Boeing Aircraft owner from Seattle, came up and bought the shipyard out. We started to build his big yacht, the *Taconite*. It's still afloat, doing charter work. They imported teak logs from the south seas and had them sawn into lumber. It's practically solid teak, that boat. The frames are sawn yellow cedar, but the planking is all teak, four inches thick. It cost over $350,000, which in those days was a helluva high price! The Atlas diesels are still running good — that's after forty years. Most big heavy-duty engines in those days only turned about 325 rpm, and they just never wore out. If they got sloppy, they'd still run forever.

Bill Boeing had an aircraft plant built out in the back of the shipyard, on piles. He put in a boiler room for heating the building and the steam boxes. They knew I had a 3rd class steam stationary engineer's ticket, so they asked me if I'd be plant engineer. I was then working in the welding department of the aircraft plant. So I said O.K., I'd take that on. So they hired a fireman to fire the boilers, and my engineer's ticket went up on the wall and I was responsible for it.

The company brought the welding superintendent up from Seattle and the sheet metal superintendent from the Douglas factory, way down in California. There was very little sheet metal work on the airplanes in those days — it was linen fabric we used — but he also made up the fuel and water tanks to go into the boats built at the shipyard. They had shears and punches, quite an elaborate setup for building airplanes. In those days, they just handed you the aircraft blueprint and you had to build from that. If you were building interchangeable parts, you had to build a jig, which you got out of your own head.

In 1929, we started with building. We built four wooden flying boats. There was diagonal mahogany

Jimmy Campbell Remembers Busier Times

Boeing aircraft staff 1930.

Boeing's personal yacht Taconite drawn by Stephen Jackson.

planking on the fuselage, about an eighth inch thick and four inches wide, in two layers at right angles to each other. By the time we had built them, it was 1931 and the depression was on. We couldn't sell the flying boats, but they decided they'd build five mail planes. They were building them down in Seattle already, and had them flying down there. They were biplanes that carried four passengers, two abreast, all enclosed out of the weather. Now, behind the passengers was the pilot. He sat out there with his head in the open. The fuselage was tubular steel—very strong, all electric welded—and the wings were wooden spars with linen sewn on. They had girls working there, sewing in the wing department. They had a dope room where the linen went in and the dope was sprayed on, and that shrunk it good and tight onto the wings. We built five mail planes at Boeings, and it was well into the depression by then. We couldn't even give the planes away, far less sell them. We started taking in other work. We were doing repair work for the Royal Air Force—anything we could get. Flying boats would land in Coal Harbour and we would pick them up with our overhead crane and lift them right into the plant for overhaul or repair. Smaller land planes would be brought in by truck. There were quite a lot of them, but then business got worse. We'd do anything at all to make a little money. We installed Leyland Diesel engines in buses for New Westminster, built a Bekins van body and a travel trailer, even painted and rebuilt used cars. You never said you didn't know how in those days. It didn't matter what they handed you to build; you just went ahead and built it. When things were tough, they'd send me out to bid on jobs I knew nothing about. I just had a general knowledge of the length of time it took to do a job and how it should be done.

In 1931, Boeing built the last North Vancouver car ferry. We leased some ground where the Bayshore Inn is now. I think it rained the whole damn time that winter. When the bare hull was finished, it was towed down to the plant and fitted out there. It had a propellor at each end and a Union diesel engine. Boeing had Star Shipyards build a floating drydock, which slid up and down on steel beams attached to the aircraft building. Burrard Shipyards later bought the drydock, and they're still using it.

Around this time, I had my only try at boat ownership. Bill Moss and I bought a 'sea sled' planing hull, installed an engine on struts and mounted an airplane propellor. This airdrive contraption made forty miles an hour. Eventually the engine broke down, and we sold it to a man who wanted to power a gold dredge with it.

The lowest point of the depression would be around 1933-4. They could only afford so much oil for the steam plant, so I burned scrap wood, to keep the place warm.

IN the worst years of the depression, Tommy Fenner and Tom Hood started their business in a little empty shipyard near the Stanley Park entrance. One of their first contracts was a small tugboat, which had to be completely built in two weeks! There was nothing but men and material and hammering and walloping and guys laying over each other. God, what a mix-up! But they did it, they met the deadline. Then they had this big

Boeing assembly plant 1932.

stag party at the launching. It was a beauty. They took over Vancouver Shipyards, at the corner of Georgia and Gilford, about 1934. It was well equipped. It had a drop hammer and a forge in the blacksmith's shop and quite a bit of shipyard machinery. The big bandsaw used to sit out on the street corner there, under a great big alder tree. It all burnt down, of course.

Around 1931, Bill Langridge and Walter Scott started Simplex Engines in a little shed on piles at the back of Turner's Boat Works. There was water all around. You had no problem getting rid of refuse and garbage — you just opened a floor plank and pitched it down into the chuck. In 1932, Bill Langridge went down to Seattle to buy machinery with $1000. He came back with turret lathes, boring machines, key cutters, everything imaginable. He bought six pieces of heavy duty machinery. Everything had to be carried through the narrow passageway from Georgia Street down to the shed. Then when they built a new plant down the street ten years later, all the equipment had to go back out the same way.

Around 1937, Boeing got a contract to build some Blackburn Shark aircraft for the Royal Air Force. They sent two of their head men up from Seattle to take over the Vancouver plant. They started to build these all-metal Shark aircraft. They didn't want any of the old-timers there who had kept the place going for the past ten years. They wanted to bring up and re-hire their own men. So all the guys who had kept the company together, they just got pushed out. But I didn't get pushed out because I was still doing the welding work for the shipyard end. So I was in the shipyard exclusively after that, building mufflers and engine controls and so on. We were building quite a number of big seventy-foot seine boats, plus pleasure boats and sailboats. The marine end had picked up. Practically every spring from 1936 on, Boeing would start to build these seiners for Canadian Fish or B.C. Packers or other local fishing companies. Those boats are still around; they can last fifty years and still be sound.

I got pushed out of the steam engineer's job, which had only been a sideline for me anyway, but had kept me working steady. We were still in the doldrums and it wasn't steady work in the shipyards, so you just worked when there was work for you to do. If there was none, you just had to stay there in case something came up in those eight hours. Some days you'd be lucky and work a full shift. There was no such thing as holiday pay. You were just lucky to get a job, and nobody was objecting to not getting overtime pay. After two years of underemployment, I was repairing boat propellors as well as welding and fabricating. I knew from the amount of money I was making for them that they could afford to pay me more or keep me on steady. But they wouldn't. So that's when I decided, in 1941, that I would go into business doing marine propellor work.

During the depression, all my friends who had been laid off at Boeing and couldn't get a job anywhere had started with just a box of tools in a small shop and managed to expand later on. When the war came along, they got big contracts for all types of boats, and had hundreds of people working in their yards. Same with a lot of those men who started out on a shoestring, like Simplex Engines. Hand to mouth, they ended up with this big machine shop, and I thought I'd better get in on this racket too.

One very foggy morning Turner's Boat Works caught fire, back in the workshed. Boeing had a firewall along the west side of their property, against Turner's. The fire engines were coming, we could hear them in the distance. They were lost in the fog, trying to fight their way down Georgia Street. The fire broke through from the workshed and got into the end of Pete Pappajohn's restaurant. When it got to about twenty feet from where he was standing, Pappajohn just picked up the cash register and walked out the front door. Finally the fire engines got there, but the only thing that saved Boeing's from being burnt down was that firewall. It was a really hot fire because everything was wood, dried out. Boeing never did have a fire, except on boats.

It's surprising the amount of fires there were in those three blocks. Sangster's got burnt out three times, and Dawes Shipyard, and Sinclair's Boat Works, Benson's shipyard, it all got burnt out, some big wooden boats in there at the time all got burnt. They were bad fires, but the equipment would get down here as quick as they could, before it got a real hold on. Because everything was wood, plus all those boats tied up there too.

I worked for Boeing Aircraft for fourteen years. I started my own business in March, 1941, with less than $1000. I had all kinds of work after I got going. Since I'd been in charge of the welding at Boeing Aircraft, and since they'd had the only electric welding machines on the waterfront, we'd done a lot of jobs for other people.

typewriter for $15 and went at it two-finger-wise. Thank God I didn't know when I went in, because I'd have been too scared to start a business when I didn't know about invoices and statements and all that, plus all the government regulations. So I was already involved and I couldn't back out. But I learned. I worked day and night. We'd work through the night on rush propellor repairs in the old shop, then into the next day, and sure as hell, the next afternoon some other rush job would come in, and I'd be working half the next night. But I was younger then. I remember once I was on one of those long jobs, and Harold Turner of Turner Boat Works came past and he says, "When the hell are you going home, Campbell, you'll kill yourself!" But it never killed me. I built all the equipment for my shop, designed it myself and built it. The biggest propellor I repaired was a four-blade off an Imperial Oil local tanker. It was close to five ton, twelve foot diameter. We've had ten foot propellors, from the White Pass container freighters, come to us with a foot torn right

Boeing Totem test flight.

When I started my own business, a lot of their customers came to me. I had the knack of being able to weld certain things that other people at the time didn't know how to weld. I'd learned sheet aluminium welding on aircraft gas tanks. I can honestly say, from the day I started, I never really ran out of work. I went and approached shipyards and fishing companies. I did every kind of welding in those days. Repair and fabrication too. I built all my own equipment. It was touch-and-go for the first two years. It was the third year before I finally got some money I could leave in the bank, and hadn't already planned how I would spend it to build shop equipment. I never took any holidays for the first six years of business. Sunday was just another work day too. The wife saw very little of me until the war was over.

I didn't know anything about office work. I didn't even finish public school. I didn't have any invoices; I didn't even know what an invoice was! I bought a used

off the ends of the blades, from hitting the ice up north.

During the war, Boeing were hiring people left and right. They were the biggest employer on the waterfront, and it's surprising the number of marine people that had at some time worked there. When the war was over, Boeing's was finished. A lot of these fellas who didn't know anything about working with their hands, they had become foremen because they weren't mechanics. Then they'd gotten swelled heads. They thought they were indispensable. Well, after the war, those guys didn't have anything to do. They weren't anything after that.

THE Coal Harbour shipyards didn't get into the metal boat hulls until after the war. During the war, Vancouver Shipyards built a lot of wooden hulled boats for the air force and navy, and then landing barges. They were a going concern day and night then. But it was all wood. It was John Manley who started building steel hulls for fishboats and towboats out in New Westminster, just about at the end of the war. Most of them were steel hulls from then on. I don't know if there are any wooden boat apprentices coming up now like there used to be. An apprenticeship was taken very seriously. Training took four years and involved regular night school classes. If you were an apprentice, you didn't get very much money, but they couldn't lay you off.

It ended up that the commercial and repair yards in Coal Harbour were in the wrong place. They couldn't be this close in to town. A lot of them moved to the Fraser or North Vancouver where they've got a bit more elbow room. But when you go back forty-fifty years ago, well it's just like False Creek. When I was a boy, that was all mills, great big sawmills from one end to the other. Everything ran with great big steam engines, smokestacks pouring out smoke everywhere. Nobody worried about smoke in those days. You just dumped your garbage into the bloody saltchuck. You burnt the rubbish on the shore if you had to. When I started at Hoffar-Beeching Shipyards, they burnt their shavings and scrap wood beside the ways. Nobody said you couldn't do that. Back in those days, you just did what you wanted. And it didn't seem to hurt the water, because in the fall the commercial fishermen would come in with their dories and they'd fish for smelt, right in Coal Harbour. They'd put their nets out and they'd catch smelt, right from the causeway to the entrance. Well, now the water seems to be so polluted, I think bullheads are the only things you can catch out there. In the '20's, you could swim in Coal Harbour. And the water was full of shiners. I remember orientals used to come down here with a bucket, and they'd fish for these shiners around the wharves. You could fill a bucket with them.

Today there's no sign of the old Coal Harbour left. The city owns that property now. I think it'd be just as wise to keep it as parkland, instead of putting up apartments as they originally talked about doing. I think it does have a big future as a yacht basin, same as they've built in False Creek.

I was thirty-six when I started my own business, and I'm seventy-two now. But I like working. Eleven years ago I leased all the repair business to my son Ron, and then I have my own business, Campbell Propellor Suppliers, a one-man show selling imported propellors and making up locally an improved Campbell designed sailboat propellor. We have accumulated a lot of experience over the years, which we keep in log books. We are well known for being able to take on problem jobs. I was always content to stay here and to keep the business small. Now I'm the only one left.

Jimmy Campbell

Letter to Malcolm Lowry

These hills are browner and less
than when you penned them alive
in a jerrybuilt seaslapped shack
in the name of wonder and fear
when you wrote the gulls from the wind
caught the gist of the tide
called down sunsets to hang
in your dreams when your eyes were here.

With a book and a bottle of gin
clutched like weapons, you walk
toward eternity's lens
a vision-tormented squatter —
now just an ironic plaque
on a public toilet remains
your beach has been commandeered
the world grows older — no better.

The woods grow thinner — the deer
slip wary through what remains
The bears grow wormy with garbage
the squirrels store poisoned nuts
Hell has expanded and spread
the city gobbles the green
the air is fetid — the fishermen
trap tainted fish in their nets.

Old man of chaos who clung
to this place with a desperate love
who drank yourself up for words
when the world was a few years cleaner
your portents smoulder to truth
the dormant volcano smokes
a judgment growls in the ground —
the demons stalk from the corner.

Peter Trower

HAULING

I FIRST STARTED driving truck for a guy named Nelles in 1932, hauling milk from Abbotsford to Vancouver, and freight back. The reason why trucking sprung up all over the Fraser Valley was these milk runs. The valley had been still mainly stump ranches through the knolls, but as the depression set in these stump ranchers dug in and started to produce milk — cause there were no other jobs for them. There was this pretty desperate fight between the Fraser Valley Milk Producers Co-op and the independent dairies. A lot of these old-style farmers were both producing more milk and getting squeezed out.

All the milk had been shipped by the B.C. Electric trams going into Vancouver. But truckers could sneak in with their trucks, go and pick up right on the farms, and haul milk into town cheaper than the B.C. Electric because they could haul freight back. So right in the middle of the depression was this opportunity and trucking lines sprouted up all over the place. First they were hauling milk and then they were hauling everything.

We'd start picking up the milk around six or seven in the morning, seven days a week. Our area was mainly around Sumas Prairie. You'd hit fifteen, maybe twenty farms and then you'd beat it into Abbotsford, where we'd all meet and sort out our loads of milk going to different dairies in town.

There'd always be so many guys wanting a ride to town that you had all the help you needed. One day I counted twenty-two people that got on and off the truck. They'd ride from here to there. We were on a schedule so it was almost like a bus line. You'd maybe get two-bits or four-bits if they were going into town. It sounds like small change now, but it all helped. They'd either give you something or they worked like hell.

There were no paved roads in the valley to speak of except the Pacific Highway and we'd come rolling down that. No Patullo Bridge yet and you'd have to come across the river on the old railway bridge at New Westminster. It was the only bridge from the valley and it'd just take one line of trucks at a time. Creep up the hill and over to Kingsway and into Vancouver. Those little '32 Fords we were driving were only four-cylinder jobs, but we hauled five and six tons on them at times. Crawling back and forth, you'd just stumble along, gearing up and gearing down all the time.

Those trucks had no goddam brakes worth the name. It was all mechanical brakes. You'd just have to use the gears to do most of the braking. You'd never be able to get away with it today. We just crawled through town. When they're just set up and working perfect these mechanical brakes were fine. But the brake rods would wear and wouldn't stay adjusted. After a couple of days you couldn't depend on them. Half the time they didn't work worth a damn. The first really half-decent truck was the '36 Dodge — with hydraulic brakes — a really nice truck.

There were these bloody horrible fogs. Nobody thinks of that now. Now if it's foggy it only means you can't go fifty miles an hour. But at that time you couldn't go five. All the traffic came in on Kingsway, and somewhere before Fraser Street you'd start running into low spots. Bloody huge fog banks. You'd follow the streetcar tracks right downtown and you'd develop a kind of sense of where you should turn. Any time it was foggy it was always a big worry how to get off Kingsway over onto Fraser without nailing somebody head on. Your horn wasn't any use because nobody would know where it was coming from.

We'd have to hire kids to go in front of us, to lead us through the fog in some of the worst spots. No, I'm not fooling. Lead us with flashlights and hollering. You couldn't see anything. A lot of kids would come down to Water Street around the truck depot on a real foggy day just for that job. Usually you'd give them two-bits or so to get you out of there. And sometimes they'd lead you up on the sidewalk or off the road and laugh and laugh and run away. I had that trick played on me. Those fogs have disappeared now, but they were just yellow mud. I ran into a streetcar once and there was absolutely nothing that I saw until I hit it.

BUT what I really remember about those days is not the trucks and the driving so much as the people — the life down on Carrall and around Water Street out along Powell. That's what sticks in my mind. You got to know all sorts of people through there — drivers and shippers, longshoremen and storekeepers, well-known characters working and hanging around down there. We all knew each other, somewhat anyway. It was a smaller city; you could keep it all in your mind.

Coming into town I'd pull into Turner's Dairy on Fraser and then Crystal Dairy over on Commercial Drive. Then I'd beat it down to National Dairy and drop off the biggest part of the load, sixty and seventy cans there. It was on Glen Drive just off the Hastings viaduct. That was my main dairy and I hung onto it. Louie Powell ran it; he was a Greek and he supplied the White Lunch and a lot of the other Greek restaurants. You could always work out some sort of a deal with Louie. We were always being approached by some of these small farmers to see if we couldn't get a buyer for their milk, cause often they just had no outlet.

At this time a hell of a lot of small farmers shipping milk were near destitute. Their milk often went into the pig trough. Farmers stuck without an outlet a lot of times had to give it away for as low as four-bits or a dollar a can — a ten-gallon can. Well, we'd bring them to town and go see Louie Powell about taking some extra milk from a new shipper. You'd go down and have a drink somewhere and Louie'd say, "Well, alright, bring it in." Of course he wouldn't pay the regular rate. He

Rolf Knight and Frank White

AROUND TOWN

didn't expect to do favours for nothing. But these farmers with no place to sell their Christly milk, at least you could get them some money. Not the going rate, but something better than they'd get trying to sell it themselves. And all we got out of that was the haulage charges for bringing it in.

After seeing Louie it was over to Jersey Farms Dairy to drop off a load and then out to the cheese plant or to Clark's Dairy down in the West End. After that I'd beat it down to Gibson's Dairy that I carefully saved for the last. It'd usually be around lunch time. Gibson's Dairy was right beside the Rex Theatre on Hastings by Carrall.

A lot of us drivers coming into Vancouver had arranged to meet down at the Rainier. You'd go out the back door of Gibson's Dairy and across the alley and head into the Rainier Hotel. We all had charge accounts there. That's where we'd have some drinks and arrange who was going to make what pickups around the city. When I was driving for Les McGarva we'd meet him there and he'd tell us, "You've got this or that pickup to make." Every couple of weeks he'd go around to the dairies and collect his money and then we'd get paid. Les'd deal our wages across the table at the Rainier and we'd settle up our bar bills there. Ernie Clark would be around to collect and he'd have to send over a round.

Ernie Clark owned the Rainier then and he advertised himself as "The Loggers' Friend." He had some money sunk in different logging camps and he staked quite a few loggers over the winter shutdown. We had our own table down there and it was pretty lively. There'd be any number of people hanging around asking if you knew of any jobs out in the valley. There'd usually be some messages for me at the Rainier about some little deal or one haul or another.

We'd eat at the Baltimore cafe across the street or at the White Lunch off the alley on Columbia. At the White Lunch you'd grab a meal for two-bits, and if you had to pay thirty-five cents it was pretty luxurious. Or we'd go over to King's. That'd been a famous saloon in its time, a well-known part of the scene. It wasn't a saloon any more but they had a tremendous buffet laid out — steaks and pork chops and everything, so much a piece.

One thing about Vancouver then was you didn't have to go miles and miles to pick up every load. Everything was concentrated downtown. Our regular pickups were mainly along three blocks of Water Street and out along Powell and from the docks. Arrow Transfer on Granville Island was the other hot spot. Up town, around Granville, there was nothing much of interest to us going on.

We spent a lot of time down on Water Street picking up bulk orders from Kelly-Douglas, Malkin's, Swift's and the produce wholesalers for stores in Abbotsford. Three blocks of Water Street was by then a wholesaler's district, so plugged with trucks you could hardly get

through at times. You'd hand in the orders to Kelly-Douglas as soon as you got in. But there wasn't much point in waiting around because they would never be ready much before five o'clock. So we'd go making freight pickups.

We had to hang around Vancouver till at least six anyway for the last dispatches. So it was just some hours in the afternoon you had to yourself. Otherwise it was driving from morning to night. We'd head back and get into Abbotsford about eight, maybe nine, at night. We'd have to drop off the freight and switch around our loads again so we'd have the right milk cans to take out the next morning. It might be ten o'clock before you got home. So it was a pretty full day.

Some guys couldn't stand driving in the city; it wore them to a frazzle. But, I don't know—I liked it. It was different from today. The pace was set by the streetcars. In a way it was harder to drive deliveries than now. You had to work your way down alleys and around streetcars. You might get by one, but there'd always be another one ahead and a string of cars and trucks plugged up behind. Slow-moving traffic.

Today traffic is so goddamn adept. People are expert drivers today by comparison. But at the time most people really didn't know how to drive. They drove around the city like they were out on some country road. They hardly obeyed any rules. The few traffic lights in town were only on the main downtown corners. You just buffaloed your way across most corners, tried to get a jump on the other guy or you'd just sit there. With a truck you did a lot of bluffing. You just crawled ahead and hoped that the other guy would stop. You wouldn't dare do that today. The trouble was taxi drivers who wouldn't give anybody the right-of-way. It was like driving in Mexico today, where the guy that makes the biggest noise gets the right-of-way.

I'd often have a delivery down on (C.P.R.) Pier D. That was something, a hell of a big place even by today's standards. It was always busy. You really had to know your way around that pier. Freight for all the places along the coast had their separate locations: Jordan River, Tofino and so forth. You had to know the freight sheds perfect or you'd never come out right. We dropped off quite a few loads at the Union docks too, beef and spuds to ship up the coast.

We picked up a lot of stuff from the Mc&Mc warehouse on Columbia and Powell. It was the hardware supply house for the whole lower mainland. Then you'd head out along Powell. That was all part of our beat— but it's kind of hard for me to capture what it was like then. It wasn't a main artery like Hastings or Kingsway. It was more of a feeder street to the waterfront. It wasn't a truck route like you understand today; it was just an easy street to drive. I once picked up a donkey (engine) up in Harrison and hauled it into Arrow Transfer. It was overwidth and overheight and it was miles overweight. So I hauled it down Powell.

Buckerfield's was down there. They were a big distributor of feed for all through the valley. The bigger dairy farmers started using mixed feed instead of growing their own oats. So we hauled a lot of that. A hundred, a hundred and twenty sacks of mixed feed a load. You'd back under a chute in this shed alongside the Buckerfield's elevators. Guys working on the second floor would fire these feed sacks down, but you'd have to throw them into the back of the truck yourself. It was a bloody workhouse. The way they drove men was incredible. The men would try and grab a couple of minutes for a smoke between trucks. "Sh-sh." No talking while working was the rule there. Old Fred, the foreman, he'd be ranting and raving if you stopped two minutes. "Come on, get that truck loaded and out of there. We gotta get trucks in here."

Trucking was really just getting organized. At first there wasn't any real control of loads. Anybody hauled damn near anything if they could get the job and figured they might handle it. It was a pretty freebooting situation. Later, when they got these conditions of load licencing and started to make them stick, there was no more room for this jumping around fron one thing to another.

For some years we had a lot of hauls taking equipment from logging outfits around Chehalis and Vedder down to the docks to be shipped up-coast somewhere. I always liked a load to the docks; I don't know how to describe it. We were still experimenting with hauling different loads. You'd have to puzzle out how to get something on or off best. It seemed like we were always trying something the first time. Now with big machines the load's on or off—zip, nothing to it. But then it was all huffing and heaving and back power.

Those longshoremen, they were something. They were union and there weren't many unions around worth the name. Yes, there was a Teamsters union, but they didn't amount to a hill of beans. Us guys were always a little awed by longshoremen that earned real wages and worked eight hours a day. We didn't know what an eight-hour day was. I had some good friends that were longshoremen.

Sure, I enjoyed driving. But the way we worked could be condemned out of hand today. Do our regular hauling, hustle around and beat it back out to pick up an extra load. It often meant that you worked a stretch of thirty hours straight to earn some bucks.

There were big labour battles that were going on all around; going on in that part of Vancouver all through these years. I wasn't myself involved. Yet we were right there in the middle of it: the longshoremen's strike and the Post Office occupation. But we were working and this other stuff was just part of the scene. You'd wish them well and maybe drop some money in the tin can from time to time, but that was about it.

NELLES was the first guy I worked for. He couldn't assure us regular wages, but some of the freight was prepaid so we'd collect that much of our wages for sure. Later on I worked for Les McGarva, and wages were a little more certain. But we had different angles of using the truck to make a little money of our own. Once you had covered what loads McGarva had lined up you could try and rake in something on the side for yourself. One thing about it, you'd never know what came next; always something different. We were always looking for a load somewhere without Les McGarva finding out.

There were eight or ten of us drivers working all the angles we could. You'd maybe bring in a load for one of the farmers. Or there'd be somebody moving or wanting something hauled cheap—we'd be right in there. What we made on the side might seem like small change today, but it all added up. Mostly all those deals came through our table at the Rainier. It seems strange now, but that's the way trucking was done then.

One deal I had going on the side was with this one blacksmith. There were still quite a few blacksmiths around the valley and they used a good deal of coke. Every so often I'd haul coke from the gasworks down by the viaduct out to Harry Williams' blacksmith shop in Aldergrove. You'd duck into the gasworks and throw ten sacks of coke on the tailgate and take it along on the way home. He'd always be in the market for steel in old axles or main springs or something. He turned out wedges and sledges and loading tongs and logging shackles. They were handmade and always sort of expensive. You'd trade this coke or steel for what you could get from him, then take it down to peddle one of the hardware stores in town that handled that stuff. Whatever you made was velvet for the driver.

Or another angle was the deal I had with the Mainland Foundry, a black-looking place with flames inside. I was fascinated by it. They would always take some of this special foundry sand they used as their floor. Just this side of Abbotsford was this bunch of sand that was just right as foundry sand. So if there was nothing else I could run out there and haul in a load for them.

Other times I'd stop and pick up a load of lumber at the lumber yard on the corner of Wall and Powell. Maybe I'd have a beer with the shipper in the Princeton, which was around the corner. I'd haul loads of this third grade lumber out to Abbotsford. It sold for damn near peanuts and people would use it for barns or sheds or whatever.

Heading home, sometimes I'd drive up Wall Street just for a change. I used to go out that way to get to the Barnet Highway. Two or three times a month we'd hauled oil in drums from Union Oil on Barnet Highway. So I'd duck out east on Wall Street. It was a sort of enclave; little houses, a lot of bush still. You'd see the inlet from the cliff. I'd cut up past the shingle mill at the end of Wall. That sawmill was always in trouble with its burner throwing up ash and sparks over everything around there. Then back to Hastings and out to Union Oil below Burnaby Mountain. That was way out in the country then.

For a while we bootlegged spuds. See, there were a lot of Chinese market gardeners leasing five, ten acres of land on Lulu Island and around Sumas Prairie growing early potatoes. When the Potato Marketing Board was brought in, these Chinamen more or less all got frozen out. That was part of the idea behind forming the Board. So the only way the Chinamen had of selling their spuds was to bootleg them. That must have been before the Patullo Bridge opened because I remember sneaking across the old railway bridge at night with loads of black market spuds.

Two drivers would go together. With a five-ton truck we could make up to forty bucks a load on these bootleg spuds, which was really big money. My partner would take the milk cans in and pick up the freight and I'd duck into one of these Chinese farms, load up with spuds and run them in at night. We'd sneak the load off the valley and into town and pull into some cafe or a house off a back alley in Chinatown with this load of spuds. It got to be pretty well organized after a while. You'd pull in and twenty men would appear from nowhere and unload you in no time flat.

That produce was bought by the Chinese wholesalers; a lot of them bankrolled these Chinese farmers, put up the money for renting the land and getting seed and what not. There'd be labour contractors who'd arrange to bring out groups of Chinese women and men to do seasonal work on those Chinese farms. The spuds we brought in would go to the grocery stores or go out through town on the trucks of Chinese peddlers in their black Model-T trucks. There must have been quite some mechanics stuck away in Chinatown to keep them running because they just ran and ran. I didn't understand half the ins and outs of the politicking behind that Marketing Board and black market trade. Our part of the deal was over when we delivered the spuds. They were quite happy to get them.

Our time off we'd spend in the Rainier or one of those other places around there. The Savoy Hotel or the Columbia or the Stanley. There were a lot of them. Everyone that you knew was down there. Each one of those hotels had its own atmosphere and regular clientele. Now I wonder how we had the time to get around to all those deliveries and pickups and still have time to sit in beer parlours—Dutch and old man Parberry, Les Groat and his brother Bob, myself, Les McGarva and a bunch more. They're all gone now. Usually you had a fair amount of booze in you before you left for home.

Around Carrall Street it was a sort of tenderloin district, yes. But different than people can imagine today. There'd always be people around talking. People stopped and talked to each other a hell of a lot more. Sure enough there were alcoholics around. But yet it was a friendly place, a place where loggers came to spend their stakes after working for two or three months in camp. They came down to Vancouver—which was Carrall Street, "Smokeytown." Even if they were on their way home to Strawberry Hill or somewhere they'd spend a bit of time down at The West or the Rainier or somewhere.

Some talk about how rough it was, but it wasn't. About the worst you could say was that there were people there who wanted to get drunk and there were others that wanted to get their money. True enough, if you went down the streets roaring drunk and flashing money I suppose there'd be a good chance that you'd

get rolled. But with normal care you never had to worry about your safety down there then.

Coming from a small town to drive truck around the city, well, that was *living* as far as I was concerned. Hauling into Vancouver, that was the real life I thought. Hell, what does a young feller want anyway? Just to keep roving and wrestling things up. I hauled into Vancouver for nine years steady, till '41. Then, later, off and on to help Les McGarva. I drove close to a million miles on that job. But I don't know...I liked it. But we were pretty hard-driven too. In truth you were driving or picking up all the time and what spare time you had was spent downtown. Of course, after I got married it didn't work out any more. My wife got me off that job pretty quick. I started driving logging trucks for Bill Schnare off Vedder Mountain about that time.

I used to spend so much time down around Carrall and along the waterfront. And yet it's hard for me to come up with a description of what it was really like and how things have changed. It used to be just a lively place where the action was. But today it's sleazy, worse than sleazy. In the last twenty-five years those places have deteriorated so much that even the "no goods" don't hang out there any more. Loggers don't come into town much now. They've got a house in Port Hardy or somewhere. There's no friendliness in any of these places now, even when they take your money.

Vancouver is a new kind of clip joint town. It's not interested in loggers' stakes. It's the money of this swarm of businessmen and travellers with expense accounts that attracts the operators in Vancouver today. They spend two, three hundred a night on accomodation. Our stakes were peanuts compared to that.

I don't know if I can make that any clearer, I haven't resolved it yet. Thirty years before it had been the hub of town, it *was* the hub of our town. Now forty years later that world hardly exists any more. Certainly not down there.

203

EFFECTIVE
NOVEMBER 19, 1951

Fly

QCA
QUEEN CHARLOTTE AIRLINES
LIMITED

SERVING
VANCOUVER ISLAND
and the B. C. COAST

Authorized by the Air Transport Board of Canada
operate Scheduled, Non-scheduled and Charter Service

204

Q.C.A. The Accidental Airline

A.J. Spilsbury and Howard White

THE IMMEDIATELY striking fact I suppose about the rise of Queen Charlotte Airlines is that it wasn't planned or even foreseen, especially by myself, its founder and president. I was in the radio business and quite content to so remain. The whole aviation caper came about as an accident.

My partner Jim Hepburn and I were set up in a tiny little box of a building at the foot of Cardero Street I'd built with $1,500 borrowed from my wife, Hep doing the inside work and me running up and down the coast doing repairs and installations in my boat, the *Five BR*. Business was booming 'til the war came along with gasoline rationing and I had to tie the boat up. I would travel upcoast by any means I could after that—usually Union Steamship, or CP, but the boats became just terribly crowded with troops going to Port Hardy and Coal Harbour and York Island—you couldn't get a stateroom; you were lucky if you got a chair to sit on. So by 1942 we were just desperate for a better way to get up the coast.

Okay. Enter my cousin, Rupert Spilsbury, slightly younger than myself, a fly boy. Barnstorming, instructing, transatlantic ferry command, now test pilot for Canadian Pacific Overhaul. As they repaired various aircraft all the way from Spitfires to B-29's, he'd take 'em up, shake 'em around, see if the wings came off, sign 'em out. Rupert could fly anything, he was a natural flyer, and one of the things that went with being a serious flyer in the early days was to be a bit of an evangelist, always trying to awaken the masses to the new frontiers to be conquered by flight. Rupert had a touch of this, and between taking his junkpiles aloft he'd come over and get in our way. And listening to us bemoan the fact we couldn't get up the coast, it wasn't long before he said, "Why don't you get an aeroplane?"

"An aeroplane?" I said. "I've never been near one."

"Sure," he said, "You can get 'em for a dime a dozen now during the war, they're not allowed to fly them. Get a little four-place machine on floats, handle a pilot, three passengers, take a thousand-pound payload, go a hundred twenty-five miles an hour, and only burn three-and-a-half gallons an hour." The more he warmed to the notion the easier and better he made it sound. "You can't afford to run that boat of yours for what a plane would cost you," he summed up.

So where do we buy one? Rupert took care of that. He found an aeroplane advertised for sale in Montreal by a man named Albert Racicot, a bush flyer shut down by the war, and he allowed he wanted $2,500 for this aircraft, a Waco Standard four-place biplane. It was serviceable, claimed to be in good shape, had a valid C of A (Certificate of Airworthiness), and wheels, skis and floats. All complete. Fly it away. But *twenty-five hundred dollars!* This is what I'd paid for my boat eight years earlier and I'd just got that paid off. The whole idea might have ended right there with us counting our

pennies, but it turned out that Racicot was a lot hungrier than he first let on. He kept coming back, and finally he offered to take $500, the balance over two years, and deliver the plane himself in Vancouver.

We didn't have $500 either, but we found it thinkable. It didn't make us feel tiny and hopeless and weak at the knees like $2,500 did. But what about fuel? How get it for an aircraft when you can't get it for a boat? How do we get permission to fly when everyone else in the country is grounded? The only commercial planes that were flying, Air Canada or TCA as it was then, was flying over the Rockies with 14-passenger Lodestars and CPA was flying to Prince George, also with Lodestars, and they had a couple of old Barkley Grows (prior to that, Rapides) that they were flying up and down the coast, just keeping their license alive. So I had to look into this.

IT WAS A real red tape jungle of course, the wartime bureaucracy, but we had one quite effective lever with which to pry open doors. We had just a few months earlier taken on the responsibility of looking after a chain of little low-power radio stations the government had put in all up the coast called ADC—Aircraft Detection Corps. They would sign up storekeeper's wives and so on, install this little battery set, and this was for reporting enemy aircraft. The silhouettes of various types of Japanese bombers, I can remember them very well, they were always posted alongside these sets, so any time an aeroplane of any kind went over, some panicky person would run in and alert the military. This was considered very essential in defending the entire west coast of America, and our claim now was that we had to have a plane to keep these things in service. I first of all went to the Department of Transport, and they said, "No way, the Air Force would shoot you down." So I went to the Air Force and they said, "No way, you couldn't get fuel from the oil comptroller." The oil comptroller said no, I would have to get permission from the DOT. It was a grand runaround, but I refused to give up and eventually closed the circle by getting each authority in turn to clear us within its own jurisdiction and getting a letter to this effect, which I then took around to the others.

While this was going on Racicot was getting terribly anxious, wondering why all the delay. Hepburn had nothing at all to contribute toward the $500 it turned out, but I did have a life insurance policy I'd been paying on since I was very small and I was able to raise the whole sum on that. Which got us in—we didn't worry about getting out, we'd make lots of money when we got the thing, as cousin Rupert kept reminding us.

Now it was Racicot's turn to move and our turn to be anxious. The floats arrived by rail. That was very exciting, but where's the aeroplane? Weeks go by. No word from Racicot. The skis arrive by rail. We get all excited again, then we get all impatient again. Eventually comes a CPR telegram from Princeton. He had got the aeroplane that far, he was socked in, he could not get over the Coast Range. The Rockies had scared hell out of him but the Coast Range was something else again. He'd never seen clouds so full of rocks in his life before. He had 14 children and a wife in Montreal, he'd been away three weeks, and he had to get back. Rupert found the plane under a tree and brought it down to the old Vancouver Airport.

We had Cecil Coates of Coates Aircraft put the floats on and make up beaching gear so we could haul it up the ramp, then we pegged it down on the grass and put a barbed wire fence around it. That was all the hanger it had for the first year. I think our first flight took place on the first day it was serviceable. A famous flight. We left Vancouver with a complete radio telephone station which we built for a camp operated up Sechelt Inlet by Brown and Kirkland. Rupert was pilot and had along a friend, Norman Hope, later for many years the owner of Refuge Cove Store. Hepburn went along as technician, and I went along to climb trees. In addition there was radio equipment weighing 200 pounds, two large six-volt batteries weighing well over a hundred pounds, a Johnson Chorehorse charging plant which weighed about 150 pounds, plus antenna wire and tool kits.

Miraculously Rupert got the plane to lift off, we got up there, and oh, it was a beautiful day, just a tremendous thrill. It was a successful trip. Mr. Kirkland was there himself and he was terribly impressed and thanked us, gave us a cheque for the whole job, shook our hands, we climbed into our little aeroplane, the loggers all came to push us off, Rupert cranked it over and away we went back to Vancouver, extrememly pleased with ourselves. It had been more costly and difficult than we'd dreamed, certainly more so than we'd have undertaken if we'd had an inkling, but at this moment we had no doubt that Rupert was a wise and farsighted man and that a great new dawning had opened up for all of us.

This euphoric state was rather rudely punctured when we landed and found waiting for us Mr. Carter Guest, regional director of the DOT's Air Regulations Branch, and his assistant Mr. "Uppy" Upson. They wished to know what was going on. This was the first they'd heard of us getting an aeroplane. We'd failed to notify them. We'd gone over their heads, to Ottawa, and their noses were very much out of joint.

They demanded our Certificate of Airworthiness (C of A) but that was alright, Rupert knew where to look for it, it was in the glove compartment; he dug it out and there it was, valid, signed out in Montreal. The only problem was the weights—tare weight, fully loaded weight, net weight and so on. If you figured it out, it wasn't anything like I'd thought. Far from being able to carry three passengers and one thousand pounds of freight, it turned out that if you filled the fuel tanks there was no capacity left over even for the pilot. On wheels, alright, but with floats on, all that extra weight, you had to leave out a hundred pounds of fuel just to get the pilot on board.

This of course delighted Mr. Guest, and he raised particular hob with us. If it ever happened again, he said, they'd cancel everything including Rupert's pilot licence. Furthermore they advised us that when the C of A expired the next April they wanted a *full* inspection, and just the way they said "full" sent shivers down my spine.

So we had to be very cautious after that. I don't mean we curtailed our use of the plane in any way. We were just *cautious*. In fact we did much more flying than we'd

Vickers Flying Boat, radio service boat 5BR at Savary Island

The WACO at Nootka Cannery

Bill Peters refuelling WACO

planned, and this came about in a way quite unexpected to all of us. Our logger friend Mr. Bob Kirkland of B & K called us one day and said he had a bunch of timber to cruise, and he was wondering, did we charter out that aeroplane of ours? I didn't know about this, but I talked to cousin Rupert and he was all for it. "Tell him it's sixty bucks an hour," he said. I did as advised, Mr. Kirkland was agreeable, the plane was gone for a few hours, came back, and Mr. Kirkland handed us $300. Almost what we'd paid in our own down payment! It revolutionized our whole way of thinking about money, just considering the ease and rapidity with which we'd acquired this $300, a good month's wages for both of us.

And after that, more and more charters. It was as if we'd discovered a little vein of gold under the floor-boards in back of the shop. It gave us the confidence to hire some technicians, a parttime stenographer, a janitor, possibly half a dozen employees.

WACO on radio service call

I**T WAS JUST** a little too good to be true, and who better to bring us back to earth than Mr. Carter Guest?

True to his promise, there was an inspector to see us from the AID (Aircraft Inspection Department) the very day our C of A expired. Norm Terry, very good inspector, very well known, said where is this aeroplane, walked up to it, took a very sharp knife out of his pocket, went under the wing, and started slitting the fabric. To look at the ribs. Took out a notebook, made some notes, and took another great slash. Made some more notes, went over to the next wing, did both lower wings, then he opened up both upper wings. And then he cut a great long slash in the fuselage, and he looked in there and he noted that there was rust on the tubing. Went away, totalled it all up, came back and delivered the verdict: we had to replace three of the four spars; at least 50% of the ribs—these were spruce—had to be replaced; all fabric had to be replaced—it was what they call ringworming, you could poke it with your finger and it cracks in circles because the dope has petrified—and the engine was due for an overhaul. Left us the list of things to be complied with, and when you've done this come back and we'll inspect it again.

Looking at our pretty little aircraft, that had become such a key to our financial security and future hopes, sitting there in tatters looking like an absolute worthless wreck was quite a comedown for us, but Terry had done his work with such a casual assuredness we kind of

shrugged and said to ourselves, well this must be a fairly normal sort of occurence in this world of aviation, now let's go over to Cecil Coates Aviation and see what it's going to cost us to get out. Harold Rogers was engineer in charge. They gave us a minimum estimate, which they wouldn't guarantee, of $9,200.

This was possibly the worst setback I can ever remember. We still hadn't paid Racicot.

We then went around scratching our heads trying to come out of the shock and wondering what to do, I forget how, but I came in touch with Stan Sharpe, who was then operating Brisbane Aviation in the same area—what is now the south airport. Brisbane Aviation was a flying school but during the war they were training air engineers for the Air Force. Stan was a sportsman, he was damn good to us, very sympathetic to our predicament and very anxious to take a job away from Coates, and this is what transpired: He badly needed an aeroplane for his students to work on. It was agreed if I paid for materials he would supply the labour free, bringing our cost for the overhaul down to around $4,800, about half of Coates' estimate. A bargain you see. There's nothing to egg you on like a bargain, even when you're getting into something way over your head. It seemed a godsend, but $4,800 was still more money than Hepburn or I had ever had in our lives, probably combined. But we were too deeply invested now, we had to get this money. So where? Enter Jack Tindall.

I'd met Jack over ham radio years before and by this time he owned the store at Refuge Cove, which he had been running for fourteen years. He'd bought the store, as far as I recall, from Eddy Moyer, who previously bought it from Ives, and Ives bought it from the man that had originally started it, who was Donnelly from Pender Harbour. And it was Jack who sold to Bus and Norman Hope, who retired only in the past few years. Jack was far more interested in his hobby, in radio, than he was in running the general store by this time. He was terribly keen to get into the radio business.

I went and had a talk to Jack and he agreed he'd put the store up for sale, and if successful he'd come down and buy into the firm of Spilsbury and Hepburn. The price was $5,000. The store sold, Jack moved to West Vancouver and we went to Stan Sharpe with a cheque for $4,800. We were ready to go ahead—again.

All we had to do was wait for Sharpe to get the plane repaired. I went out to the airport evey week and it was so strewn around the shop I couldn't even find it. Completely stripped apart. They were doing a terribly thorough job. All the tubing was being sand blasted and it had to be treated and all the ribs were being formed up on jigs on great long tables with dozens of students working on it and all glued together and varnished and it went on and on and on. In the meantime we needed the aeroplane, our work upcoast was at a standstill, and we were badly in need of money. Months went by and it was very difficult to see any progress. Stan Sharpe, for all that his heart was in the right place, did not have a manager who knew anything about getting aeroplanes out on the line again. The work was excellent but it was just not getting done fast enough. I was worried sick, dashing back and forth to the airport, putting off customers—"yes, yes, yes, we'll be up there with our aircraft, we'll do this, we'll do that"—no money was coming in, payrolls rolling around, and things were looking really bad.

Only a miracle could have saved us at this point. I mentioned before that we had this janitor, Charlie Banting. Charlie had come to us through an ad in the papers. He was middle-aged or more, rather scruffy looking, he reminded me very much of Will Rogers in his appearance and speech, and he had the same sense of humour. Very dry. I grew to just *love* it. Well, Charlie was useful. He would never know much about radio, but he drilled holes in boats, strung wire, swept up the shop and did all we asked of him.

One day as I was just about to set off on another of my despairing forays out to check on our aeroplane Charlie said, "Do you mind if I come out with you, I'd like to see this aeroplane."

I said, "Sure, Charlie, are you interested in aeroplanes?"

"Well, yeah, I'd kinda like to have a look at it," he said.

I asked Hepburn, he didn't need him that afternoon, so we jumped in my old 1930 Plymouth and we rattled all the way out there. Stan Sharpe came out to meet us and I told him Charlie was just a helper at our shop who probably hadn't seen a plane before and thought he'd like to, so Stan took us all through the shop, showing how they were coming on with the wings, how the crew were working on the fuselage, somebody else had the engine pulled apart—I couldn't see much progress, and Stan just said well I think it'll be coming along pretty soon now... Then he pulled me off to the side and said, "You know I'm getting pretty worried about this job, I know I made a deal with you and I want to stick to it, but this is coming close to breaking me!" This shook me up pretty good—the whole thing was starting to get a black hopeless feeling about it and I'm afraid I wasn't in very good humour driving back to Cardero Street. Charlie didn't say anything for a few miles, then he turned and looked at me over his glasses with his big sad eyes and said in his slow way, "You know, them fellas ain't never gonna get that airplane flyin'".

"What makes you say that Charlie?" I asked, a little bit annoyed, but curious, that he would venture such a comment.

"Hell, they don't know what they're doin'," he said.

"What do you know about it?" I snapped.

"Well dammit all, I wasn't going to tell you what I know about it," he said. "I shouldn't tell you. But I guess we're into something here bigger than both of us." And so saying he reached into his inner pocket and dragged out his wallet and handed me one of the dirtiest, most worn little pieces of paper I'd ever seen. It was an air engineer's licence, classes A, B, C and D combined. He was one of Canada's top aviation mechanics. He'd been superintendent of maintenance for M and C Aviation, a large bush flying outfit at The Pas in northern Manitoba. But drinking was his problem. And he associated his drinking with planes. So he quit his job, took his wife and daughter, moved out to Vancouver and decided he'd do some other kind of work, never again go near an aeroplane. And by pure fluke ended up with us.

I turned around and drove back out again and introduced Charlie to Stan Sharpe, formally this time. Well Stan was just about floored when he saw that licence. There wasn't another one like it in B.C. I said okay, this is the deal. Charlie will work here for you and I will pay his wages, it'll cost you nothing, but let him boss the job. Less than a month later the aeroplane was out there with nine coats of hand-rubbed dope, just gleaming. Beautiful job. The inspector just shook his head and signed it out. Charlie had saved us and his reward, much to the dismay of his wife, was to become superintendent of maintenance for an even larger flying outfit than he'd run away from in Manitoba, but that is getting just a bit ahead of ourselves.

ONTO THE next crisis. What we didn't realize at this point is that we were being watched every move by the Big Brother of the west coast air business, CPA. We didn't have the plane back in service long enough to get caught up on our own calls when we had a visit from a department of government I'd never heard of before, the Air Transport Board. It had been formed just before the war to regulate commercial flying, and we were now informed that if we were going to continue chartering we would have to obtain a Class 4 charter licence. The catch was that we were by no means guaranteed of getting the licence if we did apply, because anyone else could intercede and try to get it for themselves. We had no choice by this time but to plunge onward and apply, we were so far in debt, so Esmond Lando, our lawyer, got out a very formal-looking document, shipped it away to Ottawa, and we began a nervous 30-day wait to see if anyone would intercede. We made it to the 29th day and almost started celebrating, then a telegram arrived to notify us Canadian Pacific Airlines was interceding. This was a blow to us naturally, but what annoyed us particularly was that we had not received a copy of their grounds for objection as provided in the procedure. Just this telegram mentioning something about a delay, I supposed it was deliberate on their part, to give us no time to respond or amend our application. Finally their package arrived. At our little office down on Cardero Street. I remember it so well. Very formidable-looking envelope, 8½ by 14, about an inch thick. Registered, insured, everything else, had to sign for it. Hepburn and I opened it up and read the covering letter, the table of contents, found all the different parts to it—but there was something wrong. There was all sorts of material that didn't seem to belong—original letters between CPA's western manager "Transcanada Tommy" Thompson and Punch Dickens, the general manager in Montreal, detailing every charter we had taken, discussing our business, discussing their strategy against us. Slowly it dawned on us that there had been a mistake and what had happened there, was somehow in the rush to beat the deadline, some poor secretary had inadvertently slipped the entire CPA file on us into this letter.

We had to think about this for a while. We were very aware of the stakes. If we couldn't get this licence we'd lose our aeroplane, we couldn't make any money, we couldn't keep in business, it would spell the *end*. But the whole CPA case against us was here in this file, we were holding it in our hands, and unless we shipped it back to them all threat to us was ended.

We decided to be noble about it. If we sent it back that poor secretary would be found out and lose her job, and we didn't want that. So we dropped the entire file in the furnace.

The hearing was held in the old courthouse. The Air Transport Board came out and listened as Mr. Lando presented our case, then called the opposition. CPA was represented by a sharp young lawyer from Montreal, but he was completely lost. In their embarrassment they would be uttering statements such as one I recall to the effect that Port Hardy was an important coal mining centre, when there hadn't been a piece of coal dug there in a hundred years. But they'd read this somewhere in an old history book. When the poor fellow was finished the board rather tersely announced approval of our licence and left. We were now in business legitimately.

SO HERE we were with an overhauled aeroplane, a charter licence, in debt up to our ears, but raring to go. I hired a full-time pilot, Bill Peters, an ex-CPA-TCA man who was working his way down, and we didn't quite wear the wings off the plane but by the end of the year we did have the engine worn out. Demand was such that we began to feel very strongly the need for another aircraft, perhaps a larger, twin-engine machine that could be flown as an Instrument Flight type of aircraft on a scheduled run. The Powell River Company and Kelley Spruce had come to us urging that we start a scheduled service from Vancouver to the Queen Charlotte Islands and it was clearly the way to go.

Now, at this time, over at the Jericho seaplane base on English Bay were 24 Stranraer flying boats. This big hangar they used for the Habitat conference was full of them and around it outside was a virtual forest of these things. They had been brought in for coastal patrol early in the war but later were stood down for the new Cansos. Now here they were sitting, all the way from old and worn out to new and never used. Twin engine biplane with 1200 HP Pegasus engines, carry twenty-five passengers, wonderful aeroplanes.

My cousin Rupert was convinced they would make just wonderful apparatus for carrying passengers up and down the coast. A friend of his, another Trans-Atlantic Ferry pilot, Wally Siple, had started a used aircraft business on Cote de Liesse Road in Montreal and he was buying and selling mainly military equipment. This was before War Assets was formed, and he managed to buy all 24 of these Stranraers, as is. He was selling them to South America, and my cousin came to me and said, "Look, these goddam machines are just exactly what you want, every week we're taking two more down to South America, my God, you oughta grab a couple."

Well the logging companies were still pushing for a scheduled service and we knew if we didn't do something pretty soon someone else would. We had a talk to this Wally Siple and yes, he said he'd sell us a couple of Stranraers, at a very friendly price—$25,000 each, which for an aeroplane of that size seemed reasonable. The trouble with these Stranraers was they were military aircraft and had never been licenced in any part of the world for carrying passengers. I took the notion rather nervously to our "friend" Carter Guest and he took a very positive position on it. "Positively not," he roared and thumped the table until the ashtrays jumped around. "Spilsbury, if you ever fly a passenger in a Stranraer, it'll be over my dead body!" Siple, on the other hand, with his fly-boy hustler's way of looking at things, didn't seem to think this would be a problem. In fact he was so sure he could wangle a licence one way or another he made a proviso—no licence, no pay.

At this point it was still all a pipe dream because $50,000 might as well have been $50 million as far as ourselves being able to raise it, but I knew the logging companies were pretty serious about wanting steady air service to their camps—crew turnover was getting to be such that the boats couldn't keep up anymore—so we decided to see how serious they were. If they would back a loan or give us a contract we could take to the bank, the whole thing would start to look dangerously possible. Pacific Mills at Ocean Falls, the Powell River Company, the Kelley Logging Company and the Morgan Logging Company were the main ones who were promoting this regular service idea and it turned out they were willing to put money into it but being big corporations they chose to advertise and go the formal route, inviting all interested applicants, rather than just make a friendly deal with us.

A number of outfits bid. The whole basis of *our* proposal was the use of Stranraers flying boats, where the other outfits proposed DC-3's on wheels with seaplanes distributing from the main stops to the camps—which as we see it now was certainly the best way to go. But at that time we were sold on flying boats and we did what we could to sell them. We made a great thing of their *seaworthiness*. In case of engine failure, in case of anything else, they could land anywhere between here and Prince Rupert. Up and down this coastline, all the inlets with low ceiling and so on, what sense does it make flying around there with landplanes. The Air Force had lost hundreds of them up and down the coast but here were these flying boats, they never got into trouble. Well, they bought it. The companies decided in our favour. And the deal we made was they'd loan us $52,000. *But* first we had to make one flight to Cumshewa Inlet and back with twenty passengers and meet their approval all around before we could collect.

Now the fix was in, providing Siple could perform his magic. "Fine," he said, he was on. "If it all depends on that, the aeroplane'll do it and I'll get a licence on it." So he takes one of these things, flies it back to Montreal, which was nothing for a Stranraer, put it into his shop, bent up twenty seats of aluminum tubing, and—that's about all he did to it. Then he called in Miss Jackson. Miss Jackson was the real key to Wally Siple's system. She had two unbeatable things in her favour. Firstly she was an aeronautical engineer, which is the person with the authority to draw up actual aircraft designs, and secondly her father was the director of aircraft inspection in Ottawa, which gave her very good luck in getting anything she designed approved. As soon as Siple had the last seat screwed down he turned the thing over to her, she drew up a blueprint, and the next week it was approved for commercial use. So hardly three weeks after my little encounter with Mr. Guest one of these great birds flutters over the Rockies and lands in Vancouver with a valid C of A, ready to load up with passengers. We changed the numbers, from Air Force #947 to CF-BY, and painted out the Rondels, and left the rest raw aluminum. We would have liked to have painted it but we couldn't afford to. They were big machines. They used to say it looked like the Marpole Bridge had taken off, when one of them went by.

W E NOTIFIED the Powell River Company and they sent out about sixteen passengers including Jackson, general manager of Pacific Mills, Jim Murphy, logging superintendant of Kelley Log, and George O'Brien Sr., who was the head of the Powell River Company—three of the most important men in B.C. logging—plus a bunch of flunkies and fallers and chokermen chewing snoose. I went along to see if I could keep the radio running, which was one of ours put in illegally, Rupert was pilot, Bill Peters was co-pilot and Hank Elwin was flight engineer. It was in February and not a nice day. We were terribly nervous. We had never flown the aeroplane before. We couldn't afford to fly it ourselves. We just hoped everything would work.

We left Vancouver in a southeast gale bound for Sullivan Bay where we had arranged previously for a cache of fuel in 50-gallon drums, and the first thing we discovered was that none of the instruments—turn and bank, airspeed, etc.—was working. Immediate panic. We could probably make it without them, but it wouldn't be safe. On the other hand to call off the flight with all this brass aboard, and admit to malfunctioning equipment, would likely be the end of our contract hopes. I poked around pretending to be working on the radio but couldn't see anything obvious. Then I went back to my station, and gave myself up to nerves. No one spoke. Rupert kept going ahead. I looked out the

Stranraer

window and found myself looking at my old home, Savary Island, from the air for perhaps the second time in my life, but I was too tied up inside to pay much attention. Then I noticed it was coming up toward me. We were losing altitude and banking. For whatever reason, Rupert had decided to land. He taxied up on the west side out of the strong S.E. wind and shut everything down a couple hundred yards off the wharf. None of the passengers knew what was up, and neither exactly did I. Then we saw Hank Elwin climb out onto the lower wing, take out the collapsible aluminium ladder, set it in sockets in the lower wing, climb up onto the upper wing twelve feet above, walk out along the upper wing to where the pedo head was — this is a tube sticking out of the leading edge of the wing like a boathook, that supplies air pressure to the instruments — and very carefully pulled over the pedo head and taped on was a french safe. This had been done to keep dirt from getting in it when the aircraft was in storage, and no one had ever bothered to take it off. Elwin peeled it off and bingo, the needles sprang to life.

With wind steadily rising and the sky steadily lowering we made Sullivan Bay and took off for the Charlottes, and by the time we got to Calvert Island it was very bumpy and right down on the deck. Now, for all his goofiness on the ground Rupert was very, very cautious in the air. He never got into trouble, never bent an aeroplane. So he came back, told me he wasn't going to head out into Hecate Straits with weather like this, and asked me where I wanted to put down for the night.

Meanwhile our passengers were rapidly becoming acquainted with some of the reasons Carter Guest didn't think "The Strainer" was just the best thing for commercial flying. It wasn't lined, it was just single-skin aluminium, and it was freezing. I mean literally. There was no heat aboard. Our breath was freezing to the windows, there were icicles all over everything, everybody was blue with the cold. There was no can, no facilities of any kind, outside of a suction tube the crew used in the Air Force, just a short rubber hose to the outside with a funnel on your end, and when you opened the little cock it would whistle, there was a helluva suction on it. It became famous later and earned our planes the nickname "Whistling Shithouses". We used to wonder how the women made out — we put a curtain across behind the last seat and every once in awhile when there was absolutely no recourse, you'd see some woman passenger rather painfully make her way back there, draw this curtain, and you'd hear this whistling sound — I guess somehow they managed, because they always came back.

I felt terrible of course. I was just beginning to face the fact all was lost and found it quite hard. I was also terribly air sick. George O'Brien took over as wagon master at this point and directed us to Coal Harbour on Vancouver Island, where there was a wartime seaplane ramp being used by the Gibson Brothers to haul up dead whales. We got the big Powell River Company camp at Port Hardy on the radio and a crummy was waiting for us when we landed. So we spent a comfortable night, and we made the Queen Charlottes the next day without further trouble, but our overall time wasn't much better than it would have been on a good straight-through boat and the first day had been just a dreadful ordeal.

O'Brien was ominously silent about our contract on the way down, but as soon as he was safely on ground in town he broke into a big smile, pumped my hand and then pressed into it a cheque for $52,000. He thought our new air service was just wonderful!

WITH THAT we bought the second Stranraer, and we flew under contract for the first year. We increased our fleet in this period with a couple of Norsemen purely for charter work, but we were thwarted in our other ambition, to run the scheduled service into Rupert, because we didn't have a Class 1 licence which, as the worthy Carter Guest had explained, was required before we could run scheduled service. Finally we screwed up our courage and had Esmond Lando draw up the papers and apply. This was quite the most serious hearing we'd ever been in for and again we were opposed by the CPA. We had people from all up the coast come down and testify Spilsbury and Hepburn were giving excellent service, the first they'd ever had, they wanted them to run the Prince Rupert service. CPA was taking the hearing in deadly earnest, because if you know anything of Grant McConachie's early plans for CPA, it was to make it the first trans-Pacific air carrier using short land-hops over the Polar route to the Orient, and Sandspit and Prince Rupert were to be key stops. For all his vision he hadn't seen that larger aircraft would soon eliminate the need for all these in-between stops. However we had a very well-prepared application, we had very good grounds because we had been providing service up the coast where CPA hadn't bothered, and we had tremendous

Stanraer interior

Stranraer in flight

Loading collapsible canoe

Stranraer over Sechelt peninsula

Stranraer, Pilot Rupert Spilsbury, Copilot Bill Peters, Flight engineer 'Armi' Rancheaux,
Supt. of Maintenance Charlie Bunting.

Floating Stranraer to beach after a dunking

Tofino Agent Ian McLarie, Pilot John Hatch with Norseman

public support. After the first day of the hearing it looked very rosy for us and very bleak for CPA.

When the court adjourned for lunch good old Grant McConachie came waltzing over to me with his great beaming smile, threw his arm over my shoulder and said, "Jim, let's you and me have a talk." Well he talked to me like a Dutch uncle and I'm glad he did. He said, "Look, we are in for big things, we need this, we need it badly, we have the aircraft to carry it out. You're doing a darn good job on the lower coast where you've gone, but you haven't got the kind of money to get the aircraft you need for Rupert, and you can't get it. You're out of your class. But I tell you what you do. You withdraw your application and I will give you all our coast licences, Vancouver-Powell River, Vancouver-Nanaimo, Vancouver-Alert Bay, Vancouver-Tofino, Vancouver-Zeballos and Ocean Falls—everything." He was giving us the whole coast. So the thing was, shall we say, settled out of court. We then became a Class 1 scheduled operator on the old CPA routes. We incorporated as Queen Charlotte Airlines in 1945 and we operated as Queen Charlotte Airlines until 1955. It was in 1946 we reached the point of being the third largest airline in Canada, with over twenty aircraft and several hundred employees.

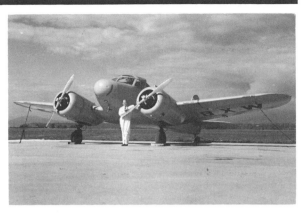

Jim Hepburn and Cessna T-50

THAT'S HOW fast it grew. CPA had been quite willing to give up the coast routes because they considered them money-losers, and in their experience no doubt they were. But in the post-war period the upper coast became active to a degree that is hard to realize now. Just looking at a place like Minstrel Island, which today boasts about three families total, in the late forties we were hauling twenty and forty people a day in and out of that place. The same with Alert Bay, the same with—I could name a dozen places that were really booming in those years. And we were there, we couldn't help but boom along with it. Tahsis and Zeballos were great revenue producers on the west coast and we instituted new routes like Vancouver-Comox—which was a natural—and Vancouver-Powell River, once we got the various governments talked into building the airport there. We put Mark V Ansons in first, then DC-3's.

That was a great day when we took delivery of our first DC-3. We felt we were then a real airline.

Anson over Vancouver

Vancouver-Nanaimo we had inherited from McConachie who figured it couldn't be made to pay, and we found out how right he was. The CPR ferry service was too good, we couldn't compete. They ran many trips a day into Nanaimo Harbour right down town and we were landing out at Cassidy Airport which was much less convenient. We did want to start harbour to harbour—Vancouver Harbour to Nanaimo Harbour and Vancouver Harbour to Victoria Harbour using our Stranraers, but we could never get permission to fly an aeroplane into Vancouver Harbour. Carter Guest was dead against it. He would always refer back to an incident 20 years before where some pilot had hit a tug's towline taking off and doused a bunch of people. We knew it was a moneymaker and we applied over and over again, but we couldn't get to first base as long as Guest was there. So it's very interesting to see Air West doing the very thing today, with 20-passenger aircraft and many times the traffic congestion in Vancouver Harbour than there was then.

DC-3 and PBY

It's not an overnight matter to build a scheduled airline with 20 aircraft and 300 employees. It's *unbelievably* complex. I had originally become involved in the thing, don't forget, as a way simply to get around to service my radio customers. Now it was remaking my life in the most revolutionary fashion, but I was

Cassidy Airport

213

determined to meet the challenge. I was determined not only to prevail but to create the finest little airline in the country. I've told about the fun side of the thing getting started, but the real hard work came now in trying to mold this ragtag bunch of aircraft and sky bums into a slick, reliable modern airline.

It was hard. It was as hard as calling up my Cousin Rupert, who with his ingenuity and ability saved our bacon on so many occasions, who was in every sense responsible for the airline starting up, and saying, "Rupert, you're fired." But I had to. Rupert would never drink on the job and he never bent a plane but he'd drink at night. He'd go into a small place like Prince Rupert or Stewart and hit the bars and bullshit and scare hell out of people and I had so many complaints I simply had to get him on the mat and say, "No."

I was trying to enforce the same rules that TCA had; no alcohol 24 hours before takeoff, but it was an uphill battle with the gang I had then.

And poor old Charlie Banting, who had plucked us from the teeth of disaster back when we were rebuilding the Waco and without whose vast engineering expertise we could never have gone on. The dearest guy you could ever want to meet. But his suspicions about the cause of his drinking trouble proved all too true. Here he found himself as Superintendent of Maintenance in a far bigger airline than he'd ever been in before, and the responsibility took a cruel toll. He'd get so goddamn plastered for a week you wouldn't see him. He couldn't make it out to the airport. It wouldn't matter even if we had an aircraft coming up for licencing, we'd have to make excuses to the DOT: "Sorry our Chief Engineer is 'indisposed'." I can't say what it did to me to drop the axe on poor Charlie. I loved the guy. But this is what I'd got myself in for. It was better than killing people. As it turned out, I wasn't half tough enough.

In 1951 we dropped a Canso with 23 people aboard on top of Mount Benson near Nanaimo. We'd had some smaller crackups, but this was the worst aviation disaster in Canadian history. Ours. I couldn't believe it.

Apart from the personal anguish we all had to face over the loss of friends and colleagues, the Mt. Benson crash exposed QCA to a long period of very nasty public criticism. Our licences were placed under review by the Air Transport Board and business went into a tailspin from which we were just recovering in 1955 when I gave in to the urging of my financial partners and sold out to the group who renamed the company Pacific Western Airlines.

I could end on this note and say, much as I would have liked to have stayed in aviation at the time, the future of QCA would have lain along the same path PWA has taken — to world charter and all this sort of thing, and frankly, I was never interested in that. My whole interest was the coast of British Columbia. More than that , I am quite certain that if I hadn't gotten away from the aviation business and all its headaches when I did, I wouldn't have survived to talk about it nearly this long.

I returned to the radio business where I have been able to put in a quarter century of quite fruitful work without having another serious thought about aeroplanes, and I can now say quite honestly that I have no regrets. Still, whenever I hear an aircraft fly over I invariably look up and wonder if he's got a payload, and whether he's going to complete his flight without incident.

Union Steamship 'CHELOHSIN' and Rapide — Sullivan Bay

Anatomy of a Legend

ONE notable hole in Vancouver's mystique as a great city is its lack of a criminal legend to stand beside the likes of Chicago's Al Capone, Paris' de Sade or London's Jack the Ripper. Others have recognized this fault and tried to repair it, but frankly I get a bit impatient reading about the quiet hermit who may have been the aged Quantrille, the petty stick-up artist who may have been the Flying Dutchman's one-time sidekick, or yet another go-round with Bill Miner, who was yet another American spending his quiet days on the safe side of the border. Gun-an-noot was homegrown, but he was really just a put-upon Indian and not of the criminal ilk at all. Andy Bruce is the latest local boy who made bad but his reputation as a low-budget hit man never quite blends with the subsequent bleating about social justice and humane treatment in a way that ultimately satisfies. Somehow all of our great bad guys come up short.

We can do better. There is one Vancouver villain who has never been touched by a CBC docu-drama, whom Pierre Berton has never dared to mention, and yet who remains so infamous among those who remember him some readers will feel the impulse to slap the book shut as soon as they see his name. Frederick Ducharme, who was hanged in 1950, remains our only unmentionable criminal, and yet he has been unmentionable in the curious way that has permitted his secret reputation to become firmly established as folklore from one end of British Columbia to the other.

And most assuredly, Ducharme does not come up short.

DUCHARME

Howard White

Word of Ducharme first reached me when I was a small boy, much too small in fact to know what to make of the tale. This would be about the time our family was at the logging camp on Nelson Island and I would be somewhere under five, just the age a little boy is getting to know enough about the grown-up world to start making his own tentative and usually disastrous forays into it. The camp wives used to get together for gab sessions—in the laundry, at the cookhouse, while cleaning the bunkhouses—wherever they found themselves together without men around, and proceed to talk with great absorption and not the slightest embarrassment about the most personal matters, especially if Aunt Edna was there. She was the sort of aunt who delighted in telling you your father got stinking drunk the night you were born and didn't bother to come home for two days, and unlike the other women she gossiped in such a loud voice you could eavesdrop at a safe distance with no risk of being sent outside to play. Still, it was pretty dumb, boring stuff, for the most part hardly worth a boy's trouble listening to. One time I remember hearing her holding forth about another of the wives not present that day whose husband, she claimed, refused to use rubbers with the result this pitiable woman was forced to wear a diaphragm, which luckily fit her well.

I happened to know what a diaphragm was, because my father had given me lots of them to play with, and even made me a slingshot from one. They were made of black rubber, about the size of a dinner plate, came out of the airbrake pots on logging trucks, and only a moron would wear one, whether it fit her or not. As for rubbers, I had seen the man in question wearing them often. They were all he did wear, when he wasn't wearing his caulk boots. Only a vivid anticipation of some sort of humiliating rebuff which would surely result prevented me from rushing in with this information and denouncing my aunt's lie.

I didn't hear the whole story about Ducharme. In fact it was only many years later I realized he was the one they had been talking about. Of course it was Aunt Edna who did the talking. It was her kind of story. By the rapt silence and clucking of tongues I could tell I'd missed out on a good one, but what I did hear was thought-provoking enough.

"They finally caught him just down there on Cornwall Street," she was saying. "He was going along in just gumboots and a raincoat with nothing underneath, and whenever he met a lady, he'd fling open the raincoat."

"Goodness. How dreadful," my mother said.

"Yeah, imagine walking home to dinner and seeing that. You wouldn't have much appetite."

"Depends. Some would have more."

"Oh, you. You wouldn't have the nerve to look."

"Darn tootin'. I'd of paid to get to see it, and so would you, if you thought nobody'd catch you."

"Sure, I'd walk up and say, well Buster, what's this you got you're so proud of, lessee here. Not bad, not bad. I've seen better in the fallers' shower, but not bad."

"Mike says he had ribbons tied to it."

"Goodness. How dreadful."

Here was something for a boy to think about. Most of the things grown-ups talked about doing, like having babies or fixing machinery, were terribly boring. But here was a man doing something that sounded like a lot of fun, and if the camp ladies disapproved, it was hard for me to tell.

A few days later when I was having my weekly bath in the galvanized laundry tub in the back room, Aunt Edna came over, and I had my chance. I jumped into my gumboots, wrapped myself in a towel and scooted out.

"Howie! What are you doing out here!" my mother shrieked when she saw me. "People will see you!"

I held the towel open.

The response was both more and less than I'd counted on.

"Oh look," Aunt Edna hooted. "He wants us to see him!"

"Howie! That's bad!"

Aunt Edna couldn't believe her eyes. "Look! look! look!" she kept hollering and pointing at me. "He's flashing us! Your kid is a flasher!"

My mother seldom raised her voice at her children, much less laid a hand on them, but this time she made for me like an angry mama bear and snagged my ear so hard it felt like it was going to tear off.

"That's BAD!" she kept repeating as she quick-marched me back to the tub. "You're very bad. Now finish washing your neck or I'll tell your father!"

The swiftness and force of this reaction caught me completely by surprise, and I burst into bitter, despairing tears. They were obviously amused and captivated by the story of the man in the raincoat in a quite extraordinary way, and yet when I did what he did it was bad and not funny. It seemed so unfair, and gave me occasion to momentarily hate all adults, the raincoat man especially. I had no way of knowing that the moral confusion of the fifties had cost him dearly also.

It was in the schoolyard that the legend of Ducharme really flourished, and that is where I met with him next. Our family had by this time moved to the fishing village of Pender Harbour. A city kid named Mickey Stillwell moved in to town, bringing with him an exotic store of back-alley folklore, including this story of a fabulous marauder with a giant dink which he kept strapped to his leg and sometimes employed to kill ladies. This quickly became the sensation of the neighbourhood, and assured Mickey Stillwell of ready acceptance into our very closed little group. Day after day we would spend the whole lunch hour over in the frog swamp across the creek regaling each other with imagined adventures of this new hero, whom we understood to be named Dushawn. He would be visualized in his early years, sitting at his school desk admiring the wondrous bee-zonkers of our singing teacher, Miss Caesar, whereupon he would fall victim to that constant schoolboy peril, the involuntary erection, just as Miss Caesar was commanding him to stand and sing a chorus from "The Walloping Window-Blind". Mickey would leap about acting out poor Dushawn's predicament as he engaged in a secret battle to subdue the constrictor—like appendage, all the while gasping out a few words of the song—"no wind that blew...dismayed her crew..." (popping of bolts and splintering of wood as the *thing* destroys his desk, begins walloping around the room like a firehose. Miss Caesar runs out screaming, the girls behind her) "or troubled the captain's...mind." This was quite the funniest thing we'd ever heard in our lives. I remember laughing so hard everything went into a spin and I actually blacked out for a few moments.

Hopalong Cassidy, even Audie Murphy, were soon banished from our thoughts. We began to see signs of Dushawn everywhere. There was another scenario where Dushawn would try to avert embarrassment by roping the errant member to his leg, as he was supposed to have done in life, but this would backfire in a number of remarkable ways. Sometimes it would appear out of his pantleg and slowly raise him up off the ground like a hydraulic jack. Other times it would cause his leg to fly up in front of him like a chorus girl's, and he would try to cover up by affecting the goose-step. Mickey would fall in behind Miss Caesar in the hall, goose-stepping, as the rest of us bayed mercilessly. Deanna Knight, a grade seven girl with breasts who occupied a prominent place in our thoughts, would come to the classroom door with a message for our home-room teacher—a pompous young stick with the interesting name of Mr. Dick—and as they whispered Tiffy Reid would break the hush with a noise like splintering wood, filling the room with grunts and wheezes of stifled hysteria. I don't know what the girls in class must have thought about any of this, but their instincts saved them from trying to find out.

There was one boy in class, a big, drawly fisherman's son with even bigger feet, a L'il Abner walk and the inexhaustible good nature of a Newfoundland pup—the type whose inevitable fate it is to be the butt of every joke within a ten-mile radius—who had the dreadful misfortune to be named Shane. The trouble with "Shane" was that it resembled "Dushawn". Not a lot, but kids don't need a lot. It was no time before some blazing wit picked up on the resemblance and Shane was re-christened "Du-Shane". There was no other pretext for linking him to the legendary molester, but the image seemed to fit; perhaps it was the big feet. In any case the tag took root and we began concocting adventures for Shane as if he possessed the same marvelous physical attributes as his mythical namesake.

It went on for years, and made a nightmare of the poor kid's school days. With constant use the nickname first became shortened to "Doosh" but when some older person pointed out the unsavory associations this might evoke in the public mind, we modified it to "Duke". By Junior high everyone called him Duke, even his mother, who seemed to take it as a mark of esteem. One way or another the girls in school found out the real story behind the name, but with a significant detail missing. They assumed the rest of us boys chose the name Shane after the fabled flasher because we knew something about him they didn't. Naturally we did everything we could think of to encourage them in this misapprehension. Eighteen inches was whispered as the secret statistic, and the number eighteen became code. If Mr. Segec, the earnest little Jehovah's Witness who served as our science teacher, asked us to open our physics texts to page eighteen, the room would instantly be filled with snickers.

"Hey, Duke, what page was that again?" the gorgeous dreamboat with even bigger bee-zonkers than Miss Caesar's would stage-whisper across the aisle.

"Very funny! Booby!"

During study period Tiffy Reid would ask Freddy Pockrant in a small clear voice, "hey did you hear what kind of shakes Duke's father is using on their roof?"

"No, what kind?"

"Straight-eighteens." This would be sufficient to convulse the entire class with squeaks and titters for another ten minutes, by which time someone would have a better one.

It's a wonder poor Shane survived. In senior high school it got so bad I once saw him running around holding his fly open hollering at everyone, "Look! Look you idiots! It's normal—small!" So, in the end, we made a flasher out of him anyway.

Having grown up in a small town you tend to look back on all your formative experiences as atypical, and for many years it never occurred to me that the Ducharme story was more than an elaborate private joke. I remember my astonishment and delight, having moved to Vancouver to attend university, when I came across a mention of Pender Harbour in one of my texts. It was Homer G. Barnett's old tome on the Coast Salish, and Pender Harbour was only mentioned in a list of midden sites, but in this great outer world where you could offer a thousand-dollar reward to the first person who could tell you where Pender Harbour was and never lose your money, just seeing the name down in black

and white seemed to confirm something surprisingly important for me. It was the same the first time I heard someone from outside mention Ducharme. I forget the circumstances now—it might have been the poet Patrick Lane, whose school days in Vernon were enlivened by rumours of the phallic phantom in a way similar to my own in the Harbour.

From another writer I learned our not-so-private joke was known to school populations as far up the coast as Prince Rupert and another friend, Joe Harrison, told me he heard the stories repeated inland as distantly as Nelson, where he and his buddies used to play at goose-stepping precisely as Mickey, Tiffy and the gang had. People whose schooling began more recently than about 1959 seem to have missed all knowledge of the Ducharme legend while those who were adult at the time remember it vividly, but disturbingly, through a veil of period morality. Initially they seem shocked to hear the name mentioned out loud, and may mumble something about "smut" or "bad taste". But there is always a second part to this reaction, especially if you give them any reason to think you are in possession of new information on the subject. Invariably they find a way to sneak back up and find out what you know.

The reason for this awkward fascination is that the legend of Ducharme is one that somehow managed to grow from the private conversation of a few eyewitnesses and spread out across the province, instilling itself permanently in the minds of at least two generations of British Columbians, without once having been confirmed as fact or fiction by any sort of authoritative medium.

The Ducharme legend has spawned any number of variants but there are four consistent elements which everyone who knows it seems to have heard. The central one is that sometime in the recent past Vancouver was inhabited by a bizarre exhibitionist who was freakishly suited to his calling by giantism of the penis. The critical statistic varies somewhat, with the most common guess being eighteen inches. Next, one hears that this Ducharme was in the habit of restraining his oversize member using rope or string. Thirdly one will be told that a woman died after having intercourse with him. Finally, it is said he was arrested on the street parading himself in nothing but gumboots and a raincoat.

The more I came to understand how widely distributed the Ducharme stories were and at the same time how uncomfortably the whole legend rested upon the public mind, the more I became convinced that Raincoast Chronicles would be failing in its duty if we didn't step into the breech and lay people's minds to rest one way or another. To record, bolster and above all to confirm the emergent regional mythology against the mass cultural onslaught was, after all, our *premiere raison d'etre*. My own lifelong curiosity about Ducharme had nothing to do with it.

EVEN three decades after the fact and even dealing with disinterested professionals it can be awkward opening a discussion about Ducharme. For the most part I resolved this problem by hiring the writer John Faustmann to do it. He, in turn, got around it by saying he was only doing it because I was paying him to, which was true. Faustmann did a superb job, tracking down even the mortician who handled Ducharme's remains, but he's been giving me strange looks ever since.

If not the crime of the century, the Ducharme case was certainly Vancouver's top crime story of the fifties. The trial was the longest continuous murder trial in British Columbia history, and a number of the city's great reputations were made and unmade on it. One who doesn't mind admitting the Ducharme case did his career no harm is the Vancouver journalist-cum-broadcaster Jack Webster, who in 1950 was a brash young reporter fresh off the boat from Edinburgh. Interviewed on the set of his morning television show, Webster recalled the 30-year-old case as if quoting verbatim from some of his old stories.

The series of events which brought Ducharme to the attention of the B.C. public began on November 9, 1949, when the tenderman on the Kitsilano swingbridge discovered a woman's body floating in False Creek. It was identified as that of Blanche Ferne Fisher, a middle-aged spinster. Police initially put the incident down as suicide, but Webster, who attended the scene with photographer George Diack, disagreed. They thought it looked like murder.

"Mystery Death", ran the headline on Jack Webster's story in the *Sun* that afternoon. "Discovery of the body of a 45-year-old spinster in False Creek today posed a mystery for police. Possibility of foul play is

They established that the victim had on the night of her death gone out alone to the Rio Theatre at Commercial and Broadway and had been last seen standing in front of the theatre after the show, but after that they got nowhere. Nearly a month after the body was discovered however, Monger and Mackay were called downtown to interview a very unusual citizen who'd been picked up the night before in the Kitsilano area. Acting on a report from the employees of the Coca-Cola bottling plant at Cornwall and Burrard, the police had confronted the man as he walked along Cornwall Street at 1:15 a.m. dressed only in a shirt, scarf, raincoat and a pair of gumboots. His penis was exposed between the buttons of the coat and he appeared to be "driving it" down the street, using strings which were tied around it like reins.

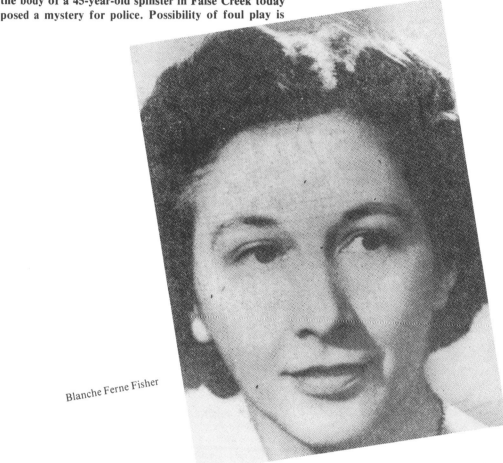

Blanche Ferne Fisher

being investigated..." But nothing developed and after a few days the papers dropped the story for reports of zoot-suit gangs and editorials about the sale of "crime comics" to youngsters.

Webster's instincts had proven right enough, however. Examination of the body found that while the quantity of water in the lungs indicated drowning as the cause of death, the woman had been strangled and sexually assaulted with a "large object" which had caused extensive injury. Two homicide detectives were assigned to the case, but recent allegations of corruption and graft on the Vancouver Force—allegations which would eventually persuade Police Chief Mulligan to seek refuge in South America—had upset press relations with the police and the two detectives weren't talking. Thirty years later, retired inspectors George Monger and C.W. (Don) Mackay seemed to welcome a chance to discuss their work on the Ducharme case.

Sorting out bad leads, following up the slightest bits of information, Monger and Mackay had begun working on the case soon after the body was found.

This strange apparition turned out to be Frederick Roger Ducharme, shown on his arrest record as being five feet seven inches tall, weighing 175 pounds and having wavy red hair. He was to be the only suspect in the case and for the next two weeks Monger and Mackay would interrogate him daily, compiling a thick file on his background, his record, his habits, and his constantly changing alibis.

Born of French-Canadian parents in Elkhorn, Manitoba, Fred Ducharme was in an orphanage by the age of nine. Described in school reports as "unpopular" and "a discipline problem", he was shifted to different institutions. In 1940 in St. Boniface, Manitoba, Ducharme was convicted of indecent exposure and given a one-year suspended sentence. 1941, Yorkton, Saskatchewan—indecent exposure; fined five dollars and costs. 1942, Yorkton—two charges of indecent exposure; six months jail sentence. 1942, Winnipeg—convicted of theft of a watch and an indecent act; six months for theft, three months for the indecent act. A stint in the R.C.A.F. ended with his being discharged as mentally unfit. A first marriage ended when Ducharme deserted his wife. A second marriage ended when he assaulted the woman, whom he had married using the alias of Farnsworth. She left him, later telling police that Ducharme had threatened her with the words: "Shut up, or I'll throw you in the creek."

"We questioned him on and off the record," George Monger recalls. "We never had any trouble with the guy. He seemed just like an ordinary Joe." Ordinary, except in one respect. On the first day of questioning, Don Mackay recalls having Ducharme remove his clothes so they could check him for scratch marks. They did find the scratch marks, but they also found, in Mackay's words, that their suspect was "hung like a stud horse. The head on that thing of his was the size of a tennis ball."

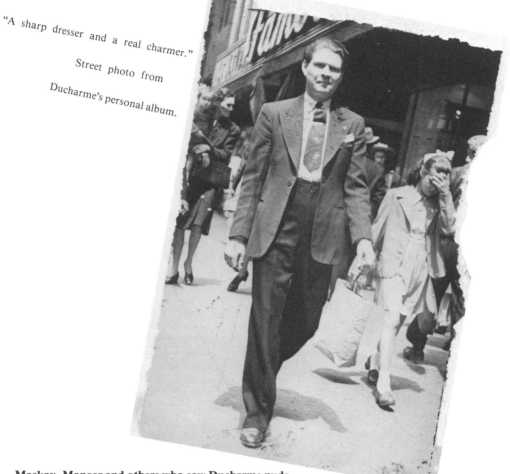

"A sharp dresser and a real charmer."

Street photo from Ducharme's personal album.

Mackay, Monger and others who saw Ducharme nude agree that the fabled organ was actually fourteen inches in length, flaccid.

It became an awkward case in that here almost at the outset the police had seen enough to know in their own minds they had the "weapon" that had been used on their victim. The trouble was, it wasn't the sort of item you wanted to end up having to exhibit before the learned gentlemen and packed press galleries of the court. They decided to take a raincheck on that one and look for something more presentable.

Ducharme lived in a tarpaper shack on floats down in False Creek, one of a great many such dwellings lining both sides of the creek in those days, comprising a neighbourhood of outcasts and fringe types in, but not of, the city. The two detectives had already spent a lot of time sniffing around among the floathouse people but hadn't stumbled across Ducharme and had found his neighbours singularly uncooperative. Now they searched Ducharme's coffin-shaped abode and came away with a dog-eared stack of *Sunbather* (the *Penthouse* of the 1950's), a diary kept in the name of

Frederick Farnsworth, a copy of the *Canada Criminal Code* with sections on sexual offences underlined, over fifty pairs of women's panties and a pair of women's shoes. From the back of his car they added a woman's bone-handled umbrella and from a neighbour to whom Ducharme had traded it, a ladies' watch inscribed with the initials B.F.F.

The shoes, umbrella and watch all proved to have been the victim's and on December 21, 1949, Ducharme was officially charged with the murder of Blanche Ferne Fisher. "Shoes Lead to Charge of Murder", ran the page one headline.

Justice A.M. Manson, whose reputation as "the hanging judge" was established partly as a result of the Ducharme case, presided at the trial. T.G. Norris, who went on to become a Supreme Court Justice, handled the case for the Crown. Dugald McAlpine, a big-name attorney who'd seen better days, defended. Taking every word down in shorthand from beginning to end, Jack Webster covered the trial for the *Sun*. "I wrote six or seven columns a day. Made three hundred dollars in overtime. That was unheard of in those days."

Webster remembers the proceedings as a contest of stubborn Scottish wills between Manson and McAlpine, a devotee of the two-martini coffee break. "McAlpine would invariably come in late after the 2:30 adjournment, and Manson would become infuriated with him. There were a number of nasty scenes." None of this was calculated to serve the best interests of the defendent, but McAlpine's worst disservice to Ducharme was in allowing him to testify on his own behalf.

Ducharme was one of those semi-literate men who tended to respond in formal encounters by adopting stilted, unnatural speech full of malapropisms and ostentatious displays of false learning, altogether giving him an air of moronic pretentiousness. "I am a victim of *circumstantea* evidence," he would claim, or say, "there seems to be a *monopoly* between two *divergent* stories." Explaining the cache of panties discovered in his shack, he said, "Every time I see a clothesline I have a yearning to collect them just like a kleptomaniac has a yearning to collect articles of the same meaning..."

Throughout the trial he grinned, fawned and played to the gallery as if he were an object of admiration with absurd emphasis, "I still say I am not guilty."

Jack Webster recalls with pride how he surrounded the courthouse with photographers to get one last picture of the condemned man. It shows a tall plainclothes cop shoving a small, hunched figure toward the door of a waiting prowl-car. Ducharme was hanged on July 14, 1950 and four days later buried in an unmarked grave just outside the gates of the old B.C. Penitentiary.

George Diack's photo of Ducharme leaving the courthouse after being sentenced to hang.

rather than repugnance and not repentant in the slightest. At the same time he was incapable of keeping to one line of thought, and blithely committed the grossest contradictions. T.G. Norris homed in on Ducharme like a wolf on a lame sheep. Described as "blunt" and "forceful" in Jack Webster's reports of the time, others prefer words like "bullying" and "brutal", remembering how he would lash out at witnesses and leave them in tears if it suited his purpose.

Referring to Ducharme only as "witness", Norris badgered him until he became hostile and evasive, shifting desperately from one preposterous claim to the next. At one point, when Norris began reading from the secret diary the defendant had kept under the name of Farnsworth, Ducharme had to be restrained from attacking the attorney, yelling, "I'll go down there and bash your blasted head in, you rat!"

In his summation McAlpine pleaded for a reduced verdict of manslaughter, stressing that Blanche Fisher had gone with Ducharme willingly and had been alive in the water. According to the only witness they had of events connecting these two circumstances—Ducharme—she also consented to have sex, withdrew that consent, and finally in a fit of guilty remorse hurled herself off the bridge.

This scenario could not be proven true beyond doubt, but neither could it be proven false beyond doubt, therefore, according to the defense, the jury was bound to reject the irrevocable penalty of death. McAlpine introduced further arguments touching the question of sanity and responsibility, but Ducharme had already hanged himself in the witness box. His final statement could only have convinced the all-male jury they had rid society of a dangerous lunatic.

"Gentlemen," Ducharme said to them, "the woman which I was referring to is still alive and well contented I was out with her that particular night." He then trailed off into gibberish, admitting for the first time he'd actually had the body in his floathouse, and finishing up

IN retrospect it isn't difficult to recognize Ducharme as a psychopath who was not responsible for his actions and probably should never have been hanged. By night an exhibitionist and rapist, possibly a killer, by day he was charming, cheerful, and well thought of by all who knew him, particularly women.

Occasionally during their pre-trial interrogation, Monger and Mackay would let Ducharme out of his cell and take him to a restaurant across the street. Monger recalls the night a waitress brought Ducharme a bowl of cold soup. "Hey, this is cold," Ducharme told her. "I'll see if I can get it warmed up," the waitress replied. "Why don't you just sit on it for a while," Ducharme said, "That'll warm it up."

"Now if I'd said that," Monger observes, "I'd have gotten my face slapped. Ducharme, he could get away with it. He had that about him."

Little Joe Holmgren, a feisty ex-Creek type who lived next door to Ducharme, remembers him as a sharp dresser and always the perfect gentleman. "He could charm the pants off any woman. He could have married a millionaire lady there one time." The detectives discovered that Ducharme had female admirers all over the city, none of whom believed him capable of the violence he stood accused of. He and Holmgren used to collaborate on "a bit of piracy"—lifting things from tied-up tugboats and parked cars out at the golf course, but Ducharme "wouldn't take nothing from anyone on the Creek. Everybody there really liked him. No one would believe he murdered that girl." On one of several trips the court made to the scene of the crime during the trial, Holmgren remembers that as Ducharme passed by a woman neighbour called to him, "Keep your pecker up!" After appearing for the prosecution at Ducharme's trial—perhaps as part of a deal respecting some of his own activities—Holmgren was denounced back on the Creek as a "Judas" and was forced to beat a hasty retreat out of town.

Of Ducharme's mental derangement there is no question. When first arrested in front of the Coke plant he told the desk Sergeant, "I get blank spells. They last about six or eight hours. I must have blacked out." This claim gained credence from testimony by psychiatrists at the trial who stated that Ducharme "exhibited a psychopathic personality" and suffered from "idiopathic" epilepsy, which would cause him to act in an automatic fashion. During the investigation and trial he was observed at various stages along the well-travelled circuit between his two personalities. There were times when he seemed on top of the world, a man in full control of his destiny. Mackay tells a story about one of the court excursions to False Creek to exhume details of the crime. These visits would have been stressful for the accused man and he could have been excused for showing it. Instead, on this occasion, Mackay remembers him spotting Dugald McAlpine, who had stepped behind a log to urinate. "Aha!" Ducharme explained, and in a loud voice quoted the exact wording of the law that was being broken.

At such a time it was hard to see much wrong with Ducharme's mind, but there were other times when his mental processes seemed to collapse, leaving him stammering and incoherent like some pathetic modern-day Caliban.

Whether Ducharme's mental problems were a result of his physical abnormality is not for the layman to say, but there was some connection. George Monger, who recalls the case with an overall sense of sadness, remembers Ducharme's obsession with his penis, and shakes his head. "He told me once," Monger says, "that 'it' went for a walk the night he was caught. It was as if 'it' had given him an order." Ducharme told him, "I had to keep a string tied around 'it'; when 'it' comes up, I get hysterical."

Jack Webster, too, recalls the case with some regret. "I used to talk with Ducharme during the trial," he says. "I got the feeling that here was a friendly, slightly retarded soul, who'd started out his public life by masturbating on street corners, and I still don't know if it was a brutal murder or an accidental death." Inspector Mckay remembers the case without remorse while admitting, "It was one of the worst from a technical point of view." Harry Rankin, the well-known Vancouver lawyer and alderman, who was a student in McAlpine's office at the time of the trial, has written in his book I Beg to Differ that the case still troubles him "because it was loaded with contradictions". Rankin believes that Ducharme panicked on the night of November 8 and did not wilfully murder Blanche Fisher. Monger agrees: "If the darn fool had taken her to hospital, she probably would have lived. Instead he lost his head, and dumped her in the drink." Webster was on holiday at Horseshoe Bay the day of the hanging, and when his editor phoned him to cover it, he refused. "There's no way I'm going to see that man hanged," he said. "He's off his nut."

As a criminal Ducharme doesn't stack up as one of your Biggs or Mesrines, even as one of your Boston Stranglers. His career outside the law was one of stinky little misdemeanors capped by a vicious blunder that cost two people their lives. Nevertheless I find the story a remarkable one on several counts. Faustmann disagrees with me here, saying the only remarkable thing about Ducharme was he happened to have a "big dick".

Okay. For starters, let me confess, I am thoroughly amazed by the simple bare fact of Ducharme's preposterous abnormality. To me it stands as most welcome proof that the Beloved Creator has a sense of humour—a devilish one at that—and when He makes a joke we needn't consider ourselves too good to enjoy it. There's too many people around these days working overtime finding ways to be serious.

Beyond this, while I recognize Ducharme's violence was abhorrent, I think society's reaction to him was classic, and tells us more about ourselves than we probably want to know. He was put to death on roughly the same impulse as people stomp on a snake. In fact that was almost precisely the process of fascinated attraction, followed by guilty recoil, which transpired. As Webster recalls when Ducharme was arrested, "the city was instantly rife with speculation and salacious rumours about the size of his organ." No word touching this delicate matter could be printed in the paper of course, and George Monger and Don Mackay remember being sidled up to in so many ways by so many different people they began to make a joke of it.

On one occasion one of the policemen involved in the case was having his mother-in-law over for an afternoon visit. He happened to mention his involvement in the highly-publicized case during tea and afterward went out to work in the garden, leaving the women to talk. Before long the mother-in-law, a well-bred middle-aged lady, appeared at the back door and made her way over to the garden where he was just in the process of rooting out his big woody winter turnips. "I didn't think to ask at dinner," she began with a little blush, "but, this Ducharme character, well, I'd heard, you know you hear some dreadful stories and I was well, wondering..." He let her hang for a moment, then without saying a word yanked out the biggest, buggiest turnip he could find and held it up to her. "Oh!" she gasped, and hurried back inside, shaking her head.

The trial itself, as one reporter wrote on the day it began, "was like a crowd at a bargain sale." Women from all over Vancouver began lining up in front of the Georgia Street courthouse as much as three hours early, hoping to get a gallery seat. Hundreds were turned away. Inside, sheriffs had their hands full trying to restrain the crowd and continually rebuked the women for their behaviour. "I just had to get a look at this fellow Ducharme," one breathless matron explained to reporters.

There is a famous poem by D. H. Lawrence called "Snake" in which he studies mankind's powerful subconscious fascination with the image of the phallus, and demonstrates how in the case of modern middle-class man with all his civilized hangups the initial entrancement is characteristically followed by a guilty awakening, causing him to lash out and from a sense of "duty" destroy the object that inspired it. At Ducharme's trial prosecution tried to impress the jury that it had a duty to see this man who'd become everyone's phallic fantasy exterminated, and played skillfully upon the prevailing atmosphere of sexual hysteria to incite jurors to vote on sentiment rather than logic. Rankin, in his book, comments, "the final outcome was as much a result of the mood of the times as it was the nature of the crime."

Annie of the Corridors.

Madonnas of the fogged past
you move through endless passageways
interminable rooms
constant among the transience
of transient hotels
aging hennaed women with much English
pretty Slavic girls with little
Betty   Olga   Doris   Petruska
and the nervous one with the unpronounceable name

lost ladies of morning corridors
like displaced mothers   amnesiac sweethearts
triggering vague dreams
of love or guttering lust
in the drifting minds of lonely men.

Annie of the corridors
queen of the Marble Arch chambermaids
how I imagined I loved you
in the pinched alienated days
when nothing like love seemed likely again.

Annie, of the fine roan hair
and the full proud man familiar body
the fortyish worldwise sensual face
you ran your troops like a kindly madam
and my fantasies like a succubus.

Annie, my seamstress of dreams
who once sewed two buttons on my one shirt
after a drunken scuffle
Who sometimes shared a drink with me
but never my bed.

Annie, immovable Annie
rejecting my clumsy advances
telling me with enormous finality:
"You're young enough to be my son.
And you drink too much."

Annie, empress of linen-closets
in visions, I stride surely back to you
no longer a boy or drunk   King of the Janitors
with coveralls and an amorous moustache
We are made for each other   we make love
in all the empty rooms
are married by the Manager
and rule that dusky corridor empire forever.

Peter Trower

ELI VISITS THE BIG SMOKE
Excerpt from a novel in progress by Hubert Evans

Hubert Evans, whose novel Mist on the River *(1954) is probably the best study of rural west coast life ever written, published his first book of B.C. fiction in 1926. Now in his 90th year, he is hard at work on a new novel recounting his first two decades in B.C., from 1911 to the early thirties. Like his acclaimed 1979 novel* O Time In Your Flight, *the new book can be seen as an historical memoir as much as a work of imagination, showing today's generations how vastly the world has changed within the span of one man's life. Where* O Time In Your Flight, *was recounted entirely in the words of a nine-year-old boy, the current work, tentatively titled* Buckethead, *is recounted from the viewpoint of an aging and simple-minded bachelor whose eternal naiveté gives the period portrait freshness and a nice ironic counter-current.*

In the following excerpt Eli Gimbal, the subject, has been taken under the wing of an ambitious young newspaperman named Jeff Purcell—Hubert Evans himself in thin disguise—and removed to New Westminster from his accustomed Nelson where he was "high pillow man" (a favoured regular) at a sporting house and carried on a somewhat fanciful romance with a girl named Effie. The year now is 1913 and Jeff is waging a one-man campaign to awaken New Westminsterites to the great opportunities presented by the opening of the Panama Canal, due the following year. It is also the year of the last great salmon run on the Fraser, tragically blocked by a rockslide in Hell's Gate Canyon, and the author of North America's last train robbery, Bill Miner, has just escaped from the New Westminster Penitentiary under mysterious circumstances...

Even before Thanksgiving Day rolled around, Eli was beginning to feel almost as much at home in New Westminster as ever he had in Nelson. In fact, when you got right down to it, except for the L.D., the back room of the cigar store and of course, Effie, he could honestly say he felt more at home than ever he had in all his wandering years since Gran died. Here he was with a well-stocked kitchen which was as good as his, and with a house and three young fellows to take care of. Sitting up week nights into the wee small hours waiting for the three to come from work, the tea-kettle singing on the stove, a snack or a full meal for each and all to be had for the asking, he sometimes let his thoughts go leaping from limb to limb, almost making himself believe he had by some miracle or other, become the father of a family and that his on-again, off-again camp cook days were over and done with.

Jeff's piece about the big things the Panama Canal would do for New Westminster did not get printed. Another subject Jeff wrote about that summer was the Fraser River salmon run, so many salmon you could almost believe the yarn about walking across the river on their backs. Eli had never seen anything like it, not in all his born days. He expected it to be Jeff's biggest story of the year. But no such thing. It did get printed on the front page of the News but it did not make much of a stir. The part of it most talked about was the short-lived strike down at Steveston, fishermen having the nerve to want up to twenty-five cents for a single solitary salmon! When any Tom, Dick or Harry with a gaff hook or a piece of net could catch them by the tubful. According to Vince, salmon bellies were the best part. You salt-pickled the bellies in kegs and threw the rest away.

The strike was a short one. According to some, the Wobblies were behind it, a man from down in Washington State where the Wobblies were out to make trouble in sawmills and logging camps. The end came shortly before six o'clock of a sunny Sunday afternoon and thanks to Jeff, Eli was on the spot to see it. If Al and Vince had stayed put that Sunday for a change he probably would not have left the house in case there was something he could do for them. But since neither of them had so much as showed his face the previous night, and since the day was a fine one, Eli decided to take up Jeff's offer for him to come along. As things turned out, if he had had so much as a glimmer of what he was to see from the Imperial Cannery wharf at six o'clock that Sunday minutes after the starting gun went off, wild horses could not have kept him away.

Right up to the minute the starting gun went off, each of the boats with its boat-puller and its fisherman standing ready beside his pile of net, were lined up at the cannery wharves like so many runners on their toes, all set to go. All of the boats had masts and sails - sprit sails was the name they had for it - in case a wind came along and there was no need to row. Some of the boats had a sort of a cubby-hole at their front end, dog houses was a name the fishermen had for them - where the two men could stretch out when they were not rowing and either putting out or pulling in their nets. One boat Eli took a close look at had what he took to be an old pail punched full of holes and set in a box of sand so the fishermen could have charcoal fires and cook their meals.

Eli had no idea how many canneries there were but from what he could make out as he stood with Jeff on the Imperial Cannery wharf there must have been at least a dozen, with boats galore lined up at the wharves of each, two men to a boat, the boat-pullers standing ready at their oars, the fishermen at the back end of the boats, all ready to throw out their nets. The very second the starting gun went off away the boats went, the boat-pullers standing and pushing on their oars, not sitting down and pulling as in your ordinary rowboat, the fishermen throwing out their nets for all they were worth, spreading their arms at every throw to separate the float line from the lead line. Minutes later, within a few chain-lengths of the wharves, the float lines began to sink under the weight of struggling salmon gilled in them. Right off, some fishermen began pulling in their nets and taking out the fish. Others made a quick turn-around, bunching their nets and heading back to the wharves for all they were worth. Talk about your excitement! Men hollering back and forth and the catches being forked out of the boats and onto the wharves, here and there a salmon still alive and kicking. In next to no time the price of a salmon dropped from two-bits to five cents, but still the boats kept coming, some loaded down with salmon, others rowing out for a second load. By the time Jeff and Eli headed for the late interurban, the canneries were chock-a-block with tons more salmon than they could handle, and had stopped buying. Even so, many of the boats kept fishing. The last Eli saw of them was their riding lights all along the river. On the Monday afternoon when Jeff went to Steveston to find out what came of it, a cannery boss showed him three scows, loaded with unwanted salmon, twenty thousand salmon to each scow, about to be towed to the river mouth and dumped. When Jeff asked if nothing could be done to prevent the waste, the man said the same thing had happened back in nineteen-three, only more so, so many unwanted salmon, drifting ashore and rotting that the Vancouver health authorities closed the beaches. It made Jeff hot under the collar just ot hear about it. He even went to the Dominion Government fisheries office a block or so from the News office and asked if nothing could be done to stop the waste. A man behind the counter as good as told him not to get his shirt in a knot. But when Jeff managed to get in and talk with Colonel F.H. Cunningham, the Chief Inspector, Colonel Cunningham more or less put in with him. Later that week, there was a story going around town about an old Scotchman and his grown son who had been staying at the Russel. According to the bartender there, the two owned fish canneries in Scotland and had been sizing up the Fraser with a view of buying out a Steveston cannery or building one of their own. But after what went on at Steveston, so much waste, they dropped the idea then and there. "God will punish them, He will, He will," the old gentleman declared and they left for Scotland, the pair of them, Aberdeen or Peterhead, the bartender could not rightly remember which. At the house when Jeff told the two others this, Vince had a good laugh over it. He said the Fraser was the world's greatest salmon river, always was and always would be.

When Jeff took Eli with him to visit Doctor McQuarrie it was not a case of killing two birds with one stone, as some might think, although a person in the know could easily have jumped to that conclusion. As well as being one of the town's doctors, Doctor McQuarrie was the penitentiary doctor. As luck would have it, while he was earning the money to become a doctor, he took the job of mail clerk on trains travelling back and forth across the country. Wellsir, the very night Bill Miner and Shorty Gunn held up the CPR train at Notch Hill or thereabouts, who should be on duty all by himself in the mail car but young McQuarrie. Years later while Bill Miner was serving time in New Westminster penitentiary who should come into his cell one fine day? Why none other than Doctor McQuarrie, safe and sound, fit as a fiddle, let bygones be bygones, shake hands and all the rest of it. Until the day Bill Miner went over the prison wall — or under it, depending on whose story you listened to--the two had some good talks and more than a few chuckles over their first meeting in the mail car years before. Nobody in his right mind could call Jeff Purcel a snooper but he could see around corners and he did not need to be told on which side his bread was buttered. Which was why he had struck up an acquaintance with Doctor McQuarrie from the very first. That spring when the *New Westminster News* ran its clean-up campaign, Jeff had written a piece which Doctor McQuarrie said hit the nail on the head. Between the two of them it was not a case of you scratch my back and I'll scratch yours or even of one good turn deserving another. All the same, when Jeff got onto the trail of the Bill Miner story it was only natural for Doctor McQuarrie to tell him things no other reporter knew. Which in the long run ended up with Jeff Purcel shaking the dust of British Columbia off his feet and making a name for himself in Toronto as a magazine writer. And all because his Bill Miner story, as he got it from Doctor McQuarrie, was printed in magazines half way around the world, England to Australia. The part of the story Eli heard Doctor McQuarrie tell Jeff that spring evening was about what

took place while Bill was making the mail clerk open the registered mail sacks. What Bill was looking for was a big shipment of money from back east which he had been led to believe would be on the train. But wasn't. One of the registered parcels held a sample bottle of some new-fangled cough medicine. Although Bill did not say so in so many words, that medicine came like an answer to a prayer. And for the reason that Bill was bothered by a troublesome cough. (Years later that cough turned out to be consumption, not the galloping kind but consumption all the same and which finished him in Georgia State prison where he was held after committing what one newspaper said was the last train robbery in the U.S.A.or in Canada, for the matter of that.) Bill told the mail clerk to hand over the bottle. He uncorked it, cool as a cucumber and took a swig. The very first time Doctor McQuarrie visited Bill in New Westminster penitentiary and told him who that mail clerk was they had a good laugh about it. Doctor McQuarrie reminded Bill that while he was uncorking the medicine bottle and taking a swig he had laid down his gun. "I was going to reach for mine but thought better of it." Bill said it was just as well he hadn't, that Shorty had him covered through the door at the far end of the car.

There was more to the Bill Miner story than Doctor McQuarrie told about. Yes, and there was more to it than Jeff wrote about and for the reason he could not be certain-sure all of it was true. If you went by what Jeff heard, Bill Miner's escape from New Westminster penitentiary was a put-up job. The way Jeff heard it, when Bill and Shorty held up the train they made off with four million dollars worth of Australian government bonds. They knew they could not sell the bonds but they cached them back in the hills somewhere just in case. Well sir, only a few months before Bill made his so-called escape, several Australian Government men registered at the Russel Hotel which is almost within the shadow of the courthouse, as you might say. They paid several visits to the penitentiary. And anyone who believed they did so just for the scenery would believe the moon is made of green cheese, as old Miss Schiller would have said. The penitentiary wall was made of planks. Lo and behold, one day when Bill was stretching his legs in the yard, he discovered a loose plank. So out he went, three other prisoners close behind him. The three did not get far before they were caught. Bill did not get far either, only to Abbotsford. But according to talk he stayed around Abbotsford for a time with nary a policeman coming for him. No person in the know came right out and said Bill was turned loose in return for telling where the bonds were cached but this did not stop people from putting two and two together.

A report Jeff did use to end some of his Bill Miner stories was that when Bill was escaping from Georgia State Prison he might not have been caught if he had been willing to shoot the guard or policeman who was hot on his trail. People who remembered Bill Miner said that was Bill all over. He was a soft-spoken little man, one of nature's gentlemen, a sort of Wild West Robin Hood.

The Saturday before his store clothes came, Eli made up his mind to have a day in Vancouver just as he was, bib overalls, old mackinaw and all. If he had asked, Al would have taken him and maybe shown him around, but Eli would just as soon have his first look at Vancouver all by himself. Al and Jeff were still asleep, Vince, as usual had not come home. So without disturbing the sleepers, Eli took three dollars - a two dollar bill and one in silver and a shin plaster from the chip-in box on what had been the clock shelf on the kitchen wall back of the stove, and headed down Sixth Street for the tram station

as fast as his legs would carry him. He got there in the nick of time. Half a minute later and the door would have been closed against him. Not that there would have been any weeping and wailing and gnashing of teeth like in the Bible, or when the door was slammed in the faces of those ten foolish virgins. But all the same he would have had an hour or more to wait.

All the regular seats were filled so he found a place for himself between two men on a side seat in the smoker. One of the men had the looks of the compass man of a survey party Eli had cooked for one season out from Hazelton as far north as Poison Mountain, though of course he wasn't the same man grown older. The other man Eli squeezed in beside wore one of those flat-topped, broad-brimmed felt hats the like of which you sometimes see on the prairies. The man sat there sort of twiddling his thumbs and gazing off into space. Eli did not know what to make of him. A man straight across from Eli had his head buried in a copy of that morning's *New Westminster News*. Eli could see it was the News on account of one of the front page headlines, the one about more money needed from Ottawa to speed up harbour improvements before ships from the Panama Canal began piling in to unload, have the seaweed and stuff cleaned from their bottoms free of charge, then load up with lumber or whatever else they came for. So the sooner the improvements were finished the sooner the port of Vancouver would be playing second fiddle to the ports of New Westminster and Port Mann. It was another of Jeff's harbour improvement stories and Eli felt proud of him for writing it.

When Eli got to the waterfront, the harbour of Vancouver was a sight to see. Right off, Eli could tell New Westminster had its work cut out for it to put Vancouver's harbour in the shade. Dock after dock with ships of every size and shape, by far the largest, the ocean liner. One of the CPR's White Empresses, Al told him later. From where he stood, Eli could not get a full view of it, but it was at least as big as the ocean liner Effie had the picture of. Away to his right, toward what he took to be the head end of the harbour, a regular sea of masts, most of them taller than the buildings beyond. It might just be that some of these masts were those of the square-rigger Jeff was given the chance of sailing around the Horn on but at the very last had changed his mind about going. And no wonder! Imagine being ordered to climb to the top of the mast in a howling gale, the ship rolling from side to side and you holding on for dear life with one hand and trying to fold the sail with the other!

After sizing up the harbour, Eli moseyed on back to Hastings Street. Talk about delivery rigs! By far the toniest was one with "Gordon Drysdale" in fancy letters on the side of it. Every last thing about it was so shiny you would think it had come from a carriage paint shop that very morning. Truth to tell, his father would have needed to have his wits about him to turn out a niftier job. On top of everything, the rig was drawn by a spanking team — dappled greys they were — high-steppers but without check-reins.

Twice coming up Granville Street - once at the corner with Hastings and once on the same side part way, he passed men plunked down on the sidewalk. One had the looks of a crippled back. The other had both legs off below the knee. One had pencils for sale, the other what Eli took to be boot-laces. Both were a pitiful sight to see. Not that they were weeping and wailing and gnashing their teeth. Like as not if they had up and weeped and wailed and gnashed their teeth, people would have paid them more heed. Back east, any town on the main railroad line, you would have taken them for brakies who had got the worst of it. But according to both Vince and Al you could be pretty sure they were loggers or sawmill men. Al said there was supposed to be a legless logger living in a hollow tree somewhere out of the way in Stanley Park, though you could not prove it by him. The mere sight of those two hunkered down on the cold sidewalk, took Eli back to the one-armed brakie who acted caretaker for the Gospel Hall, spry as a cricket and raising his voice in song with the best of them.

Granville Street had clothing stores galore and sure enough a few corners along, the Gordon Drysdale Drygoods Store with one of its shiny rigs standing at the curb and Eli would have gone still farther but it was high time he kept his wits about him. First and foremost, it was the zoo in Stanley Park he had come to see. So at the corner he asked a policeman how to get there. The policeman gave him a quick look-over and told him what number streetcar to take and not to get off until the end of the line.

Eli would never have said that Stanley Park Zoo was not all it was cracked up to be. But by the end of the afternoon he wished he had spent the time seeing the sailing ships at Hastings Mill. The sight of all those animals and birds cooped up behind bars or in cages was something he would just as soon forget. Even the monkeys did not seem to be getting any fun out of life. Probably he was allowing his imagination to run away with him as he sometimes did but the sad puzzled expressions on their faces was as if they were trying to bring back long-ago things they could not quite remember. The bears had cement hide-out rooms instead of caves or hollow trees in which to den up for the winter. And that big grey timber wolf pacing back and forth, back and forth across the front of his cage! Or the hunched up white headed eagle moveless on its high perch inside its roofed cage with never the sky to look at! In front of the cougar cage he watched a dressed-up city man with his little lap dog on a leash, telling it go sic the cat, the dog yapping and the man egging it on, the cougar not turning its head but looking down at the yapping little dog with one half closed eye. What one swipe of that cougar's paw would have done to the man's lap dog would have left him laughing on the other side of his face. To Eli's way of thinking, the wild ducks and geese and even the peacock had all the best of it.

Instead of following the car tracks back downtown, Eli decided to take in the side streets along the way and see what he could see. Which wasn't much because of the fog and the shrubbery in front of the houses even though the street lights had been turned on. From somewhere out in the harbour, a foghorn was bellowing and grunting with a voice which would make a bull moose play second fiddle. The air had the smell of soft coal smoke. It made him think of trains and machinery or of the time he took a look inside the Roger's Pass tunnel after a train came out. Wood smoke was altogether different. It reminded him of people, of crews he had cooked for, of evenings around a friendly fire. Fir, cedar, hemlock, jackpine, alder, birch, cottonwood, willow, each had its different smell and place in your remembering. Coal smoke was fine for making wheels go around. It did not make you think of people.

The walk from Stanley Park to the interurban tram station took Eli a good deal longer than he had expected it would, partly because he made several wrong turnings and had to back-track and partly because he had never before walked that distance on hard pavement, which is easy as rolling off a log for your dyed-in-the-wool city man but which took some of the starch out of him by the time he got to Hastings Street. One after another those city men went swinging past him heel and toe, never so much as glancing down to see where they were stepping which in the woods or on a side-hill would mighty soon have brought them down a cropper. Some city women - by no means all of them, the young ones mostly, tippy-tapping on their high heels, little chicken steps only from the knees down, wriggling their behinds like some cat or other having a conniption fit, others though walking from their hips, heads up and shoulders back which Effie said a girl must do to be a dancer on the Gold Coast or on what she called the Five-a-day.

There were as many people coming and going on Hastings Street as you would find on Columbia Street on your average New Westminster market day. Which is the same as saying Hastings Street had about all it could handle late that December afternoon. As he stood there sizing it up, a man brushed past him and started across. He could have been run over, and most likely would have been if the driver had not yelled at him to watch where he was going. It was plain to see the man must be from back east, or from down in the states and had not got it into his head that in British Columbia the rule was to keep to the left-hand side of the road.

The rain water soup and so-called apple pie he had taken on hours ago had done him no more good than a slap on the belly with a frozen fish, which was what he once heard a man from the Lardeau say about a certain mining recorder he was dead set and determined to whittle down to size.

By the time Eli had found his way back to Hastings Street it was getting on to suppertime, so the first good-looking eating place he came to he would treat himself to a sit-down meal, one that would stick to his ribs.

If you had backed Eli Gimball into a corner and pinned him right down to it he would have admitted without the shadow of a doubt that as he back-tracked along Hastings Street the two men he had seen that morning sitting on the cold damp sidewalk - the cripple and the legless logger - were farthest from his mind, or at least so far behind that they played second fiddle to his thoughts of a sit-down meal. Truth to tell it was not until he was sitting in an eating place in the next block that the fact of what he had done caught up with him. He had downed a thick roast beef sandwich and was polishing off a good-sized wedge of mince pie - flaky crust, spiced just right but short of the meat and suet Gran used in here - that the fact of what he had done and failed to do smacked him straight between the eyes. The pie hit the spot but even so he did not finish it. He paid his bill and hurried back. As he walked he counted the change in his pocket. There was enough and to spare for his tram fare, so he took out the two dollar bill, wrapped it around the extra two-bit piece all ready to drop in the cripple's cap as he walked past. Better late than never. But the poor fellow's place was empty, no sign of him anywhere. The rest of the way to the tram station, no sign of the legless logger either.

BOOK REVIEWS

Rolf Knight:
Indians at Work:

An Informal History of Native Indian Labour in British Columbia: 1858-1930.

ARE NORTH AMERICAN INDIANS the people of a culturally distinct internal colony, whose lands have been stolen by force and fraud? Or are they ordinary working men and women struggling to cope with an industrial society?

Obviously they are both, but Rolf Knight's book argues that a dazzling light has been focussed on their separate cultural identity; and this has blinded us to their vigorous participation as workers, proprietors and entrepreneurs.

It is time that the generations of Indian loggers, long-shoremen, teamsters, cowboys, miners (farmers), fishermen and others who labored in virtually every primary industry...were recognized. Wage work in the major industries...has been an intimate feature of Indian lives for five and more generations....
— Indians at Work: 7

The Indians did not disappear into a limbo of the unemployed as soon as the invading Euro-Canadians had them outnumbered and outgunned. Even the best of the historians seem to think so, but Knight shows that they are mistaken.

In making these points, he adds another interesting dimension to the store of working-class history that he has compiled in *A Very Ordinary Life,* 1974; *A Man of Our Times,* with Maya Koizumi, 1976; and *Stump Ranch Chronicles and Other Narratives,* 1977; *Along the Number Twenty Line,* 1980; and two annotated bibliographies that are linked with this body of writing: "Work Camps and Company Towns in Canada and the United States," 1975; and a bibliography of working-class fiction which he is now putting together.

The Indians in Knight's second latest book are not simple children of the wilderness who are bewildered by time-clocks, machinery and "white man's" ways. They are quick learners who make an early and effective adjustment to industry.

It is not the case that Indian workers were employed only in unskilled labor or in pursuits slightly modified from the traditional rounds. They learned...the highly complicated and novel skills associated with team freighting, with sailing in the most treacherous waters in the world during the last days of sail, and with the cornucopia of harness, gear and machinery required for horse-powered farming. Some Indian entrepreneurs acquired their own gas boats, steam tugs, logging donkey engines and steam threshers. The conditions under which many Indian workers, men and women, were employed from the 1870's on were as industrial as you could get in B.C.
— Indians at Work: 179

The Indians are not noble savages or passive victims; the Euro-Canadians of Knight's earlier books are not faceless oppressors or heroic pioneers or any kind of standard product. They are individually varied human beings, all striving to get along. Most of them are plain working people rather than celebrities.

...Our own stories are more alive, more meaningful and more capable of providing strength and support than any of the biographies of 'great' men or the National Dreams of statesmen and captains of industry. The experiences reported here are part of a hidden heritage....
— A Very Ordinary Life: ii

For some years Knight has been waging war against a variety of literary and social enemies, from certain politically conservative cultural anthropologists to outright history-fakers. This is more than the usual genteel sparring of the intellectual arena: it is Knight's campaign against the writers who portray people as non-human stereotypes.

His sharpest words are aimed at vendors of shallow ethnic histories and bogus profiles of the Canadian working class:

Here, tricked out in the latest styles of social concern, are the old, hackneyed views of ordinary people by

hucksters on the make. They portray working people as reactionary, stupid, racist, culturally and intellectually illiterate — but 'the salt of the earth.' Immigrants are the horny-handed sons of toil: the old Tory stereotypes of 'the common man.' Apart from being scurrilous and patronising, these caricatures are nothing more than a version of the noble savage by writers who are contemptuous of the lives of real people.
— A Very Ordinary Life: ii

However, Knight does not waste much time attacking these enemies head-on. His life and work are his argument.

He spent some of his early youth rambling about the world and working in camps. More recently, he was an anthropologist and teacher at the University of Toronto for seven years; then, in 1977, after a long leave of absence, he voluntarily quit his tenured position and dropped out of organized academic life. He did it because he could no longer endure what he saw as the narrowness of some of his colleagues and the know-nothingism of students on the University of Toronto's suburban campuses.

Now he is driving a taxi in Vancouver and writing informal social history at the average rate of one paper-back every 18 months, which is a better speed than he was able to reach when he was entangled in the university routine.

In each of his books he delivers a few cuts and thumps to "Barry Babbitts" and "Pierre Bertonesque heroes," and the makers of social science myths; and then he gets on with the job of producing a documentary record of ordinary people's lives, which he prefaces with statements of purpose like this:

This book is dedicated to those generations of migrant camp workers, stump ranch philosophers, sometimes union organizers and jacks-of-all-trades who inhabited the backlands and cities of Western Canada only yesterday. It is a tribute also to my father, who was one of them, and so to many of our friends during my youth. It is dedicated to them and to the hundreds and thousands of others like them whose lives and stories never were and now never will be told.
— Stump Ranch Chronicles: iv

"Indians at Work" does not pretend to be a full history of sociocultural change among Indians since the European invasion began. Knight hopes his book will stir others to produce such studies on a regional basis. His main purpose was to gather evidence to set the record straight about Indian participation in the economy; and he achieves this purpose in quite a convincing way.

When Crazy Horse and Sitting Bull were wiping out Custer, he observes, certain other Indian groups were growing prizewinning wheat. (But many Indian farmers were as badly clobbered as Indian warriors, eventually.)

Some Indian groups became world travellers. Members of a Bella Coola group spent 13 months demonstrating their way of life in Germany. Their presence helped influence Franz Boas to do his Northwest Coast research. B.C. Indian sealing-ship crewmen wintered in Japan. An Owikeno man from Rivers Inlet ended up as the captain of a military vessel on the Euphrates in World War I.

Among notable B.C. campaigners for native rights and restitution for stolen lands, Rev. Peter Kelly was once a logger; Andy Paull was once a sports writer. George Clutesi, who survived residential-school brainwashing to become a conserver of Nootka traditions, worked as a pile-driver operator before he made his name as a writer, artist and actor. Chief Dan George was a longshoreman.

In "Indians at Work," Knight spends more than his usual amount of space to attack what he sees as spurious models of history and society. He has previously opposed individualist romantics who interpret all events as the deeds of over-inflated heroes; now he turns his scorn on collectivist romantics who write anthropological fiction in the guise of fact.

Some. . . will claim that Indians remains tribal people with their inner values and outlook unchanged from time immemorial—that Indian labor was in the world of industrial work but not of it. It is a popular view, well suited to the romanticism of our times. It is a view based upon faith in the inherent unchangeability of human societies. Let those who pursue quintessential cultural spirits hunt away to their hearts' content —there's no arguing with them anyway.
— Indians at Work: 178

Even if one was to grant this outspoken argument, it only leads to a larger problem: the book deals mainly with the period from 1858 to 1930. If the Indian was so well adapted as a participant in European economies, what happened after that?

Knight explores the question in a preliminary way, as others have done. Accepting his analysis and carrying it further, the answer seems to add up to this:

Many Indian groups and individuals did make a successful adaptation, and many are still doing so; but discriminatory laws and practices put the Indians at a special disadvantage and destroyed their coping devices; and, second, the depression of the 1930's and its aftermath hit the Indians particularly hard, because they were particularly vulnerable.

"Indians at Work" differs from Knight's earlier books in that it is a compound of many individual life-histories rather than one or two; and the life-stories are drawn from written records and from biographies and autobiographies rather than first-hand narration; but this book is complementary to all the others. They are valuable both for what they contain and for the debates they stir up.

REVIEW: THE PROTECTED PLACE by Gilean Douglas

Travelling up the desolate and glowering reaches of B.C.'s coast, one suspects that people like Gilean Douglas exist. The only sort of people who could live there by choice, and not for reasons of transitory, thoughtless exploitation; hermit-like people with character strong as the landscape around, reposing in their coves like the ancients of the Himalayas in their caves. One hopes they exist, one hears rumours that they do, people like the Leask brothers, a legendary trio of retired Scots bachelors, one of whom had been a distinguished judge, another an engineer and the other a scholar in the old country, who dwelt for years amidst a mountain of books, bizarre labour-saving inventions and idiosyncrasy in the Patagonian remoteness of a place called Fawn Bluff, halfway up Knight Inlet.

People like Harry Roberts, author, painter, philosopher, entrepreneur and founder of Roberts Creek, B.C. whose magical hermitage, "Sunray", at Cape Cockburn, Nelson Island today lies abandoned and horribly desecrated by a monstrous powerline, the only evidence of the great life lived there a scattering of papers blowing about the yard inscribed with treatises on life, meaning and the folly of industrial progress.

One doesn't visit such places without suffering regrets, personal ones, that one didn't come while the occupants were still to be met or that there is not something more of them left to shed light on the intriguing mystery of how their days were passed.

Gilean Douglas' lonely homestead, "Channel Rock" on the Cortes Island side of twisting, treacherous Uganda Pass, is certainly one of the remaining personality landmarks of the coast, and while the occupant is still very much to be met, no one ever need ponder how she spends her days because she also happens to be a wonderfully expressive writer and she has just given us a book which directly addresses that question.

The Protected Place tells us that Douglas came to the coast over thirty years ago after a similar period of hermitage in an isolated part of the Cascade Mountains, that she lives by herself operating a Weather Observation Station, that she is a Search and Rescue agent, that she provides most of the surrounding territory with its plants, flowers and summer vegetables and that she has mixed her hermitting with a full measure of participation in mainstream society, serving as the official Cortes Island delegate to regional government, as a national officer of the International Womens Institute, a touring lecturer, as editor of the giant Lever Brothers Corporation's house organ, as a newspaper columnist, and above all as an author whose poems, songs and stories have appeared and been honoured all over the western world.

The book tells us this, but only incidentally, because its primary focus is on the sounds of the seasons, the characteristic habits of the months that sift across her view, the wonderful secure feeling she has about her place and the friendly ghosts that flicker through its woods. More than that even, the book tells us how all of these phenomena play on Gilean Douglas' astonishingly broad intellect. She has no hesitation about invoking St. Thomas Aquinas or Agobard, ninth-century Bishop of Lyons, to elucidate some inspiration triggered by a breeze riffling over the waters of Uganda Pass, but she does so in a way that gratifies us with insight about Agobard as well as Uganda Pass.

There are a number of things about The Protected Place that catch the modern reader by surprise and will no doubt put a few off. It doesn't fit any of the fashionable categories; it is neither a manual of rural skills, nor a conservationist tract, though there are nicely subdued elements of both. It belongs to that almost forgotten class of literature known as belles lettres. Its language takes no notice of stripped-down newspeak fashionable in current nonfiction prose; it is unashamedly ornate. Douglas' universal perspective, taking images from Chinese paintings and Sanskrit poetry, may seem overreaching to readers who have become accustomed to moose-and-beaver metaphors from their Canadian writers. It is an uncompromising book from an uncompromising life, but if one gives one's eyes the chance to adjust to its rich interior light, many memorable visions are to be seen.

The Protected Place by Gilean Douglas.

Mostly Coast People

Hubert Evans

Ratings

TV aerials among weathered totem poles.
The poles too have matters of importance
to communicate.
But is anybody listening?

Progress

When he was a boy
he worked with his father in the woods.

When he had a boy
they walked in the woods of a Sunday.

Now that boy has a boy.
But the woods are gone.

December Twenty-Fourth

I miss the sleigh bells and the sparkling snow
which marked this season long ago.
But now my heart is gladdened
for beyond the reef I see
a passing ship, and through the rain
its masthead Christmas tree.

Night Watch

Foreboding cloaks the shoreline cedars.
Off shore, cradled in ground swell,
A murrelet pipes "all's well."

THE BIBLE BARGE TO KINGDOM COME

by Gilean Douglas

"WHAT SCANDALOUS hours you missionaries keep!" exclaimed Reg Halliday when we woke him up at one a.m., warping into the Simoom float after an emergency night run.

Simoom, in those days, was a whole community on floats: post office, store, restaurant, warehouse, chicken coops. It was originally in Simoom Sound, but every now and then this "town" would call a tug and move somewhere else. Once it went looking for the sun for a sick Simoom child and the weekly steamer had to hunt for it in order to deliver the mail and supplies. We found it at Powell Bay, where it had moved so the folks at Echo Point could get their mail more easily.

Crazy? Well, not really. It's just that in saltchuck country things didn't happen conventionally. (They still don't.) How could they, when the distances were so tremendous, the people so few and so isolated? Not one city between Vancouver and Prince Rupert, six hundred miles north, and only a couple of towns. It was big timber country up there (it still is) and land churches, like hospitals, were few and far between: a handful of mission-built buildings in millions of square miles of water and uptilted soil.

There were great inlets stretching far back into mountain ranges, with perhaps a solitary cabin at the head of them. Maybe a couple of logging floats supporting houses and workshops, with boomsticks holding them off from the sheer cliffs towering overhead. Islands might contain two or three tiny communities with no roads connecting them. Long rivers might have only a few scattered settlers on their banks. Mainland bays were often occupied by lone fishing families, out of sight and sound and reach of everyone except those who travelled the saltwater road.

So if you couldn't get at these pioneers by land, and the air was too expensive for anything except emergen-cies, what did you do? You got yourself a boat and took to the highways and byways of the sea. Everyone did it: ministers, doctors, lawyers, merchants and some beggermen and thieves too. There were dental dories, hospital ships, barber boats and craft which carried salesmen selling everything from pots to photographs, groceries to garments. Buying boats too: mostly old junk such as discarded batteries and scrap metal.

Mission ships plied the coast from a short distance north of Vancouver to the Alaskan border. Their chaplains baptized, confirmed, married and buried by tide table, for there are skookum chucks you can't run except at slack tide and channels you can't navigate except at flood. As the chaplains were usually notaries too, it was all in a day's work for them to help engaged couples such as Joan Wren and Walter Rudd swear to the fact that logging—or fishing, or some other urgent occupation— prevented them from travelling perhaps three hundred miles to the nearest licence bureau.

In the early 1950's I began making trips on the mission ships of the Columbia Coast Mission, an Anglican Church organization started by John Antle in the middle and south coast area some forty years earlier. I had taken up residence near Whaletown on Cortes Island after a career in public relations and writing of various kinds, and became active in the small Anglican parish there. When an essay contest was held as part of the never-ending campaign for fund-raising publicity on the mission's behalf, I entered an article entitled "Saltchuck Salvation" and won a trip aboard the mission's hospital ship *Columbia* around her ports of call. I took photographs, wrote more articles, and gradually became a kind of regular lay publicist for the mission, shipping at various times on all the CCM vessels.

On this particular voyage I was again the guest of Captain MacDonald on the *Columbia*, along with John Young, one of Vancouver's top-flight commercial movie photographers, who was making a film of the mission. His wry Scots humour added to the pleasure of the voyage. Meal times in the mess were merry. The captain filled the head of the table and growled genially if his coffee wasn't strong enough to jump out of the cup. On his right sat Engineer Bob McCrea—that is, if we were tied up, so he could leave his beloved diesel. Then came Chaplain Heber Greene, Dr. W.A. McTavish and Canon Alan Greene at the bottom.

John particularly wanted to film some of the Indian villages which the *Columbia* visited regularly. So we went looking for the lay reader, Ernest Christmas, and his energetic and voluble wife, a practical nurse, who operated the sixteen-foot *Gwa-yee* for the mission. They were based in the Indian village in Kingcome Inlet, but their "parish" included all the other villages to the south, east and west. The previous year they had treated over two hundred patients on these reserves and in their dispensary at Kingcome. The *Columbia* took care of the emergencies and the more serious cases.

"See, the flags are flying," said Bob, pointing to the lines of washing at Guayasdums on the northwest shore of Gilford Island. This is a very old village, built on a huge midden, and we had been told we would find the *Gwa-yee* there. Sure enough, there she was, looking very small against the huge backdrop of mountains, sea and sky which is the British Columbia coast. Immediately the Christmases began ferrying patients out to the *Columbia*. Heber had a fine time playing with the children, but when the lines of patients waiting to see the doctor got longer and longer he became very serious.

"I hope," he said, "that those doctors and x-ray technicians who inspected the villages recently will be so impressed with the unsanitary conditions that they will insist on a radical cleanup, right at the source of tuberculosis. It seems silly to spend millions on cure

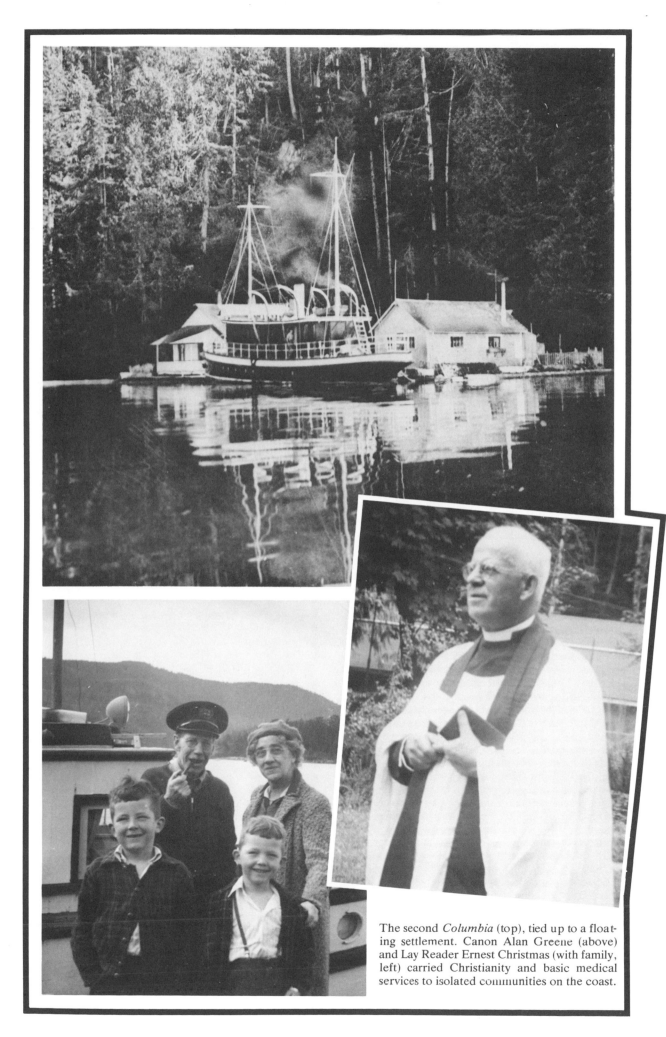

The second *Columbia* (top), tied up to a floating settlement. Canon Alan Greene (above) and Lay Reader Ernest Christmas (with family, left) carried Christianity and basic medical services to isolated communities on the coast.

instead of a few thousand at the source."

The people were certainly clean, but many of their houses looked drab and neglected, though there was a new school building and some new homes. Differences in language made learning difficult. Mrs. Christmas said that after she had carefully told one group the story of Christ's betrayal by Peter, a man muttered, "Miz Christmas say we forget cut wood for mission." I wondered, not for the first time, why none of these missionaries seemed interested in trying to learn the language of those they wished to teach.

Tuberculosis was still on the rise in the villages when I was there, killing off many young girls and mothers of small children. Sanitary facilities seemed far away. The danger to others was enormous as infected people used boats, planes, trains and visited coast towns. The men mingled with commercial fishermen and loggers, the women worked in canneries during the summer. The mission had been combatting this menace for years and it was the *Columbia* which had recently ferried up the doctors from the Department of Indian Affairs, who took x-rays and investigated conditions thoroughly. Some villages had recently had modern plumbing installed. But even I could see that much more needed to be done.

"A few thousand dollars spent at the source would save millions spent in care," reiterated Heber.

The Qoex'sotenox clans, members of the great Kwakiutl family, have lived at Guayasdums ("the outside place") for hundreds of years. Each autumn the Qoex' sotenox and the Lau'itsis of Cracroft Island would go to Gwa'yee ("the inside place") in Kingcome Inlet, to dry salmon. There they joined the Tsawateenox who lived there and the Haxuamis people who came from an offshoot of the inlet, Wakeman Sound. In the spring the four tribes would go outside to dig clams. No village was ever lived in for more than a few months of any year because of these annual food-gathering expeditions.

Clams were prepared for immediate use by long steaming. For winter food they were cooked in a pit about a dozen feet deep which was lined with firewood. They were piled in this pit to within about three feet of the top, more firewood was placed over them and this was thickly covered with fir branches after being lighted. When the pit cooled the clams were shucked, spitted on long sticks and dried in the sun on racks. Sometimes they were smoked in smoke houses or on racks suspended from the rafters of the big communal dwellings. Thus hung they formed a sort of inner roof or ceiling.

Some of the women at Guayasdums strung them on reeds or bits of cedar bark. Others "wove" them on three long sticks. The two outer sticks were thrust through the pillow of the clam and the neck was plaited around the third or centre stick. One clam was strung on top of another with such precision that the completed clam braid, two or three feet long and about six inches wide, looked like a piece of fancy crocheting.

Each house at Guayasdums had its name and they stood in a row facing the beach. In front of them was a carefully levelled street, the lower sides supported by an embankment of heavy logs. Steps led down to the beach where the canoes were lying. Opposite the houses, on the sea side of the street, were the summer seats, platforms on which the men of the village spent a great deal of time gambling and talking.

When I was there with the *Columbia* in the early 1950's, dock and thistle were growing in the ruins of the last communal dwelling and climbing up toward the huge beams. Fireweed blazed in the rear and salal sprouted out of the unpainted totem poles fronting the pretty bay and the islands which almost landlock it. A new yellow school with a green roof stood out in bright background to twenty-two new houses. These were built on stilts because the dam where the residents got their

St. George's Church and King George the Fifth memorial totem pole at Kingcome Inlet. The pole, church and its beautiful interior carving are the work of Kingcome Village Indians. Right; the old and new at Mamma-lilla-culla Indian Village; below, villagers poling up the Kingcome River, navigable for fifty miles.

water–brown cedar water–sometimes flooded over and young rivers ripped through the village.

Indian dugouts lined with burlap were tied up to the long float and fishnets were drying in the sun. In the fishing season all the males except the very old and the very young would be away after the salmon, like their ancestors. Many of the women worked in canneries. The men went trolling in gas boats fitted with poles and gurdies or they shipped out on gillnetters or seiners equipped with radar. Only the old men remembered the cedar fish spears, the bone hooks, the lines of spun nettle, the stone sinkers attached by wild cherry bark.

But even the youngest member of the four clans had heard, so I was told, of the great massacre at Guayasdums when everyone in the village was killed except seven members of the Crow and Scow families who happened to be away at the time. According to their descendants it wasn't much over a hundred years before that members of several Kwakiutl tribes gathered in Viner Sound, off the north coast of Gilford Island, to perform their winter dances in the village there. Among them were a clan from Guayasdums and one from Bella Bella, many miles north. One of the Bella Bella women carried a small deerskin bag which she never put down and this made a Guayasdums woman curious. One night when the Bella Bella woman was asleep she looked in the bag and found that it contained a hamatsa whistle.

A hamatsa whistle is big medicine. It is heard outside during the hamatsa or cannibal ceremonies which mark initiation into this highest of the many secret organizations of the Kwakiutl. Supposed to represent the voices of spirits, these whistles are small and usually made of red cedar although a number are made of bone. Some are two-toned, "have two voices," a few have three or four, and ornamental carving on them is not uncommon.

The simple stealing of dance ornaments or hamatsa whistles was almost unknown and punishable by death. Nevertheless, when the woman from Guayasdums saw the hamatsa whistle in the Bella Bella woman's bag she promptly stole it. The other woman said nothing until she and her clan were leaving. Then she is supposed to have cried out: "You had better tie your children out in the water because they are going to be drowned anyway."

When she got back to Bella Bella she told the chief and elders that the whistle had been stolen. Three war canoes set out secretly from the northern village and Guayasdums almost ceased to exist. The houses were set on fire after the slaughter, which took place at night with the Bella Bella warriors covering every exit and sparing no one. For months no one could go into the pretty Guayasdums Bay because of the dreadful stench which hung over its waters.

Through the remnants of the Crow and the Scow families the village came back to life again but when I was there the old traditions this story came down from were dying out and the younger generation laughed at the crests and ceremonies which meant so much to their ancestors. Nevertheless you could, I was told, still hear Guayasdums people taunting those of Bella Bella because their hamatsa whistle was stolen and, they say, never recovered. I was told that the descendants of the woman who stole it then lived in another Kwakiutl village and that the hamatsa whistle was still with them.

I liked Guayasdums. I liked the people there who were so patient with my ignorance. But there were other Indian villages to visit with the *Gwa-yee*; some worse, some better than Guayasdums, but all with many patients for Dr. McTavish. At mug-ups in the mess the Christmases told us about potlatches and earthquakes, tribal lore and Christian practice, of going thirty-six hours without sleep in a winter storm and shepherding a very collapsible harmonium over epileptic logs.

"Well, now the Bible barge can go to Kingdom Come,"

Dr. W.J. McTavish thinks out a medical problem in the *Columbia*'s surgery.

Transferring a seriously injured logger from camp boat to the hospital ship Columbia.

said Bob McCrea when we were heading for Kingcome Inlet and the Indian village there. The Christmases had left us, Mrs. Christmas for Vancouver and further medical treatment for her eyes. This cheery, courageous woman had been fighting blindness for years, yet no one who met her would have known it.

But we weren't to go to Kingcome yet. A call came in from Mackenzie Sound for marriage licence forms for Joan Wren and Walter Rudd. As the Sound is close to Kingcome it was decided to go there first.

I T WOULD BE rather overwhelming if a whole city turned out to a wedding. But upcoast it's the usual thing for an entire community to be present, from squalling infants to tottering great-grandparents. Sometimes the ceremony itself is held in the cabin of a mission boat, with as many guests crowding in as possible and the rest standing on deck or dock. But every now and then a logger, used to solving knotty problems, comes up with a better solution. At least 150 guests were expected to be at this wedding, so the Sullivan Bay community hall was put on a moving float borrowed from a nearby camp and a fleet of gas boats brought the church to the bride, after a day's towing. That was a wedding! All the old time logging spirit was there, bottled and otherwise. Some of the guests arrived on the *Columbia*, others by the Queen Charlotte or B.C. Airlines. But most of them came in their own gas boats, until a whole fleet was tied up around the hospital ship at the camp float.

As Heber had gone east on his annual holiday, Alan Greene performed the ceremony. "Mendelssohn should have composed some simple melody announcing the arrival of the parson," he declared, "I find it difficult to play an appropriate tune on the limited range of a ship's air whistle, but I do manage a few extra flourishes on such occasions."

The community hall's bareness had been masked by evergreen branches, flowers and crepe paper. It was filled with people and when the ceremony was over the health-drinking, cake-cutting and serious eating began; what seemed a thousand sandwiches, cakes by the dozen, gallons of tea and coffee. By the dawn's early light there would be more coffee, mounds of toast, eggs, flapjacks, sausages and good old porridge. Then chug-chug-chug would go the gas boats, zoom would go the planes and the guests would be on their way back to making a living.

But the festivities had hardly begun when Tony Berg, who had played the Wedding March on his accordion, suffered a severe heart seizure and had to have first aid

from Dr. McTavish. Gas boats were hurriedly set adrift so the *Columbia* could move out and take Tony to Alert Bay.

In the hall four fiddlers and two accordion players continued tuning up for the dance, which went on till daylight. "Merrymaking and tragedy are shipmates on the saltchuck," said Alan.

W ELL *now* the Bible barge can go to Kingdom Come!" repeated Bob as we pulled out of Mackenzie Sound. We sailed through Sutlej Channel and into Kingcome Inlet, where Alan, Dr. McTavish. John and I transferred to the ship's dinghy. We had kit for an overnight stay, robes for a church service, the doctor's black bag, plus photographic equipment galore. We were heading for the Kingcome River, which the *Columbia* could not navigate.

Huge horseflies—commonly called bulldogs, and with good reason—were on hand to greet us, and so, we found, was the saltchuck. It came pouring in through the seams of the sun-dried boat which our load had left with only about four inches of freeboard. With only a small tin for bailing and the *Columbia* sailing serenely off in the opposite direction the situation became quite desperate before we were even halfway to the river. The glacier water of the inlet is cold enough to stop your heart. "Anybody got a piece of blotting paper?" asked John, hauling cameras into his lap.

Fortunately Bob had been wondering about our boat and once the *Columbia* was underway stepped out on deck to check up on us. What he saw was the dinghy coming right after him, with all occupants waving frantically. So the *Columbia* turned around and came back—to give us more tins for bailing. But by this time our wooden craft was already beginning to take up and the sinking process had slackened its pace enough for us to concentrate on battling bulldogs while our outboard chugged us up the river.

Our progress against the tidal current was so slow that Mrs. Dick of the Indian village came sweeping down in a thirty-foot dugout with a much more powerful outboard to circle us and ask if we wanted a tow. She was laughing as she did so, this being a scene that she and Alan had played more than once.

The Kingcome is a tidal river running roughly north from the head of thirty-mile-long Kingcome Inlet. No one, I was told, had ever travelled to its source. I was skeptical because I knew that the Kingcome Indians had canoed up it for over fifty miles, passing by great waterfalls and through deep canyons. Above tower the Kingcome Mountains, averaging around 5,500 feet in

Canon Alan Greene shows his varied talents by piggy-backing Dr. McTavish ashore at Kingcome.

The flags are flying—washing hung out to dry at Kingcome Indian Village. Canon Alan Greene, centre.

height and always slashed white with snow. Usually clouds are drifting across their evergreen slopes. "It always rains at Kingcome," outsiders will tell you. But the residents—as all residents do—claim that really wet spells are quite unusual.

The day we boated up the river it was bright with sunshine. The flags were flying here too and a washing machine stood on the river bank with a girl putting clothes into it. At St. George's Church, built entirely by the Indians and with some beautiful carving inside, Alan donned hip boots and packed the doctor, John and myself ashore. Later a Toronto friend wrote saying that my violent kick when a bulldog attacked my ankle while I was riding upon Alan's back was making a hit all over eastern Canada in John's movie *Fishers of Men*.

After a church service to which all the children came in their bright summer dresses, the doctor examined a sick boy in the village and treated some minor ills. All the men were away fishing and many of the women were working in canneries.

We were told, with great glee, a saga of the snows in which Alan Greene and the Reverend Rollo Boas were joint heroes. It seems that they had a call to make the previous winter at Kingcome Village, when the snow was five feet deep. After their dinghy was nearly crushed in the ice they took to the land, using their cedar oars as hand-snowshoes to keep them from sinking completely in the soggy white stuff.

It was grim going for two miles. They crawled on hands and knees, "cooning it" over sloughs on old snags and once barely extricating Rollo's foot from between two logs. When they finally glimpsed the thunderbirds and salmon on the burial totems near the village Rollo said, "Look up and see if you can spot any vultures." Finally, soaked with perspiration and melting snow, they reached the hard-packed village path with colour from their heavy winter clothing dripping a rainbow path behind them.

Ernest Christmas was reported to have said, "I never thought I'd see the day when the superintendent of the mission would come to me on hands and knees!"

This story reminded Alan of an Indian man who, intrigued by a property sign *Trespassers will be prosecuted*, decided to erect a duplicate over his wife's grave. But he left out the second *r* in *Trespassers* when he was printing the sign, which resulted in an excellent text of which the mission thoroughly approved.

The children gave us a fine sendoff and the current swept us swiftly down river through the sunset to Ernest Halliday's homestead ranch near the head of Kingcome Inlet. Here a good supper was spread for eleven people and we heard tales of those days when the Hallidays

took up this big homestead by the mountain-guarded Kingcome River. In 1873, not long after this wild country was named for Rear Admiral Sir John Kingcome, Ernest's parents and their family came west from Ontario to live in Yale, New Westminster and Victoria, his father teaching school in each place. A dozen years later they moved to Comox, where young Ernest was married. In 1894, hearing about free land at Kingcome which could be had for the staking and proving, he sailed north in a sloop with some friends who were also looking for land.

Two miles up the Kingcome River he found a wild valley of natural grazing land lying between hills and water; an almost treeless treasure in a country where settlers usually have to gallop to keep up with wilderness growth. Here Ernest built a log cabin, planted vegetables and fruit trees and smoked fish and game for winter eating. His friendly and informative Indian neighbours helped him and the other homesteaders to be self-sufficient. So it made little difference that it took fourteen hours steady rowing to get to the nearest settlement of any size, the Indian village of Alert Bay. They went there for supplies only once a month at most.

"Our assets when we began homesteading," said Mrs. Halliday, "were one rowboat, six head of cattle and fifty-five dollars worth of groceries."

Two years later, when their third child was coming, the Hallidays rowed to Comox, a three-week trip. This was in December and they camped out on shore as they went. On March 1, 1897 a second son, William, was born and the Hallidays made the return trip to their pioneer kingdom.

"I remember," Mr. Halliday said, "thinking one day in a storm that there was only a thin plank between us and eternity. Then I remembered that God was there too—and I kept on rowing."

He had a great deal more rowing to do before acquiring a gas engine and before a coastal steamer began to make trips up the inlet. For seventeen years he made the four-day rowboat trip to and from Alert Bay to sell beef at ten cents a pound. For seventeen years his beef and butter book showed no surplus at all. The Hallidays swapped and bartered with other homesteaders and the Indians of Kingcome Village.

Then came that wonderful day when Ernest Halliday realized that he actually had a profit of twenty-eight dollars to spend as he pleased. It pleased him most to spend it on a six-foot kitchen cabinet for his wife. He loaded it into his rowboat and started for home, but a southeaster blew up and man and cabinet had to camp ashore for three days. Meanwhile his wife imagined the boat sunk, her husband drowned and herself left penniless

Three generations of the Halliday family at Kingcome with Heber Greene: back row, left to right, Reg, Lil, Ernest and Lily Halliday; Heber Greene. Front: Alan, Jim and Gordon, sons of Reg and Lil.

with the children. Neither of them will ever forget that moment when she, still watching the river with grim hope, saw her man tiredly rowing a piece of top-heavy furniture up to the home landing.

That kitchen cabinet seemed to mark a turning point for this courageous family. Steamer service came to the inlet, loggers moved in to cut the big river alders, more homesteaders arrived. There was a steady market for vegetables, fruit, meat and butter.

"But we'd have made it through even without that!" declared eighty-three-year-old Ernest Halliday with a flash of his youthful blue eyes. Of course they would. A real pioneer will win through anything and live to laugh about it.

Seven children were born, five of whom (two boys died young of tuberculosis) were sent outside to schools and colleges. In 1918 a comfortable two-storey house was built next to the original cabin. The garden rioted with roses, sweet peas, honeysuckle and all the other flowers Mrs. Halliday had planted around her first small home to spice work with beauty. Upstairs in the new house was a modern bathroom and many bedrooms. A wide porch led into a hall which opened into a spacious living room. It was lighted by electricity, but seemed more at home when firelight danced on a wall of books and on delicate china and old silver.

In this still-remote wilderness we found the latest magazines brightening low coffee tables, and soft chairs invited the visitor. For visitors also were the many pairs of house slippers which sat under the kitchen stove after the rains began. Kingcome summers can be glorious— except in the deerfly season—but winters mean heavy snow, damp cold and a wind that knifes your bones. The Indians say that years ago the inlet used to be frozen over for several miles from its head. The Kingcome River still freezes and can still crush a dugout or a gas boat in its icy jaws, as Alan Greene and Rollo Boas found out.

In autumn the half-dozen well-oiled rifles on the kitchen wall were taken down by the Halliday men who came back to the old homestead for another feast of venison, grouse and mountain goat. But they told me that game was harder to find because of the wolves and cougars.

In the old days it was nothing out of the way for the table to be spread for thirty or forty people. Even the eleven of us who were there when I was were enough to make eighty-four-year-old Mrs. Halliday remember the times of feasting, when no one came into the Kingcome country without visiting the Halliday farm. It was not much different in the 1950's, for the family never knew when they would see neighbours, friends from down-

coast, tourists, missionaries, photographers or journalists walking up through the hay-sweet fields from the river to where the spreading white house sat calmly below its protecting mountains. One and all they joined in morning and evening worship, while the organ in the living room accompanied voices strong in faith and endurance.

The Reverend John Antle wrote in the Halliday guest book on the senior Hallidays' thirty-fourth wedding anniversary: "The rains descend and the floods come, but the House of Halliday stands because it is founded upon a rock. May it ever stand and may there be many happy returns of this New Year's Day." And again in 1946: "Here we are again after twenty-one years and the house still stands and may it stand."

When Reg Halliday, his wife and three sons came to live with the senior Hallidays a few years before I was at Kingcome, more cattle were bought and the homestead changed from mixed to stock farming. It was a hard change for the pioneers, just as it was difficult for them to see loggers felling the forests around them and "civilization" creeping like a tide farther and farther up their beloved and solitary land.

"It is not easy to see things go. It is not easy," said trim, erect Mrs. Halliday, who had borne children in a log cabin with only her husband to help her. Nor was it easy the previous summer when, on August 29, her grandson Jim—laughing twenty-six-year-old son of the Reg Hallidays—was drowned after his speedboat capsized in Kingcome Inlet. The Indians, who had been his friends, dragged the deep glacial waters for days but never found his body. Nine months later Jim's grandparents celebrated their diamond wedding anniversary. Other days, other ways, but joy and sorrow will always be shipmates on the saltchuck.

There were four generations of Hallidays on the coast then. Ernest Jr. and his family had a floathouse in Kingcome Inlet. Alan, Reg Halliday's second son, lived about a mile away from the old farm with his wife and child. Some of the younger generation liked the new things. They liked speed and glitter and "guaranteed security." But I wonder if we moderns will ever know as much about real security as the elder Hallidays had learned.

"I'd like to start all over again," sturdy, gentle-faced Mr. Halliday said to me as we stood on his float with the Kingcome River whispering softly by beneath mountains crowned with sunset. "Sometimes I sleep in the old log cabin and the years go by like this river. Good and bad years, births and deaths—I never want to forget any of them. They were living."

the STARFISH TELEGRAPH

DURING THE summer of 1920, I went on a vacation on an island up the British Columbia coast named Aristazabal and while there I moored my boat at a place locally known as Borrowman Bay.

As I gathered a bucket of pilchards, I noticed a starfish that had one ray broken off close to its body. It lay in two parts. About two weeks later I walked along that part of the beach in search of clams. I was amazed to find a change had undergone the two parts of the starfish. The part that contained four rays had started to grow a fifth ray. But what really amazed me was that the single ray had a small central body and four miniature rays attached and growing on it.

I had a friend by the name of Barney who had a shack in the vicinity and from him I obtained some wire netting and fashioned a fence around the area where the starfish lay. In about seven weeks the two starfish were hardly distinguishable from each other.

One day I noticed one had its rays curled around a piece of fish, while the other also had its rays curled under in a feeding position. I gently straightened the rays out and to my surprise the other starfish straightened its rays out in a time lapse of thirty seconds. Then I took the tip of the ray of one and gently bent it slightly and the corresponding tip of the ray of the other responded in a like manner. The impact of this strange phenomenon on my mind was staggering. Here were two bodies that seemed to have an invisible nervous system in common.

Following this discovery I constructed two pegboards by which I could fix (outlining with pegs) the rays of one starfish. Barney's shack was about two hundred yards distance from my boat and I would outline one starfish on a pegboard while Barney at his shack would lay the other starfish on a pegboard and do the same. Then we would compare the two. Invariably the two starfish would be in an identical position. Late in the fall, we devised means for communication by various combinations of bending the rays of one starfish on the pegboard. The other starfish always assumed the same position on the other pegboard. Later we were able to communicate this way for a distance of about five miles.

It was at Kettle Inlet in October, 1920, that fate ended the study. After no response from Barney for twenty-four hours, my starfish spelled, "Help bloo." I hoisted the anchor and arrived at Barney's to find him collapsed and hemorrhaging. I took him in my boat to the nearest settlement, leaving the two starfish in a bucket of sea water in the shack. Barney later died in the Prince Rupert hospital.

When I got back to Kettle Inlet, the starfish were dead. The water should have been changed every twenty-four hours or oftener.

The years have passed and I've never related this story for fear that I might become a candidate for the funny house. Quite recently I read an article similar in regard to plants which gave me the courage to contribute my story at this time.

by C.H. Doane

Searching for Cape St. Elias

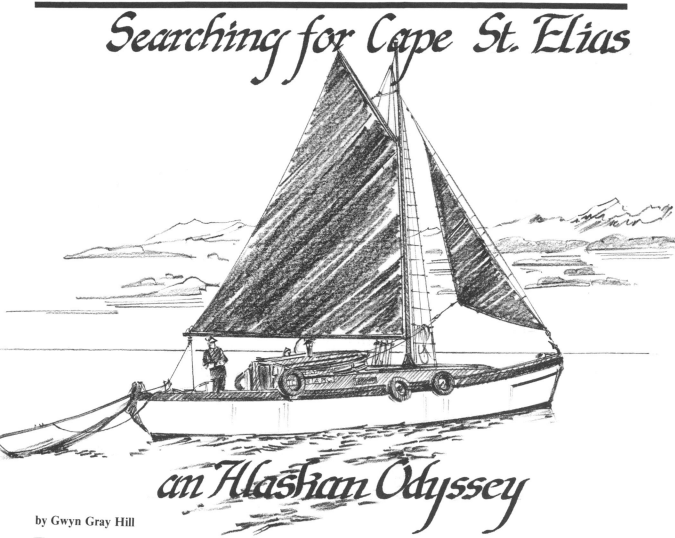

an Alaskan Odyssey

by Gwyn Gray Hill

In June, 1946, sailing on my boat, the *Cape St. Elias,* I found myself nearly nine hundred miles from my home port, Victoria, on my way to Cape St. Elias, in Alaska. It is three hundred miles or so in along the shores of the eastern half of the Gulf of Alaska, and I was now at Icy Point, about seventeen miles out from Cape Spencer, quite definitely at the end of the coast-range scenery, with its heavy forest and fjord-like inlets, Indians and totem poles. It is the northern end also of a thousand crooked channels and inlets that extend from Cape Flattery at the southern tip of British Columbia to southeast Alaska.

I rounded Icy Point expecting to see more rocks. Instead a curved sandy beach stretched for miles to an overhanging cape on the horizon. This cape proved to be made of dark discoloured ice shattered into the most curious serpentine formation; as I moved slowly, to the west it revealed the glittering blue wonder of its south and west sides. For this whole headland is but the snout of a glacier descending from Mt. Crillon. In all Alaska, I believe it is the only glacier which descends directly and discharges into the open Pacific Ocean. Its face, three to four hundred feet high, is an array of sapphire shafts and needles, two miles in length, the full sweep of the sea spouting and thundering in its violet caverns with such force as to create a low fog about its base. The glacier is far too fearsome to allow of close examination and at a distance of three quarters of a mile I watched as one of its vast spindles of ice commenced to topple over. A herd of seals scurried seaward and, the gulls in thousands rose with discordant cries. Very slowly it seemed from where I was, the spindle fell into the sea like a cathedral of blue glass. Long green spears of water shot upward and as it hit the sea, there was a detonation as from a big gun that wound away in distant thunder midst the bare mountain peaks. The ground swell, always heavy on these shores was doubled by the waves raised by the berg. This amazing glacial forest of ice spires recedes from the shoreline in vast aisles and depressions, lit by their own fiery blue light. Here and there are curious discolourations caused by moraines and heaps of colossal red boulders carried down from the mountains. In an inlet called Lituya Bay, about eighteen miles further on, I saw small icebergs only just able to displace their own weight of water. They seemed infused with a black substance, possibly coal, so ingrained as to appear to be pure black ice. On melting some pieces I obtained water which contained the black grains in suspension. Of all the extraordinary scenes to the westward, Mt. Crillon Glacier was the most brilliant. I was so absorbed in what I was seeing that my camera was quite forgotten.

The entrance to the six miles of Lituya Bay inlet is a mariner's nightmare. The tide rushes out at twelve knots to meet the ocean swell, creating tremendous seas through which no small vessel could survive. It was here that the fishing vessel *Manhatten* was lost in 1917 with all hands. In the middle of the inlet lies Cenotaph Island, small and round with a dense growth of trees. A monument or cenotaph raised by La Perouse in 1786 in memory of men who were lost in the race at the entrance, has long since disappeared. A few ruined fox farmers' cabins are on the shore and bears swim over to the island; but nobody lives in the bay. Only a few fishing vessels are to be found offshore, in the summer months.

The anchorage is poor; the bottom slopes rapidly down and is composed mostly of gravel and coarse sand. It was this and my carelessness that all but lost me the *Cape St. Elias* when I left her at anchor and visited the fishing boat *Neptune* at anchor close by. The tide carried her as far as the bar, where the anchor again took hold. Fortunately I have a good masthead light and, though it was dark and cloudy, *Neptune's* skipper managed to land me alongside my boat. But the race was running hard at the time and had the *Cape St. Elias* gone out through the entrance I doubt if I should ever have seen it again.

Three small glaciers discharge into the head of Lituya Bay. Their faces descend into the sea, but not at uniform speed. Only in some places were there rents and walls of ice occasionally dropping a berg off into the water with a resounding bang. I let my boat drift, as it was dead calm and everywhere it was too deep to anchor. Then I rowed back toward the face of one of these glaciers in the dinghy. I rowed and rowed and seemed to get no closer. Finally I found myself, as I thought, directly beneath a great flat wall of ice which seemed solid enough and I put out an oar expecting to push off it only to see a flight of gulls pass between. I was nowhere near! From somewhere came a sharp report and a long swell came out from the glacier face. What I thought were cliffs of ice rising about thirty feet were a hundred and fifty, but for all I had to compare them to they might have been five feet tall or five hundred. I had a weird sensation of unreality. Not a shrub grew upon the mountains that disappeared into the clouds fifteen thousand feet above. The only sound was the sudden and unexpected bangs emerging from the glacier, and there was a funny little tinkling sound everywhere caused by the movements of innumerable berglets, some no bigger than a teacup, lying in the water several hundred yards off from the face of the ice.

Eighteen miles beyond the glacier is Lituya, and from there it is eighty-eight miles to Ocean Cape, the entrance to Yakutat Bay. Sand beaches are continuous all the way to Dry Bay, twelve miles wide and almost entirely filled with sand bars. I had hoped to put in there; one look at those bars convinced me to proceed to the great bay of Yakutat. With the eastern end of Dry Bay about three miles away, by the time I brought the west end abeam I was fully eight miles off shore, pushed out to sea by the current of Alsek River, whose delta is in Dry Bay.

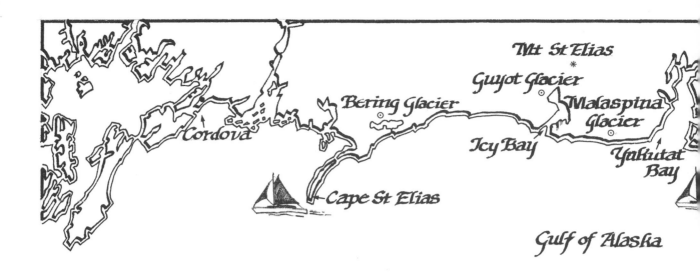

Logs, roots and chunks of muskeg floated past, and the water was dark reddish brown. The Alsek must have been in flood, but all I could see were great dry sands with the swells climbing over them in towers of foam and spray.

From Dry Bay to Yakutat, about forty-five miles, the coast is not even six feet high, and two or three miles off shore is an area of heavy surf breakers. Fifteen miles inland lie the mountains, and between them and the sea is a low wooded plain, quite flat and mostly forested, with some areas of open grass land. Endeavouring to see as much as possible, I came within three miles of the shore; every so often I could feel the increased swell on the shoals and once I had to get well out of sight of the shore to get round breakers which appeared ahead. I soon gave up and set a course a safe six miles off.

These shores were uninhabited and desolate beyond words. The weather was not good; I had never seen such ominous clouds. They were not the grey they are towards the south but black as jet, rolling along in great heaped-up masses before the east wind. Under the stygian black canopy the lower spurs of the St. Elias range and innumerable coiling rivers of ice had an evil glitter in the sea beyond the wooded plain.

As my boat rose to the crests of these huge seas, the grim black coast and sky seemed to stretch on forever. This was the real Alaska I had imagined from the story book. The last frontier indeed; and never so named in jest. After being shaken like a pea in a box for hours during which I somehow managed to stay awake on a diet of cream puffs and cheese, I rounded Ocean Cape into great Yakutat Bay, nineteen miles wide and about thirty deep, anchored off Libby's cannery, five miles within Monti Bay.

Libby's cannery which I had been told had been in that same spot for fifty years, operated a railway extending back from the bay over the wooded plain to the mouth of the Situk River. I was offered a ride. The distance was ten miles, the fare nothing. The whole settlement entrained a hundred strong at 7 p.m., returning for supper at 9 p.m.

In 1741, Vitus Bering sailed to Yakutat. He must have seen many wonders, but never anything like this. At 6:30 a heavily moustached Greek at the depot commenced to haul on a wire which tolled a bell in a distant tower. Out from the sheds rolled the train, the "Yakutat and Southern", three red boxes on wheels and a gem of a yellow coach from the days of '98. Birds nested in its faded roof but nobody minded. A concourse of natives then entrained, some in the red boxes designed to carry fish back from the river and some in the yellow coach. With a squeal from the tiny engine we were off. There were beards and pigtails, mosquito nets suspended from straw boaters and one man even wore spats. A fusillade of gunfire from our passengers greeted every old can that we passed and the squawk of a dozen phonographs on board rose above the gentle rumble of the little wheels as we slowly trundled across the plain. The engineer set the throttle at 10 m.p.h. and retired for a game of cards. Woe betide the pedestrian who encountered the Snail. But there were no wayfarers upon that lonely plain. There were no fish at the Situk either, but a number of natives disembarked and made off in flat boats followed by a great cloud of bees.

And so it was from this hilarious conveyance that I first saw Mt. St. Elias, for rolling black clouds finally parted for the first time in a week. The natives all peered from the yellow carriage at their ancient God of the ice and snow, looking down upon them still. *Yatsetahshak* they called it, but I could never find out what it meant. I had come a thousand miles to see it; even further, for in my youth in England I was something of a prodigy at geography, ever fascinated by this towering giant with the curious name at the end of the world. Right now only the top was visable, a squat silver pyramid towering into the Alaskan sky seventy miles away. With hardly a turn, the "Yakutat and Southern" waded window-high through acres of beautiful blue flowers sprouting up from the muskeg and rank grass. The phonographs phoned and the flies flitted out, biting everybody so unwise as to be unnetted. The tracks were ancient, the expansion gaps wide. "Clackerty-flap-clickerty-clap" went the Slow Snail over the wooded plain beneath great St. Elias.

I stayed in Yakutat and the weather became very bad, blowing furiously out at sea. The thought of those lonely rivers, the low wooded plain and the hundred and twenty-eight miles back to Cape Spencer and safety caused me no little concern. But, it was July and I supposed it to be a day or two's tempest and no more.

I took on quantities of supplies and a charming Roman Catholic priest sold me oil which he poured as if it was communion wine, never spilling a drop. I asked him how the Church of Rome fared so far afield; apparently, it did not. "The natives are not enthusiastic," said he, "I am leaving this season in disgust."

Poor man! He was under five feet tall and the rain poured off his little nose as it did off mine; indeed for two solid days and nights it never ceased its relentless downpour.

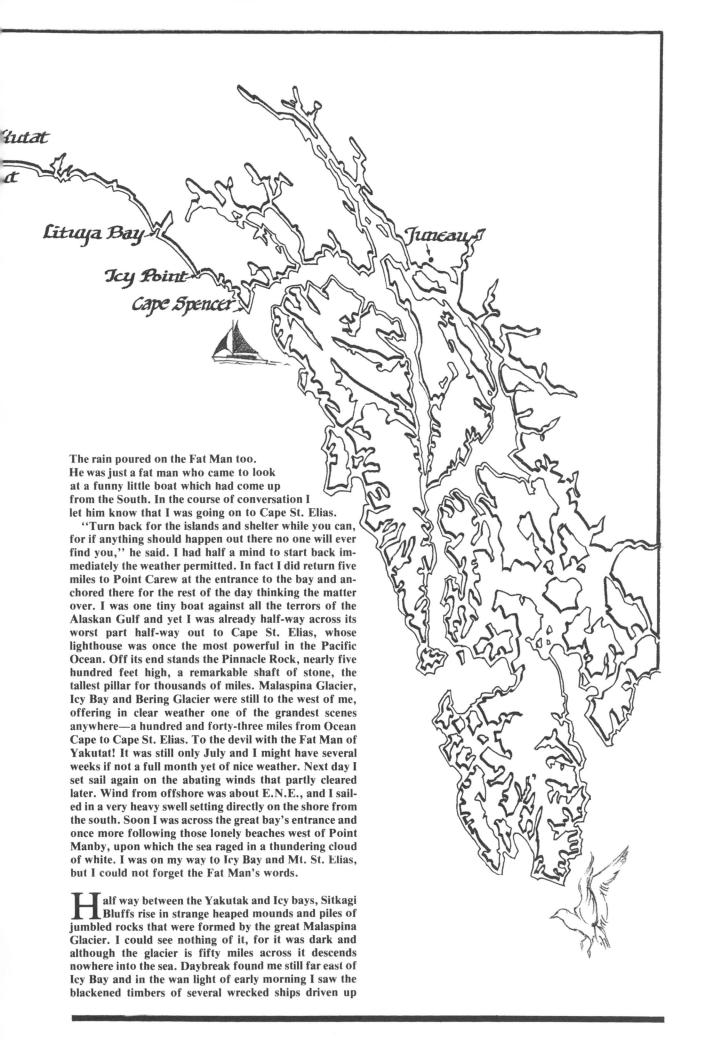

Lituya Bay

Icy Point
Cape Spencer

Juneau

The rain poured on the Fat Man too. He was just a fat man who came to look at a funny little boat which had come up from the South. In the course of conversation I let him know that I was going on to Cape St. Elias.

"Turn back for the islands and shelter while you can, for if anything should happen out there no one will ever find you," he said. I had half a mind to start back immediately the weather permitted. In fact I did return five miles to Point Carew at the entrance to the bay and anchored there for the rest of the day thinking the matter over. I was one tiny boat against all the terrors of the Alaskan Gulf and yet I was already half-way across its worst part half-way out to Cape St. Elias, whose lighthouse was once the most powerful in the Pacific Ocean. Off its end stands the Pinnacle Rock, nearly five hundred feet high, a remarkable shaft of stone, the tallest pillar for thousands of miles. Malaspina Glacier, Icy Bay and Bering Glacier were still to the west of me, offering in clear weather one of the grandest scenes anywhere—a hundred and forty-three miles from Ocean Cape to Cape St. Elias. To the devil with the Fat Man of Yakutat! It was still only July and I might have several weeks if not a full month yet of nice weather. Next day I set sail again on the abating winds that partly cleared later. Wind from offshore was about E.N.E., and I sailed in a very heavy swell setting directly on the shore from the south. Soon I was across the great bay's entrance and once more following those lonely beaches west of Point Manby, upon which the sea raged in a thundering cloud of white. I was on my way to Icy Bay and Mt. St. Elias, but I could not forget the Fat Man's words.

Half way between the Yakutak and Icy bays, Sitkagi Bluffs rise in strange heaped mounds and piles of jumbled rocks that were formed by the great Malaspina Glacier. I could see nothing of it, for it was dark and although the glacier is fifty miles across it descends nowhere into the sea. Daybreak found me still far east of Icy Bay and in the wan light of early morning I saw the blackened timbers of several wrecked ships driven up

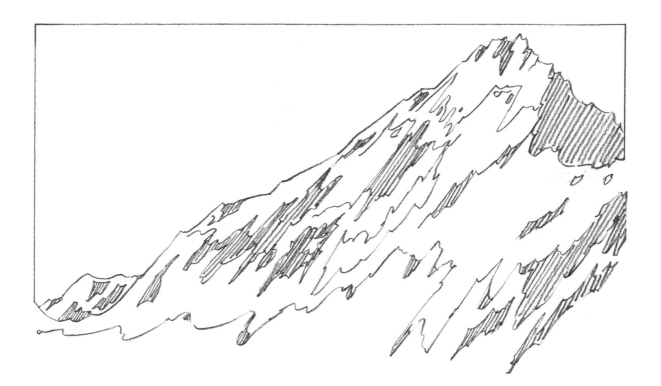

high onto the sands beyond the surf breakers. One ship-wreck seemed to be of great size, every rib showing high above the sands. The wind soon came off shore and, on rounding Riou Spit, I found it blowing with some force out of Icy Bay at whose head I could see Guyot Glacier. A great array of icebergs were making out from its face. I anchored on the east side behind Moraine Island intending to stay until I could get a good look at Mt. St. Elias twenty-six miles inland. The mountain's lower spurs to eleven thousand feet were partly clear of clouds, hinting at the grandeur beyond, as they rose from black rock to ice filled chasms above. At only twenty-six miles distance, a mountain eighteen thousand feet high should be a sight to behold, but I was not prepared for what I saw next day as the west wind rolled a great black canopy of cloud from the face of St. Elias at sunrise. Across the eastern battlements there stretched what appeared to be a vast bird, its wings spread wide, with a leering visage aslant at its centre. It was chance lodgement of snow and the steep black rocks; but a more sinister spectre of mountains I have never seen. It is said that these huge shoulders of stone stamped with that indelible centre visage form the greatest landmark on the shores of the seven seas; for nowhere does the land rise so abruptly, so high, so close to any coast, and I'd be the last to doubt it.

The Duke of Abruzzi was the first man to climb St. Elias. The year was 1897. I have a photo of him, elegantly attired and calling himself Luigi Amadeo, Prince of Savoy and Duke of Abruzzi. Whether or not he wore his high collar and sash, medallions and sword upon the approaches to this mountain I have no idea. But he did ride in a sedan chair supported upon the shoulders of a considerable number of minions to the base of the mountain. I spoke to two very old natives of Yakutat who remembered the excitement attendant upon the Duke's arrival. He was then a young man and this was his first expedition. The natives seemed to think it unsporting to start off on such a climb in so soft and comfortable a manner. The Duke lived to be one of the boldest explorers into strange lands of his day and to be a statesman as well. More than half a century has gone by and the name of the Duke may be forgotten but not his chair.

The west wind rose off Guyot Glacier and a fleet of icebergs threatened to block off my exit from the cove in which I was anchored. I at once started out, bumping and crunching slowly through masses of little berglets that tinkled and clinked together over an area of several square miles. Here and there great massive ice blocks rose high above the others, with spires, cornices, arches and blue caverns in their sides. The ocean swell gurgled and spouted through blow-holes and fissures which filled with air as the berglets swayed and heaved in the body of the bay.

It was ninety-five miles to the next shelter behind Cape St. Elias past another low plain over which Bering Glacier descends. Beyond Cape Yakataga to the Ugalenka River no shrubs were to be seen beyond a mile from shore. Yet along the land within the beach were miles and miles of red flowers, appearing as a red mist in the distance. This stretch of the coast had many wrecks scattered along it. Beachcombing parties working east from Controller Bay and using ski-like boards to cross

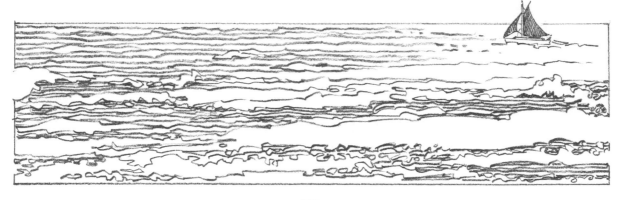

242

the quicksands reported every conceivable kind of flotsam; jeeps on their backs with their rusty wheels in the air like dead bugs; and near Tsivat River a huge pink water tank stood like a monarch in the lonely sands. No bodies were found, the dunes told no tales; neither did the packs of wolves that roamed the plain. There were no settlements of any kind. All progress east or west was effectually cut off by impassable terrain; a man might as well face Bering Glacier or walk back into the sea. West of Tsivat River the dunes were covered with beautiful green verdure; here and there white, perched stones seemed like sub-arctic players addressing the ball. Beyond I could see the St. Elias Range, gable behind gable, trailing ever further inland to the northwest, on into the mysterious heart of Alaska.

How strange this whole scene was! The distant glacier seemed made of huge cakes and cliffs, smoother than others I had seen. All the way from Cape Spencer I had passed only one other boat. The east wind hurried me along under full sail but the empty desolation, mile after mile, frightened me. I was a solitary voyager in a very small boat going nowhere fast. "No one will ever find you!" the Fat Man had said. I began to see why.

Cape St. Elias is the name given to the outer end of the narrow island of Kayak that points out from the coast for seventeen miles, but is little more than a mile wide, with two-thousand-foot-high hills in a jagged backbone down the middle.

I anchored on the inshore side of the island facing Controller Bay, which is at the mouth of Bering River. It is about twelve miles wide and twelve miles deep, and filled by drying flats at low tide. The neighbouring island of Wingham gives but feeble protection from the west, likewise Kayak from the south east.

Next day I crossed Controller Bay to what I was told was the town of Katalla with adjacent oil wells. Going in to the river over the bar I saw at once I had been falsely informed, for nothing was there but several dilapidated sheds half hidden in grass. Where were the oil derricks? Where was the wharf? Alas, time and Alaska had long since swallowed them up. What I did see was a group of people gathered on the sand to find out who I was. Anchoring, I hastily rowed over and approached a tall figure in front. I quickly backed away. Around and on the whole group, inches thick, was a crawling mass of little flies. I had seen mosquitoes before, I had seen no-see-ums and deer flies in clouds, but never anything like this.

Then insects rose in a blue fog about four feet high over all the surrounding land and out of it those people loomed in vague shapes like nebulous ghosts of the dead. Returning to my boat I dressed in net, gloves and scarf saturated in coal oil and again landed, to face yet another of Alaska's jokes. The tall man led me over some rising ground and into his tidy tin shack. Brushing off the slime of flies we went in quickly and shut the door. He turned out to be Mr. Nelson Larsen, an elderly white-haired Swede with rather fine features and a giant frame, the last remaining person from the days when Katalla boasted eight saloons and, in one night of Saturnalian orgy, burnt to the ground. He was, he said, a combination of fisherman and trapper. The other five or six people were the wives of similar men and with their children had collected to witness my arrival, which caused great excitement, as no strangers ever came this way. Larsen had lived for forty years in Alaska and travelled from south to north; from Ketchikan to Kotzebue. Nowhere, he said, had he seen flies any worse than at Katalla; but his chief complaint was the water pressure in his tap.

"It is not what it was in the old days," he said. I timed it to fill a kettle in four minutes.

"In these remote regions, things are very uncertain," he said.

Braving the flies once more, we went out and looked at the surf rollers tumbling over the bar. The tide had gone down since my arrival, and there in the narrow channel were the rows of rusty spikes which marked the engine of the wreck of the steamer *Portland*. Like the devil's claws, I thought at the time. How I missed them on the way in I shall never know, and neither will Nelson Larsen. A foot less water or an inch to one side and the Fat Man's words would have been a fact and Alaska would have had me yet.

I then went out, twenty-five miles from Katalla, to see Cape St. Elias. It proved to be a high ridge of rock falling abruptly into the sea from a height of sixteen

hundred feet. At its base was the low, squat lighthouse, unapproachable through the continuous surf. Off the Cape's extremity and connected to it by a sand bar stood the towering Pinnacle Rock. At times clouds were down, black as night, across the headlands and the great shaft rose from the sea with its summit lost in swirling mist.

The weather became increasingly unsettled so I returned to my former anchorage between Wingham Island and the Cape. The wind blew from the east with gale force for four days. That masterpiece of understatement, *Alaska Pilot Vol. II* stated, "No sea enters but there is some local chop." The local chop was over six feet from trough to crest and the rain drove with such force that I could not face it. Fortunately my tackle was oversize, I had the best of clothing. My boat is low, and though every so often the waves would come aboard and I could no longer stay in my bunk, I still held my ground. There was nothing to be seen but flying spindrift, and the wind howled dismally through the shrouds. They call that Russian Anchorage; better perhaps than being driven ashore on the open coast but it was absolutely Siberian. Nobody knew where I was and I had no idea how long the gale might continue. As for Katalla, it might have been a thousand miles away for all the encouragement its proximity gave me. In quaking horror I saw that the Fat Man of Yakutat had been indeed right. I should have gone back while the weather permitted.

I struck a foreign object near the Pinnacle Rock in the trough of the swell, and when I eventually did start back as the winds abated and reached the Tsivat River, my outboard water cooling pipe fell off in the rough sea. A lot of water came in around the engine with the added pressure overflowing the tank. After securing matters I decided it best to try and effect repairs further on at Cordova. I steered a dud course at night, and dawn found me looking up once more, in great alarm, at the extreme end of the Cape, with its tall pillar of stone shining like pink coral in the rays of the rising sun. When would I see the old navigators' anchorage again? Would I ever find Cordova? I had no charts west of Katalla. Fuel oil was getting low, and I was down to smoking tea leaves at last, but not eating them yet. Would I ever escape from this awful place for which, in past enthusiasm, I named my boat? I doubted then and, looking back, I still remember how I felt. It's the abode of all the devils of the deep.

Somehow I managed to turn in to Katalla. Once I thought I saw white boats but they disappeared as I approached, some figment of the mist and fog or my imagination. Larsen gave me what information he could about the voyage to Cordova. It was not very encouraging, but I started out nevertheless and arrived at Hinchinbrook Island about forty-five miles west and entered Boswell Bay round Hook Point after back-tracking several miles to get inside a long line of breakers making out from the point. Fortunately the weather had improved. The estuary of the Copper River, about forty miles wide and fronted by a crescent of low sand islets, looked no better than the coast to the eastward. Somewhere in a long chain of dark and saw-toothed mountains the main river enters the sea but I had nowhere seen it in passing, though the day was fine and the sun had dried the land to a crystal clearness under a pale turquoise sky. For nearly a hundred miles I could see the curious peaked capes of Montague Island trailing off over the horizon. Entering Boswell Bay I anchored near chimney-like rocks about a hundred feet high, cut into bulges and globes. At first I thought they were pillars of white quartz; but no, they were seagull rookeries smothered with nests, and all about them a million white birds shrieked and fluttered, making these white rocks conspicuous in fair weather by their presence and in fog by their constant cries.

I was now in Prince William Sound and soon I got to that little city I shall never forget, Cordova, of which Mr. Larsen had said, "Beware, it's a den of thieves and a robbers' roost." He may have been right but the people I met were very kind to a stranger far from home. Of one thing I am convinced: the spirit of Old Alaska still lives on beyond the Copper River.

Up Orca Inlet, in a setting of green mountains streaked with snow, lies Cordova. The first thing I saw was a fire engine attacking a flaming pile-driver. How the fire fighters ever managed to turn out I could not imagine as, like everyone else, they enjoyed their spirits to the full. Getting to the fire they had one object in view, and it sits on the bar under the label of "Old Overholt" or even "Old Mr. Boston." From all over Prince William Sound people come to bottle up at Cordova. Drunkenness is a man's own concern and nobody else's, but fear at some time is the concern of all, and the saying goes that a magnum of old, be it "Overholt" or "Grandad," will make the odds against you seem a trifle less.

I saw men with beards gobbling pots of marmalade, and there was a bespectacled cook who wept as he munched handfuls of wedding cake. A globular blob rolled at the entrance to a vegetable store where men were moving produce with a spade.

At sometime someone had enthusiastically attempted to pave parts of the streets, but the pavement was worn out and on the muskeg of Alaska wobbled like black blanc-mange.

After completing repairs and meeting many kind people who presented me with strawberry pies and boxes of tobacco I started south again. The east wind raged day and night and I could make no progress against it whatever. The air began to have a distinct nip. August was drawing to a close, and the aurora lit the heavens with flaming swords of light beyond the Copper River. After futile maneovering about the river flats, I gave up and tried either to get my boat aboard a steamer bound for Seattle, or to get a tow behind someone going back to southeast Alaska.

A group of curious people from Los Angeles arrived in Cordova by plane and at once set out for home in two ex-Coast Guard launches, followed by a fisherman in a flat-bottomed boat. I have often wondered how they made out. Small craft do not return along those shores and in six hundred miles of cruising I had passed only three boats, all large halibut vessels.

No one was going my way. The steamer, loaded with a thousand cannery hands, sailed south, and there I was, left with no escape. I might have stayed on for months at Cordova, but the tales I had heard of the winter winds that rush down from the mountains, rolling cars over and whirling whole buildings from their foundations, made me quake like an aspen. Those three hundred miles of rolling breakers with never a sign of a soul! I had to leave, and fast, somehow.

I wandered all over the waterfront, asking the skipper of every boat of good size whether he was going my way. At length I found a roly-poly man on a new halibut boat, surrounded by hundreds of bottles. He was a friendly fat man, very nice and solid, but his words were nicer still, for he said, "Just tie alongside. We are leaving now." Three other gentlemen arrived and were about to cast off my lines when Carl, the captain, got them interested in a case of beer instead—the first of thirty-six cases. Only ten miles out fog shut everything from view.

We stopped and drifted, made away with a bottle of the best and an excellent beef stew. Then the halibut boat started off again, towing me four hundred feet astern through the swirling fog, and for seventy-two hours an almost continuous trail of glass bottles drifted past across the Gulf of Alaska. There was Carl; his friend from Seward, who had not been outside in twenty-five years; and a Roman Catholic fox hunter from the island of Afognak whence they had all come after the season's fishing. There was also a vague character from Seattle, who seemed as keen to get out as I was.

Only for fifteen minutes did we see anything but fog and it was then, perhaps thirty miles off Icy Bay, that fog settled down very thick and low on the sea. There, in the light of the setting sun, across the mauve fog blanket, appeared Mt. St. Elias, the colour of old wine. Captain Carl and his friends would have surely fallen asleep at a performance of *Carmen* or the *Halleluiah Chorus,* unless it had heralded the arrival of "Old Grandad." Yet at this spectacle we came to a stop and gaped in awe. It was my last sight of those grim shores and the ageless spectre of the mountain seemed to wave its great wings in

farewell. "Never again; not for a King's Ransom, Fat Man," I thought, and I still do. We rolled on, day and night. At times I thought the tow line must surely part, or pull my boat under water, as Carl, his bottles and sixty tons of boat sank into the great green valleys of the sea and took up the slack.

One night from the tops of the highest waves we saw the light on Cape Spencer flaring out over the tumbling wastes of water. At three the next morning we were home, in Seattle's back yard, returned from the nameless terrors of those remote Alaskan regions. Death, the grimmest spectre of all, was postponed a little longer. At least three bottles of "O.O." were disposed of right there and then.

Next day I awoke at anchor and my recent companions had gone, leaving a faint trail of corks to mark their passing. That was the last I ever saw of the four men from Afognak. May the spirit of Old Overholt go with them yet; like themselves, one hundred proof.

Such was the Alaskan Coast from Cape Spencer to Cordova, as I saw it in 1946. I never returned.

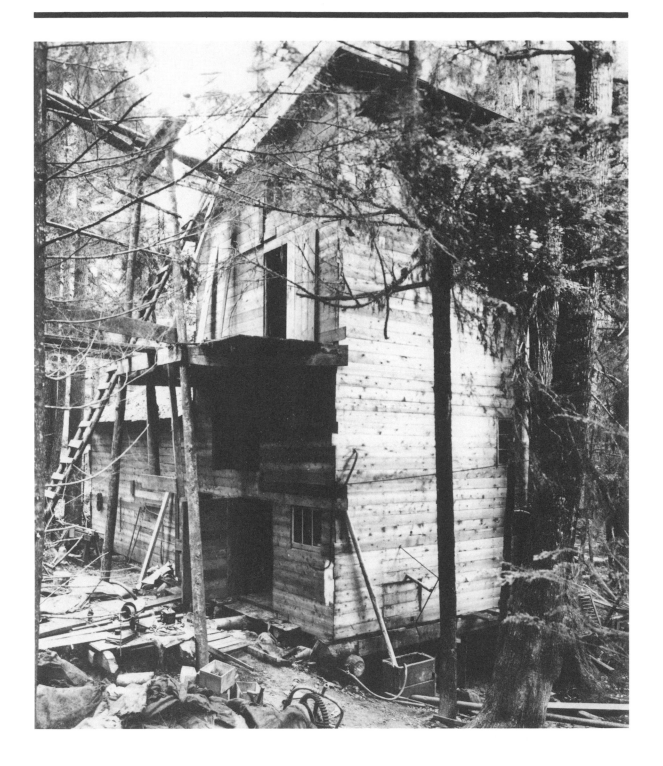

the POCAHONTAS CAPER

Back in 1972 *Raincoast Chronicles* ran the above photo as part of an article on rum-running, identifying it, "High-production still on the west coast of Texada Island." High production it was, but, as a legion of Texada readers have protested, the operation was actually located in Pocahontas Bay, halfway up the island's east coast. The great Pocahontas Bay moonshine caper is remembered as a sort of watershed event in island history, as one long-time resident explains in the following account.

by Stewart Brinton

BET YOU DIDN'T know that Texada once had the largest moonshining operation north of San Francisco. Yep, that's true. It was over in Pocahontas Bay. That was in '29 at the beginning of the Depression. The still was run by Vancouver men—three owners and two wage men who'd been hired as sentinels. Pocahontas was the perfect place. It was a distance away from things. Even the islanders rarely went there. The Perry boys used to have a logging operation out there. They had a sawmill too. But that was years before and it was thick with second growth, especially along the creek. And the creek had good, clear water year round.

So the boys barged everything up—all the boilers and lumber and other equipment—and set up operation. They built what amounted to a small barn. Half of it was over the creek. They disguised everything. They pulled the tops of the firs down over the building and tied 'em off with cable. They had a six-inch cast iron pipe that carried the runoff from the still, and they buried it all the way out to the low tide mark on the beach, just so they wouldn't be detected. And they had holes dug above the beach with poles over the top, and dirt fill over that. There they hid the product: five-gallon kerosene tins of moonshine, packed in crates and lined with paper so they wouldn't vibrate when they were being shipped in the hold of the rum runner.

Ya gotta remember that this was a commercial operation with a 500-gallon-a-week capacity. It wasn't a pot still with a copper coil condenser; it was a reflux still with a Scotch boiler and a stripper. The mash was cooked by steam and the temperature and pressure gauges had to be always right on the mark. It was a tricky operation, but it produced 96% pure grain alcohol . . . that's 192 proof. Just sniffing the bung on a tin of that stuff would set your eyes to crossin'. They say they sold the stuff in the States. That's hard to say, but the centre of the operation was False Creek. That was where they shipped the grain from and where they brought the moonshine to. Don't know who all was in on it. Some say the Tolmie government—as far as politicians go you can believe almost anything.

Vancouver Barge and Transportation did the shipping. They'd bring a scow up to Pocahontas loaded with a couple of tons of barley and some sacks of rye. At False Creek it was labelled AGRICULTURAL USE—that was their front. Pig feed, hah! The tugs *Trucilla* and *Etta Mack* were carrying about everything possible in those days, stopping at every logging camp from Vancouver to Powell River. It wasn't unusual to carry pig feed to some hell and gone place. The company was up and coming and needed the business, so they must have been paid off to keep quiet. Both tugs' history was a little shaded. Both were World War I sub-chasers that became rum runners and were finally converted into tugs. Whichever tug was delivering would leave the barge at Pocahontas. The boys at the still would quickly unload it and take it around to Raven Bay and tie it up. That was so it didn't draw any attention.

Well, the government agents knew a still was operating somewhere up north, but they didn't have a clue as to where. It took about nine months before they got their first lead: the captain of a salmon troller got drunk and passed out on the wharf at False Creek. The agents nabbed him and checked the hold of his boat. They found forty gallons of alcohol in five-gallon kerosene tins. The captain squealed. So they knew a still was operating somewhere on Texada Island. They sent word out to the Forestry Department to keep an eye out for any suspicious activity. Well, it wasn't long before a forestry plane was passing over Pocahontas Bay and spotted a grey horse. They wondered what it was doing there, since there was no evidence of a farm around. So they reported it to the agents. Well, actually the horse was used to unload the grain from the scow and take it up to the mash tanks. The revenuers, knowing a bit about the business, knew that horse was clear cut evidence of a still, so they sent a boat up to Pocahontas to investigate. They still wouldn't have found it if the sentinel hadn't seen the government boat turn into the mouth of the bay. He got shaky and fired a warning shot. They caught the sentinel, a guy named Brody. The others fled to the west side of the island and caught a ride on a fishing boat. Brody took the rap for 'em. He claimed he was only hired help so he only drew nine months on a twenty-year sentence. Twenty-year sentence! For selling moonshine! Nowadays you can kill somebody and get only two years.

Well, the government put the equipment in the still up for bid—everything but the boiler and the stripper. A few of the boys—Hadden, Burnett, Tate and Robbins—got wind of it and went down to the city and won the bid. It took 'em about a week to dismantle it and barge it all to Vananda. People'd pretty well heard about it by then and they were all amazed by the size of that distillery. The boys got tools like chain pipe wrenches and lengths of cast iron pipe, pumps, even an outboard motor. The best of the lot was the mash tanks—four of 'em. They were made of fir staves. They were about ten feet high and six feet in diameter with about a 2,200-gallon capacity. You can still see it at Hadden's place behind the shed; there's another one at Lowther's old homestead.

Hadden got a lot of stuff from that still. He built a two-storey farm house out of the lumber. Dismantling the still also gave him the notion to build one of his own. Times were hard in '29, and he was anxious to put his daughter through college. So he built a still out of a ten-gallon copper barrel. He had a four-pound jam tin soldered on top. A copper coil came out of that. The jam tin sort of channeled the alcohol into the coil and kept it from condensing too early. The coil ran through a forty-gallon oil drum filled with lake water. The brew that dripped out of the end of the coil was filtered through a cannister of charcoal. It took about four to seven runs to get a good fix. Hadden made a five-gallon tin of moonshine a week when he worked at it. My brother said it was damn good stuff; it gave ya a kick in the head without all the headache. Hadden used cracked corn for his mash. He used to feed the leftovers to his pigs. You should have seen 'em! Jesus! A drunken pig is just like a drunken man. Half the pigs'd be snorting and kicking up the dirt; the other half'd be sitting on their haunches singing to beat hell.

Well, pretty soon Hadden, Fleming and a few others were all running pot stills. Texada was a nice place for that type of private enterprise. It was isolated. A still makes a helluva stink when it's cookin' and you don't want any strangers snooping around. Bill ran the water taxi and he was in on the deal. He was sort of the middleman—shuttling it over to Powell River, hiding it in the bilge. Buck lived out in Wildwood. He was what they called the *blind pig*. He sold a lot of it to the whorehouse. Eventually the police came over to investigate. But the minute they stepped off the taxi and onto the dock the word was out, everybody knowing everybody and the taxi driver being in on it. They never got a chance to find out anything. Hadden got wind of it and threw his pot and coil into the lake behind his place. You could probably take a grappling hook and find it.

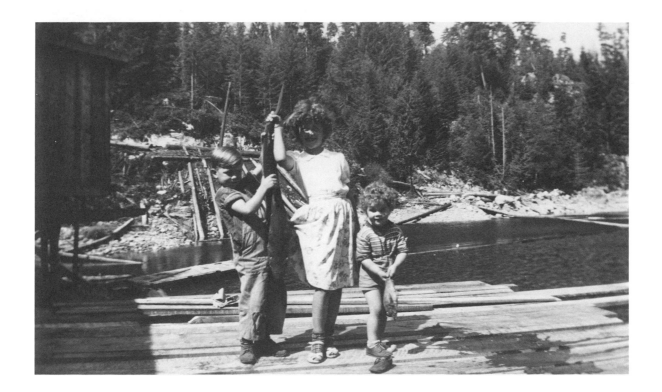

THE BOMB THAT *MOOED*

Memories of a logging camp childhood

by Howard White

MY FATHER first set foot on Nelson Island some
time in 1949, as near as I can figure. To this day
I think he may thoroughly regret that move, but none of
us kids do. How could we? To him and Mom it was a
tough luck show that robbed them of their prime years;
to us it is the mold that formed us – to reject it would be
to reject a basic part of what we now are.

Charlie Philp was to blame for Green Bay. Charlie
was a rich guy who lived in Vancouver. He'd been a
lowly car salesman at one time but then he got the Mack
Truck dealership just as truck logging was sweeping the
coast and made a million. He enjoyed his surplus wealth
by funding ambitious young loggers like Dad to go
out and set up hard-scratch gyppo shows, then slowly
tormenting them into bankruptcy.

The camp itself was already set up when we arrived. It
consisted of three small board-and-batten shacks on posts
just above tideline and three somewhat more permanent
shacks farther up from the beach, located on the west
side of the bay beside a waterfall that roared like a
rushing freight train all winter and disappeared in the
summer.

It was in 1950, on May 24 as I inexplicably recall,
that Dad decided to move the rest of the family, consisting
of my mother Kay, my older sister Marilyn, eight,
myself, five, and my baby sister Cindy, three, into camp.
We had just moved out of a failed camp at North Bend,
after weathering the record-setting winter of 1948 in one
of the worst areas of the province for extremes of climate,

spent a few months of respite in the comfortable family
seat at Abbotsford, then moved with all our effects
aboard the fish packer *Moorpack*, owned by the keeper
of Pender Harbour's main store, Royal Murdoch.

The house we kids slept in at Green Bay was practically
at the foot of that waterfall and that eternal roaring still
goes on somewhere in the back of my mind; whenever I
hear the rush of falling water now it does strange things
to me. That house wasn't a part of the camp; it was
finished on the outside with real siding and lined inside
with birch veneer like a real house in the city, built as a
wilderness home by a family named Yates who still
owned the twenty acres the camp occupied. All we kids
knew of these mysterious Yateses was that they were
Christian Scientists; the closets and attic of their abandoned house were packed with innumerable issues – not
of the *Christian Science Monitor* – but of a lesser true-
believer publication on octavo-size pages, the covers
decorated with Roman columns intertwined with vines.

I suppose Dad chose the Yates house for us because it
appeared at first glance to be the most comfortable; it
had two private bedrooms, a large living room, a kitchen
with nice cabinets, an old wood range and hot water, and
an inside bathroom with a chemical toilet, all finished
in handsome birch plywood; in contrast to the other
bunkhouses, which were just bunkhouses, with the usual
beaverboard and spiked-to-the-wall orange-crate appointments. But the Yates house was totally accursed. I still
dream about it regularly; it provides my subconscious

with a purgatory symbol that can't be improved upon. It was always dark, dank and cold. It was built in a kind of muddy hole in one of the few locations with no view of the bay and was so overhung with droopy cedars the sun never shone. It was always wet; glossy magazines left in that house for more than a few days would turn to mush and clothes gathered mildew hanging in the closet. Dampness was endemic. A cool steam wafted over from the waterfall, filtering through trees burdened down with Spanish moss. Periodically the wetness would gather its energies and erupt into the open; during spring and fall rainstorms, an impromptu river might break down the back door and flood the whole house to a depth of six inches. I recall being delighted the first time I awoke to find my gumboots bobbing against the wall, then later when the waters subsided discovering the plywood floor blistered into a series of springy hills that made for good jumping until Dad caught us. I remember him looking underneath the house and roaring, "They actually dug the goddamn thing down into a hole! How could anybody be so goddamn stupid as to build a goddamn house in a goddamn mudhole! They must have blasted to get it so bloody low!"

Everything had been done wrong in that house. Doors opened the wrong way, the steps were pitched to make you trip every time, the water pipes couldn't be made to stop leaking in the summer or freezing in the winter, so they were simply never hooked up. As a result the bathroom was inoperative, the kitchen sink was only good for trapping spiders and the stove couldn't be lit because that would burn out the unused water coil. And yet here were all these good intentions: dish cabinets with glass doors, leaded windows, pretentious archways, laboriously built dry-stone terraces, all useless. It was like an arrested dream. We very much envied the wife of the camp foreman, who occupied the boxy shack on the

ads for '52 Plymouths and Chryslers from the *Saturday Evening Post*, projected on the wall with Marilyn's opaque projector. After lights out she would read to us by flashlight from risque bestsellers such as Edna Ferber's *Giant* and John Steinbeck's *Cannery Row*, which served us in place of *Mother Goose*.

By day we lived in a world of pretend that with time developed a Byzantine elaborateness. Each of us had one main pretend persona. Marilyn's was Marilyn-of-the-Stores, so named because we originally began by setting up pretend stores stocked with beachcombed bottles and cans. I was a straight-laced masculine hero named Sevward Billington, and tag-along Cindy was a ne'er-do-well named Mrs. Bad Keeky. During most of our waking hours we lived in these made-up roles, snapping out only when confronted by grownups, and frequently branching off into innumerable lesser roles that altogether comprised a pretend world of such highly developed interrelatedness the adults in camp were continually astonished by the glimpses they caught of it.

In the course of our play we transformed the geography of Greenzbay into a fantasyland. Our parents were of the enlightened generation who followed the indulgent dicta of Dr. Spock and went him one better, allowing us the free run of the place as long as we kept our bulging kapok lifejackets – which we dressed in automatically as soon as we got out of bed – firmly buckled in place. We were provided with a rowboat my father had built for us, using plans from *Popular Mechanics*, his hands-down favorite reading material. The skiff was a blue-painted, high-sided, V-bottomed, blunt-nosed thing called a "pram", hand-made out of half-inch plywood, and we wore out one set of oarlock holders after another exploring the local landscape. Across the bay from camp was a sheer bluff which nevertheless contained a cave with eerie signs of previous occupancy. Part way down

hill which had none of these pretentions but was warm, dry, functional and commanded a clear view of the bay. The only good thing about the Yates house was that we kids had it all to ourselves, after Mom and Dad moved down the trail to less gracious but more livable quarters in the back of the cookhouse.

We kids loved Green Bay, or as we invariably call it, Greenzbay. There was nothing there for us – no schools, no playmates, no television, no radio, not even regular mail or newspapers, but for us it was paradise. We lived basically on our own in the Yates house, our parents were so preoccupied with business. Our entertainments, in spite of the lack of modern amenities, seemed endless. At night we would stay up as long as the light plant stayed on, enjoying movies which consisted of new car

the bay toward the north end was an equally evocative abandoned campsite and boat-beaching grid where I found a five-inch barnacle that grownups told me could only have come from the west coast. Legend was that this site had been previously occupied by an old hermit who beached his sailboat there. Later another vagabond found it: the legendary Allen Farrell, who built his famous ketch *Native Girl* there some years after we left.

Unlike settlers who lived up on the Blind Bay side of the island, we down at Green Bay felt virtually without neighbours. Technically speaking we had one, the Henrys. The Henrys were an old-world Finnish couple and I think the term for them was "hard-bitten". They had the old cannery site in the little hole-in-the-wall just to the right as you came out of the bay. They called this little lagoon, which becomes landlocked at about half-tide, Hidden Basin, in memory of their first homesite up at Hidden Bay, which they had left some years earlier following persecution by the "unreasonable people" who lived up there, as they explained it.

Unlike our bay, it got sun, it had a bit of flat land where they could run their solitary brush-fed cow, and there were still a number of cannery cabins scattered along the beach bluffs which the Henrys promptly organized into a sort of low-budget summer resort, mainly for Finn millworkers from Fraser Mills.

The early history of Green Bay was a pattern of decisive failure and abandonment—a pattern that persisted through our experience, and ultimately through the Henrys'. As Finns tend to be, the Henrys were inexhaustibly hard-working, especially Mrs. Henry. Boats leaving camp at daybreak would always discover her out before them, jigging cod off the bay mouth in one of the curiously designed sampan-like boats they used. During the spring she toiled until dusk in the large garden they had built up on a rock knoll near their house, laboriously packing soil in pails and fertilizing it with starfish, dogfish and seaweed until it blossomed into a heartbreaking jungle of fruits, berries and vegetables—heartbreaking because, gawk and drool as we might, we can-fed urchins never got to sample a bit of it. Every scrap of food Mrs. Henry could lay her hands on went into jars to feed her summer guests. Again following the Finnish stereotype, everything about the Henrys' place was clean, orderly and well kept. The house itself was quite striking, with large windows, crisp white-painted siding, a bright green roof in the shape of a curved arch and odd projections at each of the four corners where the eaves continued clear down to the ground—the way we always assumed the houses in Finland must be, although I suspect now it was just another of Captain Henry's quirks. In the midst of all that enclosing coniferous jungle they maintained a neat lawn with trained shrubbery and charming flower plots that gave the place the aspect of a toy village in the Alps—or in Finland, I suppose. It was a kind of magic

country all of its own to us kids, just because its civilized charm was such a contrast to the bunkhouse and bulldozer universe we occupied; but on the few occasions we were admitted to the house with its fragile furnishing, porcelain trinkets and unearthly cleanness, we felt suffocated.

The locals warned Dad that the two old Finns were "mesatchie" and troublemaking—a reputation resulting no doubt from their dispute in Hidden Bay—so, true to his perverse nature, Dad set out to win them over.

This proved less than simple. Those first-generation Finns had a very hard face which they turned to the non-Finnish world, a peculiar blank expression which seemed so devoid of human feeling as to be completely intimidating, and this was the face we would be met with on any attempt to stop the Henrys for a chat on the Irvine's Landing dock, or to drop in on them for a casual visit. One's business would be crisply asked, and there being none of note, no quarter would be given. The seven-mile trip to Pender Harbour and back was a day's undertaking in those slow-moving days, particularly with the Henrys' snail-like little sampans, but all overtures toward collaborating on shopping runs were dismissed. The initial attempt by us to deliver their accumulated winter mail was received with something akin to shock, and resulted in the postmistress being rudely dressed down for giving it to us and ordered not to do it again. They were also extremely jealous of the boundaries of their large tract of mostly worthless bush and would be seen lurking behind trees whenever logging operations came anywhere remotely in the vicinity. If we kids ventured out that way in our rowboat we would be shooed home, and once when one of the men fired a shotgun at some mallards they were stalking down the beach from the Henrys', the old lady popped out of a crevice in the rock and gave them such a ferocious tongue-lashing that they withdrew without attempting to retrieve the good-sized drake they'd hit. They had been unable to determine whether Mrs. Henry was upset by the noise, didn't approve of killing or just wanted to chase them off so she could put the duck in jars.

There were two cracks in the Henry's heavily armoured independence: their cow, and the internal combustion engine. Old Otto was a deep sea mariner but his experience was all in sail and he had never really gotten the hang of keeping gas engines going. Since in the summer they depended on the boat to meet guests coming up on the Gulf Line steamers to Pender Harbour, this was a serious problem, and finally one morning Mrs. Henry appeared in her skiff at our wharf in a dreadful state, pleading for help. She had the better English of the two and was normally quite comprehensible, but when she got worked up you had to have a lot of Finnish to decipher what she was saying. This Dad couldn't do, but it was clear enough the problem was over at their place, so he towed the old girl home with our camp boat, a coffin-like ex-rumrunner entitled the *Suez*, and found the old captain almost dead of exhaustion from heaving on the one-cylinder Easthope in his sampan. He was just purple and gasping and his hands were raw to the point of bloody. A quick check showed the gas line to be running straight rusty water, and after draining the tank and cleaning the carburetor, the engine performed like it was made to. The old boy was effusive in his thanks, and Mrs. Henry appeared to insist Dad accept a King George dollar bill, neatly folded in quarters. She was so upset when he declined that he offered to take "something for the wife" from their garden, and came home with four carrots and a bit of lettuce.

The trouble with Henrys' cow was that it was Canadian. They wanted a Finnish cow as frugal and orderly as they were, but this cow was haywire. For one thing, it

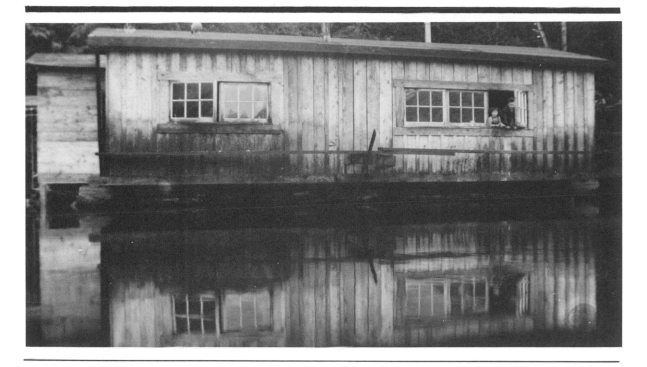

gave too much milk, always at the wrong time, so Mrs. Henry always had lots when there were no guests to feed and none when there were lots. This led to Mrs. Henry's next actual attempt to acknowledge our neighbourly existence, which took the form of approaching my mother with an offer to provide the camp with fresh milk. Mom of course happily agreed, even when it turned out the old lady wanted the same price per ounce as we paid for canned milk at Murdoch's store. Mom took it and even kept taking it after we discovered it was so queer-tasting, a result of the cow's peculiar diet of seaweed and salal brush, that no one would drink it; so anxious was Mom to establish something approaching a normal human relationship with her only neighbour.

The other thing about Mrs. Henry's cow that helped bring us together was its propensity for wandering. There was no real road connecting our two places—the Henrys wouldn't let Dad make one—and Mrs. Henry desperately tried to keep that cow fenced and roped in, but it was over at our place every time you turned around. I don't know why. It just hung around. Maybe it longed to hear its own language spoken. We kids naturally liked it and made a big fuss over it and snuck it pocketfuls of rolled oats, but Mom and Dad made a neighbourly effort to send it home. Dad was afraid a logging truck would run over it and he'd have to pay Mrs. Henry its worth in T-bone steaks at Murdoch's. The trouble was, that cow was very hard to get home. It would get bogged down in swamps, jam its head between close-spaced saplings and get stuck trying to climb over fallen logs, bawling and thrashing as spike-knots ripped into its udder. We could never figure out how it got around on its own, or why it was never killed by a cougar—or one of the area's numerous pit-lampers.

Its greatest caper was the time it ate the dynamite. Dad was a bit sensitive about the dynamite because by law it was supposed to be kept locked up miles from human habitation in a special air-tight magazine built of six-by-six timbers; while he had it stashed in a flimsy open lean-to just up the road from the shop. On top of this, you were supposed to destroy dynamite after a certain date because it becomes unstable and dangerous to handle, but he could never bring himself to just burn dynamite he'd paid good money for. Eventually our dynamite got so old and cranky everyone was afraid to

go within a hundred feet of the magazine, let alone use the stuff.

This was when Mrs. Henry's cow was discovered standing by the road chewing away on a stick of twenty-per-cent stumping powder as contentedly as Fidel Casto munching a Havana cigar. Closer inspection revealed that the beast had been living for some days at the magazine, stomping boxes open and eating case after case of dynamite, evidently enjoying the piquant taste of saltpetre- and nitroglycerine-soaked sawdust.

"Holy jumped-up, bald-headed, bare-assed, black-balled Mexican Christ!" my father shouted, twisting his cap around on his head as the implications of the discovery sunk in. "Nobody touch that cow!"

"One hiccup and we're all goners," observed Jack Spence, Dad's foreman. "Can you imagine what a time the cops would have if it blew up, trying to figure it out? There'd be just a crater full of guts, hooves and hardhats."

They were all afraid the cow would go home and blow up in Mrs. Henry's barn, or else the dynamite would get into the milk and poison half the crew of Fraser Mills. Finally they decided to drive it way to hell and gone up the logging road where it would take two weeks to get home, by which time it should have cleaned its system out. But nobody wanted to go close enough to tie a rope around its neck, so they hit on the idea of getting behind it with the logging truck and scaring it up the road with the air horn. With everyone else cowering down behind stumps, Long Tom Gray eased slowly up in the truck, but at the first honk the unsuspecting animal shot into the brush like a goosed kangaroo and was gone. We all spent the following week with one ear tuned for large blasts, actual or verbal, emanating from the Henrys' direction, but the case of the bomb that mooed closed without further incident.

The next thing I remember about that cow was Dad killing it. I think the suspense got to Mrs. Henry, after so many years of sitting home fretting about losing all that potential bottled beef to a marauding cougar, and eventually she prevailed upon Dad, who she had somehow found out was a trained butcher, to do the thing in. Being of the opinion that it was never too soon to start disabusing his male heirs of any innate squeamishness about blood and gore, Dad took me along to "help".

I remember there being a parental discussion on the

matter, where it was concluded this would be "good" for me, so the event took on a ritual air, augmented by the careful laying out of tools, the erection of the hanging beam and by Mrs. Henry's hysteria. Even before we arrived, her face had the wrung-out, red-eyed look of a person suffering through a death in a close family. However this was equalled by the excitement of the bonanza of bottled provisions which were about to land in her lap, and she couldn't pull herself away until the fatal moment was upon us; and then only with the odd request we summon her immediately the deed was done. Then she struggled off, wringing her hands, to hide in the house. Dad cocked his head in the direction of her retreat to make sure I learned my lesson.

"What's wrong with Mrs. Henry, Dad?" I said.

"Well son, she's like most people," he intoned. "They can't bear the sight of blood, but they like to eat meat. That's why there has to be men like you and me around to look after them."

Then he told me to put down a handful of hay under the hanging beam and when the cow lowered its head to munch, he quietly suggested I hand him the ball peen hammer we'd brought along in our bucket. I fetched it and he delivered the cow an easy thud on the back of its head, collapsing it in a heap exactly on the spot he wanted to hang it for skinning and splitting.

"Gee, is Mrs. Henry's cow dead now, Dad?" I said. It didn't seem like much of a spectacle, for all the buildup there'd been.

"That's all there is to it, son. Farmers, you'll see 'em get the animal rearing all around while they beat on its nose with a claw hammer, but this is the way you do it."

Coming from the Fraser Valley, Dad always used farmers as the example of people who did everything haywire, although after he'd been up the coast for a few

years he began to cite fishermen instead of farmers in this role. I grew up thinking of both the way prairie Wasps think of Ukrainians. It wasn't until I was fully grown that I heard fishermen refer to gyppo loggers in the same way.

I looked at Mrs. Henry's cow lying threre whole, unmarred, unchanged, as if it were asleep, except for the odd finality of its stillness, and I found death didn't impress me at all. Then Dad reached down and drew our butcher knife across the cow's silken brown throat and my heart stopped as an ocean of blood burst out over the dry fir needles.

"Take a stick and make a groove in the ground so it will drain over there and we don't walk in it," Dad said. But I was transfixed.

At this point Mrs. Henry came puffing up the trail. "Is it done? Is it done?" she kept calling, not wanting to get too close in case it wasn't. Then she followed my pale stare to the blood.

"Oohh!" she gasped, and began running agitatedly about. "Oohh! I wanted you to call me." She produced an enamel basin and stared from it to the brilliant puddle now dispersing amongst black fir tree roots and spongy moss.

"I–I wanted to keep it," she stammered. "We always keep it . . . in the old country." And then she knelt with the basin to her cow's clotted jugular, but the flow had stopped. This was too much for me.

"What's she doing, Daddy?" I shrieked, jumping up and down. "You told me she couldn't stand blood and now she's going to drink it!"

I survived Dad's pained explanation and the full spectacle of slaughter as it unfolded before my now thoroughly impressed eyes. My eyes, but not Mrs. Henry's. Her squeamishness forgotten, she fastened herself to my father's elbow, snatching every scrap and drip for her jars. The stupendous eruption of guts did not faze her; she hungrily seized upon the tripe, lungs, brains, lights, hustling them off to the kitchen and returning quickly for more.

"What's that?" she would demand in the angry-seeming way that was more her normal tone, with that singular Finnish blanche beginning to seize her features, as Dad went to throw another piece on the compost pile.

"Bung," he said.

"What?"

"Bung."

"What's it good for?"

"Well, Scotchmen use it for haggis . . ."

"Give it here!"

Dad gave it.

"What's that?"

"Bladder."

"What's it good for?"

"Well, when we were kids we used to blow it up and play football with it . . ."

For his efforts Dad was allowed to take home a roast of his choice, so he cut out the sirloin—she didn't know one cut from another anyway—and amid much festive feeling and dynamite-belch and exploding-oven jokes the camp crew sat down to eat it that Sunday; but true to form, Mrs. Henry's cow was completely inedible.

Captain Otto Henry was a good deal older than his wife and, once you learned how to decipher his mangled English, actually proved to be the more sociable of the two. Once or twice when Mrs. Henry was off on one of her occasional trips to Vancouver, Dad and some of the guys went over with a bottle and even discovered the old fellow to be a bit of a rounder. He could laugh, tell stories, and his history was fascinating. Finland had built up a merchant navy early in the century by buying richer countries' mothballed sailing fleets and crewing

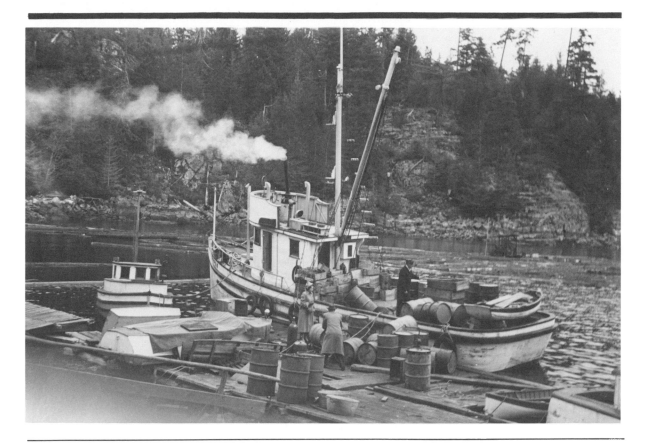

them with destitute farm boys who worked under seventeenth-century conditions. Captain Henry had begun as a cabin boy on one of these ships, and told horrific tales of the hardships the Finn sailors suffered from hard work, bad conditions and harsh discipline.

One of young Otto's tasks was to take care of the raisins—raisins were the one luxury on the ship's menu—and while he had the raisin locker open to squish weevils and count out portions he was under orders, under pain of the lash, to keep continuously whistling. It is very difficult to eat a stolen raisin when you are whistling.

Despite the hardship of life in his native land, Captain Henry never ceased to be homesick for it and scornful of his adopted one. His dream was not only to once again see the old sod, but to build himself a fine little ship that would take him back to all the wondrous places he'd seen in his youth and provide him a long retirement of leisurely drifting on the tide. The whole time we were on Nelson Island, Captain Henry worked as assiduously as his wife did with her jars on this perfect vessel. It took shape in a shed a few hundred feet down the beach from the house, but so painstakingly was he piecing this last command together, double-planking it with yellow cedar over oak ribs and teak fittings, that the progress from year to year was barely perceptible. It was a very strange-looking ship, for a dream boat, about thirty-six feet and rather tubby, with a long foredeck and a high house amidships with tiny round windows. Of course it was designed to sail—I'm not sure he even planned to bore the keel.

Not too long after we left in 1954—victims of the Social Credit government's policy of closing the woods to small free enterprise and delivering it over to the big monopolies—Captain Henry, who must have been eighty, died with his little ship still on dry land. I went up to look at it and noted that he had gotten as far as painting a name on the bows, *Esto Utopia*, which must translate as something like "This is heaven". A few years later Mrs. Henry sold it to Oscar Tahtinen of Pender Harbour, who cut off the outlandish house, bobbed the

stout mast, painted out the *Utopia* and converted it into a very prosaic gillnetter called simply the *Esto*. I never saw it tied up to the Whisky Slough fish barge without stopping to marvel at its odd fate, but Oscar only complained of its screwball design and the rot in its timbers.

By the late fifties, Green Bay had won its sunless, rockbound solitude back to itself once again, and buried another generation of settlers' dreams. My parents never forgave it and remember the period only with bitterness. For us kids, it has remained a place of dreams, and my dreams of it are the pleasantest I have. Every time I dream about it I resolve to go back for a visit, and at least once a year Marilyn and I do. But it gives us a funny feeling. The falls are still there, and Dad's old log dump, but all trace of the camp is gone. Even the one permanent structure, the Yates house, has been so thoroughly consumed by salal and elderberry we can never agree exactly where it was. The great looming bluffs across the bay are gone, replaced by an anonymous, unimposing low hump, and nothing seems mythic at all. I swear someone has moved a reef, where the otters used to romp a hundred feet closer to the shore and somehow changed the way it looks. There are traces of the intervening decades—the burned-out hulk of a west coast troller, Clarence Cook's old *Morien II*, below the falls, and around in Mud Bay is a tug in similar condition—I think the *Viking Prince*. Over in Hidden Basin the Henrys' successor, an even bigger Finn dreamer named Ken Viitanen, spent several years trying to grow exotic hothouse orchids for world-wide distribution—but he also vanished without a trace, although his son-in-law Walter Ibey still booms salvage logs in the main bay. The Henrys' house is gone too, disgracefully burned during the hippie era, which brought the most recent wave of dreamers to Green Bay. Thirteen of them went together and bought the old Yates property—but already the little shacks they dotted through the woods have been left for the ravens.

THE THIRD STIFF

from an account by George Weeks

Far as getting busted up goes it's safer on a boat
than most shore jobs   safest job there is
if you don't count drowning
Gillnetters especially
out on deck for a beer piss
boat leans one way
you lean the other—
kersplash.
Or reaching out over the rollers
to shake a log out of the web.
They find your boat idling up against a bluff
the next day, tow it into the float
nobody will tie up next to it.
One year up in Rivers Inlet
three guys went over in one week.
What happens then, they turn up a few days later
in other guys' nets. Guy'd see this lump coming up
and think it was a seal till it falls on deck
and an arm flops out to signal
shit-your-drawers time.
Two of these corpses showed up on schedule
but the third one kept us guessing for a while.
Fishermen are a spooky lot to begin with
and you have to have done it to know just how eerie
it gets out there in the middle of the night
all by yourself leaning over the stern
wondering just what sort of a ghastly item
the murk is going to puke up at you next
everybody in the inlet was just quaking in their
   gumboots
every time they saw something that wasn't a fish
come into the light figuring for sure
they'd snagged the third stiff

Sonny Iverson said this night he got so bad
he had to go knock back half a twenty-sixer
before he could get the rest of his net in
leaning over the stern to pull kelp out of the rudderpost
thinking what a damn fool he was to get so spooked
the whisky took his balance and plop
he's in the soup   his faithful boat
gliding serenely away into the night
and all he can think about is that damn stiff—
"now I'm in here with that sonofabitch!"
he's afraid to paddle, certain when he reaches out
he'll touch it and once when he brushes a chunk
he finds himself screaming like he's being murdered.
Then he hears something.
A kind of faint swishing noise.
Swish, swish, swish—
He listens real careful and reaches around a bit.
There, right under his nose, is a moving line of corks.
Somebody is picking their net past him and all he has to do
is grab on and wait to be saved.
This works fine until he comes up to the other boat
and finds he's all tangled up in the net
and before he can say anything he's up over the rollers
crashes head first on the deck and knocks himself silly.
Of course the other fisherman just cuts loose
swearing and cursing all the foul luck in the world
figuring it's the missing stiff he's hooked onto
until Sonny starts coming to and moaning a bit
then the poor guy runs howling the length of the boat
bars himself into the house
cursing God and praying to be saved at the same time
it takes Sonny fifteen minutes to calm him down enough
to go get his boat.

Howard White

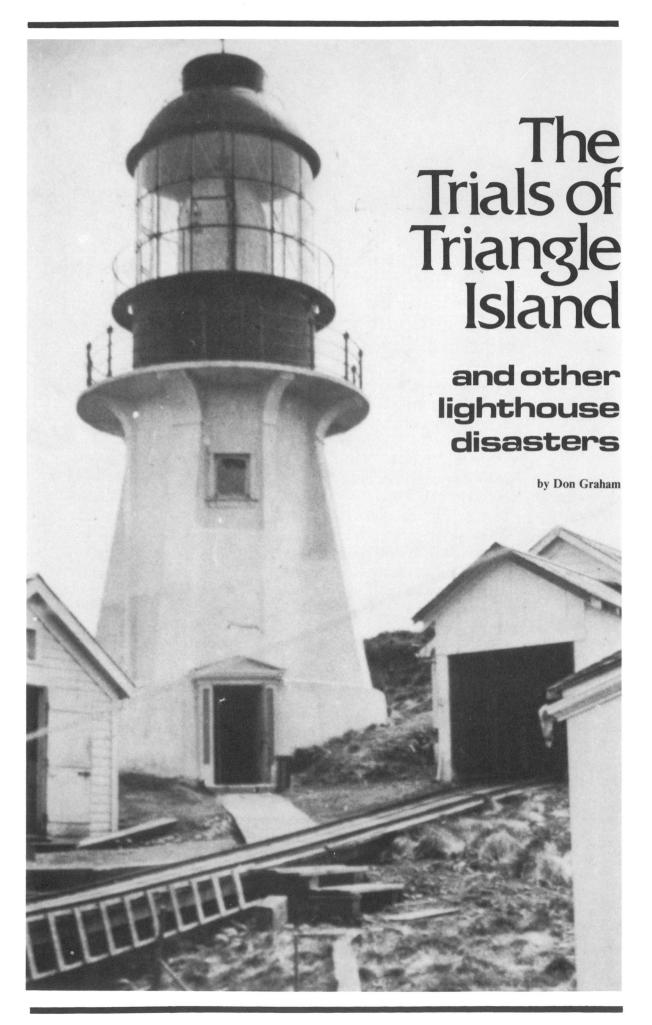

The Trials of Triangle Island

and other lighthouse disasters

by Don Graham

*E*ven considered together, the stories of the light-houses which mark the rocks and channels of the B.C. coast remain as individual and varied as the well-formed personalities of the keepers who tended them. From the first, Fisgard Lightstation (built in 1860), to the last, Bonilla Island (built one hundred years later in 1960), it is a record of engineering mastery matched by human endurance, devotion to duty and, on occasion, both heroism and tragedy.

The most notorious example of the latter circumstance is no doubt the murder of Addenbroke Island keeper Ernie Maynard, who was shot from behind while standing on the lightstation landing in 1928. The mystery of who might have been passing by that extremely remote location in one of the most unpopulated reaches of the north coast, and what his motive might have been for taking the life of a harmless lightkeeper, has remained forever unsolved. Equally imponderable is the mystery of what strange fate befell the American lightkeepers from Tatoosh Island, off Cape Flattery, whose bodies washed up within three days of each other, the first at Carmanah Point and the second at Cape Beale, in January, 1900. The body found at Carmanah was headless.

In an entirely different way, the story of the coast's tallest free-standing lighthouse at Estevan Point on the west coast of Vancouver Island, is no less mysterious. Thanks to its shelling by an unidentified vessel the night of June 20th, 1942, the Estevan light has entered Canadian history as the only part of Canada to come under enemy fire in World War II.

The cause of most lighthouse lore on this coast is nothing as exotic as murder and war however; it is the perfectly ordinary and dismayingly regular fact of stormy weather. One of the leading victims in this regard has been the Egg Island station, built at the exposed seaward entrance to Fitzhugh Sound in 1898. Storm damage to the installation the first year incited the Department of Marine and Fisheries to construct a protective breakwater, but the next winter's waves casually brushed it aside. Over the next few years, the wind and sea came calling for the house, snatching away, in turn, the porch, a good section of the roof, a wooden walkway, a steel derrick and the fog-horn building, as well as the lightkeeper and his assistant, missing and presumed drowned in March, 1934. But even these sallies were a mere foretaste of the storm which, on November 2nd, 1948, washed all of Egg Island station save the basement into the sea, leaving keeper T.R. Wilkins and his astonished family cowering in the bush for five days until the storm abated sufficiently for rescuers to find them. Rebuilt on higher ground, the new light was itself witness to tragedy, in 1950, when keeper Laurie Dupuis, distraught at the supposed desertion of his common-law wife, committed suicide at the very moment she was trying to contact him to effect a reconciliation.

But in the annals of B.C. coast lighthouse history, no other horror story can compare with that of Triangle Island, where overreaching ambition and plain human error combined with incalculable forces of nature to produce the worst calamity in the Department of Marine and Fisheries' history. Ever since, lightkeepers from Race Rocks to Green Island have consoled themselves with the thought, as they watch the wind scale shingles off their roofs during week-long winter gales, that however bad things got, they were infinitely worse at Triangle Island.

Lightkeeper Don Graham in the following account of Triangle Island focusses on the unique combination of circumstances, human and otherwise, which came into play there.

ON SEPTEMBER 23rd, 1910, the Canadian Government steamship *Quadra*—chiefly remembered now as the one-time command (1891-1903) of Captain John T. Walbran, author of *British Columbia Coast Names*—docked at Victoria after laying out plans for the ultimate lighthouse. Marine Department surveyor H.C. Killeen informed a *Colonist* reporter he had established, at the behest of Colonel William P. Anderson, Chief Engineer and Chairman of the Lighthouse Board of Canada, a spectacular 650-foot-high site for a powerful first-order light "which will ultimately develop into one of the most important of all lighthouses on this coast." Rightly predicting "great development" of steamship traffic, Killeen declared that Triangle Island "would be a leading light which will be the first picked up by the steamship captains and will give them their bearings whether they are bound to Puget Sound or Prince Rupert."

No one will ever know the particular challenge Killeen's boss Anderson saw in Triangle but, flushed with the success of his recent architectural triumph at Estevan Point, Anderson must have hoped for another, even greater one, a light so magnificent it would propel him at once into the company of his heroes, Stevenson, Douglass and Halpin, the greatest lighthouse builders of them all. A decorated veteran of the Fenian raids, a charter member of the Canadian Society of Engineers and executive member of the Geographic Board of Canada, a lover of philately and good cigars, Anderson stood head and shoulders above the stale air of petty Ottawa office politics; he was an artist bureaucrat with power. Marine Agents on both coasts and the Inland Waterway were at his bidding; he had only to bring his finger down on a map to dispatch armies of workers and tons of materials to transform an untouched wilderness forever. Five times higher than Estevan, Triangle may have stood in his mind, as it did in the mind of an anonymous writer in the Victoria *Colonist* on July 11, 1909, as "the furthermost western point of the Empire," a bookend of British Imperialism to match Bombay's great Gateway to India, a station destined to be "the key to wireless communicaton on the Pacific."

Despite its relative newness, wireless telegraphy was rapidly assuming an importance as a navigational aid to rival the lights themselves, and at the time of Triangle's selection a good deal was made of its perfection as a wireless site. "Perhaps nowhere in the world has nature so effectively congregated the essential fundamentals for a wireless station," waxed the *Colonist* writer, who went on to note the island's unique isolation, elevation, and the fact it was "absolutely barren of forestation, not a tree and scarcely a blade of grass finding lodgement on its bleak and rugged sides and windswept crown."

The importance of "barrenness" at the wireless site, the *Colonist* reported, "can only be fully appreciated by workers in wireless, who assert that it is among the mysteries of this ghostly new agency of inter-communication that it is a matter of less difficulty to project the all-important waves through rugged masses of granite than over the gently waving tops of a young forest of live pine. Indeed, the operators at the first station established in British Columbia have frequently declared that when messages were in transit across the Straits to or from Douglas Hill, one could actually see the needles of the pines all quiver nervously as they feasted upon the current designed for the speeding of the written thought."

Flying buttresses (top) grace Anderson lightstation at Estevan Point. Right: the 1,820-foot tramway. Below: Pender Harbour fisherman Ray Phillips and the squat remains of Triangle Island's light tower.

TRIANGLE ISLAND itself is a cone-shaped mountain rising above the waves some forty-two miles out in the rolling Pacific to the north and west of Cape Scott at the northernmost tip of Vancouver Island. From the outset, erecting Triangle Light was an endless struggle. Straining at her anchors in the heavy seas, S.S. *Leebro* in the summer of 1909 landed supplies and a work gang who set to work on a 1,820-foot-long tramway up the rock to a steam winch above. On the summit, workers constructed a wireless telegraph shack, dwellings for the radio operators and lightkeepers, a cookhouse, engine room, oil storage shed and light tower. They dug, drilled and blasted water cisterns under both dwellings and the cookhouse. Fierce winds ripped shingles off roofs almost as fast as they nailed them down. Buffeted by the elements, carpenters harnessed to safety belts hammered up forms for the tower, mixed, poured and tamped the concrete. Once stripped, the squat tower stood forty-six feet tall. It took all of three months battling the wind to affix the curved glass around the huge beacon; putty vibrated out of the frames faster than it would set. Inside, the lantern chamber was braced with stout beams and made fast outside by cable and turnbuckle.

Taking a much-needed break from their labours, workers exploring the island crawled into a cave on the shoreline where their lights fell upon a leering skeleton clad in a battered lifebelt, gumboots and a few shreds of clothing. No one ever learned the identity of "the sentinel of Triangle Island", as he came to be called, except that he was a white man who had somehow made his way ashore to die years before. Captain Freeman of the halibut boat *Flamingo* buried his remains in the cavern, but not before a radio operator with a ghoulish sense of humour had snatched up his skull for a souvenir.

Despite the omen of the corpse and all the construction difficulties, the light was finished by November, 1910, and the *Colonist* could proclaim TRIANGLE LIGHT IS SHOWN NOW, echoing Killen's brash confidence in the "largest and most powerful of North Pacific Coast lights." And so it was: the ponderous first-order classical lens focussed a million candlepower from incandescent petroleum vapour and, when conditions were right, threw a shaft of light thirty miles out to sea.

The trouble was, conditions were rarely right. From the beginning, lightkeepers and radio operators looked down in disbelief as bank upon bank of fog and cloud rolled in almost as soon as the winds stopped. Mariners nearly seven hundred feet below searched in vain for a light all too often obscured by cloud and fog. For reasons unknown to this day, Anderson on Triangle Island broke the most elementary rule of lighthouse construction and built a light higher than 150 feet off the water. As rumours of the light's ineffectiveness piled up, Anderson, in his capacity as the Department of Marine and Fisheries' Chief Engineer, came west to inspect Pachena, Estevan and Triangle, all constructed since his last visit. But if he had any doubts or reservations about Triangle, Anderson kept them carefully to himself.

Meanwhile, for the little colony of lightkeepers and radio operators on the island itself, life soon became unbearable. James Davies, whose father George had been the province's first lightkeeper, officially took over the station in July, 1910, with his wife and three daughters. The assistant keeper Holmes and the two wireless operators, Jack Bowerman and Alex Sutherland, doubled as school teachers. For all, sleep was often impossible, thanks to the shrieking gales and constant "evil lament of the huge sea lions." Seven-foot deposits of guano made Triangle's soil so caustic it burned like lye, making a garden impossible; occasional halibut dropped off by sympathetic fishermen were the only relief from a monotonous round of canned food. At this station as at most others, landing supplies was a difficult task at best. Davies once tried to enhance their diet by ordering a large consignment of apples, oranges, bananas and vegetables. When *Leebro* unloaded, the precious cargo was dug out from under thirty tons of coal; two apples and half a banana were all that survived. It is hardly surprising that people confined under such dismal conditions soon turned upon each other, and a trivial dispute over some coal soon escalated into a fist-fight. An exasperated Captain Robertson, the new Marine agent in Victoria, was forced to issue standing orders to Davies "that you and your family . . . have no communication whatever with the wireless station on Triangle Island, except when business necessitates it." The navy's radio telegram branch sent similar instructions to its staff.

In February, 1911, James Davies rushed next door "on business" and handed the operators a message for Victoria: MRS. DAVIES DANGEROUSLY ILL SOME TIME PAST, BAD HEMORRHAGE CANNOT STOP, ESTEEM IT A FAVOUR IF VESSEL SENT DIRECT AS MATTER IS SERIOUS. Captain Robertson wired Gordon Halkett, his superintendent of lights aboard the tender *Newington*, who in turn ordered Captain Barnes "to proceed with all dispatch to the station." As she plied her way to Triangle, a freak wave overtook the tender from the stern, filling her decks to the rails, uprooting steam pipes and sweeping away all her deck cargo. The crew, up to their chests in water, thought their ship had gone, but she rose again and made it through to the island, where Halkett scaled the tramway and found Violet Davies "very weak from loss of blood." The shore party lashed her to a mattress and lowered her down the tracks; she arrived on the beach upside-down. The seamen had a tough time hoisting her up the side and over the rails "owing to the *Newington* rolling badly." Halkett brought a doctor aboard at Alert Bay and he urged him to waste no time getting her to hospital. Fifty-six hours later an operator came across to Davies' house to tell him Violet was safe in Victoria.

But it was weather, more than anything else, that made life on Triangle unbearable. Signing on for two-month relief stints, radio operators were sometimes marooned for many months, forced to live out of the single suitcase they had brought with them. Many complained they had been "shanghaied". Even when relief ships came into sight, weeks would sometimes slip

away while crews waited for safe landing conditions, or those on land were forced to swallow their disappointment at the sight of their relief fleeing for shelter in Bull Harbour. Ashore, the simple task of getting from one building to another was a problem; all masts and structures were rigged like ships with cables and turnbuckles fastened to deadeyes grouted into the rocks; life-line cables linked all the buildings along the walkways. Despite these reinforcements, dwellings rocked so violently on their foundations that their occupants sometimes became seasick. Windows bulged inward and, as a matter of routine, no one opened a door alone. The wind roared down chimneys, making fires impossible to keep. Everything on the station stood poised to rush over the cliffs to the raging seas far below.

O N OCTOBER 22, 1912, the anemometer registered 120 miles per hour before the wind ripped it from its mounts and assaulted the buildings, shearing off six brick-and-iron chimneys clean at the roof line. One gust sent a shed end-over-end over the cliffside into the sea; another snapped the wireless mast, ending all communications. Down on the beach, raging surf reduced two storehouses to kindling, and the two-ton engine for the tramway was knocked several feet from its base. Praying and shouting encouragement to each other, the two radio operators crouched in their dwelling while the gale burst their windows and plucked doors off their hinges. Finally the house shuddered and split in two, rupturing the attic water tank, which flooded all the rooms. Preferring even James Davies' company to the threat of annihilation, they inched their way over to the keeper's house which, in its turn, "absolutely rocked in the gale . . . not safe to be inside."

By December, 1913, Davies had had enough and begged for a transfer to "more congenial surroundings" in light of his nineteen years' service. "Triangle," the former keeper from Egg Island confessed, "is a great strain on our constitutions." Only two years old, the lightkeeper's dwelling was already "unfit for habitation." Rain driven horizontally by the incessant wind "swamps us out, as the building leaks and it is an utter impossibility to keep a fire, as the place gets smoked out and we have sometimes to go a week at a stretch without a warm meal. You can imagine," he wrote Robertson, "what a trial it is to me and mine."

Davies left in March, 1914. In late January Thomas Watkins, Davies' successor, informed Victoria that a gale a week before had blown the beach storage shed over again, littering the shore with 450 oil cans and five kegs of nails. "The roof is blown about three hundred feet along the beach," he wrote, "the sides and floor about 150 feet from their original positions." Both dwellings "got a severe shaking;" the door of the spare house blew off and chimneys were blown down again. By October, Watkins was eager to transfer to a new station planned for Bonilla Island in Hecate strait, "a much more suitable place for a man with a wife and young children than Triangle Island." Watkins was succeeded by Michael O'Brien, who had spent five years in the hold of the Sandheads Lightship and contracted rheumatism "owing to the confinement and dampness;" he was "very desirous of being exchanged to Triangle Island."

Triangle Island light may have been an unending trial for its keepers, but when the verdict came in on Anderson's accomplishment his peers were unanimous. According to F.A. Talbot, whose 1913 study *Lighthouses and Lightships* (London: William Heineman) was a survey of the state of the art, "probably the most important light and certainly the loftiest on the Pacific seacoast north of the equator is that on the summit of Triangle Island, British Columbia." Talbot also had nothing but praise for the "Engineer-in-Chief of the Lighthouse Authority of the Canadian Government" for his light at Estevan Point, "placed in a most romantic setting." The two lights confirmed Anderson's revolutionary reinforced concrete designs with their graceful but functional buttresses as "the last word in lighthouse building." None could compare with Britain's Eddystone or Scotland's Skerryvore as engineering feats, yet there was no denying Anderson's "most powerful beacons [were] of commanding character, representing as they do the latest and best in coast lighting."

If expert acclaim and journalistic hoopla indicate how much the light captured the public's imagination, no record exists of the inner thoughts and feelings of its creator, who must have known it was a complete and utter failure from the time of his first visit, watching the beach below shrink to the size of one of his rare stamps as he rose up the long tramway. He may even have ascended through the grey stratus which clings to the top two hundred feet of the island most of the year. Knowing the 150-foot maximum height rule could be read on blackboards in every first-year engineering classroom in the country, what thoughts must have passed through Anderson's mind when the praise pouring in was poisoned by grumbling and (worst of all) derision in wheelhouses and shipping offices from Shanghai to San Francisco. No one will ever know. All complaints by mariners about lights were forwarded to the Chairman of the Lighthouse Board of Canada – Col. W.P. Anderson himself – in Ottawa, where they were carefully docketed and placed on the Board's agenda. Yet despite thick files of complaints on every conceivable subject during Anderson's tenure – petitions for new lights, suggestions about existing ones, handwritten notes from fishermen, detailed letters under imposing letterheads from the world's great shipping companies – not one has survived about Triangle Island. The only reference to Triangle appears in minutes to a board meeting held March 5, 1909, before the light was built, when Anderson's colleagues tried to dissuade him from the site because of its extreme height. There is no indication of what the colonel's reply might have been to this seemingly unanswerable argument.

This absence of any correspondence or mention of the Triangle Island blunder is pregnant with implications. But whatever reason exists for the Board's apparent ignorance, the island was about to loom up and confront them all with a disaster which, ironically, had nothing directly to do with the ineffectiveness of its light. Shortly after noon on October 29, 1918, the naval patrol vessel *Galiano*, on loan to the Department of Marine and Fisheries, dropped anchor off the station and sent off its workboat with supplies. For the weary island-bound radio operators ashore, it was to be a day of deliverance. Sid Elliott was scheduled to come off, and Jack Neary would visit with his brother Michael, who was a radio operator aboard the *Galiano*. But no one was permitted to go aboard, due to the risk of being infected with Spanish influenza which was then rampant in Victoria and had already caused eight members of the crew to be left behind. Sid Elliott received the disappointing news that his stint would be continued; crestfallen, he climbed back up the thousand stairs while Jack Neary caught up on news of friends and family from his brother. By 1:30 southwest winds began to muster for a fresh assault; the workboat hurriedly transferred cargo while the Neary brothers said goodbye. Seamen threw the remaining cargo onto the beach and hastily snatched up Miss Brunton, a housekeeper who had been teaching the

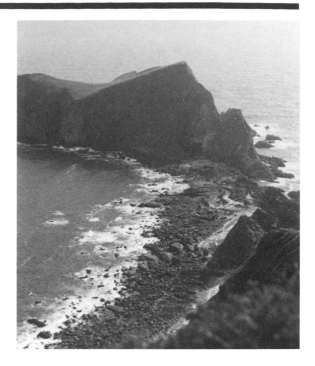

O'Brien children, and rode the gathering swells back out to the ship.

The *Galiano* wasted no time hoisting her anchors and then, inexplicably, headed for the open sea instead of seeking shelter in Shushartie Bay. In view of her tendency to have decks awash when the wind was on her quarter, the crew had long complained about their captain's preference for riding out storms when shelter was available. Two hours later, somewhere south and possibly west of Ikeda Head in the Queen Charlotte Islands, the *Galiano* foundered and sank. Art Green, the operator on watch at Triangle, strained to catch her last faint message: HOLD FULL OF WATER. SEND HELP. He called Sid Elliott over and the two took turns signalling through the night, but received no reply. Jack Neary was sleeping on his cot, unaware his brother and twenty-six others had gone to the bottom, but they let him sleep through. Fishermen aboard the halibut boat *George Foster* pulled Wilfred Ebb's body out of the water two days later, and two others were later found drifting east of Cape St. James. A distance-recording log identical to the one used aboard the *Galiano* turned up in 1939, but no other evidence of the tragedy was ever found.

Lightkeeper Michael O'Brien left that winter to keep his own appointment with tragedy at Entrance Island, where his wife drowned while rowing home from Nanaimo, and Alec Dingwell came down from Green Island to preside at the station until 1920, when the Department conceded defeat and shut it down. Ten years after the *Colonist* had written that "Triangle Island is at last to be put to the uses for which Nature apparently designed it from the beginning," some of the same men who had bolted the beacon room together scaled the island again to remove it. Today the lens and beacon room repose on the parking lot of the new Coast Guard base in Victoria, bearing mute witness to the Lighthouse Service's greatest mistake.

BUNKHOUSE BETTY

by Pat Jackson

I DIDN'T exactly hire Bunkhouse Betty. She was arranged for me, like a Chinese bride, by Oscar Eagle.

At the time, Oscar was building a sled for me and because he worked in camp he expected lunch to be provided in the cookhouse. This view was not shared by Crazy Legs, the cook, who insisted that he pack a lunch like the rest of the crew. Crazy Legs, so named by the crew because of their somewhat uncharitable contention that, "she could walk around both sides of a gas drum without scraping her knees," finally succeeded in excluding Oscar from the cookhouse at lunch. The following day he responded by heating a can of beans over a fire of chips and shavings kindled on the doorstep of the cookhouse, and within an hour Crazy Legs was on the bomber headed for Campbell River.

Oscar firmly contended that she was no loss, but after enduring my cooking for a few days he volunteered to go to Vancouver and recruit a replacement if I would stake him to the fare. His parting shot was that he would find someone who would "jazz up this stump ranch a little bit." He succeeded beyond my wildest expectations.

Within a week he called me on the radio to inform me that, "I got ya a real dandy! Ya better get down here and hire her quick before some other boss logger grabs her." A few days later I had occasion to go to Vancouver and I located Oscar and Betty in the pub of the old West Hotel. A glance at Betty was enough to inform me that there had been no necessity for haste.

Her figure resembled a gunny sack full of busted choker knobs. She sported a pair of beauteous black eyes and a butch haircut that looked like Prince Valiant in drag. The shiners, she explained, were a going away present from her boyfriend and the fright wig was a deliberate ploy, "to keep them guys at camp from getting horny, if ya know what I mean." I assured her that I knew exactly what she meant but that my boys would

treat her with the utmost respect. Privately, I opined that Betty was hardly likely to arouse unbridled lust in even my deprived crew and that even without the ultimate horror of the coiffure, her chastity was virtually assured. I little reckoned on the power of a determined woman. As diplomatically as possible I suggested to Oscar that Betty was not exactly what I had in mind when I agreed to let him recruit a new cook. He was outraged. I had entrusted him with the responsibility of hiring a cook. He had made certain commitments to Betty and under no circumstances could I ask him to go back on his word. If I did, he'd "pull the pin". Good sled builders are hard to come by so with severe misgivings I gave him a hundred-dollar "drag", told him not to bring her to camp until she sobered up and headed up coast to ready my crew for the calamity about to befall them.

My most descriptive briefing was inadequate to prepare the boys for the impact of Betty's premiere appearance in the cookhouse. The black eyes had matured into a bizarre kaleidoscope of mauves, greens and yellows. The haircut had taken on the aspect of an enraged porcupine and, with the whole thing overlaid by a very obvious hangover, the entire effect was, to say the least, startling.

The crew filed in and sat down to dinner with that silent singleness of purpose that characterizes every logging camp cookhouse. Betty stared at the crew and they stared back in frank astonishment. The silence was finally broken by Betty, who grasped a large iron skillet and, waving it aloft, menacingly declared, "The first one of you buggers who gets horny gets nailed with this!" The boys were visibly impressed. I began to wonder if having her virtue assaulted was not some sort of obsession with Betty.

It turned out that she was a passable cook and as camp life settled back into its dull routine I breathed a sigh of relief and relaxed. Not so Betty. Powerful

261

primeval forces were stirring within her breast. She was developing a carnal passion for the Horse, the boom man, a blonde Adonis who was the reigning Canadian amateur heavyweight boxing champ and whose sojourn in camp was prompted by a recent misunderstanding involving a policeman's ribs.

Following the hasty departure of the late, unlamented Crazy Legs, the Horse had reasserted the boom man's traditional privilege of eating a hot lunch in the cookhouse. As the days passed, love bloomed amidst the warmed-over spareribs until Betty coyly declared her affection one lunch hour by hurling herself across the cookhouse into the arms of the Horse as he entered for lunch, shrieking, "Horsie, I'm hot for yer body!" As the Horse described it later to an appreciative audience in the bunkhouse, "that broad almost decked my ass." He further stated most emphatically, "I wouldn't touch her with ten feet of frozen rope."

Hell hath no fury like a woman scorned. The Horse went back to eating cold sandwiches on the boom winch. Betty sulked and the cooking fell off markedly. Pressures began to build. Something, or someone, had to give soon.

Something did, but in a most unexpected manner. Irish Paddy attempted to rape Betty. As he explained later, "Bejasus now, and I was terrible drunk. I must have been!" My foreman was awakened in the middle of the night by a commotion in the cookhouse. Thinking that perhaps a bear had gotten in, he pulled on his boots and dashed over. The scenario that greeted him was, in his own words, "unforgettable." Paddy had Betty backed into a corner of the room where he was throttling her with the one hand while with the other he had torn away the front of her nightdress, revealing a snowy avalanche of breasts. It did not appear to be an occasion for gentle persuasion and, acting with admirable alacrity, he administered a clout behind Paddy's ear, which put him away for an hour or so, and packed him off to the bunkhouse.

Betty bore the affair with admirable aplomb. At my insistence, Paddy tendered an apology which she accepted most graciously, even going so far as to hint that if he would care to press his suit soberly and politely he would be warmly received. Paddy ungallantly muttered something that sounded like, "not bloody likely," and the incident was closed.

Camp life resumed the even tenor of its ways, but all was not serene. Bunkhouse Betty, or Bunkers, as the boys now called her, was becoming increasingly irritable and hinted darkly at pulling the pin and heading for town to get serviced if some stalwart in camp did not soon step forward to fill the breach, so to speak. She even asked me if the boys had some kind of grudge against her regarding her cooking, because she had done everything except hand out engraved invitations, all to no avail. I assured her that everyone was delighted with her cuisine and they were probably all just a bunch of fairies anyway. This explanation appeared to satisfy her intellectually, if not physically, but she continued to grumble, "If one of them goddamn homos don't get it up soon you can blow for the bomber for me and I'm long gone." Since no one, least of all myself, wanted to revert to my cooking again, it became apparent to us all that someone had to "bell the cat"—or ball the cook.

Events reached a climax the night the crew went to Minstrel Island to pick up the mail. I had an old tug boat called *El Toro*, which had been sunk and raised so many times that the boys referred to it as *El Yo-yo*. They used to request permission periodically to borrow it to go to Minstrel, to "pick up the mail," which seemed to come back neatly packaged in twelve-compartment boxes about two o'clock the next morning.

On this particular occasion they invited Bunkers along, and in the course of defending her from some derogatory remarks passed in the Minstrel pub they got into a glorious donnybrook with a group of indigenous native sons from Turnour Island. Paddy had his head split open and Teeth, the cat-skinner, lost the one remaining

262

cuspid gracing his smile. Through it all, Horse, the man who could have carried the day for our side, slept blissfully unaware in a bunk on *El Yo-yo* and was bitterly disappointed when he learned he had missed out on the festivities.

Bunkers' honour having been vindicated, the fallen heroes headed back to camp with an adequate supply of beer to celebrate the occasion. Upon arrival at camp, Betty grandly announced that she was going to reward her champions with a full course turkey dinner, followed by certain exotic delights.

Unfortunately the turkey was frozen solid, so she placed it in the oven of the big cast iron oil range and turned the throttle up to the top notch. Everyone applied themselves diligently to the beer and Betty archly suggested that while they were waiting for the main course, they could proceed directly to the dessert, and retired to her bedroom, which was annexed to the cookhouse.

I had heard the boat return but had decided there was nothing untoward in the happy hubbub and had gone back to sleep. I was rudely awakened by the foreman frantically shaking me shouting, "For Christ sakes, the cookhouse is on fire and the whole damn crew is in there!"

Still groggy with sleep, I stumbled outside and was jolted into full awareness by the sight of great clouds of black smoke billowing out of the doors and windows of the cookhouse. Our eyes streaming with tears, we groped our way in through the front door and discovered that the entire cookhouse was filled with dense, acrid smoke except for a layer of relatively clear air about two feet off the floor. After dropping to my hands and knees I could perceive the recumbent forms of about half my crew, flat on their backs in this safety zone, happily swilling beer. Ignoring a cheery invitation from the Lout to "lay down an' have a beer," I crawled to the stove and yanked open the oven to discover the source of the smoke. The *piece de resistance* of Betty's dinner party was a smouldering, charred mass.

I flung it out the door and crawled into Betty's room, where I was confronted by a truly bacchanalian spectacle. Shrouded in smoke, a coughing, wheezing, gloriously happy Betty was presiding queen-like over the wreckage from her bed, a barely conscious Oscar Eagle propped at her elbow.

"They're in love," a slurred voice informed me from out of the murk.

"In love!" I gasped, totally failing to show the appropriate awe and respect.

"Yer goddamn rights," Betty snapped archly. "And you can just stop yer gawkin' 'cause we're goina go ta town t'morra and tie the knot."

"Oscar, is this true?" I pleaded.

"Far's I know," he shrugged. I could see the cause was lost.

"It was love at first sight," Betty trumpeted.

"You hid it well, all these weeks," I couldn't help observing.

"I figured it was just a hangover at first, but I jus' couldn't shake it," Oscar explained.

It was obvious that it would take a squad of riot police to terminate the orgy, so, after kicking open all the windows and doors, I retired discreetly and left them all to their somewhat dubious delights.

The next day a badly hung over and rather sheepish crew stumbled out to work and the whole incident seemed forgotten. Not so! The following day the lovesick couple appeared in the office to officially invite me to the glorious event, to be held in St. James Church on Vancouver's Skid Row in honour of the many free meals both had partaken of in the soup kitchen there, and to be followed by an all-out drunk at the West.

I found a delicate way to beg off, but it was soon evident I was the only one in camp who did. By nightfall it was clear the entire crew had decided the duty of witnessing Oscar and Betty's nuptials outweighed any obligation they might feel for helping me get my boom out ahead of impending violence among my creditors. I sat down to consider the enormity of the calamity which had just befallen me.

I had painstakingly recruited some of the finest logging talent to be found in the Skid Row pubs of Vancouver, hauled them to camp, sobered them up and assembled them into one of the best gyppo crews on the coast. And now, in one night, Bunkhouse Betty had decimated the ranks as effectively as if she had used a hand grenade. Reluctantly I called a council of war in the bunkhouse and handed out cheques all round.

They were sorry I wasn't going with them and they all promised to return as soon as they could. However, I knew that the chances of rounding them up again after a couple of weeks in town with a three-month stake in their pockets was just about nil. I was seeing the last of them and we both knew it. With a heavy heart I stood on the float and waved farewell to the first planeload to take off.

Betty went out on the second plane and she left with a flourish. As I helped her into the aircraft she announced with gusto to her fellow travellers that since they could not catch the shuttle out of Campbell River until the next day, "we might as well shack up in the Willows tonight and kinda keep the ball rolling, if ya know what I mean hey!" I'll say this for her, she had no class but she sure as hell knew how to make the most of opportunity.

The next cook was a Seventh Day Adventist with a figure like a sack of deer horns. In very short order she had the cookhouse licked into shape and the new crew whipped into line and life in camp became efficient, orderly and extremely dull.

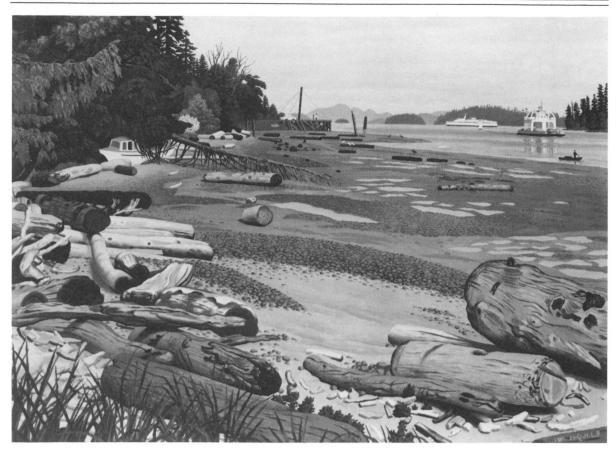

E.J. Hughes' *Low Tide at Fulford Harbour,* painted in 1982

E.J. Hughes: Painter of the Raincoast

by Patricia Salmon and Leslie Forsyth Black

THE ROMANTIC view of an artist as a solitary figure existing only for and in his work is not widely held in this age of the verbal and public painter, but Edward J. Hughes is just such a solitary figure; a quiet man who speaks only, eloquently, through his paintings. Hughes has painted for almost fifty years. He leads a secluded life on Vancouver Island, recording the landscape of his native province with a unique vision, combining intense fidelity to the physical structure with vivid hues in finely balanced compositions outside the mainstream of modern abstraction.

Hughes has never wavered from his initial commitment to paint the beauty of his land, with his private perception of that beauty. In his early landscapes he sought to capture decorative elements that occur spontaneously in nature, becoming obsessed later on with the atmosphere, the essence of the air between. After each brief excursion into other subjects, he has been drawn back inexorably to landscape painting.

EDWARD J. HUGHES, a member of the third generation of the Hughes family to reside in British Columbia, was born in North Vancouver in 1913, but spent the first decade of his life in the small, lively town of Nanaimo, surrounded by the forests and coastal waters that later were to be his primary subjects. He was the eldest of the four children of Edward Samuel Hughes and Katherine Mary McLean. His father, a professional musician, insisted that the children take music lessons but Edward never considered a musical career. He has said since,

> Every week I would carry my great leather roll of music to my piano lesson. I hated it. I was far too slow and just couldn't stand my own mistakes. To me a piano lesson was worse than the dentist. I even hated the leathery smell of the roll.

Young Edward showed an early interest in drawing, however. His mother recalls,

> Edward could draw almost before he could speak. I remember him drawing a small picture of a boat on pointy waves with smoke coming out of a funnel.

She fostered this interest by supplying him with colouring

PAINTINGS BY E.J. HUGHES

View of Cowichan Bay, by E.J. Hughes, 1975. Oil, 60 x 90cm.

Over page: *Nanaimo Harbour,* by E.J. Hughes, 1962   Oil, 81 x 114.3 cm

Comox Valley, by E.J. Hughes, 1953. Oil, 91.5 x 101.5cm.

books, but Edward rarely used them. The young boy was frustrated by the pale, uneven colours that wax crayons produced on the paper. He preferred clean black-and-white drawings.

Edward's early life was exceptional in only one respect: he liked to be alone. He shunned group activities and never had more than one friend. He spent most of his time sketching or reading boy's books. He had a youngster's enthusiasm for comic books and regularly read the *Boy's Own Annual* and *Chums*. Their illustrative comic-book style is reflected in his first original drawings.

Most young boys used to entertain heroic visions of military life, but it must have come as a shock to Edward's parents to find that their reclusive elder son was seriously interested in soldiering. He dreamed of attending the Royal Military College at Kingston, and began preparing for a military career. He joined the Seaforth Highland Cadets, the one group activity he enjoyed. Instead of being alienated by the discipline, he was exhilarated by marching, precision drills and target practice. He still keeps two small trophies he won for his skill as a marksman. He was approached locally to take what seemed like a very attractive position that, on closer investigation, turned out to be the operation of a Lewis machine gun aboard a coastal rum runner. He consulted his mother. He recalls,

I was so excited. It was at the beginning of the Depression and the money was very good. Mum didn't want me to go, though.

She was privately horrified, but carefully explained to Edward that he was still too young for the assignment. It was the one argument that he could accept. Swallowing his disappointment and pride, he passed up what seemed to him a golden opportunity.

His mother realized now that her restless son might be lured into dangerous pursuits, so she encouraged him to enroll in a program of evening drawing classes. Years of sketching on his own had made him ready for formal instruction and he found it rewarding. The teacher, Mrs. Verrall, insisted on proficiency in pencil drawing, principally still lifes. Hughes remembers long hours spent labouring over one drawing entitled *Kitchen Chair*. After mastering pencil techniques a few of the students, including Hughes, were permitted to begin classes in oils. The new medium delighted him.

Hughes began seriously to consider painting as a career. He studied art books in the Vancouver Public Library for hours on end. Gainsborough and the Renaissance painters captured his interest and ignited his desire to become an easel painter.

His father was hired to provide background music for vaudeville and the silent films at the Orpheum Theatre, and the family moved from North Vancouver to Kitsilano, into a large new home. The family future looked bright, but the year was 1929 and the Stock Market crash set off a chain reaction that soon engulfed Vancouver and brought young Edward's training in oils to an abrupt stop. The Depression struck suddenly and viciously. Theatre musicians were among the hardest hit, for the new talking pictures were already threatening their existence. The Hughes family had to give up the fine house in Kitsilano and move to Princeton, where Edward and his father found work in the mine.

For young Hughes, the Depression meant abandoning any thought of attending the Royal Military College. Gone too was a long nurtured private dream. He secretly had hoped to combine his two passions, painting and the army, by becoming an army artist.

THE YEAR 1929 marked a profound change for Canada. A review of the government agencies and foundations established during the following years reads like a checklist of national institutions: the Royal Mint, the Bank of Canada, the Canadian Broadcasting Corporation, the Dominion Drama Festival, the Governor General's Literary Awards, the National Film Board. In painting, members of the Group of Seven were still influential, with their emphasis on the Canadian land. The abstract experimentation popular in Europe did not find ready acceptance in Canada; rather, the grim reality of life during the Depression provided the dominant focus for artists and writers. Some of the most moving paintings of the decade include Prudence Heward's portraits, Jack Humphrey's children, Carl Schaefer's farmhouses. In literature too, the harsh economic conditions figure prominently in works by Anne Marriot, Claudius Gregory, Morley Callaghan and Irene Baird.

The Vancouver School of Decorative and Applied Arts was an exciting place to be during the Depression. Hughes felt fortunate when sympathetic uncles offered him financial support to art school, and, determined not to be a burden to his uncles, Hughes immersed himself in his studies. His drawing and painting instructor was Frederick Horsman Varley, member of the Group of Seven. Hughes recalls:

Self Portrait (drawing), 1978

Really he was a great painter; in fact, I rank him third of the painters at that time. Tom Thomson's colours have never been equalled. Jackson I would put second for his interpretation of the landscape. Then Varley, even though he painted mostly figures at this time. The way he used colours to express feeling and his grasp of the model's character was amazing. But as a person and a teacher, I somehow never understood him. He would stride about the classroom loudly exhorting us. "Get the mood, get the mood," he would say. I never really knew what he meant.

J.W.G. MacDonald was also an instructor at the school. He had studied at the Edinburgh School of Art and had come to Vancouver in 1926 to teach design. MacDonald was a vigorous, enthusiastic teacher. His friendly, outgoing manner made him a great favourite with the students, and the strong underlying patterns evident in many of Hughes' early landscapes reflect the influence of MacDonald.

Hughes also valued help received from other less famous teachers. Grace Melvin, who taught design and crafts, specializing in decorative work and illustrations, encouraged Hughes' love of bright, clear colours. Charles

H. Scott, director of the school, an able and active administrator, always gave time to teaching despite a busy schedule. Hughes remembers Scott as a selfless, dedicated man and a gifted teacher. Scott and Grace Melvin encouraged Hughes to continue into post-graduate studies, and they arranged financial support for the final two years.

The curriculum at the art school was built around basic techniques. In the first and second years, the students took drawing and design; their only choice was between clay modelling and architecture. Hughes elected sculpture, taught by Charles Marega, who later made the lions for the Lion's Gate Bridge in Vancouver. In the third and fourth years they could major in drawing and painting, design and commercial art, sculpture or architecture. Hughes specialized in painting for the last two years of the diploma course and continued in this area for his post-graduate studies. He says now:

I have done no sculpture since art school. I admire sculpture and think the work of Rodin is magnificent. But for me sculpting always seemed too much of a craft. There are so many steps before you can see what you have done. Painting is so immediate. You can work more directly with colour.

He further remembers,

In our last years at the school John Varley, Orville Fisher, John Avison and I decided to let our hair grow long. I don't know why. I guess we thought we were a bit smart. For a long time no one mentioned it. Mine just kept growing longer but Orville's was curly and grew straight up and out. One day, walking along the hall, we met Jack Booth, who watched us go by, then said, "Hey Fisher, where did you get your fur cap?" We weren't sure if he was kidding or not but we all went to the barber's.

Edward thought seriously about becoming a teacher. In his post-graduate years, he taught Saturday morning children's art classes and soon discovered that he was unsuited for it. Teaching exhausted him emotionally, and he spent an inordinate amount of time preparing for each class.

It was awful. The classes were Saturday morning. On Sunday I was all right, but on Monday I began worrying. It increased all week and by the next Saturday I felt a wreck. The children were talented, but I had such trouble making them behave. The minute I turned my back, the little monkeys would start throwing balls of clay at each other.

It was his only attempt at teaching. Many artists rely on teaching to supplement their income, but for Hughes it was just not possible. When he taught, he was unable to paint.

H IS FORMAL training behind him, Hughes had to earn a living. Together with Paul Goranson and Orville Fisher, he began work as a freelance commercial artist. They rented space in downtown Vancouver in the Bekins Building for fifteen dollars a month. While waiting for commissions, they made dry point etchings and tried to sell them at small exhibitions. Many of Hughes' etchings from this period foretell his later paintings. Times were lean and Hughes recalls the trio's jubilation after an unusually successful sale:

We closed the office a bit early that day and went

to a nearby beer parlour. We celebrated with several beers, followed by some very cheap wine. Then we walked around Vancouver, laughing our heads off. Then we went back to the office and all that night we were very sick. The next morning I couldn't move. Fisher and Goranson opened the office as usual. When they heard a customer coming, they quickly tucked me under the counter out of sight. I remember lying there. My mind was perfectly clear. I just couldn't see.

Their first major commission was six panels for the walls of the First United Church in Vancouver. All three painters had a strong commitment to realism in murals. They drew lots to determine the assignment of the various panels. Hughes was delighted when he drew the Nativity scene for the central panel, and struggled to reconcile the spiritual, transcendental qualities of the Virgin with the physical strength of a young Jewish mother. Existing preparatory work for this portrait indicates he was successful.

The three felt honoured to receive this commission, although the pay consisted only of meals and a small cash allowance. Execution of the work was lengthy, full of setbacks. The cream manilla paper on which preparatory sketches were drawn attracted rats that inhabited the building. They had a constant battle to keep their work from being devoured; some of Hughes' sketches then bear the marks of the rats' teeth.

In 1936 they received another commission; to decorate the W.K. Oriental Gardens in Vancouver's Chinatown. Although the pay was better, their patron insisted they copy favourite scenes from an old Chinese calendar, and working conditions were not ideal. Renovations were being made only a few feet from where the artists worked. Even then, Hughes found noise so disruptive that he could hardly work. This experience may have convinced him that he must paint in solitude.

In 1938 the group did a mural for the Malaspina Hotel in Nanaimo, painted in oil on shellacked walls. It portrayed the history of Nanaimo and the surrounding area, featuring early explorers: Lieutenant Malaspina, Captain Galiano, Captain Quadra and Captain Vancouver. Unfortunately their mural has been covered by later construction.

Although survival during the Depression years was difficult, the young painter became determined to marry, after meeting Fern Smith in the autumn of 1937. On October 15, in Stanley Park, he was sketching a group of trees near Second Beach when Fern walked by with her dog and stopped to look at his drawing. They had a relaxed, easy conversation and he asked if he could walk her home. This was the beginning of the relationship that was to sustain Hughes for many years. Soon after, Hughes persuaded Fern to sit for a sketch. The pencil drawing *Fern in Stanley Park*, a delicate line drawing, reveals the vibrant inner strength of this quiet woman.

During the summers of 1937 and 1938, commissions were so scarce that Hughes rented a fishing boat and nets. Although born on the coast and raised near the ocean, he was unsuited to be a fisherman. During his first days out alone on the boat he remembers being desperately seasick and adds,

The fishermen were paid per fish. The exception was the large red salmon which was paid by the pound. Everyone hoped to catch a large red salmon. One night I caught this really large fish; it must have been well over forty pounds. I could scarcely lift it into the boat. I thought it was too big to turn in as a single fish so I kept it to eat. I cut it into pieces and gave some away to other fishing boats. They thought I was crazy—it was a red spring

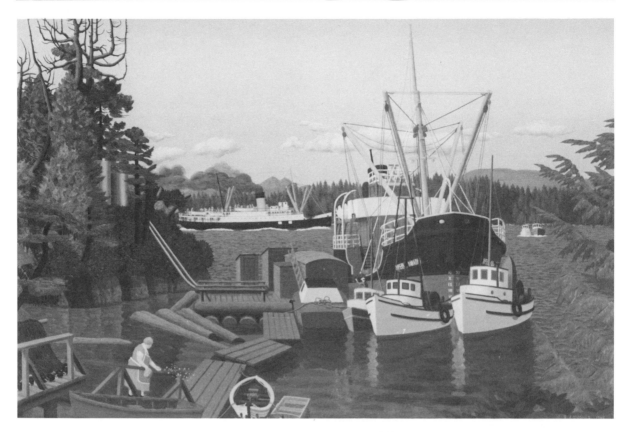

Christie Pass, Hurst Island, 1962

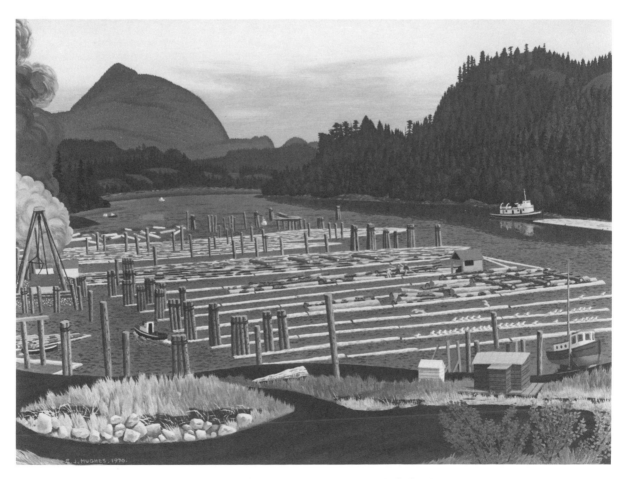

View from the Old Coal Dump, Ladysmith, B.C., 1970

Fern in Stanley Park (drawing), 1937

Edge of Wood, Gabriola Island, 1965

Abandoned Village, 1947

salmon. That fish must have been worth more than I earned the whole first month.

In several months, Hughes cleared only a few hundred dollars, but he considered himself lucky. Some men didn't make any money or ended the season with a loss after paying boat rental charges.

While fishing in 1938, Hughes received word from his colleagues that the provincial government wanted them to paint murals of British Columbia for the San Francisco World's Fair. He joined Goranson and Fisher in Vancouver, where they rented a large warehouse and began work on the murals. They were directed to show the commercial, agricultural and recreational aspects of B.C., set against the oceans and mountains of the province. Goranson did shipping, lumbering, mining and mountaineering scenes. Orville Fisher devoted his panels to industry, featuring railroads, highways, agriculture and commercial fishing. Hughes painted Indian life, tractor logging and outdoor sports—big game hunting and fishing. They painted in the same realistic style developed in earlier commissions, although current trends in painting were beginning to emphasize abstract design. Paul Goranson, the eldest and their usual spokesman, commented in the Vancouver *Province* at the time:

It is quite possible to have strong design without loss of detail. Lovers of the abstract have been leaving out detail unless it conformed with the composition they had in mind. It is our belief that the artist receives his inspiration from nature, and he does not have to leave out what is in nature in order to get good design.

Hopkins Landing, Howe Sound, 1952

The work was favourably received, but it was their last large commission. Their commercial association was dissolved, but they were together later as part of a much larger group—the Canadian war artists.

The Car Ferry at Sidney, British Columbia, 1952

Old Baldy Mountain, Shawnigan Lake, 1961

Cowichan Bay Road, 1962

An Arbutus Tree at Crofton Beach, 1973

In spite of these commissions, their years together had been lean. They were frequently on relief, and Goranson, as well as Hughes, tried commercial fishing without success. Hughes was engaged to Fern and needed financial security to marry. While executing the San Francisco murals, he applied to several branches of the army in the hope of a more stable income. In August of 1939 he was accepted by the Coast Artillery.

W ITH THE OUTBREAK of hostilities, Hughes, an artillery man, was posted to various batteries along the coast. While stationed in Vancouver, he heard that the Historical Section of the Department of National Defence wanted artists to record war activities. Hughes applied, his dream of becoming an army artist reborn. His commanding officer, through whom such a request should have been forwarded, was angry when Hughes applied directly to the Historical Section and reprimanded him. However, after viewing Hughes' work, he recommended him for the position. Hughes says:

The Freighter Ringstad at Crofton, 1971

> I was sorry to have gone above his head; it was good of him to help me but there wasn't much that could happen. He couldn't have demoted me. There was no lower step to go.

Hughes' early work during the war was for the Historical Section of the Department of National Defence. During World War I, the Canadian War Records Program had been established by Lord Beaverbrook, to record Canadian military activities overseas. In 1943, after agitation from the National Gallery and artists, the Canadian War Records Program was revived and Hughes became one of the first official war artists.

Edward Hughes married Fern Smith soon after the outbreak of war. They had only a brief period together before he was transferred to Eastern Canada, then to

Looking North over Finlayson Arm, 1973

Steamer at the Old Wharf, Nanaimo, 1958

Osborn Bay, 1978

Britain and thence, with the Canadian Forces, to the Arctic. Hughes' paintings from these years form an impressive visual record of Canada at war.

In the First World War, artists such as F.H. Varley, A.Y. Jackson and Arthur Nantel focussed on how war affects the individual. During the Second World War, Edward Hughes continued this concern for the ordinary man caught up in world-wide holocaust.

Freed from the confines of commissions, Hughes explored a variety of styles and techniques as he struggled to capture the scenes of war. He was influenced by other artists: Tom Thomson, John Constable, Paul Cezanne, the Renaissance masters—especially Raphael and Leonardo da Vinci—and the Mexican painters, Diego Rivera, Siqueros and Orozco. Later Hughes formulated his own style; his war art was not so much adaptation as total absorption of these styles, with an incredible range of technique.

HUGHES returned from the war determined to become a full-time painter. With government aid, he and Fern bought a large rooming house in Victoria. Fern would look after the boarders and Edward would paint. However, the noise and pressure of boarders so disrupted his painting that they had to abandon the enterprise. They moved to several smaller houses in Victoria, trying to get away from city sounds.

Hughes' flight from noisy neighbours, teeming traffic and barking dogs continued for several years. Fern, having finally exhausted the quieter spots in Victoria, finally found Edward the sanctuary he needed at Shawnigan Lake, twenty-five miles north. It was an environment that suited Hughes for over two decades.

These were happy years, marred only by financial struggle. The couple had a steady income of fifty dollars a month from the sale of their former house, which was augmented by the sale of an occasional painting; but Hughes could only complete one or two paintings a year. Even the move to the relative quiet of Shawnigan Lake did not increase his output substantially.

Their house lacked plumbing and was difficult to heat. Hughes' upstairs studio was warmed by a small wood stove. He still recalls how hard it was to remember to tend that stove. Totally preoccupied with his painting, he would let the fire go out. He would realize what had happened when he began to shiver with cold, and once again he would lay a new fire, a task he abhorred.

Throughout this period Fern's faith in his ability as an artist was unwavering. Hughes remembers:

In many ways they were difficult times. But through all those years, Fern never once suggested that there wasn't enough money, or that perhaps I could find a job. One word, and I'd have put aside my paintings and found a job. One word is all it would have taken; but Fern knew what painting meant to me and she never complained.

He was also encouraged by an Emily Carr Scholarship in 1947 that enabled him to sketch the west coast of Vancouver Island and, in 1948, by his election to the Canadian Group of Painters.

The landscape of Vancouver Island was to dominate his canvas from that time on. He began to paint the beaches, the fishing boats and the ocean views, and would return to them again and again. Lacking a car, he hiked to his sketching spots, becoming familiar with the nuances of the changing seasons.

The completion of a painting was double-edged. Hughes was pleased when he had successfully finished a work, but dreaded the prospect of selling it. He was—and is—a very private man, and dealing with the public was always a problem. When he had to sell his own works,

the problem was magnified. The more he worried about selling, the less he was able to paint. Several of his pictures remained unsold.

In 1951 he was finally relieved of this burden. Dr. Max Stern of the Dominion Gallery in Montreal had come west seeking new and talented artists. He was intrigued by a Hughes painting that he had seen in Brock Hall at the University of British Columbia. Excited, he went to Victoria with the address he had received, but finding the elusive Hughes was no easy task. Stern started at the boarding house and then followed house by house the Hugheses many moves throughout the city, to no avail. Finally, with the help of newspapers and the RCMP, Stern found the artist at his Shawnigan retreat and negotiated an exclusive contract for all of his work.

In the same year an exhibition of western painters was arranged by the Dominion Gallery, which included E.J. Hughes. Robert Ayre of the Montreal *Star* reviewed the show. He wrote:

Nineteen western painters are attracting attention at the Dominion. No one is attracting more attention than Edward J. Hughes of Vancouver Island. He not only looks at the Canadian scene but feels it, with passion, and puts it down note for note, leaf for leaf and wave for wave, with the love and concentration of a "primitive". I can well believe that it takes him two months to paint a picture—I almost said carve, because some of these works look as if they had been carved out of linoleum. The result of his passion and labour is tremendous intensity.

With the assurance of a market for his paintings and the certainty of income as each work was completed, Hughes became even more involved in painting. It became the centre of his life and social contact, always minimal, became a rare event. He and Fern lived an isolated existence.

Nineteen fifty-four was a busy year. Eighteen of Canada's leading artists were chosen to paint murals of Canadian scenery for the Canadian Pacific Railroad. The murals, depicting the parks of Canada, were installed in scenic dome lounge cars used by the CPR for its transcontinental service. Edward Hughes' contribution to the CPR project was a painting of Tweedsmuir Park in northern British Columbia featuring Lake Eutsuk, his brilliant colours and decorative technique capturing the typical west coast clarity of the park. His training in mural decoration enabled him to easily and effectively present a panoramic landscape within a confined space.

In 1954 Hughes was also chosen by the Standard Oil Company to paint a series of coast scenes. He made a voyage aboard their tanker *Imperial Nanaimo* along the west coast of British Columbia, gathering material as the boat travelled the Inside Passage delivering products to small villages. In colourful pictures, he showed the life of the seamen and of the people who lived in the coastal communities.

Hughes was asked in 1957 to paint a cover for the B.C. Telephone Directory. This was the special Centennial Directory, and Hughes painted the arrival of the first stern wheeler, the *S.S. Umatilla*, in *Yale, B.C., July 21, 1858*. This gold rush scene was something new for Hughes—an historical painting. The public reaction was favourable and he was requested to do a second cover. *View of the Cowichan River in July* appeared on the directory for 1961.

In 1958 Hughes was commissioned to paint a mural in oils for the British Columbia Room of the Royal York Hotel in Toronto, which became *A View from Qualicum Beach*. This was by far the most lucrative commission

Edward Hughes had yet received, and he recalls:

> I was forty-five years old, and for the first time able to afford a car. I bought one with an automatic transmission and our neighbour, Mr. Hamilton, agreed to teach me how to drive. Owning a car made a wonderful difference to our life. Fern's health had been failing for several years and by then she was unable to walk. How I enjoyed taking her along on my sketching trips!

The convenience of a car also made new sketching sites accessible that had previously been too far away.

For the 1966 centenary of British Columbia, Ocean Cement Limited contracted with Hughes to paint *HMS Discovery and HMS Chatham 1792*. In this picture, the ships are journeying north to Nootka. A dark background contrasts with the neutral tones of the ships. Hughes did several preparatory sketches in order to combine historical and topographical exactitude with an effective composition. The painting was the first in a collection, *Building B.C.*, which celebrated major events in the history of the province.

By now Hughes was receiving recognition generally, with Canada Council Awards in 1958, 1963, 1967 and 1970 to sketch the coast and interior of B.C. He also appeared on a CBC programme, *The Lively Arts,* that featured four other western artists—Jack Shadbolt, B.C. Binning, Gordon Smith and Takao Tanabe—besides himself. Hughes was elected a full member of the Royal Canadian Academy of Art in 1968.

The peaceful pattern of Edward's life was shattered by the sudden death of Fern in 1974. For the first time in his life he was unable to paint, and for six months remained idle. Slowly he returned to painting as his major solace, but the house which had shared with Fern held too many memories. Once more he started the restless search for a new home. He has had three houses since 1974, but the feeling of home eludes him. Hughes now lives in Duncan, an hour's drive from Victoria.

HUGHES has done a variety of paintings not usually associated with his style, many of which have never been exhibited. They include portraits, still lifes and cityscapes, but, of course, are far outnumbered by his landscapes.

Hughes made several portraits of Fern besides the pencil sketch *Fern in Stanley Park*. A sadder period was recorded in *Portrait of Fern*, 1941, after she had been gravely ill and their infant son Edward had died shortly after birth. Hughes expressed her courage and his gratitude at her recovery in this very finished pencil sketch. An introspective Fern is revealed in *The Painter's Wife*, 1945. Her windswept hair and quiet features are shown with a loose brushstroke. The couple had been separated during the war and this romantic portrait study was executed after their reunion.

Years later, in 1956, Hughes made his only self-portrait, entitled *Portrait of the Painter*, at the request of Max Stern. Like many painters he showed himself at work at the easel, but the actual self-portrait is only a small portion of the canvas, with Hughes gazing rather shyly at the viewer. The work was completed in the spacious studio of his Shawnigan Lake home and a prominent feature is the surrounding land seen through the window.

Hughes' preparatory sketches are filled with detailed studies of driftwood, boats and flowers, incorporated later into large finished canvases. Only rarely is an oil completed as a still life, featuring an inanimate object.

Cityscapes, in which actual land form is secondary, are a genre that Hughes has rarely handled; but the changes in his style over time parallel those in his landscapes. Early works feature the juxtaposition of circular and angular forms with a dramatic variety of perspectives; later works are calmer and more classical. Examples are the busy *Street Scene, Courtenay* of 1949 and the peaceful *University Avenue, Toronto, Looking South* of 1957. Between 1949 and 1957, Hughes had not only physically retreated to Shawnigan Lake but had also withdrawn from outside social contacts. The distance that he puts between himself and the town can clearly be seen in his later paintings. He paints large cities clinically, faithfully recording the buildings and the topography; the most startling feature is the absence of people and activity. In his landscapes he frequently adds isolated figures at ease in their surroundings, but in the bustle of a city, he paints no one. He disliked sketching in cities because of proximity to crowds and the straight lines required for architectural renderings; his last cityscapes were executed on a cross-Canada trip in 1955-56.

The one consistent theme of the Group of Seven had been the domination of the land over man; the powerful rhythms of the land loom larger than the scenes of human habitation. Hughes, who studied under Varley, admires Thomson and even titles his paintings in the same descriptive manner as the Group of Seven, tends to grant man and his works a more significant position in the landscape, but one feels nonetheless the encroaching presence of the trees and forests, the overwhelming immensity of the sea. Foreground area frequently contains blades of grass or shrubs which the artist seems to have been unable to push out of the way. Grass grows along the beach. Towns and villages huddle along the edge of an island. Small boats seem even smaller on a large ocean. Highways and roadways are invaded by growing vegetation. In terms of space, the land and the sea have the upper hand.

Hughes had three distinctive post-war landscape phases. Paintings immediately after the war are noisy, jarring and demanding. During the 1950's they are quieter, more composed, featuring bright, clear colours; in the late 1960's, colours are softer and lighter as he became more interested in atmosphere; an object is bathed in light and surrounded by air (*An Arbutus Tree, Crofton Beach*, 1973).

A Hughes canvas is clearly, carefully structured; organized so that land, sky and water achieve a harmonious balance. Several paintings from the 1940's and 1950's have unusual simplicity; they are landscapes using elements of nature in their most basic forms, freeing the artist to explore colour, perspective and the effect of light on land, water and sky. Typical of this type of painting is *Hopkins Landing*, 1952. These works were to serve as preliminary studies for later, more complex paintings.

Osborn Bay, 1978, is just such a painting. The coherence of colour, atmosphere and composition bespeak an intense, quiet affair between artist and subject. Calm stillness and a skillful blend of horizontal elements produces serenity. Major tonal areas are balanced; there are regulated steps from foreground to background—the light, bleached driftwood, the dark sand, the clear water, the grey reflection, the dark mass of foliage, the bright sky. Repetition is avoided by a distant view on the left, by grey clouds in the sky. These elements are united by the decorative tree on the right that joins beach, sea, distant shore and sky. The crystal clarity feels fresh and charming.

The combination of clarity and stillness gives a Hughes painting a super-real, other-world aura. At a time when our best natural images are being exhausted by the voracious demands of commercial media, E.J. Hughes' unique vision renews the visual experience of everyday life in the coastal B.C. landscape.

Eustace Smith:
The Last Authority

IN THE EARLIER years of the west coast forest industry when there was a seemingly endless choice of standing timber to buy, sell and log, the most important man in the woods was the cruiser, who could walk through a given tract and, just by looking at the growing trees, make an accurate and honest estimate of their value for logging. A good cruiser not only required the physical stamina to spend weeks in the bush covering long distances on foot, he had to understand all the things that can make otherwise sound-looking timber uneconomic to cut—conk, windshake, powderworm and a thousand and one other biological subtleties. In addition he had to know everything there was to know about the process of logging itself, since the amount of breakage to be expected in falling or the cost of building road all had to be factored into the final estimate. Perhaps the most important quality required in a good cruiser was trustworthiness, since the loggers or timber traders guarded their timber discoveries more jealously than pirates did their buried treasure.

In all of these categories there was one man who stood clearly above all others and achieved the status of a living legend throughout the west coast forest industry: Eustace Smith. Born in England in 1876, Smith emigrated to Canada with his parents in 1887, helping his father establish a farm near Comox on Vancouver Island. He began his logging career on the lowest rung of the ladder—as a "PF man", or skid-greaser—in 1890, and followed this with ten years of hand logging in Kingcome Inlet, Wakeman Sound, Mackenzie Sound and Simoom Sound. Still labouring under the illusion that logging was only a preparatory stage for turning the valleys of the B.C. coast into farmland, Smith married in 1900 and took up land at Beaver Cove. After four years of unmitigated disaster, he began returning to the woods as a cruiser part-time. After some initial successes trading timber himself he moved his family to Vancouver and set himself up in the profession that earned him a place in B.C. history. In time he came to know the forests of the Pacific Northwest—both in Canada and the U.S.—more intimately than any man before him or since, and many fortunes were built on his sound advice. Vancouver's H.R. MacMillan, for one, used Eustace Smith so often many still think of him as the key to MacMillan's early dominance of the B.C. forest industry.

The following oral accounts by Eustace Smith and men who knew him were recorded before Smith's death in 1964 and prepared by David Day from tapes in the Aural History Archives in Victoria, B.C.

NAME: **Eustace Smith**

Yes. He was tall, just about six feet. Lean... always lean. Well, in very late years he took on flesh, but when I knew him—in his hey-days—he was lean, kind of hungry-looking, you know, but he could run through the woods like a **wolf.**

He had a slightly long face, fair hair, medium fair, straight. Powerful. He was very powerful.... the outstanding cruiser of the time. I mean, the **last** *authority...*

It really begins at eleven with me, when we came out from the Old Country to Black Creek. My father wished to begin again—in a place that would support our large family, in a country that would grow as we grew. We found this place near Comox, enough cleared land for a house and the beginning of a farm.

But even here, we would be closed in, held in this small pasture. There were twelve in our family and we all wanted to be farmers then, but the land was crowded with mountains, and what seemed to us then the equally immovable timber. For the small farmer this land clearing was a massive work.

So we, all farmer's sons, set out alone. Left the farm to make our own way in this new wilderness. My brothers went out, scattered across the islands of the coast, and I found my way to a gyppo camp of horse team loggers.

That was the first job, near Courtenay. I was known as "the kid" by the axemen. I was the skid-greaser. Carrying that great stinking bucket of dogfish grease. Walking up and down the skid-row slopping down the ties before those big hoofed horses, as they dragged the big logs. And the bull puncher holding a long whip but directing, controlling with only his slow deep voice. He would say "Up, up", I think it was. No, it was some other word for forward. But "Come here" just to come toward him. "Back, back. Come here, Wally." Yes, I can hear that kind of cry.

I remember that—the first job, not much of a job really. I mean, you didn't stick to it if you could get another one. For one thing, you could never make any friends. Not with that stench of rotten stewed dogfish reeking from every pore. The skid-greaser wasn't even allowed in the bunkhouse, slept alone in a little shed out in the back. No, I got out of that one.

Yes, that's what he did at first. Before he was fourteen years old... and from then on, he had different jobs at the logging camps, and finally became adept... He did some falling and bucking, I think. That was about the best at that time.

It was with axes and saws and oxen and horses that I, my brothers and most of the young sons of the immigrant families, carved out a life in this country. But like many others, I wanted my own land – farmland. Land for raising cattle and growing crops and bringing up a family. So when I worked, I always had this dream of being a farmer. I wanted a farm as I remembered farms to be in England. Many here worked hard at making an England out of Vancouver Island. Make these the British Isles of the west. I guess we all had that idea, "gentlemen farmers". In the Old Country a big farm would make you landed gentry, land was associated with wealth. Here it meant toil. You became a serf to your own land. The wilderness gripped it, held on to the farmer's dream of wide green pastures with the massive dark roots of the great forest. It seemed then that we could never break that grip, could never make it loosen and give up the land to us.

But we were young and stubborn. I worked at logging in season, then with the money made would go with others, other settlers who wanted to be farmers, and carve a home out of this wild coast. The first time was at Kingcome, then later briefly at Knight's Inlet. Both ventures failed. The settlements dwindled, then disappeared. It seemed the land would not have us. And so I would go back to the timber camps and work out what was left of the year.

It was while I was logging up at Nimpkish that I met the daughter of a big Irish logger. Her name was Sissy Mather. At the end of the season, I took her to my parents' farm in Comox and introduced her. Meet my wife, I told them. Yes.

After that I wanted the farm even more. I had begun to build my life now in earnest, I didn't want this wandering, I wanted a place to build on. I was twenty-four and married. I had been a wandering logger for ten years by then. I'd had enough, I thought. I wanted some place to establish a stable life – again, it was the Old World dream. Trying to make a little England here, "a green and pleasant land." Well, it's green here all right, but by God, it's fierce.

Still, I had decided. I left Comox in the winter months with my new bride in a rowboat. We had decided to take land at Beaver Cove. We knew others had begun to settle nearby, and I had staked out a piece for a homestead lot the year before. This was where I was going to lay my foundations. Build a home and have a family. I would dig into the earth – and it was such rich black earth, more than a foot of good black topsoil. No one in the Old Country would believe such earth, but still if one was to have a farm of any size, there was a need to push back the forest.

So we set out in that rowboat full of goods and a small sail, left Comox for Beaver Cove. Sounds almost crazy now, setting out in that little boat with my child-bride and following that fierce ragged coastline all the way up, through the riptide at Seymour Narrows. (How many ships went down there? I can't remember. A lot of big ones.) Yes, through the Narrows, past – or rather wide around – the great whirlpool at Ripple Rock. Up the coast – and this was winter, so we'd have to lay in quite often because of the bad storms. Then when it would clear, we'd shovel the snow out of the boat and start up again. It took us more than a month to end that odyssey. I guess that was our honeymoon. Come to think of it, it wasn't such a bad honeymoon at that.

When we arrived I thought: this is it, this is where our lives will be lived out. But it seemed the very nature of

the land was against us. Was it hostile? I don't know, I don't really know what it was, but even when timber was cleared, the land somehow still seemed to belong to the forest. Something about the spirit of the place. At times I felt a kind of watching presence—at dusk, at the dark edge, where the timber met my own cleared land.

As I say, it was only a feeling, because there was no one for miles, not even the Indians came this way. I've always refused those superstitions and stories of the Indians. I've never *seen* anything that would give substance to their stories, yet I must admit there was a presence in that place.

It was from Beaver Cove, of course, that he— ranging around there, hunting and one thing and another— that he discovered Bonanza Lake. There was a taboo amongst the Indians about that area. They never went hunting there at all. There were no villages at Beaver Cove. So he had it all to himself, and he went ranging up there, and found that chain of three lakes: Ida, Bonanza. . .I forget the other one.

That was one area in which no white man had ever been. No Indian, as far as we knew, had ever been there.

As I say, it was taboo country. There was something about it that the Indians didn't like. There was such a thing as—what they call it now—the Sasquatch.

There was, among the Indians, a myth. I think it was called a Tsuniquah and he was a man like a Sasquatch. He was described the same. They described him as. . .if he ever got his eyes on you or you looked at him, you'd turn to stone. . .which, I suppose, was hypnosis, if there ever was such a thing. But they did have this fetish, or whatever it was.

Well, I stuck in there. I was young. I *wanted* that land. I built a house near the sea and worked the land: clearing, then going out to camps to make money for food, then returning to clear the land some more. I was determined. And in the second year came the first child, a boy, and I felt, yes, it has begun now—a wife, a farm and a male child. But I was wrong, for the child was born premature and was weak and began to fade. Within the month he returned to that deep sleep from which he came. I cannot even remember him having a voice, crying aloud; just his infant movements. Now even his features have faded. Perhaps I refuse to remember. I will not speak his name. Perhaps no one really remembers such pain, and I will thank God for that.

After the child's death, I worked the land with something like hatred. I would *not* allow it to break me. I would fight it out. Again I shifted from the logging camps to the farm, but always my mind was on the farmland.

It was in the numbing drudgery of the next two years that the two girls were born, but as a farmer I could not succeed. Too much rain, or not enough sun, or early frost, or too much wind. It just would not go!

I remember when I went down to visit him. He had two little girls there—Dorothy and Kathie—and he had taken out a big spruce tree, and that spruce tree. . .he had all the roots piled up there.

It must have been a terrific job, you know. It was probably about six feet in diameter, and he'd taken out every vestige of roots, and it was piled up there. It seemed to cover almost an acre of ground—this stack of roots, which he would later burn.

But this was nearing the end for me, at Beaver Cove.

274

The end of my thoughts about being a farmer. All along, I now believe, it was the wrong thing for me. Farmer's son or not, I was never meant to be a farmer. It really wasn't in me, I was learning that. I was learning—as a logger, as a hunter, as I ranged the forests, that these great woodlands were somehow more natural to me. Not that I could settle there, not that I could really *myself* settle anywhere, but my transience itself, my movement through the timber was the experience I was made for, had been trained for—from the day I arrived in this country.

I was ranging out by one of the upper lakes one day, quite deep in the timber. I don't know why, but I remember it exactly. It was like a photograph or a dream that I simply walked into. I stopped and everything seemed suddenly calm, unmoving. I remember thinking it was like a great cathedral with huge pillars running to the sky, and shafts of sunlight pouring down. It was big, fine timber and the tall cedars twisted their long, gnarled trunks toward the light. And of course spruce, hemlock, fir . . . yes, like great pillars in a vast cathedral. It was then, near the base of a huge swell-butt cedar, that I saw the grey timber wolf. It was strange, but it didn't startle me. Somehow I expected it to be there. I didn't move, I was in some way held. (I didn't have a gun. I hadn't come to hunt.) And it didn't move toward me. It just stood there and looked at me. I was so close I could see its eyes, and I swear to you they were blue, as blue as my own. I don't know how long we stood like that, but finally it slowly turned from me and stalked away.

It's strange, I'll always remember that, although I don't know why. It's come back to me often.

It seems it was after that, around that time anyway, that I began timber cruising—in earnest, I mean. Being a logger, of course, I always had an eye for good timber. I knew it when I saw it, and I had a good sense of woodlore. In fact, I began to learn I belonged there more than I belonged anywhere, I suppose. Well, I staked out that area up at Bonanza Lake and went to Vancouver with the timber cruising estimates and made a quick turnover profit on the land. Not a great deal of money, but more than I could ever expect to eke out on the farm. I believe it was then that I *knew* my calling. Who I was. What I was. Still, I thought I might hold on to the farm. Make Beaver Cove my headquarters. But then young Kathie died, and I knew I must get what was left of my family out. My wife was to have another child in the fall. I felt I had to guard them, to hold them where I could be sure they would be safe.

We buried the second child and then moved out, leaving nearly everything behind. I took them down to Vancouver, where our home has been ever since. No idea of owning a farm ever entered my mind again. More children came and grew up safely in the city, but I found that although that was where the family would live, I did not belong. I had known this before I came. I knew that I would spend the rest of my life as a timber cruiser, tracking the big timberlands of the coast.

*When Eustace turned full time to timber-cruising, he was lean, and probably at the peak of his strength and ability. He could travel like a **wolf** in there, and very few people could keep up with him.*

Sometimes he would go alone—yes, he did—I know. He was such a good cruiser, you know, that he was taken over, on more than one occasion, over as far as Oregon, to cruise timber over there for them. He was quite outstanding as a cruiser, you see. He was employed so much, altogether by purchasers and by banks, looking at timber, checking it over, you know. He got practically all that trade.

*Later in life he became **the** outstanding cruiser of the time. I mean, the **last** authority.*

Country of the Bull

for Gordon Gibson, Sr.

Beyond the blacktop's end
the road runs wild
through raw and ravaged land
from duncecap peaks
rambunctious rivers crash
beneath log bridges
the rough way twists and climbs
tips, dips and sheers.
The gravel slides like ice
beneath the wheels—
blind corners veer—
we fear for logging-trucks
The last hills wave us past
we crest the summit of a final ridge
through parting trees, the ancient inlet blinks
and we are in the Country of the Bull.
This limberlost
remote aloof exhilarating land
was once his bailiwick
Across these slopes
along these waterways when youth ran strong
he beat his measured path
the gawky boy became the looming man

he squared off with the trees
spat on his hands and taught himself to log
Bull of the Woods
they called him for his stormblast of a voice
and his ox-stubborn ways unquenchable
his thirst for timber (and the other stuff)
he slaked it to the full
In his spare time, he fished and flew a plane
ran sawmills, captained ships and carved his mark
then by a wild river, he sat down
and breached a crock of scotch
and dreamed a town.
The Bull has long forged on
to other schemes in places far removed
The town he dreamed remains
around the sawmill at the valley's mouth
those first rude shacks
have burgeoned into modern houses now
a bullish legacy
this thriving outport at the inlet's head
a monument to that unflinching man
who thundered it from nothing long ago.

Peter Trower

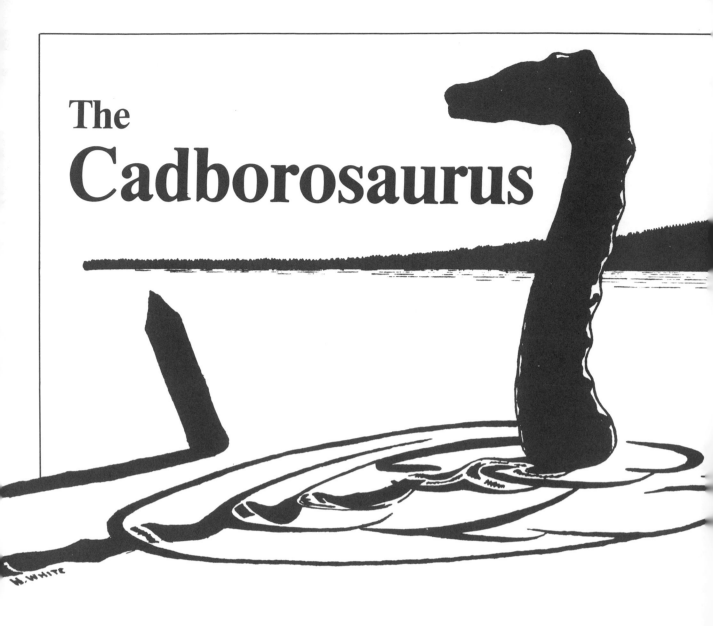

The Cadborosaurus

I DON'T BELIEVE in flying saucers. I don't believe in ghosts. I don't believe the 18th-century concept of free enterprise can be revived by wishful thinking to cure all the complex ills of our time. I never did believe in Pierre Trudeau's charisma. I'm skeptical. Believe me.

But I do believe in the Cadborosaurus.

No, I've never seen one. I've got something better than that.

Hubert Evans saw one.

I knew Hubert a long time before he revealed this to me. Some people, if they saw a sea serpent, would try to make a career out of it. With Hubert, I don't think I ever would have found out if I hadn't been sitting in his front room in Roberts Creek one day, looking out across the glassy calm gulf towards Nanaimo when a new report of the Loch Ness monster happened to come on the radio.

"What do you think of that?" Hubert asked, very evenly.

Hubert, as anyone who has spent even ten minutes in the healing balm of his presence will aver, is one of the most admirable beings currently dwelling amongst us. You can tell just by looking at the picture on the back of his latest novel, *O Time in Your Flight*, published when he was eighty-eight, recounting with scientific precision what life was like back in 1899 when he was eight—surely one of the greatest feats of pure memory in literature. Hubert has a gorgeous mane of fine white hair and a visage reminiscent of Mark Twain's except with

compassion in place of Twain's conceit, and whereas Mark Twain became bitter after he got to be about fifty and wrote nothing more of consequence, when Hubert turned ninety in 1983—sixteen years older than Mark Twain ever got to be—he had just finished publishing another fine optimistic book about his wide-awake life in the twentieth century. His body is truly the proverbial tattered coat upon a stick, but his mind is better than yours or mine ever was.

"Bunch of malarkey," I said, going back to my first impulse after some thought. It was unusual for him to make mention of something so frivolous.

"We had one here, you know."

"One what?"

"A sea serpent. Or some sort of sea creature quite similar to the way they describe that one over there."

"No!"

"Well I've never told many people, but it's a fact," he said. "It was in 1932, right out there where you're looking. I was up on the back lot with Dick Reeve, our neighbour, working on the road—that same one you drove in on to get here. Bob Stephens, the old Scot from down the beach—he's dead these many years—came puffing up the hill and said, 'By God now, you've got to come down and see what you make of this. We've had the glass on it for half an hour. It's the damnedest thing.'

"It was late afternoon with the water dead calm just as it is now, and the sun was low so the water was just a

276

Meets
Hubert Evans

by Howard White

sheet of gold. And here, out just beyond that deadhead, was a series of bumps breaking the water, all in dark silhouette, and circled with ripples.

" 'Sea lions,' I said. 'They run in a line like that sometimes.'

" 'Just you keep watching,' old Scotty said. And just a minute or so later, along at the end of this series of bumps, up out of the water comes a shaft–this was all in silhouette, so we couldn't see detail, although the outlines were very clear–up, up, up until it must have been six or eight feet out of the water. There was a spar buoy out on the reef then, which was about twelve inches through, and I could see this thing was about the same thickness– certainly no smaller.

" 'You know, it could be a log,' I said. I'd seen a crooked log sometimes catch in the current and roll, so a limb comes up like that–when you see something you don't know what to make of, you keep trying to explain it by the things you know.

"But right there as we stood watching, none of us breathing a word, the top end of this shaft began to elongate horizontally, until we were presented with the profile of a head, very much like a horse's in general shape, with eye bumps, nostrils, and something in the way of ears or horns. The neighbour down the way said it had stuff hanging down like hair but I didn't see that. I tell you, it was a feeling, watching that head come round as if to look at us. It just put the hair up on the back of your neck".

When Hubert finished telling me this I was just as speechless as he must have been at the original event. Knowing him as I did, it was not possible to disbelieve. Apart from the fact he is a very reliable observer of west coast nature, I don't think I have ever encountered a person more careful of his reputation for getting things right.

I had to accept the facts as given. The problem was a matter of re-ordering the suddenly fractured cosmos around them. How could such a thing occur and not be known? How could any person, even one of Hubert's character, look upon such a thing and not have it mark him in some way for the rest of his days? Had he ever tried to write about it?

No, he made a point of not doing so, although he told the kids at the time, "If you can find a camera and get a picture of this, it might be the biggest thing that ever happens to you." So they went rummaging all over Roberts Creek and found a camera, but no film. After a few minutes Hubert went back up to work on his road, but his daughter Elizabeth, who was about eleven then, had come home from school and watched it for half an hour more as it worked its way down the beach towards the mouth of Roberts Creek. When Hubert's neighbour Dick Reeve came up from taking a look, Hubert said, "Well, what did you see?"

"I know what I saw but I'm not telling anybody," Reeve said.

"There were reports after," Hubert continued. "The police boat saw it and got a good description, accurate measurements and all. There were many sightings. You could look it up."

I'd heard of the Cadborosaurus before, but I'd always dismissed it as an attempt by the Victoria Chamber of Commerce to borrow yet another of the beloved mother country's tourist attractions. As I now learned from a search of the newspaper file at the Provincial Archives, the legend rested on reasonably impressive factual ground. The first records, if they can be accepted as such, are prehistoric. Salish Indian mythology is rife with appearances by a friendly Caddy-like creature called by the Sechelts *T'chain-ko*, and there are a number of very ancient petroglyphs at Petroglyph Park in Nanaimo and at other sites around the Gulf of Georgia recording shapes remarkably like the one described by Hubert. At the other end of the time scale there have been scattered sightings as recently as the late 70's. But Caddy's credibility rests mainly on a flurry of sightings which took place on the lower B.C. coast between August, 1932 and late 1934.

The first reported sighting in this series, and the one which gave the creature its most enduring name, was made October 8, 1933 off Victoria's Cadboro Bay by Major W.H. Langley, a prominent barrister who was then clerk of the legislature.

Sailing past Chatham Island one Sunday in October, 1933, with Mrs. Langley in their sloop *Dorothy* at about 1:30 in the afternoon, the couple got a close view of the monster's back, which was "nearly eighty feet long and as wide as the average automobile." It was greenish brown, serrated and "every bit as big as a whale but entirely different from a whale in many respects," according to Major Langley, who added that he had spent time on a whaling ship and knew his whales.

His report in the Victoria *Times* elicited another from Mr. F.W. Kemp, an employee of the Provincial Archives, who had seen the monster in the same location the previous August but kept quiet about it, fearing ridicule. Mrs. Kemp had been sitting on the beach when she saw "a commotion in the water which threw a wash against the rocks similar to that caused by a motorboat."

Mr. Kemp was summoned, and as the party watched from a distance of three or four hundred yards, the beast "slid about ten feet of its head and body onto the rock and commenced to rub itself against the rough surface." They could plainly see its serrated back, which near the tail "resembled the cutting edge of a saw," and the sun, glistening on its body, clearly showed its colour to be greenish brown. After two or three minutes the animal slid off the rock and went on its way down the channel, "thrashing the water into a lather with its tail."

In the following two years there were dozens of Cadborosaurus reports from Cowichan Bay, Nanaimo, Pender Island, the north arm of the Fraser, Sooke, Campbell River, Alberni Inlet and the Queen Charlotte Islands—by fishermen, steamer captains, quarry owners, an excited news photographer who ran after it without taking his camera, the assistant accountant of the CPR's coastal operations and a wealthy businessman with a steam yacht full of distinguished guests.

All of the sightings reported a long looped body with a cow-like or camel-like head mounted on a long, slender neck. One of the most convincing later reports was made in February, 1950 by Chief Justice James T. Brown of Saskatchewan's King's Bench.

Impressive evidence, but in all these great questions like the existence of God or the Sasquatch, the crucial thing is not the mass of evidence that almost convinces you, it's the sliver of doubt that remains, holding the verdict forever open. To remove that final obstacle to conviction takes something special, and that's why I feel compelled to spill Hubert's special secret after all these years. After hearing him I *know* sea monsters exist. This in itself is a sufficiently important fact that it needs to be said; it changes a lot of things. But I am equally excited by the realization that I may have stumbled upon the ultimate description of Hubert: he is the sort of person who, if he tells you the Cadborosaurus exists, you suddenly discover you believe in Cadborosauruses. I would be hard put to say which is more remarkable.

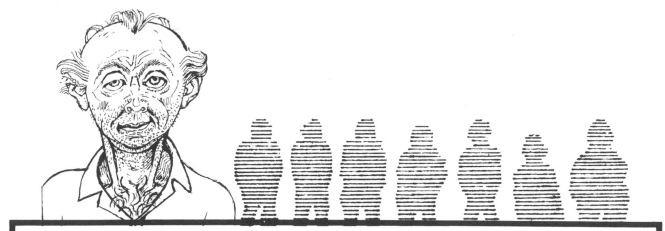

Marco

by W.P. Kinsella

MARCO FERLINGHETTI spends his life getting picked out of police lineups. The police collar Marco nearly every day. He is not hard to find, for he is virtually never more than two blocks from the corner of Hastings and Main in Vancouver at any time in his life. Marco stands sullen in the middle of the lineup, eyelids drooping, while behind two-way glass, victims and witnesses scrutinize. On one especially productive day Marco was positively identified as a flasher, a hit-and-run driver, a burglar, a dope pusher and a peeping tom.

The rationale of the police is that if a potential witness can pass over Marco for someone else, then the identification is likely to stick. The reason that Marco is such a popular choice is that he looks exactly the way people think a criminal should look. He has scraggily, receding hair, protruding eyes, no chin to speak of, and is always in need of a shave. His teeth are yellow, his nose hooked; he wears a dirty trenchcoat, baggy pants and sneakers. Marco Ferlinghetti is an incarnation of the middle-class idea of a child molester, pimp, pusher and petty thief.

Marco did indeed do time a few years ago for selling a marijuana cigarette to an undercover cop. While he was in prison, Marco was treated rather harshly, partly because of his looks and partly because the undercover cop was standing outside an elementary school when he made the buy. Marco decided to learn a trade. Behind the walls he learned to be a cannon (a professional pickpocket), and now practises his trade with a solemn efficiency. His stall (an assistant who distracts the intended victims, usually by bumping into them) is his girlfriend, whom he calls Jackson, a bedraggled little hype in jeans, boots and a halter that exposes most of her breasts. Jackson always looks as if she is about to ask someone for directions.

The police know of Marco's profession, but live and let live as long as he keeps himself available for daily lineups.

A few weeks ago, Marco, in all his grimy splendor, crab-walked into the Toronto Dominion Bank on Granville Street, several blocks away from Hastings and Main, and presented the teller with a note.

The note was clearly printed but poorly spelled and punctuated. It was enough to produce a coronary in a grammarian. Marco, the proud holder of a B.Comm. from the University of British Columbia, walked away with several thousand dollars.

The police pulled in an assortment of known bank robbers; they also pulled in Marco Ferlinghetti.

"That's him!" said the robbed teller.

"That's him!" said the assistant bank manager.

"That's him!" said an elderly lady who had been in line behind Marco.

The police politely thanked them for their trouble.

A few days later Marco limped into the Main Street Police Station and approached the sergeant in charge of police lineups.

"I'd like to take a little time off," he said deferentially. "I think I picked a rotten pocket, if you know what I mean. Came into a large amount of bread but the empty pocket belonged to the mob. There are nasty rumours on the street."

"You go ahead, Marco," said the police officer. The sergeant had a soft spot in his heart for petty criminals like Marco. He didn't like the mob either. "Just be sure you settle around here when you come back. You're very valuable to us."

Marco and Jackson caught the next flight for Honolulu. But even in paradise, dressed in a Hawaiian shirt, with a lei of waxen orchids around his neck, Marco Ferlinghetti looked like a criminal. His third day on Waikiki, Marco was picked up and displayed in a police lineup. Late at night, wallets, picked clean as fish skeletons, glow whitely in the alleys of Honolulu.

in Paradise

BOOK REVIEWS

AGAINST WIND AND WEATHER
The History of Towboating in British Columbia

Review by A.C. (Fred) Rogers

THE BRITISH COLUMBIA towboat industry has gone without a published history of its own for an unaccountably long while and this handsome book, commissioned by the Council of Marine Carriers of British Columbia, should appeal to tugboat men and armchair mariners alike. It is well illustrated with fine photographs and with many salty quotations by tug owners and skippers which illuminate the basic text.

In writing of the B.C. tugboat industry the researcher faces a particularly challenging task. Early B.C. tugboat history only occasionally crops up in Lewis and Dryden's *Marine History of the Pacific Northwest* (1895) and its sequel *McCurdy's Maritime History*. In the matter of B.C. boats particularly, these standard source-books are incomplete, and great numbers of tugs go unrecorded except for the scanty information in steamship inspection reports. Given the difficulties of his task and the length of time he had to do it, author Ken Drushka has done a commendable piece of work.

The absence of information about the early evolution of B.C. tugboats and their jurisdictional disputes with American tugs is disappointing however, particularly since that conflict characterized relations between the two fleets until a truce was finally achieved in 1890-91. B.C. tugs were forbidden by American law to tow sailing vessels into Puget Sound ports past Port Townsend; to go farther was to risk seizure and heavy fines. Similarly, to tow any vessel out of a U.S. port was tantamount, in the American view, to piracy. Yet American tugs with relative impunity towed vessels in and out of British Columbia ports in violation of the Canada Shipping Act, in effect from B.C.'s entry into Confederation in 1871. The mighty *Lorne* and several other deep-sea tugs, the *Pilot* among them, were seized for daring to tow ships from Cape Flattery to Tacoma. The issue finally came to a head in 1891 when Ottawa seized an American tug that wrongfully towed a sailing vessel from Victoria to Nanaimo, and it was only in the wake of this watershed incident that B.C. tugboating came into its own.

A more distressing disappointment concerns Drushka's lack of caution in approaching the very tricky subject of vessel histories. Just one example of the trouble he makes for himself in this area concerns the question of B.C.'s oldest working tugboat.

There are few issues more certain to start an animated discussion among maritime history buffs, and any writer new to the subject would be well advised to make sure of his facts before venturing to offer an opinion. As stated in *Raincoast Chronicles Number Eight*, the expert consensus was that up to her sinking in 1979, the title of oldest working tugboat on the B.C. coast was held by the 36-ton ex-steam tug *Brunette*, built at Fraser Mills in 1890. Drushka blitheley dismisses the body of opinion backing the *Brunette* and summarily awards the honour to a vessel called the *Swan*, owned by Alfred Talbot, which he fearlessly states was built in 1888.

As shown in the annual steamship register, there was a *Swan* built in the year 1888, but the register also records three other *Swan*s built in later years. How Drushka has proven that the first is the *Swan* owned by the Talbots is a matter he keeps to himself, but certainly to other authorities it would not appear to be the case. In May, 1896 this advertisement appeared in the Vancouver *Province:* "Tug *Swan* for sale, owner J.A. Cates, speed 8 mph, eight years old." Cates did not report selling her until 1900 and both the selling price — $850 — and contemporary reports indicate she was nearing the end of her usefulness. Another clipping I have, dated September 21, 1899, reports: "Tug *Swan* reg. New Westminster sank while lying at the city dock of Vancouver and has been raised." These clues as to her poor condition all substantiate the report by oldtime towboater W.A. (Bill) Henry (Vancouver *Sun*, July 5, 1972, in a column by Charles M. Defieux) stating, "The last time I saw the original *Swan* she was lying on her beam ends on the mud flats in Coal Harbour about the foot of Cardero Street. This was her final resting place. She was beyond any chance of repairs. I took her teakwood steering wheel and installed it in my boat *Redwing I.*" All of this evidence amounts to a fairly solid case for the argument that the 1888 *Swan* met her demise early in this century.

The next *Swan*, somewhat larger at 36.32 tons, turns up on the register in 1893, built for Shotbolt and Drainey, to be used in the Rivers Inlet fishing industry. This is apparently the boat Drushka claims as pre-dating the *Brunette* but it is difficult to say since he gives two different dates, stating on page 51, "She was a 45-foot steam tug built at Rivers Inlet in 1891 by the manager of Rivers Inlet Cannery, Bob Drainey", then contradicting himself on page 211 by stating "There have been several *Swan*s; this one was built in 1888 at the head of Rivers Inlet by Bob Drainey." He identifies this vessel as the *Swan* Captain Don Peck once chartered, but in a letter published in *Raincoast Chronicles First Five* (page 193) Captain Peck gave the launch date of that *Swan* as 1891. Captain Peck's letter was in reply to an earlier query by Mrs. Talbot, who wrote, "We have been told she was built in 1888 but we have been unable to confirm this."

Another *Swan* was built in 1894 at Nanaimo as a yacht — a small steamer of seven gross tons. A fourth and final *Swan* was built in 1897 — register number 122340 — by George W. Roberts of Vancouver and jointly owned by the builder and Herman Thorsen. This tug was 46.4 feet long with an 11.8-foot beam. I believe this, and not the 1893 *Swan*, is the boat now owned by Alfred Talbot. The steamship register number 122340 is the same as the register number I located from the original register now in the Vancouver Customs Office.

Drushka also has the tug *Comet* misplaced in history. He states that the *Comet* was towing for the Hastings Mill before the tug *Active* began her distinguished reign in 1889. The 85-foot *Comet* was not launched until 1891, making her trial run up the Fraser to Port Kells. If Drushka wants a predecessor to the *Active*, he can have the *Belle*, launched in 1884. But there were two *Belle*s — there's more rope for his wheel.

To some, all this argument over precise dates, names and specifications no doubt seems so much hair-splitting, but to those who have spent years trying to get the facts in order, the prospect of having them get mixed up again can be positively alarming. To those not afflicted with this worry however, *Against Wind and Weather* should prove an uninterrupted pleasure.

THE MEN THERE WERE THEN

Review by Dale Zieroth

HOWARD WHITE writes an elegant introduction to his own first book of poems *The Men There Were Then*. Perhaps this should become standard practice for all poets: it gives his book a focus that enables us to enter into the spirit of the poems more quickly. He says,

Some of the poems included here were written as long ago as the mid-sixties, but clashed so violently with the literary taste of that time that I spent the next decade convinced they were unpublishable. . . . Today I find the same poems held up as examples of what has come to be called industrial writing.

If you're the kind of reader who isn't familiar with "industrial writing", or if your unfamiliarity has led you to expect poems that pay little attention to control of language, then reading *The Men There Were Then* will be a delightful corrective.

"Accidents", the first half of the book, is described by White as:

stories of ingenious death
details honed to a
murderous edge
to make you forget how
many times you heard
that one before.

He captures not just the story, but the story-teller, and through the narrator we discover the fascination that the industrial working man has with the death and near-death that walks through his day-by-day. We hear the various ways that he deals with this death: he laughs in nervousness; he ignores or lashes out; he withdraws into bitterness. Or he becomes a story-teller spinning out his lunchtime yarn about the kid who displaced his brains with high-pressure grease, the man who fell into a vat of caustic. We laugh and recoil at the same time, caught up in the suspense and shock of the poem. "Accidents" presents a macabre view of working, but only if we forget that these are also tall tales, intended not only for the ears of the startled greenhorn but for the listener who has heard the story before and who is willing to suspend his disbelief again. And no one is exempt from the story-teller: listen to this fellow talking about "These Here Poets":

now it's these Christly poets
trying to get you to repeat everything
gotta do your job and their job too
babysit the useless bastards
until the first plane goes out
Canada Council gives 'em ten thousand dollars
to write about what it's like
to be a workingman
tiny little book comes out
cost you half a day's pay to buy it
and here's all your words
all phonied up—

White knows how to turn the words back on himself, and he knows he has the responsibility to catch, not distort, the speech of the place.

In the second part of the book, "Bulldozer Joke", we see a continued concern with the boredom and horror of working:

in a place where nothing ever happens
except the same thing about
seven thousand times a day.
It's the danger that keeps you alive.

Often the poems come out of the battleground between men and machines "hungry for human limbs;" as a truckdriver says,"now the genius has all been put into the machines." We see comparisons between different workers:

The logger has a new tinsel shirt he will tell you
how outrageously he paid for, but it will
be on the floor, once used and ruined when he
leaves.
The fisherman has on wool and tweeds bagged to
his shape.

There are several occasional poems here, about his family and co-workers, and throughout we hear White's concern with the tug-of-war between the work-weary body and the fantasizing mind. But what I remember finally is not this theme of the brain seeking to know its place in the world as much as the world itself—the men and their deadly machines, the gurdy drives and gillnet drums, the fields of dandelions, the fishing boats, the cold and the rain. As White says,

What we seek is
not a beyond world
but an angle on this one.

In his introduction, White claims:

The makers of the great primitive legends, the authors of the great epics, the troubadors, the Elizabethan playwrights, didn't consider it beneath themselves to tell a story, but modern poetry does, and this has made it the preserve of an incidental minority while the mass of people are abandoned to Warner Brothers.
It doesn't have to be that way.

Indeed. If I thought of modern poetry as a distant battle, this would be a shot close at hand. What is important here is not just White's assertion of narrative, but the skill with which he handles the voices, whether they belong to redneck catskinners or lone wolf trollers or poetry editors. White shares the world with his narrators; he catches up their speech in his own lightly ironic humour that always illuminates the men and women behind their work. He is not separate from them; as he says in "Lunching on Myth", each of the story-tellers becomes:

in turn
a poet for the moment.

MOSTLY COAST PEOPLE

Review by Margaret Laurence

I have never met Hubert Evans, but I feel privileged to call him my friend, for I have met him through his books and through letters. *Mist on the River*, his splendid novel about the native peoples in northern B.C., was first published in 1954, but I did not read it until later, in the New Canadian Library edition, which fortunately brought the book back into print and assured its continued availability. This novel moved me a great deal and taught me a great deal, not by any didacticism but by the simple power of the writing and the ways in which the reader is given the sense of truly living characters caught up in the conflict between the old ways of the villages and the new and oppressive ways of the fish canneries. This is a tragic novel, but it also proclaims the strength of the human spirit.

Enthusiastically, I mentioned *Mist on the River* to Silver Donald Cameron, writer, colleague and friend, and asked him if he had read it. Not only had he read it, but he was actually planning soon to go to B.C. and interview Hubert Evans. He suggested that I write and tell Evans how much I admired the novel. Rather hesitantly I did so, not knowing what the response might be. I need not have worried. Very soon I got a cordial letter back. Hubert was then in his late eighties and was being forced by failing eyesight to learn touch-typing. He apologized for the errors. It was then that I began to realize the marvellous nature of the man. Learning touch-typing, under such conditions, was no big deal for him. As a very long-time writer, fisherman, union volunteer, a builder of his own house at Roberts Creek, partner in a long and loving marriage, a father, grandfather and great-grandfather, learning to touch-type, with minimal eyesight and at that age, was just something to be dealt with in a commonsense way, with the wisdom and sheer determination acquired over many years.

I subsequently came to know that Hubert Evans had published his first book in 1926, the year I was born. Throughout his writing life, a large number of stories, serials and children's books have appeared. For years he earned his living partly as a writer and partly as a fisherman. *Mist on the River* must now be regarded as a Canadian classic. The publication of his novel *O Time in Your Flight*, in 1979, was a very special event. This fine autobiographical novel tells of one year in a boy's life, that year being 1899, when the century turned. The picture of life in those times is done vividly and in fascinating detail. The book is a true gift, not only to my generation but to my children's generation and all generations to come.

I recall Silver Donald Cameron saying once, when he was about forty, that when he grew up he would like to be Hubert Evans. Well, at fifty-six I have some of the same feelings. Hubert is now ninety, and has kept the faith all these years. In this terrifying world, we must try, as writers, to proclaim life and its worth for as long as it is given to us to do so. Hubert Evans has done this and he continues to do so.

The poems in this present collection speak directly to me, and to the deepest parts of my belief. Frequently, they contain a compassionate humour, and this kind of humour is a gift of grace. They are wise and they are caring, caring in the widest sense about human beings and all creatures dwelling on our earth and the earth itself. He is no tourist in this life. He is a person who undertakes responsibilities and who gives and can receive that basic love which is at the heart of faith. His view of life is essentially, I feel, a religious one, by which I mean a sense of sharing in the holy spirit, of celebrating life and trying to honour and protect it.

Hubert, being himself, would probably laugh at my statement that I believe him to be a truly great human being, and a fine writer who has given so much to so many of us. He signs his letters "The Old Journeyman." He is, indeed, that. I like, respect and agree with someone who regards writing not in any pretentious way as his "art" but rather as one's craft, one's trade—which also encompasses the sense of vocation. I think of the words of St. Paul, and although Hubert Evans would never use them in reference to himself, they do apply. "I have fought a good fight; I have finished my course; I have kept the faith."

Many of these poems stay in my mind, but I think of one especially, now:

Many times in life I too have forgotten
whence I came and have beaten my wings
against barriers which would not yield.
Whose the hand which guided me to the light?

Old Journeyman, thanks. We go on learning. We go on journeying.

Index

286